Learning Photoshop CS2

by
Pete Watkins

Publisher
The Goodheart-Willcox Company, Inc.
Tinley Park, Illinois
www.g-w.com

Copyright © 2007

by

The Goodheart-Willcox Company, Inc.

All rights reserved. No part of this work may be reproduced, stored, or transmitted in any form or by any electronic or mechanical means, including information storage and retrieval systems, without the prior written permission of The Goodheart-Willcox Company, Inc.

Manufactured in the United States of America.

Library of Congress Catalog Card Number

ISBN 978-1-59070-773-9

1 2 3 4 5 6 7 8 9 – 07 – 11 10 09 08 07

The Goodheart-Willcox Company, Inc. Brand Disclaimer: Brand names, company names, and illustrations for products and services included in this text are provided for educational purposes only, and do not represent or imply endorsement or recommendation by the author or the publisher.

The Goodheart-Willcox Company, Inc. Safety Notice: The reader is expressly advised to carefully read, understand, and apply all safety precautions and warnings described in this book or that might also be indicated in undertaking the activities and exercises described herein to minimize risk of personal injury or injury to others. Common sense and good judgment should also be exercised and applied to help avoid all potential hazards. The reader should always refer to the appropriate manufacturer's technical information, directions, and recommendations; then proceed with care to follow specific equipment operating instructions. The reader should understand these notices and cautions are not exhaustive.

The publisher makes no warranty or representation whatsoever, either expressed or implied, including, but not limited to, equipment, procedures, and applications described or referred to herein, their quality, performance, merchantability, or fitness for a particular purpose. The publisher assumes no responsibility for any changes, errors, or omissions in this book. The publisher specifically disclaims any liability whatsoever, including any direct, indirect, incidental, consequential, special, or exemplary damages resulting, in whole or in part, from the reader's use or reliance upon the information, instructions, procedures, warnings, cautions, applications, or other matter contained in this book. The publisher assumes no responsibility for the activities of the reader.

Library of Congress Cataloging-in-Publication Data

Watkins, Peter N.
  Learning Photoshop CS2 / by Peter N. Watkins
        p. cm.
     Includes index.
     ISBN 978-1-59070-773-9
     1. Computer graphics. 2. Adobe Photoshop
     I. Title.

Introduction

Photoshop: A Powerful Image-Editing Program

Open an image in Adobe® Photoshop® CS2, and endless possibilities await you. You can adjust the color, brightness, or contrast of the image. You can create a variety of special effects, such as making a photo look like it is covered with plastic wrap, or making it look like it is under water. You can remove scratches from an old photo, or make out-of-place hairs disappear from a portrait. You can add fancy text to an image or even create artwork from scratch with a wide variety of painting and drawing tools.

Photoshop has an amazing collection of tools, options, and commands. Often, there is more than one way to accomplish the same task. After you become more comfortable with the program, you will develop favorite tools and techniques. However, you should continue to experiment with other tools and techniques, because flexibility will help you create innovative designs.

This book is written for beginning to intermediate Photoshop users. As you become a more serious Photoshop user, you can keep building your knowledge by tuning in to the thousands of tips and tricks other Photoshop users discover and share on websites. You can also find such Photoshop tips in magazines related to digital photography or other publications written at the intermediate to advanced level.

Apple Computer Users

The illustrations in this book are from a Windows version of Photoshop CS2, but the Mac version is almost identical. Occasionally, there are slight differences between the menu selections in the Windows version of Photoshop and the Mac version. Such cases are pointed out throughout the text. The following key combinations are also different for Apple and Windows users. In the text, the first three instances of each alternate keystroke are noted for Apple users. After the third instance, a note is no longer added:

Windows Action	**Equivalent Action in Mac**
Right click	[Ctrl] + click
[Alt] + click	[Option] + click
[Ctrl] + click	[Command] + click

About the Author

When Pete Watkins started teaching Photoshop several years ago, he searched for an expansive, beginning-level Photoshop text that included a significant amount of easy-to-follow tutorials and other classroom activities. Seeing a need for such a book, Pete began working on this project.

Pete holds a master's degree in Instructional Technology from Utah State University. He is an Adobe Certified Expert in Photoshop CS2. Pete has taught technology-related subjects at the high school and college levels for over a decade. He currently teaches Photography, 3D Graphics and Animation, and Computer-Aided Drafting at Bear River High School in Garland, Utah.

Using This Book

Since you are reading a book about a specific computer program, it is assumed that you already have basic computer skills, including the ability to use a mouse, open and close computer applications (such as Photoshop), and open, save, and close files within an application.

Whether you are a beginner or intermediate-level Photoshop user, this book will help you understand Photoshop's tools and commands. You will learn a variety of image-editing techniques. The fundamentals of graphic design will also be discussed. Tutorials are included at the end of each chapter, giving you a chance to practice what you have learned.

Table of Contents

Introduction 3

Chapter 1—The Work Area 13

Introduction 13
The Default Work Area 13
The Welcome Screen 14
The Toolbox 14
    Foreground and Background Colors 14
    Screen Modes 16
    What Is Image Ready? 17
The Options Bar 18
Menus 18
    Keyboard Shortcuts 20
Palettes 21
    Arranging Palettes 21
    Saving the Workspace Arrangement 22
Working with Multiple Image Windows 22
Using the Help Menu 22
Using the Undo and Step Backward Commands 25
GRAPHIC DESIGN: An Introduction 25
Summary 26
CHAPTER TUTORIALS 27
Review Questions 31

Chapter 2—Resolution 33

Introduction 33
    Will the Image Be Printed or Displayed on a Computer Screen? 33
    Image Capture Devices 34
    Pixels and Resolution 36
The Zoom Tool 37
    Zoom Percentage 37
    Print Size 37
    Zoom Tool Options 37
    Zooming In by Dragging a Box 39
The Hand Tool 39
    Hand Tool Options 40

Image Resolution and Size   40
   The Image Size Dialog Box   41
   Resizing an Image (Resampling Off)   42
   Resizing an Image (Resampling On)   43
   Printing Resolution   44
   Resizing Images for Printing   44
   The Resize Image Wizard   45
Scanning Tips   46
Digital Camera Tips   47
Images for E-mail, Websites, Multimedia   47
   The Save For Web Dialog Box   47
Creating Images for Video   50
GRAPHIC DESIGN: The Mood of a Design   50
Summary   51
CHAPTER TUTORIALS   52
Review Questions   63

Chapter 3—Selection Tools   65

Introduction   65
Selection Options   65
   Fine-Tuning Selections   66
   Feathered vs. Normal Selections   68
   Anti-Aliasing   69
The Marquee Selection Tools   69
   The Rectangular Marquee Tool   70
   The Elliptical Marquee Tool   71
   The Single Column and Single Row Marquee Tools   71
The Crop Tool   72
   Initial Crop Tool Options   72
   Cropping an Image   73
   Secondary Crop Tool Options   74
The Lasso Tools   74
   The Lasso Tool   74
   The Polygonal Lasso Tool   75
   The Magnetic Lasso Tool   76
   Useful Keyboard Shortcuts for the Lasso Tools   78
The Magic Wand Tool   79
Quick Mask Mode   80
The Type Masking Tools   81
The Select Menu   82
   The All Command   82
   The Deselect Command   82
   The Reselect Command   83
   The Inverse Command   83
   Selecting by Color Range   83
   The Feather Command   84
   The Modify Submenu   84
   The Grow and Similar Commands   85
   The Transform Selection Command   85
   Saving and Loading a Selection   86

Temporarily Hiding a Selection   87
Removing a Fringe   87
GRAPHIC DESIGN: Choosing Photographic Images   88
Summary   89
CHAPTER TUTORIALS   90
Review Questions   108

Chapter 4—Introduction to Layers   111

Introduction   111
The Layers Palette   112
Creating a New File   113
The Move Tool   114
    Scenario 1: Using the Move Tool to Move Selected Pixels within an Image   115
    Scenario 2: Using the Move Tool to Copy Selected Pixels to Another
        Location in an Image   115
    Scenario 3: Using the Move Tool to Copy a Selected Area or an Entire
        Image to Another File   116
Transforming with the Bounding Box   116
    The Transform Options Bar   117
    The Edit > Transform Submenu   122
Using the Cut, Copy, and Paste Commands   123
Aligning Image Elements Using Grids, Guides, Rulers, and Snaps   124
    The Grid   125
    Rulers   126
    Guides   126
    Smart Guides   127
    Using Snap to Align Layers   127
Working with Layers in the Layers Palette   128
    Making Layers Active   128
    Selecting the Content of a Layer   128
    Duplicating a Layer   129
    Layer Properties: Renaming and Color-Coding Layers   130
    Changing the Stacking Order of Layers   131
    Creating a New, Blank Layer   132
    Deleting a Layer   132
    Layer Visibility   132
    Grouping Layers   133
    Linking Layers   134
    Merging Layers   135
    Flattening an Image   136
    Layer Opacity   136
    Layer Transparency   136
    Locking Layers   138
    Layers Palette Menu   138
    Right Clicking on the Layers Palette   139
GRAPHIC DESIGN: Text Basics   140
Summary   141
CHAPTER TUTORIALS   142
Review Questions   159

Chapter 5—Text, Shapes, and Layer Styles   161

Introduction   161
Two Kinds of Graphics: Vector vs. Bitmap   161
Text in Photoshop   162
    The Horizontal Type Tool and the Vertical Type Tool   162
    The Type Masking Tools   164
    Inserting Special Text Characters   165
    The Character Palette   165
    The Paragraph Palette   170
    Rasterizing Text   172
Shape Tools   173
    The Options Bar for Shape Tools   173
Paths, Pen Tools, and Path Selection Tools   181
    Creating a Path with the Pen Tool   182
    Creating a Path with the Freeform Pen Tool   184
    Modifying a Path with the Path Selection Tools   184
    Modifying a Path with the Pen Tools   186
The Paths Palette   187
    Converting a Path into Brush Strokes   188
    Converting a Path into a Filled Shape   189
    Converting a Path into a Selection   189
Text on a Path   190
Layer Styles   190
    The Styles Palette   190
GRAPHIC DESIGN: Fonts   194
Summary   195
CHAPTER TUTORIALS   196
Review Questions   214

Chapter 6—Painting Tools and Filters   217

Introduction   217
The Brush Tool   218
    The Brush Preset Picker   219
    Brush Tool Blending Modes   220
    The Brushes Palette   223
    Creating a Custom Brush Tip   231
The Pencil Tool   231
The Pattern Stamp Tool   232
    The Pattern Stamp Tool's Options Bar   232
    Defining Your Own Patterns   233
The Gradient Tool   233
    Editing Gradients   236
The Paint Bucket Tool   238
    The Fill Command   240
    The Smudge Tool   240
The Eyedropper Tool   240
The Canvas   242

Filters   242
- *The Filter Menu*   243
- *The Filter Gallery*   244
- *The Liquefy Filter*   245
- *The Pattern Maker Filter*   248
- *Other Filters in the Filter Menu*   251

GRAPHIC DESIGN: Focal Point and Visual Hierarchy   251
Summary   253
CHAPTER TUTORIALS   254
Review Questions   273

Chapter 7—Erasing, Deleting, and Undoing   275

Introduction   275
Eraser Tools   276
- *The Eraser Tool*   276
- *The Background Eraser Tool*   278
- *The Magic Eraser Tool*   282

The History Palette   283
History Brush Tools   285
- *The History Brush Tool*   285
- *The Art History Brush Tool*   285

The Extract Filter   287
- *Extracting an Image*   288

Finding Extra Pixels with the Reveal All Command   290
The Trim Command   291
GRAPHIC DESIGN: Balance in Symmetrical and Asymmetrical Designs   293
Summary   294
CHAPTER TUTORIALS   295
Review Questions   313

Chapter 8—Restoring and Retouching Photos   315

Introduction   315
Sharpening an Image   316
- *The Usharp Mask Filter*   316
- *The Smart Sharpen Filter*   317
- *Other Sharpening Filters*   318
- *Sharpening Tips*   319
- *The Sharpening Tool vs. the Blur Tool*   319

Filters That Remove Dust, Scratches, and Noise   319
- *The Despeckle Filter*   320
- *The Dust & Scratches and Median Filters*   321
- *The Reduce Noise Filter*   321

Blemish-Removing Tools   322
- *The Spot Healing Brush Tool*   323
- *The Healing Brush Tool*   324
- *The Patch Tool*   324
- *The Red Eye Tool*   325
- *The Clone Stamp Tool*   326

The Vanishing Point Filter 328
    Creating and Adjusting Planes 329
    The Vanishing Point Filter's Marquee Tool 330
    The Vanishing Point Filter's Stamp Tool 332
    The Vanishing Point Filter's Brush Tool 332
    Other Tips for Working with the Vanishing Point Filter 333
GRAPHIC DESIGN: Using a Grid 334
Summary 335
CHAPTER TUTORIALS 336
Review Questions 353

Chapter 9—Introduction to Color Correction 355

Introduction 355
    Before You Read On… 356
The Variations Command 357
    Adjusting Shadows, Highlights, and Midtones 358
    Adjusting Saturation 359
The Brightness/Contrast Command 360
The Hue and Saturation Command 361
    Adding a Tint to an Image 362
The Replace Color Command 364
The Color Replacement Tool 364
The Sponge Tool 366
The Dodge Tool and The Burn Tool 366
The Shadow/Highlights Command 367
Blending Modes 369
One-Step Color Correction Tools 370
    The Auto Color Command 370
    The Auto Contrast Command 370
    The Auto Levels Command 370
    The Desaturate Command 370
    The Invert Command 370
    The Equalize Command 370
Other Easy-to-Use Color Correction Tools 371
    The Photo Filter Command 372
    The Gradient Map Command 373
    The Posterize Command 373
    The Match Color Command 374
    The Color Balance Command 376
    The Selective Color Command 376
Adjustment Layers 377
GRAPHIC DESIGN: Color and Mood 379
Summary 381
CHAPTER TUTORIALS 382
Review Questions 392

Chapter 10—Advanced Color Correction Techniques   395

Introduction   395
Different Shades of Color   396
    Red, Green, and Blue Light (RGB Color)   396
    Cyan, Magenta, Yellow, and Black (CMYK Color)   397
    Color Modes   398
Identifying and Matching Color in Photoshop   399
    How Photoshop Measures Color   399
    Non-Web-Safe and Out-of-Gamut Colors   403
Channels   404
    The Channels Palette   404
    The Channel Mixer   408
The Histogram Palette   410
    The Histogram Palette Menu   410
    Viewing Color Adjustments in the Histogram Palette   412
The Threshold Command   413
The Levels Command   414
The Curves Command   416
    Adjusting Color in the Curves Dialog Box   417
Color-Related Palettes   418
    The Info Palette   418
    The Color Palette   420
    The Swatches Palette   421
Recommended Sequence for Color Correction   422
Color Management   422
GRAPHIC DESIGN: Color Harmony and Contrast   423
Summary   425
CHAPTER TUTORIALS   426
Review Questions   433

Chapter 11—Additional Layer Techniques   435

Introduction   435
Blending Modes   435
    Using Blending Modes with Layers   436
    Using Blending Modes with Filters and Color Adjustment Tools   437
Layer Masks   437
    Displaying Layer Masks   438
    Linking Layer Masks and Layers   440
    The Layer Mask Shortcut Menu   440
    The Layer > Layer Mask Submenu   440
    Adjusting Layer Masks with Filters   442
    Creating Layer Masks with the Paste Into Command   442
Vector Masks   442
    Creating a Vector Mask   443
    Converting a Path into a Vector Mask   443
    Setting the Areas to Display and Hide   444
    Converting a Selection into a Vector Mask   444
    Working with Vector Masks   444

Clipping Masks   445
    Controlling the Visible and Hidden Areas of a Clipping Mask   447
    Releasing Clipping Masks   447
Using Blending Options to Hide Portions of a Layer   447
    General Blending   447
    Creating a Knockout   447
    Using Layer Style Blending Options to Mask a Layer   450
Deleting the Masked Area of a Layer   452
Layer Comps   452
    The Limitations of Layer Comps   452
    Creating a New Layer Comp   452
    Editing Layer Comps   454
    Presenting Layer Comps   455
Aligning and Distributing Layers   456
    The Align Commands   456
    The Distribute Commands   457
    The Align and Distribute Buttons on the Options Bar   459
Artwork Created in Other Applications and Smart Objects   459
GRAPHIC DESIGN: The Prepress Process—Preparing Documents for Print   460
Summary   463
CHAPTER TUTORIALS   464
Review Questions   471

Chapter 12—File Management and Automated Tasks   473

Introduction   473
File Formats   473
    JPEG Images and Compression   474
    Common File Formats   475
    Camera RAW   476
Scripts and Actions   477
    Using Scripts   477
    Recording and Using Actions   478
    The Automate Menu   480
Organizing Files with Bridge   486
    Viewing Options   486
    Metadata   487
    Sorting   487
    Rotating Images without Opening Them   487
Audio Annotation and Notes   487
GRAPHIC DESIGN: FAQ—Graphic Design Careers   489
Summary   493
Review Questions   494

Glossary   495

Index   503

1
The Work Area

Learning Objectives

After completing this chapter, you will be able to:
- Identify different features of Photoshop's work area, including menus, tools, tool options, and palettes.
- Modify Photoshop's work area using a variety of methods.
- Reset Photoshop's work area.
- Change and reset the foreground and background colors.

Introduction

Photoshop has a vast number of tools and commands, and there just is not enough room to display all of them on a single computer screen. Many tools and options are hidden from view until you need them. This chapter will acquaint you with Photoshop's work area—the tools, menus, and windows you see when you first open the program. You will find there are many different ways to arrange the work area to fit your work style.

The Default Work Area

If you open Photoshop just after it has been installed, you will see the *default* work area, **Figure 1-1**. Default means "how a computer program looks before any settings are changed."

> **Note**
>
> If your work area does not look like this example, it is recommended that you restore Photoshop's default settings before working through this book. This procedure is explained in a tutorial at the end of this chapter.

Figure 1-1.
If you have not changed any of Photoshop's default settings, the work area looks like this.

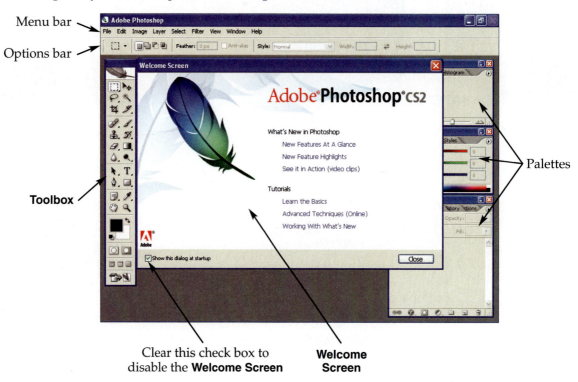

The Welcome Screen

The **Welcome Screen**, shown in Figure 1-1, contains links to several tutorials and information about Photoshop CS2. You can disable this window by clearing the **Show this dialog at startup** check box and picking the **Close** button.

The Toolbox

The **Toolbox** (also called the **Tools** palette) contains most of Photoshop's tools. Some of the tool buttons have a small arrow in the lower right corner. This arrow tells you that additional tools will appear if you click and hold the mouse button on the tool button. For example, when you click and hold the mouse button on the **Brush Tool** button, the **Pencil Tool** and **Color Replacement Tool** appear, no longer hidden from view, **Figure 1-2**. These tools will remain visible on the **Toolbox** until you click the mouse button. You can drag the **Toolbox** to any location on your screen by clicking the title bar area (at the top of the **Toolbox**) and dragging it to a new location.

Foreground and Background Colors

While working in Photoshop, you should be aware of two colored boxes about a quarter of the way up from the bottom of the **Toolbox**, **Figure 1-3**. These two boxes show what colors are currently selected for the foreground and background colors. The *foreground color,* the top color box, is used by Photoshop's painting and drawing tools. The *background color* (the bottom color box) appears when you erase something.

Figure 1-2.
This is Photoshop's **Toolbox**. Some tools are hidden until they are chosen. For example, the **Pencil Tool** can be found "underneath" the **Brush Tool**.

Figure 1-3.
The **Foreground Color** and **Background Color** buttons are used to define the colors used by Photoshop.

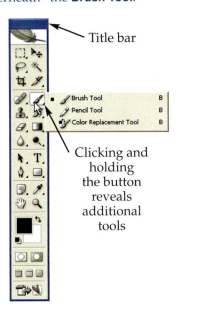

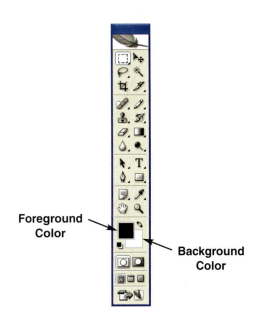

To change either the foreground color or the background color, click on the corresponding color box in the **Toolbox**. This opens the **Color Picker** dialog box, **Figure 1-4**. Next, click on the desired hue in the color slider. Then, click on the desired shade of color in the color field. Notice that a preview of the selected color appears in the **Color Picker** dialog box. Directly below the preview of the selected color is a sample of the original color so you can compare the two. You can adjust the hue by picking a new color in the color slider, and you can adjust the shade by picking a different point in the color field.

The other settings in the **Color Picker** dialog box will be discussed in a later chapter.

Figure 1-4.
The **Color Picker** provides an interface for defining a new color.

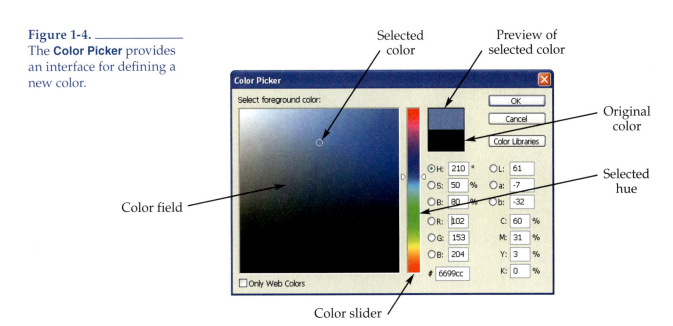

Resetting the Colors to Black and White

In Photoshop, "white" means "no color." When you print a Photoshop project, white areas are not printed. Instead, the white paper shows through. This is why Photoshop's default background color is white. You can think of your image's white background as the paper itself as you create your project.

Since black is often used for text and lines, Photoshop provides an easy way to reset the foreground color to black and the background color to white. You can easily do this by clicking the **Default Foreground and Background Colors** icon, **Figure 1-5**.

Switching Foreground and Background Colors

The other small icon next to the foreground and background color boxes is the **Switch Foreground and Background Colors** icon. This handy icon looks like a curved arrow and, when it is clicked, switches the colors used for the foreground and the background.

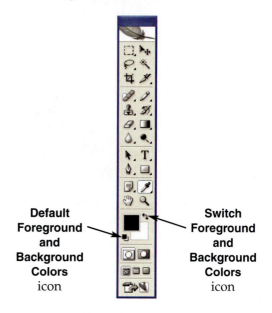

Figure 1-5.
Clicking the **Default Foreground and Background Colors** icon in the **Toolbox** resets the foreground color to black and the background color to white. These can be switched by clicking on the **Switch Foreground and Background Colors** icon.

Default Foreground and Background Colors icon

Switch Foreground and Background Colors icon

Screen Modes

There are three screen mode buttons on the **Toolbox** that change how your image fits on your screen. The **Standard Screen Mode** button (left button) activates the default setting, which you are already familiar with. Menus, the options bar, palettes, the **Toolbox**, and any images you have opened are all displayed on your screen.

The **Full Screen Mode with Menu Bar** button (middle button) sets the next mode. This mode creates a little more room for your image by hiding the image window title bars, **Figure 1-6**.

The last screen mode, set by picking the **Full Screen Mode** button (left button), hides the title bars *and* the menu bar. The menus are hidden, but can still be accessed by clicking the tiny arrow that appears at the top of the **Toolbox**. See **Figure 1-7**.

There is a quick way to hide everything except your open image. Press [Tab] to hide the **Toolbox**, the options bar, and all of the palettes. Press [Tab] again to turn everything back on.

> **Note** The three screen modes discussed in this section can also be chosen from the **View** menu.

Figure 1-6. Clicking the **Full Screen Mode with Menu Bar** button resizes your image so it fills the entire screen.

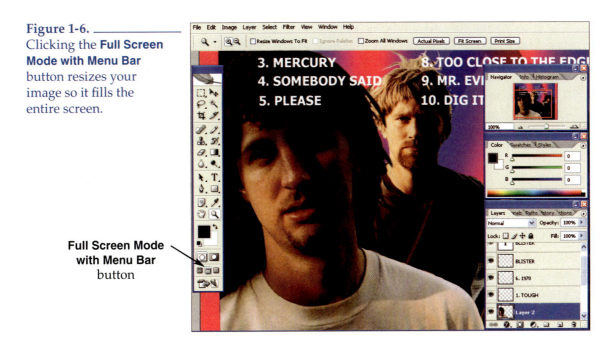

Full Screen Mode with Menu Bar button

Figure 1-7.
Clicking the **Full Screen Mode** button hides the menus, but puts a small menu shortcut button (look for the arrow) at the top of the **Toolbox**.

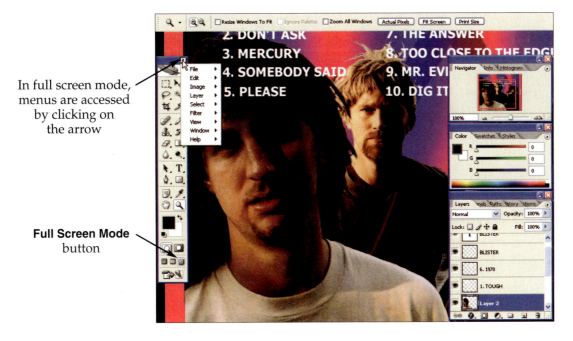

In full screen mode, menus are accessed by clicking on the arrow

Full Screen Mode button

What Is ImageReady?

ImageReady® is another software application that is included with Photoshop. It contains tools that allow web page designers to create complex web page layouts, animations for web pages, and other website-related graphics.

At the bottom of the Photoshop's **Toolbox** is a button called **Edit in ImageReady**, **Figure 1-8**. Clicking this button allows you to jump back and forth between Photoshop and ImageReady's tools while working on an image.

The focus of this book is on learning Photoshop, so ImageReady's tools and features will not be discussed. You should know, however, that you can use Photoshop to prepare and create images for web pages or e-mail. ImageReady allows you to create more complicated content for viewing on the Internet.

Figure 1-8.
Clicking the **Edit in ImageReady** button launches ImageReady and loads the current image file to that program.

The Options Bar

The *options bar* is located just below the menu bar. When you click on any tool in the **Toolbox**, the tool's options (or settings) appear here. If you hold the mouse for two seconds over any section of the options bar, a *tooltip* appears. A tooltip is a brief description of each option. See **Figure 1-9**.

At the far left side of the options bar, the current tool's *icon* appears. An icon is a picture or symbol that represents the selected tool. If you right-click on the tool icon, you can reset the tool to its default settings by selecting **Reset Tool** from the pop-up menu. And, if you click the small arrow pointing downward (right next to the icon), the **Tool Preset** dialog box appears, **Figure 1-10**. As you grow comfortable with Photoshop and find that you are setting options the same way over and over, you can use the **Tool Preset** dialog box to save your favorite settings and quickly recall them any time.

When the **Create new tool preset** button is clicked, all of the settings in the options bar are saved, and you are asked to name the settings. Once the settings are saved, you can retrieve them at any time by clicking the small down arrow in the options bar and selecting the desired preset name in the **Tool Preset** dialog box.

Menus

As a general rule, *menus* are lists of commands that are related to each other. When you click on a menu, the list of commands appears, allowing you to select the desired command. For example, the **View** menu contains commands that help you *see* things by displaying a grid, or by displaying a ruler around the border of your image, or by causing your image to fill the entire screen so you can see it better. Photoshop's menus are located at the top of the work area in an area called the *menu bar*.

Some entries in a menu will have an arrow to their right. This arrow tells you that entry is not a command, but a subcategory that contains a cascading submenu. When you position the cursor over an entry that contains a cascading menu, a submenu appears listing all of the commands available in that subcategory, **Figure 1-11**.

Figure 1-9.
In this example, the **Horizontal Type Tool** (text tool) has been clicked in the **Toolbox**. The options bar shows the settings for this tool, including font style, font size, justification, etc.

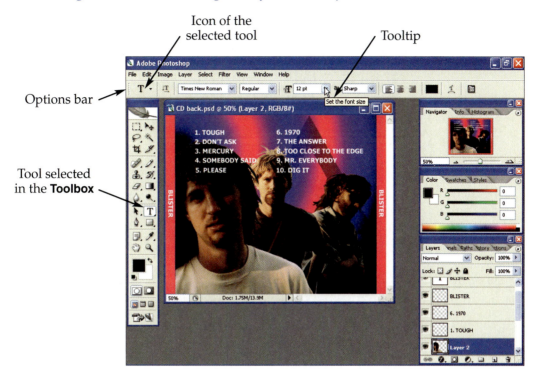

Figure 1-10.
When the **Create New Tool Preset** button is clicked, all of the settings in the options bar are saved, and you are asked to name the settings. You can retrieve your saved settings at any time by clicking the small down arrow in the options bar and selecting the desired preset.

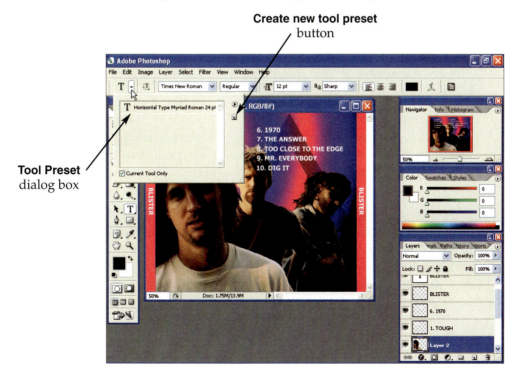

Figure 1-11.
The **View** menu is shown here with **Show** cascading submenu. If a keyboard shortcut is available for a menu command, it appears at the right side of the menu.

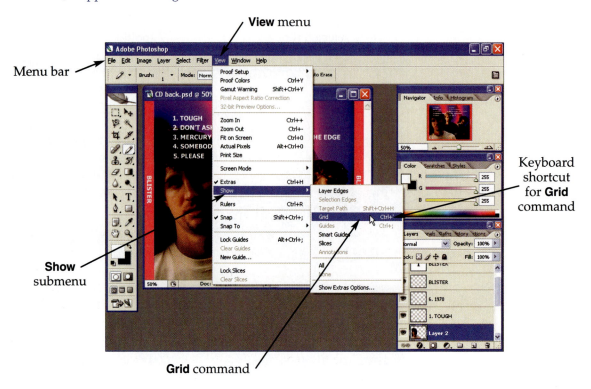

Keyboard Shortcuts

Many commands found on the menus can also be executed by pressing a combination of keys, known as keyboard shortcuts. In Figure 1-11, the menu command **View > Show > Grid** is being chosen. The keyboard shortcut **Ctrl+'** appears to the right of the **Grid** command. This means that instead of using the menu, you can turn the grid on and off by pressing the control key and the apostrophe key at the same time, [Ctrl][']. If you are working on a project and need to show and hide the grid again and again, using this keyboard shortcut will save you a lot of time.

> **Note**
> In this text, menu selections are indicated by the menu title, subcategory (if applicable), and command separated by greater-than signs. In the example of **View > Show > Grid**, you would select the **View** in the menu bar, then the **Show** subcategory in the menu, and finally the **Grid** command from the cascading submenu.

Photoshop offers many other time-saving keyboard shortcuts that are *not* listed in the menus. You will become familiar with many of these shortcuts as you progress through this book. Users that are more advanced at Photoshop can customize menus and keyboard shortcuts to fit their particular work style. This can be done by selecting **Edit > Keyboard Shortcuts** or by choosing **Edit > Menus** and then picking the **Keyboard Shortcuts** tab.

Note In this text, keyboard keys are identified by the character or function of the key enclosed in brackets. For example, [Ctrl] indicates the control key, [Shift] indicates the shift key, [P] indicates the P key. If a combination of keys appear side by side, such as [Ctrl][Shift][P], it indicates that all of the corresponding keyboard keys should be pressed at the same time.

Palettes

Imagine an artist working on a painting. He holds a brush in one hand and a palette in the other. He uses a *palette* to hold and mix gobs of paint as he creates his artwork. Photoshop's palettes serve a similar purpose. They are small windows that contain a variety of settings. Many Photoshop users do not have large computer monitors, and palettes can easily take up too much precious space.

Arranging Palettes

There are several ways to arrange palettes on your screen. To keep your workspace from being cluttered, you can hide the ones you do not use very often. The name of each palette appears on a *tab*, just like a tab on a folder in a filing cabinet. See **Figure 1-12**.

- The **Window** menu shows a list of all of the palettes. Each palette can be turned on or off using the **Window** menu. If a check mark is next to a palette's name, it is displaying somewhere on your screen. The **Window** menu even includes the **Toolbox** and the options bar as items that can be turned on or off.
- Palettes can be moved to another location by clicking and dragging their tab.
- Palettes can be *zipped shut* and restored by double-clicking on their tab. When a palette or group of palettes is zipped shut, its window is minimized and only the palette tab(s) are visible.

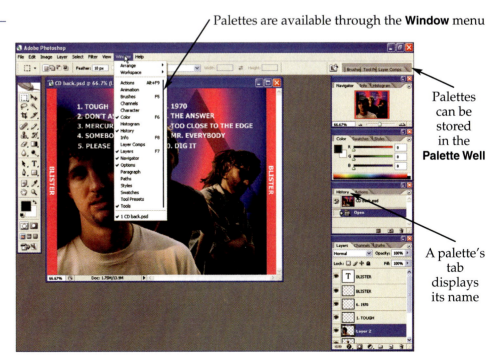

Figure 1-12. The **Window** menu can be used to hide or display palettes. In this example, three palettes are visible in the **Palette Well**. Each palette has a tab that displays its name.

- A palette can be *stretched* taller by dragging its bottom-right corner to resize its window.
- A palette can be *stacked* with another palette by dragging its tab just to the right of the other palette's tab. A palette can be *separated* from a stack by dragging its tab clear of the other palettes' window.
- Palettes can be dragged to the **Palette Well**, a storage area that shows only the palettes' tabs. When you click on a palette's tab, the entire palette temporarily displays until you click somewhere else on your screen.

> **Note** The **Palette Well** is only available when screen resolutions are set to 1024×768 or higher.

Saving the Workspace Arrangement

You can arrange palettes as desired and save their location by choosing **Window > Workspace > Save Workspace**. You will be asked to name your workspace configuration. You can recall it later by returning to the **Window** menu and selecting the desired workspace name in the bottom section of the menu. At any time, you can choose **Window > Workspace > Default Workspace** to restore everything to its default location.

Working with Multiple Image Windows

You have learned that the **Window** menu can be used to show and hide palettes and reset Photoshop's workspace. If you have more than one image file open in Photoshop, you can also use the **Window** menu to quickly arrange your images. The following is a detailed discussion of some of the commands found in the **Window** menu.

The **Cascade**, **Tile Horizontally**, and **Tile Vertically** commands in the **Arrange** subcategory of the **Window** menu provide different ways to neatly arrange multiple images that you have opened. The **Cascade** command stacks the images on top of each other, in such a way that each image's title bar is easily seen, **Figure 1-13A**. Choosing the **Tile Horizontally** command resizes the image windows so they all fit on the screen to provide the maximum horizontal working space with minimum overlap, **Figure 1-13B**. The **Tile Vertically** command resizes the image windows so they all fit on the screen to provide the maximum vertical working space with minimum overlap, **Figure 1-13C**.

Choosing **Window > Arrange > New Window** opens a second copy of an image that is already open and selected. From time to time, you may find it useful to have your image display at actual size on one side of your screen, while working in a close-up view of the same image on the other side of your screen. The changes you make in one image appear in the other image.

At the bottom of the **Window** menu, you will find a list of all the images that are currently open, **Figure 1-14**. If several images are open, they will likely be in a big pile on your screen. Selecting the file you want from the **Window** menu causes that image to jump to the top of the stack.

Using the Help Menu

The **Help** menu contains a vast amount of information about Photoshop. However, some Photoshop users find the writing style to be quite technical and not at a beginning level. That is why textbooks such as this one are written—to explain Photoshop in simpler terms.

Figure 1-13.
Six image files have been opened at the same time. **A**—Choosing **Window > Arrange > Cascade** stacks them neatly. Each image's title bar is partially visible. **B**—The same six image files are rearranged by choosing **Window > Arrange > Tile Horizontally**. Note that the image windows have more working space horizontally than they do vertically. **C**—The same image files are rearranged by choosing **Window > Arrange > Tile Vertically**. Note that with this option, the image windows provide more vertical working space than horizontal working space.

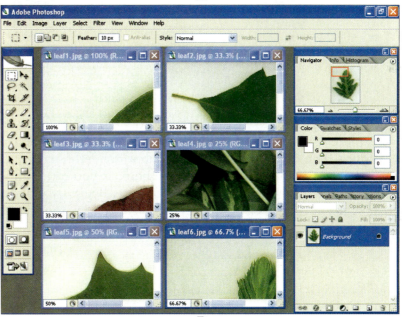

A

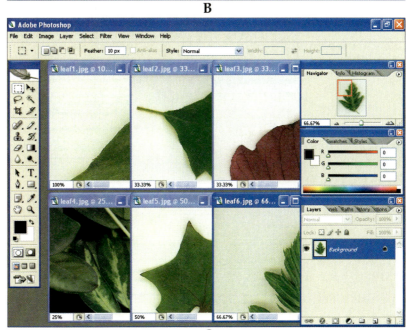

B

C

Figure 1-14.
If the work area is cluttered with images, you can use the **Window** menu to choose the image file you want to work on.

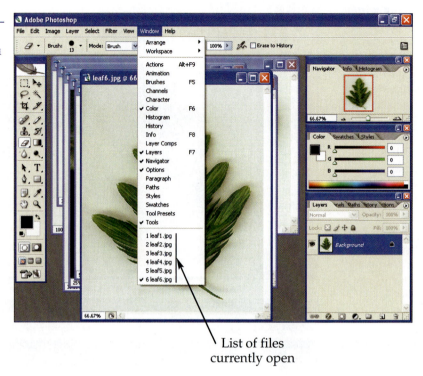

List of files currently open

If you would like further clarification on a Photoshop tool or topic, or would like to explore any feature not covered by this book, choose **Help > Photoshop Help...**. In the **Adobe Help Center**, pick the **Index** tab in the left-hand window. You can use the index just as you would use an index in a book. If you cannot find what you are looking for in the index, try using the search feature. Begin by entering keywords in the **Search** text box at the upper right of the dialog box. Pick the **Search** button to search the **Help** database for the specified words. See **Figure 1-15**.

Figure 1-15.
You can locate information in the **Adobe Help Center** dialog box by looking through the index or by keyword search.

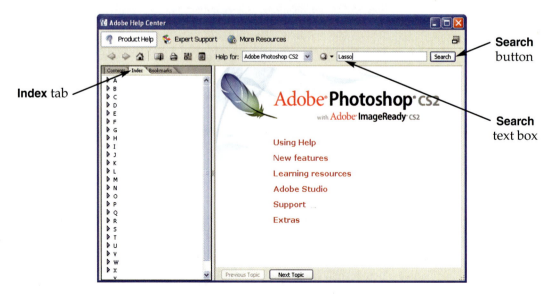

Using the Undo and Step Backward Commands

As you continue through this book, you will try out your skills as you complete the tutorials that follow each chapter. Any time you make a mistake while using Photoshop, be aware that you can always undo it by choosing **Edit > Undo** or pressing [Ctrl][Z] (or [Command] [Z] for Mac users). If you want to undo more than one mistake, choose **Edit > Step Backward** or press [Ctrl][Alt][Z] (or [Command][Option][Z] for Mac users). The **Step Backward** command can erase up to twenty actions by default. If your computer has plenty of RAM, you can raise this to a higher number by selecting **Edit > Preferences > General…**. When the **Preferences** dialog box opens, change the value in the **History States:** textbox and pick the **OK** button.

GRAPHIC DESIGN:
An Introduction

A *graphic designer* arranges images, illustrations, and text to effectively and creatively communicate some kind of message, **Figure 1-16**. Graphic designers work in many different industries and design projects that will be presented in many different formats. They create advertisements that appear in magazines and newspapers. They also create web pages and animations, brochures, posters, logos, signs, product packaging, in-store displays, greeting cards, and much more.

As you progress through this textbook, you will be introduced to several graphic design techniques that can help your designs become more visually interesting. You will encounter strategies for using color effectively, guidelines for arranging design elements in attractive ways, and tips for using text effectively in a design.

Figure 1-16. _____
Graphic designers often use two computer displays, allowing them to easily switch between computer applications.

There is never one correct way to create a design, and there are occasions where designers do not follow recommended techniques. The fundamental rule of graphic design is this: if the design is interesting and pleasing to the eye and the reader can glean the intended message with little or no effort, a good design has been created.

The first step a graphic designer must take before beginning any design is to *understand clearly what the design needs to communicate*. Most designers work for **clients** (businesses or individuals that hire outside services). It is important to communicate with the client throughout the design process. Often, clients do not know exactly what they want at the beginning of a project. However, at your first meeting, you should try to get as clear of a picture as possible of what they envision. Then, effective communication (such as sending proofs or samples of your work via e-mail, etc.) throughout the design process saves time-consuming and costly do-overs later.

A graphic designer must *become familiar with various professional printing techniques*. Photoshop has tremendous power and flexibility when it comes to preparing images for printing presses. You will learn some fundamentals about the printing industry as you progress through this textbook. Thankfully, you do not have to know everything about the professional printing industry to be a successful graphic designer. Professional printers at the printing service center with whom you do business will be happy to answer your questions—after all, you will be bringing them business!

Summary

You are now familiar with Photoshop's workspace, and you have learned several ways to arrange palettes and image windows on your screen. The more you use Photoshop, the more you will want to control the workspace environment to make your work style as efficient as possible.

CHAPTER TUTORIALS

In the tutorials that follow, you will learn how to reset Photoshop to its default settings. You will try out some of the commands discussed in this chapter. You will also be introduced to the **Navigator** palette.

Tutorial 1-1: Resetting Photoshop's Default Preferences

Photoshop CS2 Icon

In this tutorial, you will restore Photoshop's tools and palettes to their default condition.

1. To reset Photoshop's default preferences, hold down three keys on your keyboard just after double-clicking on the Photoshop CS2 icon on the desktop to launch the program:

    - **For Windows users, hold down** [Ctrl][Alt][Shift].
    - **For Mac users, hold down** [Command][Option][Shift].

2. In the **Delete the Adobe Photoshop Settings File** dialog box, click **Yes**.
3. If another message appears, asking if you want to set up your monitor, click **No**.
4. If the **Welcome Screen** appears, you can prevent it from appearing again by clearing the **Show this dialog at startup** check box. Then, click the **Close** button on the **Welcome Screen**. See **Figure T1-1**.

    Photoshop CS2 should now be open and using default settings.

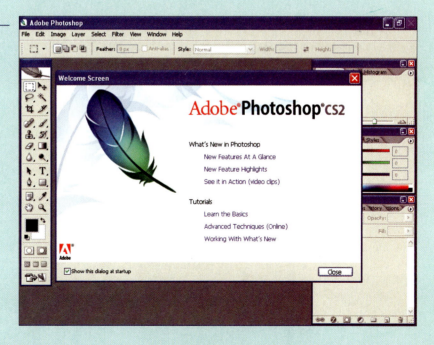

Figure T1-1. The **Welcome Screen** appears when Photoshop is first launched.

Tutorial 1-2: The Work Area

In this tutorial, you will become familiar with Photoshop's work area. You will use the **Navigator** palette to move around in the open image. You will also practice arranging multiple image windows.

1. Locate the folder named leaves on your hard drive. This folder should have been copied to your hard drive from the Student CD accompanying this book. Open all six leaf files in this folder.
2. If the red leaf (leaf3.jpg) is not on top of the other images, select **Window > leaf3.jpg**.
3. Click the **Navigator** palette tab and drag it to the location shown, **Figure T1-2**.
4. In the **Navigator** palette, click the **Zoom In** button.

Zoom In

Zoom Out

The Zoom In button is on the right end of the Zoom slider and looks like two large mountains. The Zoom Out button is on the left side of the Zoom slider and looks like two smaller mountains.

5. Click the **Zoom In** button two more times. See **Figure T1-3**.
6. Position the cursor over the red box in the **Navigator** palette and click and hold the mouse button. Drag the red box around the image. Moving the red box allows you to scroll around your image. When you have positioned the red box where you want it, release the mouse button.
7. A small box that shows the zoom percentage can be found in the lower left corner of the **Navigator** palette. Change the value in the zoom percentage text box to 25% and press [Enter]. This is another way to quickly zoom in and out.
8. Enter 300% in the zoom percentage text box to magnify the image again.

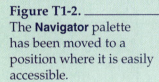
Hand Tool

9. Choose the **Hand Tool** in the **Toolbox** (or press the [Spacebar] to temporarily use the **Hand Tool**).
10. Choose **Window > Arrange > Tile Horizontally**.
11. Close all of the leaf files except for leaf3.jpg.

Figure T1-2.
The **Navigator** palette has been moved to a position where it is easily accessible.

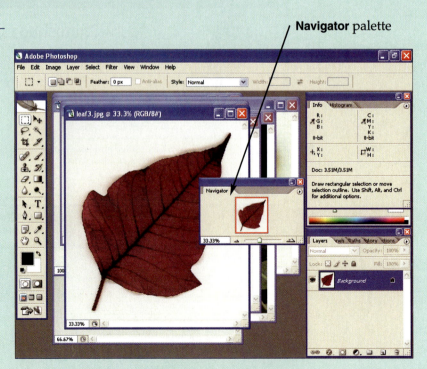

Figure T1-3.
The **Zoom In** button is on the right side of the **Zoom Slider**.

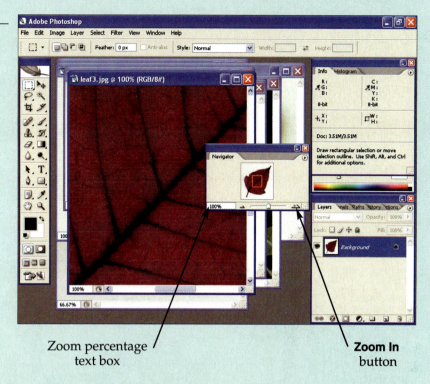

Zoom percentage text box

Zoom In button

12. Choose **Window > Arrange > New Window for leaf3.jpg**.
13. Choose **Window > Arrange > Tile Horizontally**.
14. Using the **Hand Tool**, adjust the view of the magnified (300%) leaf until it looks like the example in **Figure T1-4**.
15. Click the **Brush Tool** in the **Toolbox**.
16. Click the **Foreground Color** button and change the color. Choose a color other than black or white.

Brush Tool

Figure T1-4.
Use the **Hand Tool** to reposition the image in the window.

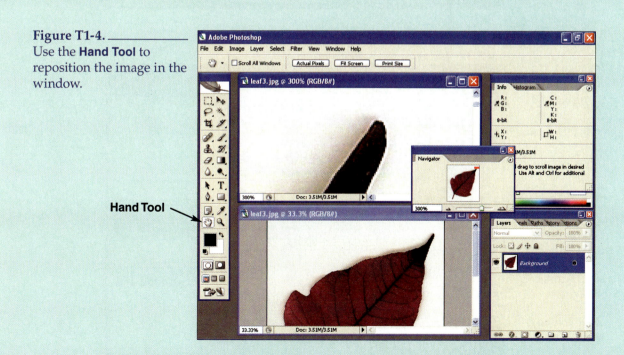

Hand Tool

30   Learning Photoshop

17. Paint a few lines in the 300% magnified view of the leaf. Notice that both image windows display your work, **Figure T1-5**.
18. Choose **Edit > Undo**. This command erases the last line of paint you created.
19. To erase the rest of the paint, choose **Edit > Step Backward**. Notice a keyboard shortcut for this command is shown at the right side of the menu. Continue stepping backward until all the paint is gone.
20. Close the new window that you created (the window that is *not* magnified at 300%).
21. Click the **Full Screen Mode** button.

Full Screen Mode

22. Press the [Spacebar] to temporarily activate the **Hand Tool**. Scroll (adjust the view) until your image looks like the example in **Figure T1-6**.

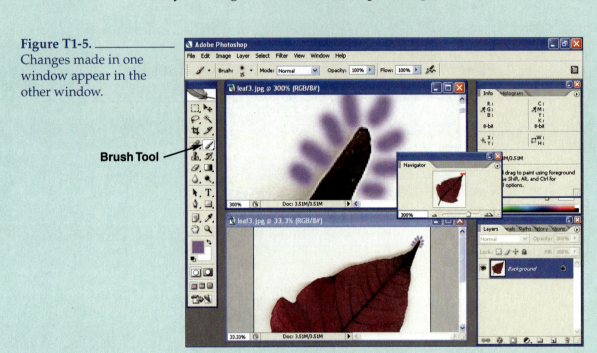

Figure T1-5. Changes made in one window appear in the other window.

Brush Tool

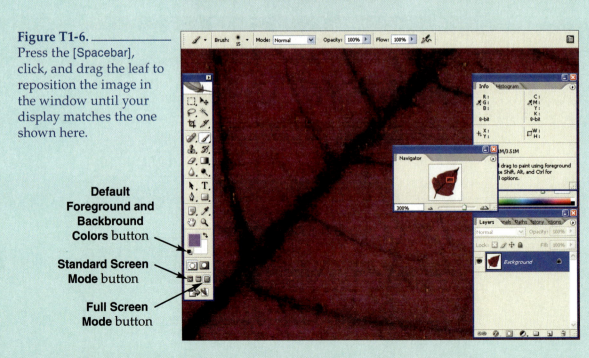

Figure T1-6. Press the [Spacebar], click, and drag the leaf to reposition the image in the window until your display matches the one shown here.

Default Foreground and Backbround Colors button

Standard Screen Mode button

Full Screen Mode button

Standard Screen Mode

23. Click the **Standard Screen Mode** button.
24. Click the **Default Foreground and Background Colors** button to change the colors back to black and white.
25. Choose **Window > Workspace > Reset Palette Locations**.
26. Most of the tutorials in this book will ask you to save your changes. This tutorial, however, is an exception. Close the leaf3.jpg file without saving changes.

Key Terms

background color
clients
default
foreground color
graphic designer
icon

menu bar
menus
options bar
palette
separated

stacked
stretched
tab
tooltip
zipped shut

Review Questions

Answer the following questions on a separate piece of paper.

1. What does the term "default" mean?
2. Some of the tool buttons found on Photoshop's **Toolbox** have a small arrow in their lower right corner. What does that arrow tell you?
3. When you click the **View** menu (as shown in Figure 1-11), how many of the entries have additional cascading submenus available?
4. How do you reset a tool back to its default settings?
5. What button do you need to click before you can see the **Create New Tool Preset** button?
6. When does Photoshop's background color appear?
7. How do you reset Photoshop's foreground and background colors to black and white?
8. What menu shows a list of all of Photoshop's palettes?
9. How can you zip a palette shut and unzip it again?
10. What is the difference between choosing **Window > Arrange > Tile Horizontally** and **Window > Arrange > Cascade**?
11. What happens if you choose **Window > Arrange > New Window**?
12. How do you reset Photoshop's palettes to their default locations?
13. If several image files are open in Photoshop, how can you bring a particular image to the "top of the pile?"
14. How can you hide all of Photoshop's tools, palettes, and the options bar?
15. What happens if you click on the **Edit in Image Ready** button at the bottom of the **Toolbox**?

Learning Photoshop

The various tools available in the **Toolbox** flyouts are shown here.

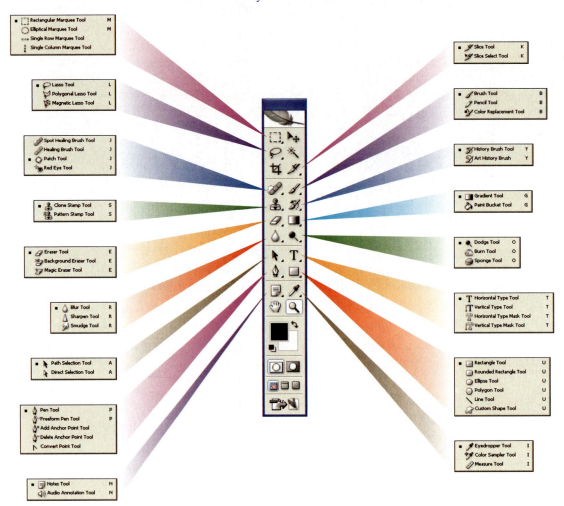

2 Resolution

Learning Objectives

After completing this chapter, you will be able to:
- Explain the relationship between pixels and resolution.
- Use the **Zoom Tool** and **Hand Tool** to magnify and scroll around an image.
- Resize images using multiple methods.
- Differentiate between image resolution and printing resolution.
- Describe how to use a scanner to capture an image at a desired resolution.
- Describe how to use a digital camera to capture an image at a desired resolution.

Introduction

When you work with images in Photoshop, they will have different *resolutions*, or quality levels. Resolution is a complicated topic, and many Photoshop users struggle to understand it. An average person may need to read this chapter more than once before feeling knowledgeable about resolution.

Will the Image Be Printed or Displayed on a Computer Screen?

Many people use Photoshop to create images that will be *printed*. But some images are meant to only be *displayed on a computer screen*, such as an image on a web page or a multimedia project that plays from a CD ROM.

If you look closely at a computer monitor when it is turned on, you will notice that the screen is made of thousands of tiny, colored, glowing dots, Figure 2-1. Because your eye can see these tiny dots, computer screens are considered to have a low-quality resolution. Therefore, images created for onscreen use are created as low-resolution images in Photoshop, because that is the only quality level that a computer screen can display.

Creating images that will be printed is a more difficult challenge. The printing industry is amazingly complex. There are many different kinds of commercial-grade printers and printing presses. Furthermore, different projects are printed at different resolutions. For example, a newspaper ad is printed at a lower resolution than a typical magazine. Full-color books and brochures are printed at higher resolutions.

Figure 2-1.
A—A monitor displays an image by illuminating tiny groups of red, green, and blue dots. B—A digital image is made up of tiny blocks of color called pixels.

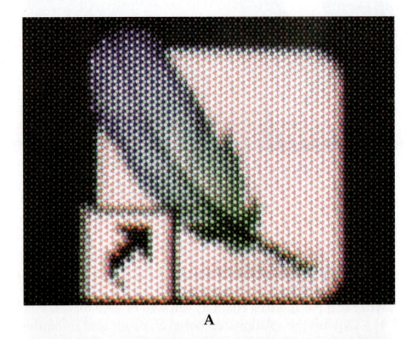

A

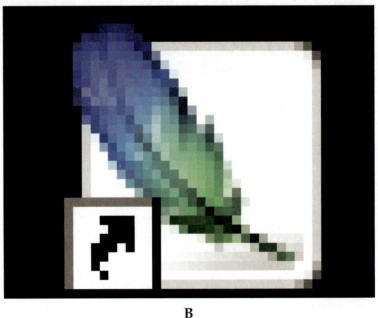

B

To use Photoshop effectively, you will need to know how to set and adjust, if necessary, the resolution of your images. If you plan on creating a lot of work that will be professionally printed, you will also need to regularly communicate with your printing company. They will help you understand what resolution settings you should use when preparing your images for a particular project.

Image Capture Devices

Which of the following statements is most accurate?
"I took some pictures."
"I shot a roll of film."
"I captured a few images."

All three statements describe the act of creating photographs with a camera. But if you use a ***digital camera***, the *last* statement is technically correct. A digital camera can also be called an ***image capture device***. The term *capture* means "to cause data to be stored in computer memory." Instead of storing the image on film, digital cameras convert an image to a ***digital*** format (a format that a computer can recognize). Then, the digital data is stored in some kind of computer memory, such as a compact flash card, **Figure 2-2**.

A *scanner* is another image capture device. A scanner is a digital copy machine: it shines a strong light on an image and analyzes the image with its sensors. A digital version of the image is created, which can be saved into computer memory, **Figure 2-3**.

Later in this chapter, you will learn more about using digital cameras and scanners, but first, you will learn what digital images are made of.

Figure 2-2. The Nikon D70 digital camera (front and rear views) and a compact flash memory card are shown here.

Figure 2-3. A flatbed scanner is used to capture printed images or photographs.

Pixels and Resolution

Any image that is captured by a digital camera or a scanner is made up of tiny, colored squares called *pixels*. The word "pixel" was created from two words: "picture" and "element". Computers have to keep track of what color each pixel is and where it belongs in the image. There can be *millions* of pixels in an image, so file sizes can be very large.

If an image has a **high resolution**, its pixels are so small that the human eye cannot make out the individual pixels when the image is printed. On the other hand, **low-resolution** images look fine when displayed on a computer screen, but when printed, they appear a little rough and out of focus. This is because the pixels are large enough to be visible. If your eye can see pixels in an image, the image is ***pixilated***, Figure 2-4.

High-resolution images are used in professionally printed projects, such as books, magazines, and brochures. These files are often too large to attach to an e-mail, so professionals must either ship them to printing companies on CD, or use Internet FTP (file transfer protocol) accounts or other web upload services to transfer them.

If you are using Photoshop to create an image for a web page or to send to a friend over e-mail, you need to set the image's resolution to a lower setting. Low-resolution images display quickly on web pages and can be sent quickly over e-mail because of their small file size.

Figure 2-4.
As the zoom percentage increases, the difference between high-resolution and low-resolution images becomes more pronounced. **A**—This is a high-resolution image of an ostrich. **B**—When you zoom in on a high-resolution image, the image remains crisp. **C**—When a low-resolution image is zoomed the same percentage, the pixels become noticeably larger and the image loses some of its quality.

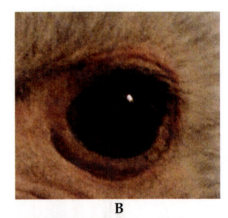
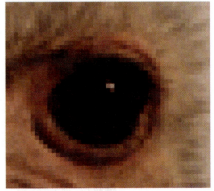

The Zoom Tool

The **Zoom Tool** is used to magnify an image so you can see it better. Each time you click on your image with the **Zoom Tool**, you can zoom in (make your image appear larger) or zoom out (make your image appear smaller). Zooming does not change the *actual size* (print size) of your image, it only changes *your view* of the image.

Zoom Percentage

When an image file is open in Photoshop, the title bar shows the *zoom percentage*, which can be between .01—1600%, **Figure 2-5**. A zoom percentage of 100% *is not the actual print size* of the image. Instead, it means that the pixels in your image are currently the same size as the tiny glowing dots on your computer screen. This is helpful information if you are creating images for the web, because at a zoom magnification of 100% the image appears the same size in Photoshop as it will appear on a website.

Print Size

If you are designing images for *print*, be aware that the zoom percentage has nothing to do with how large your image will be when printed. To see how large your image will be when printed, click the **Print Size** button on the **Zoom Tool**'s option bar, or choose **View > Print Size**. Your monitor settings may cause the print size setting to be a bit inaccurate, but it is usually close to actual size.

Zoom Tool Options

In the tutorial at the end of Chapter 1, you learned that the **Navigator** palette can be used to zoom in and out on an image. The **Zoom Tool** offers additional options. When you click on the **Zoom Tool** in the **Toolbox**, the options bar displays the available options, **Figure 2-6**.

Figure 2-5.
The zoom percentage always appears in the title bar of an open image.

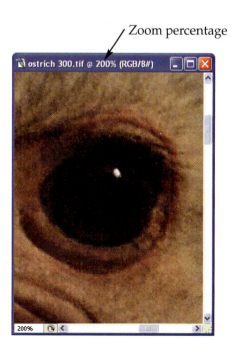

Figure 2-6.
This figure shows the options bar features that are displayed when the **Zoom Tool** is selected.

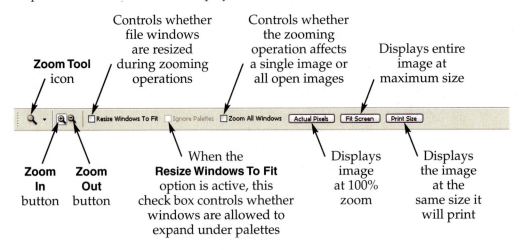

The Zoom In and Zoom Out Buttons

The **Zoom In** and **Zoom Out** buttons allow you to change the function of the **Zoom Tool**. When the **Zoom In** button is pressed, you will magnify your image every time you click on it. The **Zoom Out** button has the opposite effect.

Regardless of whether the **Zoom In** or **Zoom Out** button is selected, the location of the **Zoom Tool** cursor is the center point of the zooming operation. When you click the mouse button, the image is zoomed and repositioned in the window so that the cursor's location is as close as possible to the center of the window. If you click in the center of your image, the center area of your image will be zoomed. If you click in a corner, the corner area will be zoomed.

To quickly switch between zooming in and zooming out, you can press [Alt] instead of clicking the buttons on the options bar.

Resize Windows to Fit

When the **Resize Windows To Fit** check box is checked, the image window increases or decreases in size as the image is zoomed. The image window is resized with every zoom operation until the available space is filled up or the window has reached its minimum usable size.

If the **Resize Windows To Fit** check box is left unchecked, the image window will not change sizes as you zoom in and out. Leaving this setting off is recommended, especially if you have two or more image files open.

Ignore Palettes

The **Ignore Palettes** option only becomes available if the **Resize Windows To Fit** option has been turned on. If you are zooming in on your image, this option allows your image window to become larger by spreading it underneath any palettes on your screen.

Zoom All Windows

The **Zoom All Windows** option is available if you have two or more image files open. When this check box is checked, zooming in or out on one image causes the other images that are currently open to be affected the same way.

The Actual Pixels Button

Click the **Actual Pixels** button to view the image at 100% zoom. This is a quick way to "reset" your image if you have zoomed in very close. The phrase "actual pixels" means that the pixels in the image are the same size as the tiny glowing dots on the computer screen. Double-clicking the **Zoom Tool** in the **Toolbox** will also reset the zoom magnification to 100%.

The Fit Screen Button

Clicking the **Fit Screen** button quickly zooms your image so it appears onscreen at the maximum size possible, without any portion of the image being hidden within the window. The image window is also resized until it fills all the space available horizontally or vertically.

When the **Fit Screen** button is clicked, the image window is resized, regardless of whether the **Resize Windows to Fit** check box is checked or not. If the **Ignore Palettes** check box is checked, the images and windows are stretched to the very edge of the screen, and part of the image may be hidden under any palettes onscreen.

The Print Size Button

Click the **Print Size** button to see the actual size of your image. When you click on the **Print Size** button, the image appears onscreen at approximately the same size as it would if it were printed. For more information about print size, refer to the *Print Size* section presented earlier in this chapter.

Zooming In by Dragging a Box

Perhaps the easiest way to zoom in is to *drag a box* in your image with the **Zoom Tool**. To zoom in on an area of the image, begin by making sure the **Zoom In** button is selected on the options bar. Next, position the cursor at one corner of the area you want to zoom in on. Click and hold the mouse button and drag the cursor to the opposite corner of the area you want to zoom in on. Whatever you include in your box will be magnified. The zoom percentage will depend on the resolution of the image and the size of the box you create.

The Hand Tool

When you are zoomed in close to your image, or if your image is too large to fit in a window, *scroll bars* (sliders that allow you to reposition the image in the window) appear at the side and bottom of the image window, Figure 2-7. Say you wanted to stay zoomed in on the ostrich shown in Figure 2-7, but you wanted to see his beak instead of his eye. One way to adjust the view is to move the scroll bars on the image window. However, there is a faster way to do this. The **Hand Tool** lets you "grab" your image and move it around.

Photoshop provides a convenient keyboard shortcut for the **Hand Tool** because the tool is so frequently used. Hold down the [Spacebar] to temporarily activate the **Hand Tool**. When you release the [Spacebar], the tool you were previously using becomes active again.

Figure 2-7.
If the view of your image is larger than the image window, you can adjust the view with the **Hand Tool** (simplest method) or by dragging the scroll bars.

Hand Tool Options

Using the [Spacebar] shortcut for the hand tool is convenient if you want to make a quick adjustment. However, if you want to access the options available with the **Hand Tool**, you must select the tool from **Toolbox**. When the **Hand Tool** is clicked in the **Toolbox**, its options display in the options bar. See **Figure 2-8**.

The **Scroll All Windows** option is available if you have two or more image files open. If this check box is checked, as you adjust one image with the **Hand Tool**, the other images that are currently open are affected the same way.

The **Actual Pixels, Fit Screen,** and **Print Size** buttons are the same buttons found on the **Zoom Tool**'s options bar. The functions of these buttons were described in the **Zoom Tool** section of this chapter.

Image Resolution and Size

When you are working with digital images, resolution is measured by *pixels per inch (ppi)*. If you measure an image and count a single row of pixels along one inch, you know the image's resolution, or ppi. You will never need to use a ruler however, because Photoshop can tell you what the resolution is if you choose **Image > Image Size…**.

The standard resolution for images on websites is 72 ppi. If you printed one of these images and laid a ruler on top of it, you would count 72 pixels along one inch, **Figure 2-9**. In this example, Photoshop's built-in *rulers* were displayed by choosing **View > Rulers**. If desired, you can change the units of measurement on the ruler by choosing **Edit > Preferences > Units & Rulers…** (Windows) or **Photoshop > Preferences > Units & Rulers…** (Mac).

Figure 2-8.
Most of the **Hand Tool**'s options are also found on the **Zoom Tool**'s option bar.

Figure 2-9.
A—This is the original 72 ppi image. B—This is a close up view of the same image, showing 72 pixels between the 0″ and 1″ marks on the ruler, both horizontally and vertically.

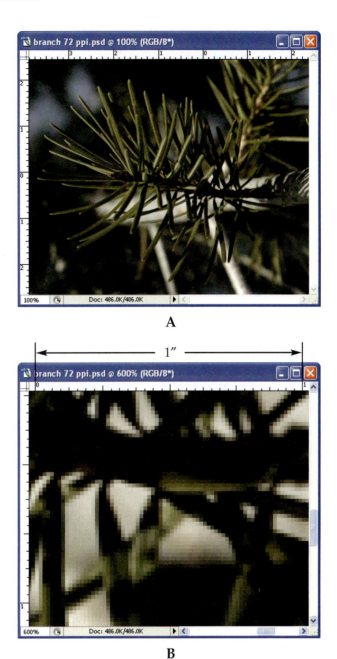

The Image Size Dialog Box

Choose **Image > Image Size...** to display the **Image Size** dialog box, Figure 2-10. These settings, if adjusted, will change the size and/or resolution of your image. There are several ways to do this. First, notice that the dialog box is divided into two sections, with three options at the bottom.

The **Pixel Dimensions:** section shows how many pixels wide and tall your image is. This is helpful information for web designers, because images that will be displayed on a computer screen are measured by pixels, not inches. You can change the value from pixels to percent if you are resizing the image (explained later). The current *file size* is also displayed at the top of the **Pixel Dimensions:** section.

Figure 2-10.
The **Image Size** dialog box shows the size and resolution of an image.

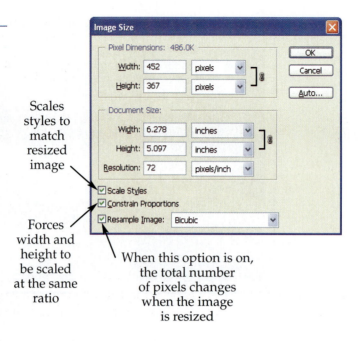

The **Document Size:** section shows the actual size of the image. Actual size refers to the size of the image when it is printed. You can view the size of your image in inches, centimeters, millimeters, and other units of measurement used by the printing industry. The resolution of the image is also listed here. You can display the resolution in pixels/inch or pixels/centimeter.

The **Constrain Proportions** option is usually left on. This option prevents you from "squishing" your picture when you resize it. When the **Constrain Proportions** check box is checked, a chain link appears to the right of the **Width:** and the **Height:** settings, reminding you that the two settings are locked together and Photoshop will force the image to stay in proportion. If you change the width of your image to smaller size, for example, Photoshop automatically changes the height for you.

The **Scale Styles** option is also left on most of the time. It is only available if the **Constrain Proportions** option is also on. Styles are special effects that you can add to an image, such as shadows or borders. When the **Scale Styles** check box is checked, any styles you have added are resized along with your image. Styles will be discussed in greater detail in a later chapter.

The final check box available in the **Image Size** dialog box is the **Resample Image:** check box. *Resampling* is the term for changing the total number of pixels in an image. For more information, see the *Resizing an Image (Resampling On)* section in this chapter.

The **Auto...** button, on the upper right side of the **Image Size** dialog box, is used as a calculator to determine certain resolution settings. For more information about how to use the **Auto...** button, refer to the *Printing Resolution* section in this chapter.

Resizing an Image (Resampling Off)

The **Image Size** dialog box can be used to resize, or change the actual size of, images. Resizing occurs when you enter new size values in either the **Document Size:** section or the **Pixel Dimensions:** section of the **Image Size** dialog box. Be sure to turn the resampling option off before changing any other settings. The following changes are made to an image when you resize it with the resampling option turned off. In both cases, the actual number of pixels making up the image remains constant:

- You can change the resolution of your image to a higher or lower quality. When you do this, the actual size of your image will become larger if you select a lower resolution, or smaller if you select a higher resolution.
- You can change the width and height of your image to a larger or smaller size. If you do this, the resolution of your image will increase if you make the image smaller and decrease if you make the image larger.

Resizing is especially necessary when you use a digital camera. Some digital cameras create images at one resolution: 72 ppi. What if you wanted a high-quality, 300 ppi image from your digital camera? First, you would adjust your digital camera so it captures a large image size. Then, after uploading the image to your computer, you would use Photoshop to change the resolution to 300 ppi. All of the pixels would become smaller, causing your entire image to shrink. Your much smaller image would become a high-quality, 300 ppi image, with pixels too small to be seen individually by the human eye. The trick is to start with a large-enough image size setting on your digital camera so you end up with your desired size after you change the resolution.

Resizing an Image (Resampling On)

The following changes are made to an image when you resize it with the resampling option turned on.

- You can change the resolution of your image to a higher or lower quality. When you do this, your image size will remain the same (unless you change it also).
- You can change the width and height of your image to a larger or smaller size. When you do this, the resolution of your image will remain the same (unless you change it also).

Another word for "resampling" is "recalculating." When you use this option, Photoshop adjusts the resolution or size of your image, but to do so, pixels need to be added or taken away from your image.

What will happen if you open a low-quality, 72 ppi image, turn on the resampling option, and change the resolution to 300 ppi? Photoshop *will not* change the size of the image when you enter 300 as the resolution. Instead, a large number of new, tiny pixels will be created. In other words, Photoshop must create the image again, using much smaller pixels than before. When this happens, images usually end up looking fuzzy, since Photoshop has to do some guessing. Sharpening the image (discussed in a later chapter) can help, but the resampled image will never look as good as the original. The bottom line is, *you cannot make a usable high-resolution image from a low-resolution image of the same size.*

Next to the **Resample Image:** check box is a drop-down list that contains several resampling methods. If you resample an image, leave this setting on **Bicubic**, which is the highest-quality resampling method.

> **Note** A word of caution, resampling usually weakens the quality of your image. If you want to change the resolution of an image to a higher quality, the best method is to capture your image at a large size, leave the resampling option off, and change the resolution to a higher quality. However, if you prepare images for the printing industry, you may need to occasionally resample images so they print at optimal resolution. In these situations, consult with your print service provider.

Printing Resolution

Up to this point in the chapter, you have been reading about image resolution. Printing resolution is a bit different. ***Printing resolution*** refers to the quality level that a printer is capable of producing. A printed image is made up of tiny dots of ink. These specks of ink can be round, but they can also be other shapes. Printer resolution is measured one of two ways, depending on the printer: dots per inch (dpi), or lines per inch (lpi).

There are many different kinds of printers. ***Inkjet printers*** create an image by spraying microscopic dots of ink on paper. If you have ever shopped for one of these printers, you probably noticed that the printer's maximum resolution is advertised. For example, some printers have a maximum resolution of 4800 x 2400 dpi. A printing resolution of 1200 x 1200 dpi is adequate to produce a high-quality print. Even though many printers can produce resolutions significantly higher than this, it can be argued whether image quality is significantly better when printing above a resolution of 1200 x 1200 dpi.

Some commercial printing presses also print rows of tiny dots, but the technology is different. These dots can be square, diamond-shaped, circular, and even cross-shaped. These small shapes are often printed at an angle. This is called *halftone* printing, and it is measured in lines per inch (lpi). Lpi is measured just like dpi or ppi, by counting how many dots are along one inch, **Figure 2-11**.

Resizing Images for Printing

Your goal should be to create Photoshop files that have an image resolution that is appropriate for the printing resolution. Newspapers are printed at resolutions of 85–100 lpi. Magazines and brochures are printed at roughly 133–170 dpi. So, what if you were using Photoshop to create a newspaper ad? Photoshop has a built-in calculator to help you convert lpi into ppi. Your first step should be to check with the company that will print the newspaper and ask them what resolution the image will be printed at.

Assume for a moment the answer to that question is 85 lpi. To convert this to pixels per inch, choose **Image > Image Size...**. Before continuing, you should know that you

Figure 2-11.
This is a magnified view of a grayscale (black, white, and shades of gray) halftone print, showing thousands of tiny diamond-shaped dots. This image has a resolution of 85 lpi.

will be changing the resolution of your image as you progress through these steps. To avoid changing the actual size of your image during this process, make sure the **Resample** check box is checked. Then, click the **Auto...** button. See Figure 2-12. In the **Auto Resolution** dialog box, enter 85 in the **Screen:** text box. Make sure that **lines/inch** is selected in the drop-down list and then choose a radio button in the **Quality** area of the dialog box. Again, check with your print provider in order to select the appropriate quality level. When you click the **OK** button the **Auto Resolution** dialog box closes, and Photoshop automatically enters the adjusted values in the **Width:**, **Height:**, and **Resolution:** text boxes in the **Image Size** dialog box. The **Auto Resolution** dialog box shows that for the best quality output at a print resolution of 85 lpi, the image should have a resolution of 170 ppi.

> **Note**
>
> As a general rule of thumb, an image intended for halftone printing should have a resolution of at least *twice* the resolution at which it will be printed. Lower resolutions will result in poorer print quality.

As a general rule, Photoshop documents with a resolution of 300 ppi are entirely capable of producing a print of the highest quality. For the nonprofessional, there is really no need to use resolutions higher than this to produce high-quality prints, because at 300 ppi, pixels are already microscopic in size. Some people are perfectly happy printing and even exhibiting work that has a resolution of 150 ppi. If you are printing your own Photoshop projects, experiment within these ranges and decide what your eye likes the best.

If you are preparing images for professional printing, you may need to use higher resolutions. You should consult with the printer for the exact image resolutions needed. Keep in mind that you can always reduce an image's resolution, but you cannot turn a low resolution image into a high resolution image and expect satisfactory results.

The Resize Image Wizard

Now that you have learned about resizing, resampling, and printing resolution, you should know that Photoshop has a built-in wizard that will resize and resample images for you! Choose **Help > Resize Image...** to display the **Resize Image Wizard**. The wizard asks you several questions about the way your image will be used, including what lpi the image will be printed at. A duplicate, resized copy of your image is made automatically for you, preserving your original image.

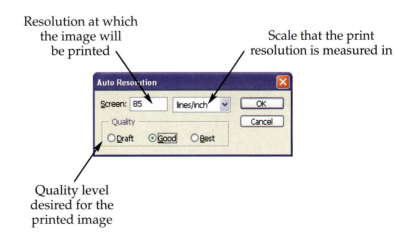

Figure 2-12. In the **Auto Resolution** dialog box, enter the resolution at which the image will be printed and the desired output quality and pick the **OK** button. Photoshop will automatically calculate the required settings.

Scanning Tips

When you prepare to scan an image, you can set the image resolution before you scan. This is the same image resolution that Photoshop recognizes—how many pixels are along one inch. The technical term for scanner resolution is *samples per inch (spi)*, but it is often called *dots per inch (dpi)* instead.

The image resolution setting is found in the software program that operates your scanner. Some consumer-level scanners will not ask you to enter a resolution setting. They will scan at the same resolution (often a medium quality, like 150 spi) unless you find the setting and change it.

Say you want to scan a 4×5 inch photo, but you need it to be larger when you add it into a Photoshop project you are working on. If you know the actual size and image resolution that you want to end up with, you can set your scanner resolution setting appropriately. Study the following table carefully, **Figure 2-13**. Use it as a guide when you scan images at other sizes and resolutions.

If your goal is to retouch or repair damaged photos (discussed in a later chapter), you should scan at a resolution of at least 300 spi. When repairing photos, you often need to zoom in on your image to repair tiny scratches, dust marks, and other problems. The higher the resolution, the smoother your repairs will look.

Figure 2-13.
This table explores the relationship between scan size and resolution and print size and resolution.

If the image you are scanning is this size…	…and you want the actual printed size of the image to be…	…and you want the image to have this resolution…	Printer you will use…	Set the scan resolution to…
4"×5" photo	4"×5"—same size as the original	300 ppi	Inkjet	300 spi/dpi
4"×5" photo	8"×10" (twice as big)	300 ppi	Inkjet	600 spi/dpi
35 mm slide	4 times bigger than the original	300 ppi	Inkjet	1200 spi/dpi
35 mm slide	4 times bigger than the original	150 ppi	Inkjet	600 spi/dpi
4"×5" photo	4"×5"—same size as the original	Good quality (for a halftone print)	Printing press with resolution set at 135 lpi	270 spi/dpi (multiply the lpi by 2 to find an adequate ppi setting), *or* use the **Auto…** button in the **Image Size** dialog box *or* the **Resize Image Wizard** to figure this out
4"×5" photo	8"×10" (twice as big)	Good quality (for a halftone print)	Printing press, 135 lpi	540 spi/dpi (multiply the lpi by 2 to find an adequate ppi setting), *or* use the **Auto…** button in the **Image Size** dialog box *or* the **Resize Image Wizard** to figure this out

Digital Camera Tips

When you use a digital camera, you will not find a resolution setting. Instead, your camera will give you several different *image sizes* (measured in pixels) to choose from. Some cameras (such as the Nikon D-70) capture all images at a resolution of 72 ppi, regardless of the image size setting you choose on the camera. After uploading the images to your computer, you can change the image resolution by resizing it in Photoshop. For example, the Nikon D70's image size settings are shown in the following table, Figure 2-14. The table also illustrates what the final print size of images will be when resized to 200 or 300 ppi. For additional information about this topic, refer to the *Resizing an Image (Resampling Off)* section of this chapter.

Digital cameras are rated in megapixels. The term *megapixel* refers to one million pixels. The largest image a Nikon D70 can capture is 3008 pixels wide and 2000 pixels high. Multiply those two numbers to find the total amount of pixels that this camera can produce in one photo—just over 6 million. The Nikon D70 is referred to as a 6 megapixel digital camera.

If you wanted to print 8"×10" images with a resolution of 300 ppi, you would need a camera with a higher megapixel rating. The table in Figure 2-14 reveals that the largest 300 ppi image you can produce, using the Nikon D70, is slightly smaller than 8"×10".

Images for E-mail, Websites, Multimedia

You have read that images that will be displayed on a computer screen are most often created with a resolution of 72 ppi. To adjust an image for display on a computer screen, you can manually resize the image to 72 ppi or use the **Resize Image Wizard**. However, Photoshop has a command called **Save for Web** that makes it easy to convert any image into a 72 ppi image and optimize it for use on the web.

The Save For Web Dialog Box

To use this feature, open the image you want to adjust. Then, choose **File > Save For Web...** to display the **Save For Web** dialog box, Figure 2-15. The **Save For Web** dialog box includes controls for displaying the original image and optimized variations of the image, adjusting image properties, and selecting a file format.

Figure 2-14.
This table lists the Nikon D70's image size settings. These settings vary from camera to camera.

Image size setting on Nikon D-70	If Photoshop is used to resize (change the resolution) from 72 to 200 ppi, the actual printed size will be approximately:	If Photoshop is used to resize the image from 72 to 300 ppi, the actual printed size will be approximately:
3008 x 2000 pixels (72 ppi)	15"×10"	10"×6.5"
2240 x 1488 pixels (72 ppi)	11"×7.5"	7.5"×5"
1504 x 1000 pixels (72 ppi)	7.5"×5"	5"×3.5"

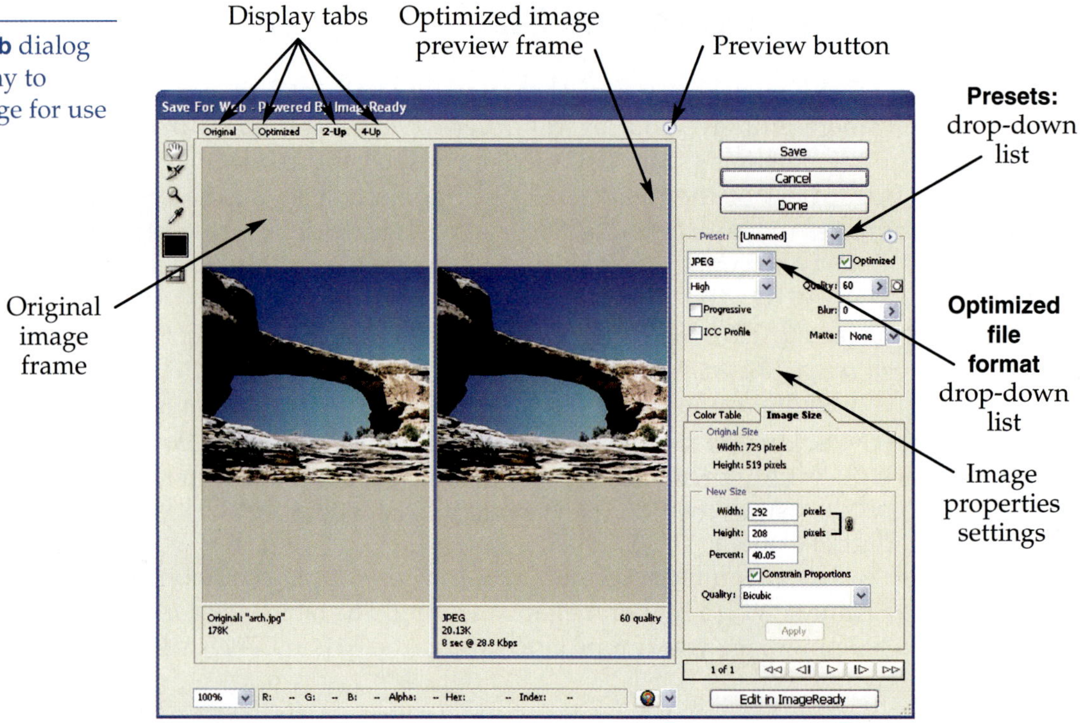

Figure 2-15.
The **Save For Web** dialog box is a quick way to optimize an image for use on a website.

The Display Tabs

Four tabs appear at the top of the **Save for Web** dialog box. When the **Original** tab is selected, the original image is displayed in a single frame in the dialog box. The filename and file size are displayed below the image. Changes made to the image properties settings on the right side of the dialog box do not affect the original image, but changes made to the image size settings do.

When the **Optimized** tab is selected, an optimized version (a small, compressed version that still exhibits decent quality) of the original image is displayed in a single frame in the dialog box. The appearance of this image is based on the settings made on the right-hand side of the dialog box. Information about the optimized image is displayed at the bottom of the frame, including file format, size, approximate download time (time it would take to display in a web browser), and color and dithering information.

When the **2-Up** tab is selected, the original image is displayed on the left, and a view of how it will look when it is changed appears on the right. The appearance of the optimized image on the right is based on the settings made in the controls to the far right of the dialog box. In Figure 2-15, the image has been changed to a 72 ppi JPEG image, which will be explained in the following section. Information about the original image and optimized image appear at the bottom of each frame.

When the **4-Up** tab is selected, the original image and three different optimized versions appear in separate frames in the dialog box. Changes made to the image properties settings on the right side of the dialog box affect only the currently selected image. For this reason, the **4-Up** option can be used to compare the results of various image settings.

If you pick the **Preview** button to the far right of the display tabs, a pop-up menu appears. This pop-up menu allows you to *toggle* (turn on and off) certain display properties in the optimized image preview frame. In this menu, you can also choose between different connection speeds, ranging from typical dial-up to typical broadband speed, to be used in calculating the approximate download times displayed at the bottom of the optimized image preview frames.

Image Properties Settings

In this section, you can save the image in a file format that will compress the image, making its file size even smaller. The image file format can be selected in the **Preset:** drop-down list at the top of this section or from the **Optimized file format** drop-down list, below it and to the left. The **Preset:** drop-down list provides a number of predefined image formats and settings to choose from. Using this list, you can convert to one of the following file formats:

- **GIF** or **PNG-8:** These formats are used to optimize non-photographic images (such as logos and other graphics).
- **JPEG:** This is the most common file format used to optimize digital photos for display on the web. You can compress JPEG files in a low, medium, or high quality level. If you compress a JPEG image at a low level, the file size becomes very small, but the loss in image quality is very noticeable. You will learn more about the JPEG file format in a later chapter.
- **PNG-24:** This format is used to optimize images that contain areas of transparency.
- **WBNP:** This is a black-and-white format that is used to optimize images for cell phones and other hand-held devices.

Beneath the **Preset:** drop-down list is a group of drop-down lists, check boxes, and sliders that allow you to tailor the image properties to your needs. The types of settings available depends on the image format selected in either the **Preset:** drop-down list or the **Optimized file format** drop-down list. These settings can be adjusted to modify one of the presets or to define file properties from scratch.

The Color Table Tab

If a GIF or PNG-8 image file format is selected, clicking on the **Color Table** tab displays the colors used in the optimized image. If you select a color in the table and double click, you can select a new color in the **Color Picker** dialog box. The original color will be replaced with the newly selected color. You can also edit a color by selecting it in the table and picking one of the tool buttons at the bottom of the tab, **Figure 2-16**.

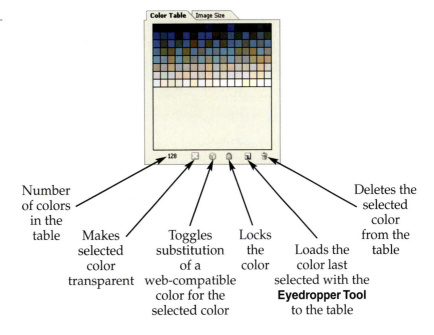

Figure 2-16.
All of the colors used in the optimized image are displayed in the **Color Table** tab.

Number of colors in the table

Makes selected color transparent

Toggles substitution of a web-compatible color for the selected color

Locks the color

Loads the color last selected with the **Eyedropper Tool** to the table

Deletes the selected color from the table

The Image Size Tab

In the **Image Size** tab, you can adjust the pixel dimensions or percentage of the image, just as if you were using the **Image Size** dialog box. Since the image being saved is optimized for web use, all resizing performed in this tab is done with resampling.

Creating Images for Video

You learned earlier in this chapter that a computer monitor has thousands of tiny, glowing dots that produce an image. These glowing dots are often referred to as pixels, but should not be confused with pixels that make up a digital image (also introduced earlier in this chapter). The glowing pixels on a computer monitor are typically square in shape. Because any Photoshop document or digital photo is made up of perfectly square pixels, computer monitors accurately display these images with their tiny, glowing square-shaped pixels.

The pixels on video displays (such as televisions or video monitors) are more rectangular in shape. With that in mind, images created in Photoshop that will appear in a video production or a television broadcast must be adjusted or they will appear out of proportion.

Pixel aspect ratio describes how wide a pixel is compared to how tall it is. You can use the **Image > Pixel Aspect Ratio** menu to instantly convert an image into a number of different video formats. Pixel aspect ratios are presented in simplified form on this menu. If the pixels on a particular type of TV are two times wider than their height (a ratio of 2:1), the pixel aspect ratio will be expressed as 2 (the first number divided by the second number) on the **Image > Pixel Aspect Ratio** menu. You can also specify a custom pixel aspect ratio using this menu.

GRAPHIC DESIGN:
The Mood of a Design

After you understand exactly what message a design needs to communicate, the next step is to plan on what kind of mood and feel the design will have. Just as a musician can create different moods using various combinations of rhythms, chords, scales, instruments and even silence, a graphic designer can manipulate **design elements** (images, graphics, text, colors, and empty space on the page) to create different feelings or moods. Designs can portray many different moods, including:

- Happiness or sadness.
- Creativity or boredom.
- Tension or relaxation.
- Energy or calm.
- Stability or chaos.
- Beauty or ugliness.

Two different designs for a CD insert are shown in **Figure 2-17**. These designs were created for the same band. Version A of the design gives the viewer the impression that the band is somewhat experimental and unpredictable. Version B paints a picture of a rock band that is more

Figure 2-17.
Do you agree with the author's description of the different moods that these designs create?

A

B

aggressive, loud, and full of attitude. The text in each design is the primary element that helps establish these moods. The colors in each design help a bit, too.

As you learn more about graphic design fundamentals (look for a section at the end of each chapter), you will discover specific tips about how both text and color can be used to enhance the mood of a design.

Summary

Resolution is a very technical subject. Many readers will not understand everything they have read in this chapter after reading it only once. Give yourself time to review this information and experiment, especially with resizing images. It is particularly important to understand the difference between resizing with the resampling option *on* and with the resampling option *off*.

CHAPTER TUTORIALS

As you complete the following tutorials, you will become familiar with the **Image Size** dialog box as you compare the same image at two different resolutions. You will also use the **Save for Web** dialog box to prepare an image for use on a website. Lastly, you will resize an image taken with a digital camera. These tutorials will help you become more comfortable with many of the concepts introduced in this chapter.

Tutorial 2-1: Image Resolution

In this tutorial, you will use the **Zoom Tool** and other commands to compare two images. One image has a resolution of 72 ppi, and the other has a resolution of 300 ppi.

1. Open the file named oak300.jpg.
2. Click the **Zoom Tool** in the **Toolbox**.
3. With the **Zoom Tool** active, drag a box around the stem. Click and drag from point A to point B to create the box. See **Figure T2-1**.
4. Click the **Zoom Out** button on the options bar.
5. Zoom out by clicking on the leaf five times, **Figure T2-2**.
6. Click the **Zoom In** button on the options bar.

As you perform the next step, watch the title bar in the image window.

Zoom Tool

Zoom Out

Zoom In

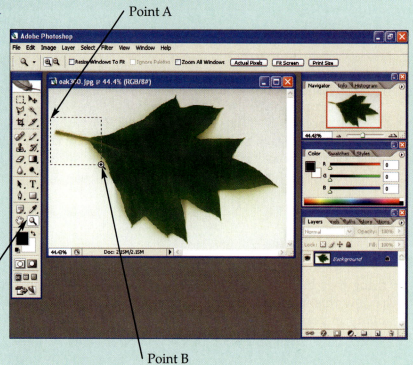

Figure T2-1. Zoom in on the leaf stem by dragging a box with the **Zoom Tool**.

Point A

Zoom Tool selected

Point B

Figure T2-2. ⎯⎯⎯⎯⎯⎯
Zoom out on the leaf.

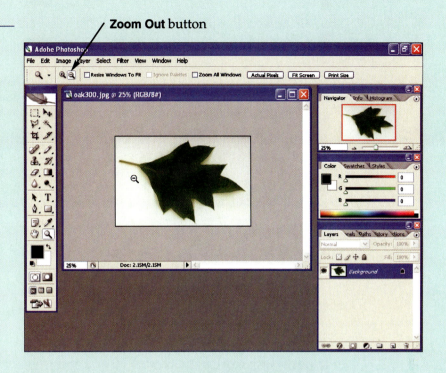

7. Zoom in (click) on the stem until the title bar displays 1600%. See **Figure T2-3**.

   Now that you have zoomed in, you can see that this image is made up of thousands of small squares. These squares are called pixels, or dots.

Figure T2-3. ⎯⎯⎯⎯⎯⎯
Zoom in on the leaf 1600%. Note that the plus sign disappears from the zoom cursor, indicating that the image cannot be zoomed further.

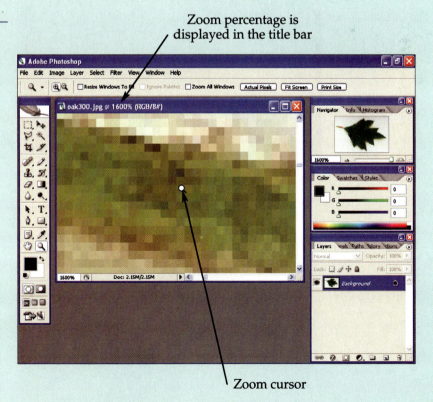

8. Click the **Fit Screen** button on the options bar. The oak300.jpg window fills the empty area on your screen, and the image is zoomed out so that it fits entirely in the window.

   The oak300.jpg file was created by placing a leaf on a scanner and setting the resolution setting to 300 spi (ppi), **Figure T2-4**. As the scanner passed over the leaf, it created 300 pixels per inch, both across and down!

   The scanned oak300.jpg image is shown at actual size in **Figure T2-5**. One square inch (the area within the dotted lines) contains 90,000 pixels! "Resolution" means "how many pixels are in one square inch." But instead of saying that the oak300.jpg file has a resolution of 90,000 pixels, it is correct to say that it has a resolution of 300 pixels per inch (ppi). It should be noted that many people use the terms dpi and ppi interchangeably.

9. Choose **Image > Image Size…**. This opens the **Image Size** dialog box, **Figure T2-6**.

   The **Pixel Dimensions:** section shows how many pixels are in the image. Multiply the width (1078) by the height (696) to discover the total number of pixels in this image: 750,288!

   The **Document Size:** section shows that this image is 3.593″ wide and 2.32″ tall.

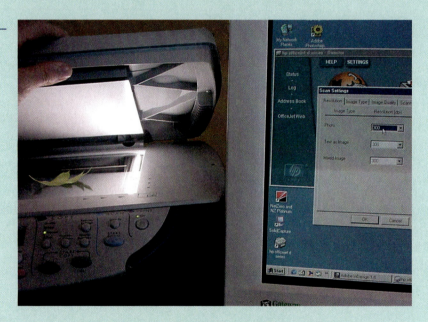

Figure T2-4.
A leaf was scanned at 300 spi in a flatbed scanner to produce the oak300.jpg image.

Figure T2-5.
The horizontal resolution is multiplied by the vertical resolution to determine the number of pixels in an area.

Chapter 2   Resolution

10. Click the **Cancel** button.
11. Without closing oak300.jpg, open the file named oak72.jpg.

    The oak72.jpg image has a resolution of 72 ppi.

12. Choose **Window > Arrange > Tile Horizontally**.

    If your image windows are not arranged as shown in **Figure T2-7**, move them by grabbing and dragging their title bars. If necessary, resize the windows by clicking and dragging a corner of the window to be resized.

    The oak72.jpg image should be active. When an image is referred to as *active*, that means it is selected and ready to work on. To make a image active, click on its title bar.

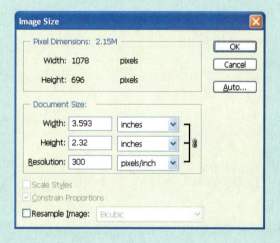

Figure T2-6.
The **Image Size** dialog box displays the image's size and resolution.

Figure T2-7.
When the image windows are tiled horizontally, they should appear as shown here. Windows can be resized and moved as needed.

You can move a window by clicking and dragging its title bar

You can resize a window by clicking and dragging a corner

13. Enter 200 in the zoom text box at the bottom left of the image window and press the [Enter] key. This is another way to quickly zoom in or out.

    Now the leaves are about the same size on your screen. Notice the difference in quality between the two leaves. The oak300.jpg leaf looks more in focus.

14. With the oak72.jpg image active, choose **Image > Image Size…**, **Figure T2-8**.

    In the **Document Size:** section, notice that this image is exactly the same size as the oak300.jpg image: about 3.6" wide and 2.3" tall. This section also shows the image has a resolution of 72 ppi.

    The **Pixel Dimensions:** section shows this image is 259 pixels wide and 167 pixels high, for a total of 43,771 pixels. Remember, the oak300.jpg image contained over 750,000 pixels!

15. Click the **Cancel** button.
16. Make sure the **Zoom Tool** is still selected and the oak72.jpg is still active.
17. Click the **Print Size** button on the options bar.

    The print size refers to the actual size of the image when its printed. This image is 3.5" wide and 2.3" tall, but it may appear a bit larger or smaller than this, depending on your monitor display settings.

18. Click on the oak300.jpg image to make it active.
19. Click the **Print Size** button again.

    Both images are displayed at their actual size.

20. Use the **Zoom Tool** to drag a box around the stem in the oak72.jpg image, as shown in **Figure T2-9**.

    Look closely at the pixels. Notice that a pixel only contains one shade of color. In the oak72.jpg image, the pixels (dots) are quite large. Because the pixels are so large, you cannot see any detail on the stem.

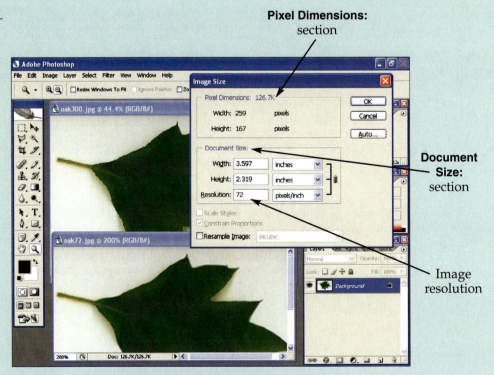

Figure T2-8. Image size and resolution information for oak72.jpg is displayed in the **Image Size** dialog box.

Figure T2-9. ―――――
Zoom in on the stem in the oak72.jpg image.

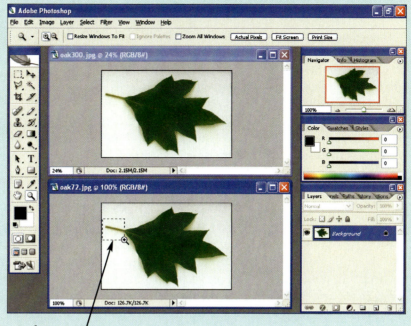

Zoom in on the stem

21. Activate the oak300.jpg image and use the **Zoom Tool** to drag a box around the stem. Make sure the box is the same size and in the same relative location as the one you drew around the stem in the oak72.jpg image.

   Note that in the oak300.jpg image, you can see individual hairs on the stem. The pixels are much smaller in this image—that is why it is sharper and more detailed. See **Figure T2-10.**

Figure T2-10. ―――――
The same area is magnified in oak300.jpg and oak72.jpg, images. Note that the oak72.jpg image is pixelated.

Image is crisp

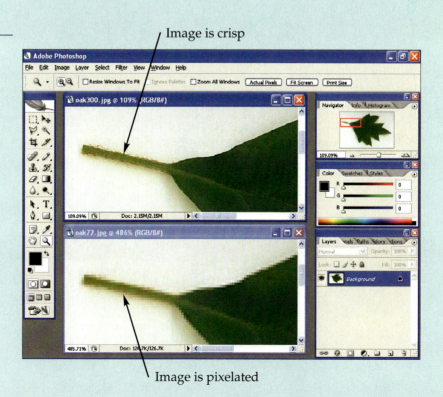

Image is pixelated

22. Now, zoom in on the oak300.jpg image until you can see individual square pixels.

    Because it has so many pixels, the oak300.jpg file takes up sixteen times more disk space than the oak72.jpg file.

23. With the oak300.jpg image active, click the **Actual Pixels** button.
24. Activate the oak72.jpg image and click the **Actual Pixels** button again.

    Clicking the **Actual Pixels** button is a quick way to zoom to 100%. This causes each pixel to appear at the same size as a single glowing square or your monitor. Your images should look like the example in Figure T2-11.

25. Close both files. If you are asked if you want to save changes, click **No**.

Tutorial 2-2: The Save For Web Dialog Box

It is recommended that all digital images used for e-mail and web pages on the Internet have a resolution of 72 ppi. Images at this resolution look good on a computer screen, and 72 ppi images do not take up much file space, so they attach quickly to e-mail messages and display quickly on a web browser. This tutorial will demonstrate a quick way to change an image to 72 ppi so it is ready to attach to an e-mail message or be uploaded to a web page.

1. Open the oak300.jpg file.
2. Choose **File > Save for Web…**.

    This opens the **Save For Web** dialog box.

3. Click the **Original** tab.

    The oak300.jpg image is shown. Near the lower left corner, the size of the oak300.jpg file is displayed. The image file is 2.15 MB (2,100 kilobytes). See Figure T2-12.

4. Click the **2-Up** tab.

    The original image is shown on the left. The right side will show any changes that are made to the file.

Figure T2-11. When both images are displayed at 100%, its easy to see that the oak300.jpg image contains many more pixels.

Both images displayed at 100% zoom

Actual Pixels button

Figure T2-12.
The filename and file size for the oak300.jpg image are displayed at the bottom of the image frame.

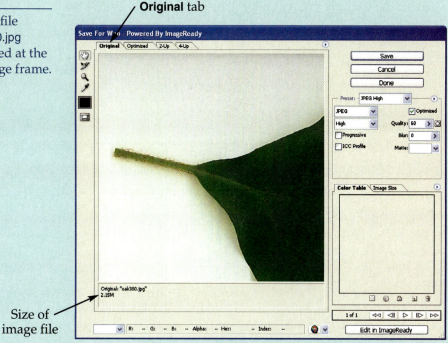

Size of image file

5. In the **Optimized file format** drop-down list, choose **JPEG**, **Figure T2-13**.

   Photographs (whether scanned or captured with a digital camera), are often saved as JPEG files before e-mailing or using them on a website. This makes their file size smaller. When an image is saved as a JPEG file, it can be compressed to make the file size even smaller.

Figure T2-13.
The controls in the **Save For Web** dialog box are used to fine tune the properties of the optimized image.

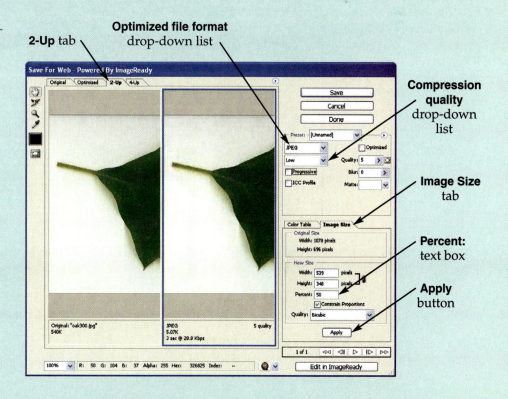

6. In the **Compression quality** drop-down list, choose **Low** (low quality).

   Note that selecting Low in the Compression quality: drop-down list also changes the value to 10 in the Quality: slider. If you want to change the quality from that provided by the preset value, you can enter a new value in the Quality: slider.

7. Enter a new value of 5 in the **Quality:** slider.

   You can do this by typing a new value in the text box or by picking on the arrow button and then clicking and dragging the slider to the desired value. Click away from the slider to hide it again. This lowers the compression quality from the Low preset level of 10.

8. Click the **Image Size** tab on the right side of the **Save For Web** dialog box.
9. Enter 50 in the **Percent:** text box to make the image width and height 50% smaller.
10. Click the **Apply** button.

    The image on the right now looks blurry, because the quality is so low. The new file size and the time the file would take to load through a 28.8 Kbps (dial-up) Internet connection is displayed at the bottom of the optimized image's window.

    If you would like to see how quickly this file would load over a faster Internet connection, click the Preview Menu arrow at the top of the dialog box and choose a different connection speed. See **Figure T2-14**.

11. Change the compression quality setting to 40 (see step 7).

    Note that the level selected in the **Compression quality:** drop-down list changes from Low to Medium.

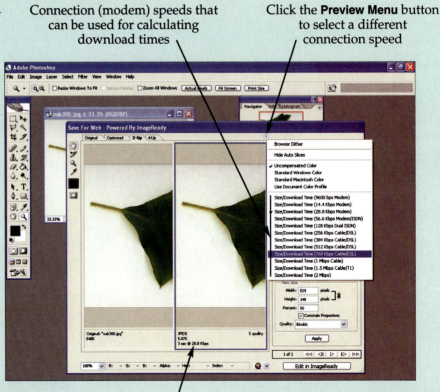

Figure T2-14. A new connection speed can be specified for calculating download time for the image. The connection speed and approximate download time are displayed in the lower left corner of the optimized image frame.

Connection (modem) speeds that can be used for calculating download times

Click the **Preview Menu** button to select a different connection speed

File size and approximate time required to download the image at the selected connection speed

12. Click the **Save** button in the upper right corner of the dialog box.

    This opens the **Save Optimized As** dialog box.

13. Name the file 02web and choose a location in which to save it. Then, click the **Save** button to save the file and close the dialog box.

    When the optimized image is saved, the **Save For Web** dialog box automatically closes.

14. Close the oak300.jpg image. If asked to save changes, click **No**.
15. Open the 02web.jpg file you just created.
16. Choose **Image > Image Size…**. In the **Document Size:** section of the **Image Size** dialog box, notice the resolution of the 02web.jpg file has been automatically changed to 72 ppi.
17. Click the **Cancel** button to close the **Image Size** dialog box.
18. Choose **File > Close** to close the 02web.jpg file.

Tutorial 2-3: Resizing an Image Captured by a Digital Camera

If you want to print a digital image, an image resolution of at least 150 ppi is recommended. If you are using a scanner, all you have to do is set the resolution at 150 spi (ppi), scan, touch up the image if necessary, and print. If you are using a digital camera, after sending the image to your computer, you need to adjust the image resolution. This tutorial will step you through the procedure.

1. Open the file named 640x480.jpg, 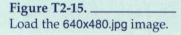 **Figure T2-15**.

    This image was captured with a digital camera. Before taking the picture, the image size setting on the camera was set to 640×480 (pixels).

Figure T2-15.
Load the 640x480.jpg image.

2. Choose **View > Print Size** from the menu bar or click the **Print Size** button on the options bar.
3. Click **Image > Image Size....** This opens the **Image Size** dialog box, **Figure T2-16**.

   In the **Pixel Dimensions:** section, you can confirm what you already knew, that the image dimensions (in pixels) are 640×480. In the **Document Size:** section, you can see that the actual size of this image is about 6.7" wide by 8.9" high and the resolution is only 72 ppi. If you print this 72 ppi image, it will not look sharp and crisp because the pixels are so large.

4. Make sure the **Resample Image:** check box is unchecked.
5. Enter 150 in the **Resolution:** text box.
6. Click the **OK** button.

   The image is resized and the **Image Size** dialog box closes automatically.

7. Choose **View > Print Size** from the menu bar, or pick the **Print Size** button on the options bar.

   Notice the size of the image got smaller when you changed the resolution. This is because all of the pixels got smaller—small enough for 150 of them to fit in a 1" width.

   The printout on the left in **Figure T2-17** shows the 640x480.jpg image printed at its original resolution of 72 ppi. The quality is poor because the pixels are so large that the viewer can distinguish between individual pixels.

   The printout on the right was printed after changing the resolution to 150 ppi. The image is smaller because the pixels are smaller. In fact, the pixels are so small that individual pixels cannot be seen, which is why the image looks sharp and crisp.

   If you are using a digital camera and you want to end up with larger printouts at 150 ppi, you need to start with a larger image size setting on your camera. As a general rule, you should not try to make a small image bigger. You should start with a larger, high-quality image and make it smaller for best results.

8. Choose **File > Save As....**
9. In the **Save As** dialog box, name the file 02ppi150, pick a location in which to save the file, and click the **Save** button.
10. In the **JPEG Options** dialog box, accept the defaults by picking the **OK** button.
11. Close the 02ppi150.jpg file.

Figure T2-16. File size and resolution information for the 640x480.jpg image are displayed in the **Image Size** dialog box.

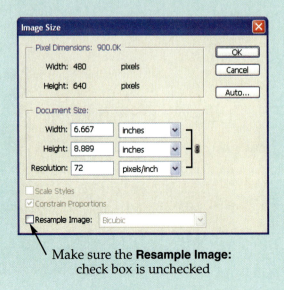

Make sure the **Resample Image:** check box is unchecked

Chapter 2   Resolution

Figure T2-17. _____
The same image has been printed out in two different resolutions. In the sample on the left, the image is printed at its original resolution (72 ppi). The image resolution was increased to 150 ppi before the example on the right was printed. The left print is a larger, but a lower quality print than the print on the right.

Key Terms

capture
design elements
digital
digital camera
dots per inch (dpi)
drag a box
halftone
high resolution
image capture device

inkjet printers
low-resolution
megapixel
pixel aspect ratio
pixels
pixels per inch (ppi)
pixelated
printing resolution

resampling
resolutions
rulers
samples per inch (spi)
scanner
scroll bars
toggle
zoom percentage

Review Questions

Answer the following questions on a separate sheet of paper.

1. A digital camera is an image capture device. What does "capture" mean?
2. What are pixels?
3. What is a "pixelized" or "pixelated" image?
4. Why does a low-resolution image not use as much file space as a high-resolution image?
5. When an image's zoom percentage is at 100%, what does it mean?
6. What button (or menu command) shows you how large your image will be when printed?
7. List two ways you can reset the zoom magnification of an image to 100%.
8. The book suggests that the easiest way to zoom in on an image is to do what?
9. Using the **Hand Tool** is the same as doing what?

10. If you are using another tool, what keyboard shortcut enables you to temporarily use the **Hand Tool**?
11. What is the standard resolution for images on websites?
12. What menu command shows or hides Photoshop's rulers?
13. If you change the width of an image in the **Image Size** dialog box and the **Constrain Proportions** option is on, what happens to the height of the image?
14. Explain how to resize an image in the **Image Size** dialog box without changing the total number of pixels in the image.
15. If you change the width and height of an image to a smaller size with the **Resample Image:** option turned off, what will happen to the pixels in your image?
16. With the **Resample Image:** option on, if you change the width and height of an image to a smaller size and leave the resolution setting the same, what will happen to your image?
17. What is another term for "resampling?"
18. Describe the differences you would see if you used a magnifying glass to compare a halftone print and a print produced by an inkjet printer.
19. If you know the lpi that an image will be printed, how can you use Photoshop to help you figure out a compatible image resolution?
20. Scanners often measure the resolution they capture by dpi. What is the technically correct term to measure scanner resolution?
21. If you are scanning a 4"×5" photo, and want to resize it to 12"×15" at a resolution of 300 ppi, at what resolution (spi) should you scan the image?
22. Since digital cameras do not have a resolution setting, how can you control the resolution of images that you capture with your digital camera?
23. If a camera can take a photo that is 4000×3000 pixels, what megapixel rating does that camera have?
24. What two things happen to file when JPEG compression is applied to it?
25. If a TV has a pixel aspect ratio of 2, what does this mean?

3

Selection Tools

Learning Objectives

After completing this chapter, you will be able to:
- Explain the purpose of Photoshop's selection tools.
- Describe how to use the **New selection**, **Add to selection**, **Subtract from selection**, and **Intersect with selection** buttons that most selection tools have.
- Identify situations in which you may want to feather a selection.
- Explain what anti-aliasing does to the edge of a selection.
- Create rectangular and square selections with the **Rectangular Marquee Tool**.
- Create oval and circular selections with the **Elliptical Marquee Tool**.
- Trim images with the **Crop Tool**.
- Create selections with the **Lasso Tool**, **Polygonal Lasso Tool**, and **Magnetic Lasso Tool**.
- Describe a situation in which each of the three lasso tools would be the best choice to create a selection.
- Select similarly-colored areas with the **Magic Wand Tool**.
- Describe the selection commands found in the **Select** menu.
- Remove a fringe from a selected portion of an image.

Introduction

Photoshop's selection tools are used to choose an area in your document that you want to edit. After you select part of your image, it is surrounded with a dashed line. In **Figure 3-1**, a selection border has been created around the leaf, making it the *active* part of the file. Any of Photoshop's tools or commands will affect the selected leaf, but not the white background behind it. Since the white background is not selected, it is protected until the selection border is removed, or *deselected*.

Selection Options

Each selection tool offers a different way to choose part of an image. Before discussing each selection tool in detail, it is important to notice that most selection tools share some of the same options. If you click on the **Lasso Tool**, for example, the options bar contains options that most of the other selection tools have as well, **Figure 3-2**. We will discuss these commonly-shared options before explaining the differences between each selection tool.

Fine-Tuning Selections

Most of the selection tools have the following buttons on their options bar. The four buttons, in order, are called: **New selection**, **Add to selection**, **Subtract from selection**, and **Intersect with selection**:

- Click the **New Selection** button when you want to create a new selection.
- To make an existing selection larger, click the **Add to selection** button and use the selection tool to add more area to the current selection. The keyboard shortcut for this button is [Shift].
- To make an existing selection smaller, click the **Subtract from selection** button and use the selection tool to specify what areas should be removed from the current selection. The keyboard shortcut for this button is [Alt] (Windows) or [Option] (Mac).
- The **Intersect with selection** button is used to create a second selection that overlaps one that already exists. The area where the two selection borders overlap is kept as the final selection. This option is not used frequently, but it may come in handy occasionally.

An example of how the **Subtract from selection** button is used is shown in **Figure 3-3**. The image of the red floppy disk was created by scanning the disk on a flatbed scanner. Unfortunately, there is a shadow around the edges of the disk that

Figure 3-1.
A selection border is a dashed line that surrounds a portion of your file.

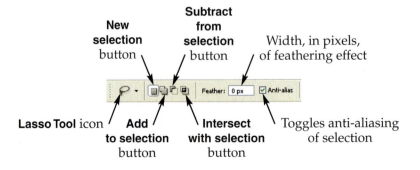

Figure 3-2.
These options are shared by most of the selection tools.

Figure 3-3. _____
The **Subtract from selection** button makes it easy to create an irregularly shaped selection. **A**—First, a square-shaped selection is drawn around the entire disk with the **Rectangular Marquee Selection Tool**. **B**—After zooming in on a corner, the **Polygonal Lasso Tool** is chosen, and the **Subtract from selection** button is clicked. The **Polygonal Lasso Tool** draws a triangle-shaped selection at the corner of the floppy disk. **C**—The triangular selection is removed from rectangular selection.

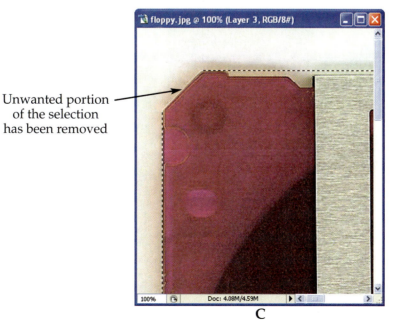

needs to be excluded from the selection. It is quicker and easier to draw rectangular selection around the entire disk and then subtract the unwanted portions than it is to draw an accurate selection from scratch.

Feathered vs. Normal Selections

Most of Photoshop's selection tools have a *feathering* option, which creates a fading-out effect at the edges of the selection, Figure 3-4. Leaving the **Feather:** setting at 0 creates a crisp-looking edge around the selection. When the **Feather:** setting is set to 10, the actual fade-out effect is a total of twenty pixels wide (ten pixels in either direction of the selection). When the feather option is used, the selection you see in your image actually shows the *midpoint* of the feather effect.

When using the **Feather:** option in the options bar, you must remember to enter the feathering value *before* selecting in your image. Additionally, you must remember to set this option back to 0 when you are finished, so you do not accidentally feather your next selection. There is a feather command available from the **Select** menu (discussed later in this chapter), that is easier to use.

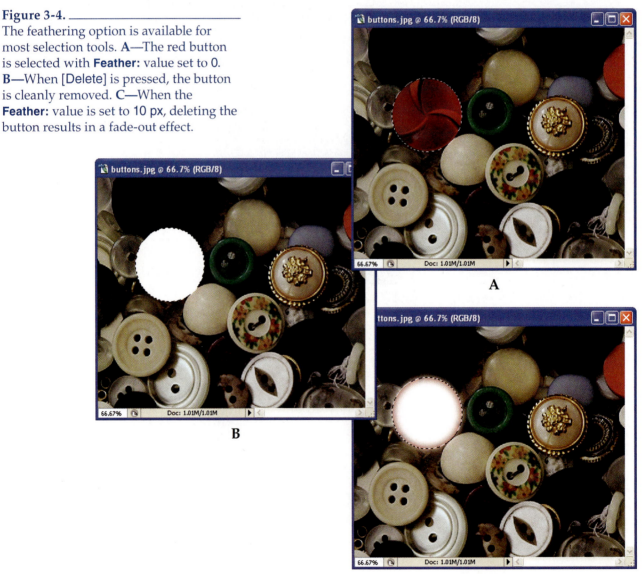

Figure 3-4.
The feathering option is available for most selection tools. **A**—The red button is selected with **Feather:** value set to 0. **B**—When [Delete] is pressed, the button is cleanly removed. **C**—When the **Feather:** value is set to 10 px, deleting the button results in a fade-out effect.

Anti-Aliasing

Most of the selection tools have an option called *anti-aliasing*, which creates a slight smoothing effect around the edges of the selection. Since pixels are square, whenever you create a selection with curved edges, those edges will be rough. You may have to zoom in to see the rough edges if your image has a high resolution (large number of pixels per inch).

Anti-aliasing helps selected pixels look less jagged at the edges by filling in related colors to create a blended look along the edge of a selection, **Figure 3-5**. Think of anti-aliasing as a feather effect that is one pixel wide. For most of your selection work, keep this option turned on for best results. However, anti-aliasing is not an option for two selection tools. Since the **Rectangular Marquee Tool** and **Crop Tool** produce square and rectangular selections, anti-aliasing is not necessary. Selections made with these tools will perfectly follow the square shape of pixels, so edges will not look jagged.

The Marquee Selection Tools

The word *marquee* refers to a large sign surrounded by blinking lightbulbs—something you might see at a movie theater. The marquee tools create selections shaped like rectangles, squares, circles, and *ellipses* (ovals). When you create a selection, it slowly "blinks" to help you clearly see it. Most people agree, however, that selections in Photoshop look more like marching ants than blinking lightbulbs.

To access all of the available marquee tools, click and hold the mouse button on the tool in the top-left corner of the **Toolbox**. The four marquee selection tools appear, grouped together in a pop-up menu, **Figure 3-6**.

Figure 3-5.
Two close-up views of the buttons image are shown here. The **Feather:** setting is set to 0 in both examples. **A**—A button has been selected and deleted with anti-aliasing on. **B**—The same button has been selected and deleted with anti-aliasing off. Notice that the edge appears more jagged.

A   B

Figure 3-6.
The **Marquee Selection Tools** are available in a pop-up menu.

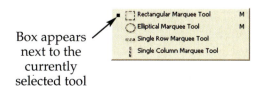

Box appears next to the currently selected tool

The Rectangular Marquee Tool

The **Rectangular Marquee Tool** is used to create rectangular or square selections. When the **Rectangular Marquee Tool** is active, the options bar appears as shown in **Figure 3-7**. Notice that the **Anti-alias** check box is grayed out.

When the **Style:** option is set to **Normal**, you can create selections a number of different ways. See the table in **Figure 3-8**.

The second setting listed in the **Style:** drop-down list, **Fixed Aspect Ratio**, allows you to control the proportion of rectangles. When this option is selected, the **Width:** and **Height:** text boxes become available. Enter the proportions that you want the selection to maintain in these text boxes. For example, if you enter 2 in the **Width:** text box and 1 in the **Height:** text box, you will only be able to drag a rectangle that is twice as wide as it is high.

When you select the **Fixed Size** option in the **Style:** drop-down list, you are able to enter an exact width and height for the selection. For example, to create a 1" square-shaped selection, enter "1 in" in both the **Width:** and **Height:** text boxes, then click in your image and move the selection where you want it. To specify width and height in pixels instead of inches, enter px instead of in. Other possible units of measurement are centimeters (cm), points (pt), and picas (pica).

Figure 3-7.
The options available for the **Rectangular Marquee Tool** appear in the options bar.

Figure 3-8.
This chart describes the different ways to create and move selections with the **Rectangular Marquee Tool**.

Selection Method	Keyboard/Mouse Actions
Create a rectangular selection, corner-to-corner.	Click and drag with the mouse.
Create a rectangular selection, center-to-corner.	Press [Alt] (Windows) or [Option] (Mac) after you begin clicking and dragging with the mouse.
Create a square selection, corner-to-corner.	Press [Shift] while clicking and dragging.
Create a square selection, center-to-corner.	Press [Shift][Alt] (Windows) or [Shift][Option] (Mac) after you begin clicking and dragging.
Move and resize a selection while it is being created.	Press the [spacebar] after you begin clicking and dragging.
Move a selection after it has been created (without moving the selected pixels).	1. Use the arrow keys for 1-pixel movements. 2. Press [Shift] and use the arrow keys for 10-pixel movements. 3. Click and drag inside of the selected area (make sure the **Rectangular Marquee Tool** is active).

The Elliptical Marquee Tool

This **Elliptical Marquee Tool** is used to create elliptical (oval) or circular selections. When this tool is active, the options bar offers the same options as those in the **Rectangular Marquee Tool**'s options bar, with one exception: the **Anti-alias** check box is available, **Figure 3-9**.

The table in **Figure 3-10** explains various ways to create elliptical or circular selections with the **Elliptical Marquee Tool**. These methods are almost identical to the **Rectangular Marquee Tool**'s methods.

The Single Column and Single Row Marquee Tools

These two tools are specialized rectangular marquee tools. They create a rectangular-shaped column or row that is only one pixel wide. These tools can be used to create "picture-frame" effects around images, since their width and height can easily be expanded by using the **Select** menu (discussed later in this chapter).

Clicking the mouse button once creates a column or row that extends from one edge of your document to the other. If you hold the mouse button down, you can drag the column or row you just created to another location.

Because the **Single Column Marquee Tool** can only draw a selection that is one pixel wide and the same height as the image, and the **Single Row Marquee Tool** can only draw a selection that is one pixel high and the same width as the image, most of the options are unavailable (grayed out) on the options bar, **Figure 3-11**.

Figure 3-9.
The **Elliptical Marquee Tool**'s options bar is almost identical to the options bar for the **Rectangular Marquee Tool**.

Elliptical Marquee Tool icon — Anti-aliasing is available for elliptical selections

Figure 3-10.
This chart describes the methods of creating and moving circular and elliptical selections.

Selection Method	Keyboard/Mouse Actions
Create an elliptical selection, corner-to-corner.	Click and drag with the mouse. You may wish to display Photoshop's grid (**View > Show > Grid**).
Create an elliptical selection, center-to-corner.	Press [Alt] (Windows) or [Option] (Mac) after you begin clicking and dragging with the mouse.
Create a circular selection, corner-to-corner.	Press [Shift] while clicking and dragging.
Create a circular selection, center-to-corner.	Press [Shift][Alt] (Windows) or [Shift][Option] (Mac) after you begin clicking and dragging.
Move and resize a selection while it is being created.	Press the [Spacebar] after you begin clicking and dragging.
Move a selection after it has been created (without moving the selected pixels).	1. Use the arrow keys for 1-pixel movements. 2. Press [Shift] and use the arrow keys for 10-pixel movements. 3. Click and drag inside of the selected area (make sure the **Rectangular Marquee Tool** is active).

The Crop Tool

The **Crop Tool** is *not* a selection tool, but it is included in this chapter because it is similar to the **Rectangular Marquee Tool**. The term *crop* means "to cut off." The **Crop Tool** is used to make a document smaller by cutting away parts of it. Selection tools, on the other hand, can be used to erase part of a document (by pressing [Delete] after selecting an area), but the document remains the same size. The **Crop Tool** can also be used to straighten an image that was placed crookedly on a scanner.

Initial Crop Tool Options

When the **Crop Tool** is first selected, the options bar appears as shown in **Figure 3-12**. You should use the **Width:** and **Height:** text boxes *only* if you want to specify an exact size for the crop. If you enter an exact size for the crop, the resolution of the image will change to accommodate the new size. You can enter a new value in the **Resolution:** text box to change the resolution of the cropped image. The size of the cropped image will be adjusted to accommodate the new resolution. If you enter new values in the **Width:**, **Height:**, *and* the **Resolution:** text box, the image will be resampled when the crop is performed. To quickly delete the values in the **Width:**, **Height:**, and **Resolution:** text boxes, click the **Clear** button.

The **Front Image** button is used to copy the width, height, and resolution settings from another image. If you want to crop an image so it is exactly the same size and resolution as another image you have already edited, open the edited image first and click the **Front Image** button. The width, height, and resolution data is copied into the options bar. Close the image file. Open the file you want to crop, and the width, height, and resolution settings remain in the options bar.

Figure 3-11.
Few options are available in the options bar when the **Single Row Marquee Tool** is selected. It should be noted that although the **Feather:** option is available, it does not work with the **Single Row Marquee Tool** or the **Single Column Marquee Tool**, because the selections are only one pixel wide.

Single Row Marquee Tool icon

Figure 3-12.
The initial options appear in the options bar when the **Crop Tool** is selected.

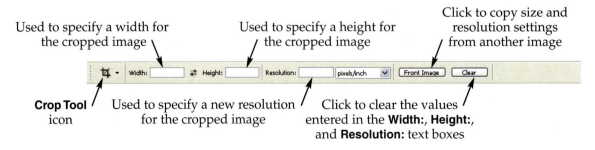

Chapter 3   Selection Tools

Cropping an Image

Begin the cropping process by dragging a rectangle cropping box on your image, without worrying about its size. When you release the mouse button, the options bar changes, revealing additional options, which will be discussed shortly. Small squares called *handles* appear around the selected area, **Figure 3-13**. You can click and drag those handles until the rectangle is exactly the size you want. If you specified a crop

Figure 3-13.
Trimming away unwanted portions of an image is made easy with the **Crop Tool**. **A**—With the **Crop Tool** selected, drag a cropping box and press [Enter] to crop the image. **B**—The portion of the image within the crop box is retained, the rest is discarded.

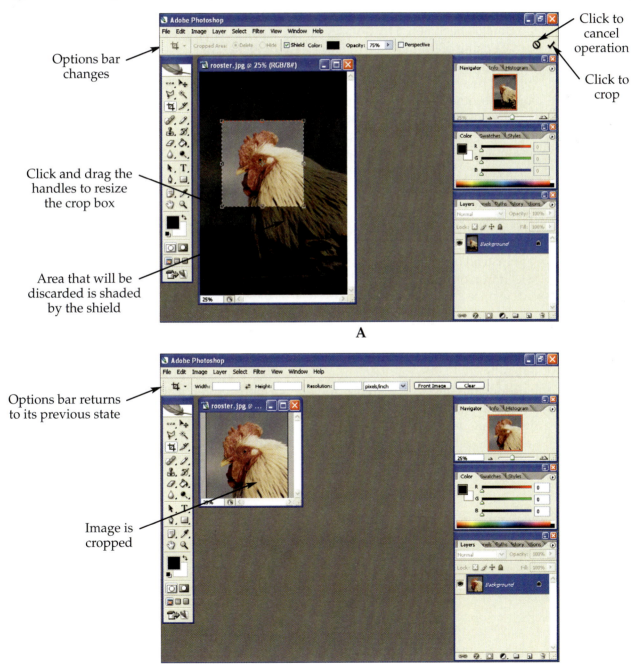

size before drawing the crop box, you will be able to adjust only the size of the box, not its width-to-height ratio. The area outside of the crop box is covered with a partially-transparent black shield, indicating what will be deleted. Then, press [Enter] or [Return], or click the **Commit** (check mark) button on the options bar to crop the image.

If an image was scanned crookedly and needs to be straightened, drag a rectangle close to the desired size. Then, position the cursor just outside one of the corner handles until the cursor turns into a curved arrow. Click and hold the mouse button, then drag the crop box until it has rotated to the desired position.

Secondary Crop Tool Options

As mentioned earlier, when you draw a cropping box, the options bar changes, Figure 3-14. The shield settings are among the new options that become available after the cropping box is drawn. The shield can be turned on or off by checking or clearing the **Shield** check box. The **Color:** color swatch appears to the right of the **Shield:** check box. Clicking on this swatch opens the **Color Picker** dialog box, from which a new shield color can be selected. The value entered in the **Opacity:** slider (to the right of the **Color:** swatch) determines how solid the shield appears. As the **Opacity:** value decreases, the shield becomes more transparent.

When the **Perspective** check box is checked, you can adjust the cropping box to an unusual shape before cropping. When the crop is performed, the final result is resampled to fit in a rectangular shape. The perspective looks like it has changed, but as you can see in Figure 3-15, too much resampling causes the result to be distorted.

The Lasso Tools

Instead of creating fixed-shape selections like the marquee selection tools, the lasso selection tools create freehand-drawn selections.

The Lasso Tool

The **Lasso Tool** draws a selection beginning where you click the mouse and following the cursor as you drag the mouse, Figure 3-16. If you let go of the mouse button while selecting with this tool, Photoshop automatically finishes the selection for you by drawing a straight line from the point where you release the mouse button to the starting point. For best results, you should zoom in 200% or more so you can draw selections as accurately as possible. Use the **Add to selection** and **Subtract from selection** buttons to clean up any mistakes.

Figure 3-14.
The **Crop Tool**'s second options bar appears after the cropping box has been drawn.

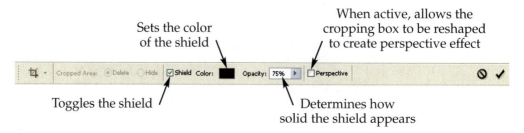

Figure 3-15.
After the crop box is drawn, checking the **Perspective** check box in the options bar allows you to create a perspective effect. **A**—The perspective effect is created by adjusting the cropping box handles. **B**—When [Enter] is pressed, everything within the crop box is resampled to fit into a rectangular area, creating a perspective look.

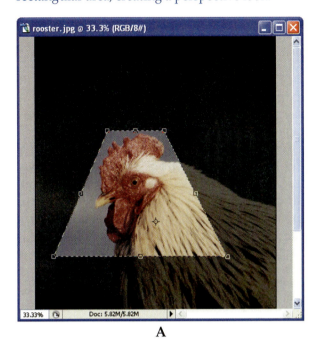

A   B

Figure 3-16.
To create a selection with the **Lasso Tool**, hold the mouse button and drag the mouse. The selection border is created along the cursor's path.

The **Lasso Tool** icon

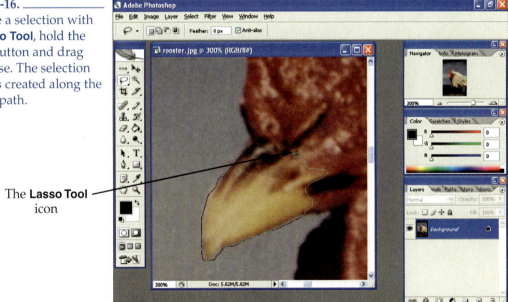

The Polygonal Lasso Tool

The **Polygonal Lasso Tool** is similar to the **Lasso Tool** and has the same available selection options. The major difference between the tools is that the **Polygonal Lasso Tool** creates only straight lines. Every time you click the mouse, you can change directions and create another straight line segment.

To finish creating a selection with the **Polygonal Lasso Tool**, you can click exactly where you began, the starting point of the selection. A small circle appears at the lower left corner of the **Polygonal Lasso Tool** cursor when it is positioned over the starting point, making it easier to select. See Figure 3-17. Another way to complete the selection is to press [Enter] or [Return]. A straight line will be drawn between the cursor's position and the starting point, closing the selection.

The Magnetic Lasso Tool

The **Magnetic Lasso Tool** finds the edge of objects in an image. This tool works well only if the area you want to select does not blend in with the colors around it. The **Magnetic Lasso Tool** looks for places where there are contrasting colors, and draws a selection where the two colors meet.

As you create a selection border, the **Magnetic Lasso Tool** generates *fastening points*, which hold the selection border in place, Figure 3-18. If the **Magnetic Lasso Tool** seems to get a bit confused, press [Delete] or [Backspace] as you backtrack the cursor over the selection. Then, move forward again, keeping the **Magnetic Lasso Tool** on track by clicking the mouse at key points along the object, such as the apex of curves or places where the selection path must change directions sharply. This creates additional fastening points.

As with the **Polygonal Lasso Tool**, you can complete the selection by clicking the starting point of the selection. A small circle appears at the lower left corner of the **Magnetic Lasso Tool** cursor when it is positioned over the starting point of the selection. You can also complete the selection by pressing [Enter] or [Return]. This draws a straight line between the cursor's position and the starting point, closing the selection.

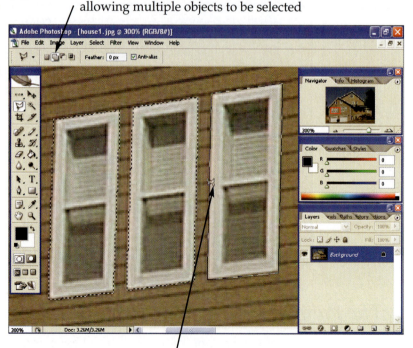

Figure 3-17. These three windows have been selected using the **Add to selection** option in the **Polygonal Lasso Tool**'s option bar. The small circle at the bottom of the cursor indicates that clicking the mouse will complete the selection.

The **Add to selection** button is active, allowing multiple objects to be selected

A small circle appears on the **Polygonal Lasso Tool** cursor, indicating that clicking will close the selection

Figure 3-18.
The **Magnetic Lasso Tool** creates fastening points. The fastening points hold the selection border to the edges in the image.

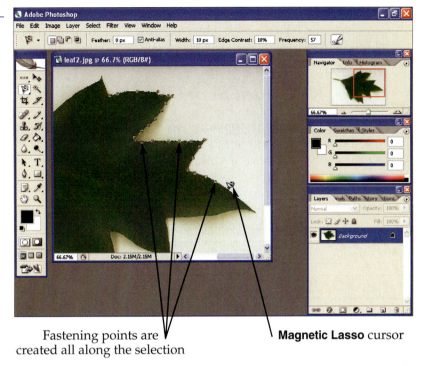

Fastening points are created all along the selection

Magnetic Lasso cursor

The Magnetic Lasso Tool Options Bar

The **Magnetic Lasso Tool** has all of the selection options available for the **Lasso Tool** and **Polygonal Lasso Tool**. In addition to these options, the options bar for the **Magnetic Lasso Tool** also contains several settings that control the tool's sensitivity, **Figure 3-19**.

The **Width:** setting determines how wide of an area the **Magnetic Lasso Tool** analyzes while trying to find an edge to select. For example, if the **Width:** value is set at 10 px, the **Magnetic Lasso Tool** tries to find an edge within ten pixels (in all directions) of itself. Edges more than ten pixels away are not detected in this case.

Enter a high percentage in the **Edge Contrast:** setting if the area you wish to select contrasts sharply with the color of the background behind it. This lowers the sensitivity of the **Magnetic Lasso Tool** and makes it work a bit more efficiently. Enter lower percentages if you are trying to select areas of your image that do not contrast as much with surrounding colors.

A high number (up to 100) entered in the **Frequency:** text box causes fastening points to be created more frequently. More fastening points can be helpful when selecting an area that does not sharply contrast with the colors around it.

Figure 3-19.
The **Magnetic Lasso Tool**'s options bar has controls for adjusting the tool's edge detection sensitivity and the frequency at which it creates fastening points.

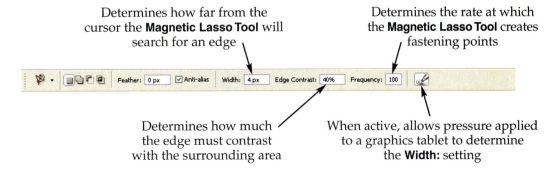

Determines how far from the cursor the **Magnetic Lasso Tool** will search for an edge

Determines the rate at which the **Magnetic Lasso Tool** creates fastening points

Determines how much the edge must contrast with the surrounding area

When active, allows pressure applied to a graphics tablet to determine the **Width:** setting

The **Use Tablet Pressure to change pen width** button is provided for Photoshop users who use a graphics tablet instead of a mouse. When this button is active, the **Width:** setting can be changed by varying the pressure applied to the stylus tablet.

Useful Keyboard Shortcuts for the Lasso Tools

As you work with the lasso selection tools, you will occasionally need to change options or make changes to the selection. The table in **Figure 3-20** describes some helpful keyboard shortcuts that can be used when creating selections with the lasso selection tools.

Figure 3-20.
This chart describes various selection methods for the lasso tools and their keyboard shortcuts.

Selection Method	Keyboard/Mouse Actions
Lasso Tool	
Add to a selection (keyboard shortcut for the **Add to selection** button in the options bar).	Press [Shift].
Subtract from selection (shortcut for the **Subtract from selection** button in the options bar).	Press [Alt] (Windows) or [Option] (Mac).
Switch from the **Lasso Tool** to the **Polygonal Lasso Tool** and back again while creating a selection.	While creating a selection, press [Alt] (Windows) or [Option] (Mac) and then release the mouse button. Hold the [Alt] button while using the **Polygonal Lasso Tool**. To switch back to the **Lasso Tool**, hold the mouse button and release [Alt]. If you release both [Alt] and the mouse button, the selection closes.
Polygonal Lasso Tool	
Add to a selection (keyboard shortcut for the **Add to selection** button in the options bar).	Press [Shift].
Subtract from selection (shortcut for the **Subtract from selection** button in the options bar).	Press [Alt] (Windows) or [Option] (Mac).
Switch from the **Polygonal Lasso Tool** to the **Lasso Tool** and back again while creating a selection.	While creating a selection, press and hold [Alt] (Windows) or [Option] (Mac) and the mouse button. Drag the mouse to change to the **Lasso Tool**. Release the mouse button or [Alt] to return to the **Polygonal Lasso Tool**.
Back up (erase line segments and fastening points) while drawing a selection.	Press [Delete] or [Backspace]. This must be done before the selection is closed.
Magnetic Lasso Tool	
Back up (erase line segments and fastening points) while drawing a selection.	Press [Delete] or [Backspace] and move the mouse backward along the selection path.
Switch to the **Lasso Tool** and back again while creating a selection.	Click and hold the mouse button, press and hold [Alt] (Windows) or [Option] (Mac). Drag the mouse to switch to the **Lasso Tool**. To return to the **Magnetic Lasso Tool**, release [Alt] and then release the mouse button. Note: if you release the mouse button first, the **Polygonal Lasso Tool** is activated. Click the mouse and release [Alt] to return to the **Magnetic Lasso Tool**.
Switch to the **Polygonal Lasso Tool** and back again while creating a selection.	Press and hold [Alt] (Windows) or [Option] (Mac) and click the mouse button. To return to the **Magnetic Lasso Tool**, release [Alt] and click the mouse button.

The Magic Wand Tool

When you click a pixel with the **Magic Wand Tool**, Photoshop looks for other pixels that are similar in color and selects them, as well. This tool enables you to select complicated areas of similarly-colored pixels, such as blue sky showing through tree branches. However, for this tool to work well, the colored areas you select need to contrast with their immediate surroundings.

The **Tolerance:** setting on the options bar controls how "tolerant" the **Magic Wand Tool** is of different shades of color. See **Figure 3-21**. If a low value is entered and you click on a pixel, only pixels that are very similar in color are selected. Entering the maximum **Tolerance:** value of 255 would result in all pixels being selected, no matter what color they were. Tolerance settings from 5 to about 75 are most commonly used.

Pixels that are touching or bordering each other are *contiguous*. When the **Contiguous** check box is checked, the **Magic Wand Tool** selects similar-colored pixels only if they are touching each other, **Figure 3-22**. When the **Contiguous** check box is unchecked, similar colors in the entire image are selected. Notice that with contiguous option turned off, the blue sky showing between the branches was also selected.

Figure 3-21.
The controls in the **Magic Wand Tool**'s options bar determine how sensitive the tool is. A higher tolerance setting will allow a greater range of colors to be selected than a low tolerance setting.

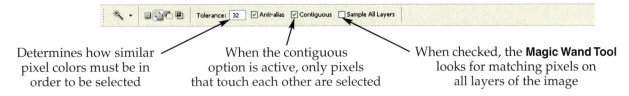

Determines how similar pixel colors must be in order to be selected

When the contiguous option is active, only pixels that touch each other are selected

When checked, the **Magic Wand Tool** looks for matching pixels on all layers of the image

Figure 3-22.
The **Magic Wand Tool** was used to select the blue sky near the top of the house in both of these examples. **A**—The blue sky selected with the **Magic Wand Tool** with the **Contiguous** option off. Areas of blue in the window and showing through the tree are selected along with the open sky. **B**—When the same color is clicked with the **Contiguous** setting on, only the open sky is selected.

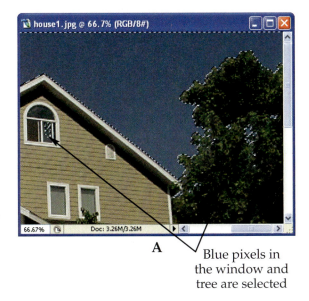
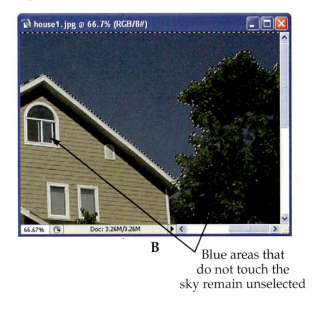

A — Blue pixels in the window and tree are selected

B — Blue areas that do not touch the sky remain unselected

However, part of a window that is blue-gray was also selected. This could easily be fixed by choosing the **Lasso Tool**, clicking the **Subtract from selection** button, and selecting the problem area to remove it from the selection.

A Photoshop image can be made up of several layers (layers will be discussed thoroughly in Chapter 4). When the **Sample All Layers** check box is checked, the **Magic Wand Tool** will select pixels of similar color on all visible layers. When **Sample All Layers** check box is unchecked, pixels will be selected only on the active layer.

Quick Mask Mode

The quick mask mode enables you to select an area in a very different way. You use Photoshop's **Brush Tool**, with its various brush styles, to "paint" a semitransparent color over your image. This colored area is really a protective shield called a mask, and it is painted over the portions of your file that you do *not* want to select. Press the **Edit in Quick Mask Mode** button near the bottom of the **Toolbox** to activate this mode, **Figure 3-23**. Press the **Edit in Standard Mode** button to change the selection mode back to the "marching ants" style. As you create a selection, you can jump back and forth between standard mode and quick mask mode at any time.

To create a selection in quick mask mode, select the **Brush Tool**, choose a brush style and diameter, and set black as the foreground color to paint the mask, **Figure 3-24**. The **Brush Tool** will be discussed in detail in Chapter 6, *Painting Tools and Filters*. For the purpose of drawing a mask, simply click the **Brush Tool** in the **Toolbox**, and then select the desired brush from the **Brush Presets** drop-down list in the options bar. When selecting a brush preset, keep in mind that "soft" brush styles create a feathered selection.

Zoom in close (200% or more) to paint your mask accurately. To erase parts of the mask, if necessary, change the foreground color to white. When the foreground color is set to white, the **Brush Tool** acts as an eraser. When you have finished creating the mask, the entire image except for the areas that are covered by the mask are selected.

You can use any combination of selection tools and quick masking to create a single selection. Keep in mind that quick mask mode is especially helpful for viewing feathered selections, since the "marching ants" cannot show how the feathered effect is going to look.

Double-clicking on the **Edit in Quick Mask Mode** button brings up the **Quick Mask Options** dialog box, **Figure 3-25**. In this dialog box, you can specify whether the mask represents selected areas instead of non-selected areas (default setting), select a new color for the mask, and adjust the transparency of the mask.

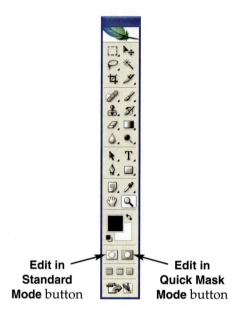

Figure 3-23.
The **Edit in Standard Mode** button and **Edit in Quick Mask Mode** button are used to switch between quick mask mode and standard mode. Standard mode is the mode in which selections are made using the selection tools such as the lasso tools, the marquee tools, and the **Magic Wand Tool**.

Edit in Standard Mode button — **Edit in Quick Mask Mode** button

Figure 3-24.
This image is being edited in quick mask mode. The **Brush Tool** is being used to paint a mask, telling Photoshop what part of the image should *not* be selected.

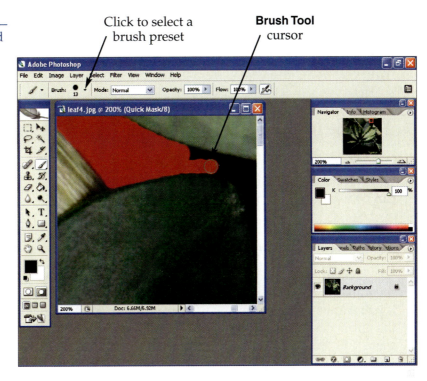

Figure 3-25.
You can adjust the properties of quick mask mode in the **Quick Mask Options** dialog box.

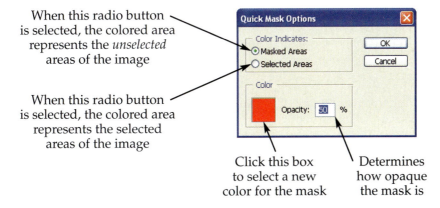

The Type Masking Tools

The **Horizontal Type Mask Tool** and the **Vertical Type Mask Tool** create selections shaped like text. These tools are accessed by clicking on the **Horizontal Type Tool** (or other active type tool) button and holding the mouse button until the other type tools appear in a pop-up menu.

After selecting the desired type masking tool from the pop-up menu, you set the font, size and style in the options bar. The options available are the same as those available for the other text tools. These options are discussed in detail in Chapter 5, *Text, Shapes, and Layer Styles*. Using these options, you can change the font, change font style, adjust the font size, select an anti-aliasing method, change justification, warp the text, and fine-tune a number of typesetting properties.

A pink mask appears as you click on your image and begin to enter your text. Notice that the text is cut out of the mask, meaning that it will be selected. After you finish entering the text, click the **Commit** button (check mark button) in the options bar to turn the text into a selection, **Figure 3-26**.

The Select Menu

The **Select** menu contains commands that can adjust selections in many useful ways. The following sections explain the commands found in this menu and how they can be used to create, modify, and save selections.

The All Command

The **All** command selects the entire image. However, if your file is made up of several layers, only the contents of the active layer are selected. This command is useful if you want to select large areas of the drawing. With one menu selection, you can select the entire image, and then use the selection tools or quick mask option to deselect the areas you do not want included.

The Deselect Command

The **Deselect** command clears any selections in your image. This command is used frequently, so it is useful to memorize the keyboard shortcut, [Ctrl][D]. Occasionally, you will try to use one of Photoshop's tools and it will not seem to work. It is easy to forget that a part of your file may be selected, preventing Photoshop's tools from working anywhere else in the image. Choosing **Select > Deselect** clears up this problem.

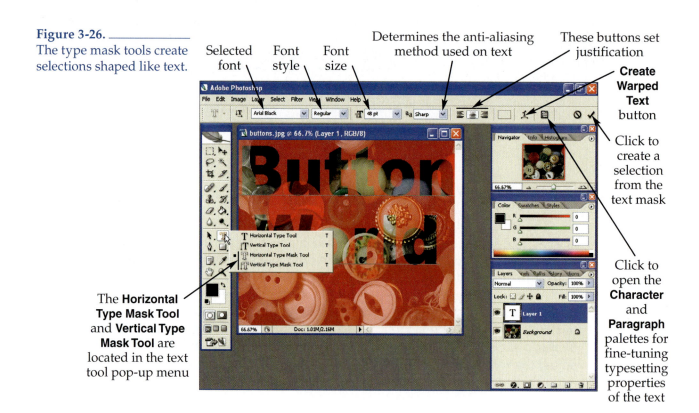

Figure 3-26. The type mask tools create selections shaped like text.

The **Horizontal Type Mask Tool** and **Vertical Type Mask Tool** are located in the text tool pop-up menu

Selected font

Font style

Font size

Determines the anti-aliasing method used on text

These buttons set justification

Create Warped Text button

Click to create a selection from the text mask

Click to open the **Character** and **Paragraph** palettes for fine-tuning typesetting properties of the text

The Reselect Command

If you deselect an area, the **Reselect** command can bring it back for later use. You can use this command to restore a selection any time after it has been deselected but before a new selection is created. Since this command is often used with the **Deselect** command, you will want to learn its keyboard shortcut, [Shift][Ctrl][D].

The Inverse Command

The term *inverse* means "the opposite of." With some images, it is easier to select the parts you do not want to include first, and then invert the selection. For example, the leaf in Figure 3-27 can be quickly selected by first using the **Magic Wand** to select all of the white background and then choosing **Select > Inverse** to invert or "flip" the selection so it surrounds the leaf instead of the background.

Selecting by Color Range

The **Color Range** command is similar in function to the **Magic Wand Tool**. When you choose **Select > Color Range...**, the **Color Range** dialog box appears and your cursor becomes an **Eyedropper Tool**, Figure 3-28. Click on a color in your image, and a preview of your selection appears in the dialog box. Click on the **Add to Sample** (eyedropper with a plus sign) button and then click on additional colors in the image to add more shades of color to your selection. Click on the **Subtract from Sample** (eyedropper with a minus sign) button and pick colors in the image to remove from the selection.

If you want to include a smaller range of colors with each selected color, drag the **Fuzziness:** slider to the left. If you want to include a greater range of colors in the selection, drag the **Fuzziness:** slider to the right. You can see the effects of the **Fuzziness:** setting in the preview window.

When you click the **OK** button, the **Color Range** dialog box closes and the colors are selected in your image. Be aware that high **Fuzziness:** settings cause some pixels to be only *partially* selected (similar to the effect created by feather-selecting an area). These partially selected areas may not have a visible selection border around them when you click **OK**. Partially selected areas will be partially affected by Photoshop's tools and commands.

Figure 3-27.
The **Inverse** command is used to quickly select this leaf. **A**—The **Magic Wand Tool** is used to select the white background. **B**—After choosing **Select > Inverse**, the leaf is selected and the background is not.

A　　　　　　　　　　　　B

Figure 3-28. The **Color Range** dialog box is used to select parts of an image based on color. It is similar in function to the **Magic Wand Tool** with the **Contiguous** option turned off.

The Feather Command

The **Feather** command allows you to feather a selection that has already been created. Even though most of the selection tools have a feather option on their respective options bars, using the **Feather** command is often more convenient. If you use the **Feather:** option on the options bar, you must enter the feather value *before* you create the selection. You must also change the feather value back to 0 before you can make a nonfeathered selection. If you use the **Feather** command, you do not have to worry about either of those problems.

To use the **Feather** command, begin by making a selection. Next, choose **Select > Feather....** This opens the **Feather Selection** dialog box. Enter a value in the **Feather Radius:** text box and pick the **OK** button. The **Feather Selection** dialog box closes and, in the image window, your selection is adjusted for the new feathering setting. The "marching ants" around the selection indicate the midpoint of the feathering effect.

The Modify Submenu

The **Select > Modify** submenu contains four helpful commands that are used to adjust selections. These commands can be used to create a border from a selection, smooth a selection, or change the size of a selection.

The **Border** command creates two new edges on each side of the outside edge of the original selection. The command then deselects everything not within the two new edges, creating a border effect. Choosing this command opens the **Border Selection** dialog box. If you enter a setting of 6 in the **Width:** text box, the outside edge of the border is located three pixels out from the outside edge of the original selection. A new inside edge is created three pixels in from the original selection's outside edge. The area between the two new edges is selected.

The **Smooth** command is used to smooth out sharp angles and corners on a selection. Choosing this command opens the **Smooth Selection** dialog box. The value entered in the **Sample Radius:** text box of this dialog box is the radius used to round the corners.

The **Expand** command makes the selection larger (based on the original shape). Choosing this command opens the **Expand Selection** dialog box. The selection grows outward by the value entered in the **Expand By:** text box. It should be noted that in addition to increasing the size of the selection, the **Expand** command also has a smoothing effect on the selection.

The **Contract** command makes the selection smaller while keeping its original shape. Choosing this command opens the **Contract Selection** dialog box. The selection shrinks by the amount entered in the **Contract By:** text box.

The Grow and Similar Commands

The **Grow** and **Similar** commands are directly related to the **Magic Wand Tool**. In fact, the **Tolerance:** setting in the **Magic Wand Tool**'s options bar controls these two commands. The **Grow** command functions like the **Magic Wand Tool** with the **Contiguous** setting on. The **Similar** command works like the **Magic Wand Tool** with the **Contiguous** setting turned off (similar colors are selected throughout the entire file). One advantage of these commands over the **Magic Wand Tool** is that they can be used to select numerous colors at one time.

To use these commands, begin by creating a selection that contains the color or colors that you want to select. Next, click the **Magic Wand Tool** in the **Toolbox** and set the **Tolerance:** setting in the options bar to the desired value. Then, choose either **Select > Grow** or **Select > Similar**. The colors in the original selection are included in the new selection, just as they would have been if they had been individually added to a selection with the **Magic Wand Tool**.

The Transform Selection Command

The **Transform Selection** command creates small, square handles around your selection. These handles allow you to adjust the scale (by holding [Shift] and dragging a corner handle) or size (by dragging any handle) of your selection. If you position the cursor outside of the selection, the cursor will change into a rotation cursor (curved arrow). You can then rotate the selection by clicking and holding the mouse button and dragging the mouse until the selection is rotated to the desired position, **Figure 3-29**.

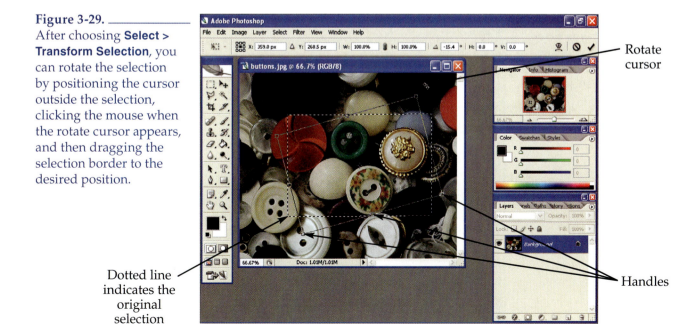

Figure 3-29. After choosing **Select > Transform Selection**, you can rotate the selection by positioning the cursor outside the selection, clicking the mouse when the rotate cursor appears, and then dragging the selection border to the desired position.

Dotted line indicates the original selection

Rotate cursor

Handles

When you select the **Transform Selection** command, the options bar contains settings that allow you to input precise width and height scaling amounts, angle of rotation, skewing (distorting) amounts, and actual location of the selection in the file (X and Y reference points).

While you are transforming a selection, right-click (or [Ctrl]+click for Mac) to bring up a menu that lists additional transformation options.

Saving and Loading a Selection

Some complicated selections take hours to create, and you may need to save your work and continue refining your selection later. To save a selection for further use, choose the **Select > Save Selection…** command. In the **Save Selection** dialog box, enter a name for the selection in the **Name:** text box and pick the **OK** button. The saved selection is stored in the **Channels** palette, which is discussed later in this book. See **Figure 3-30**.

If you have previously saved a selection, you can add the current selection to the saved selection. To do this, choose **Select > Save Selection…**. In the **Save Selection** dialog box, select the name of the saved selection from the **Channel:** drop-down list. In the **Operation** section of the dialog box, select the appropriate radio button. If you select the **Replace Channel** radio button, the new selection replaces the saved selection. If you select the **Add to Channel** radio button, a single selection is created by adding the new selection to the saved selection. If you select the **Subtract from Channel** radio button, a single selection is created by removing the area in the new selection from the saved selection. If you select the **Intersect with Channel** radio button, a single selection is created by keeping overlapping areas from both selections and discarding areas that do not overlap.

Each time you save a selection, you also need to save the image in order to record the new channel containing the selection. When you save the file, make sure your file is saved in Photoshop (PSD) format. The PSD file format saves the channel containing the selection without changing the image. TIFF or PDF formats can also be used. If the file is saved in a format other than PSD, TIFF, or PDF, the selection will be lost.

When you open your file to continue adjusting the selection, choose **Select > Load Selection…**. In the **Load Selection** dialog box, choose the selection from the **Channel:**

Figure 3-30.
This layer is being saved as a new channel. Note that another selection has previously been saved.

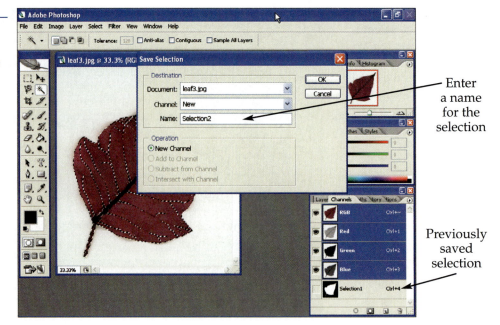

drop-down list. You can invert the selection by checking the **Invert** check box. If there is currently no selection in the image window, simply click the **OK** button to load the saved selection into the image window.

However, if you currently have a selection in the image window, there are four different ways you can load the saved selection. In the **Operation** section of the **Load Selection** dialog box, choose the appropriate radio button. Choosing the **New Selection** radio button will completely replace the current selection with the saved selection. Choosing the **Add to Selection** radio button will combine the saved selection and the current selection. Choosing the **Subtract from Selection** radio button will remove the area included in the saved selection from the current selection. Choosing the **Intersect with Selection** radio button causes the overlapping areas of the saved and current selections to remain selected, but areas of both selections that do not overlap are deselected. Once you have selected the appropriate radio button, click the **OK** button to load the saved selection.

Temporarily Hiding a Selection

When you have made a selection and it blocks your view (sometimes those marching ants get in the way), you can temporarily hide it by choosing **View > Show > Selection Edges**. The selection will be hidden until you choose this command again.

Removing a Fringe

The leaf in **Figure 3-31** was selected and copied to another image that has a different background. Part of the white background along the leaf's edge was selected along with the leaf, causing a fringe or halo to be visible when the leaf was placed against the different background. In situations such as this, you may be able to remove the fringe by selecting **Layer > Matting > Defringe…**. In the leaf example, the **Defringe** command copies green pixels from the leaf and expands them outward, replacing the light colors in the fringe. You specify the distance (in pixels) in the **Defringe** dialog box. Usually a distance of one or two pixels is enough to remove a fringe.

Figure 3-31.
In many cases, a light colored fringe can be easily removed from a pasted-in selection. **A**—This leaf was selected and moved to another file with a contrasting background. White pixels along the edge are clearly visible. **B**—The **Defringe** command replaces the light-colored pixels with green pixels, eliminating the fringe.

GRAPHIC DESIGN:
Choosing Photographic Images

Photographic images that are used in graphic designs must be chosen with care. Some designers capture their own images. Many designers purchase images from *stock photo agencies*. Stock photo agencies are companies that keep large libraries of images, usually categorized by subject, that can be purchased for use. At times, professional photographers are hired to capture needed images.

The following are factors that should be considered when selecting images.

- Focus: Images should be clearly in focus, unless a blurred effect is desired. Photoshop can only sharpen images with very minor blur problems (discussed in a later chapter).

- Lighting: If the photograph has a main subject, the lighting should adequately illuminate the subject. In other words, details in the image should not appear washed out because the lighting is too bright or the shadows are too black. The lighting in an image should fit the overall mood and strategy of the design. If several photographs are to be used in the same design, the lighting in each photograph should be similar.

- Posing of the Subject: Look for images where the subject is posed in a way that allows the designer some flexibility when incorporating the image into the design. Keep in mind that images can influence the actual format of the design. For example, tall subjects (such as skyscrapers or statues) in an image may influence the designer to create a more vertically-oriented design.

- Image composition: In the photographic sense, composition means "what the photographer chose to include in the image." As you select photos, keep in mind that a photo's appearance may be improved if it is cropped or rotated. If an entire photo will be used in a design, judge the photo by how well-composed it is. If you are not familiar with tips for creating better photos, search the web using "photographic composition" as keywords for more information.

The band members shown in **Figure 3-32** wanted a CD insert design that had a "backstage" look and feel. The photographer captured images of the band members outdoors, just before sunset. The summer sun was low in the sky and shining through a bit of haze, creating warm-colored side lighting on each band members' face—a lighting condition that would fit well with a stage lighting design scheme. One of the band members was posed sideways to avoid a redundant, forward-facing trio. This gives the designer more flexibility—the image could be flipped either way as the designer arranged the images with the other design elements.

Lighting conditions can make an incredible difference in image quality. The ostrich image on the left in **Figure 3-33** was captured in the early morning hours, just after sunrise. The early morning sun was filtering through some clouds, causing the ostrich to be illuminated by very soft light. There are no bright highlights or dark shadows on the ostrich, unlike the second photo which was shot around noon on a hot, cloudless summer day. You can see some detail on the ostrich's neck, but most of the subject's detail is drowned out in harsh, bright highlights or black shadow areas.

Figure 3-32.
The photos of these band members were captured in a parking lot early on a summer evening.

Figure 3-33.
These images show the dramatic effects that different lighting can offer. **A**—Soft lighting preserves the details of a subject. **B**—Harsh lighting drowns out image detail.

A　　　　　　　B

Summary

Using the selection tools discussed in this chapter is a fundamental Photoshop skill. Take the time to review the keyboard shortcuts—they can make a selection task much easier. For example, when creating a selection around a circular object in an image (such as a coin), you may find yourself holding down three different keys simultaneously: [Shift] to force a circle, [Alt] to create the selection from a center point, and the [Spacebar] to adjust the position of the circular selection as you create it.

Chapter Tutorials

In the tutorials that follow, you get a chance to practice using the selection tools discussed in this chapter. You will use these tools to begin creating projects, which you will continue to refine as you progress through this book.

Tutorial 3-1: The Marquee Selection Tools

In this tutorial, you will combine various photos to create the front and back of a postcard. You will use a variety of the selection methods discussed in this chapter. You will also be introduced to layers, which will be discussed in detail in Chapter 4.

1. Open the file named Gilia.jpg, located in the flowers folder.
2. In the **Layers** palette, double click the Background layer.
3. In the **New Layer** dialog box, accept the name Layer 1 by clicking **OK**.

   This step is necessary because you will be adding a new, white background layer in the following steps. Layers allow you to keep different parts of your design seperate from each other.

4. Select **Layer > New > Layer…** and click **OK** in the **New Layer** dialog box to accept the default settings.
5. Click the **Paint Bucket Tool** in the **Toolbox** and set white as the foreground color.
6. Make sure Layer 2 is active, and click anywhere in the image window to fill the image with white.
7. With Layer 2 still active, select **Layer > New > Background From Layer…** (**Photoshop > Preferences > Grids, Guides, & Slices...** for Mac users).

   Layer 2 becomes the background layer and is moved behind Layer 1.

8. Choose **Edit > Preferences > Guides, Grid & Slices…**.
9. In the **Grid** section of the **Preferences** dialog box, enter 1 in the **Gridline every:** text box and select **inches** from the drop-down list. Enter a value of 4 in the **Subdivisions:** text box.
10. Click the **OK** button.
11. Choose **View > Show > Grid** to turn on the grid.

    1" squares appear, subdivided into 1/4" sections.

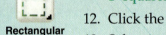

Rectangular Marquee Tool

12. Click the **Rectangular Marquee Tool** in the **Toolbox**.
13. Select Layer 1 in the **Layers** palette, and then drag a selection border the same size and in the same location as shown in **Figure T3-1**.
14. Choose **Select > Feather…**. In the **Feather Selection** dialog box, enter 10 in the **Feather Radius:** text box and click **OK**.

    The rectangular selection now has rounded corners because of the feather effect.

15. Press [Delete], **Figure T3-2**.

    A white area is created for the postal service to print a bar code.

16. Choose **Layer > New > Layer…**. In the **New Layer** dialog box, name the layer Stamp Box and click **OK**.
17. The **Rectangular Marquee Tool** should still be active. In the options bar, choose **Fixed Size** from the **Style:** drop-down list.
18. In the **Width:** text box, enter .65 in ("in" is an abbreviation for inches). In the **Height:** text box, enter .9 in.

Figure T3-1.
The selection is created along the grid lines.

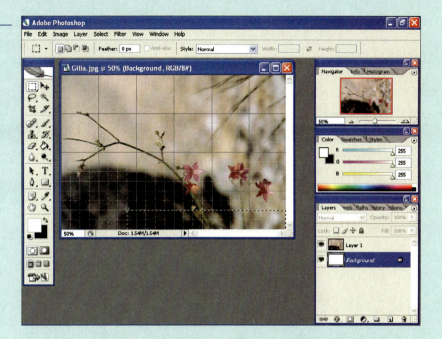

Figure T3-2.
When [Delete] is pressed, a blank area is created for printing a bar code.

Corners of the selection are rounded, indicating the selection is feathered

Default Foreground and **Background Colors** button

19. Click to place the rectangular selection, then move it to the location shown in **Figure T3-3**. To move the selection, use the arrow keys or click inside the selection and drag.
20. Make sure the Stamp Box layer is still selected in the **Layers** palette and that white is set as the foreground color.
21. Click the **Paint Bucket Tool** in the **Toolbox** and then click inside the selection to fill it with white.
22. Choose **Select > Modify > Border....**
23. In the **Border Selection** dialog box, enter a value of 5 in the **Width:** text box and click **OK**.

Figure T3-3. Move the selection to the upper right corner of the image.

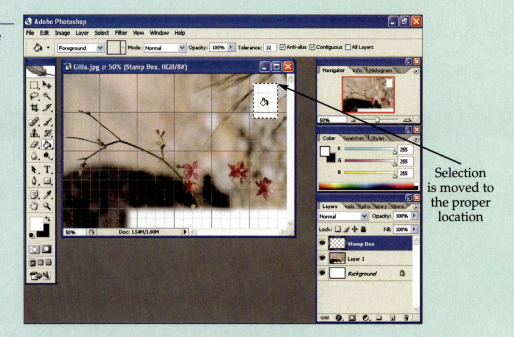

Selection is moved to the proper location

Brush Tool

24. Set the foreground color to black and click the **Brush Tool** in the **Toolbox**.
25. In the options bar, click the **Brush Presets** button. In the control panel that pops up, choose a round brush and drag the **Master Diameter** slider to 30 px and the **Hardness** slider to 100%.
26. Paint over the selection border until it fills with black. See **Figure T3-4**.

    The black color bleeds outside of the selection. This is because Border command automatically applies a slight feather effect.

27. Zoom in to check the accuracy of your painting.
28. Without closing the Gilia.jpg file, open the Dusty.jpg file. This image is located in the flowers folder.

Figure T3-4. The **Border** command changes the rectangular selection into a border.

An oval selection is drawn around the flowers

A black border is painted around the rectangular selection

Elliptical Marquee Tool

29. Click the **Elliptical Marquee Tool** in the **Toolbox**.

   Remember that the **Elliptical Marquee Tool** is accessed by clicking on the **Marquee Tool** button and holding the mouse button until the shortcut menu with the additional tools appears.

30. Create a oval-shaped selection around the flower. Press the [Spacebar] as you create the selection to move it to the location shown in Figure T3-4.

Move Tool

31. Click the **Move Tool** in the **Toolbox**.
32. In the options bar, place a check mark in the **Show Transform Controls** check box.
33. Drag the selected flower over to the Gilia.jpg image and release the mouse button.

   The oval-shaped selection is copied from the Dusty.jpg image and pasted into the Gilia.jpg image, which is made active and brought to the front.

34. Choose **Edit > Transform > Scale**.
35. In the options bar, enter 24% in both the **W:** (width) and **H:** (height) text boxes.

Commit

36. Click the **Commit** (check mark) button at the far right end of the options bar to complete the **Scale** command.
37. Use the **Move Tool** to drag the purple flower to the location shown in **Figure T3-5**.
38. Close the Dusty.jpg file. Do *not* save the changes.

   The Dusty.jpg image closes, and the Gilia.jpg image becomes active.

39. In the **Save As** dialog box, name this file 03cardback and select **Photoshop (*.PSD, *.PDD)** from the **Format:** drop-down list. Pick the **Save** button to save the file.

   You will work again with this file later.

40. Close the 03cardback.psd file.
41. Open the Paper.jpg file.

   This 6" × 4" image will become the front of a postcard.

42. Open the Beauty.jpg file.
43. Click the **Elliptical Marquee Tool** in the **Toolbox**.

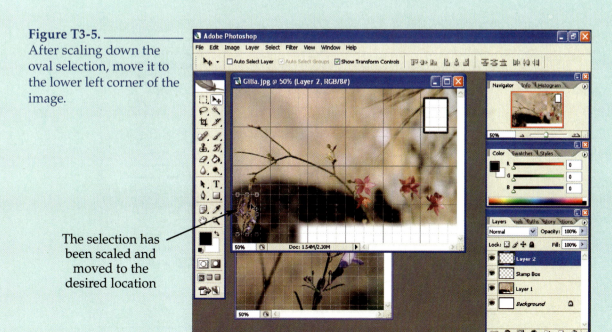

Figure T3-5. After scaling down the oval selection, move it to the lower left corner of the image.

The selection has been scaled and moved to the desired location

44. Hold down [Shift] and drag a circle around some of the pink flowers, as shown in **Figure T3-6**.
45. Click the **Move Tool** in the **Toolbox** and use it to drag the selected flowers over to the Paper.jpg image.
46. Close the Beauty.jpg file and do not save changes.

    The Beauty.jpg image closes and the Paper.jpg becomes active and moves to the front.

47. Choose **Edit > Transform > Scale**. In the options bar, enter 60% in the **W:** and **H:** text boxes.
48. Move the selection to the location shown in **Figure T3-7**.

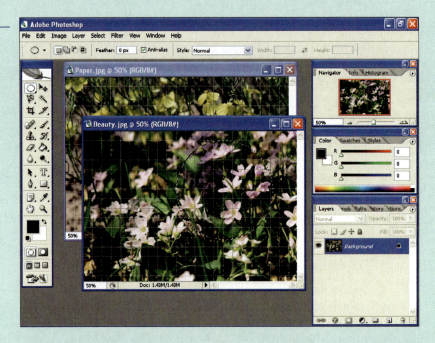

Figure T3-6.
Draw a circular selection around the flowers in the location shown.

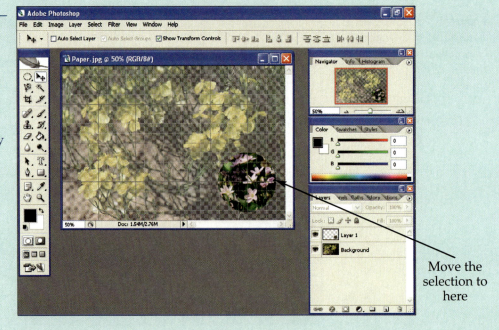

Figure T3-7.
Move the selection to the lower right corner of the image. Note: In this figure, the opacity of the background has been lowered to make it easier to see the selection. Your image should look slightly different.

Move the selection to here

49. Open the file named Mountain.jpg, located in the flowers folder.
50. Create a circular selection around the purple flowers, **Figure T3-8**.
51. Click the **Move Tool** in the **Toolbox** and drag the selection over to the Paper.jpg image and release the mouse button. Use the **Edit > Transform > Scale** command to scale the selection to 50%. Then, move it next to the pink flowers, **Figure T3-9**.
52. Close the Mountain.jpg file and do *not* save the changes.
53. Choose **View > Show > Grid** to turn off the grid.
54. The Paper.jpg image should still be on your screen. Choose **File > Save As…**.

Figure T3-8.
Draw a circular selection around the flowers, in the location shown.

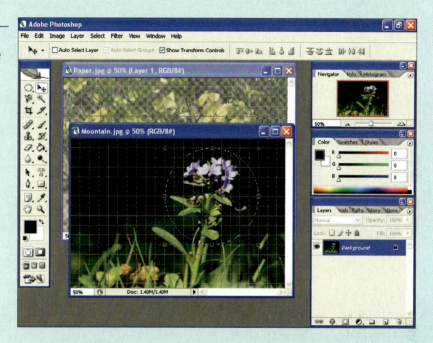

Figure T3-9.
Move the purple flowers next to the pink flowers, as shown here. Note: In this figure, the opacity of the background has been lowered to make it easier to see the inset flowers. Your image should look slightly different.

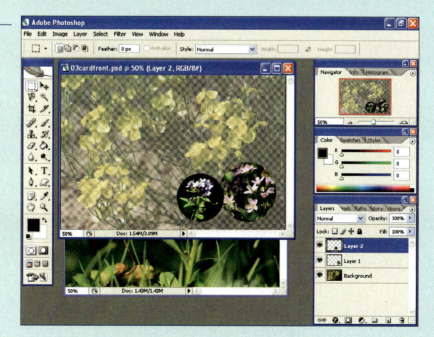

55. In the **Save As** dialog box, name this file 03cardfront and select **Photoshop (*.PSD, *.PDD)** from the **Format:** drop-down list. Pick the **Save** button to save the file.

   You will add more to this file in later tutorials.

56. Close the 03cardfront.psd file.

Tutorial 3-2: Create a Vignette Effect

In this tutorial, you will feather-select an image to create a vignette effect. A vignette is a soft, faded-out edge around a portrait.

1. Open the Henry.jpg file.

2. Select the **Elliptical Marquee Tool** from the **Toolbox** and use it to create the selection shown in **Figure T3-10A**.

   Use the [Spacebar] and [Shift] keys as needed to help you create the selection.

3. Choose **Select > Inverse**.

   Now, the background is selected instead of Henry.

4. Choose **Select > Feather**. In the **Feather Selection** dialog box, enter 14 in the **Feather Radius:** text box and click the **OK** button.

   The selection is feathered to soften its edges.

5. Press [Delete].

   This deletes the background, creating a vignette effect. Note that the feathering option causes the image to fade in from a point seven pixels outside the elliptical selection to a point seven pixels in from the elliptical selection. The size of this fade-in region is controlled by the **Feather Radius:** setting. See **Figure T3-10B**.

6. Choose **File > Save As...**. In the **Save As** dialog box, name the file 03vignette and select **Photoshop (*.PSD, *.PDD)** from the **Format:** drop-down list. Click the **Save** button to save the image.

7. Close the 03vignette.psd file.

Figure T3-10. Creating a vignette from this image is a simple process. **A**—Create an elliptical selection around the portrait. **B**—The selection is inverted and feathered. The background is then deleted, creating the vignette effect.

Selection is at the center of the feathering effect

A   B

Tutorial 3-3: The Crop Tool

In this tutorial, you will use the **Crop Tool** to straighten and discard unwanted portions of an image.

1. Open the file named bball.jpg.

   This damaged photo was placed crookedly on the scanner. It needs to be cropped and rotated.

Crop Tool

2. Click the **Crop Tool** in the **Toolbox** and drag a box in the image as shown in **Figure T3-11A**.
3. Move the cursor just beyond the lower right corner handle until the rotate cursor appears.
4. Rotate the crop selection box slightly, so it looks like the example in **Figure T3-11B**.

   You can change the position of the crop selection by clicking inside the crop area and dragging the selection or by using the arrow keys. You can resize the crop selection as needed by clicking and dragging the handles surrounding the selection.

5. Click the **Commit** (check mark) button at the far right of the options bar *or* press [Enter] to crop and rotate the image.
6. Choose **File > Save As…**. In the **Save As** dialog box, name the file 03bball and select **Photoshop (*.PSD, *.PDD)** from the **Format:** drop-down list. Click the **Save** button to save the image.
7. Close the 03bball.psd image.

Figure T3-11.
This image, which was not placed on the scanner squarely, can be straightened with the **Crop Tool**. A—Draw a rectangular crop box around the image. When the box is properly sized and positioned, the image overlap on opposite corners should mirror one another. B—Rotate the crop box until it is squared up with the image.

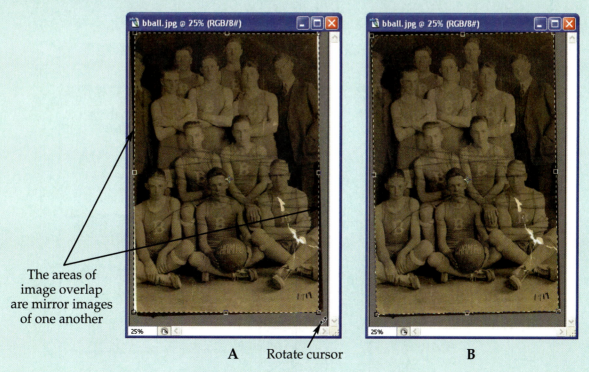

The areas of image overlap are mirror images of one another

A   Rotate cursor   B

Tutorial 3-4

This tutorial is divided into several parts. In each part, you will practice using a different selection tool. You will select several images of leaves and then move each leaf to a new file. In later chapters, you will create a design out of the selected leaves.

Part 1: The Lasso Tool

The **Lasso Tool** is typically used to create selections that are more complicated than the selection in this example. However, following these steps will strengthen your **Lasso Tool** skills.

1. Open the file named leaf1.jpg.

   If you make a mistake as you work on this file, choose Edit > Undo.

2. Click the **Lasso Tool** in the **Toolbox**.
3. Click the **New selection** button on the options bar.
4. Using the mouse, draw a selection border near the edge of the leaf, as shown in **Figure T3-12**.

   Do not worry about making a smooth selection or getting the selection as close as possible to the edge of the leaf. You will improve the accuracy of the selection in the steps that follow.

5. Click the **Zoom Tool** in the **Toolbox**.
6. Drag a box to zoom in on the stem as shown in **Figure T3-13**.
7. Click the **Lasso Tool**.
8. Click the **Add to selection** button in the options bar.
9. Draw a selection border around the part of the stem shown in **Figure T3-14**. Be accurate when you select along the edge of the stem.

   *Your selection border is now larger. It should look similar to the example in **Figure T3-15**.*

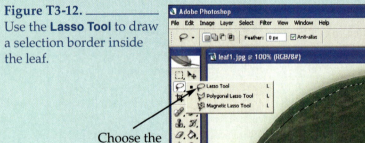

Figure T3-12. Use the **Lasso Tool** to draw a selection border inside the leaf.

Choose the **Lasso Tool**

Figure T3-13. Draw a zoom box to zoom in on the stem of the leaf.

Drag a box to zoom in on the stem

Figure T3-14. With the **Add to selection** button active, carefully draw a small selection around the area shown. The new selection border is shown in yellow and red.

Figure T3-15. The new selection is added to the previous selection.

Subtract from selection

10. The **Add to selection** button should still be active. Add an area like the one shown in **Figure T3-16** to your selection border.
11. If you make the selection border too big, click the **Subtract from selection** button, and create a selection like the one shown in **Figure T3-17**.

The newly created selection is subtracted from the original selection. See **Figure T3-18**.

Figure T3-16. Draw another small selection to add to the existing selection. The new selection border is shown in yellow and red.

Figure T3-17. If the selection border strays outside of the area you want selected, click the **Subtract from selection** button and then draw a new selection around the area you want to remove. The new selection is shown in yellow and red.

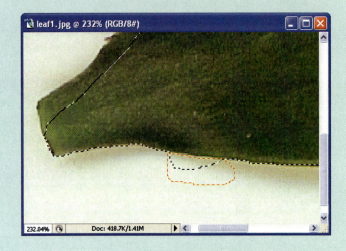

Figure T3-18. The new selection is subtracted from the existing selection.

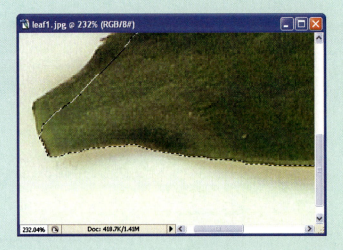

12. Continue using the **Add to selection** and **Subtract from selection** buttons until you have adjusted the selection border snugly around the leaf.

   Hand Tool

   Use the Hand Tool or the Navigator palette to move around your leaf as you work.

13. Choose **View > Actual Pixels** to zoom in at 100%.

Chapter 3   Selection Tools

14. Without closing the leaf1.jpg image, choose **File > New…**.
15. In the **New** dialog box, enter the settings shown in **Figure T3-19**.
16. Click the **OK** button.

    You have just created a new file, named 03leafy, that is 7" tall by 7" wide. Your selection border in the leaf1.jpg image window has disappeared, but do not worry—it is still there.

17. Move the image windows to the positions shown in **Figure T3-20** by clicking and dragging their title bars.
18. Click once anywhere on the title bar of the leaf1.jpg image to make it active.
19. Select the **Move Tool**.

Figure T3-19.
Enter these settings to create the new image into which the leaf will be pasted.

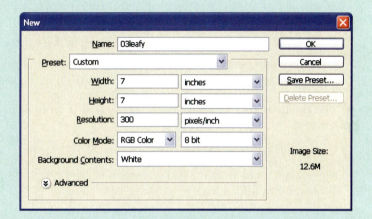

Figure T3-20.
Move the image windows to the positions shown here.

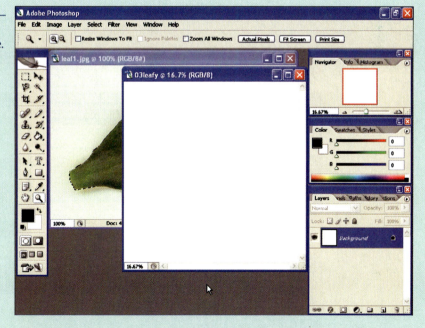

20. Click on the leaf, drag it over to the 03leafy image, and release the mouse button.

    The leaf appears smaller here because the files are zoomed differently. See **Figure T3-21**.

21. Choose **File > Save**. In the **Save As** dialog box, make sure the image is named 03leafy. Select **Photoshop (*.PSD, *.PDD)** from the **Format:** drop-down list.

22. If you are going to continue on with the other tutorials in this chapter, leave the 03leafy.psd file open. If you are not going to continue on with the other tutorials in the book right away, close the 03leafy.psd file.

23. Close the leaf1.jpg file. Do not save changes.

Part 2: The Magnetic Lasso Tool

When making selections, the **Magnetic Lasso Tool** is a better choice than the **Lasso Tool** in many situations. In Part 2 of this tutorial, you will gain some experience in using the **Magnetic Lasso Tool** to create a selection.

1. If the 03leafy.psd file you created in Part 1 of this tutorial is not open, open it now.
2. Open the leaf2.jpg file.
3. Choose **Image > Rotate Canvas > 90° CCW** (counterclockwise).

   The image is rotated so the stem of the leaf is more or less pointed at the bottom of the screen.

4. Choose **View > Fit on Screen**.

   The image window increases in size to fill the vertical work space available. The image is zoomed to fill the image window.

Figure T3-21.
The leaves appear in very different sizes because of the difference in the zoom percentages of the two image windows.

The images have different zoom percentages

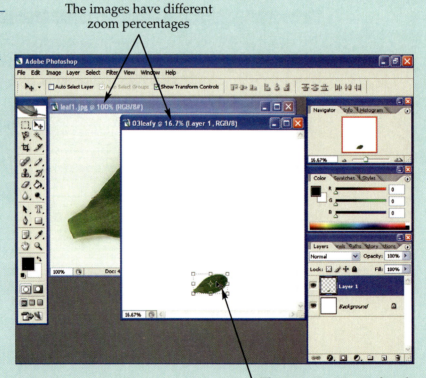

The **Move Tool** is used to drag the selection from one image to the other

Magnetic Lasso Tool

5. Click and hold the mouse button on the **Lasso Tool** in the **Toolbox**. When the pop-up menu appears, choose the **Magnetic Lasso Tool**. See **Figure T3-22**.
6. Enter the following settings in the options bar:
   - Click the **New Selection** button.
   - **Width:** 8 px
   - **Edge Contrast:** 40%

   The edge of the green leaf contrasts with the white background behind it. However, the Magnetic Lasso Tool might become confused where the shadow is darkest. The settings you entered increase the width and decrease the edge contrast required for a selection. This makes it easier to select the edge of the leaf in shadowed areas.

7. Click anywhere at the leaf's edge.
8. Release the mouse button and move the mouse cursor slowly around the leaf's edge.

   If the Magnetic Lasso Tool makes a mistake, you can backtrack by pressing [Delete] or [Backspace] repeatedly while moving the cursor backward along the selection path.

9. Press [Enter] after you have moved the **Magnetic Lasso Tool** all the way around the leaf.

   The selection is closed and the familiar marching ants appear at the selection border. Your selection border will probably not be perfect. The Magnetic Lasso Tool gets "confused" in places, such as the leaf tips (which are less than eight pixels wide) and the stem.

10. Zoom in, switch to the **Lasso Tool**, and use the **Add to selection** and **Subtract from selection** buttons to fix the selection border where necessary.
11. Use the **Move Tool** to drag the selected leaf over to the 03leafy.psd file.
12. Close the leaf2.jpg file. Do *not* save changes.
13. With the 03leafy.psd image active, choose **File > Save**.
14. If you are going to continue on with the other tutorials in this chapter, leave the 03leafy.psd file open. If you are not going to continue on with the other tutorials in the book right away, close the 03leafy.psd file.

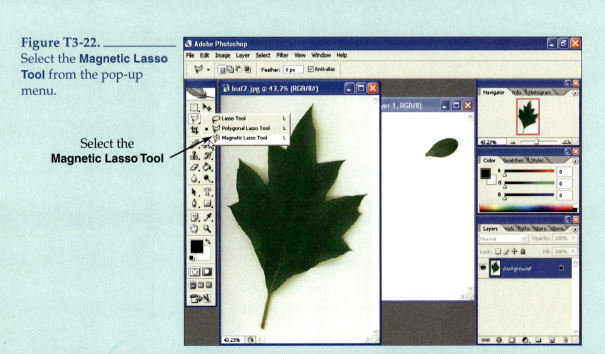

Figure T3-22. Select the **Magnetic Lasso Tool** from the pop-up menu.

Select the **Magnetic Lasso Tool**

Part 3: The Magic Wand Tool

As you will see in this tutorial, the **Magic Wand Tool** is useful for selecting objects that have a limited range of colors. It is even more useful if the object to be selected appears against a strongly contrasting background.

1. If the 03leafy.psd file you created in Parts 1 and 2 of this tutorial is not open, open it now.
2. Open the file named leaf3.jpg.
3. Choose **View > Fit on Screen**.
4. Click the **Magic Wand Tool**.

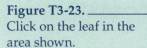
Magic Wand Tool

5. Make sure the **New selection** button is activated in the options bar.
6. In the options bar, change the **Tolerance:** setting to 20.
7. Click on the part of the leaf indicated in **Figure T3-23**.

   When you click with the **Magic Wand Tool**, it looks at the color of the pixel you clicked on. Then, it selects similar colors around that pixel.

8. Choose **Select > Deselect**.
9. Change the **Tolerance:** setting to 50.
10. Click in the same place you did in step 7.

    The **Magic Wand Tool** now selects a broader range of red pixels because the **Tolerance:** setting is higher. However, there are still parts of the leaf that are not selected. You can continue to pick colors with the **Add to selection** button selected in the options bar until you have selected all of the colors in the leaf, but there is an easier way. In the following steps, you will pick the background and then invert the selection.

11. Make sure the **New Selection** button is selected in the options bar. Change the **Tolerance:** setting to 100.

    By increasing the **Tolerance:** setting, you are allowing more colors to be selected at one time. A high tolerance setting is required to avoid selecting the pink shadow areas around the edge of the leaf. Fortunately, the leaf and the background contrast enough that parts of the leaf will not be selected by mistake.

Figure T3-23.
Click on the leaf in the area shown.

Click on this general area of the leaf

Chapter 3   Selection Tools

12. Click on a white or near-white part of the background.

    The entire background is selected and the leaf remains unselected. See **Figure T3-24**.

13. Choose **Select > Inverse**.

    The leaf becomes selected and the background is unselected.

14. Use the **Move Tool** to drag the selection over to the 03leafy.psd file.
15. Close the leaf3.jpg file. Do not save the changes.
16. With the 03leafy.psd image active, choose **File > Save**.
17. If you are going to continue on with the other tutorials in this chapter, leave the 03leafy.psd file open. If you are not going to continue on with the other tutorials in the book right away, close the 03leafy.psd file.

Part 4: Quick Mask Mode

Quick mask mode allows you to use the **Brush Tool** to paint a selection. This is helpful when selecting portions of an image that has similar colors throughout, making other selection tools more difficult to use.

1. If the 03leafy.psd file you worked on in Parts 1–3 of this tutorial is not open, open it now.
2. Open the leaf4.jpg file.
3. Choose **View > Fit on Screen**.
4. Click the **Lasso Tool** in the **Toolbox**.
5. Click the **New selection** button on the options bar.
6. With the mouse, draw a selection around the outside of the longest leaf, as shown in **Figure T3-25**.
7. Click the **Edit in Quick Mask Mode** button. A pink mask covers the area of the image that is not selected.
8. Click on the **Brush Tool** in the **Toolbox**.

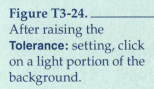
Edit in Quick Mask Mode

Figure T3-24. After raising the **Tolerance:** setting, click on a light portion of the background.

Figure T3-25. ──────
Use the **Lasso Tool** to draw a rough selection around the leaf. The selection will be refined in quick mask mode.

9. In the options bar, click on the **Brush Presets** (arrow) button.
10. Hold your mouse over any of these brushes for two seconds, but do not click. A brief description of the brush appears.
11. Click on the brush with the description **Soft round 13 pixels**. See **Figure T3-26**.

"Soft" means the brush will have a feathery edge. The feather effect will be slight, however, because the brush size is small.

Figure T3-26. ──────
Select the **Soft Round 13 pixels** brush to paint the selection mask.

Brush Tool icon

Brush Presets button

Soft Round 13 Pixels brush preset

Edit in Quick Mask Mode button

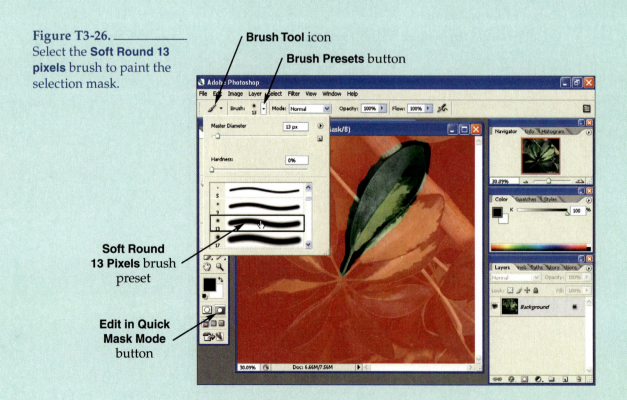

Chapter 3   Selection Tools

12. Click the **Zoom Tool**.
13. Zoom in on the stem of the leaf, **Figure T3-27**.
14. Click the **Brush Tool** again. Paint the area around the leaf, right up to its edge.

    If you make a mistake, change the foreground color to white. Then, the Brush Tool will act like an eraser. Switch the foreground color back to black to resume painting the mask. Change to a smaller brush size as needed to paint accurately. Use the Hand Tool or the Navigator palette to grab and move your leaf as you continue to paint.

Edit in Standard Mode

15. When you have painted a mask around the entire leaf, zoom in even further and check your work.
16. When the area surrounding the leaf is cleanly masked (painted with pink), click the **Edit in Standard Mode** button.

    Everything that was not masked is now selected.

17. Choose **View > Fit on Screen**.
18. Use the **Move Tool** to drag the leaf over to the 03leafy.psd file.
19. Click anywhere on the leaf4.jpg image to make it active and then close the file. Do *not* save the changes.
20. With the 03leafy.psd image active, choose **File > Save**.
21. If you are going to continue on with the other tutorials in this chapter, leave the 03leafy.psd file open. If you are not going to continue on with Part 5 of this tutorial right away, close the 03leafy.psd file.

Part 5: Select and Move the Remaining Leaves

In this part of the tutorial, you will gain experience evaluating an area that needs to be selected, choosing the best selection tool for that area, and using the tool to make the selection.

1. There are two more leaf images that need to be copied to the 03leafy.psd image, leaf5.jpg and leaf6.jpg. Use any method you have learned to select and move the leaves over to the 03leafy.psd file.

Figure T3-27.
Zoom in on the leaf so you can paint the mask accurately.

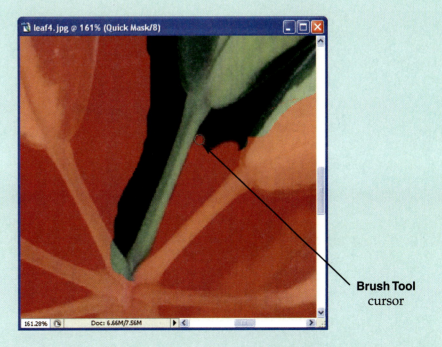

Brush Tool cursor

2. When you are done copying each leaf to the 03leafy.psd image, close the original leaf image without saving the changes. Keep the 03leafy.psd file open.
3. Click the **Move Tool**.
4. In the options bar, click to place a check mark in the **Auto Select Layer** check box.

   Normally, the Move Tool will only affect objects on the selected layer. When the Auto Select Layer option is active, the Move Tool will affect objects regardless of which layer they are on.

5. Use the **Move Tool** to arrange the leaves as shown in Figure T3-28.
6. Save and close your 03leafy.psd file.

   You will use this file in the next chapter.

Figure T3-28.
After activating the **Auto Select Layer** option, arrange the leaves as shown here.

Key Terms

active	deselected	handles
anti-aliasing	ellipses	inverse
contiguous	fastening points	marquee
crop	feathering	stock photo agencies

Review Questions

Answer the following questions on a separate piece of paper.

1. When making a selection, if you set the **Feather:** option to 6 px, how wide will the total feathered effect be?
2. If you create a feathered selection using the options bar instead of choosing **Select > Feather…**, what two things do you need to remember?
3. Define "anti-aliased."
4. Explain why the **Rectangular Marquee Tool** does not have an **Anti-Alias** option.
5. When using the marquee selection tools, how do you move and resize a selection while it is being created?

6. Describe the areas selected by the **Single Row Marquee Tool** and the **Single Column Marquee Tool**.
7. How is the **Crop Tool** different from the **Rectangular Marquee Tool**?
8. How is the **Polygonal Lasso Tool** different from the **Lasso Tool**?
9. There are two ways to increase how quickly the **Magnetic Lasso Tool** creates fastening points. What are they?
10. If you make a mistake while selecting with the **Magnetic Lasso Tool**, how do you backtrack without starting over?
11. How does the **Tolerance:** setting affect the **Magic Wand Tool**?
12. Define the term "contiguous" as it applies to pixels.
13. What happens when you choose **Select > Inverse**?
14. There are three commands found in the **Select** menu that are directly related to the **Magic Wand Tool**. What are they?
15. How do you save a selection in Photoshop?

In later tutorials, you will combine the leaves you have isolated into a composite design.

4 Introduction to Layers

Learning Objectives

After completing this chapter, you will be able to:
- Create a new file.
- Explain how the **Move Tool** is associated with layers.
- Transform a layer, selected area, or image using a variety of methods.
- Use Photoshop's grid, guides, and **Snap** command to line up elements of a design.
- Create layers using several different methods.
- Organize layers in the **Layers** palette using several different methods.
- Describe the difference between grouping, linking, and merging layers.
- Differentiate between merging layers and flattening an image.
- Control the opacity of a layer.
- Protect layers by locking their content.

Introduction

A Photoshop file can be made up of several *layers*. Layers keep different parts of your design separate from each other. In **Figure 4-1**, each ostrich is on a separate layer. This makes it possible to move, edit, or delete each ostrich without affecting the rest of the design.

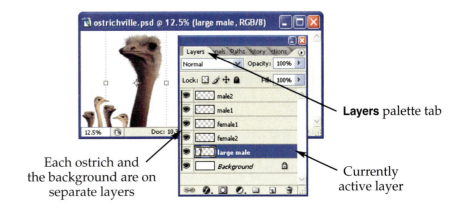

Figure 4-1. This partially-completed project is made of six layers. Each ostrich is on a different layer, and a white Background layer is behind all of the ostrich layers.

Each ostrich and the background are on separate layers

Layers palette tab

Currently active layer

There are often different ways to accomplish a task in Photoshop, and working with layers is no exception. For example, you will find the **New Layer** command on two different menus *and* as a button on the **Layers** palette.

The Layers Palette

A layer must be active before you can make any changes to it. To make a layer active, it must be highlighted in the **Layers** palette. In Figure 4-1, the layer named "large male" is active. That is the only layer that can currently be edited with Photoshop's tools. It is possible to highlight more than one layer in the **Layers** palette, but when this occurs, most of Photoshop's tools and commands become unavailable until only a single layer is again highlighted in the **Layers** palette.

The **Layers** palette is one of Photoshop's most frequently used palettes. If a project has more than one layer, you should keep the **Layers** palette visible on your screen. If you find that one of Photoshop's tools is not working, check the **Layers** palette first to see if the correct layer is active.

There are many Photoshop commands that relate to layers. This chapter will cover the basics. More advanced techniques will be discussed in a later chapter. But before discussing layer basics, we need to discuss two fundamental Photoshop skills that are directly related to layers: creating a new file and using the **Move Tool**.

Creating a New File

When you create a new Photoshop file by choosing **File > New...**, it only has one layer. As you progress through this chapter, you will find there are several ways to create additional layers in a Photoshop file.

The "ostrichville" design you will see throughout this chapter is intended to be placed on a billboard. The actual size of the billboard is 50′ wide by 20′ high. The best way to begin this project is to create a much smaller file that will help the client and the designer choose the final design for the billboard. A file that is 10″ wide by 4″ high has the same proportions as the billboard, and is much easier to work with. A resolution of 300 ppi will ensure high-quality printouts to show the client. This requires that a new image file be created.

Choosing **File > New...** brings up the **New** dialog box, Figure 4-2. Use this box to specify any of the following:

- In the **Name:** text box, enter a name for the new file.
- The **Preset:** drop-down list contains several preset image sizes. The entries in the first half of the list, from **Letter** through **B3**, correspond to common paper sizes. The entries in the bottom half of the list, from **NTSC DV 720 x 480 (with guides)** to **Cineon Full** correspond to common video sizes. If applicable, you can choose one of these preset sizes instead of entering width and height information. If you want to enter your own size, leave this list set to **Custom**.
- The values entered in the **Width:** and **Height:** text boxes specify the size of the new image. When entering width and height values, be sure that the desired units of measurement are chosen in drop-down lists directly to the right of the **Width:** and **Height:** text boxes. When you create a new document, you have a choice of several units of measurement: pixels, inches, centimeters, millimeters, points, picas, and columns.

Figure 4-2.
The specifications for a new image, such as image size, color mode, color bit depth, and background color, are set in the **New** dialog box.

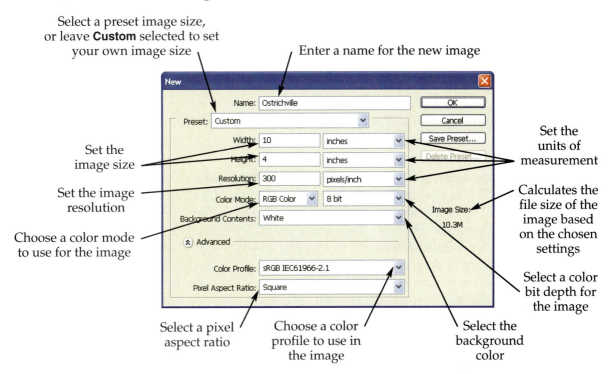

- In the **Resolution:** text box, enter the resolution you want the project to be. You must also specify the units of measure from the drop-down list directly to the right of the **Resolution:** text box. If your project will be in inches, choose the **pixels/inch** setting. For projects using metric units of measurement, choose the **pixels/cm** option.

- In the **Color Mode:** drop-down list, choose the color model that you want to use in the new image. In most cases, you will choose **RGB Color** for new files that will be full color. Use **Grayscale** for files that will be black and white. In the drop-down list directly to the right of the **Color Mode:** drop-down list, specify a color depth for the image. *Color depth* is total number of colors that can be used in the image. This is expressed as the number of bits of data used to describe each color. For now, leave this drop-down list set to **8 bit**. There are several different color modes and bit depths available, and they will be explained in a later chapter.

- The **Background Contents:** drop-down list controls the color of the **Background** layer that is created when you create a new file. Remember that "white" means "no color" in Photoshop. For this reason, **White** is usually the preferred background color, because many projects are printed on white paper, and printers simply ignore white areas of your image. If you select the **Background Color** option, your new file will be created using whatever color is currently selected in the **Background Color** box (see Chapter 1, *The Work Area*). Selecting **Transparent** creates an invisible background.

- The **Image Size:** area, in the lower right corner of the dialog box, will automatically adjust to show you how much file space your new file will consume. The file size of the image will vary depending on the settings chosen.

- Clicking the **Advanced** toggle reveals the **Color Profile:** drop-down list and the **Pixel Aspect Ratio:** drop-down list. In the **Color Profile:** drop-down list, you can choose from various color profiles, which will be discussed in a later chapter. In the **Pixel Aspect Ratio:** drop-down list, you can choose the pixel aspect ratio to use in the image, which may be necessary if you are preparing an image to be included on some type of video production. See Chapter 2, *Resolution* for more information on pixel aspect ratios.

The Move Tool

The **Move Tool** can be used to grab and move a selected area of an image, an entire layer, or an entire image. Because the **Move Tool** is used often, you can temporarily switch to it by pressing [Ctrl] (or [Command] in Mac).

A good strategy when moving anything in Photoshop is to use the **Move Tool** to drag content *approximately* where you want it. Then, use the arrow keys on your keyboard to nudge the content *exactly* where you would like it. Each time an arrow key is pressed, the active area in your file is moved one pixel in the direction of the arrow. If [Shift] is pressed while using the arrow keys, the active area moves ten pixels at a time.

There are two options and several odd-looking buttons on the **Move Tool**'s options bar, **Figure 4-3**:

- When the **Auto Select Layer** option is on, the **Move Tool** looks at the pixel you click on, determines what layer that pixel is assigned to, and makes that layer active. In complex projects with many layers, you may need to hide other layers that may be "on top" of the layer you are trying to click on. More information about hiding layers is found in the *Layer Visibility* section of this chapter.

- When the **Auto Select Groups** option is on, clicking on a pixel will activate the layer that the pixel is on and all layers that are grouped with that layer. Grouped layers are discussed in more detail later in this chapter.

- When the **Show Transform Controls** option is on, a rectangular box appears around all of the pixels in the layers highlighted in the **Layers** palette. This is called a *bounding box*, and it shows you which layer(s) are active. It also helps you transform the layer's content in several different ways. Transforming layers is discussed later in this chapter.

- The align and distribute buttons are available only when you are aligning and distributing layers. These techniques are discussed in a later chapter.

As you read the remainder of this section, you will discover that the **Move Tool** behavior varies, depending on the situation. Several common scenarios are presented in the next three sections. Familiarize yourself with the way the **Move Tool** works in each of these common scenarios.

Figure 4-3.
The **Move Tool**'s options bar contains tools that help arrange layers or selections.

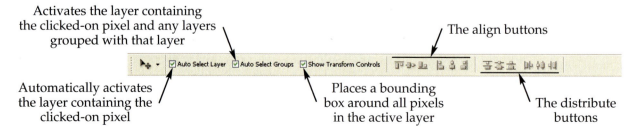

Scenario 1: Using the Move Tool to Move Selected Pixels within an Image

Place the **Move Tool** *inside* the selected area and drag the selected pixels to another location. This leaves behind a hole that will either be the background color shown on the **Toolbox** or a transparent area if the layer transparency is not locked (locking layers is discussed later in this chapter). Transparent areas in Photoshop appear as a checkerboard pattern. See **Figure 4-4**.

> **Note** Be aware that if the **Move Tool** is placed *outside* of a selected area and then dragged, the selected area is ignored. The entire image will be moved, if the layer is not locked.

Scenario 2: Using the Move Tool to Copy Selected Pixels to Another Location in an Image

Hold down [Alt] (or [Option] for Mac) while dragging a selected area to make a *copy* of the selected area. The original selected area will remain as it appeared before. This option does not automatically create a new layer, however, so the copy you make will permanently cover up whatever is behind it. A better alternative is to Choose **Edit > Copy** and then **Edit > Paste**. The copied pixels are automatically placed on a new layer, which can then be easily moved. See the section in this chapter called *Using the Cut, Copy, and Paste Commands* for further explanation.

Figure 4-4.
When a selected area of an image is moved, the background appears in the hole where the selection used to be. **A**—The ostrich is selected. **B**—When the selected ostrich is moved, the white background shows through. **C**—If a checkerboard pattern appears, the area behind the ostrich is transparent. This occurs when layer transparency is not locked.

A	B	C

Scenario 3: Using the Move Tool to Copy a Selected Area or an Entire Image to Another File

Drag the selected area and release it on top of the *destination image*, the image to which you want to copy the selection. The selected area is automatically copied and placed on a new layer created in the destination image. In the original image, the selected area remains unchanged. See Figure 4-5. If the destination image is zoomed differently than the original image (you can tell by checking the magnification percentage in each image's title bar), your copied pixels will appear larger or smaller than the original.

> **Note**
>
> If the **Move Tool** is placed *outside* a selected area and then dragged, the entire image will be copied over to the destination image.

You may find that as you move something with the **Move Tool**, it jumps around, preventing you from moving it exactly where you want to. When this happens, Photoshop's snap function needs to be turned off. Refer to the section in this chapter called *Using Snap to Align Layers*.

Transforming with the Bounding Box

A bounding box allows you to *transform* the active part of your image in several different ways. The active part of your image can be either an active, unlocked layer or a selected area of a particular layer. Rotating, bending, or making the active part of your image larger or smaller (scaling) are common transformation commands.

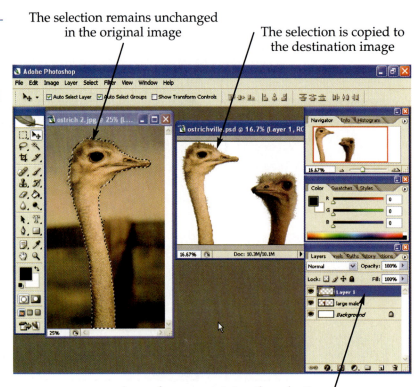

Figure 4-5. When the **Move Tool** is used to drag content from one image to another, the pixels are copied in the original image and pasted onto a new layer that is automatically created in the destination image.

The selection remains unchanged in the original image

The selection is copied to the destination image

A new layer containing the selection is created in the destination image

A bounding box appears around a layer when it is clicked with the **Move Tool**, providing the **Show Transform Controls** option is on. You can also choose **Edit > Free Transform** or **Edit > Transform > (desired transformation)** to display the bounding box. Remember, if part of your image is selected, the bounding box will only appear around that selected area.

The Transform Options Bar

If you click on or near any of the square handles at the sides and corners of the bounding box, the **Transform** options bar appears. There are numerous controls on the **Transform** options bar, **Figure 4-6**. Many of the tasks that can be performed in the **Transform** options bar can also be performed by manipulating the bounding box. In the following section, the options available in the options bar are explained. If the same task can be performed by manipulating the bounding box, that alterative method is also explained.

The Transform Icon

The **Transform** icon simply shows you that a transform command is currently active. If you cause the **Transform** options bar to appear by mistake, click the **Cancel** button or press [Esc].

The Reference Point Locator

By clicking one of the nine squares on the **Reference point locator**, you can change the point around which transformations are made. By default, the center of the bounding box is the reference point, and all transformations are centered on that point. For example, if you leave the center box clicked and rotate your layer, the layer will pivot around the center of the bounding box. You can pick a corner or side of the bounding box to be your reference point instead, if desired.

The Reference Point Coordinate Text Boxes

The **X:** and **Y:** text boxes show how far the current reference point is from the left edge and top edge of your image (or document). In these boxes, you can enter an exact location, in either pixels (**px**) or inches (**in**), for a new reference point. Instead of using the

Figure 4-6.
The **Transform** options bar replaces the **Move Tool**'s normal options bar when a selection is being transformed.

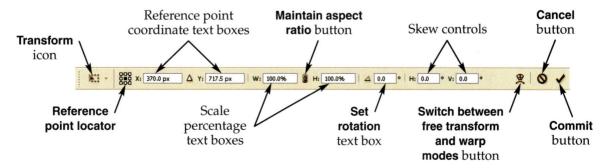

left and top of your file to generate reference values, you can click the triangle-shaped button. Photoshop looks at the handle you have selected as a reference point and resets the **X:** and **Y:** values to 0, 0. This allows you to reposition the reference point relative to its current location rather than to the upper left corner of the image.

You can also adjust the reference point by dragging the center point of the bounding box anywhere in the image. The values in the **X:** and **Y:** text boxes are automatically updated to match the new reference point location. Often, Photoshop users drag this center point by mistake while using the **Move Tool** to move the active layer. If this happens, you can reset the reference point location by clicking one of the small boxes on the **Reference point locator**. As an alternative, you can press [Esc] or click the **Cancel** button on the **Transform** options bar. However, pressing [Esc] or the **Cancel** button will close the transform mode. You will need to reselect the transform command or click on one of the small squares on the bounding box to reload the **Transform** options bar.

The Scale Controls

The term *scale* means to make larger or smaller, **Figure 4-7**. Scaling is done by entering percentages in the **W:** and **H:** text boxes. For example, if you want to make something half as large as it currently is, enter a percentage of 50%. In most cases, the width and height should be the same percentage to avoid a stretched or squashed look. Clicking the **Maintain aspect ratio** (chain link) button between the **W:** and **H:** text boxes forces the image to stay in proportion—whatever value is entered in one box is automatically entered in another.

You can also use the bounding box to scale your image. If you drag a corner handle of the bounding box, the **Transform** options bar will appear and the scaling width and height values in the **W:** and **H:** text boxes will automatically change. Hold down [Shift] after you start dragging to keep the image in proportion. Forgetting to hold [Shift] during this process is one of the most common errors made by new Photoshop users.

Figure 4-7.
Scaling is used to reduce or increase the size of the content in the selection or layer. **A**—The original layer is shown here. **B**—After scaling the width and height to 25%, the resulting image is one-quarter the size of the original.

A

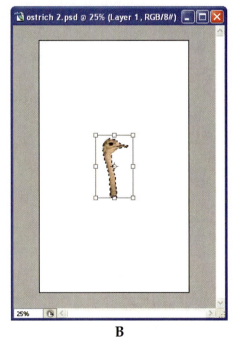

B

> **Note**
>
> When you scale part of your image to a larger size, you are really resampling it. This will result in a loss of image quality. Remember, it is always better to start with a larger image and make it smaller.

Set Rotation Text Box

To rotate a selection, enter a value from 0° to 360° in the **Set rotation** text box. All of the pixels contained within the bounding box will be rotated around the reference point you have chosen.

As an alternative, you can use the bounding box to rotate your image. Position the cursor just outside any of the bounding box handles, and it will turn into a curved arrow. When the rotate cursor appears, click and drag to rotate your image, Figure 4-8. Holding down [Shift] as you drag causes the bounding box to rotate in 15° increments.

You can also drag the center mark in the bounding box to a different location. This changes the reference point, or center point, of the transformation. The content in your bounding box will rotate around the new center point.

The Skew Controls

Skew means "to slant at an angle." Skewing can make an image look like the perspective has changed. You can skew a selection by entering values in the **H:** and **V:** text boxes. The image is skewed by moving the selected edge of the image and leaving the opposite edge stationary. The value entered in the **H:** text box determines the angle of the slant along the vertical edges, created when the selection is skewed horizontally. The value entered in the **V:** text box determines the angle of slant of the horizontal edges, created when the selection is skewed vertically. Enter an amount in degrees from –180 to 180 in these text boxes.

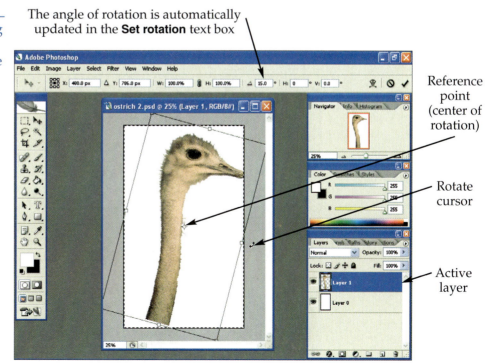

Figure 4-8. The bounding box is being rotated, using the center of the bounding box as the reference point (center of rotation).

You can also use the bounding box to skew the selection. With the **Transform** options bar active, right click anywhere in the drawing. Select **Skew** from the shortcut menu. Position your cursor over a side handle to skew the selection vertically, or a top or bottom handle to skew the selection horizontally. The cursor will change to an arrow with double arrowheads. Then, click and drag the mouse up or down or left or right to skew the selection, **Figure 4-9**.

> **Note**
> You can also grab a corner handle after selecting **Skew** from the shortcut menu. However, this will cause you to scale and skew the image at the same time, resulting in a nonsymmetrical effect. The effect is identical to choosing **Edit > Transform > Distort**.

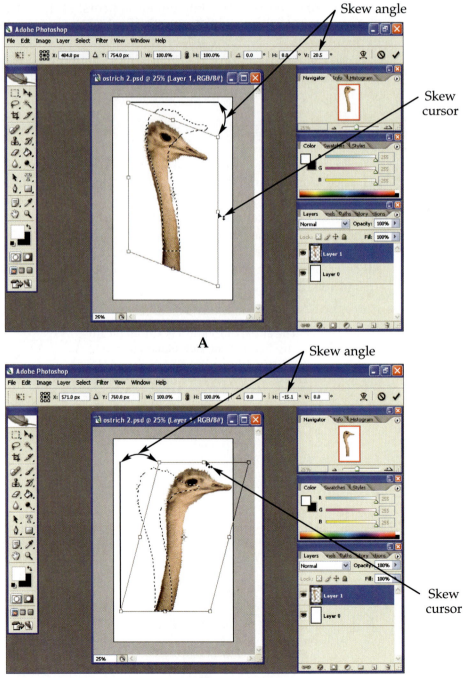

Figure 4-9.
The bounding box is being skewed, using the center of the bounding box as the reference point. **A**—If the image is skewed vertically, the skew angle describes how far the top and bottom edges are rotated away from horizontal. **B**—If the image is skewed horizontally, the skew angle describes how far the left and right edges are rotated away from vertical.

Switching between Free Transform and Warp Modes

Clicking the **Switch between free transform and warp modes** button jumps you back and forth between transform mode and warp mode. Warp mode is extremely useful when adjusting a layer so it "wraps" to the surface of an object on another layer (such as applying a design on a cup).

In warp mode, a grid appears over your layer instead of the bounding box. Four boxes appear at the corners of the grid. These boxes can be clicked and dragged to a new location. The selection can also be adjusted by moving the two bezier handles attached to each of the boxes. By moving these handles, you can adjust the curvature of the edges of the selection. See **Figure 4-10**.

In warp mode, a new options bar appears. You can choose from several predefined warps in the **Warp:** drop-down list on the options bar. After selecting the desired warp, you can adjust the settings if desired by changing the numbers in the **Bend:**, **H:**, and **V:** text boxes. The **Bend:** text box sets the overall strength of the warp. The **H:** and **V:** text boxes determine the amount of perspective effect applied to the image. The **H:** text box setting controls the horizontal perspective and the **V:** text box setting controls the vertical perspective. When the **Change warp orientation** button is unselected, the effect of the predefined warp is applied vertically. When this button is selected, the effect of the warp is applied horizontally.

Clicking the **Switch between free transform and warp modes** button again returns Photoshop to the transform mode, with the bounding box and the **Transform** options bar.

The Cancel and Commit Buttons

After applying any of the transforming commands, press [Enter] or [Return] on your keyboard *or* click the **Commit** button, which looks like a check mark. To cancel any transform command, press [Esc] or click the **Cancel** button next to the **Commit** button.

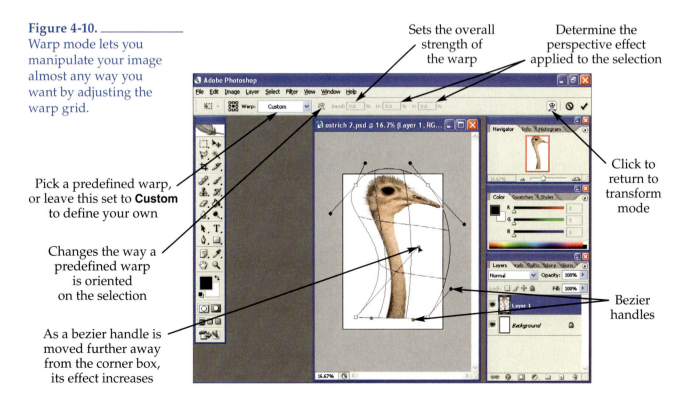

Figure 4-10. Warp mode lets you manipulate your image almost any way you want by adjusting the warp grid.

The Edit > Transform Submenu

Choosing the **Edit > Transform** submenu brings up a list of all of the transform commands. This menu choice is not available unless an unlocked layer is active or part of your image is selected. Some of the commands listed in the **Edit > Transform** submenu are not found on the **Transform** options bar. A brief description of these commands follows.

The Again Command

Choosing the **Again** command duplicates the last transformation that was applied to the selection. The effects of the transforms are cumulative. For example, if you scale the selection to 50%, and then choose **Edit > Transform > Again**, the selection will be one-quarter of its original size.

The Distort Command

Choosing the **Distort** command lets you move one or more of the selection's bounding box handles in any direction. To distort the image, choose **Edit > Transform > Distort**. Click a corner handle on the selection box and drag it to the desired position. Keep in mind that too much distortion can result in a low-quality image, because of the amount of resampling Photoshop has to do. See **Figure 4-11**.

> **Note** If you click a side, top, or bottom handle instead of a corner handle after choosing the **Distort** command, you will scale or skew the selection rather than distort it. You must choose a corner handle in order to distort the selection.

The Perspective Command

The **Perspective** command is similar to the **Distort** command. The difference is that when a corner handle is dragged, the opposite corner handle is also moved proportionally, **Figure 4-12**. If you click a side, top, or bottom handle instead of a corner handle, the selection is skewed rather than having the perspective effect applied.

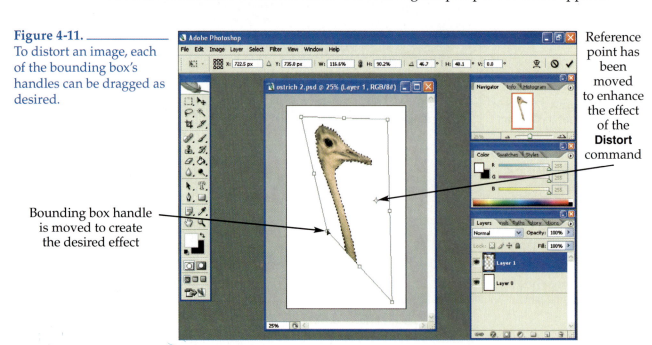

Figure 4-11. To distort an image, each of the bounding box's handles can be dragged as desired.

Bounding box handle is moved to create the desired effect

Reference point has been moved to enhance the effect of the **Distort** command

Figure 4-12.
The **Perspective** command is used to change the perspective of an image.

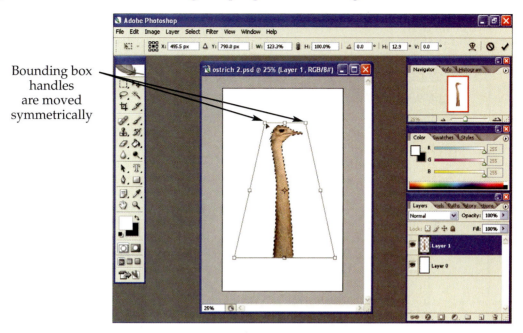

Bounding box handles are moved symmetrically

The Rotating and Flipping Commands

Also listed in the **Edit > Transform** submenu are rotating and flipping commands. The **Rotate 180°** command turns the contents of a bounding box upside down. You can also choose to rotate the selection using the **Rotate 90° CW** command, which rotates the selection 90° clockwise, or the **Rotate 90° CCW** command, which rotates the selection 90° counterclockwise.

To *flip* an image in Photoshop means to mirror the image, so it appears as if you were looking at it from the other side. As you might expect, the **Flip Horizontal** command flips a selection horizontally and the **Flip Vertical** command flips the selection vertically. See **Figure 4-13**.

> **Note** To rotate or flip an entire image, including all layers that make up the image, choose **Image > Rotate Canvas…** and either the **Flip Canvas Horizontal** or **Flip Canvas Vertical** command.

Using the Cut, Copy, and Paste Commands

Photoshop's **Edit** menu contains **Cut**, **Copy**, and **Paste** commands. These commands are similar in function to the same commands found in a word processing program. They are most often used to copy and paste a selected area.

Once you have made a selection, you can copy it by selecting **Edit > Copy** or pressing [Ctrl][C]. The selected area on the active layer is copied to the *clipboard* (temporary computer memory), but remains unchanged in the image.

The **Cut** command is similar to the **Copy** command, but removes the selected area from the active layer, revealing whatever is behind the selection. Choosing **Edit > Cut** or pressing [Ctrl][X] cuts the selected area from the active layer and copies it to the clipboard.

Figure 4-13.
When content is flipped, a mirror image replaces the original. **A**—The original ostrich image is shown here. **B**—The ostrich has been mirrored horizontally. **C**—The ostrich has been flipped vertically. Note that flipping the ostrich vertically is *not* the same as rotating it 180°. The ostrich faces in a different direction.

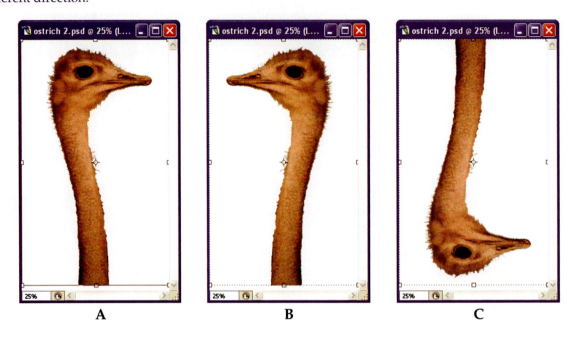

Once you have copied a selection to the clipboard with the **Copy** or **Cut** command, you can paste it by choosing **Edit > Paste** or pressing [Ctrl][V]. When the selection is pasted into the image, a new layer is automatically created. If you are copying and pasting on the same image file, the new, pasted layer is sometimes placed exactly on top of the old area. It looks like nothing happened unless a bounding box appears around the pasted selection. For this reason, it is a very good idea to enable the **Show Transform Controls** option in the **Move Tool**'s options bar. After pasting, immediately move the new layer as desired so you do not forget it is there!

The **Layer > New > Layer via Copy** and **Layer > New > Layer via Cut** commands are similar to the **Copy** and **Cut** commands. These commands are used to copy or cut a selected area and place the result on a new layer. Unlike the **Cut** and **Copy** commands, they do not require the **Paste** command; the selection is automatically pasted. Also, these commands can only be used to copy a selection back into the same image, whereas the **Cut** and **Copy** commands can be used to copy a selection from one image to another.

If an image has several layers, **Cut** and **Copy** commands only work for one layer at a time, unless you make an exception. If you want to copy and paste content from *all* the different layers simultaneously, select the area and choose **Edit > Copy Merged**. The selected area in all layers are combined and copied to the clipboard as a single selection, which can then be pasted into an image.

Aligning Image Elements Using Grids, Guides, Rulers, and Snaps

If your project contains several small shapes that need to be lined up perfectly, Photoshop's grid or guides can help you quickly accomplish this. The use of rulers and snaps makes it easy to position selections exactly where you want them.

The Grid

Photoshop's *grid* is a pattern of horizontal and vertical lines that appears on your screen but does not print. The grid is turned on or off by choosing **View > Show > Grid**. You can control the spacing and appearance of the gridlines by choosing **Edit > Preferences > Guides, Grid & Slices...** (or **Photoshop > Preferences > Guides, Grid & Slices...** for Mac). Set the desired grid properties in the **Grid** section of the **Preferences** dialog box, **Figure 4-14**.

- Using the **Color:** drop-down menu, you can change the color of the gridlines. You can select one of the preset colors, or choose **Custom** to select your own color in the **Color Picker** dialog box. You can also create a custom color by clicking in the color swatch to the right of the **Color:** drop-down list and defining the new color in the **Color Picker** dialog box.
- In the **Style:** drop-down list, you can choose between three styles of gridlines: solid lines, dashed lines, or dots that show where the gridlines intersect.

Figure 4-14.
To make the grid useful for projects of all sizes, its settings can be adjusted in the **Preferences** dialog box. **A**—These grid settings work well for projects using inches as the unit of measurement. **B**—With the **Subdivisions:** setting at 4, minor gridlines appear every 1/4″.

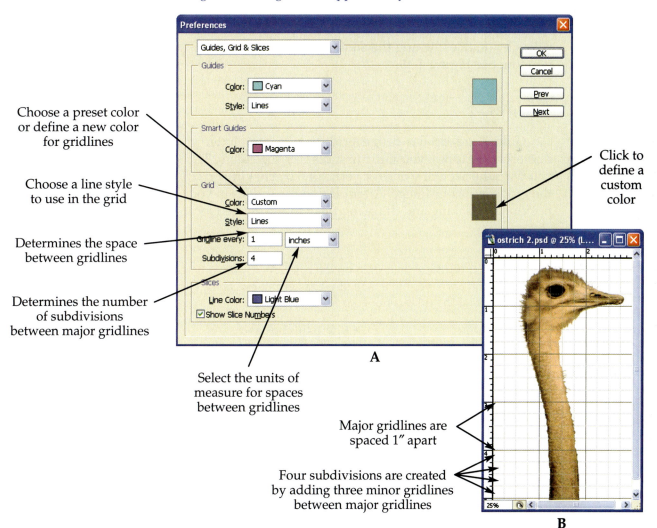

- The **Gridline every:** setting controls the number of major gridlines on your screen. The value entered into this text box determines the exact distance between major gridlines. You can set the grid to display in inches, millimeters, or numerous other units of measurement.
- The **Subdivisions:** setting determines the number of empty spaces that are created between major gridlines. These spaces are created by adding minor gridlines between the major gridlines. The minor gridlines appear lighter than the major gridlines. The number of minor gridlines added to the grid will be equal to the **Subdivisions:** setting minus one.

Rulers

Photoshop's rulers are often used with the grid. They are displayed or hidden by choosing **View > Rulers**. You can specify what units of measurement appear in the ruler (inches, centimeters, pixels, etc.) by selecting **Edit > Preferences > Units & Rulers...** (or **Photoshop > Preferences > Units and Rulers...** for Mac). In the **Units** section of the **Preferences** dialog box, select the desired units from the **Rulers:** drop-down list. You can also change the units of measurement for a particular image by right-clicking on either the horizontal or vertical ruler and selecting the desired units from the shortcut menu.

The zero point on each ruler can be adjusted by clicking and the small square in the upper left corner of the rulers, dragging it to the desired location in the image, and releasing the mouse button. If you make a mistake while doing this, you can reset the rulers by double-clicking the same small square in the upper left corner of the image window. See **Figure 4-15**.

Guides

Guides are similar to the grid, but do not clutter your image as much. To use Photoshop's guides, you must first display the rulers. Then, create as many guides as you wish (horizontally and/or vertically) by clicking on one of the rulers and dragging the guide into your image. After placing the guides in your image, you can adjust their position by clicking and dragging them to the desired location with the **Move Tool**.

Figure 4-15.
The zero point can be moved to a different location on the ruler. **A**—By default, the ruler's zero point aligns with the upper left corner of the image. **B**—The zero point can be changed by dragging the upper left corner of the rulers onto your file.

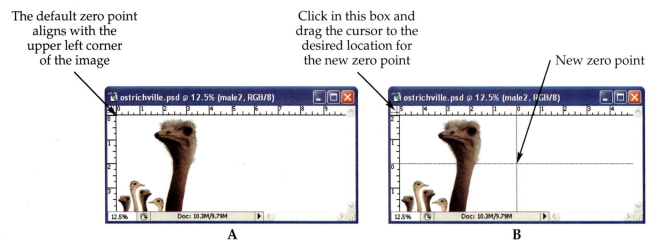

A guide can be placed at a precise distance from the left or top edge of the image by choosing **View > New Guide...**. In the **Orientation** section of the **New Guide** dialog box, select either the **Horizontal** or **Vertical** radio button, depending on which way you want the guide to run. In the **Position:** text box, enter the distance you want the guide to be from the edge of the image. For horizontal guides, this setting determines the distance between the top edge of the image and the guide. For vertical guides, this setting determines the distance between the left edge of the image and the guide.

Guides can be locked into place so they cannot be moved accidentally. To do this, choose **View > Lock Guides**. If you need to reposition locked guides, you will need to unlock them first by selecting **View > Lock Guides** again.

To remove a single guide from your image, simply drag it back to the ruler and release the mouse button. To remove all of the guides from the image, choose **View > Clear Guides**.

If desired, you can change the color and appearance of the guides by selecting **Edit > Preferences > Guides, Grid & Slices** and making the desired changes in the **Guides** section of the **Preferences** dialog box.

Smart Guides

Smart guides are temporary guides that automatically appear as you use the **Move Tool** to adjust the position of a layer or move a selection in the image. Once you release the mouse button, the guides disappear.

Smart guides can be turned on or off by choosing **View > Show > Smart Guides**. When smart guides are turned on, you will see guides pop up that show the center and edges of other bounding boxes as you move content on your screen. Smart guides also appear as you create selections or shapes (discussed later).

Using Snap to Align Layers

If you hold a magnet close to a piece of metal, the magnet snaps, or jumps, over to the metal and sticks to it. When Photoshop's **Snap** command is turned on, you can use the **Move Tool** to snap the bounding box that appears around a layer's content to gridlines, guidelines, or the edges of your image (called the *document bounds*). When using this feature, make sure the **Move Tool**'s **Show Transform Controls** option is on.

The **Snap** command does not affect how the arrow keys on your keyboard move the contents of a layer. You can always use the arrow keys to precisely adjust the location of a layer's content.

To turn the **Snap** command on or off, choose **View > Snap**. The **Snap** command is often *toggled* (turned off and on), so you will probably find it helpful to memorize the keyboard shortcut, [Shift][Ctrl][;].

The **View** menu also contains the **Snap To** submenu, Figure 4-16. From this submenu, you can choose exactly what object the **Snap** command will snap to. For example, you can specify that only guides are snapped to—not gridlines or the edges of your image (document bounds). You can also choose to snap to *slices*, which are invisible boundaries that are placed on web images.

> **Note** In addition to using the snaps to accurately place image content, you can also use the snaps to create accurate selections. This technique is especially helpful when you are using the **Rectangular Marquee Tool** or the **Elliptical Marquee Tool**.

Working with Layers in the Layers Palette

The **Layers** palette is packed with features. It is used to organize multi-layered projects in several different ways. It also shows information about styles and layer masks (discussed in later chapters) that have been applied to layers. And instead of using Photoshop's **Layers** menu, you can access many commonly used layer commands by using the buttons at the bottom of the palette, by right-clicking on different areas of the palette, or by using the palette menu.

Making Layers Active

More than one layer can be active at the same time. You can select more than one layer in the **Layers** palette by holding down [Ctrl] (or [Command] for Mac) as you click. If you press [Shift], you can select an entire group of layers by clicking on the first layer you want included and then clicking on the last layer you want included. All layers in between the two selected layers become selected automatically.

You can also select multiple layers by choosing **Select > All Layers**, and then pressing [Ctrl] and clicking all the layers you did *not* want to select. You can select all similar types of layers by choosing **Select > Similar Layers**. This command is useful for selecting all type layers, all adjustment layers, all fill layers, or all layers that contain pixels in an image.

Occasionally, you may want *none* of your layers to be active. To do this, click the blank area in the **Layers** palette just below the bottom layer or choose **Select > Deselect Layers**.

Some, but not all, of Photoshop's commands can be applied to more than one active layer simultaneously. These commands include transforming, moving, copying and pasting, applying layer styles, and aligning. Commands that can only affect one layer at a time include color correction and painting.

Selecting the Content of a Layer

In Chapter 3, you learned that to select something in Photoshop means to create a selection border around it. Yet, when you work with layers, making a layer active is almost the same as selecting it. However, there are occasions where you may need to create a selection border around the content of a layer instead of only a bounding box.

This is done by holding down [Ctrl] and placing the cursor over the appropriate layer thumbnail (small image that represents the layer content) in the **Layers** palette. When you see the cursor change to a hand with a square-shaped selection over it, click the layer thumbnail. This places a selection around the layer content in your Photoshop document. See **Figure 4-17**.

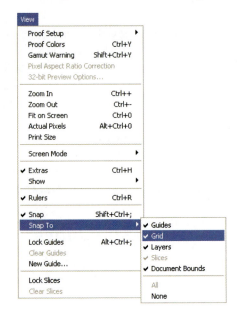

Figure 4-16.
The **Snap** command toggles snapping on and off. The options in the **Snap To** submenu allow you to pick the things that a layer or selection will snap to.

Chapter 4 Introduction to Layers

Figure 4-17.
Hold [Ctrl] and position the cursor over the layer's thumbnail. When the special cursor appears, click on the thumbnail to select the layer's contents.

Marching ants surround all non-transparent areas on the layer

When this cursor appears, click on the thumbnail to select all objects on the layer

Duplicating a Layer

There are several ways to duplicate, or copy, a layer. The easiest way to duplicate a layer is to drag the layer from its place in the **Layers** palette to the **New Layer** button at the bottom of the **Layers** palette, Figure 4-18. You will know when to release the mouse button because the cursor will change into a fist. A new layer appears in the **Layers** palette directly above the layer that was copied, and the content is placed in the image exactly on top of the layer that was duplicated.

You can also choose **Layer > Duplicate Layer...**. This opens the **Duplicate Layer** dialog box. In the **As:** text box, enter a name for the new layer you are creating. In the **Document:** drop-down list, specify the image that you want to copy the layer to. All of the currently open image files are listed in this drop-down list. You can also choose to create a new document and save the layer to that document. If you choose to create a new document, you must enter a name for the new image in the **Name:** text box.

If you need to copy a layer from one file to another, simply drag the layer from the **Layers** palette and release it on top of the destination image's window. The copied

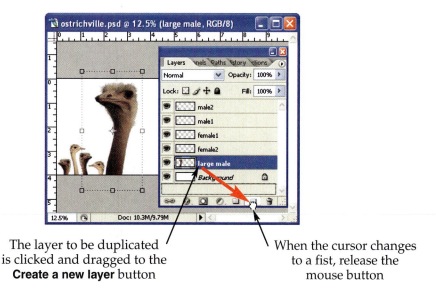

Figure 4-18.
Dragging a layer on top of the **New Layer** button is the fastest way to duplicate a layer.

The layer to be duplicated is clicked and dragged to the **Create a new layer** button

When the cursor changes to a fist, release the mouse button

layer appears in the destination image and is listed in the destination image's **Layers** palette. If no layers are selected in the destination image when the layer is copied over, the copied layer is placed at the top of the layer stack. However, if a layer is selected, the copied layer is placed immediately above the selected layer. This is important to remember because an existing layer in the destination image could hide the copied layer from view.

Layer Properties: Renaming and Color-Coding Layers

The **Layer Properties** dialog box helps you keep your layers better organized by allowing you to rename them with descriptive names. For large projects that contain many layers, you can also color-code layers to keep them better organized.

To display the **Layer Properties** dialog box, do one of the following:

- If you are creating a new layer, choose **Layer > New > Layer…**. The **New Layer** dialog box appears. This dialog box is essentially an expanded version of the **Layer Properties** dialog box. Some of the settings on this expanded dialog box will be discussed in a later chapter.

- For existing layers, right-click (or [Ctrl]+click for Mac) a layer in the **Layers** palette and choose **Layer Properties…** from the right-click menu.

- For existing layers, make sure the correct layer is active and choose **Layer > Layer Properties…**.

Once you have opened the **Layer Properties** dialog box, simply type a new name for the layer in the **Name:** text box, **Figure 4-19**. The name of the layer automatically changes in the **Layers** palette as you type. If you want to assign a different color code for the layer, click the **Color:** drop-down list and select the desired color. The selected color appears in the **Layer visibility** toggle in the **Layers** palette. Click the **OK** button in the **Layer Properties** dialog box to accept the changes.

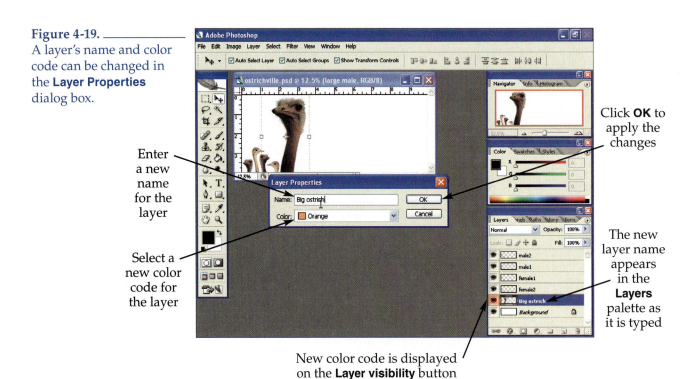

Figure 4-19.
A layer's name and color code can be changed in the **Layer Properties** dialog box.

The easiest way to rename a layer is to double-click on its name in the **Layers** palette and then type a new layer name. Press [Enter] or click on another layer to complete the renaming process. You can quickly assign a new color code to a layer by right clicking the layer's **Layer visibility** toggle in the **Layers** palette. Then, select the desired color from the shortcut menu that appears.

Changing the Stacking Order of Layers

Layers are "stacked in a pile." The layer that appears at the bottom of the list in the **Layers** palette appears behind all of the other layers in the image window. A locked **Background** layer will always be at the bottom of the stack, and you will not be able to move it from that position unless you unlock it (discussed later in this chapter).

To change how layers are stacked, simply click and drag them to a different location in the **Layers** palette. For best results when dragging layers to a new location, release the mouse when the cursor is on the borderline between two layers.

The way the layers appear in the image window depends on the way they are listed in the layer stack. Each layer in the stack appears in front of every other layer that is listed after it. The layer at the top of the list appears in front of all other layers in the list. In **Figure 4-20**, the layer named large male is first shown *behind* the smaller ostriches and then *in front* of the smaller ostriches.

Another way to change the stacking order of layers can come in handy with projects that contain many layers. The **Layer > Arrange** submenu contains commands that move layers forward or backward. Choosing **Layer > Arrange > Bring to Front** causes the selected layers to move to the top of the **Layers** palette, appearing in front of all of the other layers in your file. The **Bring Forward** command moves the selected layers up one place in the stack. The **Send to Back** command moves the selected layers to the bottom of the stack, but in front of the locked **Background** layer. The **Move Backward** command

Figure 4-20.
A layer's position in the layer stack determines whether it appears in front or behind other layers in the image window. **A**—The large male layer is listed below the other four ostrich layers in the **Layers** palette. As a result, the large ostrich appears behind the other ostriches in the image window. **B**—When the large male layer is dragged to the top of the stack in the **Layers** palette, the large ostrich appears in front of the other ostriches in the image.

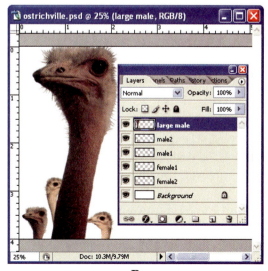

A   B

moves the selected layers down one place in the stack. The **Reverse** command reverses the order of the selected layers, but does not affect the unselected layers in the stack.

Creating a New, Blank Layer

Layers are automatically created when you use the **Cut**, **Copy**, and **Paste** commands, when you drag and drop a selection onto a different document, or when you copy a selection by pressing [Alt] and dragging it with the **Move Tool**. However, you will occasionally need to create a new, blank layer and add content to it. To create a new layer, use one of the following techniques:

- Click the **Create a new layer** button on the **Layers** palette. It is just to the left of the **Delete layer** (trash can) button.
- Choose **Layer > New Layer....** In the **New Layer** dialog box, enter a name for the new layer and pick the **OK** button to create the new layer.

A newly created layer always appears just above the layer that was previously active. Just before creating a new layer, you should make *topmost* layer in the layer palette active. The new layer will be created above it, at the very top of the stacking order. This ensures that the content you add to your new layer will not be hidden by any layers in front of it. You can then move the new layer to the desired position in the layer stack.

Deleting a Layer

The following are five different techniques for deleting a layer (and all of its contents) using the **Layers** palette.

- Make sure the layer you wish to delete is active in the **Layers** palette. Then, press [Delete] on your keyboard. This is the quickest way to delete a layer.
- Click and drag the layer on top of the **Delete layer** (trash can) button. When the cursor changes to a fist, release the mouse button, Figure 4-21.
- Make sure the correct layer is active in the **Layers** palette. Click the **Delete layer** button. Click **Yes** in the dialog box that appears.
- Right-click (or [Ctrl]+click for Mac) the layer and choose **Delete Layer** from the shortcut menu. Click **Yes** in the dialog box that appears.
- Make sure the layer you want to delete is active, then choose **Layer > Delete > Layer**.

Layer Visibility

If your project becomes too cluttered as you work, you can temporarily hide layers by clicking the **Layer visibility** (eye) toggles next to the layers on the **Layers** palette, Figure 4-22. To show the layer again, click the button to make the eye and the layer reappear.

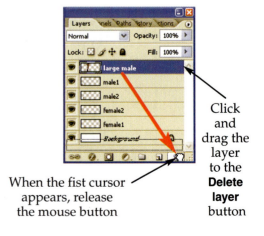

Figure 4-21. One way to delete a layer is to drag it on top of the **Delete layer** button in the **Layers** palette.

Figure 4-22. The large male layer has been temporarily hidden by clicking the **Layer visibility** toggle.

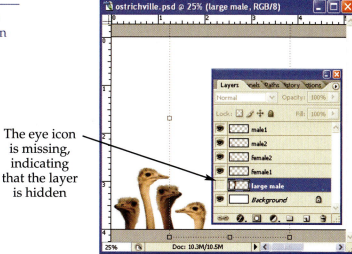

The eye icon is missing, indicating that the layer is hidden

Grouping Layers

Since large projects can contain numerous layers, a lot of time can be wasted scrolling up and down in the **Layers** palette, searching for the correct layer. Placing layers into groups is a quick way to organize the **Layers** palette. A *layer group* is really a folder that can be created in the **Layers** palette. Layers can be dragged to this folder, and, for organizational purposes, the folder can be collapsed or expanded at any time by clicking the small triangle next to it, Figure 4-23. Perhaps the biggest advantage of layer groups is that by clicking on the group, all layers within that group become active, allowing you to move or transform them simultaneously.

To create a layer group, first make the layers to be grouped active in the **Layers** palette. Then, click the **Create a new group** (folder) button on the **Layers** palette. When the group appears in the **Layers** palette, double click on it and type a new name.

You can also create a new group by selecting the layers to be grouped in the **Layers** palette and then choosing **Layer > New > Group...**. In the **New Group** dialog box, type a name for the group in the **Name:** text box and click **OK**.

Figure 4-23. The grouped layers appear together in a folder. More room can be created in the **Layers** palette by collapsing the group. This is done by clicking the small triangle next to the folder.

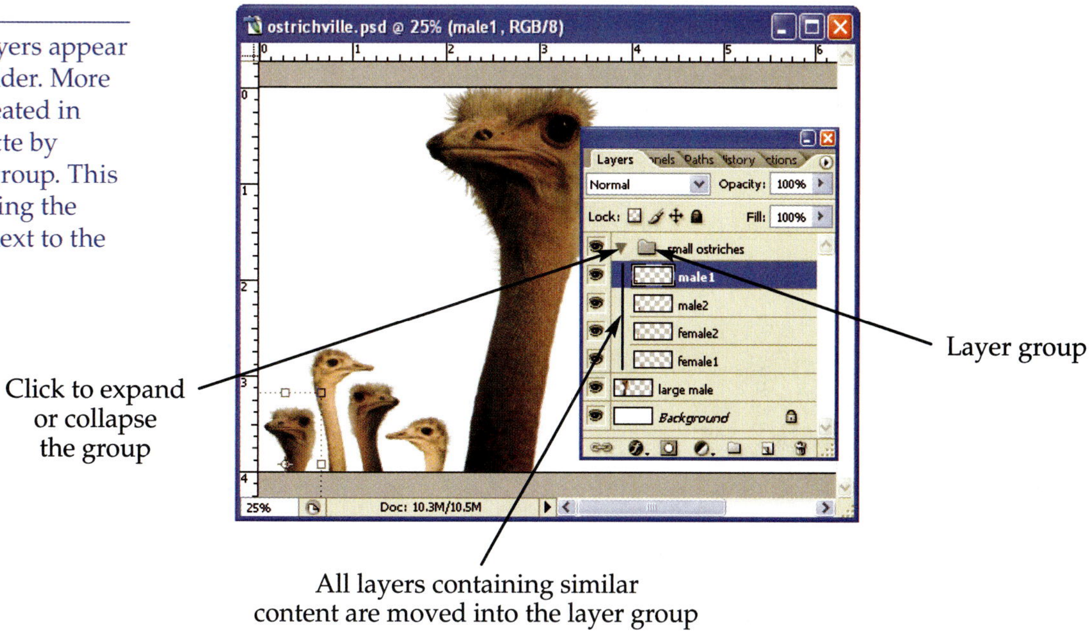

Click to expand or collapse the group

Layer group

All layers containing similar content are moved into the layer group

After you name the group, it appears in the **Layers** palette. To add layers into this new group, drag them on top of the new group folder in the **Layers** palette. You can rename and color-code the group by right-clicking (or [Ctrl]+click for Mac) on it in the **Layers** palette and choosing **Group Properties...** from the menu that appears.

In Figure 4-23, a new layer group was created to hold all the layers containing small ostriches. Any changes made to this layer group, such as turning off layer visibility or duplicating the group, will affect all layers within the group.

Layer groups can easily be duplicated and edited. The pattern of small ostriches in Figure 4-24 was created by following these simple steps:

1. The small ostriches group was duplicated four times. The group can be duplicated by selecting it in the **Layers** palette and choosing **Layer > Duplicate Group...** or right-clicking the group in the **Layers** palette. Each group was then moved to a new location.

2. Two of the duplicated groups were flipped horizontally and moved downward slightly. To flip the layers, select them in the **Layers** palette to make them active and then choose **Edit > Transform > Flip Horizontal**.

Linking Layers

Linking layers is a simple way to group layers without organizing them into folders. Once layers are linked, they can be moved or transformed simultaneously. Linking and unlinking layers is a quick, easy process.

To link layers, hold down [Ctrl] (or [Command] for Mac) as you click on the layers that you want to link in the **Layers** palette. Then, click the **Link layers** (chain) button at the bottom left of the **Layers** palette. The link icon appears at the right side of each linked layer. To unlink layers, make sure they are active, and then click the **Link layers** button at the bottom of the **Layers** palette again.

Figure 4-24.
This pattern of small ostriches was quickly created by duplicating the small ostriches layer group. Then, each group was repositioned.

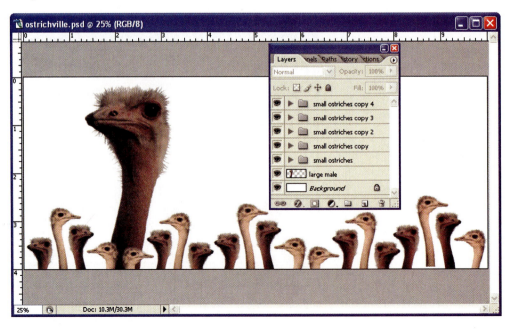

Merging Layers

Merging layers in Photoshop means to combine two or more layers into one. Merging layers is similar to grouping layers. However, when layers are merged, they become joined *permanently*. There are three ways to merge layers.

The first method is simple. Select multiple layers in the **Layers** palette by holding [Ctrl] (or [command] for Mac) as you click on each layer. Then, choose **Layer > Merge Layers**. The contents of the selected layers are copied into the selected layer that is closest to the top of the layer stack, and the other selected layers are removed. The same result can be achieved by selecting the layers in the **Layers** palette, right clicking, and selecting **Merge Layers** in the shortcut menu.

Another way to merge layers is to click the **Layer visibility** toggles in the **Layers** palette to hide all of the layers you do *not* want to merge. Then, choose **Layer > Merge Visible** to combine all the visible layers into one layer. This command will not work unless one of the visible layers is active. If only one of the visible layers is active, the content from other visible layers is copied into that layer and the other visible layers are deleted. If two or more visible layers are selected, the content from all of the visible layers is copied into the selected layer that is highest in the layer stack, and the other visible layers are deleted. The same effect can be achieved by right clicking one of the visible layers and selecting **Merge Visible** in the shortcut menu.

If you are merging only two layers, make sure the layers are next to each other in the layer stack. Then, select the layer you want to merge and choose **Layer > Merge Down**. This combines the currently active layer with the layer directly below it on the layer stack. The same effect can be achieved by selecting the layer you want to merge in the **Layers** palette, right clicking, and selecting **Merge Down** in the shortcut menu. Remember, you can reorganize the layers in the layer stack by clicking and dragging them to the desired location before merging them.

The same pattern of small ostriches shown in Figure 4-24 can be created by merging instead of grouping. See **Figure 4-25**.

Figure 4-25.
This pattern of small ostriches was created by merging, duplicating, and renaming layers.

The male1, male2, female1, and female2, layers are merged into a single layer

1. The four small ostriches were merged onto one layer.
2. The newly merged layer was duplicated four times. The duplicated layers were moved to their approximate locations.
3. Two of the duplicated layers were flipped horizontally and moved downward slightly.

Why is it necessary to combine layers using merging techniques instead of grouping them in layer groups? The answer depends on how you want to edit the merged or grouped layers. Most of Photoshop's color correction commands and many of the tools found in the **Toolbox** will only work on one layer at a time. Layer groups are the best choice to combine layers if you are only concerned about moving, transforming, duplicating, aligning, or applying layer styles to the layer group as a whole.

Flattening an Image

Images that contain layers take up a lot of file space. Images with layers can only be saved in three file formats: PSD, TIFF, and PDF. Photoshop format (PSD) is the default format that layered Photoshop images are saved in. File formats are discussed further in another chapter.

To save your file in any format other than those listed above (such as JPEG), you must *flatten* it first. To flatten an image means to merge *all* of the layers using a single command (**Layer > Flatten Image**). Photoshop files with layers take up a lot of file space, so file sizes become a lot smaller when an image is flattened.

Once you save your file in a flattened condition, you can never get your layers back again. All Photoshop users would agree that you should always save an unflattened backup copy of a file before you flatten it. This allows you to easily make changes to the file if necessary. Such unexpected changes are required when mistakes or color problems are found just before a design is ready to be printed or when a client changes their mind and requests adjustments to the look and feel of the design.

Layer Opacity

Opacity refers to an object's ability to block light. In Photoshop, the term opacity refers to how visible an image element is. If a layer has 100% opacity (its default setting), it appears completely solid, not transparent. A layer with 0% opacity is completely transparent, or invisible. Opacity values between 0% and 100% create layers that are see-through to some degree.

To change the opacity of a layer or a layer group, first select the layer or group in the **Layers** palette to make it active. Next, adjust the **Opacity:** slider to the desired value. There are actually two sliders that can control opacity: the **Opacity:** slider and the **Fill:** slider, Figure 4-26. The difference between them is that the **Fill:** slider does not change the opacity of effects that are associated with the layer, such as blending modes or layer styles.

Layer Transparency

In Figure 4-27, the Background layer, which contains the white pixels, has been hidden. A checkerboard pattern remains. Whenever you see this checkerboard pattern, it tells you that the area is transparent—there is nothing there.

The appearance of the checkerboard pattern can be changed by choosing **Edit > Preferences > Transparency and Gamut...** (or **Photoshop > Preferences > Transparency and Gamut...** for Mac). In the **Preferences** dialog box, you can change the size of the checkerboard pattern by selecting a new option from the **Grid Size:** drop-down list. You

Figure 4-26.
The opacity of the ostrich groups has been set (from left to right) to 100%, 80%, 60%, 40%, and 20%. The opacity of the large ostrich has been set to 0%.

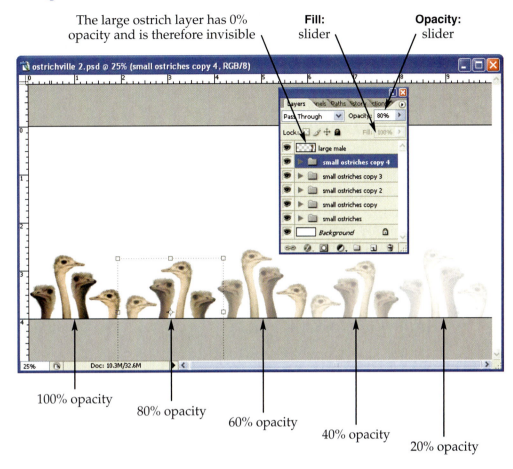

Figure 4-27.
The white background layer has been hidden. It is the only layer in this project that does not contain transparent areas (shown by the checkerboard pattern).

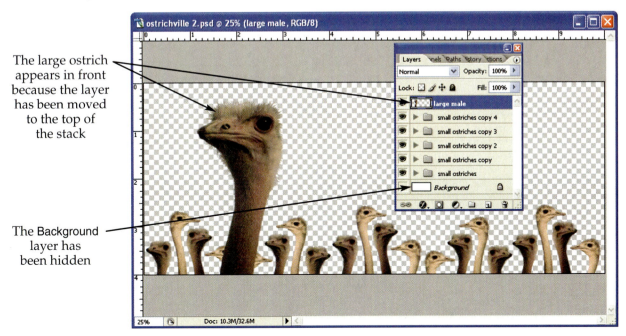

can adjust the color and shading used in the checkerboard pattern by selecting a scheme from the **Grid Colors:** drop-down list. A preview on the right side of the dialog box shows how your choices affect the transparency pattern. Pick **OK** to accept the changes.

Layer transparency is available when working with files saved in Photoshop (PSD) format. Be aware that if you save a file that has transparent areas in another format (such as JPEG), the transparent areas will not be preserved. If the file is going to be used on the web, the transparent areas can be preserved by saving files in GIF or PNG formats.

Locking Layers

To *lock* a layer means to "protect it from being changed." When you begin a new Photoshop project, the Background layer is locked automatically. It can be unlocked by double-clicking on it and giving it a new name. It can also be unlocked by selecting it and then choosing **Layer > New > Layer from Background**. It (or any other layer) can be locked again by selecting the layer in the **Layers** palette and choosing **Layer > New > Background from Layer**.

To lock or unlock a layer, other than the Background layer, first make it active. Then click one of the four different locking buttons on the **Layers** palette. See Figure 4-28.

Layers Palette Menu

The **Layers** palette has a menu that makes it easy to execute layer-related commands. The menu is accessed by clicking the small arrow at the top right of the palette, Figure 4-29. Most of the commands on this menu are also listed in the **Layer** menu. However, two of the commands are unique.

Dock to Palette Well Command

The **Dock to Palette Well** command hides the **Layers** palette so only its tab is visible in the **Palette Well** area. This option is only available if your monitor's display resolution is set to 1024×768 or higher. Refer to Chapter 1, *The Work Area* for more information on the **Palette Well**.

Figure 4-28.
The lock buttons are located on the **Layers** palette. This chart describes the function of each of the buttons.

Lock button (found on the Layers palette):	What it protects:
Lock transparent pixels	 The transparent parts of the layer are protected; nothing can be added on top of them. However, the pixels on the layer can still be edited.
Lock image pixels	 Prevents the pixels from being edited, but the layer can be moved. The transparent parts of the layer can be edited.
Lock position	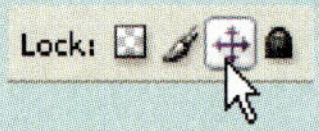 Prevents the layer from being moved, but it can still be edited.
Lock all	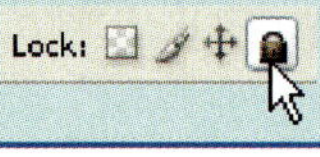 No changes can be made to the layer. All three of the previous locks are applied to the layer.

Figure 4-29.
Many of the commands listed in the **Layers** pull-down menu can also be accessed through the **Layers** palette menu. **A**—This menu is displayed by clicking the small arrow in the upper right corner of the palette. **B**—The **Layers** palette menu contains many useful commands. **C**—The appearance of the layer thumbnails can be changed in the **Layers Palette Options** dialog box.

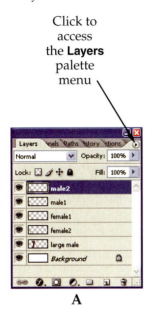

A B C

Layers Palette Options

Choosing the **Palette Options** command displays the **Layers Palette Options** dialog box. In the **Thumbnail Size** section of this dialog box, you can select a radio button to reduce or enlarge the size of the layers' *thumbnails*, the small pictures of what is contained on the layers. For large projects with many layers, change this option to a smaller size or no thumbnail image at all.

In the **Thumbnail Contents** area, you can select the **Layer Bounds** radio button to display only the content of the layer enlarged to fill the thumbnail. This option gives you the best view of the layer's content, but provides no indication of where the layer content is located in the image. Choosing the **Entire Document** causes the thumbnail to display the layer's content in relation to the extents of the image. In cases where you have many overlapping layers and position is critical, the **Entire Document** option is usually better.

Right Clicking on the Layers Palette

Many of Photoshop's palettes display contextual menus, or shortcut menus, when you right click (or [Ctrl]+click for Mac) on them. A contextual menu is a quick way to view several menu commands that are directly related to the palette you happen to be right clicking on.

The **Layers** palette is somewhat unique—there are up to four different contextual menus that can be displayed, depending on where you right click. You will get a different menu when clicking on each of the following: the layer thumbnail, the layer name, the layer visibility column, and, if a layer mask has been added, the layer mask thumbnail. Layer masks are discussed in a later chapter.

GRAPHIC DESIGN: Text Basics

In the next chapter, you will learn how to create and manipulate text in Photoshop using the type (text) tools. Photoshop also has two palettes that control the appearance of text: the **Paragraph** palette and the **Character** palette.

As a graphic designer, you will create *headings* (titles and subtitles), *lists* (bulleted or numbered groups of items), and *body text* (complete sentences and paragraphs). One of the first issues to consider is what kind of text *justification* is best. Justification refers to the way the words in the paragraph align with the edges of the document. You can choose between left, centered, right, or justified. Notice that Photoshop offers four slight variations of justified text. See Figure 4-30 and Figure 4-31.

When creating body text, lines of text should be broken (hyphenated) in well-thought-out places. Consider the two examples in Figure 4-32. At first glance, both of these paragraphs look fine—the right side of each is not too ragged in appearance. In the first example, however, two wildflower names have been broken between two lines. In the second example, no words or names are broken, making it easier for the reader to quickly comprehend the information.

Too much text per line can make it difficult to quickly absorb information from a graphic design. When creating body text, limit words per line to no more than twelve, and no fewer than four. Reading either of the examples in Figure 4-33 is more difficult than reading example B in Figure 4-32.

Figure 4-30.
There are several text justification options available in most software programs. Photoshop's text alignment buttons are shown here, however, the text alignment buttons in most other software will look very similar. Note that Photoshop has four slightly different variations of justified text.

Type of justification:		Notes
Left-aligned		Use for body text and lists. Easiest for U.S. and European audiences to read.
Center-aligned		Good for headlines and titles. Difficult to read when used for lists or body text.
Right-aligned		Some countries read from right to left. Right-justified text is difficult for U.S. and European audiences to read.
Justified		A good alternative when creating body text. Tends to create uneven spacing and channels of white space in a paragraph.

Figure 4-31.
Can you spot two or three white space channels in this justified paragraph?

When justified text is created, irregular spacing occurs between the words. Additionally, distracting channels of white space frequently appear in justified paragraphs. Both of these problems can be adjusted using Photoshop's **Character** palette. When justified text is created, irregular spacing occurs between the words. Additionally, distracting channels of white space frequently appear in justified paragraphs. Both of these problems can be adjusted using Photoshop's **Character** palette.

Figure 4-32. Line breaks affect the readability of text. **A**—The line breaks in this text have split two flower names, decreasing the readability of the text. **B**—In this example, care was taken not to split the flower names. Notice that it appears neater and is more readable.

There are hundreds of beautiful wildflower species found in the Rocky Mountains. Shown on the front: *Greenstem Paper-flower, Spring Beauty, Mountain Forget-Me-Not. Back: Car-men Gilia, Dusty Penstemon.*

A

There are hundreds of beautiful wildflower species found in the Rocky Mountains. Shown on the front: *Greenstem Paperflower, Spring Beauty, Mountain Forget-Me-Not. Back: Carmen Gilia, Dusty Penstemon.*

B

Figure 4-33. Having too many or too few words per line also decreases the readability of the text. **A**—This example has too many words per line. **B**—This example has too few words per line. Both examples are slightly more difficult to read than Figure 4-31B.

There are hundreds of beautiful wildflower species found in the Rocky Mountains. Shown on the front: *Greenstem Paperflower, Spring Beauty, Mountain Forget-Me-Not. Back: Carmen Gilia, Dusty Penstemon.*

A

There are hundreds
of beautiful wildflower
species found in the
Rocky Mountains.
Shown on the front:
*Greenstem Paperflower,
Spring Beauty, Mountain
Forget-Me-Not. Back:
Carmen Gilia,
Dusty Penstemon.*

B

Photoshop measures text in points (pt) format by default. For example, when you choose a font size of 12, it will actually be 12 point text, unless you change the type preferences. A ***point*** is a tiny unit of measure—1/72 of an inch. With that in mind, graphic designers should be aware of these recommended font sizes:

- Headings in a graphic design should be 14 pt. and up. Keep in mind that many designs (such as posters) should be easy to read from several feet away.
- Body text in a graphic design should be no smaller than 10–12 pt.

Summary

You have studied layers and selections in the previous two chapters. As you have experimented with Photoshop, you may have noticed that selections are independent of layers. In other words, if you have created a selection, you can switch to a different layer and use the same selection again.

You have learned that there are many ways to manipulate and organize layers. In this chapter, you have been introduced to the basics. Later in this book, you will encounter another chapter that will acquaint you with more advanced layer techniques, including methods of blending layers together.

Chapter Tutorials

The following tutorials will show you how to create a symmetrical design using the layer techniques discussed in this chapter. You will also create the "ostrichville" design discussed in this chapter. After completing the tutorials, you will save your designs and make further modifications to them later.

Tutorial 4-1

This tutorial will give you experience creating, organizing, and transforming layers in order to create a composited design. You will also use the grid to help you position the elements that make up the design.

Part 1: Introduction to Layers

In this part of the tutorial, you will rename the layers containing the leaves copied in previous tutorials.

1. Open Photoshop.
2. Open the 03leafy.psd file that you created in an earlier chapter.
3. Click on the **Layers** palette tab and drag it until it is next to the 03leafy.psd image window, as shown in Figure T4-1. Click and drag the bottom edge of the palette to resize it as needed.

   Each leaf is on a separate layer. Every time you dragged a leaf over to the 03leafy.psd file, a new layer was automatically created.

Move Tool

4. Click the **Move Tool**.
5. In the options bar, place a check mark in the **Show Transform Controls** check box.

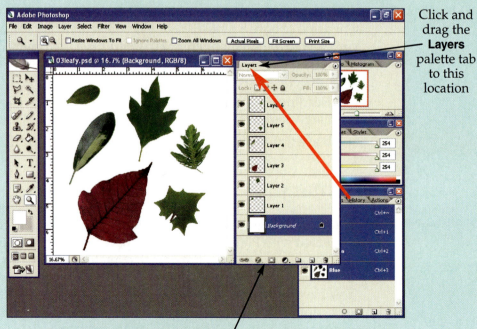

Figure T4-1. Open 03leafy.psd and drag the **Layers** palette out next to the image window.

Click and drag the **Layers** palette tab to this location

Click and drag the bottom edge of the palette to resize it as needed

Chapter 4 Introduction to Layers

6. Use the **Move Tool** to click on each of the leaves.

   As you click on a leaf, a box appears around the leaf and the leaf's layer is highlighted in blue in the **Layers** palette.

7. With the **Move Tool**, click on the large dark green leaf in the top center of the image window.

   The layer that contains the leaf is highlighted in the **Layers** palette.

8. Choose **Layer > Layer Properties…**.

   This opens the **Layer Properties** dialog box. See **Figure T4-2**.

9. Enter oak as the name of the layer and click **OK**.
10. Continue to rename the layers, using the names shown in **Figure T4-3**.

Figure T4-2. Rename the layer in the **Layer Properties** dialog box.

Click this leaf

Rename the layer oak

Click to access the **Layers** palette menu

The name of the layer changes in the **Layers** palette

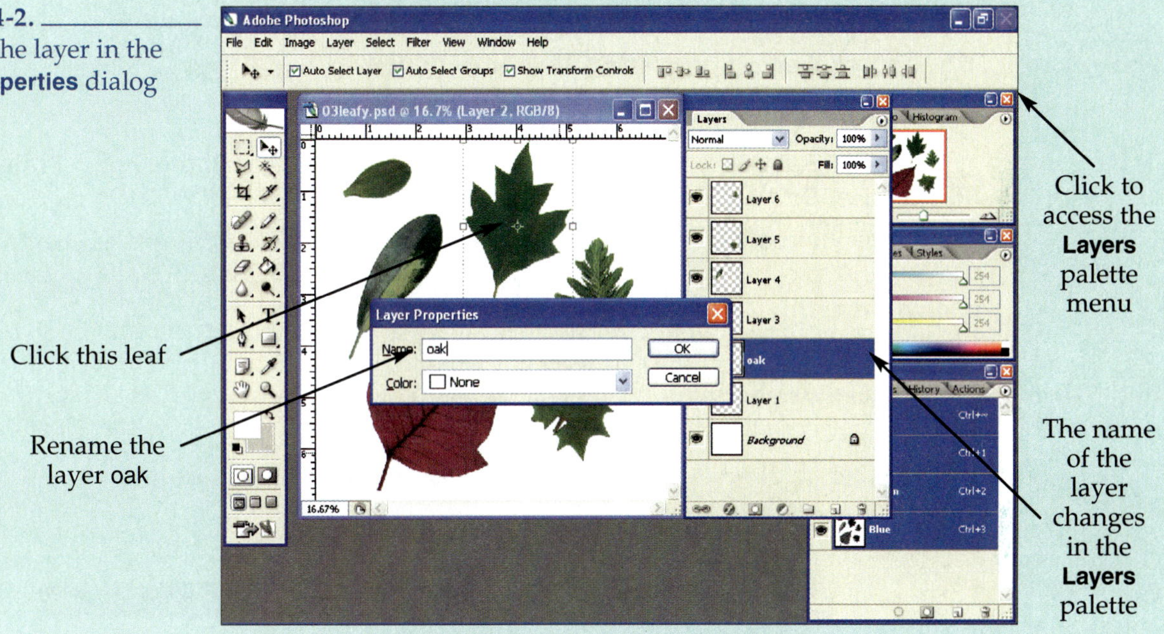

Figure T4-3. Rename the layers based on their content. Use the names shown here.

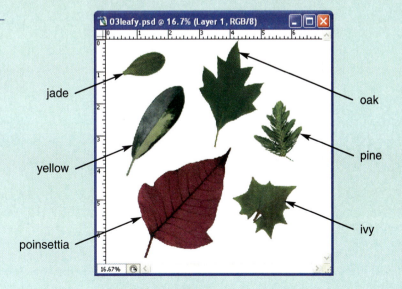

jade

yellow

poinsettia

oak

pine

ivy

11. Click on the arrow in the upper right corner of the **Layers** palette and choose **Palette Options...** from the menu.
12. If a smaller size thumbnail option is available, select it and click **OK**. If no smaller thumbnail option is available, click **Cancel**.

    If you selected a smaller thumbnail option, each layer appears a little smaller in the **Layers** palette.

13. If you are not going to continue with the remaining parts of this tutorial, save your work.

Part 2: Using the Grid

In this part of the tutorial, you will set up and display the grid to assist you in creating the design. You will also experiment with moving a layer with snap on and with snap off.

1. If necessary, open the 03leafy.psd image.
2. Choose **View > Show > Grid**.

    This makes the grid appear on your image.

3. Choose **Edit > Preferences > Guides, Grid & Slices...** (or **Photoshop > Preferences > Guides, Grid & Slices...** for Mac).
4. In the **Preferences** dialog box, enter the settings shown in **Figure T4-4** and click **OK**.
5. Use the **Move Tool** to slowly drag the jade leaf to the bottom left corner.

    As you perform this step, do not click and drag this symbol in the center of the bounding box that surrounds the jade leaf. It is used to rotate objects. If you move this symbol by mistake, press [Esc].

    Do you notice the jerky movement of the leaf as you drag it? The leaf is trying to line up with the gridlines as it is moved—this is called snapping to the grid.

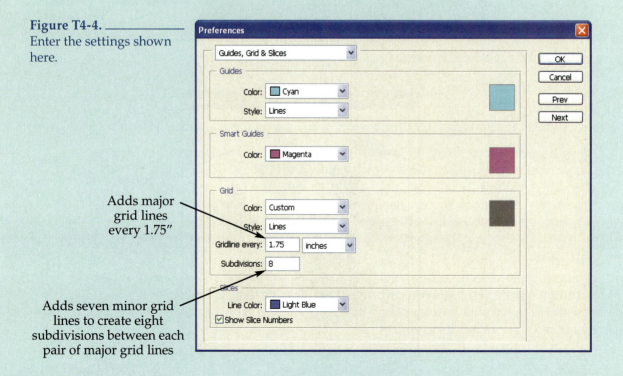

Figure T4-4. Enter the settings shown here.

Adds major grid lines every 1.75"

Adds seven minor grid lines to create eight subdivisions between each pair of major grid lines

Chapter 4   Introduction to Layers

6. Choose **View > Snap To > Grid**.

   This turns off the snap-to-grid option. You can tell the option is no longer active because the check mark is removed from the **Grid** option in the **Snap To** submenu.

7. Choose **View > Snap To > Layers**.

   This turns off the snap-to-layers option. If left on, the snap-to-layers option may also interfere with the movement of the leaf.

8. Move the jade leaf a little. Notice it moves smoothly now.

   Another way to move a selected layer is to use the arrow keys on your keyboard. When you use the arrow keys to move a selection, the snaps settings do not affect the movement.

9. Use the arrow keys to move the jade leaf so it is in the position shown in **Figure T4-5**.
10. If you are not going to continue with the remaining parts of this tutorial, save your work.

Part 3: Linking Layers

In this part of the tutorial, you will experiment with linking layers. Linking allows you to quickly and easily move or transform multiple layers and then make the layers independent again.

1. If necessary, open the 03leafy.psd image.
2. In the **Layers** palette, click on the layer named yellow to make it active.

   You know the layer is active because it is highlighted in blue in the **Layers** palette.

3. Press [Ctrl] (or [Command] for Mac) and click the pine layer.

   The yellow and pine layers should both be highlighted in blue in the **Layers** palette.

Figure T4-5. Position the jade leaf as shown.

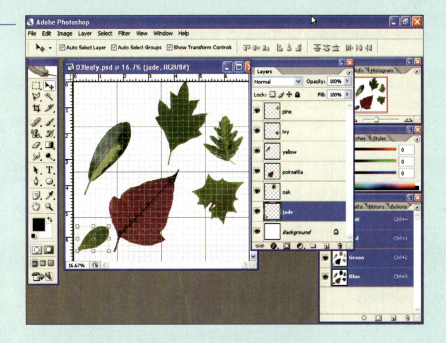

Link Layers

4. Click the **Link layers** (chain) button in the lower left corner of the **Layers** palette.

   Chain icons appear on the right side of the pine and yellow layers indicating that you have linked the yellow layer to the pine layer, **Figure T4-6**. Linking is used when you need to move more than one layer at a time.

5. Click the **Move Tool**.
6. Experiment with moving the leaves around a little.

   The leaves stick together as they are moved.

7. Move the linked leaves upward, as shown in **Figure T4-7**.

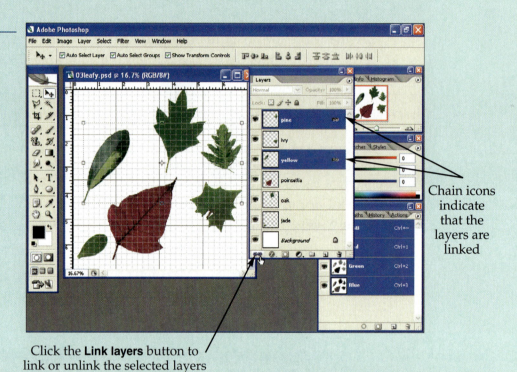

Figure T4-6. Click the **Link layers** button to link the yellow and pine layers.

Click the **Link layers** button to link or unlink the selected layers

Chain icons indicate that the layers are linked

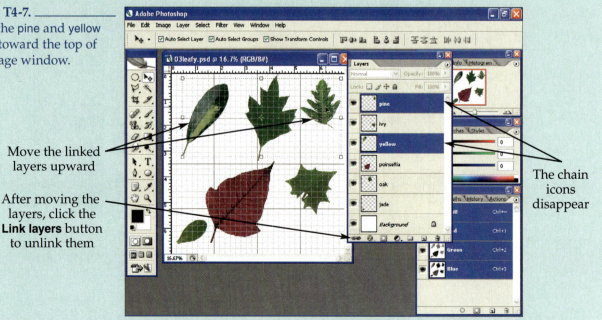

Figure T4-7. Move the pine and yellow layers toward the top of the image window.

Move the linked layers upward

After moving the layers, click the **Link layers** button to unlink them

The chain icons disappear

Chapter 4   Introduction to Layers

8. Turn off the link by clicking on the **Link** layers button at the bottom left corner of the **Layers** palette.

   The chain icons to the right of the layer names disappear, indicating that the layers are no longer linked.

9. If you are not going to continue with the remaining parts of this tutorial, save your work.

Part 4: Layer Visibility

In this part of the tutorial, you will experiment with hiding layers to unclutter your work area. Toggling visibility on and off is also useful for selecting layers to merge.

Layer visibility

1. Click the **Layer visibility** (eye) toggle next to each layer.

   This hides all of the layers.

2. Click on the jade layer to make it active.
3. Restore the visibility of the jade layer by clicking the **Layer visibility** toggle again.
4. Turn on the Background layer by clicking its **Layer visibility** toggle.
5. Move the jade leaf to the center of the 03leafy.psd image. See **Figure T4-8**.
6. If you are not going to continue with the remaining parts of this tutorial, save your work.

Part 5: Rotate (Transform) a Layer

In this part of the tutorial, you will rotate a layer using the transform controls associated with the **Move Tool**.

1. If necessary, open the 03leafy.psd image.
2. Zoom in on the jade leaf by dragging a zoom box around the leaf.
3. Make sure the jade layer is active and click the **Move Tool**.

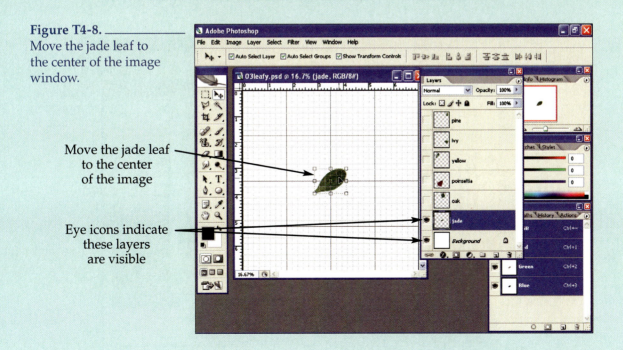

Figure T4-8. Move the jade leaf to the center of the image window.

Move the jade leaf to the center of the image

Eye icons indicate these layers are visible

4. Position the cursor outside one corner of the leaf's bounding box and keep it there until the rotate cursor appears. See Figure T4-9.
5. Click and drag the cursor until the jade leaf is rotated −85°, as in Figure T4-10.

   As the leaf rotates, it pivots around the reference point. The options bar shows you how many degrees the leaf has been rotated. You can also enter an exact amount.

Commit

6. Press [Enter] or [Return] or click the **Commit** button on the options bar to end the rotate command.

   If you make a mistake and need to start over press [Esc] or click the **Cancel** button.

Cancel

7. If you are not going to continue with the remaining parts of this tutorial, save your work.

Figure T4-9.
Position the cursor outside the bounding box.

When the cursor is positioned outside the corner of the bounding box, it changes into the rotate cursor

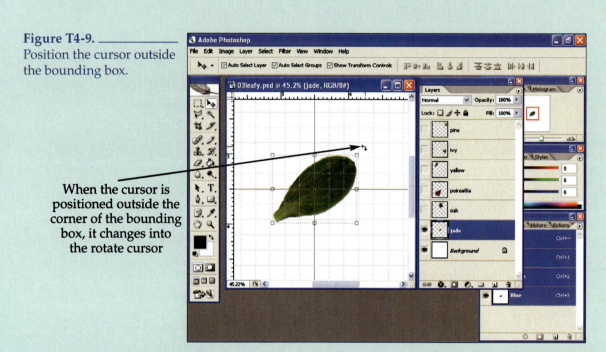

Figure T4-10.
Rotate the leaf to the position shown.

Reference point

Commit transform button

Displays amount of rotation

Part 6: Duplicate a Layer

In this part of the tutorial, you will duplicate and transform a layer.

1. If necessary, open the 03leafy.psd image.
2. With the jade layer active, choose **Layer > Duplicate Layer…**.
3. Name the new layer jade 2.
4. Click **OK**.

   A new layer is created just above the jade layer in the **Layers** palette, and a new jade leaf is created exactly on top of the old one.

5. Rotate the new leaf 31° and press [Enter] or [Return] or click the **Commit** button to complete the rotation.
6. Use the arrow keys to move it to the location shown in **Figure T4-11**.

   The leaves should barely touch where the X appears.

7. If you are not going to continue with the remaining parts of this tutorial, save your work.

Part 7: Merging Layers

In this part of the tutorial, you will create a repeating pattern by duplicating, transforming, and then merging layers.

1. If necessary, open the 03leafy.psd image.
2. Hide the Background layer by clicking its **Layer visibility** (eye) toggle.

   The jade and jade 2 layers should be visible. All other layers should be hidden, **Figure T4-12**.

3. Make sure the jade 2 layer is active (highlighted in blue).
4. Choose **Layer > Merge Visible**.

   This command merges both leaves onto a single layer.

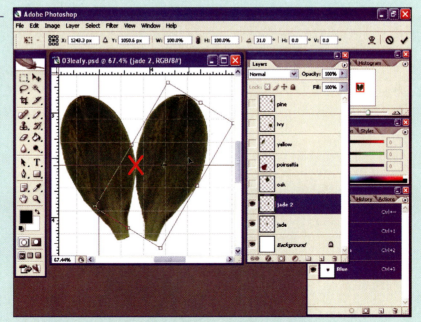

Figure T4-11. Rotate the duplicate layer and move it into the position shown.

Figure T4-12.
Hide the Background layer. Only the jade and jade 2 layers should be visible.

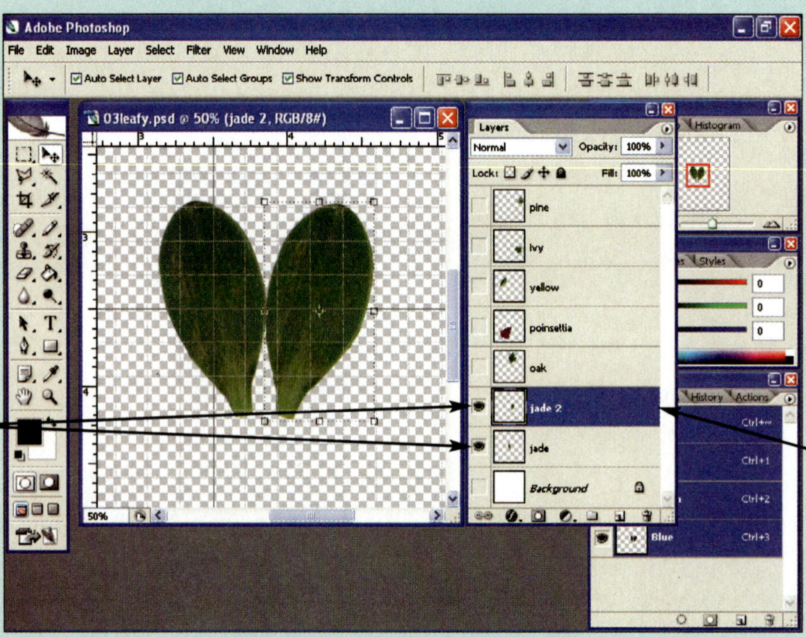

Only these two layers are visible

The Jade 2 layer is active

5. Choose **Layer > Duplicate Layer...**. In the **Duplicate Layer** dialog box, click **OK** to accept jade 2 copy as the name.
6. Zoom and adjust your view as needed. Then, rotate the new layer 60° and move it to the position shown in **Figure T4-13**.
7. Press [Enter] or [Return] or click the **Commit** button to complete the rotation.
8. Choose **Layer > Merge Visible**.

    Now, all four leaves should be on the same layer.

9. Choose **Layer > Properties...**.
10. In the **Layer Properties** dialog box, name this layer 4 jade leaves and click **OK**.

    At this point, you may want to reposition the jade leaves on the grid so that a major gridline passes between the first and second leaves and along the bottom of the fourth leaf, as seen in Figure T4-13. This will make it easier to check the leaf wreath for symmetry as you continue to assemble it.

Figure T4-13.
Move the jade 2 copy layer into the position shown here.

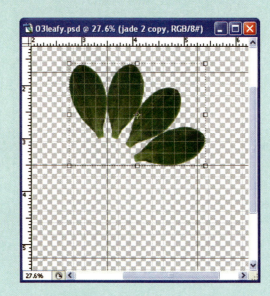

Chapter 4   Introduction to Layers   **151**

11. Choose **Layer > Duplicate Layer…**.
12. In the **Duplicate Layer** dialog box, click **OK** to accept 4 jade leaves copy as the name.
13. Hold down [Shift] and rotate this new layer until the **Rotate** text box in the options bar shows 120°.

    When [Shift] is held down, the selection rotates 15° at a time.

14. Move the 4 jade leaves copy layer to the position shown in **Figure T4-14**.
15. Press [Enter] or [Return] or click the **Commit** button on the options bar.
16. Choose **Layer > Duplicate Layer…**.
17. In the **Duplicate Layer** dialog box, click **OK** to accept 4 jade leaves copy 2 as the name.
18. Rotate the layer 120° and move it to the position shown in **Figure T4-15**.

    Move and rotate each layer as needed until your file looks like the example.

Figure T4-14. _____
Move the 4 jade leaves copy layer to the position shown.

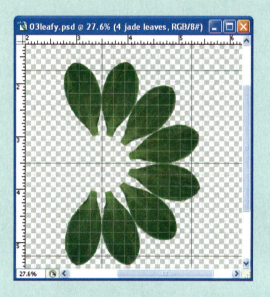

Figure T4-15. _____
Move the 4 jade leaves copy 2 layer to the position shown.

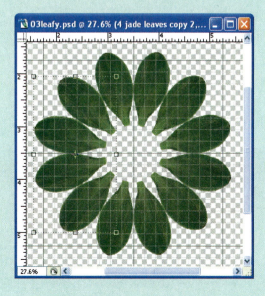

19. Press [Enter] or [Return] or click the **Commit** button on the options bar.
20. Choose **Layer > Merge Visible**.
21. Choose **Layer > Layer Properties…**.
22. In the **Layer Properties** dialog box, name the layer jade leaves.
23. If you are not going to continue with the remaining parts of this tutorial, save your work.

Part 8: Changing the Stacking Order of Layers

In this part of the tutorial, you will experiment with changing the stacking order of the layers. This will help you see how the stacking order changes the way the image appears in the image window.

1. If necessary, open the 03leafy.psd image.
2. Make the Background layer visible.
3. Move the jade leaves layer to the middle of the image. Use the grid as a guide.
4. Make the poinsettia layer visible. See **Figure T4-16**.
5. In the **Layers** palette, click and drag the poinsettia layer so it is just below the jade leaves layer in the layer stack, **Figure T4-17**.

Now, the poinsettia leaf appears to be behind the jade leaves in the image window.

6. If you are not going to continue with the remaining parts of this tutorial, save your work.

Part 9: Scale (Transform) a Layer

In this part of the tutorial, you will resize and reposition the poinsettia leaf used in the design.

1. If necessary, open the 03leafy.psd image.

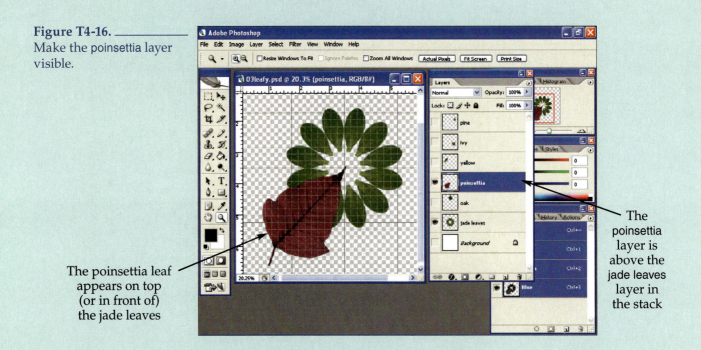

Figure T4-16. Make the poinsettia layer visible.

The poinsettia leaf appears on top (or in front of) the jade leaves

The poinsettia layer is above the jade leaves layer in the stack

Figure T4-17.
Move the poinsettia layer below the jade leaves layer in the **Layers** palette.

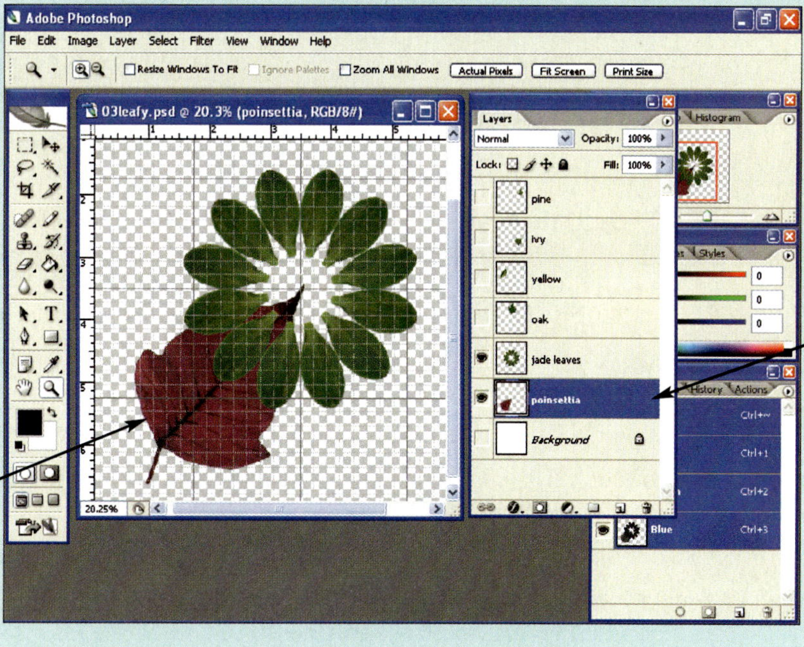

The poinsettia leaf appears to be behind (or in back of) the jade leaves

The poinsettia layer is below the jade leaves layer in the stack

2. Make sure the poinsettia layer is active.
3. Choose **Edit > Transform > Scale**.

   The option menu displays transform settings.

4. In the scaling area of the options bar, enter 60 in the **W:** (width) text box and 60 in the **H:** (height) text box.

   The poinsettia leaf is now 60% of its former size. See **Figure T4-18**.

Figure T4-18.
Scale the poinsettia layer to 60%.

The height and width are scaled to 60%

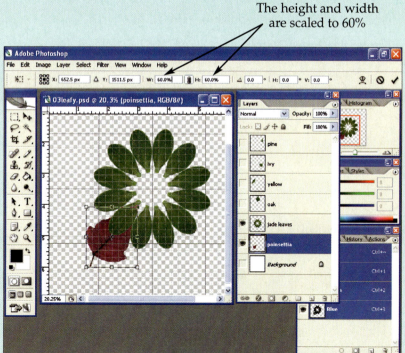

5. Press [Enter] or [Return] or click the **Commit** button to end the scaling process.
6. Move the poinsettia leaf to the location shown in **Figure T4-19**.
7. If you are not going to continue with the remaining parts of this tutorial, save your work.

Part 10: Adding More Leaves to the Design

In this part of the tutorial, you will apply the techniques you have learned in the chapter to duplicate, transform, and merge layers to add the remaining leaves to the design.

1. If necessary, open the 03leafy.psd image.
2. Make sure the poinsettia layer is active.
3. Right-click (or [Ctrl]+click for Mac) on the poinsettia layer in the **Layers** palette and choose **Duplicate Layer…** from the shortcut menu that appears.
4. In the **Duplicate Layer** dialog box, click **OK** to accept poinsettia copy as the name for this new layer.
5. Choose **Edit > Transform > Rotate 90° CCW**.

   This rotates the new layer 90° in the counter-clockwise direction.

6. Move the new layer to the location shown in **Figure T4-20**.
7. In the **Layers** palette, drag the layers until they are in the order shown in **Figure T4-21**.
8. Click the poinsettia copy layer to make it active.
9. Choose **Layer > Merge Down**.

   This is another way to merge layers. The active layer merges with the layer just below it.

10. Now that the two poinsettia leaves are on the same layer, right-click on the poinsettia layer in the **Layers** palette and choose **Duplicate Layer…**.
11. In the **Duplicate layer** dialog box, click **OK** to accept the poinsettia copy name.
12. Choose **Edit > Transform > Rotate 180°**.
13. Move the new layer to the location shown in **Figure T4-22**.

Figure T4-19. ─────────
Move the poinsettia layer to the location shown here.

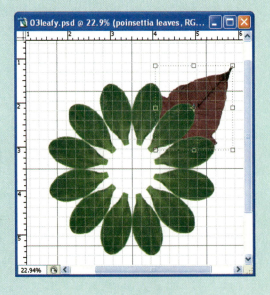

Chapter 4 Introduction to Layers 155

Figure T4-20. ———
Move the second poinsettia leaf to this location.

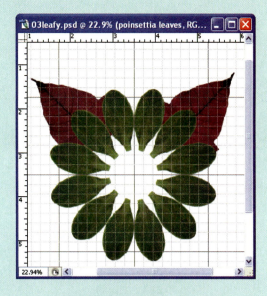

Figure T4-21. ———
Arrange the layers in the order shown here.

Figure T4-22. ———
Move the poinsettia copy layer to the bottom of the jade leaf ring.

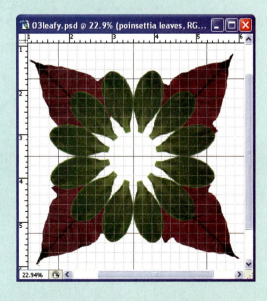

156 Learning Photoshop

14. Merge the two layers that contain poinsettia leaves.
15. Rename this layer poinsettia leaves.
16. Make the oak layer visible.
17. Rotate and move the oak layer until it is in the position shown in **Figure T4-23**. Adjust the zoom and your view as needed.
18. Click the **Lasso Tool** in the **Toolbox**.
19. Make sure the **New selection** button is pressed and that **Feather:** is set to 0 in the options bar.
20. Create a selection border around the oak leaf stem, like the one shown in Figure T4-23.
21. Press [Delete].

    Only items on the oak layer are deleted, because it is the active layer.

22. Continue duplicating, rotating, scaling, and merging layers until your design looks like the design in **Figure T4-24**.

    After adding the yellow leaves, use the **Elliptical Marquee Tool** to remove any stems that extend into the star-shaped center of the arrangement.

23. Choose **View > Show > Grid**.

    This turns off the grid.

24. Choose **File > Save As…**. In the **Save As** dialog box, name the file 04leafy.psd. You will add more to it later.
25. Close the 04leafy.psd image.

Tutorial 4-2: Layer Opacity

In this tutorial, you will lower a layer's opacity setting to mute an image. This creates a popular effect you will find in many designs.

1. Open the 03cardback.psd file you created in an earlier chapter.

Figure T4-23.
Position the oak layer as shown.

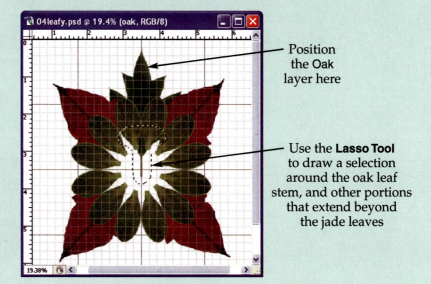

Figure T4-24.
Continue duplicating and transforming layers to create the design shown here.

2. Make the layer active that contains the large image of the Gilia flowers. This should be labeled Layer 1.
3. In the **Layers** palette, set the **Opacity:** slider to 30%.

   The white background shows through, causing the image to appear lighter. See Figure T4-25.

4. Choose **File > Save As…** and name the file 04cardback.psd.
5. Close the 04cardback.psd file. You will add more to it later.

Figure T4-25.
Set the **Opacity:** slider to 30% for Layer 1.

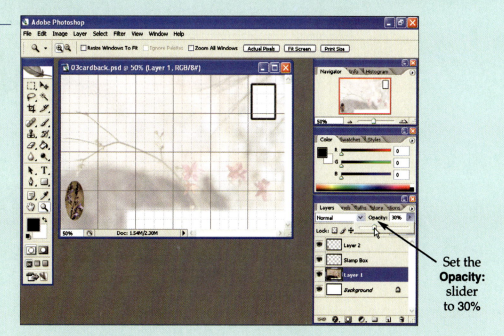

Set the **Opacity:** slider to 30%

Tutorial 4-3: Create the "Ostrichville" Design

In this tutorial, you will create a repeating-pattern design using the grouping and transforming techniques you learned in this chapter.

1. Open the file named ostrichville.psd.
2. Using the techniques learned in this chapter, create the design shown in **Figure T4-26**. Organize your layers using grouping techniques instead of merging techniques.
3. After completing the design, choose **File > Save As…** and name the file 04ostrichville.psd.
4. Close the 04ostrichville.psd image. You will add more to it later.

Figure 4-26.
Use the techniques you have learned in this chapter to create an interesting design. **A**—The original image consists of two ostriches. **B**—Use layers, transformations, and grouping to create the design shown.

A

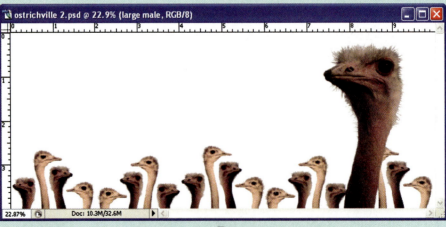

B

Key Terms

body text	grid	point
bounding box	headings	scale
clipboard	layers	skew
color depth	layer group	slices
destination image	linking	smart guides
document bounds	lists	thumbnails
flatten	lock	text justification
flip	merging	toggled

Review Questions

Answer the following questions on a separate sheet of paper.

1. What is an active layer?
2. What keyboard shortcut lets you temporarily switch to the **Move Tool**?
3. What does the **Move Tool**'s **Auto Select Layer** option do?
4. When does the **Move Tool** automatically create a new layer?
5. If you move something over to another file, and the content you moved appears smaller, what is the problem?
6. How can you cause the transform options bar to appear without choosing any menu commands?
7. What are two different ways of changing the bounding box's reference point?
8. What does the **Maintain aspect ratio button** do when clicked?
9. When using the bounding box to scale an image, what happens if you do not hold down [Shift] after you begin to drag a corner of the bounding box?
10. How can you rotate a bounding box in increments of 15°?
11. You can only copy and paste from one layer at a time unless you use what command?
12. What is the difference between **View > Snap** and **View > Snap To** menu choices?
13. How do you place a selection border around the content of a layer?
14. For a layer to appear "in front" of all other layers in your file, where should it be listed (or stacked) in the **Layers** palette?
15. When a new layer is created, where is it listed (or stacked) in the **Layers** palette?
16. Which method of deleting a layer is the fastest?
17. If you hide a layer (turn off its visibility), how do you show it again?
18. What is the difference between grouping and linking layers?
19. What is the difference between grouping and merging layers?
20. What does flattening do to an image?
21. What is the difference between the **Opacity:** and **Fill:** sliders in the **Layers** palette?
22. What file formats let you save (preserve) transparent areas of an image?
23. How do you unlock a Background layer?
24. What is the difference between the **Lock image pixels** button and the **Lock transparent pixels** button on the **Layers** palette?
25. What are layer thumbnails?

Learning Photoshop

This diagram shows all of the commands available through the **Layer** menu and its submenus.

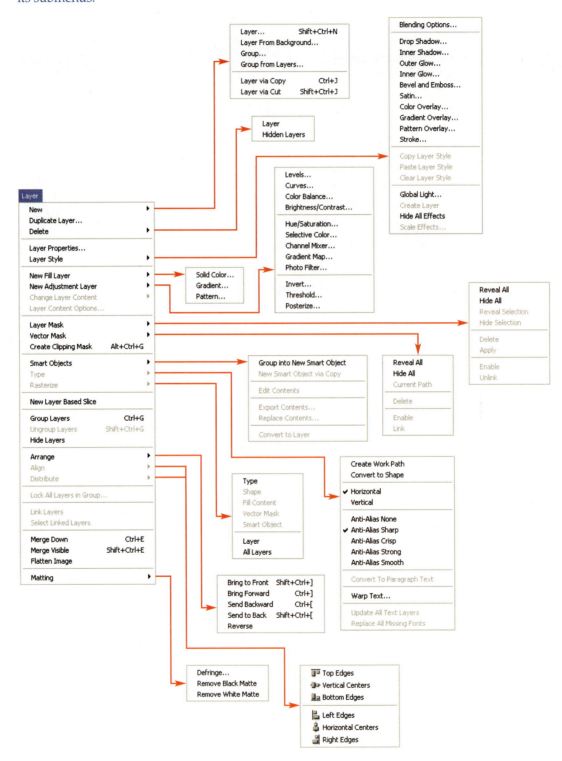

5
Text, Shapes, and Layer Styles

Learning Objectives

After completing this chapter, you will be able to:
- Explain the differences between vector and bitmap graphics.
- Enter and edit text using the type tools.
- Find special text characters and insert them into your file.
- Use the type masking tools to create a selection.
- Fine-tune the appearance of text using the **Character** and **Paragraph** palettes.
- Explain why it is sometimes necessary to rasterize text and shapes.
- Create simple and complex shapes using the shape and pen tools.
- Discuss how to create your own custom shapes.
- Use the **Paths** palette to convert paths into other Photoshop features.
- Apply layer styles to your projects using both the **Layer** menu and the **Styles** palette.

Introduction

In this chapter, you will learn about using Photoshop to draw vector graphics. With vector graphics, you can create any shape you can imagine and fill it with a color or pattern.

You will also learn how to manipulate text in many different ways. As you read through the chapter, you will discover that you can apply a variety of effects such as drop shadows and beveled edges (called *styles*) to text or shapes. See **Figure 5-1**.

Two Kinds of Graphics: Vector vs Bitmap

Any image captured by a digital camera or scanner is called a *bitmap graphic* (also called a *raster graphic*). Bitmap graphics are made up of pixels. You learned in Chapter 2, *Resolution*, that as bitmap image is enlarged, it loses quality because its pixels get larger.

Vector graphics are different. If you draw a circle that is a vector graphic, you can resize it and it will not lose any quality. Vector graphics are *not* made up of pixels—they are composed of lines that are controlled by mathematical formulas. These lines can be edited easily or filled with colors or patterns.

Text in Photoshop

Text is similar to a vector graphic—it can be changed to various fonts, sizes, and styles. But unlike a true vector graphic, the shape of each text character cannot be changed.

Type is a word borrowed from the printing industry. It refers to individual text characters that were set by hand, inked, and pressed against paper in the early days of the printing industry. Adobe chose to call text-related tools *type tools* instead of text tools. There are four type tools, the **Horizontal Type Tool**, the **Vertical Type Tool**, the **Horizontal Type Mask Tool**, and the **Vertical Type Mask Tool**.

The Horizontal Type Tool and the Vertical Type Tool

The **Horizontal Type Tool** and the **Vertical Type Tool** create text as you might expect—by clicking in your file, setting options, and entering text with your keyboard. Once you select one of the type tools, you can adjust the text properties in the options bar.

The Type Tool Options Bar

The options bar is the same for all of the type tools. See **Figure 5-2**. At the far left of the options bar is an icon that indicates which type tool is selected. Immediately to the right of this icon is the **Change the text orientation** button. Clicking this button changes the text orientation from horizontal to vertical or vice versa.

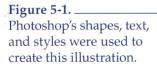

Figure 5-1.
Photoshop's shapes, text, and styles were used to create this illustration.

Figure 5-2.
The options bar for all four text tools look almost identical.

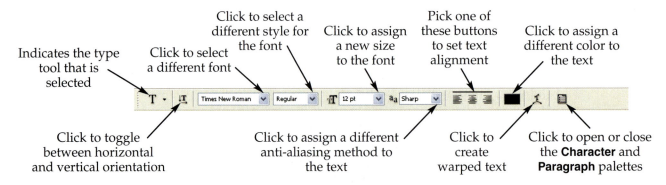

The font that the type tool uses is selected in the **Set the font family** drop-down list. When you click on the arrow, a list of available fonts appears. You can use the up and down arrow keys to scroll through the list.

The style of the font is selected in the **Set font style** drop-down list. Common font styles include regular, italic, bold, and bold italic, but will vary from font to font.

Next, select the size of the font in the **Set the font size** drop-down list. Common font sizes are included in the list. However, you can enter a custom size in the text box if the size you want is not listed.

The **Set the anti-aliasing method** drop-down list is located to the right of the **Set the font size** drop-down list. This setting controls how "soft" the edges of your text will appear. A setting of **None** creates the sharpest edge, and a setting of **Smooth** creates the softest edge. The default setting is **Sharp**, and it works well in most cases.

Next to the **Set the anti-aliasing method** drop-down list are three buttons that allow you to set the justification (alignment) of the text. The three text-alignment options available on the options bar are **Left align text**, **Center text**, and **Right align text**.

There is a small color box on the options bar. Clicking on this box opens the **Color Picker**. In the **Color Picker**, you can choose a new color for the text.

The **Create warped text** button looks like a letter T with a curved line under it. Warp effects are added after text has been created. To add warp effect to text, make sure the layer containing the text is active. Then, click the **Create warped text** button or choose **Layer > Type > Warp Text…**. This opens the **Warp Text** dialog box. Choose a warp style from the **Style:** drop-down menu, and experiment with the **Bend:**, **Horizontal Distortion:**, and **Vertical Distortion:** slider settings to change the warp effect. See **Figure 5-3**.

The last button on the options bar is the **Toggle Character and Paragraph palettes** button. Clicking this button will display or hide the **Character** and **Paragraph** palettes, which contain many controls for fine-tuning text. The **Character** and **Paragraph** palettes are explained in more detail later in this chapter.

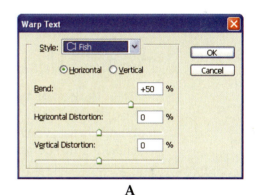

Figure 5-3. Interesting effects can be added to text by warping it. **A**—The **Warp Text** dialog box contains the settings for warping text. **B**—Select a warp style from the **Style:** drop-down list. **C**—The top line of text is normal. A fish warp has been applied to the bottom line of text.

Entering and Editing Text

There are two ways to enter text using the **Horizontal Type Tool** or the **Vertical Type Tool**. For short text entries, click anywhere in your image and start typing. You can move the text after typing because the cursor turns into a **Move Tool** automatically when you move the cursor away from the text. For longer text entries, such as a paragraph, drag a box with the cursor. The selected area becomes a bounding box. The edges of the box serve as margins, which can be adjusted by dragging the bounding box handles. To add text, simply start typing.

When you create text, a new text layer is automatically created. You can easily spot a text layer in the **Layers** palette because a large letter T is displayed where the thumbnail would be on a normal layer. See Figure 5-4. When you are finished adding text, click the **Commit** button at the far right end of the options bar. Clicking the **Commit** button completes the text layer. If you click in your file and start typing again, a new text layer will be created. Clicking the **Cancel** button is similar to choosing **Edit > Undo**.

You can easily edit a text layer. As a general rule, if you want to change the color, size, font, etc., of text after it has already been created, make sure the correct text layer is active. Then, adjust the settings in the options bar. If for any reason you have trouble doing this, try highlighting the text before changing it. To highlight the text, begin by making sure the proper type tool is active. Check to see that the correct text layer is active. Then, place the cursor on top of the first or last text character, click and hold the mouse button and drag the cursor over the text you want to highlight.

Two other familiar word processing commands, **Check Spelling** and **Find and Replace Text,** are found in the **Edit** menu. These commands will search all text layers in your file, no matter what layer is currently active.

The Type Masking Tools

The **Horizontal Type Mask Tool** and **Vertical Type Mask Tool** do not create text. Instead, they create a selection that is shaped like text. When you select one of these tools and click in your file, a pink mask covers your entire document. After entering text and clicking the **Commit** button, a selection is created in the image window, Figure 5-5. This procedure is similar to using quick mask mode, explained in Chapter 3, *Selection Tools*.

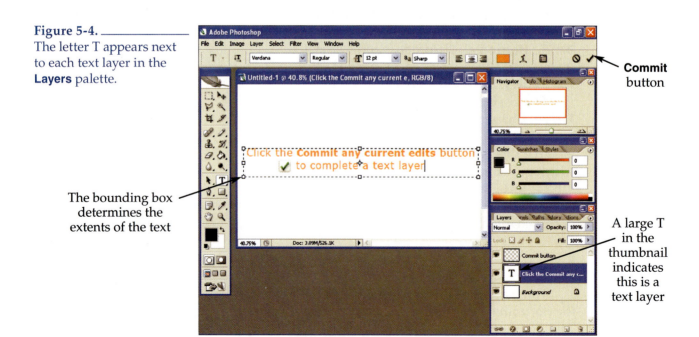

Figure 5-4. The letter T appears next to each text layer in the **Layers** palette.

The bounding box determines the extents of the text

Commit button

A large T in the thumbnail indicates this is a text layer

Figure 5-5.
The type masking tools create type-shaped selections. **A**—A pink mask covers the image as you enter text with the type mask tools. **B**—A selection is left behind after clicking the **Commit** button.

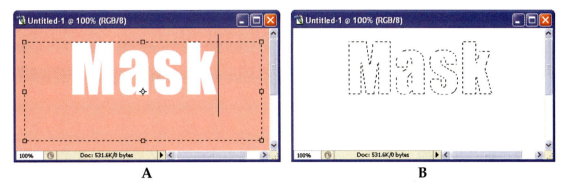

A   B

Why would you ever want to create a selection shaped like text? One situation might be to create a cutout effect by placing the text selection over an image and then pressing [Delete].

Inserting Special Text Characters

You will often need to insert special text characters such as bullets (• ◊ ▪), the copyright symbol (©), the degree symbol (°), etc.. To do this, first make sure the layer containing the text you want the symbol inserted into is active. Next, select the **Horizontal Type Tool** and click in the text line where you want the symbol to be inserted. Make sure the cursor is at the position where you want the symbol inserted. Use the arrow keys to move it if it is not.

Next, if you are using a computer with a Windows operating system, minimize Photoshop and choose **Start > Programs > Accessories > System Tools > Character Map** from Window's **Start** menu. In the **Character Map** dialog box, select the appropriate font from the **Font:** drop-down list. Locate and click the desired symbol in the symbol window. Next, click the **Select** button. The character will appear in the **Characters to copy:** text box. Finally, click the **Copy** button. Press [Alt][Tab] or pick the Photoshop icon at the bottom of the taskbar to return to your Photoshop file. Make sure the correct font is selected in the type tool's options bar before choosing **Edit > Paste**.

If you are running Photoshop on a Mac using OS 10.3 or later, use the application called Keyboard Viewer to select, copy, and paste characters. If your computer is running OS 10.2x or earlier, use the application called Key Caps. If you have trouble finding Key Caps or Keyboard Viewer, press [Command][F] and search for it. When using either of these applications, begin by choosing a font. Then, press a "modifier key" (such as [Option], [Command], [Ctrl], or [Shift]) to see what additional characters are available. When you copy and paste characters into your Photoshop document, be sure to choose the same font in the type tool's options bar before choosing **Edit > Paste**.

The Character Palette

The **Character** palette contains many settings that help you precisely control how your text appears. A description of each setting is found in the following table, **Figure 5-6**. Some of these settings will be familiar because they are also present in the type tools' options bar. However, you will see that the additional controls in the **Character** palette provide much greater control over the text.

Figure 5-6.
This chart contains brief descriptions of the settings found on the **Character** palette.

Location on the Character Palette	Description of the option	How to use the option	Examples
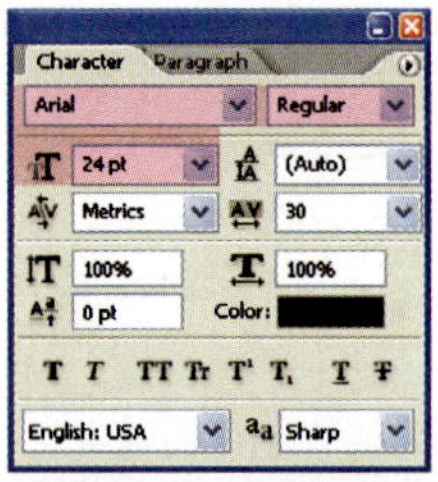 *(Character palette image)*	**Font, Style,** and **Size** These settings are also found on the options bar of any type tool.	If you want to change text that you have already created, highlight it first.	Font, style, and size **Font, style, and size** *Top: Times New Roman 12 pt regular style.* *Bottom: Changed to Helvetica 14 pt bold oblique style.*
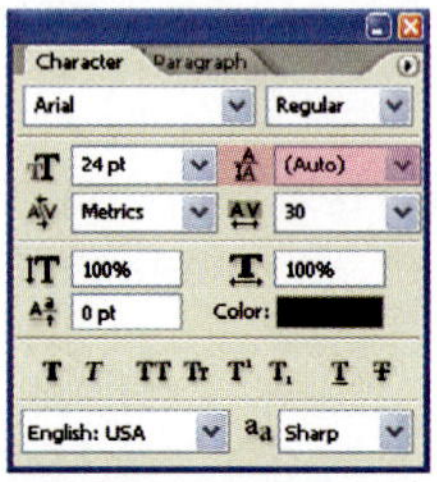 *(Character palette image)*	**Leading** Controls the space between lines of text. The **Auto** setting creates a line spacing that is the same height as the text plus 20% more.	Highlight the text and do one of the following: A) drag the leading icon, B) enter a new value in the text box, or C) select one of the presets from the drop-down list.	**Leading controls the space between lines.** **Leading controls the space between lines.** *Top: Leading's* **Auto** *setting.* *Bottom: Leading increased*
 *(Character palette image)*	**Kerning** Controls the space between *two* text characters.	Click between the letters and drag the kerning icon, enter a new value in the text box, or select one of the presets from the drop-down list.	Kerning Kerning *Top: No Kerning.* *Bottom: Kerning has been adjusted between the "k" and "e" and "n" and "g".*
 *(Character palette image)*	**Tracking** Controls the space between *all* highlighted text characters.	Highlight the text and drag the tracking icon, enter a new value in the text box, or select one of the presets from the drop-down list.	**Tracking setting: 0** **Tracking setting: 75** *Top: Default tracking setting.* *Bottom: Tracking increased.*
 *(Character palette image)*	**Vertical and Horizontal Scaling** Makes text larger or smaller, vertically or horizontally.	Highlight the text that needs to be scaled. Drag the scaling icon or enter a new percentage in the text box.	Scaling Scaling *Top: No scaling.* *Bottom: Vertical scaling at 200%.*
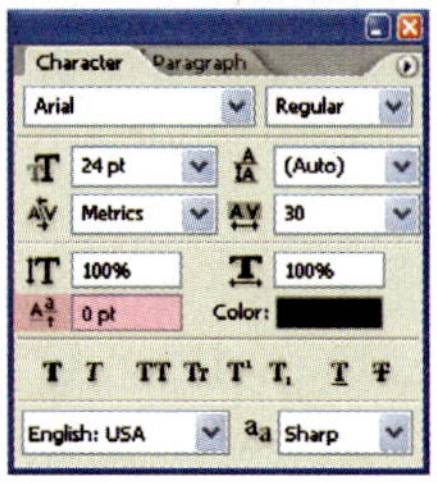 *(Character palette image)*	**Baseline Shift** Moves the baseline (bottom reference point) of the text up or down.	Highlight the text and drag the baseline shift icon or enter a new value in the text box.	$3x_2 + x = 3y$ $3x^2 + x = 3y$ *Top: The "2" was changed to a smaller font size.* *Bottom: The baseline of the number "2" has been shifted.*

(Continued)

Figure 5-6.
Continued.

Location on the Character Palette	Description of the option	How to use the option	Examples
 *(Character palette with Color highlighted)*	**Text Color** This setting is identical to the color box on the options bar of any type tool.	Highlight the text first. Click the box, and then select a color from the **Color Picker**.	**Text color** **Text color** *Top:* The font is the default black. *Bottom:* A different color is assigned to the font.
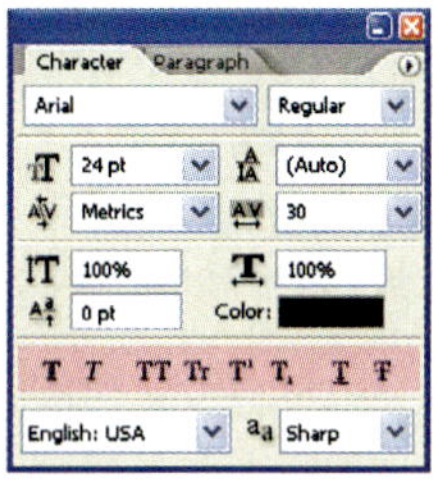 *(Character palette with style buttons row highlighted)*	The next eight entries refer to the text style buttons found on the **Character** palette.		
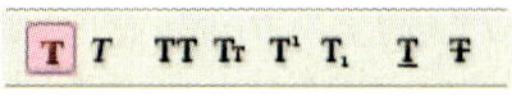 *(Faux Bold button highlighted)*	**Faux Bold** Applies a bold style to fonts that do not normally have a bold option.	Highlight the text before clicking this button.	*Regular Text* **Faux Bold** *Top:* The only style available for this font is regular. *Bottom:* The faux bold option simulates a bold font style.
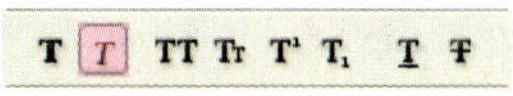 *(Faux Italic button highlighted)*	**Faux Italic** Applies an italic style to fonts that do not normally have a italic option.	Highlight the text before clicking this button.	Regular Text *Faux Italic* *Top:* Comic Sans font in the regular style. *Bottom:* The faux italic option simulates an italic font style.
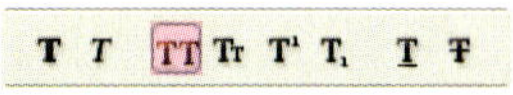 *(All Caps button highlighted)*	**All Caps** Changes text to capital letters.	Highlight the text before clicking this button.	Regular Text ALL CAPS *Top:* Text displayed in upper- and lowercase. *Bottom:* The **All Caps** option changes all characters to uppercase.
 *(Small Caps button highlighted)*	**Small Caps** Changes all letters to uppercase and uses smaller uppercase letters for the letters that were lowercase.	Highlight the text before clicking this button.	Regular Text SMALL CAPS *Top:* Text displayed in upper- and lowercase. *Bottom:* Text created with the **Small Caps** option.

(Continued)

Figure 5-6.
Continued.

Location on the Character Palette	Description of the option	How to use the option	Examples
 T T TT Tr **T¹** T₁ T ₮	**Superscript** Makes text smaller and raises its baseline.	Highlight the text before clicking this button.	**$25.37** **$25.**³⁷ *Top: A price written with regular text.* *Bottom: The dollar sign and cents are changed to superscript. This is a common practice.*
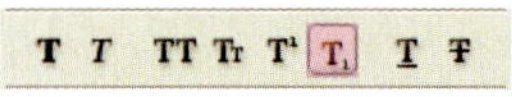 T T TT Tr T¹ **T₁** T ₮	**Subscript** Makes text smaller and lowers its baseline.	Highlight the text before clicking this button.	**Regular Text** ₛᵤᵦscript *Top: Regular text.* *Bottom: Subscript option used on the prefix. Subscript can be useful when designing simple logos.*
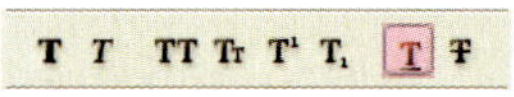 T T TT Tr T¹ T₁ **T** ₮	**Underline** Places an underline below text.	Highlight the text before clicking this button.	**$25.**³⁷ **$25.**³⁷ *Top: A price written with superscript dollar sign and cents.* *Bottom: An underline effect is placed under the cents in the price. This is a common technique.*
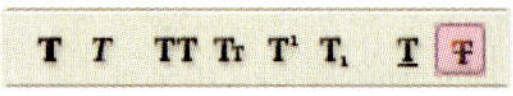 T T TT Tr T¹ T₁ T **₮**	**Strikethrough** Places a line through text.	Highlight the text before clicking this button.	**$19.95** ~~**$25.37**~~ *Top: The price written with regular text.* *Bottom: Strikethroughs can be used to cross out "old" prices on an advertisement.*
 *(Character palette image)*	**Language Setting** Selecting the appropriate language ensures that the **Check Spelling...** command works properly.	Click on the drop-down menu and select the appropriate language.	
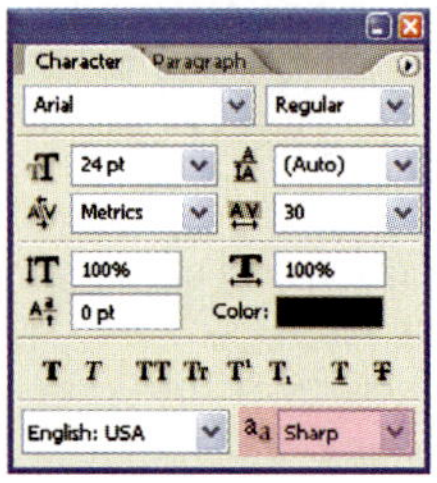 *(Character palette image)*	**Anti-Aliasing** These settings are also found on the options bar of any type tool.	Click the drop-down menu and select the appropriate anti-aliasing method.	

The Character Palette Menu

At the top of the **Character** palette is a small arrow button. Clicking this button opens the **Character** palette menu, **Figure 5-7**. Many of the commands available in this menu should be familiar to you from other menus.

The first item in the **Character** palette menu is the **Dock to Palette Well** command. This command is only available if the computer's display resolution is set to 1024 × 768 or higher. Choosing this command moves the **Character** palette to the **Palette Well**.

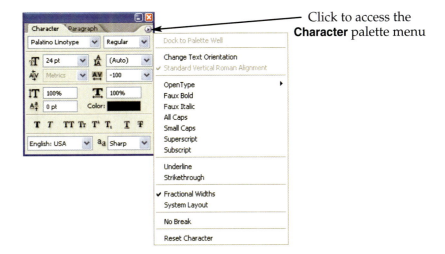

Figure 5-7. The **Character** palette menu contains a number of options for adjusting text style.

The **Change Text Orientation** command switches text from horizontal to vertical, or vice-versa. When horizontal text is switched to vertical, the characters remain vertically oriented as long as the **Standard Vertical Roman Alignment** toggle is active. If this option is turned off, the characters for vertical text are aligned horizontally instead of vertically. See **Figure 5-8**.

The **Character** palette menu also contains the **OpenType** submenu. This submenu is only available if you are using an OpenType font, designated by an "O" in the font list, **Figure 5-9**. OpenType fonts are cross-compatible with both Windows and Mac operating systems. Some (but not all) OpenType fonts have more features than other fonts, such as fractions, *ligatures* (blending two letters together), *ordinals* (the small, raised letters found in 1st, 2nd, etc.) and other alternatives. These additional features are selected from the **OpenType** submenu in the **Character** palette menu. You can choose these options before you begin typing, or edit them after the text has already been entered.

Figure 5-8. The **Change Text Orientation** and **Standard Vertical Roman Alignment** options can be used together to change the alignment of the text. **A**—This text was created with the **Horizontal Type Tool** with the **Change Text Orientation** option off. **B**—This text was created with the **Horizontal Type Tool** with the **Change Text Orientation** and **Standard Vertical Roman Alignment** options active. **C**—This text was created with the **Horizontal Type Tool** with the **Change Text Orientation** option active, and the **Standard Vertical Roman Alignment** option off.

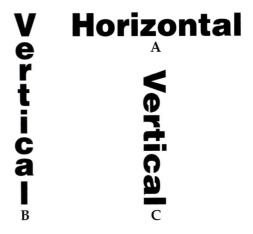

Figure 5-9.
The O next to a font means it is an OpenType font, compatible with both Windows and MacOS. **A**—The three main types of fonts can be identified by the icon that appears in front of them in the font list. **B**—An OpenType font was used to enter this text. After highlighting the fraction, **Open Type > Fractions** is chosen from the **Character** palette menu. The characters in the fraction are automatically updated. The same basic process can be used to apply the other OpenType options as well.

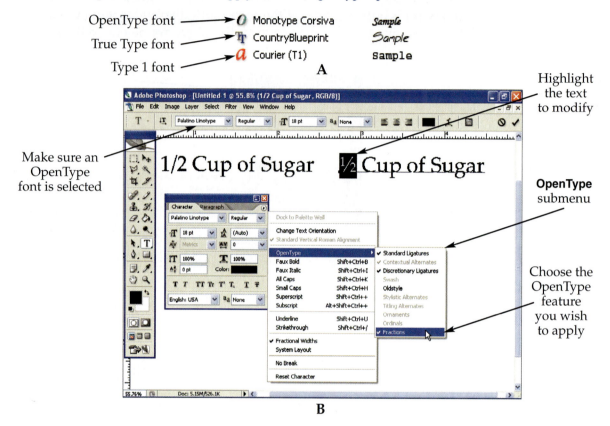

Beneath the **OpenType** submenu, you will see eight styles listed, beginning with **Faux Bold** and ending with **Strikethrough**. These styles should be familiar from the discussion of the buttons in the **Character** palette. Choosing one of these options in the **Character** palette menu creates the same effect as picking the corresponding button in the **Character** palette.

The **Fractional Widths** setting allows spacing between text characters to be less than one pixel wide in certain places. This setting is usually left on. Making the **System Layout** option active will reset any tracking and kerning to zero. It also sets the anti-aliasing method to **None**. Activate the **No Break** option in situations where you do not want words to break between one line and the next. The **Reset Character** command, at the bottom of the menu, resets the font to its default settings.

The Paragraph Palette

By default, the **Paragraph** palette is grouped with the **Character** palette. Click on the **Paragraph** tab or choose **Window > Paragraph** to access the **Paragraph** palette. When editing text using the settings on the **Paragraph** palette, **Figure 5-10**, you do not need to highlight any text. Instead, just click anywhere inside the paragraph you want to edit before changing the settings on the palette.

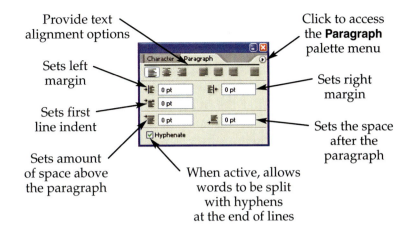

Figure 5-10.
The **Paragraph** palette contains controls for adjusting the entire body of text.

You can select between several justification options. These options are similar to those found in any word processing program.

The middle section of the palette contains some self-explanatory controls: the **Indent left margin**, **Indent right margin**, and **Indent first line** text boxes. You can enter a new value in the text box or click and drag the icon to change the values.

Below the margin and indent settings are two text boxes that adjust how much of a gap appears between two paragraphs: the **Add space before paragraph** and **Add space after paragraph** text boxes. As with the margin and indent controls, you can adjust the settings by entering new values or by clicking and dragging the icons.

The **Hyphenate** check box determines whether words can be broken at the end of lines. If this check box is checked, words can be hyphenated and split between lines of text where needed. If this check box is unchecked, words will not be broken between lines of text.

The Paragraph Palette Menu

You can access the **Paragraph** palette menu by clicking the arrow at the top right of the **Paragraph** palette. As you can see in **Figure 5-11**, the first option in the **Paragraph** palette is **Dock to Palette Well**. This command moves the **Paragraph** palette to the **Palette Well**.

The **Roman Hanging Punctuation** option is a toggle that, when active, allows quote marks to appear outside of margins. When this option is inactive (unchecked), quote marks are placed inside the margins.

Clicking the **Justification...** entry opens the **Justification** dialog box. In this dialog box, you can fine-tune the way Photoshop justifies text. When the preview check box is checked, the selected text is updated in the image window according to the new settings. Click **OK** to accept the changes, or the **Cancel** button to discard the changes and return the text to its original settings.

You can adjust the hyphenation created by word breaks by choosing the **Hyphenation...** entry in the **Paragraph** palette menu. This opens the **Hyphenation** dialog

Figure 5-11.
The **Paragraph** palette menu contains additional options that affect the appearance of text.

box. The value entered in the **Words Longer Than:** text box determines the minimum number of letters a word must have before it is allowed to be hyphenated. The location of the break within the word is influenced by the **After First:** and **Before Last:** text box settings. The **After First:** setting sets the minimum number of letters that must appear before the hyphen. The **Before Last:** text box setting determines the number of letters that must appear after the hyphen. The **Hyphen Limit:** text box setting determines the maximum number of consecutive lines of text that can end with a hyphen. The **Hyphenation Zone:** setting determines how big a gap must be at an end of a line of unjustified text before a word is allowed to be broken. When the **Preview** check box is checked, the new settings are applied to the text in the image window. Click the **OK** button to accept the new settings or **Cancel** to restore the original settings and close the dialog box.

The two composer options are different strategies Photoshop uses for structuring paragraphs as you type them. Select the **Adobe Single-line Composer** option for short text entries and the **Adobe Every-line Composer** when entering long paragraphs.

The final control available in the **Paragraph** palette menu is the **Reset Paragraph** command. This command sets the **Paragraph** palette to its default settings.

Rasterizing Text

Rasterize means "to convert a vector graphic into a bitmap graphic." For some projects, you will never need to rasterize text. However, many of Photoshop's tools and commands will work only on *bitmap* graphics. These tools and commands include the painting tools, filters, and merging layers.

> **Note** If you merge text layers or flatten an image containing text layers, the text layers are automatically rasterized. No warning occurs.

How do you know when you should rasterize a layer? A good approach is to go about your business as usual. Photoshop will display an error message if you try to do something that requires a rasterized text layer, **Figure 5-12**.

When a type layer is rasterized, you can no longer change the font, size, or style. Instead of text, you have thousands of pixels that *look* like text. Be sure to save a backup copy of your file before rasterizing, just in case you need to change a font, size, or style later.

To rasterize a layer, just click the **OK** button in the error message dialog box. If you would rather rasterize the layer at a later time, click the **Cancel** button in the dialog box. Then, when you are ready to rasterize the layer, simply right-click on it in the **Layers** palette and choose **Rasterize Type** from the shortcut menu. You can also rasterize the layer by making it active and choosing **Layer > Rasterize > Type**. A rasterized type layer looks just like any other layer that contains pixels, **Figure 5-13**.

Figure 5-12. An error message pops up if you need to rasterize a layer.

Figure 5-13.
This text layer has been rasterized. The T symbol has disappeared from the **Layers** palette. The text can no longer be edited using "word processor" techniques.

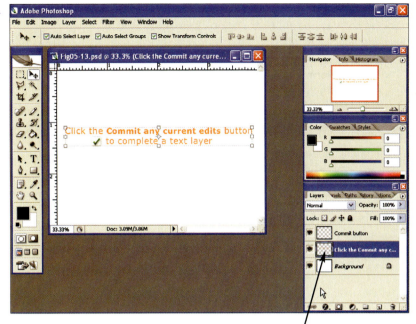

The T is replaced with a thumbnail image when the layer is rasterized

Shape Tools

Shapes are vector graphics. They can be resized as often as desired with no loss of image quality. Similar to text, shapes must be rasterized in some situations.

The shape tool button in the **Toolbox** looks like a rectangle, unless you have previously selected another shape. The **Toolbox** displays the last shape tool that was used. When you click and hold the mouse button on the shape tool button, a pop-up menu with six different shape tools appears, **Figure 5-14**.

The Options Bar for Shape Tools

When you click on one of the shape tools in the **Toolbox**, its options bar appears. There are only slight differences in the options bar for each shape tool, **Figure 5-15**. We will discuss the options that are available on all shape tools' options bars first. Then, we will discuss the unique options found on each tool's options bar. The options that are specific to a particular shape tool are found in the center of the options bar.

The first three buttons on the options bar represent three different ways that shapes can be created. The creation mode that is selected here also determines some of the options that are available on the options bar.

Figure 5-14.
There are six shape tools that can be accessed by clicking and holding briefly on the currently selected shape tool in the **Toolbox**.

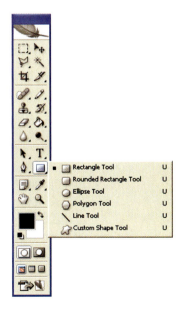

Figure 5-15.
The options bars for the various shape tools look nearly identical.

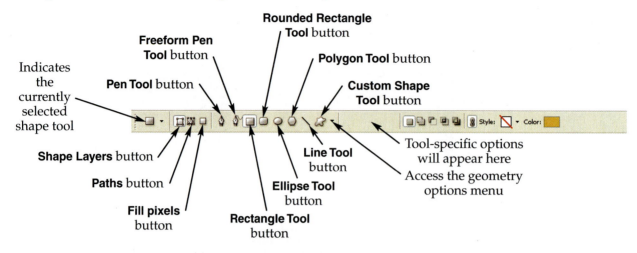

The Shape Layers Button

The **Shape layers** option is the most flexible and commonly-used option. When this button is selected, you click and drag to create a shape, which is filled with the foreground color. An outline of the shape, called a path, is also created.

When a shape is created using the **Shape layers** option, a shortcut to the **Color Picker** appears in the **Layers** palette, **Figure 5-16**. There is also a thumbnail of the shape you created. A shape layer is really a layer mask or vector mask, which you will learn more about in the Chapter 11, *Additional Layer Techniques*.

Also, when you click the **Shape layers** button, five buttons to control the way shapes are combined appear on the right side of the options bar. The first four of these buttons, **Create new shape layer**, **Add to shape area (+)**, **Subtract from shape area (-)**, and **Intersect shape areas** should look familiar from your study of the selection tools. These buttons look and act basically the same as their counterparts for the selections tools. The fifth button available, the **Exclude overlapping shade areas** button, does not appear with the selection tools, but is similar in function to the **Intersect shape areas** button.

When the **Create new shape layer** button is active, each new shape is created on a new layer. This is the only option that is initially available. After one shape has been drawn, the other options become available in the options bar. Switching to the **Add to shape area (+)** button combines each new shape with the previous shape(s) on the existing layer. Switching to the **Subtract from shape area** button causes each new shape to be cut out of the existing shape(s) on the layer. Selecting the **Intersect shape areas** button saves only those areas of the new shape that overlap with the existing shape. Areas of either the new shape or the existing shape that do not overlap are discarded. Switching to the final button in this area, the **Exclude overlapping shade areas** button, discards the areas of the new shape and existing shape(s) that overlap and keeps those that do not overlap.

Styles are a quick and easy way to apply special effects to shapes or text. You can access the **Styles** palette and **Styles** palette menu by clicking on the **Style:** box or by clicking the **Click to open Style picker** button to the right of the box. The **Styles** palette is discussed later in this chapter.

At the far right of the options bar is the **Color:** box. Clicking this box opens the **Color Picker**, from which you can pick a new color for the shape layer. Keep in mind that the new color will be applied to all of the shapes on the layer, not just the next shape created. You can also use the **Color Picker** shortcut on the **Layers** palette to change a shape's color.

Figure 5-16.
A shortcut to the **Color Picker** appears on each shape layer.

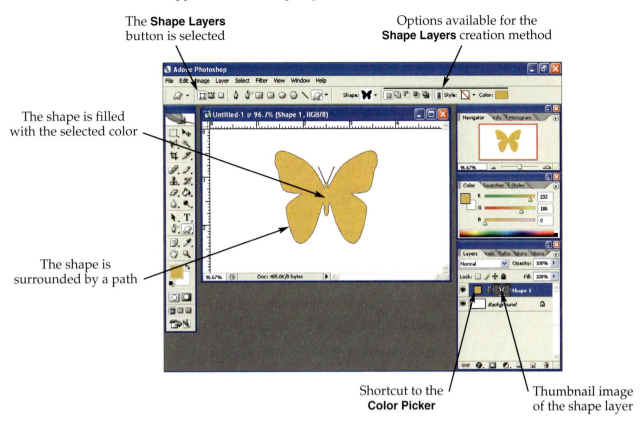

The Paths Button

The **Paths** option creates only an *outline* of the shape. This outline, called a *path*, is adjustable. When the **Paths** option is active, the outline is added to the current layer. A new layer is not created. If the **Shape Layers** option is chosen again, the outline disappears from the image window, but is still available in the **Paths** palette. Paths are discussed in more detail in *The Pen and Path Selection Tools* section of this chapter.

The **Create new shape layer** button, **Style:** box, and **Color:** box disappear when you click the **Paths** button, **Figure 5-17**.

The Fill Pixels Button

The **Fill pixels** option is really a painting tool. When you draw a shape, it is filled with the foreground color. An adjustable path does *not* appear around the edge of the shape, and a new layer is *not* created automatically. You should create a new layer before adding a shape using this option.

When you click the **Fill pixels** button, a **Mode:** drop-down list, an **Opacity:** slider, and an **Anti-alias** check box replace the settings found in the options bar when the **Shape layers** or **Paths** shape creation methods are selected, **Figure 5-18**. These settings are discussed further in Chapter 6, *Painting Tools and Filters*.

Note The **Fill Pixels** option is not available if the **Pen Tool** or **Freeform Pen Tool** is active.

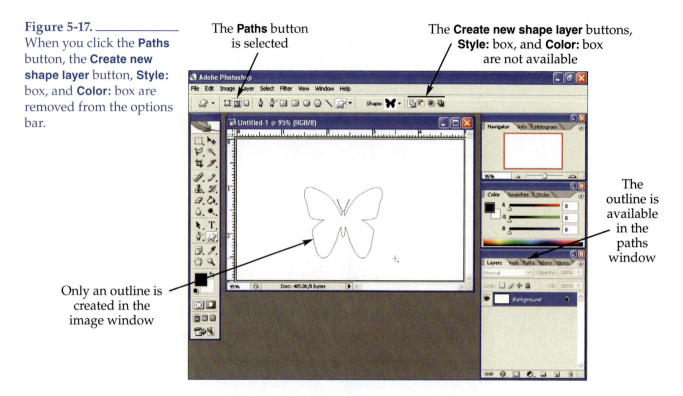

Figure 5-17. When you click the **Paths** button, the **Create new shape layer** button, **Style:** box, and **Color:** box are removed from the options bar.

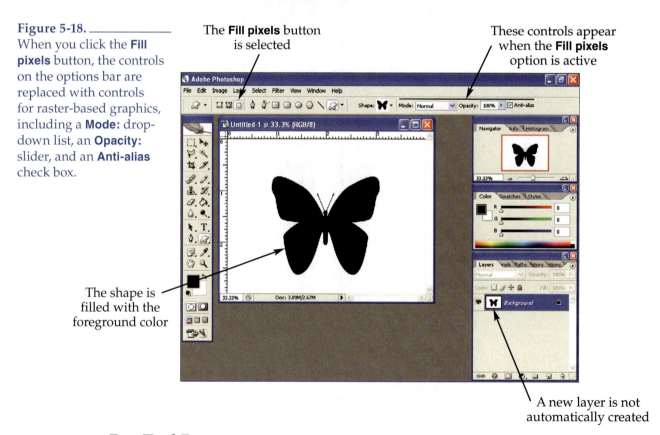

Figure 5-18. When you click the **Fill pixels** button, the controls on the options bar are replaced with controls for raster-based graphics, including a **Mode:** drop-down list, an **Opacity:** slider, and an **Anti-alias** check box.

Pen Tool Buttons

Next on the options bar, you will see two buttons that activate pen tools. These buttons override the shape tool selection made in the **Toolbox**. If you click the **Pen Tool** button, you can create a shape by clicking anchor points and adjusting the curvature of the line passing through those points. If you click the **Freeform Pen Tool**, you can draw any shape you desire by clicking and dragging the mouse. Pen tools are discussed in more detail later in this chapter.

Shape Tool Buttons

The next six buttons on the options bar activate the various shape tools. As with the two pen tool buttons, clicking on one of these buttons overrides the tool selection made in the **Toolbox**. The options bar changes accordingly.

The Geometry Options Menu

Just to the right of all of the shape tools on the options bar, you will see a small down-arrow labeled **Geometry Options**. Clicking on this arrow reveals additional options for each shape. The example in Figure 5-19 shows the geometry options for the **Rectangle Tool**. The geometry options for the **Rounded Rectangle Tool**, **Ellipse Tool**, and **Custom Shape Tool** are very similar to those for the **Rectangle Tool**:

- The **Unconstrained** option lets you draw a shape of any size.
- The **Square** (or **Circle** for the **Ellipse Tool** or **Defined Proportions** for the **Custom Shape Tool**) option forces the shape to be drawn with a preset height to width ratio. In the case of the **Rectangle Tool**, this creates a square. In the case of the **Ellipse Tool**, it creates a circle. For the **Custom Shape Tool**, this setting creates a shape that has standard proportions.
- The **Fixed Size** option lets you enter values in the **W:** (width) and **H:** (height) text boxes. A shape with those dimensions is created by clicking once in your file.
- The **Proportional** option is used when you want a shape that is, for example, two times wider than it is high. For this example, enter 2 in the **W:** text box and 1 in the **H:** text box. Then, click in the image window and drag to create the shape.

> **Note** The **Proportional** option is not available for the **Custom Shape Tool**. Instead, this tool has a **Defined Size** option. This option creates a shape with predefined size and proportions.

- The **From Center** check box determines whether the shape will be created from a center point instead of a corner as you click and drag. When this check box is checked, the location clicked in the image window becomes the center point of the shape. When the check box is unchecked, the location clicked in the image window becomes one corner of the shape's bounding box.
- When the **Snap to Pixels** check box is checked, the edges of the shape will align perfectly with pixels in the image—not cover pixels partially.

The geometry options available for the **Polygon Tool** and the **Line Tool** are considerably different than those available for the other tools. The **Polygon Tool**'s geometry options include a **Radius:** setting. The value

Figure 5-19.
The geometry options for the **Rectangle Tool**, **Rounded Rectangle Tool**, **Ellipse Tool**, and **Custom Shape Tool** are nearly identical.

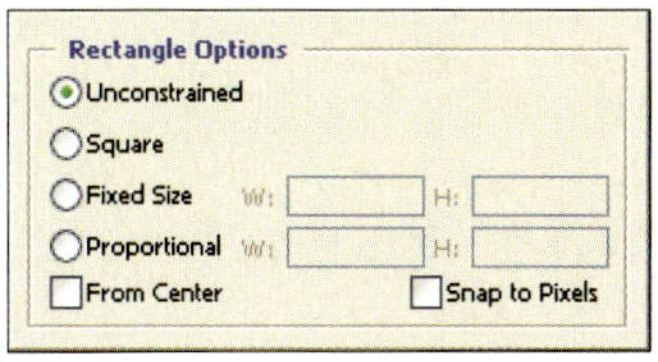

entered in this text box determines the size of the shape that is created when you click in the image window. The **Polygon Tool**'s geometry options also include the **Smooth Corners** check box. When this check box is checked, the corners of the shape are radiused, or rounded off. When the **Star** option is active, the centerpoints of the sides of the polygon are drawn in toward the center of the polygon, creating a star shape. The value entered in the **Indent Sides By:** text box determines how deeply the indented the sides are, or, in other words, how pointy the star is. See **Figure 5-20**.

The **Line Tool**'s geometry options let you add *arrowheads* to your lines and control their size. The **Start** and **End** check boxes determine on which end of the line the arrowhead is created. If both check boxes are checked, arrowheads are created at both ends of the lines. The value entered in the **Width:** text determines how wide the arrowhead is in relation to the width of the line. The value entered in the **Length:** text box controls how long the arrowhead is. Lastly, the **Concave:** setting determines how far the back of the arrow is pushed in. See **Figure 5-21**.

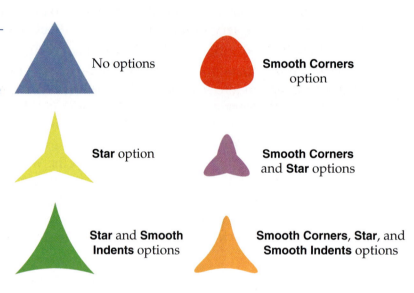

Figure 5-20.
Star shapes can be easily created using the **Polygon Tool**'s geometry options. This illustration shows the shapes that can be created by adjusting the geometry options for a three-sided polygon.

Figure 5-21.
Arrowheads can be added to lines using the **Line Tool**'s geometry options. **A**—The **Arrowheads** dialog box contains the settings that determine the appearance of the arrowheads. **B**—The effects of the arrowhead settings are shown here. **1) Start** option active. **2) End** option active. **3) Start** and **End** options active. **4) Width:** setting increased. **5) Length:** setting increased. **6) Concavity** setting increased.

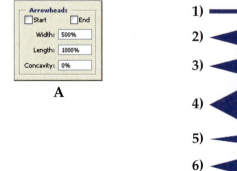

> **Note** The arrowhead's **Length:** setting does not affect the overall length of the line. When you click points to create a line, you are specifying the overall length of the line *including* the arrowheads. However, it does affect the minimum length that the line can be. The line must be at least long enough to accommodate the arrowhead. If you attempt to draw a line shorter than the length of the arrowhead, the line is cut out of the arrowhead, as shown here.
>
>

Tool-Specific Options in the Options Bar

Now that you have learned about the options bar settings available for all shape tools, we will discuss the additional controls available in the options bar of certain shape tools. These additional settings appear in the center section of the options bar, and they control the unique geometry created by the different shape tools.

- The **Rectangle Tool** and the **Ellipse Tool** have no special controls in the options bar.
- The **Rounded Rectangle Tool**'s **Radius:** option controls the appearance of the rounded corners. The value entered in this text box determines the radius of the rounded corners of the rectangle.
- The **Polygon Tool**'s **Sides:** option lets you create a polygon based on how many sides it has. For example, if you want to draw an octagon, enter 8 in the **Sides:** text box.
- The **Line Tool**'s **Weight:** text box determines the thickness of the line that is created. When you enter a width, be sure to specify the units to be used, pixels (px) or inches (in). For example, type 3 px—do not just type 3, or your line might be three *inches* wide. (It depends on the ruler setting in Photoshop's preferences.) When drawing lines, hold down [Shift] to create straight lines or lines at a 45° angle. If you create a very thin line, only one or two pixels wide, you may not be able to see it unless you zoom in.
- When the **Custom Shape Tool** is active, a **Shape:** box appears in the options bar. This box displays a thumbnail image of the custom shape currently selected. Clicking on the thumbnail opens the **Custom Shape Picker**, which allows you select from a variety of shapes. The **Custom Shape Picker** is explained in detail in the following section. When drawing a custom shape, you may need to hold down [Shift] to keep the shape in proportion.

The Custom Shape Picker

When you click on the **Custom Shape Tool**, the last of the shape tool buttons, the **Shape:** box appears in the options bar. As mentioned earlier, this box displays a thumbnail image of the currently selected shape. Click on the box or the down-arrow next to it to display the **Custom Shape Picker**. A variety of custom shapes appear in the **Custom Shape Picker** by default, **Figure 5-22**. Other shapes can be added here as well. The **Custom Shape Picker** has a menu that appears when the arrow pointing to the right is clicked. The bottom section of the menu lists several categories of shapes, such as music, nature, and symbols that can be loaded into the picker.

To load a category of shapes into the **Custom Shape Picker**, click on the category in the list. A dialog box appears, asking if you want to replace or append the currently loaded shapes. If you click the **OK** button, the shapes currently loaded into the **Custom**

Figure 5-22.
The **Custom Shape Picker** provides many predefined shapes that can be placed in the image. Additional shapes can be loaded through the **Custom Shape Picker** menu.

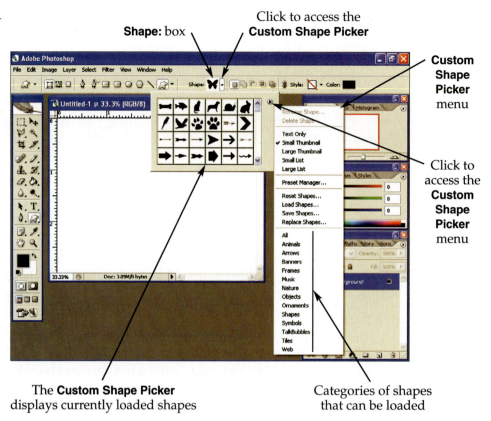

The **Custom Shape Picker** displays currently loaded shapes

Categories of shapes that can be loaded

Shape Picker are deleted and then the new shapes are loaded. If you click the **Append** button, the new shapes are added to the currently loaded shapes.

The first two commands in the **Custom Shape Picker** menu, **Rename Shape** and **Delete Shape**, are only available if you click on a shape in the **Custom Shape Picker** before opening the menu. These commands are self-explanatory and affect only the shape currently selected in the **Custom Shape Picker**.

The second section of the palette menu lists several ways that the shapes can appear in the **Custom Shape Picker**. The **Text Only** command displays only the names of the loaded shapes. The **Small Thumbnail** and **Large Thumbnail** commands display only thumbnail images of the loaded shapes. The **Small List** command displays the names (in small type) and small thumbnails of the loaded shapes. The **Large List** command displays the names of the loaded shapes in larger type and with larger thumbnails.

Selecting the **Preset Manager** command in the **Custom Shape Picker** menu opens the **Preset Manager** dialog box. The **Preset Manager** dialog box provides an optional way to organize shapes—it shows all of the shapes that are currently in the **Custom Shape Picker**. You can use the **Preset Manager** to delete and load different shapes, if desired.

Choose the **Reset Shapes** command to restore the **Custom Shape Picker** to its default state. When you modify shapes and organize them your own way in the **Custom Shape Picker**, you can use the **Save Shapes** command to save them into a file that can be loaded later using the **Load Shapes** command. The **Replace Shapes** command is very similar to the **Load Shapes** command. The difference is the old shapes are replaced (deleted) instead of appended (added to) as the new shapes are loaded into the picker.

You can create your own custom shapes and load them into the **Custom Shape Picker** by first drawing a shape using one of the shape or pen tools with the **Shape layers** or **Paths** option active. After creating the shape, choose **Edit > Define Custom**

Shape.... If you want *text* to be part of a custom shape that you create, first convert the text to a shape by choosing **Layer > Type > Convert to Shape**. After the text is converted, choose **Edit > Define Custom Shape....**

You can modify a shape before using it to define a custom shape by choosing **Edit > Transform Path** and then one of the commands in the submenu. This allows you to use all of the transform controls you learned about in Chapter 4, *Introduction to Layers* to create the shape you want.

Remember that if Photoshop alerts you that you need to rasterize a shape layer, make sure the shape is exactly the way you want it. Save a backup copy of your file at this point, if necessary. Once a shape layer is rasterized, you will not have as many editing options available to manipulate its appearance.

Paths, Pen Tools, and Path Selection Tools

In this section, you will learn about paths, the pen tools, and the path selection tools, **Figure 5-23**. The options bars for these tools will be discussed shortly, but first, some background knowledge is necessary.

The pen tools are used to draw paths. Paths are lines that have anchor points on them. The anchor points can be added, deleted, or adjusted to change the appearance of the path. Paths are vector shapes that do not print. Instead, they are used to create other features. In order to manipulate paths, they must first be selected with special tools.

Earlier in this chapter, you learned that shapes have a path around their edges (unless the shape was created in **Fill pixels** mode). So, one approach to creating a path is to use a shape tool to create a basic shape, like a rectangle, and then switch to the pen tools to edit the rectangular path. Text also can be converted to a path by choosing **Layer > Type > Create Work Path**.

Figure 5-23.
The pen tools are used to create and edit paths, which can only be selected with the path selection tools. **A**—Click on the currently selected pen tool and hold the mouse button briefly to reveal the other tools available. **B**—There are two different path selection tools available.

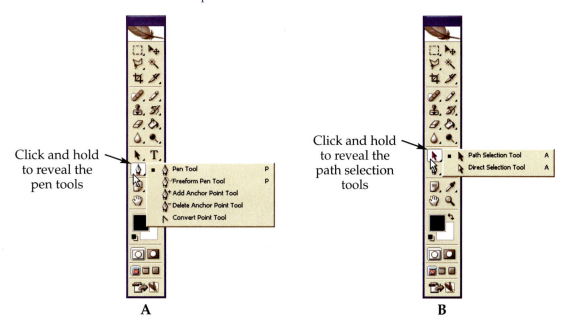

Once you have created a path, it can be converted into any of the following items. This is explained in more detail later in this chapter, after the **Paths** palette is introduced:

- A *shape* by filling the path with color.
- A *brush stroke* that follows the perimeter of the entire path.
- A *selection*. You can also do the opposite: convert a *selection to a path*.
- A *clipping mask*. Clipping paths and clipping masks are discussed in the Chapter 11, *Additional Layer Techniques*.

The pen tools can create paths three different ways: in straight segments, in curved segments, or freehand. You can use any combination of these three methods to create a single path, and you can adjust a path after you draw it.

Creating a Path with the Pen Tool

Paths can be *closed* or *open*. **Closed paths** are fully enclosed shapes. They do not have a beginning or end. An **open path**, on the other hand, is a path that is not closed, such as a zigzag line. To create a closed path, you finish by simply clicking your beginning point, just like when you use the **Magnetic Lasso Tool**.

To create a straight segment of a path, select the **Pen Tool** and make sure the Paths option is selected in the options bar. Then, use the **Pen Tool** to *single-click* points in the image window to create anchor points. As you create anchor points, lines automatically appear between the points, **Figure 5-24**. You can use the grid and snap settings to help you create precise shapes, if desired.

To create a curved segment of a path, click and hold the mouse button instead of just single-clicking. When you click and hold the mouse button, an anchor point is placed at the location and a double handle is created that controls the curvature of the path through the anchor point, **Figure 5-25**. To adjust the curvature of the path, just move the handles without releasing the mouse button. The handles move as a pair. Move them away from the anchor point to increase the length of the curve or closer to the anchor point to shorten the curve. Move them around the anchor point to change the direction of the curve. Hold [Shift] to rotate the handle in 45° increments. Release the mouse button when you have the segment's curvature set the way you want. Repeat the process to add additional segments to the path.

The type of segment that is created, curved or straight, depends on the type of anchor points that are created. If the anchor points at both ends of the segment are corner-producing anchor points, the segment will be straight. However, if one or both of the anchor points are curve-producing anchor points, the segment created between them will be curved.

If you want to create two or more *subpaths* (unconnected path fragments), press [Esc] before creating more anchor points. This causes the **Pen Tool** to create a new subpath rather than connecting the new anchor points to the existing path.

Figure 5-24.
This path was created by clicking to place each anchor point (tiny square). The lines appeared automatically.

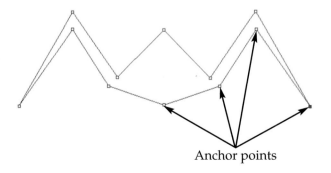

Anchor points

Figure 5-25.
Straight segments are created by single clicking to place anchor points. Curved segments are created by clicking and dragging to create curve-producing anchor points.

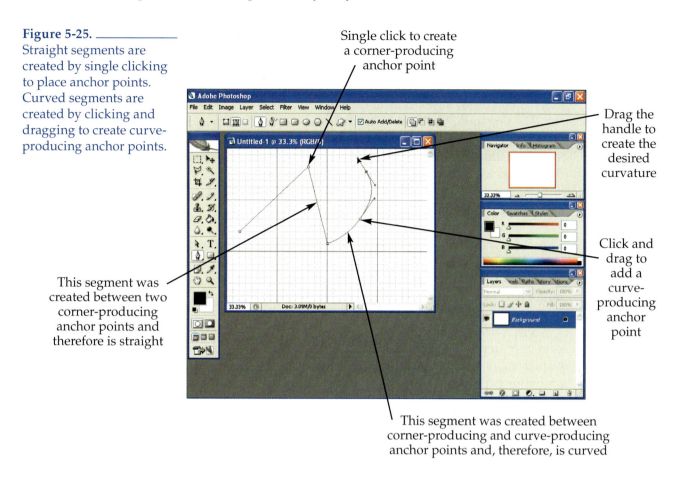

This segment was created between corner-producing and curve-producing anchor points and, therefore, is curved

The Pen Tool's Options Bar

The **Pen Tool**'s options bar is almost identical to the **Shape Tool**'s. There are two options that are unique, however. See **Figure 5-26**.

The **Auto Add/Delete** option allows the **Pen Tool** to add an anchor point by clicking on a path. This option will also allow you to delete an anchor point by clicking on it. In other words, using this option replaces the need for the **Add Anchor Point Tool** and the **Delete Anchor Point Tool**. Editing a path using the **Pen Tool** with the **Auto Add/Delete** option active is discussed in detail later in this chapter.

The **Rubber Band** option is accessed by clicking the **Geometry options** (down-arrow) button on the options bar. When clicking to create anchor points, this option causes the path to stretch from one anchor point to another instead of appearing suddenly.

Figure 5-26.
The options bar for the **Pen Tool** is nearly identical to the shape tool option bars. There are, however, two settings that are unique to the **Pen Tool**.

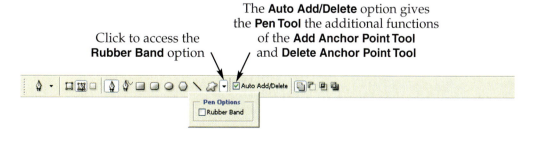

Creating a Path with the Freeform Pen Tool

You can also create a path with the **Freeform Pen Tool**. To create a path with this tool, simply click and drag the mouse. The **Freeform Pen Tool** creates anchor points along the path as you draw, although you cannot see them.

The **Freeform Pen Tool** starts a new subpath every time you click and drag rather than connecting the new segments to the existing path. If you want to connect the new segments to the existing path, position the cursor over the end of the existing path. When a small diagonal line appears at the bottom right of the cursor, click and drag to add to the path.

The Freeform Pen Tool's Options Bar

The options bar of the **Freeform Pen Tool** has a **Magnetic** option, Figure 5-27. When this option is active, it causes this tool to find edges of objects just like the **Magnetic Lasso Tool**, which was discussed in Chapter 3, *Selection Tools*. Clicking the **Geometry options** (down arrow) button in the **Freeform Pen Tool**'s options bar reveals settings that control the sensitivity of this tool.

The **Curve Fit** option controls how many anchor points appear in curves that are drawn with the **Freeform Pen Tool**. You can enter a value between 0.5 and 10. Entering a higher value causes some automatic smoothing to occur after you draw a curved path, and your path contains only a few anchor points. Entering a lower value creates a more complex path that contains more anchor points.

The remaining geometry options are identical to the controls found in the **Magnetic Lasso Tool**'s options bar. See the *Magnetic Lasso Tool* section of Chapter 3 if you need a refresher on these options.

Imagine you want to create a custom shape that looks like an elephant. Instead of drawing it from scratch, you could open an image of an elephant and trace it. If the elephant image stands out well from the background, the **Freeform Pen Tool,** with the **Magnetic** option turned on, would be an excellent choice to do this kind of work.

Modifying a Path with the Path Selection Tools

Once you have created a path, you cannot use the **Move Tool** to move it. Instead, use the **Path Selection Tool**. This tool has several options, which are described in the next section of the chapter. The main purpose of this tool is to select and move a path.

Figure 5-27.
The **Freeform Pen Tool** can be used to trace objects in an image. The **Magnetic** option causes it to function like the **Magnetic Lasso Tool**. The effects of this option can be adjusted in the **Freeform Pen Options** dialog box, accessed by clicking the **Geometry options** button in the options bar.

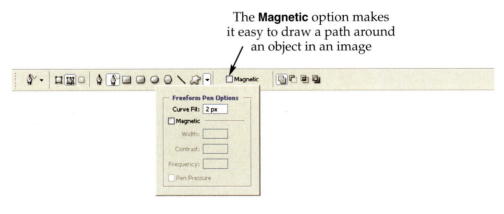

To adjust a path's anchor points, choose the **Direct Selection Tool**. Its purpose is to select and move anchor points. If the entire path has been selected, all of the anchor points will be selected. You will need to click away from the path with the **Direct Selection Tool** to reset the path. Then click and move the desired anchor point, **Figure** 5-28.

The Path Selection Tool Options Bar

The **Direct Selection Tool** does not have any options in its options bar, but the **Path Selection Tool** does, **Figure** 5-29.

The **Show Bounding Box** option lets you transform a path by dragging bounding box handles or choosing commands from the **Edit > Transform Path...** submenu. Transforming commands are discussed in Chapter 4, *Introduction to Layers*.

Similar to the shape tools and many of the selection tools, the **Path Selection Tool** has the **Add to shape area**, **Subtract from shape area**, **Intersect shape areas**, and **Exclude overlapping shape areas** buttons on the options bar. When you work with subpaths, which are explained in *The Paths Palette* section of this chapter, you can select them (and move them, if desired) with the **Path Selection Tool**. Then you can use the add, subtract, intersect, and exclude processes to modify their shape. It is a bit confusing to do this, because all of the path lines remain visible on your screen, no matter what modifier buttons you press in the options bar. You can see the changes applied to your paths, however, by watching the appropriate thumbnail in the **Paths** palette.

The **Combine** button on the **Path Selection Tool**'s options bar lets you convert two or more subpaths into a single path. To do this, select the desired subpaths while holding [Shift], then click the **Combine** button.

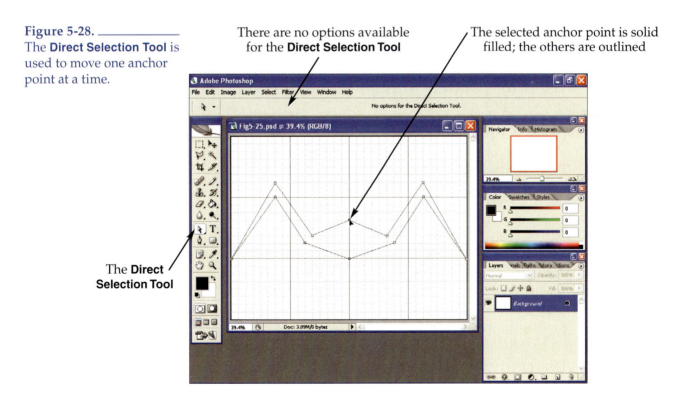

Figure 5-28. The **Direct Selection Tool** is used to move one anchor point at a time.

There are no options available for the **Direct Selection Tool**

The selected anchor point is solid filled; the others are outlined

The **Direct Selection Tool**

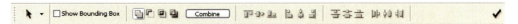

Figure 5-29. The **Path Selection Tool** options bar.

The next two sections of the options bar contain the align and distribute buttons. These buttons are used to line up and arrange objects in Photoshop. They will be discussed in detail in Chapter 11, *Additional Layer Techniques*. You can also use Photoshop's grid or guides to aid you in arranging objects.

The **Dismiss target path** (check mark) button at the far right of the options bar deselects and hides a path in the paths palette. You can also deselect a path (but not hide it) by using the **Path Selection Tool** to click next to, but not on, one of your paths.

Modifying a Path with the Pen Tools

Sometimes as you create a path, you realize that you would like to go back and add or remove an anchor point. If the **Auto Add/Delete** option is active, you can perform these functions with the **Pen Tool**. If the **Auto Add/Delete** is not active, you can perform the same tasks using the **Add Anchor Point Tool** and **Delete Anchor Point Tool**.

Using the Pen Tool to Add or Delete Anchor Points

If you want to remove an anchor point, simply make sure the path is selected and then place the **Pen Tool** cursor over the anchor point. When a small minus sign appears at the bottom right of the cursor, click to remove the anchor point. The two anchor points on either side of the deleted anchor point are adjusted to compensate for the deleted one.

If you want to add an anchor point to a path, make sure the path is selected and then place the **Pen Tool** cursor over the path at the location where you want to place the new anchor point. When the small plus sign appears at the bottom right of the cursor, click and hold the mouse button. Adjust the handles to produce the desired curvature through the anchor point by dragging the mouse. When the curvature is right, release the mouse button.

Using the Pen Tool to Adjust Curvature through an End Anchor Point

You can continue to add or remove anchor points as described, or you can continue drawing the path. To continue drawing the path, simply make sure the path is selected and then continue clicking points at which to place anchor points. However, sometimes you may want to go back and adjust the handles of the end anchor point before continuing to create the path. This is especially true if you accidentally single-clicked the last anchor point, which would create a sharp corner through that anchor point when you resume drawing the path.

You can change the curvature that the end anchor point will create by positioning the **Pen Tool** cursor over it, waiting for the small diagonal line to appear at the bottom right of the cursor, and then clicking and dragging to position the handle that is created. As mentioned earlier, this technique can be used to adjust the end anchor point's handles or to transform the anchor point from a corner-producing anchor point into a curve-producing anchor point.

Using the Convert Point Tool

The **Convert Point Tool**'s sole purpose is to change an anchor point from a curve-producing anchor point into a corner-producing anchor point or vice-versa. To change a corner-producing anchor point into a curve-producing anchor point, choose the **Convert Point Tool** in the **Toolbox** and *click and drag* on the desired point. As you drag, a double handle appears. After converting the anchor point, you can easily adjust the curve by dragging either end of the handle.

Using the Add Anchor Point Tool and Delete Anchor Point Tool

After creating a path, you can add more anchor points or delete existing anchor points to help you fine-tune it. As you learned earlier, this can be done with the **Pen Tool**, if the **Auto Add/Delete** option is active. If the **Auto Add/Delete** option is not active, you can still add more anchor points or delete existing points, but must use other pen tools. To add anchor points, choose the **Add Anchor Points Tool** in the **Toolbox** and click anywhere along the path that needs more adjustment. Then, drag to adjust the points as necessary.

The **Delete Anchor Points Tool** can adjust the path by removing anchor points, if necessary. To delete existing anchor points, begin by choosing the **Delete Anchor Point Tool** from the **Toolbox**. Then, position the cursor over the anchor point that you want to remove and click the mouse button to delete the anchor point. The path automatically adjusts for the removed anchor point.

> **Note** One advantage of the **Add Anchor Points Tool** and the **Delete Anchor Points Tool** is that these tools do not require a path or subpath to be selected before they can be used. They are capable of editing a subpath whether it is currently selected or not.

The Paths Palette

The **Paths** palette looks like the **Layers** palette, but it works differently. The **Paths** palette is used to convert a path into a filled shape, a brush stroke, a selection, or a clipping mask. You can also organize your paths using this palette.

Look at the thumbnails in the **Paths** palettes in **Figure 5-30**. In Part A of the figure, both paths are grouped together as a path called Work Path. In this state, the two paths

Figure 5-30.
Additional path segments can be drawn on the same layer or on separate layers. **A**—If you do not click the **New Path** button before drawing new path segments, subpaths are added to the existing path. **B**—An entirely new path is created if you click the **New Path** button before drawing with a pen tool. You should note that a subpath can be copied and pasted as a new path.

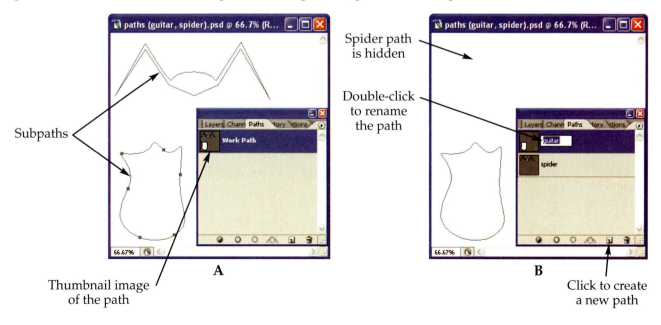

are called subpaths. However, in Part B of the figure, each shape is a separate path. To create a new path rather than a subpath in the existing path, click the **New Path** button next to the **Delete current path** (trashcan) button at the bottom of the **Paths** palette before you begin drawing. This helps keep the paths better organized. To rename a path, double-click it in the **Paths** palette, type a new name, and press [Enter].

> **Note**
>
> If you create a path on a shape layer or text layer that has *not* been rasterized, you cannot convert it to a brush stroke, a selection, or a filled shape. One solution to this problem is to create a new layer first, then create a path on the new layer, and then convert the path to one of the above options.

Converting a Path into Brush Strokes

With practice, you can use the pen tools to create paths exactly the way you want them to appear. One way to create your signature in Photoshop, for example, is to use the **Freeform Pen Tool** to sign your name in a 300 dpi-or-greater document (a graphics tablet would be easier to use than a mouse in this case). Then, adjust the anchor points as desired until your signature looks perfect to you. You can then cover your path with a stroke that applies the **Brush Tool**'s settings. You can also choose a different tool, such as the **Eraser Tool**, to create a stroke along a path.

To convert a path into a brush stroke, follow these steps. Refer to **Figure 5-31**:

- Create a new layer in the **Layers** palette. Your brush stroke will eventually appear on this new layer.

Figure 5-31.
Paths can be easily converted into brush strokes. **A**—After creating a layer for the brush stroke, select a path in the **Paths** palette. Then, select **Stroke Path...** in the **Paths** palette menu. **B**—Select the desired tool from the **Tool:** drop-down list in the **Stroke Path** dialog box. When applying a brush stroke to a path, you can choose from any of Photoshop's tools that use brushes. **C**—The brush stroke follows the path.

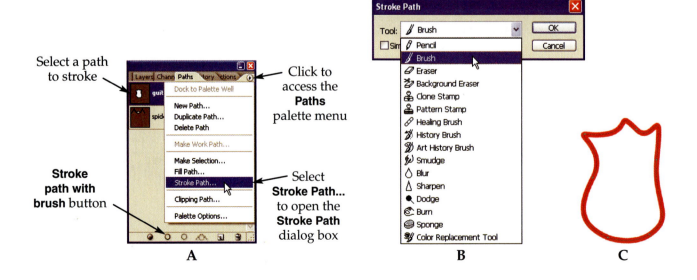

- Select the path you want to cover with a brush stroke. Use the **Path Selection Tool** or select it in the **Paths** palette (if it is not grouped with other subpaths).
- Choose **Stroke Path** from the **Paths** palette menu. As an alternative, you can right-click on the path in the **Paths** palette and select **Stroke Paths...** from the shortcut menu. This opens the **Stroke Path** dialog box.
- Choose the tool that you want to apply along the path from the **Tool:** drop-down list in the **Stroke Path** dialog box. The tool's current settings will be used. If necessary, select the tool in the **Toolbox** and change the settings *before* stroking the path.

Another way to stroke the path is to select the desired tool in the **Toolbox**, select the path in the **Paths** palette, and then click the **Stroke path with brush** button at the bottom of the **Paths** palette.

Converting a Path into a Filled Shape

Filling a closed path with the foreground color is a way to create your own custom shape. You might use this technique when drawing large block letters from scratch, for example. To convert a path into a filled shape, follow these steps:

- Create a new layer in the **Layers** palette. Your filled shape will appear on this new layer.
- Select the path you want to fill. Use the **Path Selection Tool** or select it in the **Paths** palette (if it is not grouped with other subpaths).
- Choose **Fill Path...** from the **Paths** palette menu. As an alternative, you can right-click on the path in the **Paths** palette and select **Fill Path...** from the shortcut menu. This opens the **Fill Path** dialog box.
- Change the settings as desired.

You can also fill the path by selecting the desired foreground color in the **Toolbox**, selecting the path, and then clicking the **Fill path with foreground color** button at the bottom of the **Paths** palette.

Converting a Path into a Selection

Photoshop users who become experienced with the pen tools occasionally choose to bypass the selection tools and use the pen tools to create a selection. This technique is useful when selecting objects that have a variety of straight and curved edges. First, a path (and subpaths, when necessary) are created around an object. The path(s) can quickly be converted to a selection by following these steps:

- Select the appropriate path.
- Click the **Load path as selection** button at the bottom of the **Paths** palette or choose **Make Selection...** from the **Paths** palette menu. You can also right-click on the path in the **Paths** palette and select **Make Selection...** from the shortcut menu.

Note If you attempt to convert an *open path* into a selection, Photoshop automatically closes the path, adding an unwanted segment to your selection.

Text on a Path

Text can follow a path, **Figure 5-32**. To add text that follows a path, begin by creating a path with either the pen tools or the shape tools. To add text along a path that is either open or closed, click on the path with one of the type tools and start typing. To fill a closed path with type, simply click inside the path and start typing. You will notice the text cursor changes slightly when you click on a path or inside of a closed path.

Type can be moved to a different location along a path. To do this, make sure the text layer is selected in the **Layers** palette. Then, use the **Path Selection Tool** to click at the beginning of the text. The cursor changes to a text cursor with an arrow next to it, and type will move as you click and drag.

> **Note** As you drag the text, follow the path. If you veer off of the path with the cursor, the text may jump to a different location on the path.

Layer Styles

Layer styles are special effects such as drop shadows, beveled edges, and colorful outlines that can quickly be applied to an entire layer. Layer styles can cause one-dimensional graphics such as *text* and *shapes* to appear three-dimensional, helping them stand out in a design.

To apply a layer style to a layer, make sure the correct layer is active. Then, choose **Layer > Layer Style** and select a particular style from the submenu. This opens the **Layer Style** dialog box, **Figure 5-33**, allowing you to adjust the settings for each style.

You can use more than one style per layer to create interesting combinations of effects. To do this, begin by selecting the style on the left side of the **Layer Style** dialog box. Then, click the check box to activate the style. Adjust the settings on the right side of the dialog box as desired, and then repeat the process for each style you want to add.

The table in **Figure 5-34** shows three examples of each layer style. For example, a drop shadow is shown applied to text, a custom shape, and an image. The settings for each example have been adjusted differently in the **Layer Style** dialog box to give you a sense of the possible effects you can create.

The Styles Palette

You have learned that you can combine several different layer styles to create interesting effects. Photoshop's **Styles** palette is a collection of ready-made effects that are built from layer styles. To display the **Styles**, choose **Window > Styles** or find the **Styles** tab and click on it.

Figure 5-32. Text can follow a closed path (left), follow an open path (center), or fill a closed path (right).

Figure 5-33. The **Layer Style** dialog box appears when you select any of the layer styles listed in the **Layer > Layer Style** submenu.

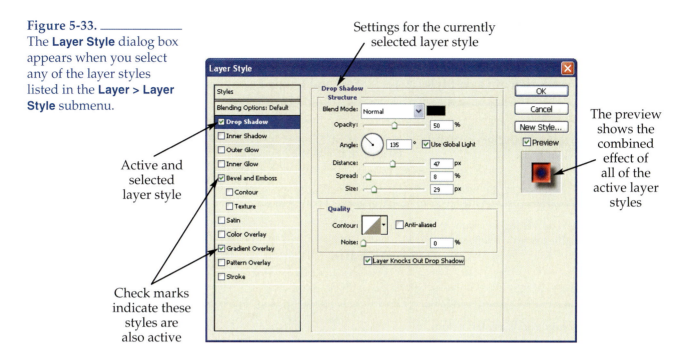

Settings for the currently selected layer style

Active and selected layer style

Check marks indicate these styles are also active

The preview shows the combined effect of all of the active layer styles

Figure 5-34. This table shows you three samples for each layer style. The name of the layer style and a brief description appear in the left column. The center column shows you the layer effect applied to text and to a filled shape. The right column shows the layer effect applied to an actual image.

Name and Description of Layer Style	Text and Shape Examples	Image Example
Blending Modes are discussed in Chapter 11, *Additional Layer Techniques*.		
The **Drop Shadow** style helps an object stand out. It can also be used to create shadows in the background behind an image that has not been flattened.		
The **Inner Shadow** style makes text and shapes look hollow, creating a moon crater effect.		
The **Outer Glow** style makes an object appear to be luminous. If you use a light color for an outer glow, you need to change the background to a dark color.		
Use the **Inner Glow** style for intense backlighting effects.		

(Continued)

Figure 5-34.
Continued.

Name and Description of Layer Style	Text and Shape Examples	Image Example
The **Bevel and Emboss** style adds shadows to make objects appear to be thicker and with rounded or beveled edges.	Bevel & Emboss 	
The **Satin** style is a darkening technique that also adds highlights to create a soft, satin look.	Satin 	
The **Color Overlay** style adds a color on top of the layer.	Color Overlay 	
The **Gradient Overlay** style adds a gradient on top of the layer. Gradients are two or more colors that blend together. You will learn more about gradients in Chapter 6, *Painting Tools and Filters*.	Gradient Overlay 	
The **Pattern Overlay** style places a pattern on top of the layer. Photoshop has many predefined patterns to choose from. You can also create your own patterns. You will learn more about patterns in Chapter 6, *Painting Tools and Filters*.	Pattern Overlay 	
The **Stroke** style places a border of contrasting color, a gradient, or pattern around an object's edge.	Stroke 	

Figure 5-35 shows a custom shape with a style from the **Styles** palette applied to it. The **Custom Shape Tool**'s options bar includes a thumbnail showing the currently selected style. Clicking this thumbnail or the small button to the right of it opens a pop-up version of the **Styles** palette. All of the shape tools have this shortcut.

Selecting any of the styles in the palette applies that style to the selected layer and to any new layers that are created. Selecting the **Default Style (None)** entry removes all of the styles currently assigned to the layer.

In the example shown, the style just to the right of **Default Style (None)** has been selected in the **Styles** palette and applied to the star shape. In the **Layers** palette, the small "f" symbol appears to the far right of the layer name. This indicates that one

Figure 5-35.
The **Styles** palette can be accessed by clicking the **Styles** palette tab or clicking the **Style:** thumbnail in the options bar of any of the shape tools.

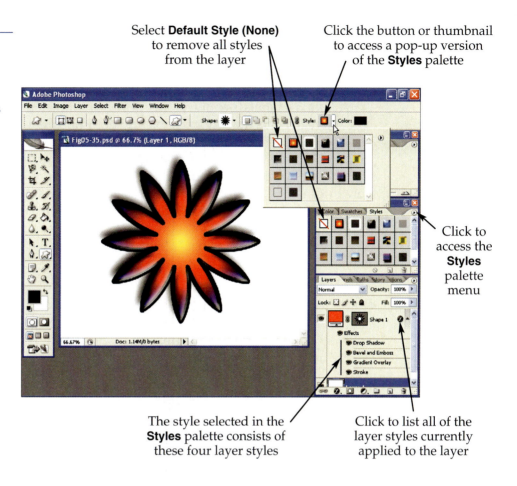

or more layer styles has been applied to the layer. The small down-arrow next to the "f" symbol has been clicked. This reveals that the style used in this example is really a combination of four different layer styles.

The Styles Palette Menu

In the upper right corner of the **Styles** palette is a small arrow button. Clicking this button accesses the **Styles** palette menu, **Figure 5-36**. The **Styles** palette menu is set up the same way as the **Custom Shape Picker** menu discussed earlier in the chapter. There are several categories of styles at the bottom of the menu. When you click on one of these groups of styles, a dialog box appears giving you the option of replacing the current styles with these new style or appending (adding) them to the current styles in the **Styles** palette. You can also use this menu to reset the **Styles** palette or create your own combinations of layer styles and save them so they can be loaded into the **Styles** palette in the future.

Figure 5-36.
The **Styles** palette menu is accessed by clicking the arrow button in the **Styles** palette. From this menu, you can load other preset styles or create your own styles from combinations of layer styles.

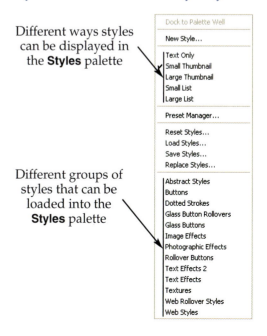

GRAPHIC DESIGN: Fonts

A *font* is a named set of text and numeric characters that share the same look and feel. Fonts that are available in Photoshop are the same fonts that are installed on your hard drive. Additional fonts can easily be purchased and downloaded online, if desired. Many fonts can be downloaded for free. Newly-acquired fonts must be placed in the correct folder on your hard drive. For more information, enter "fonts" as the search term in Photoshop Help.

Fonts can be placed into several general categories, **Figure 5-37**. When choosing appropriate fonts for a given situation, there are some guidelines to keep in mind. These guidelines are generally applicable to entire categories of fonts.

Serif Fonts

- *Serifs* are small flares or "tails" that decorate text characters. If you have never noticed serifs before, look at the bottom of the capital T in Times New Roman sample in Figure 5-37. A small tail projects from either side of the base of the T.
- Many designers agree that serif fonts are a bit easier on the eye when reading body text—the serifs help the text characters visually flow into one another.
- Serif fonts tend to create a traditional, simple, or formal mood.
- Slab serif and hairline serif are terms that are sometimes assigned to varieties of serif fonts. They describe how large or thin the serifs are.

Figure 5-37.
The four categories of fonts are shown here. **A**—In a serif font, such as Times New Roman, individual text characters have small decorative flares, or serifs, at the end of each stroke. **B**—Sans serif means "no serifs." Sans serif fonts are generally plain and easy to read. **C**—Decorative fonts help create different moods in a design. As you can see, the appearance of decorative fonts can vary widely. **D**—Symbol fonts are used to add specialized characters to a design.

A   Times New Roman is a serif font.

B   Arial is a sans-serif font.

C   Comic Sans is a decorative font.
      CommercialScript is a decorative font.

D   🎁 ✦ ? 🚌 🚲 🚭 ◄ ✦ ‖

Sans Serif Fonts

- "Sans" means "without," so *sans serif fonts* are fonts that have no serifs. In general, they have a cleaner, simpler appearance because the individual text characters do not have any added decoration. The Arial sample in Figure 5-37 is an example of a typical sans serif font.
- Sans-serif fonts are good for titles and headings.
- Sans-serif fonts can also be used for body text, even though many designers prefer using serif fonts for this purpose.

Decorative Fonts

- *Decorative fonts* can be serif or sans-serif, but they are non-traditional in appearance. There is a huge variety of decorative fonts available, including the Comic Sans and CommercialScript samples in Figure 5-37.
- Most decorative fonts are not easy to read when used for body text.
- Decorative fonts can easily help create mood in a design. For example, the Comic Sans font creates a friendly, casual, pleasant mood because it almost looks like neat handwriting. Script fonts that look like calligraphy (such as CommercialScript) create an elegant mood.

Symbol Fonts

- *Symbol fonts* are used in special circumstances in design work. Instead of text characters, symbols are inserted. The Webdings sample at the bottom of Figure 5-37 is an example of a symbol font.

A *font family* is a group of fonts that share the same name and characteristics, yet they vary slightly from one another. For example, Arial, Arial Black, and Arial Narrow make up a font family.

Using too many different fonts in a single design tends to be distracting. Here are some proven suggestions on how to limit the number of fonts in a single design:

- Avoid mixing similar-type fonts. Do *not* use different serif fonts, for example. Instead, use one serif font with different styles (bold, italics, etc.).
- Do *not* use more than two different font families in a design.
- Avoid using all capital letters for body text. This should be avoided because readers recognize both individual text characters and the *shape* of words as they read. Using all capital letters changes the familiar shape of words, resulting in slower word recognition. Also, using all capital letters is called "shouting," because of the bold, aggressive mood that is created.

Summary

You have learned that Photoshop offers many ways to add high-quality text and vector graphics to your projects. You have seen that vector graphics can be edited by adjusting the anchor points that appear around their path. You have also learned that layer styles can be applied to enhance the appearance of text or shapes.

Chapter Tutorials

As you work through these tutorials, you will refine previously-created projects by adding text and layer styles to them. You will also create a new design using the shape tools. You will also create a new custom shape and store it in the **Custom Shape Picker**.

Tutorial 5-1: The Horizontal Type Tool

In this tutorial, you will use the **Horizontal Type Tool** to add text to a design.

1. Open the 04ostrichville.psd file you worked on in an earlier chapter.
2. Choose **Window > Workspace > Reset Palette Locations**.
3. Drag the **Layers** palette to the location shown in **Figure T5-1**. If you make a mistake, repeat the previous step.
4. Click the **Horizontal Type Tool** in the **Toolbox**.
5. In the options bar, choose **Verdana** as the font.
6. Choose **Bold** as the style.
7. Type 65 in the **Set the font size** text box and press [Enter].
8. Click in the image window to place the text cursor.
9. Move the mouse away gradually until it turns into a **Move Tool** cursor. Now, you can move the text cursor exactly where you want. Move your text cursor until it is in the position shown in **Figure T5-2**.
10. Click the color box in the options bar.

    The **Color Picker** dialog box appears.

11. Move the color slider in the **Color Picker** dialog box to the green range.
12. Click in **Select text color:** window to select a medium shade of green. See **Figure T5-3**.
13. Click **OK**.

    This closes the **Color Picker** dialog box. The selected color will be assigned to any new text.

Horizontal Type Tool

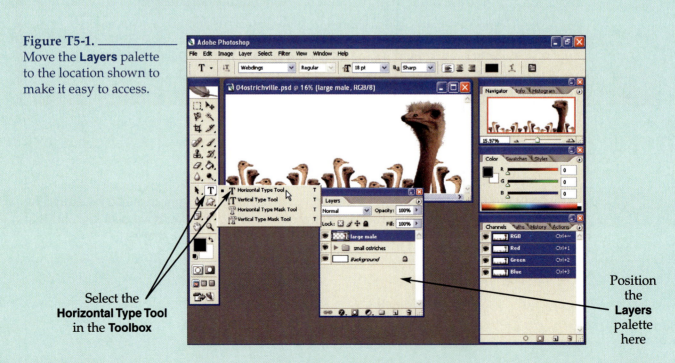

Figure T5-1.
Move the **Layers** palette to the location shown to make it easy to access.

Select the **Horizontal Type Tool** in the **Toolbox**

Position the **Layers** palette here

Figure T5-2.
Position the text cursor in the upper left corner of the image.

Position the text cursor here

Move the cursor away from the text cursor until it becomes a **Move Tool** cursor

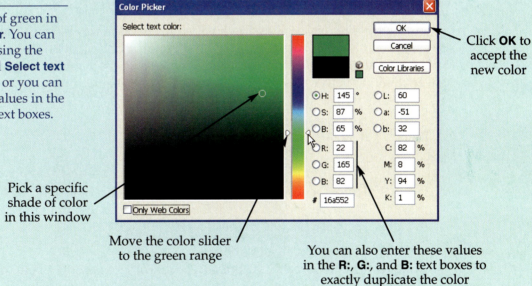

Figure T5-3.
Select a shade of green in the **Color Picker**. You can select a color using the color slider and **Select text color:** window, or you can enter desired values in the **R:**, **G:**, and **B:** text boxes.

Click **OK** to accept the new color

Pick a specific shade of color in this window

Move the color slider to the green range

You can also enter these values in the **R:**, **G:**, and **B:** text boxes to exactly duplicate the color

Commit

Cancel

14. The text cursor should still be blinking. Enter Ostrichville as the text. See **Figure T5-4**.

    If your text is not in the location shown in Figure T5-4, move your cursor just below the text until the **Move Tool** cursor appears. Click and drag to reposition the text.

15. Click the **Commit** button to accept your text settings.

    The **Cancel** button (to the left of the check mark) is used if you wish to delete what you have entered and start over.

16. Notice that a new text layer has been created automatically.

17. Choose **File > Save**. If you are going to continue with the tutorials in this chapter, leave the file open. Otherwise, close the file.

Figure T5-4.
The text is created on a new text layer.

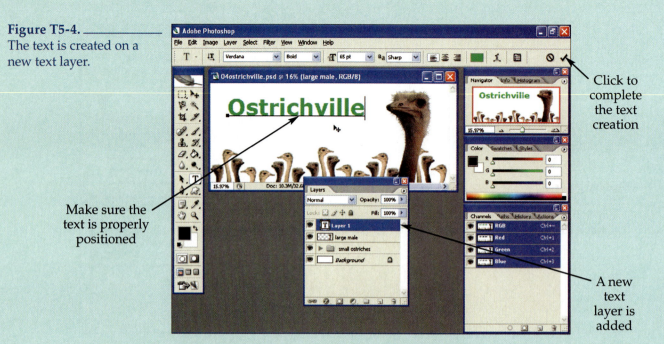

Tutorial 5-2: Layer Styles and the Styles Palette

In this tutorial, you will assign layer styles to enhance the appearance of the text you created in the previous tutorial. This will draw more attention to the text. Using the right combination of layer styles can really make text "pop out" of the design, drawing viewer attention to the most important parts of the design.

1. If necessary, open the 04ostrichville.psd file.
2. Select the text layer in the **Layers** palette.
3. Choose **Layer > Layer Style > Drop Shadow…**.

   This opens the Layer Style dialog box and selects the Drop Shadow layer effect.

4. In the **Structure** section of the **Layer Style** dialog box, enter 60 in the **Angle:** text box, move the **Distance:** slider to 22, set the **Spread:** slider to 0, and move the **Size:** slider to 10. See Figure T5-5. Notice the changes to your text.
5. Click **OK** to create the drop shadow.
6. Double-click the effects symbol in the **Layers** palette to open the **Layer Style** dialog box.
7. In the left-hand section of the **Layer Style** dialog box, click to remove the check mark from the **Drop Shadow** check box. Pick **OK** to close the **Layer Style** dialog box.
8. Make sure the text layer is active and click the **Styles** palette tab or choose **Window > Styles** to make the **Styles** palette visible.
9. Click the arrow button at the upper right corner of the **Styles** palette to access the **Styles** palette menu.
10. Choose **Text Effects 2** from the bottom section of the palette menu.
11. In the dialog box that appears, click **Append**.

    This choice will add the Text Effects 2 styles to the styles currently loaded in the Styles palette.

Figure T5-5.
Enter the appropriate values in the **Layer Style** dialog box to create the drop shadow.

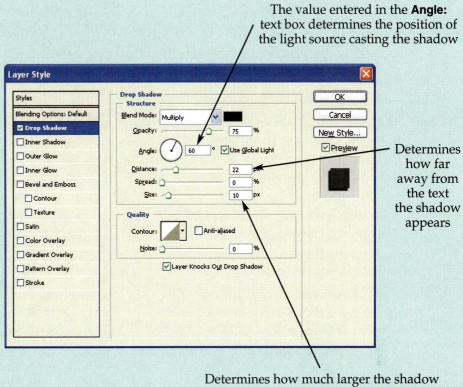

The value entered in the **Angle:** text box determines the position of the light source casting the shadow

Determines how far away from the text the shadow appears

Determines how much larger the shadow is than the object casting it—higher values result in larger but fuzzier shadows

12. Find the style named **Double Green Slime** and click on it.

    To find the names of the styles, hold the mouse over each thumbnail until the description pops up.

13. Click the **Reveals layer effects in the palette** (arrow) button next to the layer effects (f) symbol on the **Layers** palette, **Figure T5-6**.

    The **Layers** palette shows that the Double Green Slime style is really a combination of three different layer styles.

14. In the **Layers** palette, double click the **Stroke** effect. In the **Layer Style** dialog box that appears, change the size setting to 15 px and click **OK**.

Figure T5-6.
The layer styles that make up the Double Green Slime effect are revealed in the **Layers** palette.

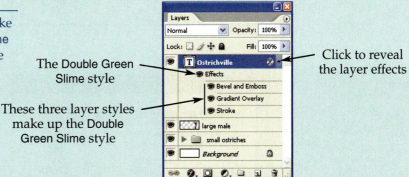

The Double Green Slime style

These three layer styles make up the Double Green Slime style

Click to reveal the layer effects

15. In the **Layers** palette, double click the **Bevel and Emboss** effect. In the **Layer Style** dialog box that appears, change the **Angle:** setting to –144 and click **OK**.
16. Your text should look like the example in **Figure T5-7**.
17. Make sure the **Horizontal Text Tool** is selected and the text layer is active.
18. In the options bar, change the font size to 70.

    Both the text and layer styles adjust to the larger font size.

Move Tool

19. Click the **Move Tool** in the **Toolbox** and use it to center the text as shown in **Figure T5-8**.
20. Click the **Horizontal Text Tool** and click just under the Ostrichville text to create a new text layer.
21. In the options bar, set the style to **Bold**, the size to 22, and the color to black. Enter this text: 1,000 Acre Ostrich Ranch.
22. Move the text as shown in **Figure T5-9**, and click the **Commit** button in the options bar.
23. Click to start a new line of text. In the options bar, set the style to **Italic** and the size to 18. Enter this text: Shuttle Tours • Restaurant • Gift Shop.
24. Highlight the text you just created and change the text color to a bright red. Click the **Commit** button when you are finished.

Figure T5-7.
Your text should look like this example.

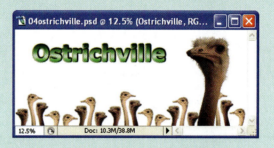

Figure T5-8.
The text is enlarged slightly and repositioned in the image.

Figure T5-9.
A second line of text is added to the image and centered under the first.

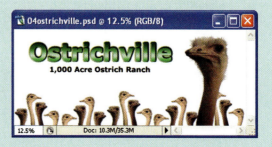

Chapter 5 Text, Shapes, and Layer Styles   201

25. Click the **Move Tool** in the **Toolbox**, and use it to position the text as shown in Figure T5-10.
26. Select one of the text layers you just created in the **Layers** palette. Choose **Layer > Styles > Drop Shadow...**. In the **Layer Style** dialog box, click **OK** to accept the default settings and create the drop shadow. Repeat this step for the other text layer. See Figure 5-11.
27. If you are going to continue on with the other tutorials in this chapter, leave the 04ostrichville.psd file open. If you are not going to continue on with the remaining tutorials right away, save and then close the 04ostrichville.psd file.

Tutorial 5-3: Warped Text

In this tutorial, you will add warped text to your design. Warped text should be used with caution. It must never be difficult for viewers to read.

1. Open the 04ostrichville.psd image if necessary.
2. Click the **Horizontal Text Tool** in the **Toolbox**.
3. Click in the lower left corner of the image window to create a new text layer.
4. In the options bar, enter the following settings:
   - **Font:** Verdana
   - **Style:** Bold
   - **Font Size:** 14
   - **Color:** Black
   - **Justification:** Center
5. Enter this text: World's (press [Enter] or [Return]) Biggest (press [Enter] or [Return]) Eggs.
6. Click the **Commit** button.
7. Click the **Create warped text** button on the options bar or choose **Layer > Type > Warp Text...**.

Create warped text

Figure T5-10. Smaller, italic text is added to the image.

Figure T5-11. Drop shadows are added to the two new lines of text.

8. In the **Warp Text** dialog box, choose **Inflate** from the menu.
9. Adjust the warp settings until your text looks like the example in **Figure T5-12**. Then, click **OK**.
10. Make sure the **Horizontal Text Tool** is selected. Click in the lower right corner of the image window to create a new text layer.
11. In the options bar, change the font size to 18.
12. Enter the following text: Next Exit - Then North 2 Miles.
13. Click the **Commit** button to create the text.
14. Add a drop shadow under the two new text layers you just created. Accept the default settings.
15. Click the **Move Tool** in the **Toolbox**. Use the **Move Tool** to move the text layers you just created to the positions shown in **Figure T5-12**.
16. Choose **File > Save As...** and name this file 05ostrichville.psd. Then, close it.

You will make some final adjustments to this billboard design in a later tutorial.

Figure T5-12. Two additional groups of text are added to the image. The text in the lower left corner is warped. Drop shadows are applied to both.

Tutorial 5-4: Stroking a Border around a Photo

In this tutorial, you will add a Stroke layer style to an image in order to draw attention to it and help it stand out from the background.

1. Open the 03cardfront.psd file you created in an earlier chapter.
2. Arrange the layers in the **Layers** palette so that the purple flowers are on top of the pink flowers. The yellow flowers should be below the purple and pink flowers.
3. In the **Layers** palette, click the layer that contains the (pink) "Beauty" flowers to make it active.

The pink, "Beauty" flowers should be on Layer 1.

4. Choose **Layer > Layer Style > Stroke...**.
5. In the **Layer Style** dialog box, enter 4 in the **Size:** text box.
6. Click on the **Color:** box. In the **Color Picker**, select a deep, bright red color, and click **OK**.
7. Click **OK** to close the **Layer Style** dialog box.
8. In the **Layers** palette, click the layer that contains the (purple) "Mountain" flowers.

The purple, "Mountain" flowers should be on Layer 2.

9. Choose **Layer > Layer Style > Stroke...**.
10. In the **Layer Style** dialog box, enter 4 in the **Size:** text box and click **OK**.
11. Choose **File > Save...**. If you are going to continue with the other tutorials in this chapter, keep the file open. Otherwise, close the file.

Tutorial 5-5: Adding the Text

In this tutorial, you will add text to a design. You will increase the visual impact of the text by using different colors and assigning layer styles.

1. If necessary, open the 03cardfront.psd file.
2. Click the **Horizontal Type Tool** in the **Toolbox**.
3. Enter the following settings in the options bar:
   - **Font:** Arial
   - **Style:** Bold
   - **Font Size:** 40 pt
   - **Justification:** Left
4. Click on the color box in the options bar.
5. Drag the **Color Picker** dialog box to the location shown in **Figure T5-13**.
6. Move the mouse cursor over to the image window.

   The cursor changes to an Eyedropper Tool, a tool used to choose a color.

7. Place the end of the eyedropper tool on the red border around the flowers and click.
8. Click the **OK** button in the **Color Picker** dialog box.

   The same red color now appears in the color box in the options bar.

9. Type the word Wildflowers and move it approximately to the location shown in **Figure T5-14**.
10. Click the **Commit** button in the options bar.
11. Choose **Layer > Layer Style > Drop Shadow…**.

Figure T5-13. _____
Move the **Color Picker** out of the way so you can access the image window with the **Eyedropper Tool**.

The cursor becomes an **Eyedropper Tool** cursor

Click **OK** to close the **Color Picker** dialog box and set the color for new text

Figure T5-14. _____
Position the text as shown. Note: A rectangular adjustment layer has been added to this image for illustration purposes only. Your image will not have the dark band behind the text.

12. In the **Layer Style** dialog box, set the **Opacity:** slider to 75%, the **Angle:** to 120°, the **Distance:** slider to 7, the **Spread:** slider to 0, and the **Size:** slider to 5. Click **OK** to create the shadow.
13. If the **Horizontal Type Tool** is not selected, click it.
14. Click just to the right of the Wildflowers text to create another text layer.
15. In the options bar, change the font size to 12 pt.
16. Click on the color box in the options bar and select a bright, golden-yellow color in the **Color Picker** dialog box. Click **OK** to close the **Color Picker** dialog box.
17. Add this text: of the Rocky Mountains.
18. Choose **Window > Character** to display the **Character** palette.
19. Adjust the tracking setting until the text you just entered looks like the example in **Figure T5-15**.

    If your text does not display correctly, make sure the two text layers are at the top of the list in the **Layers** palette.

20. Add a drop shadow (using the same settings) to the text layer you just created.
21. Choose **File > Save As…** and name this file 05cardfront.psd. Then, close the file.

Figure T5-15. _____
Adjust the tracking on the new text to spread out the characters. Place the text in the position shown.

Tutorial 5-6: Rasterizing Text Layers

In this tutorial, you will add text to a design. You will then rasterize and merge the text layers. Layers must be rasterized before they can be merged.

1. Open the file 04cardback.psd file that you created in an earlier chapter.
2. Select the Stamp Box layer in the **Layers** palette.

   This will cause the text layers to appear above the stamp box.

3. Use the **Horizontal Type Tool** to add the text shown in Figure T5-16, using three different layers. Use 10 pt Arial type, bold style, and set the color to black.

   To create the text on three different layers, click the Commit button after typing each word.

4. Use the **Move Tool** or arrow keys to center the words inside the box.
5. Right-click on one of the text layers in the **Layers** palette. Choose **Rasterize Type** from the shortcut menu.

   You can also rasterize the text by choosing Layer > Rasterize > Layer. The term "rasterize" means "to convert into pixels." You must rasterize text before you can use certain Photoshop features, such as merging (step 7).

6. Rasterize the other two text layers.
7. Hide all layers except for the three text layers and the Stamp Box layer by clicking their eye icons.
8. Make sure the Stamp Box layer is selected, and then choose **Layer > Merge Visible**.

   You now have a layer that can easily be copied to other postcards that you may create.

9. In the **Layers** palette, select the Stamp Box layer and set its **Opacity:** slider to 75%. See Figure T5-17.
10. Make the hidden layers visible by clicking the boxes where their eye icons were.
11. Click the **Horizontal Type Tool**. Change the text size setting to 5 pt and set the text style to **Bold Italic**.

Figure T5-16. Create the text on three different layers. Arrange the lines of text as shown.

Figure T5-17.
After merging the lines of text, lower the opacity of the text layer.

Set the **Opacity:** slider to 75%

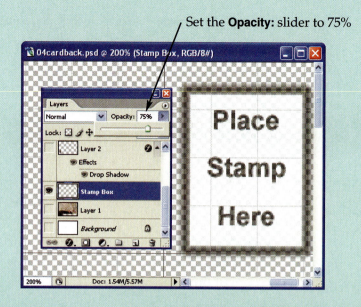

12. Click anywhere in the image window and enter text that reads "Published by" followed by your name and address *or* an imaginary design company's name and address.
13. Choose **Edit > Transform > 90° CCW** and move the text to the location shown in **Figure T5-18**.
14. Add the remaining text. Put the new text on three separate layers. Refer to Figure T5-18 for the wording, text settings, and proper positions for the additional text.

Figure T5-18.
Add the remaining lines of text to the design.

Arial 6pt Bold

Arial 6pt Regular

Arial 6pt Bold Italic—transformed 90° CCW

Arial 5pt Italic—set the tracking to 275

Chapter 5   Text, Shapes, and Layer Styles

15. Add a drop shadow to the small oval-shaped image of the purple flowers. Set the **Angle:** to 120°, the **Distance:** slider to 10, the **Spread:** slider to 0, and the **Size:** slider to 10.
16. The back of the postcard is finished. Choose **File > Save As…**, name this file 05cardback.psd, and then close it.

Tutorial 5-7: Use Shapes to Create a Design

In this tutorial, you will create a design for a CD jewel case insert by drawing, adding, and subtracting various shapes. These techniques come in handy when creating your own custom shapes.

1. Choose **File > New…**. In the **New** dialog box, assign the file the name 05CDfront and enter the settings shown in **Figure T5-19**.

   Do not forget to select inches after entering the Width: and Height: settings.

2. If the rulers are not visible, choose **View > Rulers**.
3. Click the small square in the upper left corner of the rulers and hold down the mouse button. Drag the mouse until the crosshairs are exactly in the center of the image (2 3/8" across and 2 3/8" down).
4. Release the mouse button.

   Your rulers should look like the example in **Figure T5-20**, with the zero point centered horizontally and vertically. If you made a mistake, double-click the square in the upper left corner of the rulers and try again.

Rectangle Tool

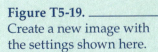
Geometry options

5. Drag the **Layers** palette next to the image window. Resize the image window and **Layers** palette as needed to give you the most room to work.
6. Select the **Rectangle Tool** in the **Toolbox**.
7. Click the **Geometry options** button in the options bar.
8. In the **Rectangle Options** dialog box that appears, activate the **Fixed Size** and **From Center** options.
9. Enter 3.75 in the **W:** (width) and **H:** (height) text boxes. See **Figure T5-21**.
10. Close the **Rectangle Options** dialog box by clicking the **Rectangle Tool** again.
11. In the options bar, click the **Color:** box. Choose a deep blue color in the **Color Picker** dialog box and click **OK**.

Figure T5-19.
Create a new image with the settings shown here.

Enter the name of the new file

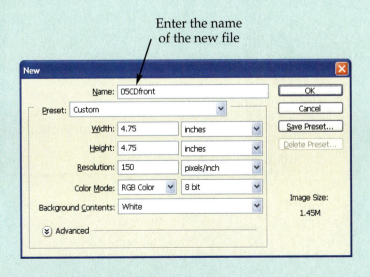

Figure T5-20.
Center the zero point in the image. **A**—Click small square between the horizontal and vertical rulers and drag it to the center of the image. **B**—The rulers are adjusted so the zeros appear in the center.

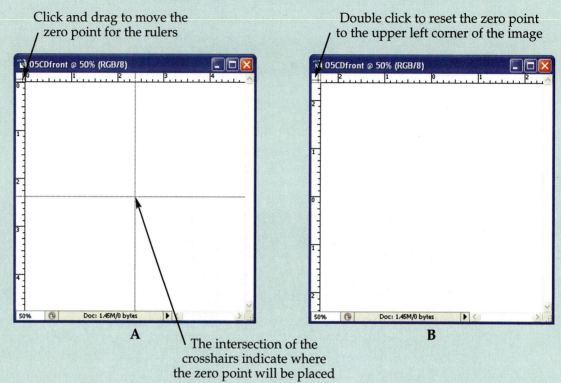

Figure T5-21.
In the **Rectangle Tool**'s options bar, click the **Geometry options** button. Activate the **From Center** and **Fixed Size** options and set the size.

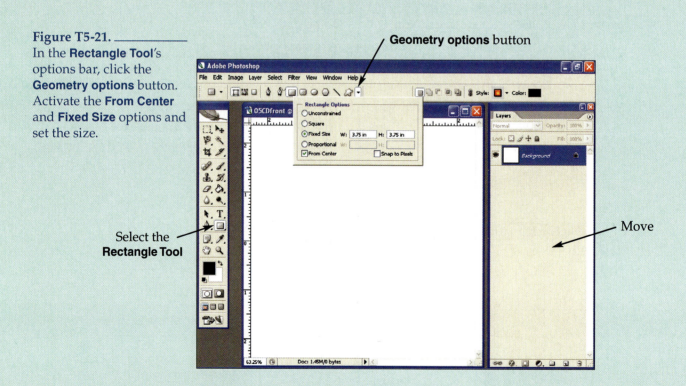

Chapter 5 Text, Shapes, and Layer Styles 209

12. Without clicking, move the mouse until the crosshairs symbol is in the center of the image.

    Watch the rulers—little guidelines will show you exactly where your crosshairs are.

13. When you are in the center of the image, click to place a 3.75" square, **Figure T5-22**.

    The **Layers** palette shows a new layer has been automatically created.

Ellipse Tool

14. On the options bar or in the **Toolbox**, click the **Ellipse Tool**.
15. Click the **Geometry options** button on the options bar.
16. In the **Ellipse Options** dialog box, activate the **Fixed Size** and **From Center** options.
17. Enter 4.25 in the **W:** (width) and **H:** (height) text boxes.
18. Click the **Add to shape area** button on the options bar.

Add to shape area

19. Move the cursor to the exact center again and click.
20. The circle is added to the square.

    The thumbnail image of Layer 1 in the **Layers** palette is updated to show the addition of the circle. See **Figure T5-23**.

21. Choose **Layer > Rasterize > Layer**.

    As with text, you must rasterize layers that contain shapes. If you do not do this, some of Photoshop's commands will not work on shape layers.

Figure T5-22.
Create a square in the center of the image.

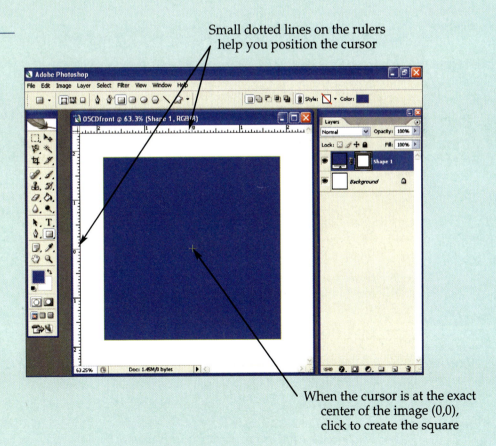

Small dotted lines on the rulers help you position the cursor

When the cursor is at the exact center of the image (0,0), click to create the square

Figure T5-23. Add a circle to the square. Both shapes should be centered in the image.

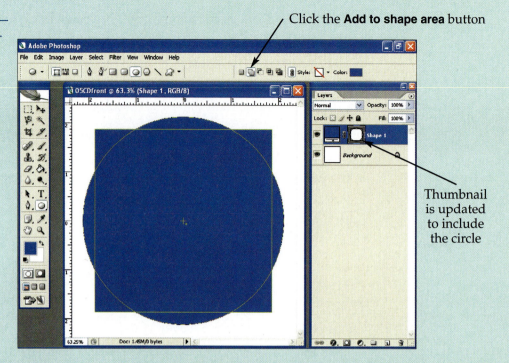

Click the **Add to shape area** button

Thumbnail is updated to include the circle

Create new shape layer

22. The next shape needs to be on a separate layer, so click the **Create new shape layer** button on the options bar.
23. With the **Ellipse Tool** still active, click the **Geometry options** button on the options bar.
24. In the **Ellipse Options** dialog box, activate the **Unconstrained** option. The **From Center** option should still be selected.
25. Click the **Color:** box on the options bar. In the **Color Picker** dialog box, choose a bright red color.
26. Click on the ruler on the left side of the image window and drag a guide to the 1.5″ mark on the right side of the image window. Then, click and drag a guide to the .75″ mark.

   These guides will help you create circles of the proper sizes in the steps that follow.

27. Position the cursor in the center of the image. When the cursor is centered, click and drag to create a circle with a radius of 1.5″, like the one shown in **Figure T5-24**.

   Since you have activated the **Unconstrained** option in the **Ellipse Options** dialog box, you must hold down [Shift] as you draw the circle. This will create a perfect circle instead of an oval.

Subtract from shape area

28. Click the **Subtract from shape area** button on the options bar.
29. Starting from the center, drag another circle with a radius of .75″, as shown in **Figure T5-25**.

   The second circle is subtracted from the first, allowing the blue shape behind to show through.

30. Right-click on this new layer in the **Layers** palette and choose **Rasterize Layer** from the shortcut menu.
31. Save the 05CDfront.psd image and then close the image window.

   You will add more to this file later.

Chapter 5   Text, Shapes, and Layer Styles

Figure T5-24.
An additional circle is created on a new shape layer.

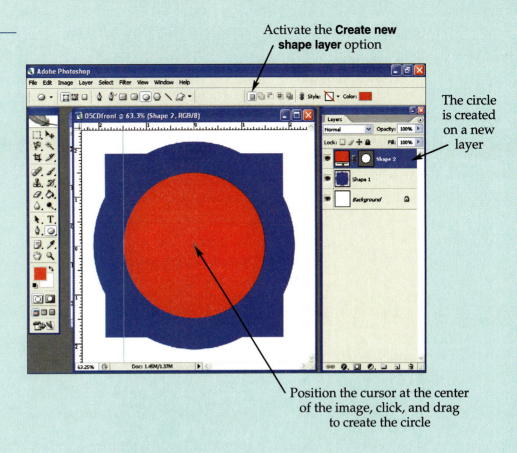

Activate the **Create new shape layer** option

The circle is created on a new layer

Position the cursor at the center of the image, click, and drag to create the circle

Figure T5-25.
A smaller circle is subtracted from the previous circle.

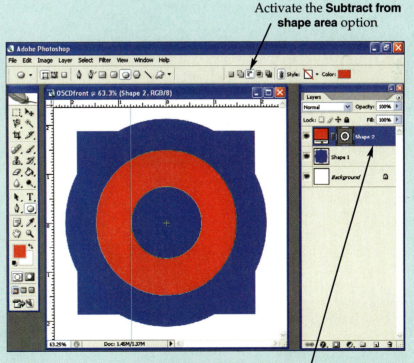

Activate the **Subtract from shape area** option

The thumbnail shows that the newest circle has been subtracted from the previous circle

Tutorial 5-8: Create a Custom Shape

In this tutorial, you will create a design that can be loaded into the **Custom Shape Picker** and quickly inserted into any document using the **Custom Shape Tool**.

1. Choose **File > New...** and enter the settings shown in **Figure T5-26**.
2. Click the **Horizontal Type Tool** in the **Toolbox**.
3. For best results, choose a font and style that creates simple, thick letters.
4. Enter 100 in the font size text box and set the text color to black.
5. Click in the image window and enter your initials. Click the **Commit** button in the options bar when you have entered your initials.
6. Choose **Layer > Type > Convert to Shape**.
7. Click the **Path Selection Tool**.
8. Hold down [Shift] and click on each of your initials to select the path that surrounds them. See **Figure T5-27**.

Path Selection Tool

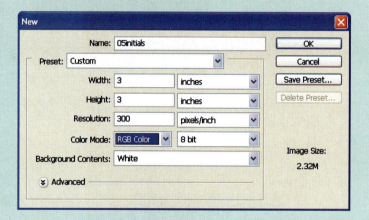

Figure T5-26. Create a new image file with these settings.

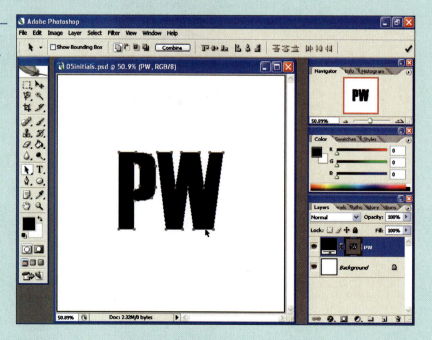

Figure T5-27. Select the paths surrounding your initials.

Chapter 5   Text, Shapes, and Layer Styles

Shape layers

9. Click the **Ellipse Tool**.
10. In the options bar, make sure the **Shape layers** button is selected.
11. Click the **Subtract from shape area** button in the options bar.
12. Make your initials look like Swiss cheese by creating a number of small holes of various sizes through the initials. See **Figure T5-28**.

    If the **Unconstrained** option is selected in the **Ellipse Options** dialog box, hold down [Shift] to create perfect circles with the **Ellipse Tool**.

13. Choose **Edit > Define Custom Shape…**.
14. In the **Shape Name** dialog box, name your custom shape Initials and click **OK**.

    This adds the shape to the very end of the list of available shapes in the **Custom Shape Picker**.

Custom Shape Tool

15. Click the **Custom Shape Tool** in the **Toolbox** or options bar.
16. In the options bar, click the **Shape:** box to access the **Custom Shape Picker**.
17. Select the Initials shape you just added to the **Custom Shape Picker**. Click the **Custom Shape Tool** button in the options bar to close the **Custom Shape Picker**.
18. Click the **Create new shape layer** button on the options bar.
19. Using the **Custom Shape Tool**, add your initials four more times into your image.

    If the **Unconstrained** option is selected in the **Custom Shape Options** dialog box, hold down [Shift] as you draw your initials to keep them in proportion.

20. Using the **Styles** palette, add a different style to each of your custom shapes. See **Figure T5-29**.

    Styles can be assigned to the shapes by clicking and dragging the style thumbnail onto the shape in the image window, or by selecting the shape layer in the **Layers** palette and then clicking the desired style in the **Styles** palette.

21. Close and save your 05initials.psd file.

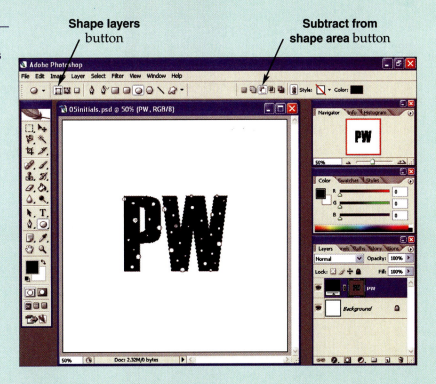

Figure T5-28. Create a bunch of small circles inside your initials using the **Subtract from shape area** option.

Figure T5-29. Assign a different style to each set of your initials.

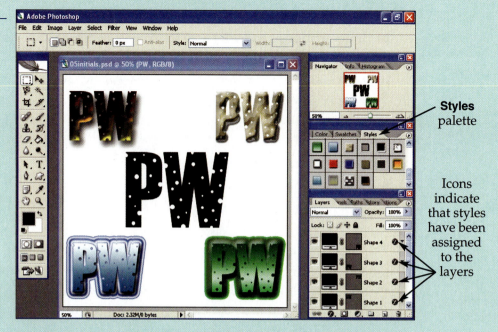

Key Terms

bitmap graphic
closed path
decorative fonts
font
font family
layer styles
ligatures

open path
ordinals
raster graphic
rasterize
sans serif fonts
serifs

shapes
styles
subpaths
symbol fonts
type
vector graphics

Review Questions

Answer the following questions on a separate sheet of paper.

1. What is the difference between vector and bitmap graphics?
2. What is another name for a bitmap graphic?
3. How can you create multiple lines of text on separate layers?
4. What program would you use to insert the copyright symbol (©) in the text in your image?
5. How are the type mask tools different from the other two type tools?
6. What setting on the **Character** palette would you adjust to create a double-spaced look between several lines of text?
7. What is the difference between the kerning and tracking settings on the **Character** palette?
8. How can you access OpenType font features such as ordinals, ligatures, and fractions?
9. What is the **Roman Hanging Punctuation** setting in the **Paragraph** palette menu used for?

Chapter 5   Text, Shapes, and Layer Styles   215

10. What does the term "rasterize" mean?
11. When using the **Line Tool**, if you want to create a line that is 10 pixels thick, what *exactly* should you enter in the **Weight:** text box in the options bar?
12. When the **Unconconstrained** option is active, how do you keep a **Custom Shape** in proportion as you draw it?
13. When using the shape or pen tools, what is the difference between the **Shape layers** and **Paths** options?
14. When using the shape or pen tools, what is the difference between the **Shape layers** and **Fill pixels** options?
15. Where can you find the settings that change a polygon into a star shape?
16. As you draw shapes, each of them will appear on a separate layer if what button is pressed in the options bar?
17. Explain the steps required to add the custom shapes in the Animals category to the **Custom Shape Picker**.
18. How do you modify a shape using Photoshop's transform and warp features?
19. A path can be converted into four different features. What are they?
20. What do you need to do differently with the **Pen Tool** to create a curved path instead of a straight path?
21. What tools are used to select paths and anchor points?
22. Describe one situation when you would use the **Freeform Pen Tool** with its **Magnetic** option turned on.
23. What are two purposes of the **Paths** palette?
24. If you are using a light-colored outer glow layer style, what must you do to the background color of your file?
25. Each of the effects on the **Styles** palette is a unique combination of what?

These are some of the popular styles accessible through the **Styles** palette

Painting Tools and Filters

Learning Objectives

After completing this chapter, you will be able to:
- Apply paint to an image using the **Brush Tool**.
- Select and modify brush styles using the **Brush Preset Picker** and the **Brushes** palette.
- Differentiate between the **Image Size** and **Canvas Size** commands.
- Paint patterns in an image using the **Pattern Stamp Tool**.
- Select and organize patterns using the **Pattern Picker**.
- Explain the difference between the **Brush Tool** and **Pencil Tool**.
- Use the **Smudge Tool** to create a "smeared" look.
- Sample a color in an image with the **Eyedropper Tool**.
- Create different styles of gradients with the **Gradient Tool**.
- Edit a gradient using the **Gradient Editor**.
- Fill an area with color with the **Paint Bucket Tool**.
- Fill an area with a color or pattern using the **Fill** command.
- Recognize how filters are organized in the **Filters** menu.
- Manipulate an image with the tools found in the **Liquify** filter.
- Create a tileable pattern with the **Pattern Picker** filter.

Introduction

You have probably used a simple painting program on a computer. Most painting programs allow you to spread color on your screen with a variety of tools, such as a paintbrush, a pencil, or a paint bucket.

Photoshop's painting tools have an incredible amount of brush styles to choose from. There are brushes that imitate any traditional art style that you can think of. There are square brushes, calligraphy brushes, and special effect brushes that let you paint anything from stars to grass, **Figure 6-1**. You can even create your own brushes, or download brushes created by other artists.

Photoshop's painting tools are used for more than just painting color on your screen. For example, in Chapter 3, *Selection Tools*, you learned that while in quick mask mode, the **Brush Tool** is used to create a mask. The shape and size of many of Photoshop's other tools are controlled by choosing from the same assortment of brushes used by the **Brush Tool**.

Figure 6-1.
This simple painting was completed in under one minute. The **Gradient Tool** was used to create the sky, and a brush shaped like a blade of grass was used to paint the grass.

Photoshop offers more than one hundred *filters*. Filters are special effects that can be applied to all or part of a file. For example, one filter makes an image look like it is coated with plastic wrap, another modifies an image so it looks like a stained glass window, and another causes a photo to appear as if it was created by an artist using colored pencils.

The Brush Tool

The primary function of the **Brush Tool** is to paint with the foreground color shown in the **Toolbox**. Painting occurs as you might expect: by clicking and dragging the mouse or using a graphics tablet. Straight lines can also be created with this tool if you press [Shift] and click (without dragging) the beginning and end points of a line. The options that appear on the **Brush Tool**'s options bar are also found on the options bar of several other painting tools. See **Figure 6-2**.

The current brush size (its diameter, in pixels) and style are shown. Next to it is a small, downward-pointing arrow that opens the **Brush Preset Picker.** The **Brush Preset Picker** is used to change the size and style of the brush. The easiest way to change brush size, however, is to press the bracket keys ([,]). The right bracket ( ]) increases the brush size, the left bracket ([ ) decreases it.

The **Mode:** setting lets you choose from several blending modes. Blending modes control the way the brush color blends with the image beneath it. Because there is a long list of modes, they will be explained a bit later in this chapter.

The **Opacity:** setting determines how solid (opaque) the paint appears. An **Opacity:** setting of 100% means you will not be able to see through the paint that the brush leaves behind. Entering a lower percentage causes the paint to appear less solid. A value of 1% in this setting results in paint that is very nearly transparent.

Figure 6-2.
The **Brush Tool**'s options bar is shown here.

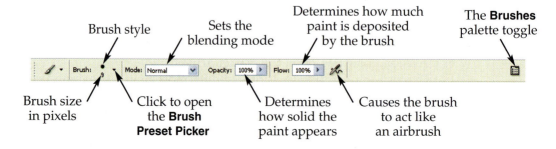

When using a lower **Opacity:** setting, you can get different results if your painting strokes *overlap*. If you release the mouse button as you paint several strokes, the paint will appear darker where the overlap occurs. See **Figure 6-3**. Holding down the mouse button continuously as you paint avoids this effect.

The **Flow:** setting determines how much paint is deposited in the image at any given time. If the **Flow:** setting is lower than 100%, the amount of paint produced by the **Brush Tool** is restricted. For example, if the **Flow:** setting is changed from 100% to 50%, only half as much paint will be produced by the **Brush Tool**.

Clicking the airbrush button causes the **Brush Tool** to act like an airbrush. An airbrush forces paint through a nozzle using compressed air. This setting causes paint to keep spraying out as long as you are holding down the mouse button. You will really notice this effect if you move the mouse very slowly or stop moving it while you paint.

At the far right of the options bar is the **Brushes** palette toggle. Activating this toggle displays the **Brushes** palette. The settings in the **Brushes** palette are more detailed than those in the **Brush Preset Picker**.

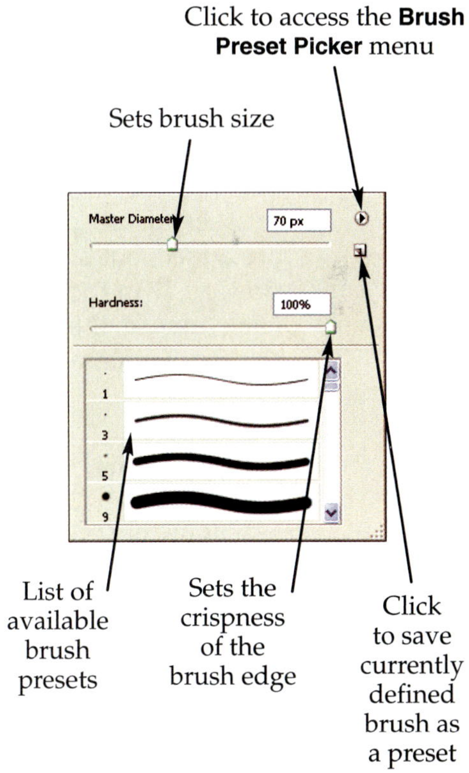

The Brush Preset Picker

The **Brush Preset Picker** displays when you click on the small downward-pointing arrow on the options bar. See **Figure 6-4**. From the **Brush Preset Picker**, you can quickly change the size (diameter) and hardness of the brush. The **Hardness:** setting controls how sharp and crisp the edge of the brush looks. A setting of 0% produces a soft, feathery edge.

Beneath the **Brush Preset Picker** menu button is the **Create a new preset from this brush** button. As its name indicates, this button is used to save the current brush settings as a preset. After you name the new preset, it appears at the bottom of the presets list in the **Brush Preset Picker**.

Figure 6-3.
When the **Opacity:** setting is less than 100%, painting in one continuous stroke does not cause a darkened overlap effect (left). Releasing the mouse button and then painting additional strokes darkens the paint in areas that overlap (right).

Figure 6-4.
The **Brush Preset Picker** is used to change the size and hardness of the brush.

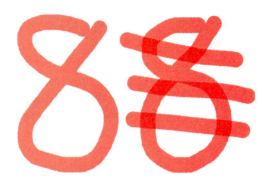

Note Keep in mind that several other tools use the same **Brush Preset Picker** to choose the size, style, and shape of the tool.

The Brush Preset Picker Menu

The **Brush Preset Picker** menu is structured just like the **Custom Shape Picker** menu that you learned about in Chapter 5, *Text, Shapes, and Layer Styles*. Most of Photoshop's picker menus are structured in the same way. See **Figure 6-5**.

The **New Brush Preset** command lets you save your current settings as a new brush in the **Brush Preset Picker**. This command is identical in function to the **Create a new preset from this brush** button in the picker. After it is named, the new preset appears at the bottom of the list of available presets in the picker.

The two commands in the next section of the menu allow you to delete and rename presets. To rename a brush preset, select the preset in the **Brush Preset Picker** and then select **Rename Brush...** from the **Brush Preset Picker** menu. To delete a preset, select the brush in the picker and then choose **Delete Brush** from the **Brush Preset Picker** menu.

The third section of the menu lists several ways the brushes can be displayed in the picker. The **Stroke Thumbnail** option is the most descriptive because you can see a sample brush stroke along with the small thumbnail image of the brush tip. The **Stroke Thumbnail** option is the default setting, and will likely never need to be changed.

Choosing the **Preset Manager** command opens the **Preset Manager** dialog box. This dialog box displays all of the brushes that are currently in the picker. You can use the **Preset Manager** to delete and load different brushes, if desired.

Choosing the **Reset Brushes** command restores the picker to its default state. When you modify brushes, you can use the **Save Brushes** command to save the current condition of the **Brush Preset Picker** to a file. This file can be retrieved later by using the **Load Brushes** command. The **Replace Brushes** command is very similar to the **Load Brushes** command. The difference is the old brushes are replaced (deleted) instead of appended (added to) as the new brushes are loaded into the picker.

The last section of the menu lists all of the available brush categories. When you click one of these categories, a dialog box asks if you want to replace or append the current brushes. If you click **OK**, the new brushes are added, but all of the brushes that were previously in the picker are deleted. If you click **Append**, the new brushes are added to the brushes already listed in the picker.

Figure 6-5.
The **Brush Preset Picker** menu is similar in layout and function to other picker menus.

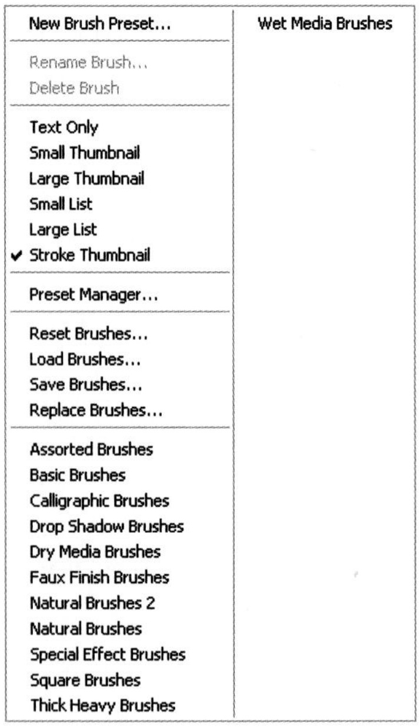

Brush Tool Blending Modes

Remember the **Mode:** setting on the **Brush Tool**'s options bar? Blending modes control how the **Brush Tool** behaves when adding color to an image. You will find these same modes on the options bar of several other painting tools (although some modes are not available with certain tools). Modes are also found on the **Layers** palette and control how layers blend with one another. This is discussed further in Chapter 11, *Additional Layer Techniques*.

The blending modes available with the **Brush Tool** are briefly explained in **Figure 6-6**. The examples that appear in the table show the result of using a soft, round

Chapter 6   Painting Tools and Filters 221

Figure 6-6.
Each brush stroke in the following examples use medium blue as the brush color (otherwise known as the blending color). The blending modes are found in the options bar of several tools. They are also found on the **Layers** palette.

Mode and Explanation	Examples
Normal mode is what you would expect—the brush paints according to the settings you have chosen.	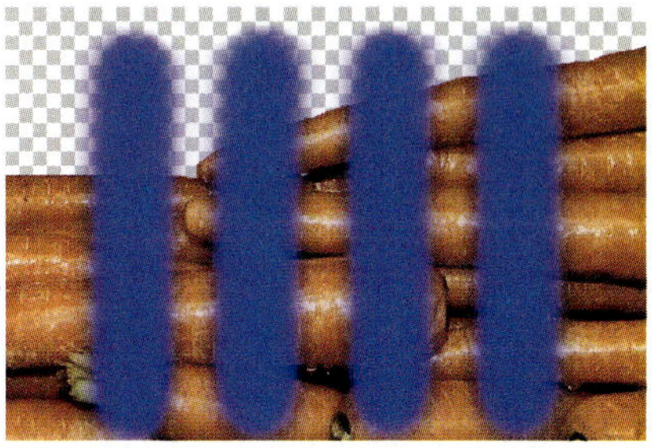
Dissolve causes the edges of the brush stroke to appear speckled and "noisy."	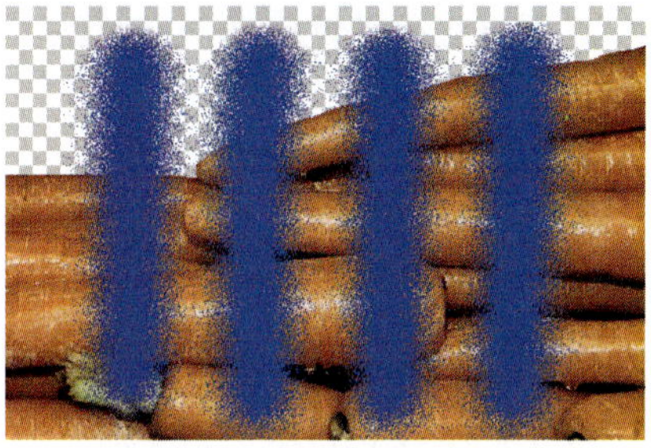
Behind mode is only available if there are *transparent areas* in the layer you are painting on. Only the transparent areas can be painted.	
Clear mode is like using the **Eraser Tool**—it creates transparent areas. The *Layer Transparency should be unlocked* when using this mode.	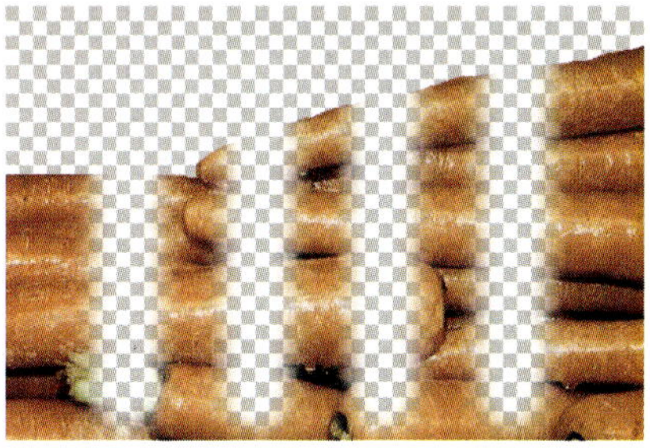
(From left to right) **Darken**, **Multiply**, **Color Burn**, and **Linear Burn** modes cause the paint color to *blend with and darken* the image. For explanations on the subtle differences between these modes, search for "blending modes" in **Help > Photoshop Help**....	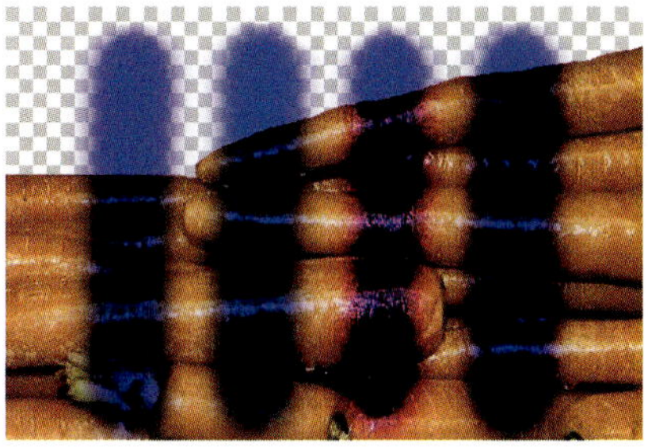

(Continued)

Figure 6-6.
Continued.

Mode and Explanation	Examples
(From left to right) **Lighten, Screen, Color Dodge**, and **Linear Dodge** modes cause the paint color to *blend with and lighten* the image. Again, refer to Photoshop's help file if you would like an explanation of the differences between each mode.	
(From left to right) **Overlay, Soft Light, Hard Light, Vivid Light, Linear Light, Pin Light**, and **Hard Mix** are found in the next section of the **Mode:** drop-down menu. Most of these modes will either darken or lighten pixels below it, depending on how dark or light the *blend color* (the color you are painting) is. The final results are computed in a slightly different manner for each of these modes.	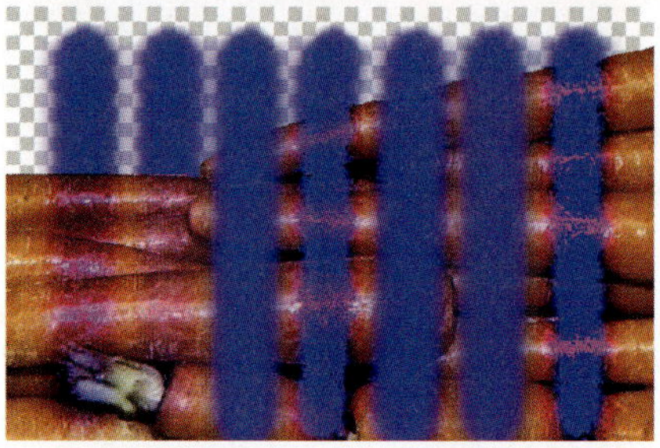
The **Difference** (left) and **Exclusion** (right) modes are similar. They create a lighter effect because they subtract the base and blend colors from each other.	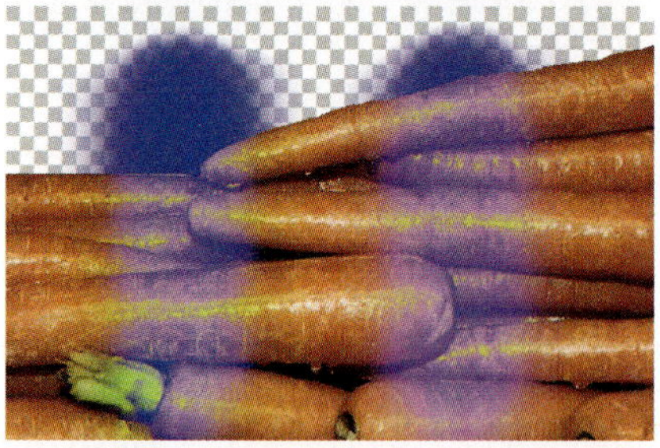
(From left to right) The **Hue** mode changes an object's color while preserving shadows and highlights (light areas). **Saturation** mode changes the saturation, or intensity, of an object's color. **Color** and **Luminosity** modes are opposite of each other. These modes combine characteristics of the base color with the blend color.	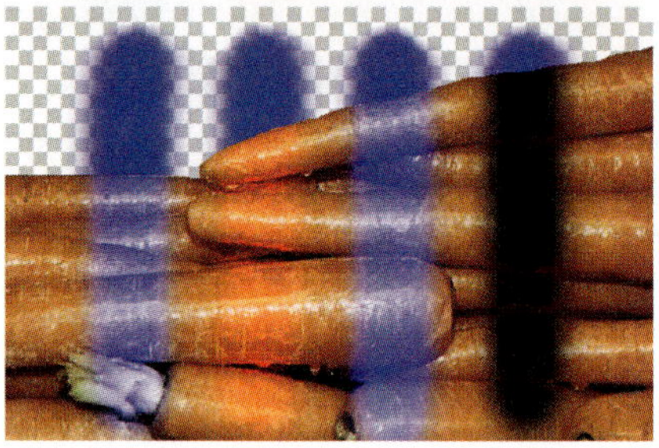

brush with a medium blue color as the foreground color. The **Opacity:** setting is 100% in all examples.

As you read about the modes in Figure 6-6, remember that you should always *create a duplicate layer before painting an image* so that the original image is always preserved. Your results will vary depending on the color of the original image and the color of the paint. You should also be aware that using black and white paint with blending modes creates unpredictable results.

The Brushes Palette

The **Brushes** palette contains many more options than the **Brush Preset Picker**. From this palette, you can customize brushes in a variety of ways. The **Brushes** palette can be displayed by clicking the **Toggle the Brushes palette** button on the options bar or by choosing **Window > Brushes**.

The **Brushes** palette contains a palette menu that is similar to the menu found on the **Brush Preset Picker**, except it contains more commands. When the **Expanded View** option is selected, the **Brushes** palette appears as shown in **Figure 6-7**. When the **Expanded View** option is not enabled, the **Brushes** palette looks very similar to the **Brush Preset Picker**.

When the **Brushes** palette is open in expanded view, the section on the left displays the different categories of controls that can be adjusted in the palette. Clicking on one of these categories places a check mark in its check box to show that it is active. The various options available for the selected category of controls are displayed on the right side of the palette. A preview window at the bottom of the palette shows the effects the current settings will have on the brush strokes.

The Brush Tip Shape Settings

When the **Brush Tip Shape** entry is clicked in the left section of the palette, the right side of the palette displays each brush tip that is currently loaded. Here, you can change the brush diameter or flip or rotate the brush tip, and adjust the spacing between brush marks.

In the example in **Figure 6-8**, one of the special effect brushes, **Dune Grass**, is selected and its spacing has been changed so that fewer grass clumps are generated

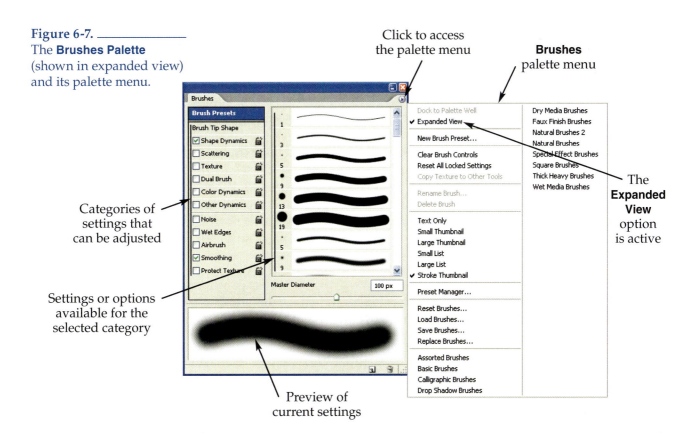

Figure 6-7.
The **Brushes Palette** (shown in expanded view) and its palette menu.

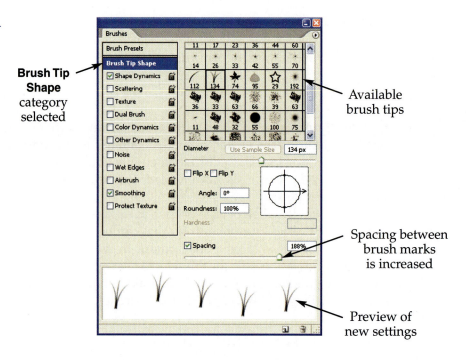

Figure 6-8.
The design, diameter, orientation, and spacing of brush tips can be changed in the **Brush Tip Shape** section of the **Brushes** palette.

while painting. The individual patterns of paint created by the brush, in this case clumps of grass, are referred to as *brush marks*. When a paint tool is being used, brush marks are created at regular intervals in the brush stroke. These intervals are called *steps*. The **Spacing** setting determines the distance between steps in the brush stroke. A path with steps that are closer together will look more solid or continuous than a stroke in which the steps are spaced widely apart. The example you see at the bottom of the **Brushes** palette shows how the brush stroke will appear as you click and drag with the mouse.

Shape Dynamics Settings

When the **Shape Dynamics** entry is clicked on the left side of the **Brushes** palette, the right side of the palette displays a group of settings that are used to add some variance to the brush stroke. The shape dynamics settings can be used in combinations to achieve the desired result.

The first control is the **Size Jitter** slider and text box. The term *jitter* means "random fluctuation." Increasing the **Size Jitter** setting causes different sizes of brush marks (grass clumps for example) to appear. See **Figure 6-9**. When this value is set to 100, the stroke is the full brush size at its widest point and the minimum allowable width (determined by the **Minimum Diameter** slider setting) at its narrowest point. When the slider is set to 50, the sizes of the brush marks may vary up to 50%. A setting of 0 results in brush marks that do not vary in size.

Note If the **Size Jitter** setting is higher than the **Minimum Diameter** setting, the **Minimum Diameter** setting determines how much the brush marks can vary in size.

The **Control:** drop-down list offers a few options for varying the stroke width. Only the **Off** and **Fade** options work without a pressure-sensitive tablet and stylus. When the **Off** option is selected, the maximum stroke width remains constant and the size jitter effect is applied to the entire stroke. When the **Fade** option is selected, the maximum

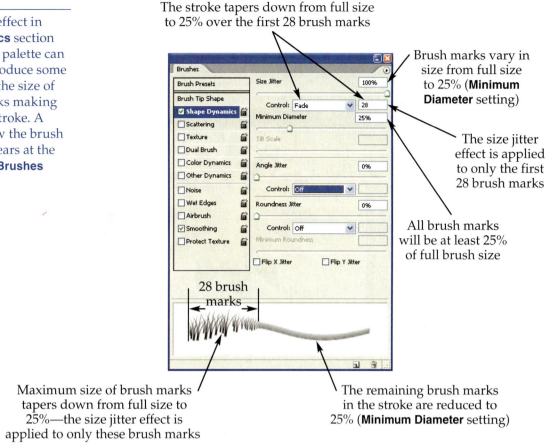

Figure 6-9. The size jitter effect in **Shape Dynamics** section of the **Brushes** palette can be used to introduce some variation into the size of the brush marks making up the brush stroke. A preview of how the brush will paint appears at the bottom of the **Brushes** palette.

width of the stroke tapers down from full size down to the minimum size over the number of steps (increments) specified in the text box to the right of the **Control:** drop-down list.

The **Fade** option also causes the size jitter effect to gradually diminish over the specified number of steps. Beyond the specified number of steps, the size jitter effect is not applied because all brush marks are already at their minimum allowable size.

The **Minimum Diameter** slider determines the *minimum* width that a brush mark is allowed to be. The value set with this slider represents a percentage of the full brush size.

The **Angle Jitter:** setting causes random fluctuation in the angles of the steps (grass clumps). The **Control:** drop-down list below the **Angle Jitter:** slider provides several options for applying the angle jitter effect and for changing the angles of stroke marks, only a few of which are available without a pressure sensitive tablet and stylus. The **Initial Direction** and **Direction** options subtly change the way the angle jitter effect is applied. When the **Fade** option is selected, the brush marks are progressively rotated from 0° to 360° over the specified number of steps. Therefore, if 10 is entered in the text box, the first ten brush marks are rotated in progressive increments of 36°. Beyond the specified number of steps, the angle jitter is applied normally. See **Figure 6-10**.

Roundness jitter changes the perspective of each brush mark. As a brush mark's roundness setting decreases, it appears as though it is rotated toward the viewer, **Figure 6-11**. The **Roundness Jitter** slider sets the amount of variation in the roundness setting of the individual brush marks. The limits of the roundness jitter effect are set with the **Minimum Roundness** slider, and the roundness setting can gradually be applied using the **Fade** option in the **Control:** drop-down list. These controls are very similar to their counterparts for the size jitter effect.

Figure 6-10. ──────
The angle jitter effect randomly tilts brush marks forward and backward.

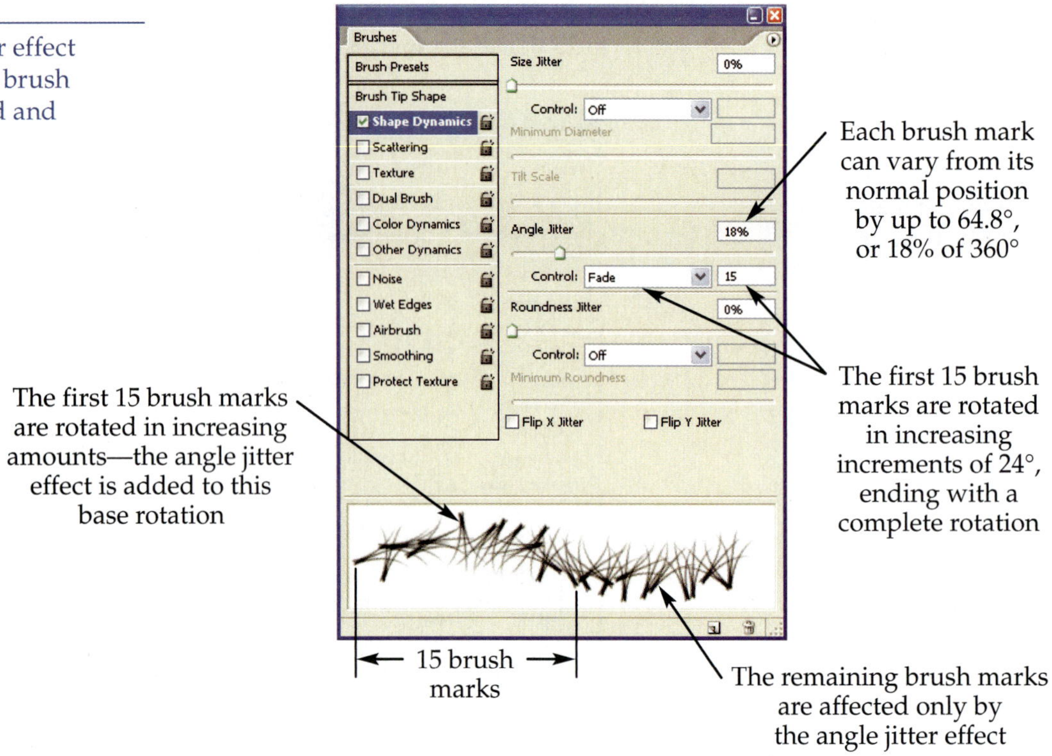

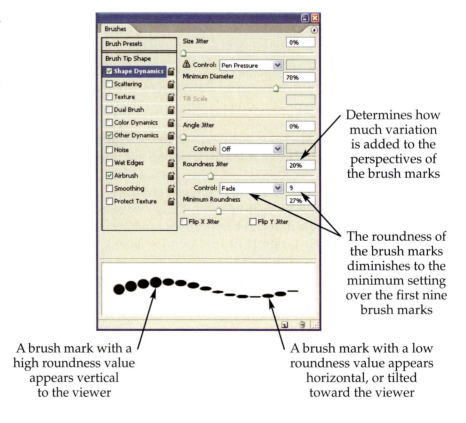

Each brush mark can vary from its normal position by up to 64.8°, or 18% of 360°

The first 15 brush marks are rotated in increasing amounts—the angle jitter effect is added to this base rotation

The first 15 brush marks are rotated in increasing increments of 24°, ending with a complete rotation

← 15 brush marks →

The remaining brush marks are affected only by the angle jitter effect

Figure 6-11. ──────
The roundness jitter effect makes the marks randomly appear to be tilted toward or away from the viewer.

Determines how much variation is added to the perspectives of the brush marks

The roundness of the brush marks diminishes to the minimum setting over the first nine brush marks

A brush mark with a high roundness value appears vertical to the viewer

A brush mark with a low roundness value appears horizontal, or tilted toward the viewer

Activating the **Flip X Jitter** check box causes some of the brush marks to be mirrored horizontally. Placing a check mark in the **Flip Y Jitter** check box causes some of the brush marks to be mirrored vertically. See **Figure 6-12**.

Figure 6-12.
The flip X jitter effect mirrors random brush marks vertically. The flip Y jitter effect mirrors random brush marks horizontally. Some brush marks will be affected by both options.

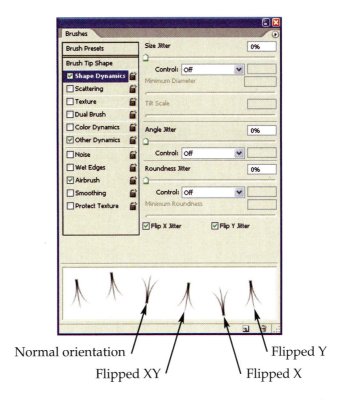

Normal orientation
Flipped XY
Flipped Y
Flipped X

Scattering Settings

When you click the **Scattering** entry on the left side of the **Brushes** palette, a set of controls appear that allow you to adjust how the brush marks are distributed in the area around the brush. Increasing the **Scatter:** setting causes brush strokes to leave paint in a ragged line instead of a straight path. If the **Both Axes** check box is checked, the brush marks will be scattered above, below, in front, and behind the cursor. If this check box is unchecked, the brush marks are distributed in a straight line perpendicular to the brush path. The **Count** setting determines the maximum number of brush marks that can be created at each step in the brush stroke. The **Count Jitter** setting determines how much variation there is in the number of brush marks created. The effect of these settings can be gradually decreased by selecting the **Fade** option from the **Control:** drop-down lists and entering a number of steps in the text box to the right. See **Figure 6-13**.

Texture Settings

When you click the **Texture** entry on the left side of the **Brushes** palette, a group of controls appear on the right that allow you to combine a texture file with the brush tip. This adds a textured look to the paint. See **Figure 6-14**. For example, with the right settings, paint can look like it was applied to a real canvas. Using texture files are discussed in more detail in the *Pattern Stamp Tool* section in this chapter.

Clicking the down arrow next to the texture preview opens the pattern picker, from which a pattern is selected on which to base the texture. Activating the **Invert** check box reverses the effect of the pattern's color on the resulting texture. The **Scale** slider setting determines the size of the texture. When the **Texture each tip** check box is checked, the texture is applied to each brush mark individually, when it is unchecked the texture is applied to the stroke as a whole. The difference between these settings can be subtle.

Figure 6-13.
Increasing the **Scattering** and **Count Jitter** settings causes paint to be applied in a more random fashion.

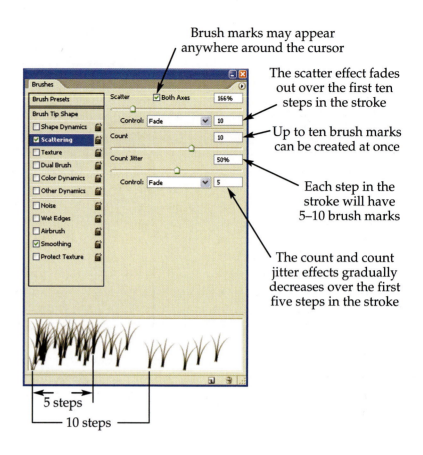

Figure 6-14.
The controls in the **Texture** section of the **Brushes** palette can be used to add a three-dimensional appearance to the brush stroke.

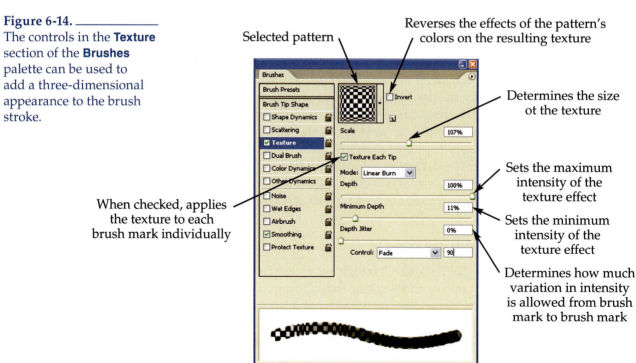

The **Depth** settings control to what degree the texture file is combined with the brush stroke. They work together to control the appearance of the image in much the same way as the other groups of controls you have studied in the **Brushes** palette.

Dual Brush Settings

In the **Dual Brush** section of the **Brushes** palette, a second brush tip can be combined with the first. Paint will appear where the two brush tips overlap. Similar to the **Texture** section, this is another way to increase the complexity of a brush tip.

To use the dual brush option, begin by defining the first brush in the **Brushes** palette. Once you have selected and adjusted the brush and activated the desired options, click the **Dual Brush** entry on the left side of the **Brushes Palette**.

Select the desired brush tip for the second brush from the picker window. Adjust the size of the second brush using the **Diameter** slider. Click the **Use Sample Size** button if you want the brush tip to be the same size as the image selected in the brush tip picker. (The size appears under the brush tip image in the picker window.) Set the method that you want to use to combine the brushes from the **Mode:** drop-down menu. Activate the **Flip** check box if you want to mirror the image being used for the brush tip.

Set the distance between stroke steps for the second brush using the **Spacing** slider. Set the desired **Scatter** value. Keep in mind that only the overlapping areas of the first and second brush will be visible. So, if you have selected a small brush size for the first brush and a high scatter value for the second brush, many of the brush strokes may not be visible.

Finally, use the **Count** slider to set the number of brush marks that you want to appear at each step of the stroke. Each additional brush mark created at a given step will be rotated slightly compared to the previous brush mark. You can see how the first and second brushes interact in the preview window at the bottom of the **Brushes** palette. See **Figure 6-15**.

Color Dynamics Settings

The **Color Dynamics** section of the **Brushes** palette contains jitter settings that create random color fluctuations. The leaf pattern in **Figure 6-16** was creating by starting with a leaf-shaped brush and setting orange as the foreground color and brown as the background color. The **Foreground/Background Jitter** setting was increased, causing the

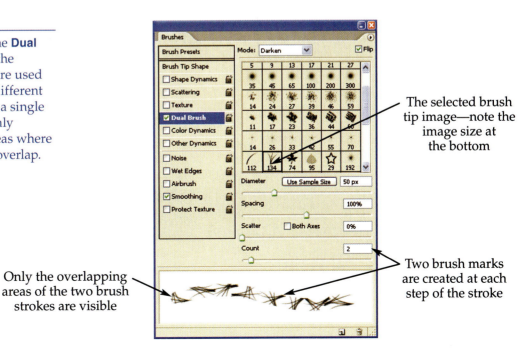

Figure 6-15. The controls in the **Dual Brush** section of the **Brushes** palette are used to combine two different brushes to create a single stroke. Paint is only applied to the areas where the two brushes overlap.

brush marks to be varying blends of the foreground color and the background color. The **Hue Jitter** was increased very slightly, allowing the leaves to have just a hint of different colors. This produces the occasional leaf that is slightly more green or yellow than the others. A higher setting would cause the brush to occasionally produce colors that are not as closely related to the selected foreground and background colors, such as a bright blue or magenta. The **Saturation Jitter** and **Brightness Jitter** settings were also increased. The saturation jitter effect causes the intensity of the colors to vary, and the brightness jitter effect causes the lightness and darkness of the colors to vary. The **Purity** slider was not adjusted. The **Purity** slider setting adjusts the saturation for all of the color created by the **Brush Tool**; the **Saturation** slider setting just sets the variation.

In addition to the changes made to the **Color Dynamics** settings, the brush was modified by changing the **Shape Dynamics** and **Scattering** settings. The **Angle Jitter** setting and **Size Jitter** settings were bumped up, as were the **Scatter** and **Count** settings.

Other Dynamics Settings

The left side of the **Brushes** palette contains one more entry, called **Other Dynamics**. Clicking this entry reveals the **Opacity Jitter** and **Flow Jitter** settings on the right side of the palette. Increasing the **Opacity Jitter** setting causes the **Brush Tool** to create brush marks with varying degrees of transparency. Increasing the **Flow Jitter** setting causes the pen to produce an inconsistent stroke. The result is very similar to the effect created by increasing the opacity jitter.

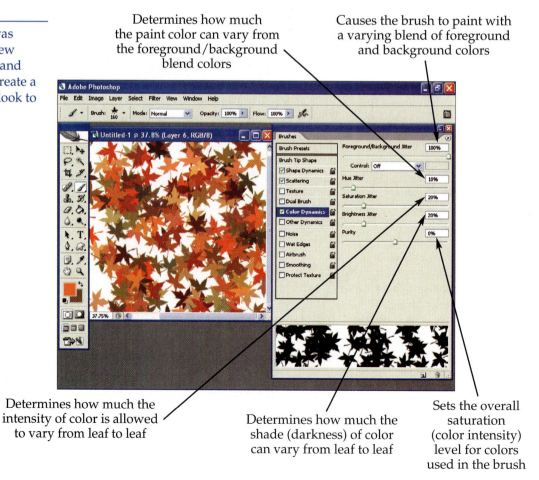

Figure 6-16. This leaf pattern was painted in only a few seconds. The jitter and scattering effects create a naturally random look to the leaves.

Determines how much the paint color can vary from the foreground/background blend colors

Causes the brush to paint with a varying blend of foreground and background colors

Determines how much the intensity of color is allowed to vary from leaf to leaf

Determines how much the shade (darkness) of color can vary from leaf to leaf

Sets the overall saturation (color intensity) level for colors used in the brush

Other Options in the Brushes Palette

The **Noise**, **Wet Edges**, **Airbrush**, **Smoothing**, and **Protect Texture** create different appearances to painted strokes. These are not further sections of the **Brushes** palette like the **Shape Dynamics** and the other entries already discussed. Rather, these are single options that are always available, no matter what other settings have been changed.

Activating the **Noise** option creates a blotching effect in the soft areas of the brush. This effect could simulate the type of spray pattern that comes from a can of spray paint that has not been shaken enough.

Turning on the **Wet Edges** option causes the paint to thin out (become somewhat transparent) in the center of the brush stroke and pool at the edges. This effect could be used to simulate excessively thinned paint, watercolors, or a coffee stain.

The **Airbrush** option, when activated, causes the brush to continue to lay down paint as long as the mouse button is held. This option works the same as its counterpart on the options bar.

When the **Smoothing** option is activated, the curves in the brush stroke are smoothed out. This option is most noticeable when you are painting with a pressure-sensitive tablet and stylus.

If you have adjusted the texture settings on various brushes, the **Protect Texture** option forces any of these brushes to use the same scale and pattern settings. This causes a uniform-looking "canvas" to appear under a painting as you switch from brush to brush.

To reset all of the settings in the **Brushes** palette, choose **Clear Brush Controls** from the **Brushes** palette menu.

Creating a Custom Brush Tip

You can create your own brush tip by opening an image or creating an image from scratch and selecting part of it. (To create a soft-edged brush, use feather settings on selection tools.) Then, choose **Edit > Define Brush Preset...**, name the brush, and click **OK**. It is added to the **Brush Preset Picker**.

The Pencil Tool

The **Pencil Tool** is found behind the **Brush Tool** in the **Toolbox**. The **Pencil Tool** is a painting tool that creates a *hard-edged* brush stroke. It does not matter what the **Hardness:** setting is in the **Brush Preset Picker**. In contrast, the **Brush Tool** creates an anti-aliased, softer edge, even when the **Hardness:** setting is changed to 100% in the **Brush Preset Picker**. Compare the two brush strokes in **Figure 6-17**. The first was created with the **Pencil Tool** with the **Hardness:** set at 100%. The second stroke was created with the **Brush Tool** with the **Hardness:** set at 100%.

The **Pencil Tool**'s options bar contains options you are already familiar with, plus

Figure 6-17.
The **Pencil Tool** creates hard-edged brush strokes (left), while the **Brush Tool** creates softer edges (right).

one more, Figure 6-18. When the **Auto Erase** option is on, the **Pencil Tool** can erase paint that it creates. It does this by painting the background color over the paint. This option only works if the exact center of your brush is over a painted area before you click the mouse button to erase. It is important to realize that this is not really erasing the stroke, as would be the case with the **Eraser Tool**, but rather is painting over it. This distinction is most notable when working on a layer that has transparency unlocked.

> **Note** The remaining tool grouped with the **Brush Tool** in the **Toolbox** is the **Color Replacement Tool**. This tool will be discussed in Chapter 9, *Introduction to Color Correction*.

The Pattern Stamp Tool

The **Pattern Stamp Tool** paints a *pattern* instead of a solid color. The **Pattern Stamp Tool** is found behind the **Clone Stamp Tool** in the **Toolbox**. The **Clone Stamp Tool** will be discussed in Chapter 8, *Restoring and Retouching Photos*.

The Pattern Stamp Tool's Options Bar

The options bar for the **Pattern Stamp Tool** contains all of the **Brush Tool**'s options, plus a **Pattern Picker**, Figure 6-19. The **Pattern Picker** behaves just like the **Brush Preset**

Figure 6-18.
The **Pencil Tool**'s options bar is shown here.

Figure 6-19.
The **Pattern Stamp Tool** is located underneath the **Clone Stamp Tool** in the **Toolbox**. It shares many of the **Brush Tool**'s options and includes a **Pattern Picker**.

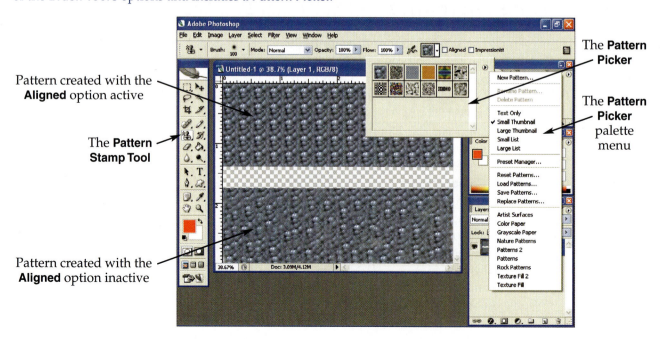

Picker. It contains a palette menu that controls the display of the picker and lets you load, save, replace, or reset patterns. The bottom section of the palette menu lists nine different pattern categories that can be replaced or appended into the **Pattern Picker**.

There are two additional settings on the **Pattern Stamp Tool**'s options bar. When the **Aligned** option is on, the pattern repeats itself over and over, side by side, as you paint it. This is called a *tiled* pattern. If the **Aligned** option is turned off, clicking the mouse occasionally as you paint creates a pattern that does not repeat—or in other words, blends the pattern into itself. Activating the **Impressionist** option causes the pattern to appear soft and out-of-focus.

Defining Your Own Patterns

You can also create your own patterns by opening an image file, selecting part of it with the **Rectangular Marquee Tool**, and choosing **Edit > Define Pattern…**. After you name the pattern and click **OK**, the pattern appears at the end of the list in the **Pattern Picker**.

The Gradient Tool

A *gradient* consists of two or more colors that gradually blend together. Gradients are used to create colorful backgrounds or shapes. They can also be used to create more complex effects, such as shadows or fade-out effects. In this chapter, you will be introduced to the basics of gradients. You will see more examples of advanced gradient effects in a later chapter.

The options bar of the **Gradient Tool** contains the **Gradient Picker**, which functions like Photoshop's other pickers, Figure 6-20. When the default gradients are loaded in the **Gradient Picker**, the first gradient is always a combination of the foreground and

Figure 6-20.
The **Gradient Picker** is set up just like the **Brush Picker** and **Pattern Picker**.

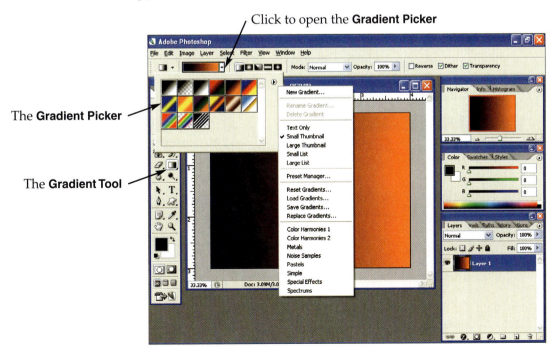

background color, and the second gradient is always a combination of the foreground color and a transparent area. The rest of the gradients are preset colors which can be replaced, deleted, or edited.

You can right-click (Mac: [Ctrl] + click) on any gradient and use the shortcut menu that appears to delete, rename, or add a new gradient to the picker. The **Gradient Picker** palette menu lists several categories of preset gradients that can be replaced or appended into the picker. You can also use the palette menu to save your own collection of gradients so they can be loaded again at a later time.

Before learning about the rest of the **Gradient Tool**'s options, you need to know how to use the **Gradient Tool**. Creating a gradient is simple—you drag a line at any angle on your screen and release the mouse button. Dragging a *long* line creates a more gradual gradient. If you drag a *short* line, the transition between colors is more abrupt. See **Figure 6-21**.

In the options bar, you can choose from several styles of gradients by clicking the buttons next to the **Gradient Picker**. The example in the Figure 6-21 was created with the first gradient style, called **Linear Gradient**, applied at an angle. Examples of all five gradient styles are shown in **Figure 6-22**.

When you add a gradient to an image, you can choose from several different blending modes in the **Mode:** drop-down list. You can control how transparent the gradient is by changing the **Opacity:** setting.

The **Reverse** option switches the gradient colors. In **Figure 6-23**, a two-color gradient (dark green and light green) was applied to a custom shape. Before the **Gradient Tool** would work, each shape layer had to be rasterized and selected.

The **Dither** option should be left on in most cases. It blends the gradient by adding "noise," making it appear smoother.

Some gradients have transparent areas, represented by a checkerboard pattern. The **Transparency** option, if turned off, will not allow those transparent areas to be created. In most cases, leave this option turned on.

> **Note** Since gradients are gradual blends of color, they do not look very good in low-resolution files. Pixelization makes the blended areas look distorted.

Figure 6-21.
The appearance of a gradient depends on how long of a line you draw when creating it. **A**—A long line creates a gradient with a gradual shift from the first color to the second. **B**—A shorter line creates a more abrupt shift from the first color to the second.

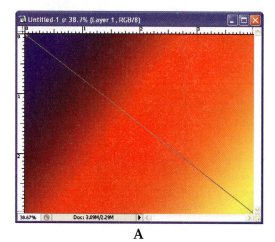
A

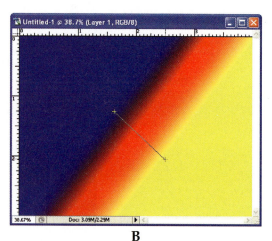
B

Figure 6-22.
Five different styles of gradients can be created.

Gradient Style	Button	Example
Linear Gradient	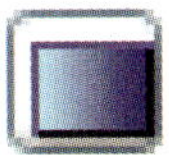	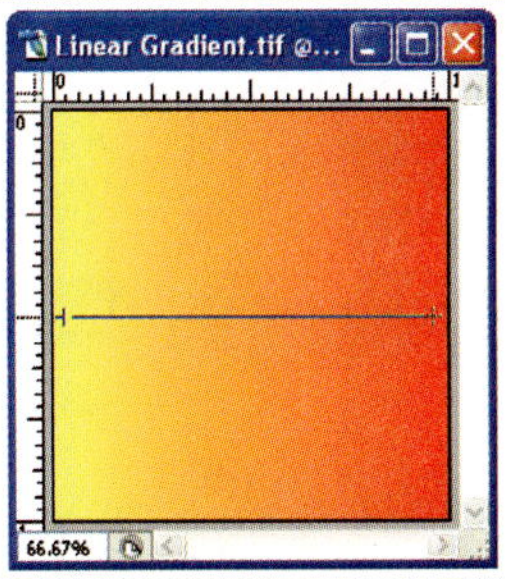
Radial Gradient		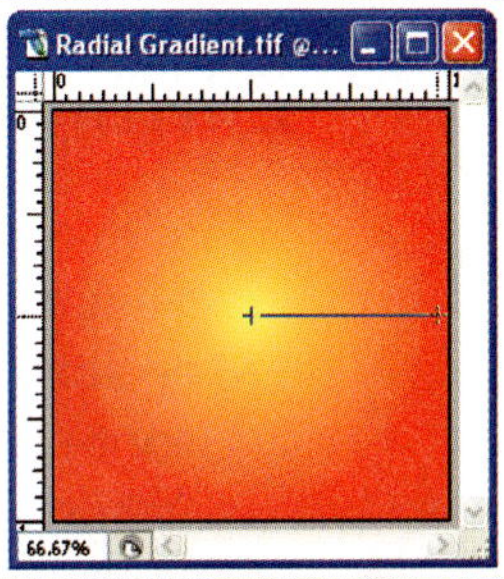
Angle Gradient		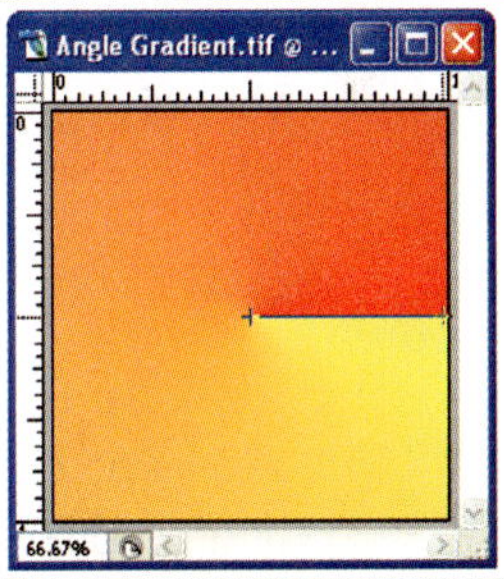
Reflected Gradient	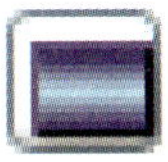	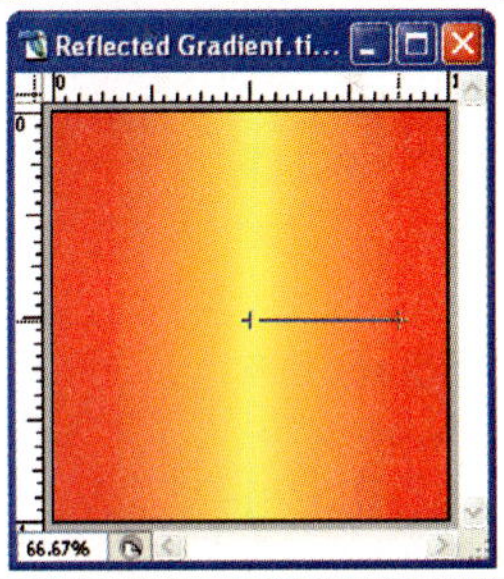
Diamond Gradient		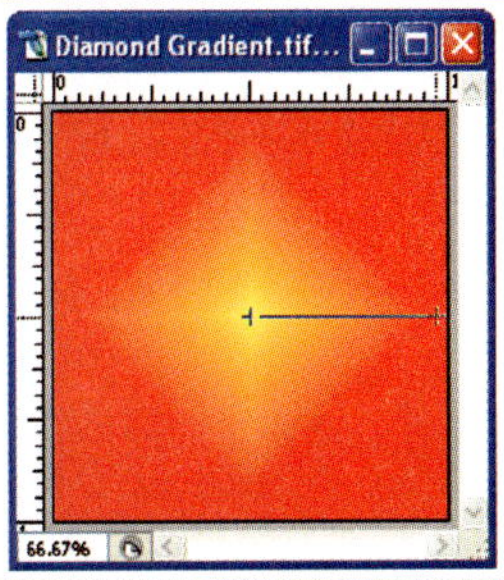

Figure 6-23.
A two-color gradient before (left) and after (right) using the **Reverse** option.

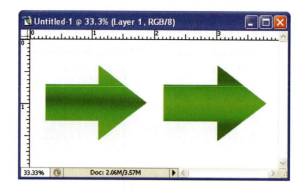

Editing Gradients

You can easily change a preset gradient's appearance or create and save your own gradient presets. To edit a gradient, double-click on whatever gradient appears on the options bar (not in the **Gradient Picker**). This causes the **Gradient Editor** to appear, Figure 6-24. Also, the **Eyedropper Tool** is activated automatically and is ready to use.

You can choose any preset gradient in the **Gradient Editor**, just like you can in the **Gradient Picker**. The palette menus for these features are almost identical. After you click on the gradient you want to edit, click the **New** button to create a copy that is ready for you to adjust.

Adjusting Color Stops

The **Gradient Editor** has *color stops* that appear along the bottom of the sample gradient box. These color stops each represent one color in the gradient and indicate where the color shifts begin and end within the gradient. The colors in the gradient blend from one color stop to the next. Each color stop can be dragged to a different location on the sample gradient box to change the appearance of the gradient. Color stops

Figure 6-24.
In the **Gradient Editor**, color stops are used to color the gradient and opacity stops are used to create transparent areas.

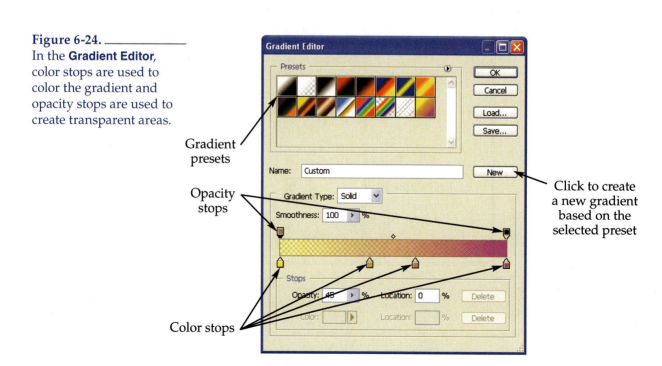

can be deleted by dragging them downward. A color stop can be added by clicking right beneath the sample gradient box. The color of a color stop can be changed by clicking on it. This causes the color picker to display, from which the new color can be selected. Remember that the **Eyedropper Tool** is automatically activated when you display the **Gradient Editor**, so you can easily choose a color from an image file, if desired.

When a color stop is clicked, two tiny diamond-shaped handles appear on either side of it. These diamonds show the midpoint between two colors. You can adjust the location of these midpoints by dragging them.

Solid and Noise Gradient Types

In the **Gradient Editor**, you can also choose between two gradient types from the **Gradient Type:** drop-down list. The **Solid** option creates a gradient with gradual blends of color. The **Smoothness:** setting lets you fine-tune how one color blends into another.

Selecting the **Noise** option creates gradients that blend colors randomly, making the gradient look choppy. See Figure 6-25. A noise-type gradient does not use color stops to determine the colors used in the gradient. Instead, the colors that will be used in the gradient are determined by first selecting a color mode from the **Color Model:** drop-down list. Once you have selected a color model, a series of sliders appear under the **Color Model:** drop-down list. Adjust these sliders to achieve the desired colors and note the changes in the sample gradient box.

> **Note** The **HSB** (hue, saturation, brightness) color model is especially good for creating monochromatic gradients. The **LAB** (luminosity, red-green, yellow-blue) color model is best for creating pastel gradients. The **RGB** (red, green, blue) is good for multicolor gradients.

You can adjust the appearance of noise by changing the **Roughness:** setting, which appears when you choose the **Noise** gradient type. You can further refine the gradient by activating the **Restrict Colors** and **Add Transparency** check boxes. The **Restrict Colors** option, when active, limits the saturation of the colors in the gradient so they are not overly intense. The **Transparency** option, when active, varies the opacity of the colors randomly, creating a gradient that fades in and out.

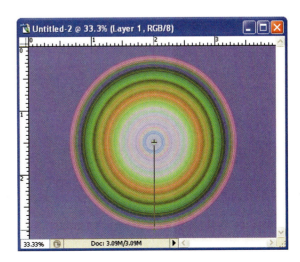

Figure 6-25.
This radial gradient was created using the **Noise** gradient type.

The Paint Bucket Tool

The **Paint Bucket Tool** is found in the **Toolbox** underneath the **Gradient Tool**. The **Paint Bucket Tool** provides a quick way to paint—it dumps the foreground color into either a selected area or an entire layer.

On the **Paint Bucket Tool**'s options bar, Figure 6-26, you can choose to dump a pattern into an area instead of the foreground color. The **Pattern Picker** appears when you choose this option.

Just like the **Brush Tool**, the **Paint Bucket Tool** has a **Mode:** setting that controls how the paint blends with the colors underneath it. The **Opacity:** setting controls how transparent the paint is.

Because the **Paint Bucket Tool** is used to fill an area that already contains other colors, it has a **Tolerance:** setting that controls how sensitive the **Paint Bucket Tool** is when spreading its color on other colored pixels. If the **Tolerance:** is set low, when a pixel is clicked with the **Paint Bucket Tool**, only similar-colored pixels are filled with the new color. This effect can be seen when dumping white on a gradient, Figure 6-27. To quickly fill a selected area, no matter how the pixels appear underneath it, set the **Tolerance:** setting to its maximum: 255.

The **Anti-alias** option is useful if the filled area contains diagonal lines or curves. Activating this option smoothes the edges of the filled area, which would normally be jagged.

Pixels that are touching or bordering each other are called *contiguous*. When the **Contiguous** option is turned on, the **Paint Bucket Tool** dumps color onto similarly colored pixels only if they are touching each other. When the **Contiguous** option is turned off, similar colors in the entire image are selected.

Activating the **All Layers** option allows you to simultaneously fill similarly colored pixels on different layers in the image. If this option is not active, you must select each layer individually to fill the desired pixels on those layers. It should be noted that when the **All Layers** option is active, paint is applied only to the selected layer. If the currently selected layer is at the top of the layer list, then when the paint is applied by the **Paint Bucket Tool**, it hides similarly colored pixels on other layers. However, if the currently selected layer is lower in the layer stack, the similarly colored pixels on layers above the selected layer will hide the paint applied by the **Paint Bucket Tool**. See Figure 6-28. For this reason, you may want to create and select a new layer at the top of the layer stack before using the **Paint Bucket Tool** with the **All Layers** option active.

Figure 6-26.
The **Paint Bucket Tool**'s option bar is shown here.

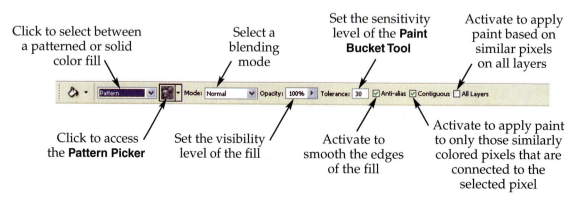

Figure 6-27. The **Tolerance:** setting determines how wide of a color range is affected by the **Paint Bucket Tool**. A—This is the original image. B—The **Paint Bucket Tool** with the **Tolerance:** set to 32 has dumped paint in the center of the gradient. C—The **Paint Bucket Tool** with the **Tolerance:** set to 80 has dumped paint in the same location on the gradient. Note that a wider range of pixel colors are affected.

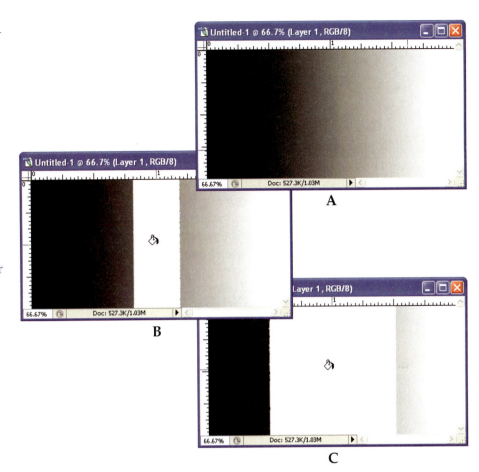

Figure 6-28. In this image, four quadrants of red pixels have been created on separate layers. Since the **Paint Bucket Tool**'s **All Layers** option is active, the **Paint Bucket Tool** applies blue paint to the entire canvas. However, since two of the red quadrants are on layers that are above the layer on which the **Paint Bucket Tool** is being used, those portions of the blue fill are hidden beneath the red quadrants.

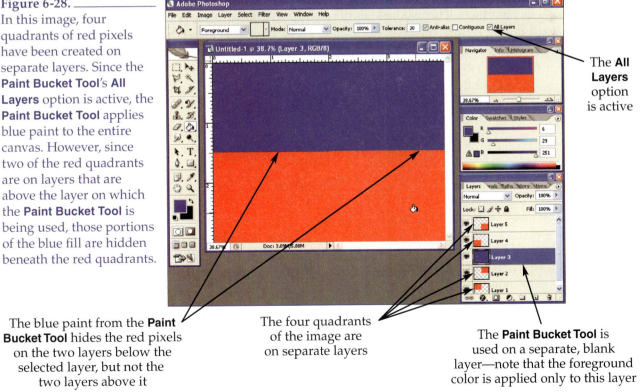

The Fill Command

Choosing **Edit > Fill...** is very similar to using the **Paint Bucket Tool**. In fact, using the **Magic Wand Tool** to select an area and then using the **Fill** command to fill it provides identical results to using the **Paint Bucket Tool**.

To use the **Fill** command, begin by making the desired selection. If you do not make a selection, the **Fill** command will fill the entire layer. Next, choose **Edit > Fill....** The **Fill** dialog box opens, letting you choose from several color options, a pattern, or history. Choosing the history option restores the area you selected to the way it looked when you first opened the image. If you created a new image rather than opening an existing image, selecting the **History** option will erase any content in the selected area.

In the **Blending** section of the **Fill** dialog box, you will find the **Mode:** and **Opacity:** settings. The **Mode:** setting determines how the fill is blended with the existing image. The **Opacity:** setting determines how visible the fill is. The **Preserve Transparency** option prevents the **Fill** command from filling the transparent portions of the selected area. This option should be active if you are working with an image that has transparent areas and you do not want those areas to be filled.

The **Layer > New Fill Layer >** submenu contains three commands that let you simultaneously create a new layer filled with a color, a pattern, or a gradient.

The Smudge Tool

Imagine using real paints to create a painting. Before letting the paint dry, you smear it with your finger. That is the effect that the **Smudge Tool** creates. You probably will not use this tool very often. One way this tool can be used is to help an object look like it is moving very fast by creating a streaked look.

The **Smudge Tool** is found behind the **Blur Tool** in the **Toolbox**. The controls found in the **Smudge Tool**'s options bar are similar to the those found in the options bar of other painting tools. The available options include a **Brush Preset Picker**, **Mode:** settings, and a **Strength:** setting, which controls how "hard" the finger smears the paint. See Figure 6-29.

When the **Sample All Layers** option is checked, all pixels under the cursor are smudged, no matter what layer they are on. The **Finger Painting** option, when turned on, adds some of the foreground color to each smudging stroke, creating a slightly messier look.

> **Note** The **Blur Tool** and **Sharpen Tool**, which are grouped with the **Smudge Tool** in the **Toolbox**, will be discussed in Chapter 8, *Restoring and Retouching Photos*.

The Eyedropper Tool

The **Eyedropper Tool** is grouped with the **Measure Tool** and the **Color Sampler Tool** in the **Toolbox**. The **Measure Tool** and **Color Sampler Tool** are discussed in Chapter 10, *Advanced Color Correction Techniques*.

Figure 6-29.
The **Smudge Tool**'s options bar is shown here.

The **Eyedropper Tool** is used to *sample*, or choose, a foreground color. With only one option in its options bar, this is one of Photoshop's simplest tools to use. The only setting that is adjustable for the **Eyedropper Tool** is the **Sample Size** drop-down list. From this drop-down list, you can select **Point Sample**, which will duplicate the color of the single pixel directly under the cursor. You can also choose **3 by 3 Average**, which looks at the nine pixels surrounding the cursor, averages their colors, and assigns that color to become the new foreground color. The **5 by 5 Average** is very similar to the **3 by 3 Average,** except it calculates an average color based on the twenty-five pixels closest to the cursor rather than the nine closest.

Imagine you want to create text that is similar in color to the purple flowers shown in **Figure 6-30**. The following is an explanation of the recommended procedure:

- Choose **Window > Arrange > New Window** to create a second view of your file (or zoom in on your original file).
- Zoom in on the second view until you can see individual pixels.
- Choose the **Eyedropper Tool** and choose one of the three **Sample Size:** options in the options bar.
- Position the tip of the **Eyedropper Tool** cursor over a pixel with the desired color. Click to set the foreground color.
- Now, you are ready to choose the **Type Tool** and enter purple text.

Note You will find that the **Eyedropper Tool** appears automatically when using some of Photoshop's features, such as editing gradients. These automatic versions of the **Eyedropper Tool** work the same as the tool selected in the **Toolbox**, but they may be used to sample a color other than the foreground color.

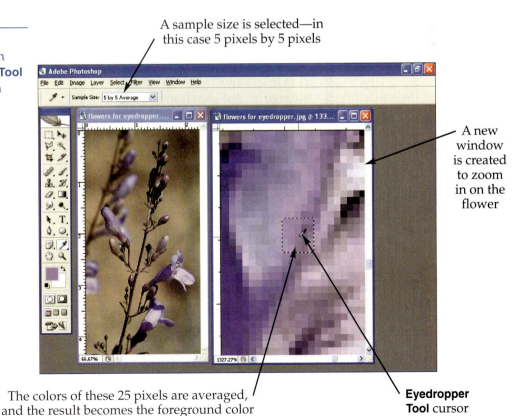

Figure 6-30. It is helpful to see individual pixels when using the **Eyedropper Tool** to pick a color from an image.

A sample size is selected—in this case 5 pixels by 5 pixels

A new window is created to zoom in on the flower

The colors of these 25 pixels are averaged, and the result becomes the foreground color

Eyedropper Tool cursor

The Canvas

A painter paints on a *canvas*. In Photoshop, the canvas is the entire area of an image. You have already learned about the image size setting in Chapter 2, *Resolution*. But what happens when you try to combine images that are different sizes? Imagine you are working on a Photoshop document that is 4″ high and 6″ wide. Then, you open an image that is 8″ × 10″. You copy it to your original document by dragging it over with the **Move Tool**. What happens? The portions of the 8″ × 10″ image that overlap the 4″ × 6″ canvas are no longer visible. All of the 8″ × 10″ image is still there (and can be moved around with the **Move Tool**), but the 4″ × 6″ canvas is not large enough to display all of it at one time. You have a couple of choices in this situation. You can use the **Image Size** dialog box to reduce the size of the 8″ × 10″ image before dragging it over, or you can enlarge the 4″ × 6″ document by adjusting the size of its canvas.

The **Canvas Size** command is most often used to create more usable space in an image by expanding its borders. With this command, you can specify a new size for the canvas and to which side of the image the additional, empty canvas will be added. Unlike the **Image Size** command, this command does not resize the contents of the image, only the space that the image occupies.

> **Note** Making an image *smaller* using the **Canvas Size** command is the same as cropping the image. It is a little easier to use the **Crop Tool** to make the canvas size smaller.

The canvas size can be made larger or smaller by choosing **Image > Canvas Size…**. This opens the **Canvas Size** dialog box, Figure 6-31. The current size of the image is displayed in the top section of the dialog box. Enter the desired size for the canvas in the **Width:** and **Height:** text boxes in the **New Size** section. Be sure to select the proper units from the drop-down lists next to these text boxes.

The **Relative** check box provides you with an alternative way to enter the desired increase in canvas size. When this check box is checked, you use the **Width:** and **Height:** text boxes to enter the amount of canvas that you want to *add* rather than the desired *overall size* of the canvas.

You also need to tell Photoshop what direction to expand the canvas. This is done by clicking the squares in the **Anchor:** section until the arrows display the desired direction(s) of expansion.

The last thing Photoshop asks for is what *color* the new canvas extension should be. Select a color from the **Canvas extension color:** drop-down list or click the color box next to select a color in the **Color Picker**. This option is only available if the image has a Background layer.

You can rotate the canvas clockwise or counterclockwise. You can also flip the canvas horizontally or vertically. The commands for these actions are found under the **Image > Rotate Canvas…** submenu and should be self-explanatory.

Filters

Filters are special effects. There are so many of them that Photoshop devoted an entire menu to filters. Some filters are similar to layer styles, and others are much more complicated. A filter can be applied to an entire image or a selected area. More than one filter can be used on the same area, or the same filter can be used more than once.

Figure 6-31.
Increasing the canvas size of an image requires entering larger dimensions, specifying an anchor point, and choosing a color for the new space. **A**—The original file is 4″ × 4″. **B**—The result of changing the canvas size to 5″ × 5″ with the anchor point in the upper left corner is shown here.

Activate this check box if you want to specify how much canvas to add rather than a new overall size for the canvas

Current size of the canvas

The additional canvas will be added to the right and bottom edges of the image

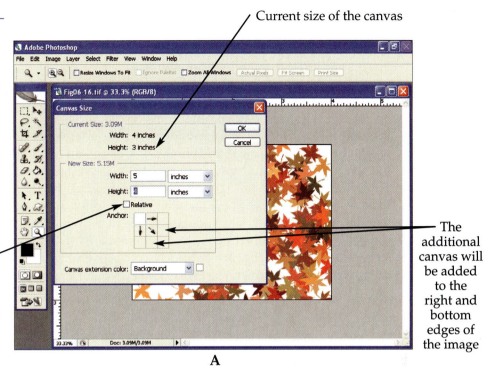

A

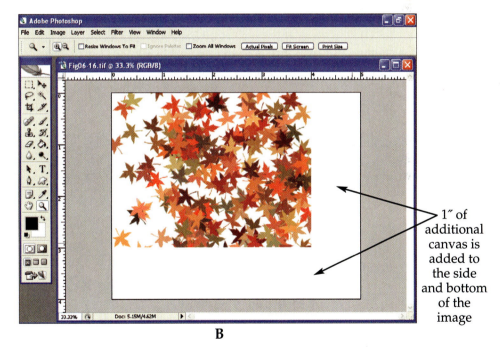

1″ of additional canvas is added to the side and bottom of the image

B

The Filter Menu

The **Filter** menu is used to apply a filter. The very first item displayed in the **Filter** menu is the last filter that was used (in case you want to apply it a second time). If you choose this filter (instead of choosing the filter from its original category), the same filter settings entered previously will be applied to your image again—you *will not* have the opportunity to adjust the settings.

The second section of the **Filter** menu lists some highly complicated filters which will be discussed near the end of this chapter. It also contains a command to open the **Filter Gallery**, which is also discussed later in the chapter.

The third section of the menu lists filters by category. The **Artistic**, **Brush Strokes**, and **Sketch** filter categories imitate traditional art practices. The **Video** category contains a filter that adjusts images for use in video (**NTSC Colors**) and a filter that corrects images captured from video (**De-Interlace**).

All of the other filter categories contain an incredible variety of special effects and image-tweaking power. There are thousands of different textures and patterns that can be created with different combinations of filters. There are many free tutorials on the Internet that will show you how to use filters in creative ways. For beginners, a good way to become acquainted with filters is to try them out, one by one. You will be asked to try out each filter and save your results in the tutorial section of this chapter.

What happens when you select a filter depends on the filter that is selected. If the filter is very basic, like the **Blur** filter, it is applied immediately, without any further user input. Some filters with adjustable settings open a dialog box containing the filter controls. This is usually the case for filters that are relatively simple (such as the **Unsharp Mask** filter) or filters that are relatively complex (such as the **Lighting Effects** filter). All other types of filters open the **Filter Gallery** when they are selected.

The Filter Gallery

When certain types of filters are selected, the **Filter Gallery** appears, Figure 6-32. In order to display the **Filter Gallery** correctly, the display resolution of your computer must be set to 1024 × 768 or higher.

If you click the small double arrow button to the left of the **OK** button, the **Filter Gallery** displays some of the available filters. All of the filters in the **Artistic** category appear in the **Filter Gallery**'s filter list, but this is not true for some of the other filter categories. Some filters are too complex or too simple to be displayed in the **Filter Gallery**. Be aware that the **Filter** menu is the only place you will see all of the filters.

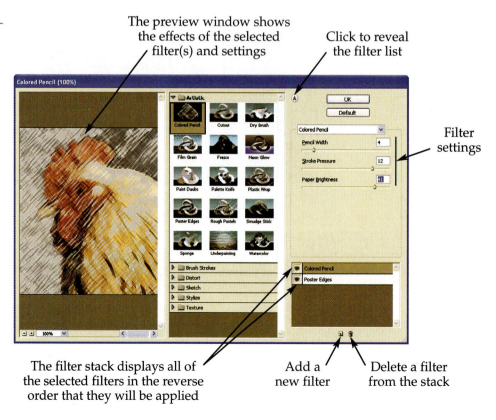

Figure 6-32.
The **Filter Gallery** displays many, but not all, of Photoshop's filters.

The filter list in the **Filter Gallery** shows thumbnail examples of what each filter does. When you choose a specific filter, its adjustable settings appear in the section at the right. For example, in Figure 6-32, the colored pencil filter's settings are displayed. This filter is designed to make a digital image look like it was created with colored pencils. You can control how fat the pencil strokes are (**Pencil Width**), how hard the pencils are pressed (**Stroke Pressure**), and whether the paper is black, gray, or white (**Paper Brightness**).

After adjusting the settings as desired, click **OK** to apply the filter. Filters are not automatically created on a new layer, so a safe habit is to always create a duplicate layer before applying a filter, leaving your original image untouched.

Assigning Multiple Filters in the Filter Gallery

If you want to add multiple filters in the **Filter Gallery** at the same time, click the **New effect layer** button instead of the **OK** button. This creates a copy of the currently selected filter and settings at the top of the filter stack. To change a filter into a different type of filter, simply select that filter in the filter stack and click the thumbnail of the desired filter in the filter list to the left. Make the necessary changes to the filter settings and observe the results in the preview window. At this point you can adjust the filter stacking order, click **OK** to accept the filters as they are, or add yet another filter.

The order that the filters appear in the filter stack influences the effect produced by the filter combination. To change the order of filters in the stack, simply click and drag them above or below each other as you learned to do with layers in the **Layers** palette. The filters are applied in order, beginning with the filter at the bottom of the stack and working upward. To remove a filter from the stack, simply select it and click the **Delete effect layer** button. When the combined filter effect is the way you want it, click the **OK** button to apply the filters to the image.

The Liquify Filter

The **Liquify** filter is complex enough to be a separate item in the second section of the **Filter** menu. This filter has several bizarre tools that let you manipulate pixels. The **Liquify** filter is often used for humorous purposes, such as modifying someone's face, but you can also use this filter to make subtle, precise adjustments to images. This filter includes tools that are used to mask (protect) areas of your image to ensure accuracy.

The Liquify Filter Tools

At the left side of the **Liquify** dialog box, is a collection of new tools, **Figure 6-33**. They are briefly described here, in order from top to bottom:

- The **Forward Warp Tool** is used to grab pixels and push them to another location.
- The **Reconstruct Tool** changes the image back to its original state. If necessary, use this tool as an "eraser."
- The **Twirl Clockwise Tool** twists pixels in a clockwise direction as you press the mouse button (hold down the [Alt] or [Option] key for counterclockwise).
- The **Pucker Tool** causes an area of pixels to appear to shrink as you press the mouse button. The effect decreases in intensity from the center of the brush out to its edges.
- The **Bloat Tool** causes an area of pixels to look larger as you press the mouse button. Again, the effect decreases in intensity from the center of the brush outward.

Figure 6-33.

The **Liquify** filter allows you to easily apply a variety of distortions to selected portions of your image while leaving the rest unaffected. **A**—The original portrait is shown here. **B**—The nose and lip areas have been manipulated with the **Liquify** filter's **Bloat Tool**. **C**—The nose, lips, and eyes have been modified with the **Pucker Tool**.

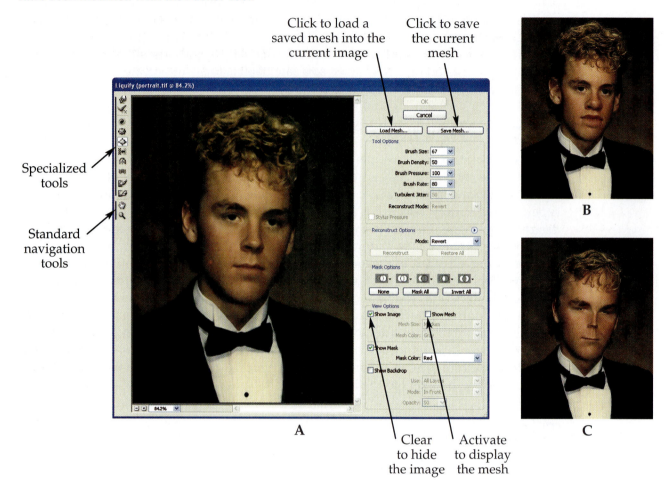

- The **Push Left Tool** stretches and moves an area to the left, creating a stretched look (hold down the [Alt] or [Option] key to push pixels the opposite direction).
- The **Mirror Tool** creates a reflection. If you drag from bottom to top, it reflects whatever is at the left of the brush. If you drag from top to bottom, it reflects whatever is at the right of the brush. A similar situation occurs when dragging horizontally—the direction you drag determines whether the area above or below the brush will be reflected.
- The **Turbulence Tool,** when applied in short strokes, is similar to the **Forward Warp** tool, but the outcome is not quite as smeared. When the tool is applied by clicking and holding over one area in the image, the tool creates a bubbling effect in the mesh, and, with prolonged use, can even tear the mesh, resulting in a hole (transparent area) in the image.
- Use the **Freeze Mask Tool** to paint a protective mask over any areas that you do not want to be affected by the various tools.
- The **Thaw Mask Tool** removes any protective masking created by the **Freeze Mask Tool**.
- Last, the **Hand Tool** and **Zoom Tool** allow you to magnify and navigate around your image as you work.

The Mesh

A *mesh* is a grid that helps you see how the image was changed with the **Liquify Filter** tools. You can view the changes you made to your file as a mesh by placing a check mark in the **Show Mesh** check box in the **View Options** section of the dialog box. You can hide the actual image by removing the check mark in the **Show Image** check box. This gives you a better view of the mesh, which is helpful in some situations. The size of the mesh can be adjusted by choosing one of the options in the **Mesh Size:** drop-down list, and you can change the color by selecting a new color from the **Mesh Color:** drop-down list.

You can also save a mesh as a file and load it later, when another image is open in the **Liquify** dialog box. In other words, you can apply saved **Liquify** filter tool effects to another image. This is done using the **Load Mesh...** and **Save Mesh...** buttons at the top of the dialog box.

Liquify Tool Options

The **Tool Options** section of the **Liquify** dialog box contains adjustable controls for the **Liquify** filter tools. Certain settings may be grayed out depending on the tool that is selected. You can use the **Brush Size:** slider to change the size of the area affected by each stroke or click of the **Liquify** filter tool. The **Brush Density:** slider controls how "thick" the brush is (similar to controlling the softness of the edges of a brush), and the **Brush Pressure:** slider controls how intensely the brush effect is applied. The **Brush Rate:** slider is available only for tools that are applied repeatedly when the mouse button is held. This setting determines the rate at which the tool application is repeated. The **Turbulent Jitter:** slider setting determines the degree of uniformity in the distortions created in the mesh by the **Turbulence Tool**. The **Reconstruct Mode:** drop-down list contains several options for the way the **Reconstruct Tool** is applied to the mesh. The **Revert** option restores the mesh to its original shape and position. The remaining options in the drop-down list restore the mesh, but use different methods to do it.

Reconstruct Options

The options available in the **Mode:** drop-down list from this section of the dialog box are nearly identical to the options in the **Reconstruct Mode** drop-down list in the **Tool Options** section. However, instead of adjusting the effect of the **Reconstruct Tool**, these settings are applied to the entire image.

After selecting the desired reconstruction mode from the drop-down list, you can click the **Reconstruct** button to apply the selected reconstruction mode to the entire image. You can also choose to click the **Restore All** button, which removes all of the distortions in the image, regardless of the reconstruction mode selected from the drop-down list.

Mask Options

The controls in the **Mask Options** section are available if you have already selected or masked the image before using the **Liquify** filter. You can then use the **Freeze Mask Tool**, **Thaw Mask Tool**, and **Mask Options** settings to further adjust the mask or selection.

> **Note** Masking is discussed in the Chapter 11, *Additional Layer Techniques.*

View Options

The final section of the **Liquify** dialog box is the **View Options** section. As previously discussed, this section has controls for displaying and adjusting the appearance of the mesh and for turning on and off the display of the image. It also contains controls for displaying and adjusting the appearance of any masks. When the **Show Mask** option is active, the mesh is displayed as a semitransparent color over the selected portions of the image. The color of the mask can be changed by selecting a new mask from the **Mask Color:** drop-down list.

When the **Show Backdrop** option is active, the original image (or only one layer from it) is displayed in the preview window of the dialog box. This backdrop allows you to see at a glance how the altered image differs from the original, or can be used as a visual aid when trying to adjust one layer of the image to match another.

You can select the layer(s) to display as a backdrop from the **Use:** drop-down list. The option chosen in the **Mode:** drop-down list determines whether the backdrop is displayed in front of the layer being modified or behind it. The **Opacity:** slider sets the level of transparency for the layer in front, regardless of whether that layer is the backdrop or the layer being modified.

The Pattern Maker Filter

This filter generates a pattern from an area of an image that you select. Some video game designers use this tool to create a pattern that can be applied to a 3D model. Some examples would be creating a grass or dirt pattern that could be applied to a planar surface representing the ground, or a brick pattern that could be assigned to a box representing a wall. You can create a pattern, save it in the **Pattern Picker,** and use the **Pattern Stamp Tool** to paint it. Or, you can apply it to a layer or selected area using the **Edit > Fill...** command.

Ideally, a pattern needs to be *tileable*, which means that it is able to blend together seamlessly when placed edge to edge. When a video game designer applies a grass pattern to a 3D environment, it is really a small grass pattern that repeats over and over and blends into itself. This uses far less computer memory than assigning one large non-repeating image, which, in turn, makes the game run more efficiently. The **Pattern Maker** filter is designed to create seamless patterns.

> **Note** To properly display the **Pattern Maker** dialog box, your computer must have the display resolution set to 1024 × 768 or higher.

To use the **Pattern Maker** filter, open an image that has interesting texture. *Duplicate the layer* you will be creating a pattern from, because the pattern will replace the layer's previous material. Choose **Filter > Pattern Maker....** The **Rectangular Marquee Tool** becomes active automatically. Select an area of your image, adjust the settings as explained in the following paragraphs, and click the **Generate** button. See **Figure 6-34**. You can click the **Generate Again** button multiple times until you get a result you like. Each time you click the **Generate Again** button, your image is sliced up and reassembled a different way.

The Tile Generation Settings

The settings in the **Tile Generation** section are used to specify how large the pattern will be. Smaller **Width:** and **Height:** settings conserve computer memory, but lack the

Figure 6-34.
The **Pattern Maker** filter creates seamless patterns that can be saved into the **Pattern Picker**. **A**—A portion of the image is selected, from which the pattern is created. **B**—A tileable pattern is created from the selected portion of the image.

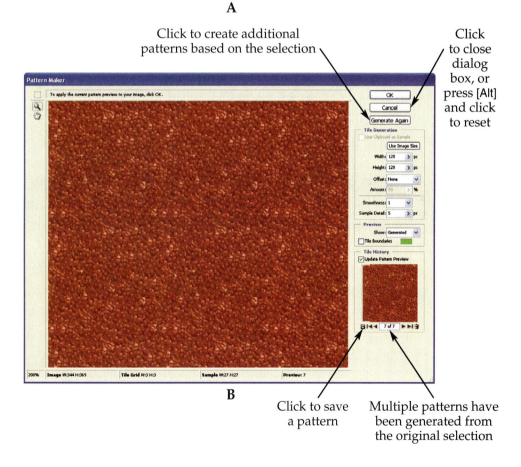

detail that larger patterns can exhibit. To start using this filter, try settings of 256 px × 256 px. Square patterns are most common.

The **Offset:** setting lets you create a tiled pattern that does not line up seamlessly. The individual tiles can be offset horizontally or vertically. The **Amount:** setting controls the degree to which the tiles are offset. For example, entering 50% on the **Amount:** slider causes each row of tiles to be offset half the distance of a tile from the rows preceding and following it.

The **Smoothness:** setting determines how well Photoshop blends any edges that may appear in the pattern. The **Sample Detail:** setting, when increased, causes Photoshop to create larger slices when rearranging the image. This usually causes the pattern to more accurately reflect details in the original image.

The Preview Settings

You can adjust the preview window display using the controls in the **Preview Settings** section of the dialog box. In the **Show:** drop-down list, you can choose what to display in the preview window. If you choose **Original**, the original image from which the pattern was generated appears in the preview window. If you choose **Generated**, the pattern appears in the window and is tiled, if possible. If you selected the **Generated** option, the **Tile Boundaries** check box is available. Activating this option lets you see how large each tile is (it matches the settings entered in the **Width:** and **Height:** boxes). You can change the color of the tile boundaries by clicking the color box to the right of the **Tile Boundaries** check box and selecting a different color in the **Color Picker**.

The Tile History Controls

Use the forward and backward buttons in the **Tile History** section to scroll through all of the patterns you generate. The thumbnail image above the forward and backward button changes as you scroll through the patterns. If the **Update Pattern Preview** check box is checked, the preview window is updated along with the thumbnail image.

You can save a pattern by clicking the **Save Preset Pattern** (floppy disk) button at the bottom of this section. In the **Pattern Name** dialog box, name the pattern and click **OK**. After saving the pattern, you will find it in the **Pattern Picker** when you use the **Pattern Stamp Tool** or the **Edit > Fill...** command and select **Pattern** in the **Use:** drop-down list.

The pattern created in Figure 6-34 looks seamless when it is tiled (placed side by side) over a large area. See **Figure 6-35**.

Figure 6-35.
The tileable (seamless) pattern created from the rooster's face has been used to fill the background layer of a new file.

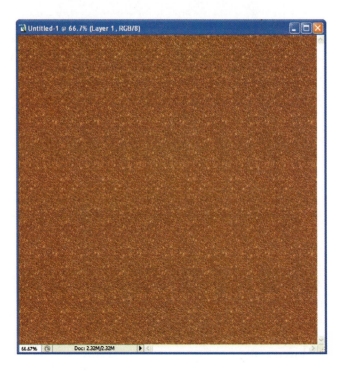

Other Filters in the Filter Menu

The **Extract** filter is a tool that removes unwanted pixels from an image. It will be explained in Chapter 7, *Erasing, Deleting, and Undoing*.

The **Vanishing Point** filter is a powerful feature that helps you edit images in almost a 3-dimensional manner. It will be explained in Chapter 8, *Restoring and Retouching Photos*.

GRAPHIC DESIGN:
Focal Point and Visual Hierarchy

Usually, one part of a graphic design is dominant. It is the center of interest; the part of the design that the viewer's eye is attracted to the most. Occasionally, a design may use repetitive patterns instead of a single focal point. Then, the entire design attracts the attention of the viewer.

The greater the emphasis, or *visual weight*, placed on part of a design, the more the viewer will notice it. The most obvious way to give more visual weight to a design element is to make it larger than the other design elements. Here are some other tips for creating more visual weight to a design element:

- Use vivid colors that contrast with the background.
- Add a special effect such as a shadow, highlight, or distortion to the subject.
- When working with text, make the text bolder or use appropriate decorative fonts.
- Rotate design elements so they are not perfectly horizontal or vertical.
- Position other design elements to effectively contrast with the element that is the focal point.

The focal point of the poster in **Figure 6-36** is the "Farmer's Market" text. It carries more visual weight than any other design element on the poster. The text is white, a color that contrasts well with the background. A drop shadow

Figure 6-36. _____
The Farmer's Market poster (actual size 11" × 17") can easily be read from several feet away because of the visual weight assigned to the text.

and a black border (stroke) were also added to help the text "jump out" at the reader. Notice that the text is sans serif – creating easily-read headlines.

After the reader's eye jumps to the focal point of the design, elements of the design should be organized in such a way that the reader does not have to search for important information. The designer should assign a visual weight to the next important item in the design. A *visual hierarchy* is the order in which design elements are presented from the greatest amount of visual weight to the least.

Designers can use color, size, and the position of objects to create a visual hierarchy. For example, lighter and duller colors carry less visual weight than bright, vivid colors. It is also important to not crowd design elements together. Some white space (empty space) is needed to make absorbing the information easy.

Imagine driving along a freeway and seeing the billboard shown in **Figure 6-37**. Most people would agree that the focal point of this design is the large ostrich—it is a huge, unusual image. The "Ostrichville" title text is the next item in the visual hierarchy. Its size, color, and special effects give it almost as much visual weight as the large ostrich image. Next, the readers eye would flow to the bold text that reads "1,000 Acre Ostrich Ranch." The text that informs drivers how to get to the ranch is also bold, and could be considered next on the list in the hierarchy. The repetitive pattern of ostriches adds interest to the entire design. Some viewers might regard it as a decorative border of the billboard; others might see all of the ostriches as a group (including the large ostrich).

Figure 6-37.
This billboard demonstrates a visual hierarchy scheme.

Summary

When you have a few extra minutes, take a close look at all of the brushes in the **Brushes** palette. You will need to choose a brush shape and size when using many of Photoshop's tools. Knowing what brushes are available can save you time—by choosing just the right tool shape for a quick, easy edit.

Filters can adjust images in amazing ways. Some filters can help clean up problem photographs. Others can be used in combination to create interesting textures and patterns from scratch. Photoshop users have discovered (and continue to discover) a vast amount of filter techniques. These techniques are shared on the Internet as Photoshop tutorials or found in more advanced books or Photography, Graphic Design, and Digital Imaging magazines.

Chapter Tutorials

You will try a couple of painting methods in these tutorials. You will be asked to try out each filter and save your results into a folder. You will also use painting tools and filters to make further modifications to projects you have already begun in previous chapters.

Tutorial 6-1 Coloring a Photo with the Brush Tool

In this tutorial, you will use the **Brush Tool** with the **Hue** blending mode to change the color of a selected part of an image. This technique is useful for calling attention to one element within an image.

Magnetic Lasso Tool

Lasso Tool

Add to selection

Subtract from selection

Brush Tool

1. Open the peppers.jpg file.
2. Choose **Layer > Duplicate Layer....** Name the new layer Paint.

   You will paint this layer and leave the original layer untouched, in case you need to start over.

3. Select the bottom center pepper, but not its stem. See **Figure T6-1**.

   To select the pepper, zoom in far enough so you can use the selection tools easily. Use the **Magnetic Lasso Tool** to start. Then, switch to the **Lasso Tool** with the **Feather:** option set to 0. Use the **Add to selection** and **Subtract from selection** buttons to fine-tune your selection border.

4. Click the **Brush Tool** in the **Toolbox**.
5. Enter the following settings in the options bar:
   - In the **Brush Preset Picker**, set the **Master Diameter:** to 45 pixels and **Hardness:** to 0%.
   - Select **Hue** in the **Mode:** drop-down list.
   - Set the **Opacity:** slider to 100%.

Figure T6-1. Select the pepper, but not the stem.

6. Click the **Set foreground color** button in the **Toolbox** and select any bright color except for red, yellow, or orange.

   Since orange is already the color of the pepper, and red and yellow are its component colors, you should not select these colors because they will produce less predictable results.

7. Without releasing the mouse button, paint the pepper.

   If you release the mouse button before you finish painting, the brush strokes will overlap and appear too dark.

8. Choose **File > Save As...** and name the file 06peppers.psd.
9. Close 06peppers.psd. You will make other changes to this file later.

Tutorial 6-2: Turn a Photo into a Painting

In this tutorial, you will use the **Find Edges** filter to essentially trace an image, and then use the **Brush Tool** to apply paint to the image. You can use this technique to quickly create a "hand-painted" design from a photo.

1. Open the Buster.jpg file.
2. Choose **Layer > Duplicate Layer...**. Accept the default layer name in the **Duplicate Layer** dialog box.
3. Choose **Filter > Stylize > Find Edges**.
4. Choose **Image > Adjustments > Desaturate**.

   Desaturate means to remove the color. See **Figure T6-2**.

5. Choose **Layer > New > Layer...**.
6. Name the new layer Paint and click **OK**.
7. Use the **Brush Tool** to paint new colors over Buster. Experiment with different brush styles and sizes.

Eraser Tool

   Because you will be painting on a separate layer, you can use the **Eraser Tool** to erase paint that goes outside of the lines. You can also use the **Edit > Undo** and **Edit > Step Backward** commands.

8. Choose **File > Save As...** and name the file 06Buster.psd.
9. Close 06Buster.psd.

Figure T6-2.
The **Find Edges** filter has been applied and the image has been desaturated.

Tutorial 6-3: The Paint Bucket and Gradient Tools

In this tutorial, you will use the **Paint Bucket Tool** to add a solid fill of the foreground color to a selected area. You will then add a gradient from foreground color to transparency to create a glow effect around the filled area.

1. Open the 04leafy.psd file that you created in a previous chapter.
2. In the **Layers** palette, click the Background layer to make it active.

Elliptical Marquee Tool

3. Click the **Elliptical Marquee Tool**.
4. Create a selection border around the "sunshine" shape, as shown in **Figure T6-3**.

   Remember to hold [Shift] to create a circle instead of an ellipse and [Alt] to create the circle from the center outward.

5. Click on the **Swatches** palette tab and click on the yellow-colored box in the top row.

   Notice that the foreground color is now yellow.

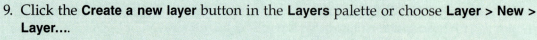

6. Click the **Paint Bucket Tool** in the **Toolbox**.
7. Click inside the selected area to dump yellow on the background layer.
8. In the **Layers** palette, click on the layer at the very top of the stack to make it active.
9. Click the **Create a new layer** button in the **Layers** palette or choose **Layer > New > Layer...**.
10. Name the new layer gradient.
11. Select the **Ellipse Marquee Tool** in the **Toolbox**.
12. Click and release anywhere in the image to clear the previous selection.
13. Select the **Gradient Tool** in the **Toolbox**.
14. In the options bar, click the small down-arrow to open the **Gradient Picker**.
15. In the **Gradient Picker**, pick the small arrow button to open the **Gradient Picker** menu. Select **Reset Gradients...** from the menu, and click **OK** in the dialog box that appears. See **Figure T6-4**.

Figure T6-3. Create a circular selection that encompasses the star shape in the center of the design.

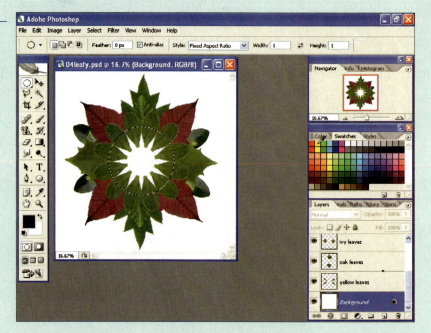

Figure T6-4.
Reset the gradients to their default settings.

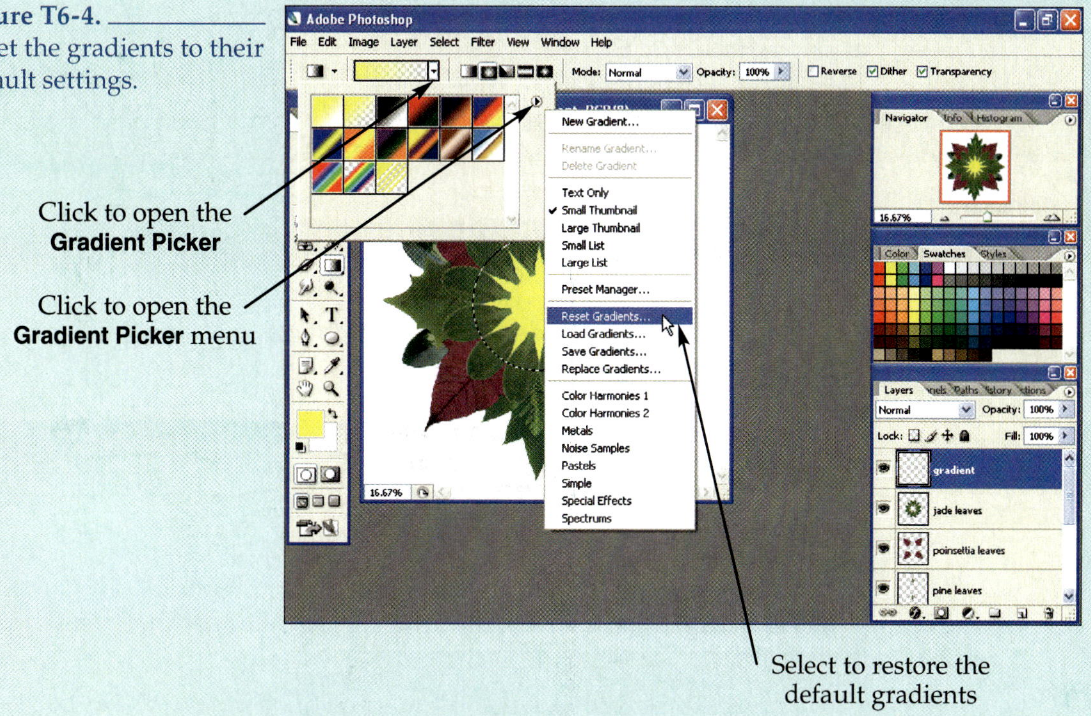

Click to open the **Gradient Picker**

Click to open the **Gradient Picker** menu

Select to restore the default gradients

Radial Gradient

16. Choose the second gradient, which is always the foreground color (in this case, yellow) and transparency.
17. In the options bar, click the **Radial Gradient** button.
18. Starting in the center of the leafy design, drag a line as shown to add a sunglow effect. See **Figure T6-5**.
19. Choose **File > Save As...** and name this file 06leafy.psd. Close the file when you are done.

Figure T6-5.
Apply the radial gradient to the center of the arrangement by dragging a line from the center of the design to a point halfway up one of the jade leaves.

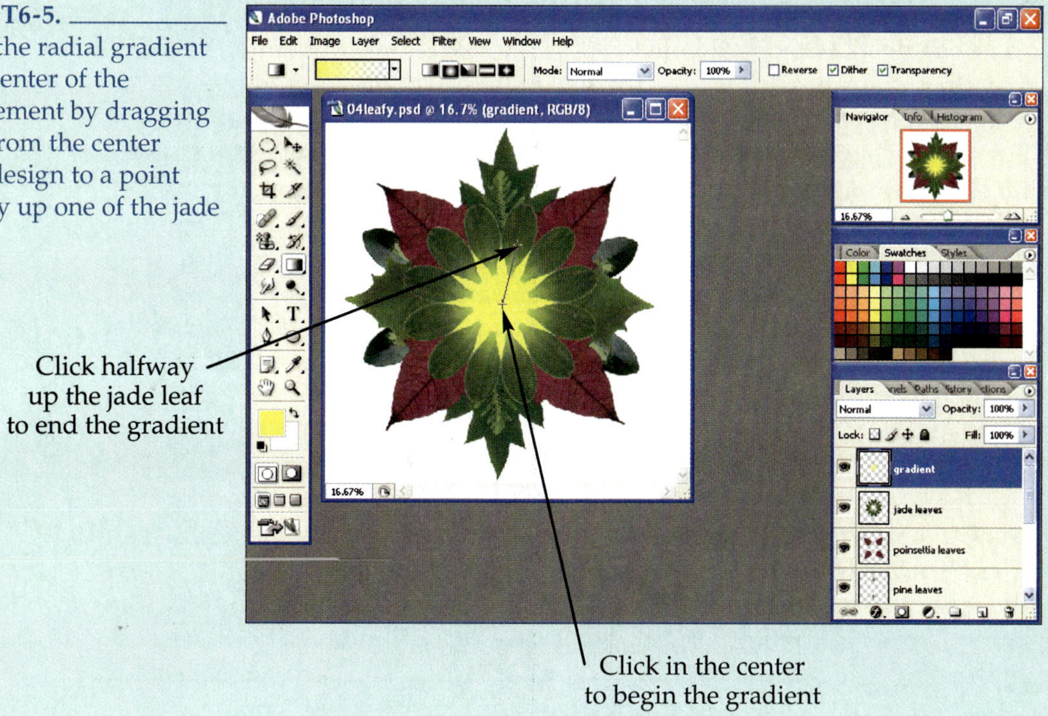

Click halfway up the jade leaf to end the gradient

Click in the center to begin the gradient

Tutorial 6-4: Exploring Filters and Styles

In this tutorial, you will be asked to save almost 100 small files. In the process, you will discover the power and flexibility of Photoshop's filters and styles. The effects produced by these tools are so widely varied that the only way to familiarize yourself with them is through hands-on experience.

Part 1: Filters

Photoshop's filters can be used to add a variety of effects to an image. The effects range from very subtle color changes to absurd distortions of the image.

1. Create a new folder named **Filters** and save each file in this new folder.
2. Open the file named Buster.jpg.
3. If the grid is showing, turn it off by choosing **View > Show > Grid**.
4. Choose **Window > Workspace > Reset Palette Locations**.
5. Choose **Filter > Artistic > Colored Pencil…**.
6. Experiment with the filter settings. Once you have the filter settings the way you want them, click **OK**.

   Choose settings that do not "destroy" the original photo. Your settings should make Buster look like he was drawn with colored pencils. See **Figure T6-6**.

7. Choose **File > Save As…**.
8. Name this file Colored Pencil.jpg, make sure it will be saved in the **Filters** folder you created, and click **Save**.
9. In the **JPEG Options** dialog box, click **OK** to accept the default settings.
10. Choose **Edit > Step Backward** to remove the colored pencil filter.
11. Choose **Filter > Artistic > Cutout…**.
12. Experiment with the filter settings and click **OK**.
13. Choose **File > Save As…** and name the file Cutout.jpg.
14. In the **JPEG Options** dialog box, click **OK** to accept the default settings.

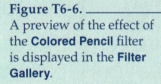

Figure T6-6. A preview of the effect of the **Colored Pencil** filter is displayed in the **Filter Gallery**.

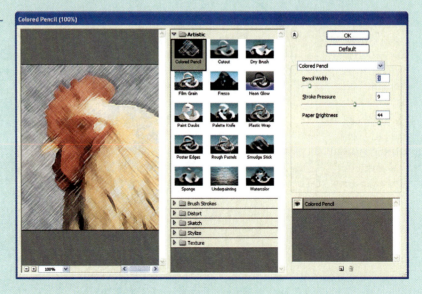

15. Try out the rest of the filters in the **Artistic** category in the same way. As you experiment with the filters, keep the following things in mind:
    - Save each file as you did in steps 7–9, using the filter name as the name of the file.
    - Change the foreground color to get different results with the **Neon Glow** filter.
16. When you have tried all of the filters in the **Artistic** category, choose **Filter > Blur > Blur More**.

    Skip the first two filters in the Blur category.

17. Experiment with each of the blur filters and save each result.
18. Continue experimenting with filters until you have tried all of the filters (except for those you are instructed to skip) in all categories and saved your results.

    The following are some special instructions to follow as you experiment with the filters:
    - Skip the **Video** category.
    - Skip the **Sharpen** category. You will learn more about the sharpen filters in Chapter 8, *Restoring and Retouching Photos*.
    - The **Stained Glass** filter and most of the filters in the **Sketch** category make use of the foreground color, so experiment with different foreground colors.
    - The **Neon Glow**, **Clouds** and **Fibers** filters use both the foreground and background colors, so experiment with different foreground and background color combinations.

    After experimenting with the filters, you should have almost 100 files saved in your Filters folder. There are several more files you will create and save to this folder.

Magic Wand Tool

19. Close all files on your screen and open the original Buster.jpg file again.
20. Use the **Magic Wand Tool** to select the sky behind Buster.
21. Choose **Filter > Texture > Texturizer**.
22. Select **Burlap** from the **Texture:** drop-down list. Set the **Scaling** slider to 115% and the **Relief:** slider to 5. Click **OK**.

    The filter is applied to the selected area. See **Figure T6-7**.

23. Choose **File > Save As…**. Name the file Buster with burlap.jpg and save it in the Filters folder.
24. Close Buster with burlap.jpg file.

Figure T6-7.
The **Texturizer** filter has been applied to the sky.

Part 2: Styles

Some of Photoshop's styles work very well with image files. Some of these styles are similar to some of the filters you have used.

1. Open the original Buster.jpg file again.
2. Click the **Styles** palette tab.
3. Open the **Styles** palette menu and choose **Photographic Effects**.
4. Click **OK** in the dialog box that appears to replace the styles in the palette.
5. Open the **Styles** palette menu again and choose **Image Effects**.
6. In the dialog box that appears, click the **Append** button to add the **Image Effects** styles to the palette without deleting the **Photographic Effects** styles.
7. Open the **Styles** palette menu and choose **Small List**.

   This changes the style list from a thumbnail display to a list of names with tiny thumbnails.

8. Click on one of the styles. Nothing happens because the layer is locked. See **Figure T6-8**.
9. Unlock the layer in the **Layers** palette by double-clicking the **Background** layer. In the **New Layer** dialog box, click **OK** to accept the default name for the layer.
10. Click each of the effects you have loaded into the **Styles** palette and save each result into the Filters folder. Use the style name as the file name.
11. When you have saved an image adjusted with each of the styles, open the **Styles** palette menu and choose **Reset Styles....** Click **OK** in the box that appears.

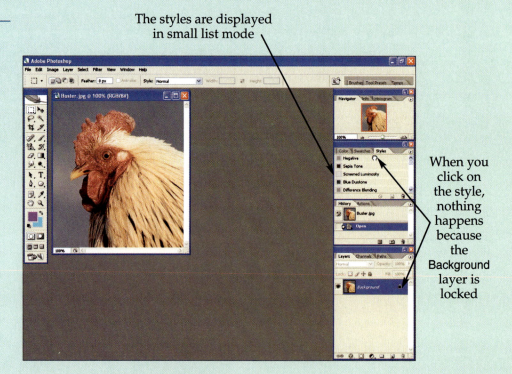

Figure T6-8.
The Background layer is locked, preventing the filter from being applied.

The styles are displayed in small list mode

When you click on the style, nothing happens because the Background layer is locked

Tutorial 6-5: Add a Filter and Layer Style to a Shape

Once a shape has been rasterized, you can apply a filter to it. In this tutorial, you will apply filters and layer styles to various shapes in a design.

1. Open the 05CDfront.psd file that you created previously.

   The layer containing the red donut shape should be active. You have already rasterized this layer in a previous tutorial. Because you have done this, you will be able to apply a filter to the layer.

2. Choose **Filter > Distort > Ripple...** and enter the following settings:
   - **Amount:** 600%
   - **Size:** Large

   These settings will cause the red donut shape to be highly distorted. See **Figure T6-9**.

3. Click **OK**.
4. Choose **Layer > Layer Style > Bevel and Emboss....**
5. In the **Layer Style** dialog box, set the **Depth:** slider to 120%, the **Size:** slider to 10 px, and click **OK**.

   The distorted red donut shape now appears to rise slightly from the background. See Figure T6-10.

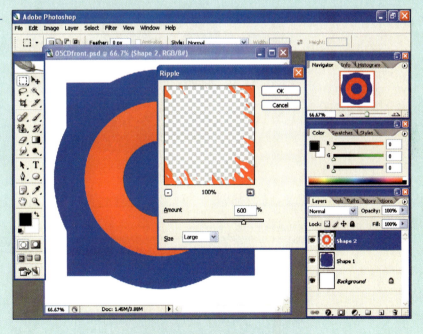

Figure T6-9.
A preview of the **Ripple** filter effect reveals that the filter will highly distort the shape.

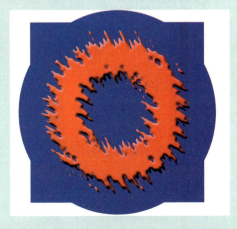

Figure T6-10.
The red donut shape appears distorted and raised up from the blue background.

6. On the **Layers** palette, click the layer containing the blue shape.
7. Choose **Filter > Distort > Ripple...** and enter the following settings:
   - **Amount:** 400%
   - **Size:** Medium
8. Add an inner bevel style to this layer by repeating steps 4 and 5.

   Your design should look like the example in **Figure T6-11**.

9. On the **Layers** palette, click the Background layer.
10. Reset the foreground and background colors to black and white.
11. Click the **Paint Bucket Tool** in the **Toolbox**.
12. Click anywhere in the image to fill the Background layer with black. See **Figure T6-12**.
13. Make the top layer active in the **Layers** palette.

    You are about to add text, and the new text layer will be created above the active layer.

14. Add the text shown in **Figure T6-13**. Use any style and font.

Figure T6-11. _____
After applying the **Ripple** filter and the **Bevel and Emboss** layer style to the blue shape, your design should look like this.

Figure T6-12. _____
With the Background layer active, click anywhere in the image to fill the background with black paint.

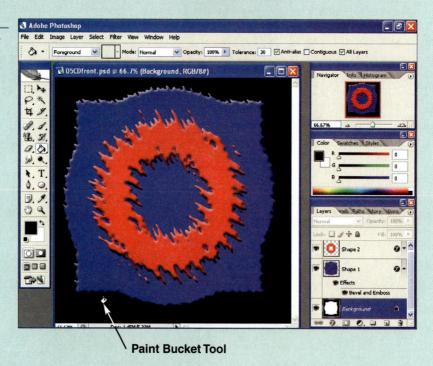

Paint Bucket Tool

Figure T6-13.
Text has been added to the design.

15. Choose **Layer > Flatten Image**.
16. Choose **File > Save As…** and name the file 06CDfront.psd.
17. If you are going to continue on to the next tutorial, leave the file open. If you are *not* going to continue on to the next tutorial, close the image.

You will sample colors from this image as you create the back insert for the CD jewel case in the next tutorial.

Tutorial 6-6: The Eyedropper and Gradient Tools

In this tutorial, you will define a gradient and apply it to a CD insert design. You will use the **Eyedropper Tool** to select colors from one image to use in creating a gradient in another image. This technique is useful for keeping color schemes consistent, visually tying together multiple documents.

1. Open the 06CDfront.psd file, if it is not already open.
2. Choose **File > New…** and enter the settings shown in **Figure T6-14**. Name the image 06CDback.
3. Move the new file window so you can see the 06CDfront.psd window behind it.
4. Click the **Eyedropper Tool**.
5. Click on the red shape at the location shown in **Figure T6-15**.

The **Eyedropper Tool** changes the foreground color to red.

6. Choose **View > Rulers**.

Figure T6-14.
Create a new file with the settings shown here and name it 06CDback.

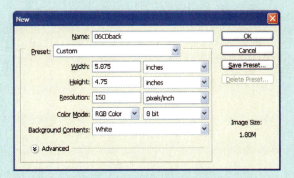

Figure T6-15.
Click on the red donut to set the foreground color.

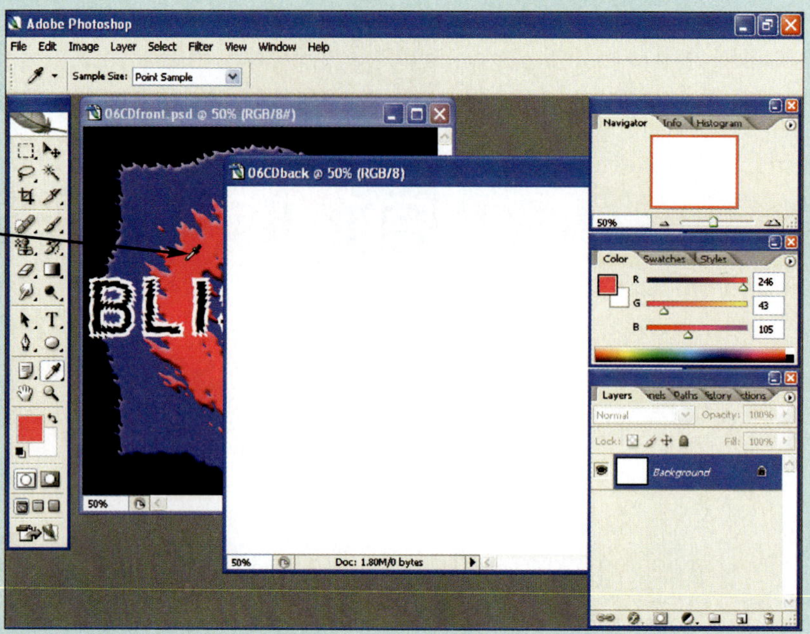

Click here to choose red as the foreground color

Rectangular Marquee Tool

7. Click the **Rectangular Marquee Tool**.
8. In the options bar, make sure that the **Feather:** option is set to 0 px.
9. Drag a rectangle starting 1/4" to the right of the upper left corner of the image and ending at the bottom left corner of the image. See **Figure T6-16**.
10. Use the **Paint Bucket Tool** to fill the rectangular selection with red.
11. Choose **Edit > Copy**.
12. Choose **Edit > Paste**.

Another red rectangle is pasted exactly on top of the first rectangle. Notice that a new layer was created automatically.

Figure T6-16.
Draw a rectangular selection as shown.

The selection should begin here...

...and end here

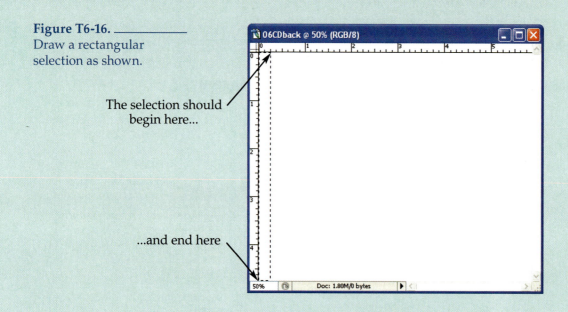

Chapter 6   Painting Tools and Filters   265

Move Tool

13. Click the **Move Tool** in the **Toolbox**, hold down [Shift], and use the arrow keys to move the second rectangle exactly into position.

    Holding [Shift] while you move the selection helps speed up the process. However, you will need to release [Shift] and use just the arrow keys to position the selection precisely at the other edge of the image. See **Figure T6-17**.

14. Choose **Layer > Flatten Image** to add the red rectangles to the Background layer.
15. Click the **Gradient Tool**, located behind the **Paint Bucket Tool** in the **Toolbox**.
16. Reposition the 06CDback image window as needed so that the 06CDfront.psd window is visible behind it.
17. In the options bar, click the down arrow to display the **Gradient Picker**.
18. Click the arrow that opens the **Gradient Picker** menu and choose **Color Harmonies I**. See **Figure T6-18**.
19. In the dialog box that appears, click **OK** to replace the gradients in the picker.

    If another dialog box asks you if you want to save changes to the current gradients, click **No**.

20. Click the first gradient listed in the picker.
21. Click the gradient in the options bar to display the **Gradient Editor**.

    When the **Gradient Editor** opens, the **Eyedropper Tool** is automatically selected.

22. Click the color stop at the far left end of the color slider. This color stop is light blue by default.
23. Click a portion of the black background in the 06CDfront.psd image to choose the black color. See **Figure T6-19**.
24. Click the next color stop.

Figure T6-17.
Move the copied rectangle to the right side of the image.

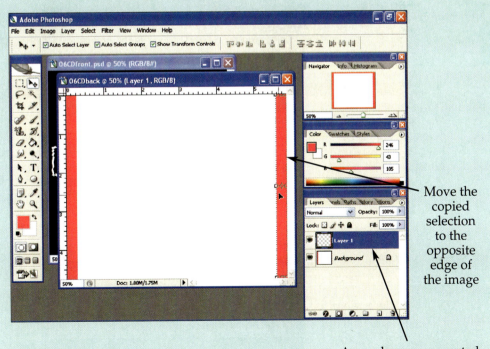

Move the copied selection to the opposite edge of the image

A new layer was created when the selection was pasted into the image

Figure T6-18. Load the Color Harmonies 1 group into the **Gradient Picker**.

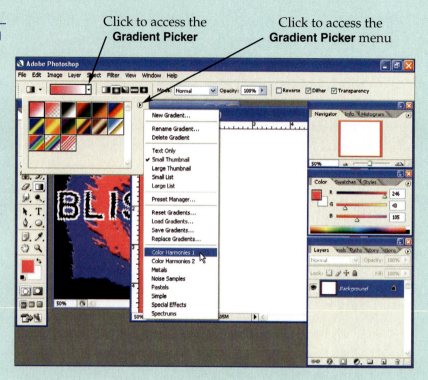

Figure T6-19. Click on a black portion of 06CDfront.psd.

Click the first color stop, and then click the background in 06CDfront.psd to select black

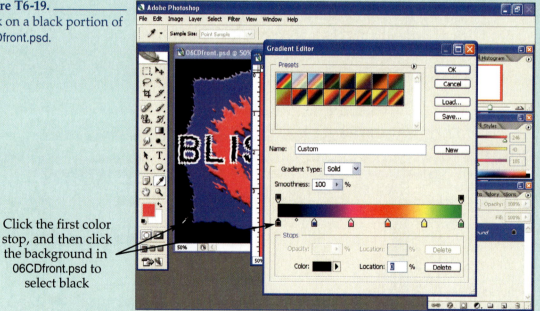

25. Click the blue area of the 06CDfront.psd image with the **Eyedropper Tool** cursor.
26. Continue changing the colors as shown in **Figure T6-20**. Use the **Eyedropper Tool** cursor to choose each color from the 06CDfront.psd image.
27. Add a color stop by clicking at the location shown in **Figure T6-21A**. Change its color to blue.
28. Drag the color stops until they are evenly spaced.

    Watch the value displayed in the **Location:** text box as you drag each color stop. The **Location:** values that will give you evenly spaced color stops is shown in **Figure T6-21B**.

Figure T6-20. Assign colors to the color stops.

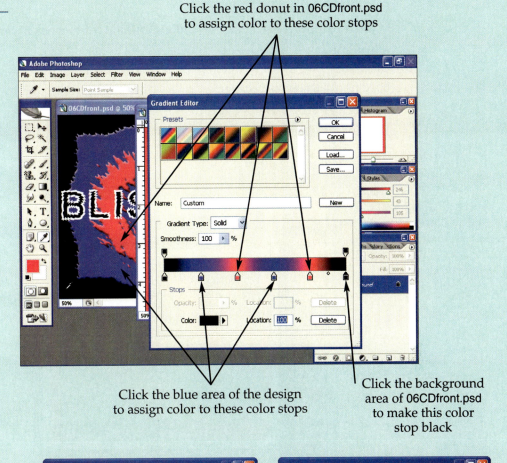

Figure T6-21. Add and adjust the color stops. **A**—A sixth color stop is added and made blue. **B**—These values in the **Location:** text boxes will produce evenly spaced color stops.

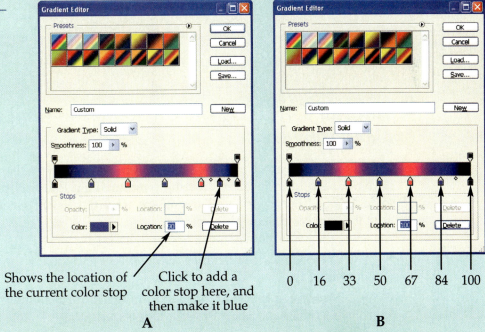

29. Click **OK** to accept the changes and close the **Gradient Editor**.
30. Reposition the 06CDback window so that it is not blocked by any other windows or palettes.
31. Use the **Magic Wand Tool** to select the white area between the red rectangles in the 06CDback image.

32. Click the **Gradient Tool**.
33. In the options bar, click the **Radial Gradient** button, select **Normal** in the **Mode:** drop-down list, and set the **Opacity:** slider to 90%.
34. Drag a line in the selected area, as shown in Figure T6-22.
35. Choose **Select > Deselect**.
36. Choose **View > Rulers** to hide the rulers.
37. Close and save the image as 06CDback.psd. You will add more to it later.

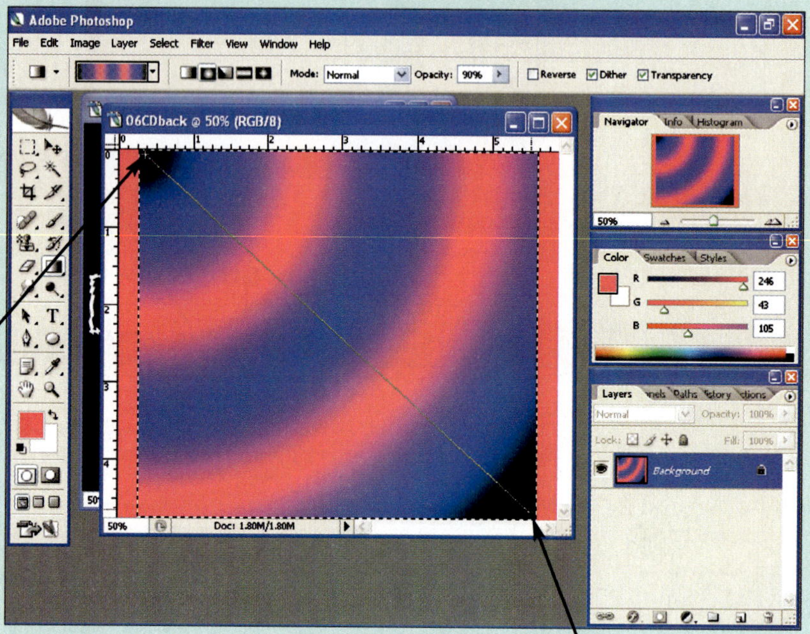

Figure T6-22. Add a gradient to the selected area. Drag the line from one corner of the area to the diagonally opposite corner.

The gradient line should begin here...

...and end here

Tutorial 6-7: Using the Clouds Filter (and Creating a Panorama)

A panorama is a large image made up of several smaller ones. Even though you have not been introduced to creating panoramas in Photoshop, you will find it is easy to do. In this tutorial, you will create a panoramic view of scenery and then fix the sky with the **Clouds** filter.

1. Find the folder named panorama and open it.
2. Click once on each of the files in this folder and look at the thumbnail image at the bottom of the **Open** dialog box. See Figure T6-23.
    - Mac users: If you do not see thumbnail images when you click on individual files, click the **Show Preview** toggle button.

   Can you tell that the photographer stood in one spot while capturing all of these images? Since the images are taken from a shared vantage point, Photoshop's **Photomerge** feature will automatically assemble all of these photos into one panoramic photo.

3. Choose **File > Automate > Photomerge...**.
4. In the **Photomerge** dialog box, click the **Browse...** button.

   This opens the **Open** dialog box.

Figure T6-23.
When a file is selected, a thumbnail is displayed at the bottom of the dialog box.

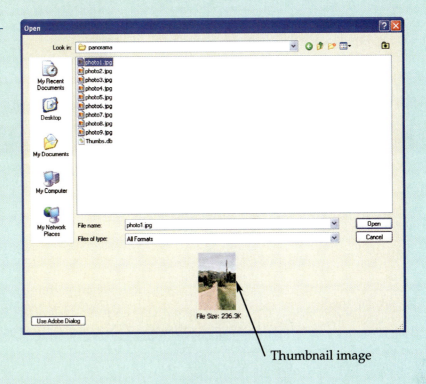

Thumbnail image

5. Once again locate the panorama folder. Highlight all of the files in this folder. You can do this by holding down [Ctrl] while you click on each file or by holding [Shift] and clicking the first and last files in the list.
   • Mac users: Hold down [Shift] as you click on each file.
6. Click the **Open** button. See **Figure T6-24**.
7. In the **Photomerge** dialog box, click **OK**. It may take more than a minute for your computer to complete this command.
8. Your panorama should look like **Figure T6-25**. If it does, skip to step 11. If it does not, continue with step 9.
9. If your panorama does not look right, click and drag each photo to the top of the dialog box, **Figure T6-26**.

Figure T6-24.
The files from the panorama file are loaded in the **Photomerge** dialog box.

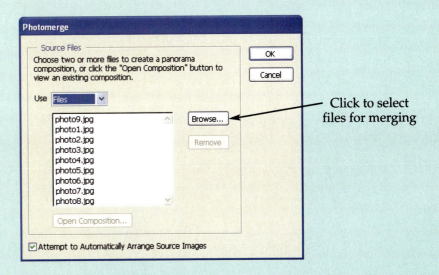

Click to select files for merging

Figure T6-25.
The nine images assembled into the panorama should look like this.

Figure T6-26.
The images making up the panorama can be moved to the top of the **Photomerge** dialog box and then reassembled in the proper order.

Drag each image to the top of the dialog box

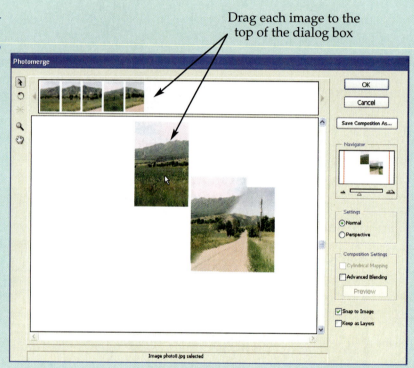

10. Drag the photos back down to the main window in the dialog box and put them together like a puzzle. Figure T6-25 shows how the panorama should look.

    You only need to get the images close to the correct position. Photoshop will automatically reposition the images so they are perfectly aligned.

11. Click **OK**.

    You may need to wait 1–2 minutes for your computer to create the final merged photo.

12. Your final image should look like **Figure T6-27**.

    The checkerboard pattern means no color is there—only transparent, empty space. Also, a common problem with panoramas is that some areas turn out too dark or too light. In Figure T6-25, you can see a line in the sky separating two areas with different brightness levels. This happens because the lighting angle was a bit different when each photo was taken.

Chapter 6   Painting Tools and Filters   271

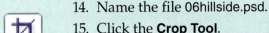
Crop Tool

13. Choose **File > Save**.
14. Name the file 06hillside.psd.
15. Click the **Crop Tool**.
16. With the **Crop Tool** selected, drag a box from point A to point B. See **Figure T6-28A**.
17. On the right side of the crop box you just created, grab the middle handle on the right edge and drag it to the right edge of the image, **Figure T6-28B**.
18. Grab the middle bottom handle and adjust the bottom of the crop box until it is flush with the bottom of the *actual image* on the right side. Grab the top left handle and drag it to the top left corner of the *image area*. Continue adjusting the crop box until it looks like **Figure T6-28C**.

The very bottom portion of the image area should be the only part that does not have the crop box around it.

Figure T6-27. _____
When Photoshop is done combining the nine images, the result should look like this. Note the transparent areas.

Transparent areas

Figure T6-28. _____
You will crop the image to eliminate the transparent area at the bottom.
A—Draw the crop box.
B—Stretch the crop box to the right side of the image.
C—Continue stretching the crop box until only the unwanted portion remains outside.

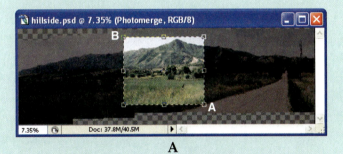
A

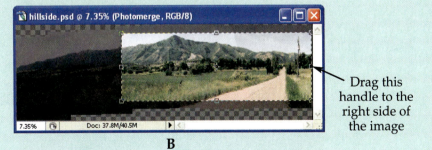
B

Drag this handle to the right side of the image

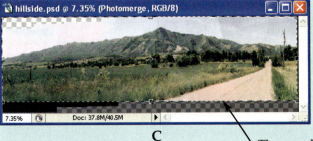
C

The crop box does not extend down to the lower portion of the image area

Commit

19. Click the **Commit** button in the options bar or press [Enter].

    The word "crop" means "to remove an unwanted portion." Everything that was inside the crop box stayed, and the rest of the file was removed.

20. Click the **Magic Wand Tool**.
21. In the options bar, set the **Tolerance:** to 20.
22. Click anywhere on the sky.
23. Click the **Add to Selection** button.
24. Continue clicking until all of the sky and the transparent (checkered pattern) areas are selected. See Figure T6-29.
25. In the **Toolbox**, click the **Set foreground color** button.
26. In the **Color Picker**, choose a very light blue color by adjusting the color slider and then picking a light blue color from the color field, Figure T6-30.
27. Click **OK**.
28. The background color box should already be white. If not, you can choose white by clicking on the background button in the **Toolbox** and then clicking the extreme upper left corner of the color field in **Color Picker** dialog box. See Figure T6-31.
29. Choose **Filter > Render > Clouds**.

    This command blends the blue and white colors into a cloud-like pattern.

30. Choose **Select > Deselect**.

    The selection border disappears.

31. Close and save the image as 06hillside.psd. You will add more to this file later.

Figure T6-29. _____
Select the entire sky with the **Magic Wand Tool**. You may need to zoom in and use the selection options.

Figure T6-30. _____
Select a very light blue in the **Color Picker**.

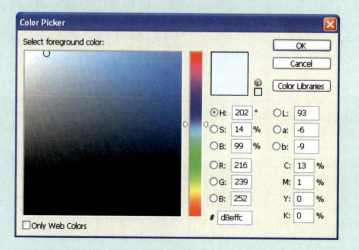

Figure T6-31.
You can select white by clicking the extreme upper right corner in the **Color Picker**, regardless of what color is selected in the color slider. When true white is selected, the **R:**, **G:**, and **B:** values will all be 255.

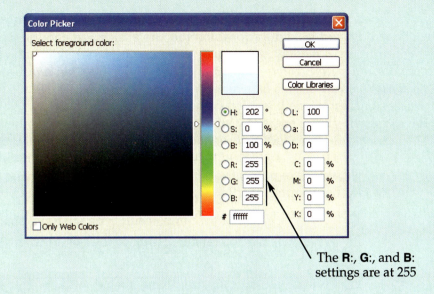

The **R:**, **G:**, and **B:** settings are at 255

Key Terms

brush marks
canvas
color stops
contiguous
filters
gradient
jitter
mesh
sample
steps
tileable
tiled
visual hierarchy
visual weight

Review Questions

Answer the following questions on a separate sheet of paper.

1. What is the easiest way to change the brush size as you are painting?
2. If you set the **Opacity:** of the **Brush Tool** under 100%, how will the paint appear?
3. When using an **Opacity:** setting of less than 100%, how can you avoid darkening areas where the paint overlaps itself?
4. What setting in the **Brush Preset Picker** controls how soft the edges of a brush are?
5. In the **Brush Preset Picker** and the **Brushes** palette, how do you restore the default brushes (the brushes that appear when Photoshop is first installed)?
6. Which blending mode only paints in transparent areas?
7. Which blending mode changes an object's color, but preserves shadows and highlights?
8. Briefly describe how the **Brushes** palette is different than the **Brush Preset Picker**.
9. What does "jitter" mean?
10. How do you reset all of the settings in the **Brushes** palette?
11. What are the five steps to follow when creating your own brush tip?
12. What is Photoshop's **Canvas Size** command used for?
13. What tool can you use to make a file's canvas size smaller?
14. When using the **Pattern Stamp Tool**, how can you create your own pattern?

15. What is the main difference between the **Pencil Tool** and the **Brush Tool**?
16. What is the difference between the **Point Sample** option and the **3 by 3 Average** option for the **Eyedropper Tool**?
17. What is a gradient?
18. When the default gradients are loaded in the **Gradient Picker**, what will the very first gradient look like?
19. What difference results from creating a gradient by dragging a long line and creating a gradient by dragging a short line?
20. Why should you avoid creating gradients in files that have a low resolution?
21. How do you open the **Gradient Editor**?
22. What two kinds of fill can you add with the **Paint Bucket Tool**?
23. What does the **Tolerance:** setting in the **Paint Bucket Tool**'s options bar do?
24. What is a "tileable" pattern?
25. How do you save a pattern you created with the **Pattern Maker** filter?

7
Erasing, Deleting, and Undoing

Learning Objectives

After completing this chapter, you will be able to:
- Remove unwanted pixels with the **Eraser Tool**.
- Explain how the **Eraser Tool**'s function is dependent on whether layer transparency is locked or not.
- Create partially-transparent areas with the **Eraser Tool**.
- Delete pixels with the **Background Eraser Tool**.
- Add a brightly-colored fill layer to easily spot "garbage pixels" after using the **Background Eraser Tool** and **Magic Eraser Tool**.
- Compare the similarities between the **Magic Eraser Tool** and the **Magic Wand** selection tool.
- Remove unwanted pixels with the **Magic Eraser Tool**.
- Describe three different ways you can use the **History** palette.
- Explain how the **History Brush Tool** works together with the **History** palette.
- Use the **History Brush Tool** to restore part of an image to a previous condition.
- Use the **Art History Brush** and the **History** palette to add paint stroke effects to an image.
- Delete unwanted pixels by using the **Extract** filter.
- Explain the purpose of the **Reveal All** command.
- Compare the **Trim** command and the **Crop Tool**.

Introduction

A common task in Photoshop is to erase or delete part of an image. The terms delete and erase mean almost the same thing. However, the term *erase* refers to using a tool to remove pixels, while the term *delete* refers to pressing a key or choosing a menu command to remove something. You have already learned that one way to delete pixels is to use any of the selection tools to select an area and then press [Delete]. Photoshop has three different eraser tools and a filter that are used to remove parts of an image. Each tool has its strengths and weaknesses. This chapter discusses these tools and other related tools and commands.

Eraser Tools

There are three different eraser tools found in the **Toolbox**, Figure 7-1. Each of the three eraser tools has different attributes, and each is the best choice under certain circumstances. The three eraser tools are discussed in detail in the following sections.

The Eraser Tool

The **Eraser Tool** functions much the same as the **Brush Tool** that you learned about in the previous chapter. The options bar of these two tools share many similarities.

If you use the **Eraser Tool** on a layer with locked transparency, it does not actually erase anything. Instead, it paints the background color over your image. If your background color is white, then it looks like it is erasing pixels, leaving white paper behind. If you erase on a layer that is not locked, all of the pixels are deleted, leaving behind a transparent area. See Figure 7-2.

The **Mode:** setting on the options bar is set to **Brush** by default. In other words, you can use the **Brush Picker** in the options bar to set the size, shape, and hardness of the **Eraser Tool**. In situations where you want to leave behind a crisp, straight edge while erasing, you can change the **Mode:** setting to **Pencil** or **Block**. The **Pencil** mode allows you to use the **Brush Picker**, but your brushes will have crisp edges, even if you change the **Hardness:** setting. The **Block** mode disables the **Brush Picker** and changes the cursor into a square brush that *does not change size* as you zoom in and out. This is a good mode to use if you want to zoom in at 1600% and carefully erase one pixel at a time, because the **Eraser Tool** becomes the same size as a single pixel at that magnification level.

When erasing around an object, zoom in so you can accurately erase along an edge. Using brushes with **Hardness:** set at 100% can make your edges look too crisp, while a **Hardness:** setting of 0% can create a bit too much of a feather effect as you erase, especially when using large-diameter brushes. Try using a **Hardness:** setting of around 50% as you begin using the **Eraser Tool**.

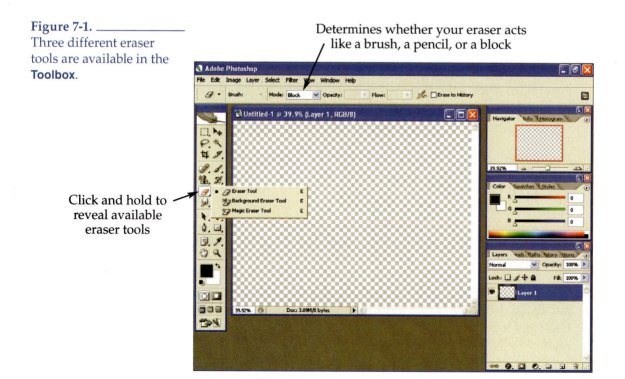

Figure 7-1.
Three different eraser tools are available in the **Toolbox**.

Determines whether your eraser acts like a brush, a pencil, or a block

Click and hold to reveal available eraser tools

Figure 7-2. The **Eraser Tool** is affected by layer transparency. **A**—When layer transparency is locked, the **Eraser Tool** paints the background color over an image. **B**—When **Layer Transparency** is unlocked, the **Eraser Tool** removes pixels, leaving behind a transparent area.

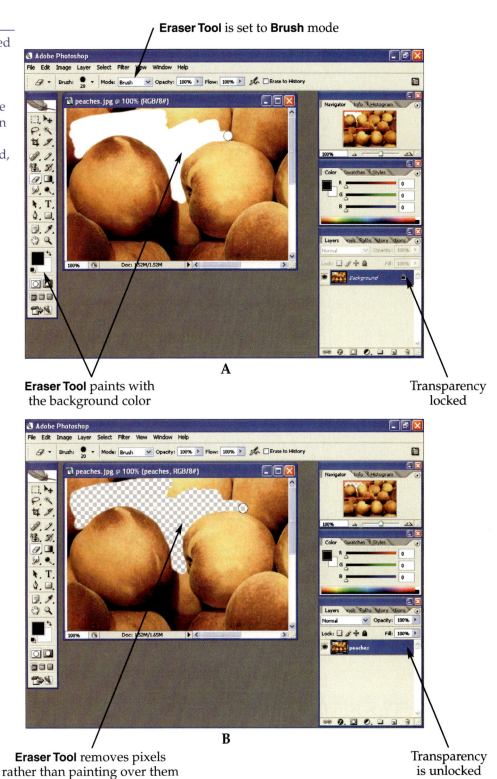

If the **Opacity:** setting in the options bar is set to 100%, the pixels in the **Eraser Tool**'s stroke are completely removed, making the area fully transparent (or completely replaced with the background color, if transparency is locked). If the **Opacity:** setting is lowered, the **Eraser Tool** causes areas to become *partially* transparent, or partially covered with the background color (if transparency is locked). See **Figure 7-3**.

Figure 7-3.
Partially transparent areas can be created by lowering the **Eraser Tool**'s **Opacity:** setting.

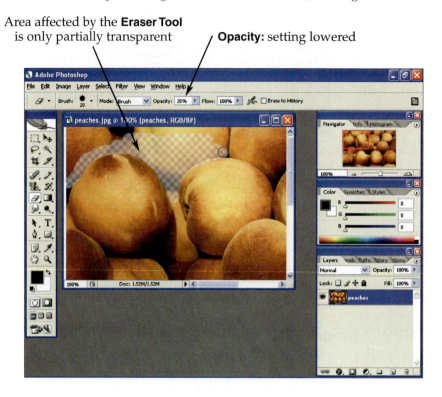

When the **Erase to History** option is activated, the **Eraser Tool** restores the image back to its original state (the state it was in the last time it was saved). If you are removing pixels and accidentally erase a bit too much, turn on the **Erase to History** option, change the brush size if necessary, and drag over the area that was accidentally erased to bring it back to its original condition.

> **Note** The **Opacity:** setting affects the **Eraser Tool** even when the **Erase to History** option is active. If you want to restore a portion of an image that was erased accidentally using the **Eraser Tool** with the **Erase to History** option active, you may need set the **Opacity:** setting back to 100%. Otherwise, the area will be only partially restored.

The Background Eraser Tool

This is the second eraser tool found behind the **Eraser Tool** in the **Toolbox**. The **Background Eraser Tool** is designed to remove the background from around an object in an image. The simpler the background, the easier it is to use this tool. However, the various controls in its options bar let you fine-tune its performance so it will work on multicolored backgrounds as well. See **Figure 7-4**.

The **Background Eraser Tool** can use only round or oval brushes. Clicking on the **Brush:** sample or the down-arrow button next to it opens a pop-up box with a variety of brush controls, **Figure 7-5**. The **Diameter:** slider controls the size of the brush, and the **Hardness:** slider controls how soft the edges of the brush appear. The **Spacing:** setting controls how often this tool samples and deletes a color as you click and drag. The **Roundness:** setting lets you transform a round brush into an oval brush. Decreasing the

Figure 7-4.
The **Background Eraser Tool** removes a selected color (and closely similar colors) from the brush area, but does not erase dissimilar colors.

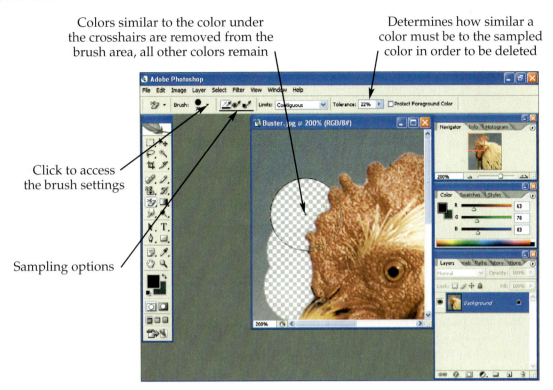

percentage entered in this text box flattens the brush, making it more oval. The value in the **Angle:** text box determines the angle of the brush. Changes to this setting are only noticeable with an oval brush. The **Size:** and **Tolerance:** settings in the **Brush:** pop-up box are functional only if you are using a graphics tablet instead of a mouse. They allow you to vary the **Diameter:** and **Tolerance:** settings of the tool based on stylus input.

When you use the **Background Eraser Tool**, you will see crosshairs (a small + symbol) in the middle of the brush. Hold the crosshairs over a color in the background that you want to delete, and then click. That background color is removed within the brush area. The **Tolerance:** setting in the options bar controls how many closely-related colors are removed when you click. See **Figure 7-6**.

There are three sampling buttons on the options bar (look for the eyedropper icons). These settings control how the crosshairs sample a color. In order, the sampling buttons are:

- **Sampling : Continuous** option (look for two eyedroppers on the button): As you click and drag the **Background Eraser Tool**, Photoshop continuously looks at the color under the crosshairs and deletes closely-related colors according to the **Tolerance:** setting. You will see the background color change continuously in the **Toolbox** as you erase. This setting works well if a

Figure 7-5.
The **Brush Preset Picker** for the **Background Eraser Tool** is shown here.

background is multicolored and the object you want to keep is a different color that stands out.

- **Sampling : Once** option (the middle button): Click once to tell Photoshop what color you would like to delete. As long as you drag the mouse without clicking again, the **Background Eraser Tool** deletes only colors that are closely related to the pixel you first clicked on. This option works well when the entire background is nearly the same color. It also works well in situations where you must click precisely on a small area of colored pixels before erasing. You may need to zoom in and out as you do this kind of erasing.
- **Sampling : Background Swatch** option: This setting is not used often. To use this setting, choose a color by temporarily activating the **Eyedropper Tool** by pressing [Alt] (or [Option] for Mac). After selecting the color, switch it with the background color by clicking the **Switch Foreground and Background Colors** icon on the **Toolbar**. When this option is active, the **Background Eraser Tool** only deletes colors that are closely related to the background color you chose.

Figure 7-6.
The **Background Eraser** tool with a large, soft (**Hardness:** 50%) brush was used to remove the background in both parts of this figure. A—When the **Tolerance:** is set to 20%, the results look good. B—When the **Tolerance:** is set to 60%, too much hair is deleted along with the background.

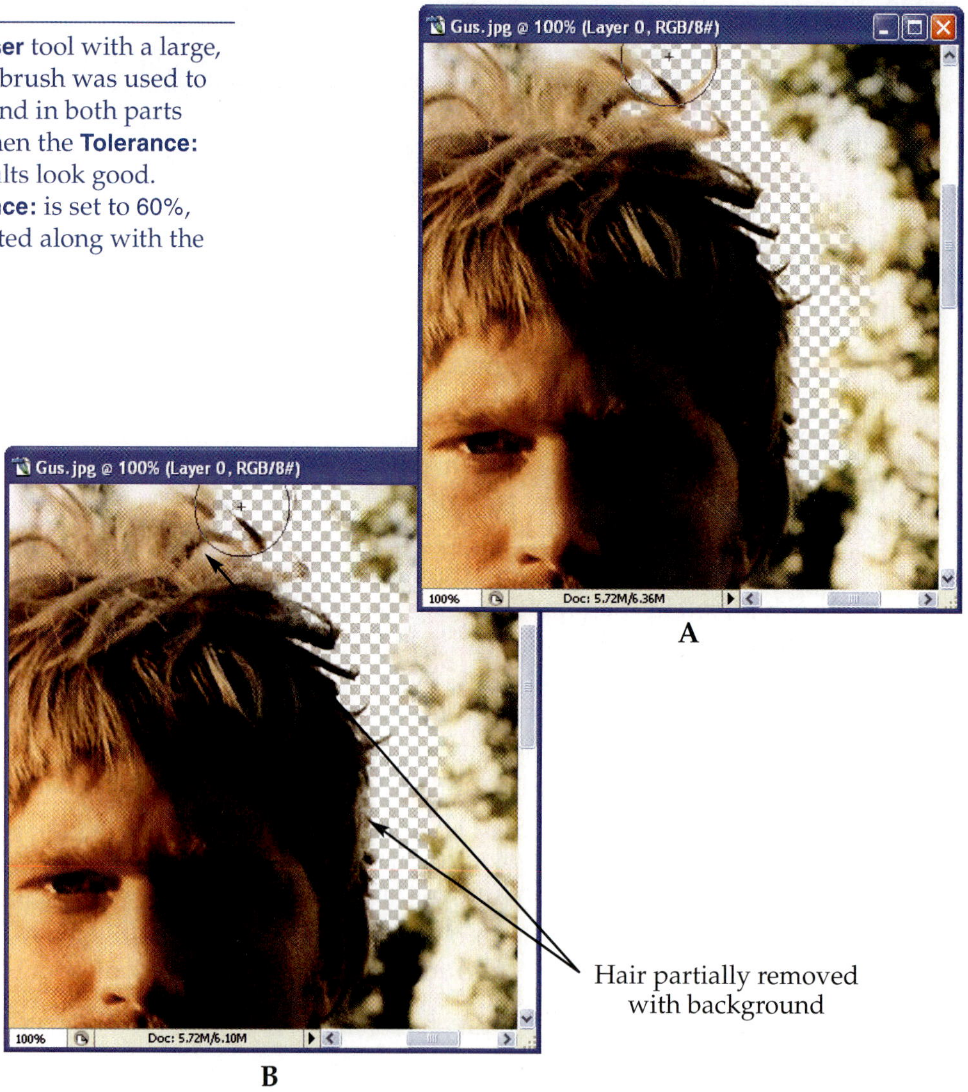

Chapter 7   Erasing, Deleting, and Undoing

The **Limits:** setting on the options bar controls how closely-related colors are deleted. You have three choices:

- The **Background Eraser Tool**'s default setting is **Contiguous**. When the colored pixel under the crosshairs is deleted, only similarly colored pixels *that are connected to the selected pixel in an unbroken group* are deleted from the brush area. Similarly colored pixels that are separated from the selected pixel by a band of dissimilar color remain in the image. See **Figure 7-7A**.
- The **Discontiguous** setting deletes from the brush area *all* pixels that are similar in color to the pixel under the crosshairs. See **Figure 7-7B**.
- The **Find Edges** option is very similar to **Contiguous**, except it preserves the edge detail of an object in the foreground more effectively. Use this option if the object you want to keep has crisp, well-defined edges.

> **Note**   Regardless of the **Limits:** setting chosen, only pixels within the diameter of the brush are removed.

The last setting on the **Background Eraser Tool**'s options bar, the **Protect Foreground Color** option, is used in tricky situations where the **Tolerance:** setting does not provide enough control. When this option is active, you can temporarily activate the **Eyedropper Tool** by pressing [Alt] (or [Option] for Mac) and sample a color that you want to protect as you erase. If you still cannot get effective results, the foreground and background colors you are working with are probably too closely related. You may need to zoom in, use the **Lasso Tool** to carefully select the troublesome areas, and press [Delete] to remove the pixels.

Figure 7-7.
The **Background Eraser Tool**, with the same brush settings, was used to delete portions of both images in this figure. The same pixel was clicked on in both examples. **A**—When the **Contiguous** option is active, fewer pixels are removed. All of the pixels that are removed border each other. **B**—When the **Discontiguous** setting is active, similarly colored pixels are removed from the entire brush area, whether they border one another or not.

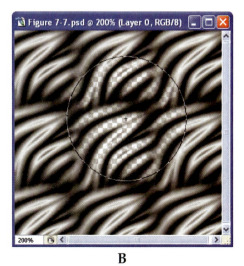

A   B

The **Background Eraser Tool** leaves behind garbage pixels that need to be cleaned up. These pixels are often hidden by the checkerboard pattern. Checking a deleted area of an image for garbage pixels only takes a moment. Begin by creating a new, blank layer. Move it below the image layer in the **Layers** palette and fill it with a bright color such as yellow, Figure 7-8. Then, select the image layer, use the **Lasso Tool** to draw a selection around the unwanted pixels, and press [Delete]. If careful deleting is needed, use the **Eraser Tool** with a small brush size.

The Magic Eraser Tool

The **Magic Eraser Tool** is similar to the **Background Eraser Tool**, except it does not use a brush and crosshairs. This tool works just like the **Magic Wand Tool**, but instead of selecting pixels, it deletes them. The **Magic Eraser Tool**'s options bar contains the same settings that are found on the **Magic Wand Tool**'s options bar, Figure 7-9.

Because this tool works just like the **Magic Wand Tool**, you should already be familiar with most of the controls in the options bar. If you would like a detailed reminder of how all of the options work, refer to the **Magic Wand Tool** section in Chapter 3, *Selection Tools*.

In addition to the controls found on the **Magic Wand Tool**'s options bar, the **Magic Eraser Tool**'s options bar also includes an **Opacity:** slider. The **Opacity:** setting, when lowered, will cause areas to appear partially transparent instead of completely removed.

You should remember from the discussion of the **Magic Wand Tool**, that when the **Contiguous** option is off, similar-colored pixels will be deleted throughout the entire

Figure 7-8.
Areas deleted with the **Background Eraser Tool** often have garbage pixels in them. **A**—The garbage pixels can be difficult to see against the transparent background. **B**—The garbage pixels can be easily spotted by adding a temporary new layer and filling it with a bright color.

A   B

Figure 7-9.
The **Magic Eraser Tool**'s options bar is shown here.

image, **Figure 7-10**. In Figure 7-10B, the **Contiguous** option was turned off before deleting the sky, and this removed the blue color showing through the trees. However, it also deleted part of the windows that were reflecting the blue sky. An easy way to restore the deleted portions of the windows is to use the **Eraser Tool** with the **Erase to History** option active.

When deleting with the **Magic Eraser Tool**, check for garbage pixels. Quite often, you will find them.

The History Palette

You have learned about using **Edit > Undo** (or pressing [Ctrl][Z]) to undo the last tool action or command you used in Photoshop. You also know about the **Edit > Step Backward** command (or pressing [Ctrl][Alt][Z]), which is used if you need to undo more than one action. The **History** palette provides another way to undo the work you have done.

Figure 7-10.
When using the **Magic Eraser Tool**, the blue sky can be deleted with a single click. **A**—When the **Contiguous** option is active, only the main part of the sky is removed. The sky peeking through the branches of the tree remains. **B**—When the **Contiguous** option is off, the blue sky is also deleted from within the tree branches. Unfortunately, the reflection of the sky in the house's windows is also removed.

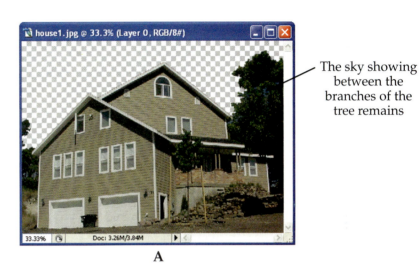

A

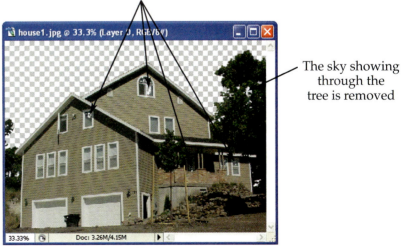

B

As you create and edit a file, the **History** palette shows you the last 20 actions (default setting) you applied to your file, Figure 7-11. Each action listed in the **History** palette is called a *state*, because your file is in a different state of existence after each adjustment you make to it. If your computer has plentiful memory, you can change the **History States** setting in the **General...** category of Photoshop's **Preferences** to have the software remember more than 20 actions.

Using the **History** palette is optional. You can use it in the following ways:

- *You can go "back in time" to any state* by clicking on its description in the **History** palette. By comparison, when you use the **Step Backward** command, you are turning off one state at a time on the **History** palette. You can also delete actions from the **History** palette by either dragging them on top of the **Delete current state** (trash can) button, selecting them and clicking on the **Delete current state** (trash can) button, or right-clicking on them (or press [Ctrl] and click for Mac) and choosing **Delete**. If you use the **History** palette to delete an action that has other actions listed below it, all actions below are also deleted.

- *You can create "snapshots" of your image.* Since the **History** palette only shows a limited number of states, you can create a *snapshot* (a temporarily-saved version of your file) whenever you are satisfied with your progress on an image. You can also create a snapshot before trying out complex effects that might ruin your work. A snapshot is created by first selecting the state of the image you would like to make a snapshot of and then clicking the **Create new snapshot** (camera) button at the bottom of the **History** palette. Snapshots can be renamed and are listed in the upper portion of the **History** palette. However, when you close your file, all information on the **History** palette is lost, including snapshots, even if the file is saved.

- You can also use the **History** palette to create a new document instead of a snapshot. This is a helpful feature because snapshots and states are deleted when you close a file. To use this feature, select a state or a snapshot in the palette and click the **Create new document from current state** button in the **History** palette. This opens the selected state in a new document window and makes it active.

At times you may want to clear the **History** palette. Choose **Clear History** from the **History** palette menu or choose **Edit > Purge > History** (this command will purge the **History** in all open documents). The **Clear History** command can be undone, but the **Edit > Purge > History** command cannot.

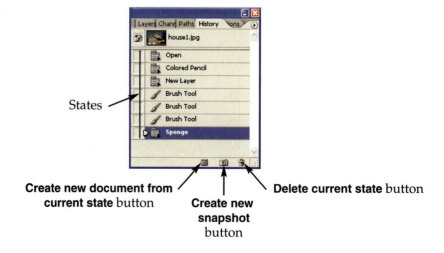

Figure 7-11.
The **History** palette lists each action performed, up to a maximum number determined by the **Preferences** settings. Each action is referred to as a state.

On other occasions, you may wish to *reset* your file and start all over. Choosing **File > Revert** resets your file to *the condition it was in when you last saved it*. When you use this command, the states are not deleted from the **History** palette. Instead, a new state named Revert is added at the end of the stack. You can jump back to a previous state (before the image was reverted) by clicking on the desired state in the **History** palette.

Some Photoshop users do not bother using the **History** palette. You should regard it as an optional way of saving your efforts while you carefully experiment with complicated adjustments on a project.

Figure 7-12.
The **History Brush Tool** is located below the brush tools on the **Toolbox**.

History Brush Tools

The history brush category of tools are found just below the brush tools on the **Toolbox**, Figure 7-12. This category includes the **History Brush Tool** and the **Art History Brush Tool**.

The History Brush Tool

The **History Brush Tool** is designed to be used with the **History** palette. Its options bar is exactly the same as the **Brush Tool**'s. However, this tool does not apply paint. Instead, its purpose is to restore an image back to its original condition or a particular state that you specify in the **History** palette.

On the left side of the **History** palette, are small squares next to each state and snapshot, Figure 7-13. The **History Brush Tool** icon can be moved from state to state by clicking on those squares. The **History Brush Tool** icon indicates that when you paint with the **History Brush Tool**, it will restore the image to that state or condition.

By default, the **History Brush Tool** restores the image to its original state. Coincidently, there is another tool and option you have learned about in this chapter that does exactly the same thing—the **Eraser Tool** with the **Erase to History** option active.

The Art History Brush Tool

The **Art History Brush Tool** does not erase or delete pixels, but it is explained in this chapter because it is closely related to the **History Brush Tool**. The **Art History Brush Tool** works like a filter that is applied to your image with a brush. This bizarre tool adds a "paint stroke" special effect as it restores an image to a state or snapshot that you select in the **History** palette.

Figure 7-13. _____ Interesting effects can be created by using the **History Brush Tool** to restore a portion of an image after modifying it with filters. **A**—The original image is shown here. **B**—Two filters have been applied to the original image. **C**—The **History Brush Tool** was used to restore the subject's face to its original condition.

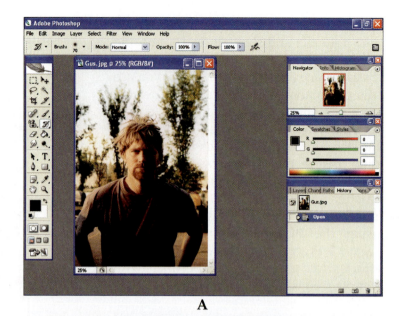

A

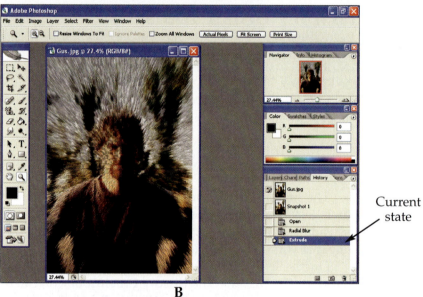

Current state

B

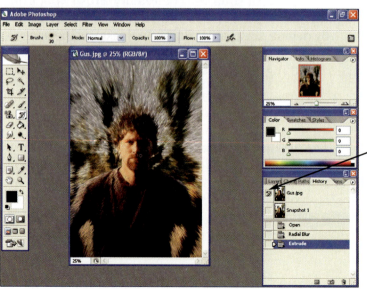

The **History Brush Tool** icon indicates that the **History Brush Tool** will restore the image to this state

C

Along with the **Brush:**, **Modes:**, and **Opacity:** settings, you will find a **Style:** setting in the options bar, **Figure 7-14**. This menu lists several methods of applying the paint stroke effect. You can get some interesting effects as you change the **Tolerance:** and **Area:** setting. The best way to get familiar with this tool is to experiment with the settings for a few minutes. It produces effects that are similar to the **Glass** filter (**Filter > Distort > Glass...**).

The Extract Filter

The term *extract* means "to remove carefully." The **Extract** filter is another method of removing the background from around an object. This filter can be the most time-saving tool to use when working with an object in an image that has wispy edges, like the small feathers on the ostrich in **Figure 7-15**. This ostrich image is particularly difficult to work with because many of the small feathers are almost the same color as the background.

Figure 7-14.
The **Art History Brush**'s options bar is shown here.

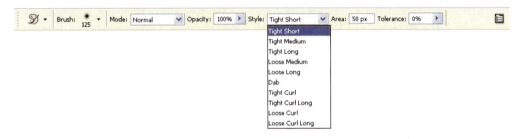

Figure 7-15.
The **Edge Highlighter Tool** is used to define the edges of the object you wish to extract.

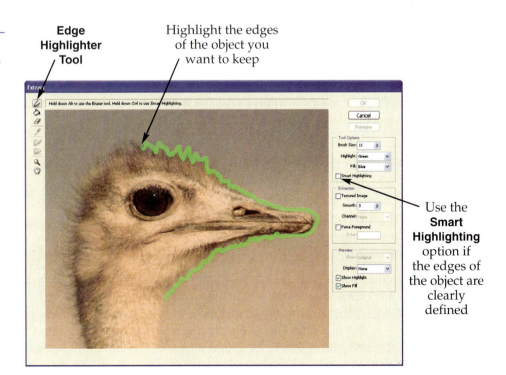

Extracting an Image

To begin using this filter, choose **Filter > Extract...** to display the **Extract** dialog box. You will find several tools at the left side of the dialog box. Use the **Extract** filter's **Zoom Tool** (found at the left side of the dialog box) to move in close to your image. As you work, use the **Hand Tool** to move around the image. You can also press [Spacebar] to temporarily activate the **Hand Tool**.

Highlighting the Edges

The first step in extracting an object from an image is to highlight the edges of the object you wish to extract. Use the **Edge Highlighter Tool** (the tool at the top of the **Extract** dialog box' toolbar) to trace over the edges of the object you want to keep. Let the **Edge Highlighter Tool** stroke overlap the background a little and just barely cover the edge of the object. Change the brush size if necessary. Refer to Figure 7-15.

The purpose of highlighting is to tell Photoshop where the edge of your extracted object should be. If you are extracting a wispy portion of an image, like someone with wild hair, accurately highlight each wisp. You can use the bracket keys ([,]) to change brush sizes as you work.

Your highlighted border needs to be continuous (no gaps). You do not need to highlight the outside edges of your image, however. If the highlighting is too thick or plentiful, Photoshop is less likely to accurately detect the edge of the object. If necessary, use the **Eraser Tool** (the third tool) to remove excessive highlighting.

Activate the **Smart Highlighting** option if the edge you are highlighting stands out clearly. This option senses the edge and uses an appropriate amount of highlighting, no matter what the brush size is.

Activate the **Textured Image** option if the object you are extracting is similar in color to the background, but has a different texture. This can help Photoshop figure out what to keep and what to throw away. The **Smooth:** setting is used to create a blur effect along the edge of your object as it is extracted. Keep this setting at or near 0 unless the edges of your extracted object look too sharp in places.

Filling the Outline

When your highlighting completely surrounds the object you want to keep, use the **Fill Tool** (paint bucket) to fill the highlighted area with color. This tells Photoshop what part of the image you want to keep. See **Figure 7-16**.

> **Note** If the **Fill Tool** fills the entire image, there is a break somewhere in your highlighting. If the object you are extracting extends to the very outside edges of the image, make sure that you did not leave a small gap between the edge of the image and the end of your highlighting stroke.

If the object you are extracting is composed entirely of very similar colors, you may consider using the **Force Foreground** option. When this option is active, the **Fill Tool** becomes unavailable. You define the area you want to extract by highlighting the entire object instead of highlighting the edges and filling of the outline.

To use the **Force Foreground** option, pick a color from your image with the **Eyedropper Tool.** Photoshop looks at the areas you highlighted and extracts pixels that are similar to the color you selected with the **Eyedropper Tool**. For this reason,

Figure 7-16.
Use the **Fill Tool** to dump color in the area you wish to keep.

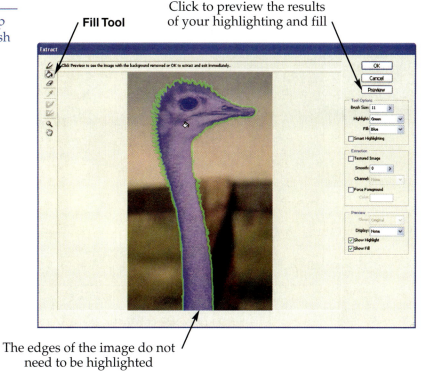

you need to completely highlight the portion of the image you want to extract, not just the edges. You should be aware that this option is difficult to control unless the area you extract contains only closely-related colors.

Once you have defined the area you want to extract, click the **Preview** button at the right side of the dialog box to check your results.

Previewing and Cleaning up the Area to be Extracted

After clicking the **Preview** button, you will probably find that the **Extract** filter did not do a perfect job. The checkerboard pattern displays behind the ostrich. To better see your results, make the background a different color by setting the **Display:** setting to **Other...** and choosing a color. See **Figure 7-17**.

Two additional tools become available when you switch to preview mode. The **Cleanup Tool** lowers the opacity of an area as you paint over it. With a few strokes, you can erase pixels completely. If you hold down [Alt] (or [Option] for Mac), this tool does just the opposite—it increases the opacity of an area, bringing back areas that were mistakenly deleted.

You can change the pressure of the **Cleanup Tool** by tapping a number key on your keyboard: [1] for light pressure and [9] for heavy pressure. With patience, images with the most complicated edges can be cleanly extracted, **Figure 7-18**.

The **Edge Touchup Tool** is also available in preview mode. It is not always necessary to use this tool, especially if the edges of your object have a wispy or feathery look. When this tool is dragged along the edge of an object, it causes the edge to be more defined. Holding down [Ctrl] (or [Command] for Mac) causes a crosshair symbol to appear in the center of the brush. The crosshairs should touch the actual edge of your object as you paint with this tool.

Figure 7-17. When the **Extract** filter is used, the initial result is seldom perfect. Some touch up is usually necessary.

To better see the areas that need to be cleaned up, select **Other...** in the **Display:** drop-down list and pick a bright color

Figure 7-18. The individual feathers were created using the **Cleanup Tool** with a very small brush size and various brush pressure settings (using the 1–9 keys).

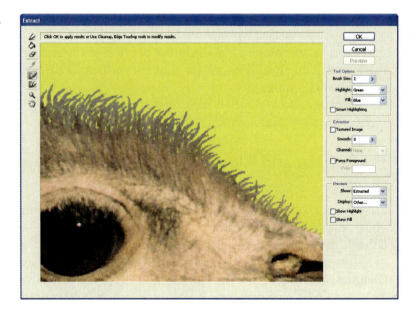

Finding Extra Pixels with the Reveal All Command

When you drag images from one file to another, Photoshop remembers the entire image even if part of it extends past the edge of your canvas. Choosing **Image > Reveal All** shows you all layers that extend past the document's bottom edge, **Figure 7-19**.

To save hard disk space, you can crop the image by first undoing the **Reveal All** command. Next, choose **Select > All**. Lastly, choose **Image > Crop**. This permanently removes the portions of the image that extend beyond the canvas, making the file size smaller. However, today's hard drives are large enough that you will probably never need to worry about this issue.

Figure 7-19.
Layers that are moved to another image and extend past the canvas take up unnecessary file space. **A**—Portions of the layers extend past the canvas are not visible. **B**—The **Reveal All** command causes the image to become large enough to display all pixels.

A

B

The Trim Command

The **Trim** command is nothing more than a fancy version of the **Crop** command that considers objects in your image and the background color before cropping. Choosing **Image > Trim...** opens a dialog box that lets you crop one or all four sides of an image. The setting in the **Based On** section of the dialog box tells Photoshop what color to trim away. The settings in the **Trim Away** section determine what part(s) of the image the selected color is trimmed from.

For example, the design in **Figure 7-20** was begun by drawing some custom shapes. A decision was then made to make the canvas size smaller. In Figure 7-20A, the **Top Left Pixel Color** option is selected in the **Based On** section of the dialog box. This means that all areas that are white (because that is the color of the top left pixel) will be cropped to the edge of the custom shapes, except for the top of the image, Figure 7-20B. The top of the image is not cropped because it was deselected in the **Trim Away** section.

Figure 7-20.
Choosing **Image > Trim...** lets you crop your image according to how objects in your image are positioned. **A**—In the **Trim** dialog box, you specify a corner of the image to use as a color reference and the areas of the image that are to be cropped. **B**—After you click **OK** in the **Trim** dialog box, the background is trimmed away on the specified sides of the image.

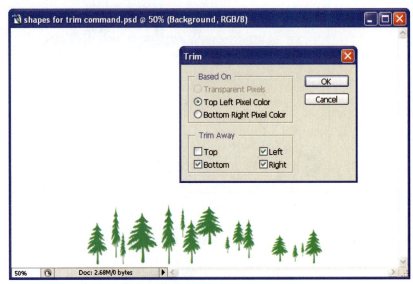

A

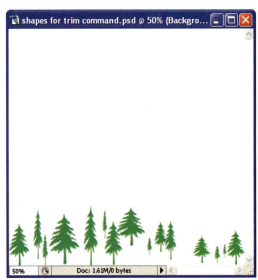

B

GRAPHIC DESIGN:
Balance in Symmetrical and Asymmetrical Designs

A graphic designer should be concerned about *balance* (the equal distribution of visual elements) as the design takes shape. It is visually pleasing if design elements in one area of the design are complemented by other elements in the opposite area of the design. There are two fundamental types of designs that portray different balance strategies.

If a line were drawn down the center of a *symmetrical design*, both sides of the design would appear equal. This creates a visual harmony—one side perfectly balances the other side of the design, Figure 7-21. Symmetrical designs create a more conservative, formal, and calm mood.

Asymmetrical means "not symmetrical," and many designs fall into this category. Comparatively speaking, asymmetrical designs evoke dynamic, energetic, and even tense moods. The postcard design in Figure 7-22 is an asymmetrical design. However, a sense of balance is maintained because the bright red "Wildflower" text in the upper left corner is balanced by the two inset images in the lower right corner. Applying a bright red stroke around each inset image helps create a visual weight that approximates the weight of the "Wildflower" text.

Figure 7-21.
The "leafy" design is symmetrical—if a line were drawn down the middle, one side would be a mirror image of the other.

Figure 7-22. Balance is created in this asymmetrical design by positioning design elements with significant visual weights opposite from one another.

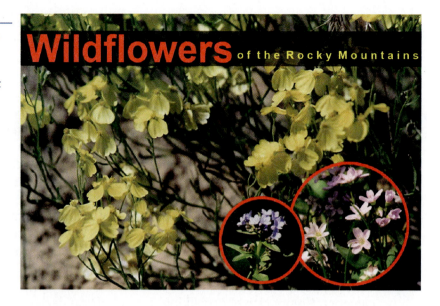

The postcard example in **Figure 7-23** is an asymmetrical design that is not balanced. Most of the visual weight sits heavily at the left side of the design.

Figure 7-23. This version of the postcard is not balanced.

Summary

Even though the three eraser tools and the **Extract** filter are powerful ways to remove unwanted pixels, they are not the only way. There are situations where the most effective way to delete a challenging area of pixels is to zoom in, use the **Lasso Tool** to select the area, and then press [Delete].

There are additional ways you can isolate parts of your image. You will learn those techniques in Chapter 11, *Additional Layer Techniques*.

CHAPTER TUTORIALS

Removing unwanted pixels requires a lot of patience. These tutorials will give you plenty of practice using the tools discussed in this chapter. There are several images that you will delete portions of and then add to projects you have started in previous chapters.

Tutorial 7-1: Create a Blended-Photo Poster with the Eraser Tool

In this tutorial, you will combine several images into a single composite image. You will use the **Eraser Tool** to remove partially cut off objects in each image so that they blend together naturally when they are combined.

1. Open Photoshop.
2. Choose **File > New…**.
3. Name the new file 07poster and enter these settings shown in **Figure T7-1**. Click **OK** when you are finished.

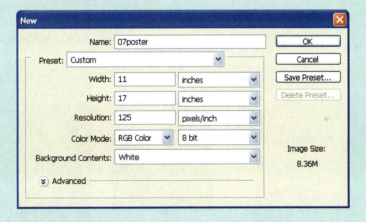

Figure T7-1. Create a new image, named 07poster. Use the settings shown here.

Move Tool

Zoom Tool

Eraser Tool

4. Open the apples1.jpg file, located in the food folder.
5. Use the **Move Tool** to drag the apples to the location shown in **Figure T7-2**.
6. Close the apples1.jpg file.
7. Use the **Zoom Tool** to enlarge the 07poster image until you see 200% in the title bar.
8. Click the **Eraser Tool**.
9. In the options bar, select **Brush** in the **Mode:** drop-down list. In the **Brush Preset Picker**, change the **Master Diameter** slider setting to 13 px. Change the **Hardness:** slider setting to 50%.
10. Begin erasing apples that are cut off along the bottom and right side until the apples layer looks like the one in **Figure T7-3**.

Figure T7-2.
Move the apples to the upper left corner of the image.

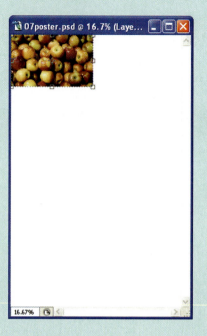

Figure T7-3.
After erasing the partially cut off apples along the bottom and right edges of the apples1.jpg image, open and drag the apples2.jpg image over to the poster.

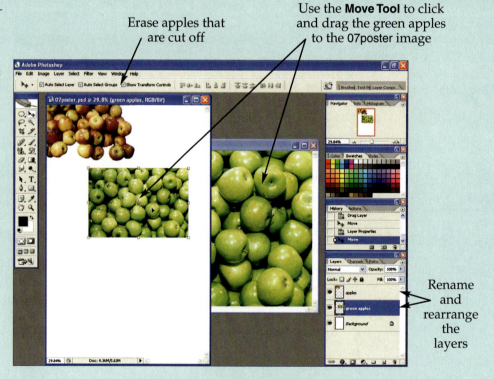

Erase apples that are cut off

Use the **Move Tool** to click and drag the green apples to the 07poster image

Rename and rearrange the layers

11. Open the apples2.jpg file and drag the apples over to the 07poster image, as shown in Figure T7-3.

12. Drag the green apples layer to upper right corner of the image.

13. Rename the layers and arrange them so the green apples layer is below the apples layer.

14. Zoom in and begin erasing the green apples that are cut off along the bottom. See **Figure T7-4**.

    As you work, change your brush size as needed. Brush **Hardness:** settings of about 50% work best for this type of work, because they leave a slightly feathered edge. The feathered edge is good for overlapping and blending with another photo.

15. Open the melons2.jpg file and drag it over to the 07poster image.

16. Since all of the cantaloupes along the bottom of the photo are cut off, rotate the image by choosing **Edit > Transform > Rotate 90° CCW**. See **Figure T7-5**.

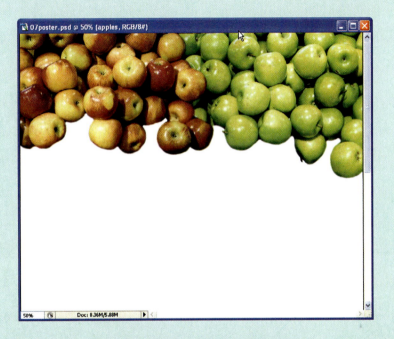

Figure T7-4. Erase any incomplete apples along the bottom edge of the green apple layer.

Figure T7-5. Drag the melons2.jpg image to the poster and rotate it as shown.

17. Rename the new layer melons2 and move it below the green apple layer in the **Layers** palette stack.
18. Move the melons2 layer to the location shown in **Figure T7-6** and erase the cantaloupe layer as shown.
19. Continue adding, positioning, and erasing parts of the other photos in the food folder. Try to make your poster look as close as possible to the example shown in **Figure T7-7**.

    The carrots.jpg image needs no erasing, because it is positioned at the very bottom of the **Layers** palette stack. Remember that each layer's position in the **Layers** palette stack determines how it will overlap adjacent layers. You will also need to rotate some of the images to match the orientations shown in the sample.

Horizontal Type Tool

20. Add the text shown. Because this is a poster, use text that can be easily read from 10' away.

    In this example, after text was entered with the **Horizontal Type Tool**, two layer styles were added: a stroked border (black) and a drop shadow.

21. After you are satisfied with how the text and images are arranged on your poster, choose **Layer > Flatten Image**.
22. Choose **View > Actual Pixels** to view your poster at actual size.
23. Save the 07poster image in PSD format and then close it.

Figure T7-6. Erase any incomplete melons from the left and bottom edges of the layer.

Figure T7-7. _____
Your completed poster should look like this.

Tutorial 7-2: Removing the Background from an Image

In this tutorial, you will use a number of methods to remove the backgrounds from around key objects in an image. You will then combine the objects in a single design.

1. Open the file named Frankie.jpg.
2. Choose **Select > All**.
3. Click the **Lasso Tool**.
4. Click the **Subtract from selection** button in the options bar.
5. Drag a selection border all the way around Frankie, as shown in **Figure T7-8**.

Lasso Tool

Subtract from selection

Figure T7-8. _____
Open the Frankie.jpg image, select the entire image, and then subtract Frankie from the selection.

6. Press [Delete].

   The background color (white) replaces the deleted part of the file. If your file does not look similar to the example in Figure T7-9, choose File > Revert and try the preceding steps again.

7. Double click on the Background layer in the **Layers** palette.
8. In the **New Layer** dialog box, click **OK** to rename the layer Layer 0.

   You have just unlocked the layer transparency by renaming the background layer.

9. Press [Delete] again.

   Instead of white, a checkerboard pattern shows around Frankie. This pattern means there is no color there.

10. Clear the selection.
11. Zoom in on Frankie's head, as shown in Figure T7-10.
12. Click the **Background Eraser Tool** and enter the following settings in the options bar:

    Background Eraser Tool

    - Set the brush **Diameter:** to 80 px (use the bracket keys to change brush sizes as you work).

    Sampling: Continuous

    - Set the brush **Hardness:** to 60%.
    - Make sure the **Sampling: Continuous** button is selected (depressed).
    - Select **Discontiguous** in the **Limits:** drop-down menu.
    - Set the **Tolerance:** slider to 20%.

13. Place the crosshairs that appear in the center of the **Background Eraser Tool** cursor on the background right next to Frankie's hair and click.

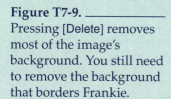

Figure T7-9. _____
Pressing [Delete] removes most of the image's background. You still need to remove the background that borders Frankie.

Figure T7-10.
Zoom in on Frankie, and erase the background with the **Background Eraser Tool**. Be careful not to accidentally position the crosshairs on the subject.

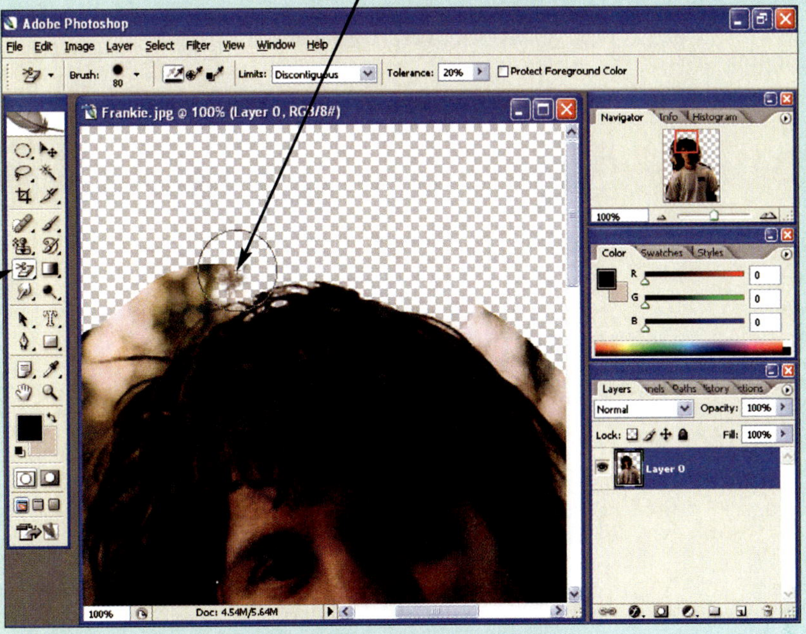

Position the crosshairs over the color you want to remove

Background Eraser Tool

14. Continue erasing the background around Frankie, observing these tips.
    - Erase one click at a time. If too much is deleted when you click, press [Ctrl][Z] to undo the action, lower the **Tolerance:** setting, and try again. Also, experiment with making the brush size smaller or setting the **Limits:** setting to **Contiguous** in problem areas.
    - In areas where the background is the same color as Frankie's hair, use the **Lasso Tool** to select and delete the background.
15. Choose **Layer > New > Layer…**. In the **New Layer** dialog box, accept the default name by clicking **OK**.
16. In the **Layers** palette, drag the new layer so it is below the layer that contains Frankie.
17. Make sure the new layer is active, and then choose **Edit > Fill…**.
18. In the **Contents** section of the **Fill** dialog box, choose **Color…** from the **Use** drop-down list.
19. In the **Color Picker**, choose a bright, vivid color and click **OK**.
20. In the **Fill** dialog box, click **OK** to fill the layer with the selected color.
21. Check closely for any garbage pixels that appear around Frankie. Use the **Eraser Tool** to delete them. See **Figure T7-11**.

    Make sure the layer containing Frankie is active, or you will only succeed in erasing the fill. You can also use the feathered edge of the **Eraser Tool**'s brush to smooth out any jagged edges on Frankie, such as edges of his T-shirt and wisps of hair.

22. When you have removed all of the garbage pixels, delete the new, color-filled layer.
23. Open the 06CDback.psd file you created in the previous chapter.
24. Move Frankie over to the 06CDback.psd image and scale him to 80% (choose **Edit > Transform > Scale**).

Commit

25. Click the **Commit** button in the options bar to end the scale command.

Figure T7-11.
After a brightly filled layer is added beneath Frankie, garbage pixels are easier to spot. Carefully use the **Eraser Tool** to remove these unnecessary pixels.

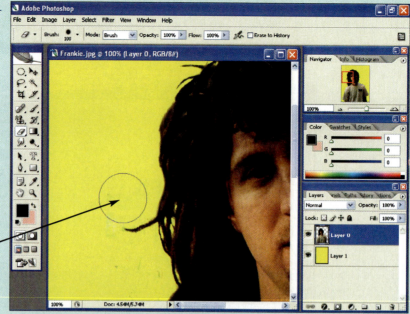

Use the **Eraser Tool** to remove garbage pixels

Rectangular Marquee Tool

26. Move Frankie to the location shown in **Figure T7-12**.
27. Use the **Rectangular Marquee Tool** to select the part of Frankie that covers the red rectangle at the left. Again, refer to Figure T7-12.
28. Press [Delete].
29. Close the Frankie.jpg file. Do not save the changes. Leave the 06CDback.psd file open.
30. Open the file named Gus.jpg.
31. Choose **Filter > Extract...**.
32. Using the **Zoom Tool** in the **Extract** dialog box, click on Gus two times.

Edge Highlighter Tool

33. Click the **Edge Highlighter Tool**, set the **Brush Size:** to 12, and highlight the edge of Gus as shown in **Figure T7-13**.

Since you are zoomed in, press [Spacebar] to activate the Hand Tool to move around the image as you outline the edges.

Figure T7-12.
Drag Frankie onto the 06CDback.psd image, scale him to 80%, and position him as shown. Remove any portions that overlap the colored bar on the left side of the image.

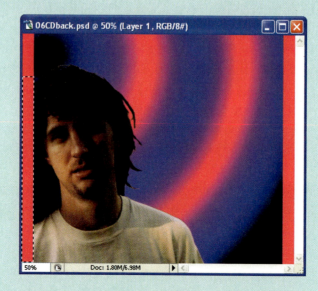

Chapter 7   Erasing, Deleting, and Undoing

Figure T7-13. _____
Highlight the edges of Gus with the **Edge Highlighter Tool** and then fill the area with the **Fill Tool**.

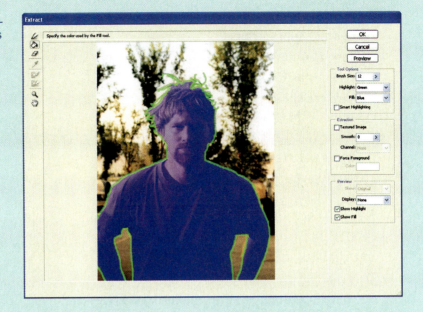

Fill Tool

34. Use the **Fill Tool** to dump color on Gus.

    This tells Photoshop what part of the image you want to keep.

35. Click the **Preview** button.

36. In the **Preview** section of the **Extract** dialog box, select **Other...** in the **Display:** drop-down list. Pick a bright color in the **Color Picker** and click **OK**.

Cleanup Tool

37. Click the **Cleanup Tool**. Look for, and repair, areas of Gus' hair that are partially deleted or unwanted areas of the background that should be removed. See **Figure T7-14**.

    To restore areas that were accidentally removed, press [Alt] (or [Option] for Mac) as you paint. To delete areas, do not press any keys as you paint. To change the pressure of this tool, type a number between 1–9.

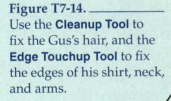
Edge Touchup Tool

38. Use the **Edge Touchup Tool** to repair the edge around Gus' shirt, neck and arms.

Figure T7-14. _____
Use the **Cleanup Tool** to fix the Gus's hair, and the **Edge Touchup Tool** to fix the edges of his shirt, neck, and arms.

Cleanup Tool
Edge Touchup Tool

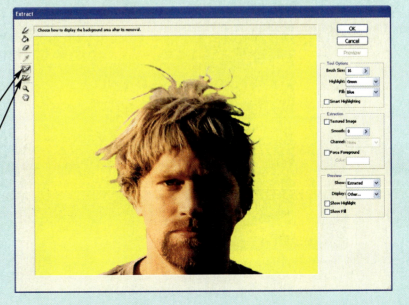

39. When you have repaired the edges around Gus using the **Cleanup Tool** and **Edge Touchup Tool**, click **OK**.
40. Move Gus over to the 06CDback.psd image, scale him to 40%, and move him to the location shown in **Figure T7-15**.

   Gus's arms were cut off in the image. Make sure you position him so that the missing portion of his arm is hidden behind Frankie.

41. Make sure the layer containing Gus is below the layer containing Frankie in the **Layers** palette stack.
42. Close the Gus.jpg file. Do *not* save the changes. Keep the 06CDback.psd image open.
43. Open the file named Chris.jpg.
44. Use any method to remove the background from around Chris.
45. Move Chris over to the 06CDback.psd image, scale him to 40%, and move him to the location shown in Figure T7-15.
46. In the **Layers** palette stack, make sure the layer containing Chris is between the layer containing Gus and the Background layer.
47. Close the Chris.jpg file. Do not save the changes. Leave the 06CDback.psd file open.
48. Click the **Custom Shape Tool**.
49. Click the down arrow next to the **Shape:** box in the options bar to open the **Custom Shape Picker**.
50. Click this arrow button on the **Custom Shape Picker**.

   This opens the **Custom Shape Picker** menu.

51. Choose **Shapes** from the **Custom Shape Picker** menu, **Figure T7-16**.
52. Click **Append** in the dialog box that appears.
53. Select the Triangle Frame shape in the **Custom Shape Picker**.
54. In the options bar, click the color box and choose black.
55. Hold down [Shift] while dragging a triangle the size shown in **Figure T7-17**.

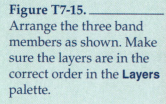

Custom Shape Tool

Figure T7-15.
Arrange the three band members as shown. Make sure the layers are in the correct order in the **Layers** palette.

Chapter 7   Erasing, Deleting, and Undoing

Figure T7-16.
Append the **Shapes** category of shapes to those currently loaded in the **Custom Shape Picker**.

Click to open the **Custom Shape Picker**

Click to open the **Custom Shape Picker** menu

The **Custom Shape Tool**

Append the **Shapes** category to the shapes currently loaded in the picker

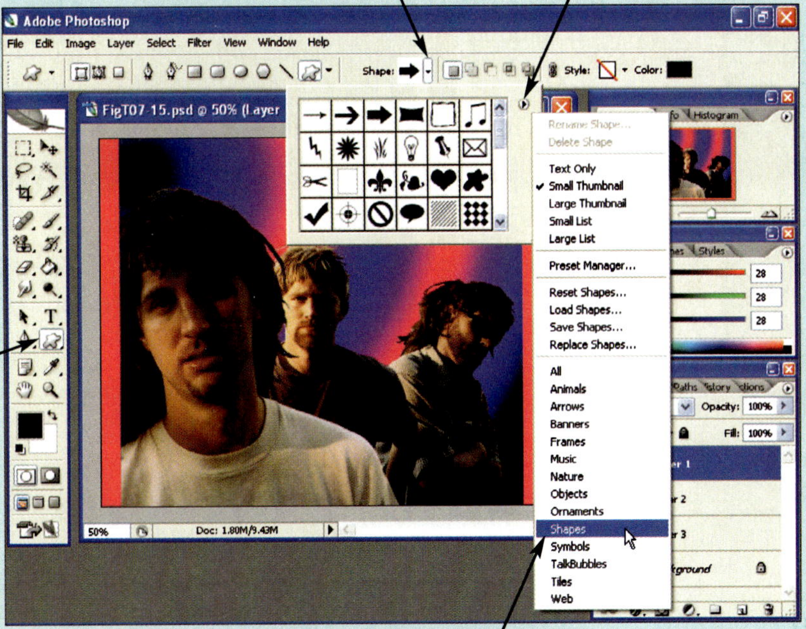

Figure T7-17.
Draw the triangle frame as shown.

Select the **Triangle Frame** shape in the **Custom Shape Picker**

Click here to begin drawing the triangle

With [Shift] pressed, drag the triangle here and release the mouse button

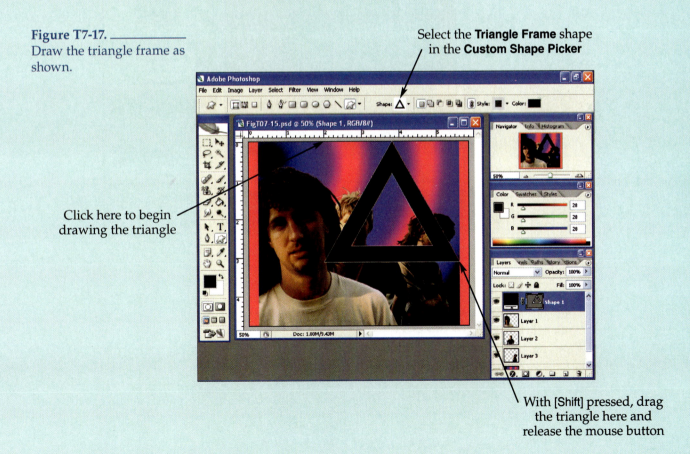

56. In the **Layers** palette, right-click on the shape layer that was just created and choose **Rasterize Layer** from the shortcut menu.
57. In the **Layers** palette, drag the new shape layer so it is just above the bottom layer in the stack.
58. On the **Layers** palette, set the opacity of the shape layer to 30%.
59. Before adding text, click the top layer in the **Layers** palette.

    You click the top layer on the stack so that your new text layer will be created on top of all the other layers.

60. Click the **Horizontal Type Tool** in the **Toolbox**.
61. In the options bar, choose the Arial Black font and set the font size to 12 pt.
62. Click the color box on the options bar and select white in the **Color Picker**.
63. Type Blister in the location shown in **Figure T7-18**.

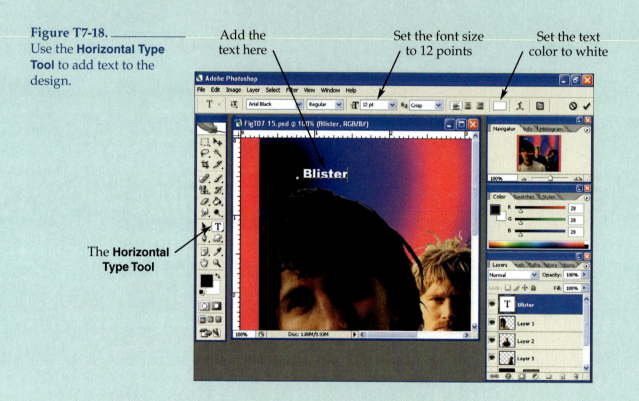

Figure T7-18. Use the **Horizontal Type Tool** to add text to the design.

64. Choose **Edit > Transform > Rotate 90° CW**.
65. Drag the rotated text to the location shown in **Figure T7-19**.
66. Choose **Layer > Duplicate Layer…**. Accept the default name.
67. Drag the text you just duplicated to the location shown in Figure T7-19.
68. Add the song titles shown in Figure T7-19.

    Use the grid to help you line the elements up evenly. In the example, major gridlines are spaced every 2″, with eight subdivisions. This creates a minor gridline every .25″.

69. Hide the grid by choosing **View > Show > Grid**.
70. Choose **File > Save As…** and name this file 07CDback.psd. Then, close the file.

    This design will be completed in a later chapter.

Figure T7-19.
Using a properly spaced grid makes it easy to line up the text elements.

Tutorial 7-3: The Magic Eraser Tool

This project will show how an undeveloped area will look with several homes built on it. You will use a variety of methods to remove the backgrounds surrounding the homes.

1. Open the 06hillside.psd file that you created in an earlier chapter.
2. Open the file named house1.jpg.
3. Click the **Magic Eraser Tool**.

Magic Eraser Tool

The Magic Eraser Tool is found behind the Eraser Tool in the Toolbox.

4. In the options bar, set the **Tolerance:** to 35.
5. Make sure the **Contiguous** check box has a check mark in it.
6. Click the blue sky above the house.

Notice that the Magic Eraser Tool deletes the blue sky color until it reaches the outside edge of the tree. However, some blue sky is still showing through the tree branches, Figure T7-20.

7. Choose **Edit > Undo Magic Eraser** to bring back the sky.
8. In the options bar, remove the check mark from the **Contiguous** check box.
9. Click in the same spot (see step 6) to delete the sky.

The blue sky color is deleted from the entire photo. See Figure T7-21.

10. Zoom in on the windows of the house and check for blue pixels that were accidentally removed.

You will likely find that some blue pixels were accidentally deleted from the windows. If the image were going to be used at somewhere near full scale, the missing pixels in the house windows would have to be fixed using the Eraser Tool with the Erase to History option active. However, in this tutorial, the house is going to be scaled down to the point where the missing pixels will not be noticeable.

11. Use the **Move Tool** to drag the house over to the 06hillside.psd image.
12. Choose **Edit > Transform > Scale** and enter 30% in the **W:** and **H:** boxes.

Figure T7-20.
The sky has been removed using the **Magic Eraser Tool** with the **Contiguous** option active.

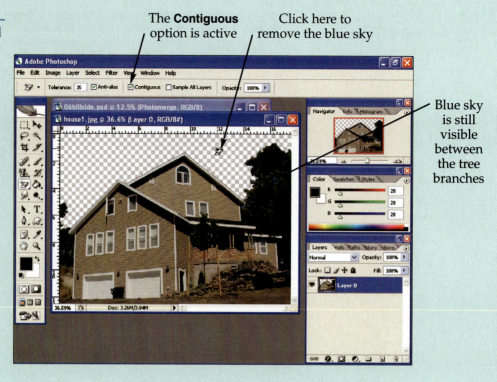

Figure T7-21.
The sky has been removed using the **Magic Eraser Tool** with the **Contiguous** option off.

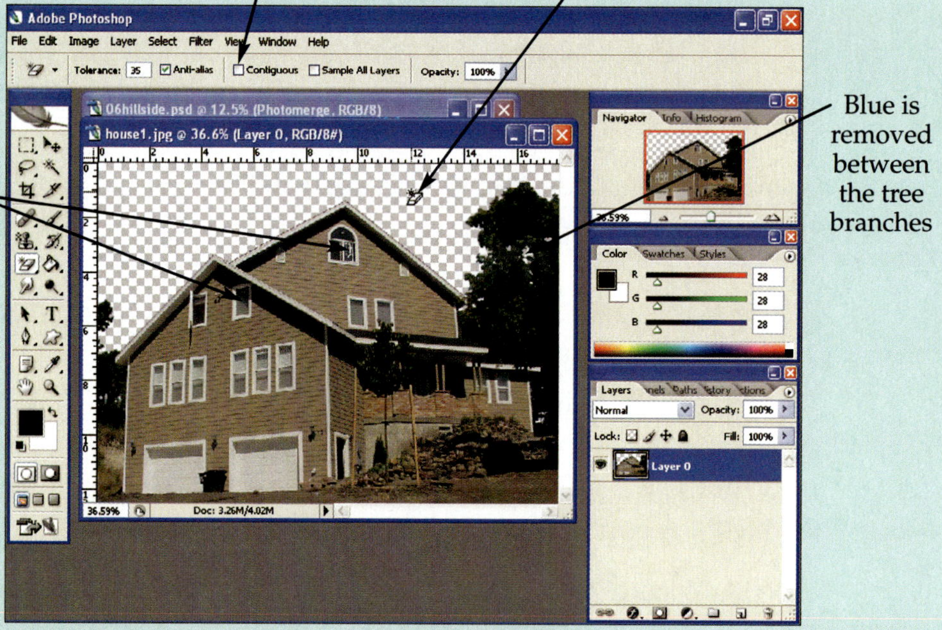

13. Click the **Commit** button in the options bar to end the scale command.
14. Move the house to the location shown in **Figure 7-22**.
15. Close the house1.jpg file. Do not save the changes.
16. Open the house2.jpg file.

   Look at the **Layers** palette. Notice the layer that opened automatically with this image is named Background and is locked.

Figure T7-22.
Scale the house to 30% and position it as shown.

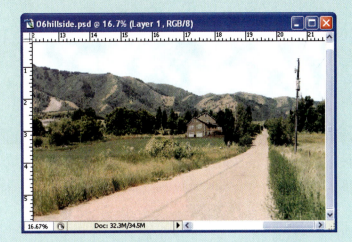

17. Click the **Magic Eraser Tool** in the **Toolbox**.
18. In the options bar, set the **Tolerance:** to 25.
19. Make sure the **Contiguous** option is not active (no check mark).
20. Click in the upper left corner of the image to delete some of the sky.

    When you use the **Magic Eraser Tool**, the Background layer is unlocked automatically (the padlock symbol is gone).

21. Delete the rest of the sky with the **Magic Eraser Tool**.
22. Click on the road to delete it.

    Some parts of the house were deleted too, because they were similar in color to the road, Figure T7-23.

23. Choose **Edit > Undo Magic Eraser**.
24. Turn on the **Contiguous** option (place a check mark in the check box).
25. Delete the road and the mountains.
26. Create a new layer and use **Edit > Fill…** to fill it with a bright color.
27. Look for pixels that were not deleted. Use the **Eraser Tool** or the **Lasso Tool** to draw a selection border around the garbage pixels, then press [Delete].

    Make sure the layer with the house is active, otherwise you will delete the brightly colored fill.

Figure T7-23.
The road was removed with the **Magic Eraser Tool** with the **Contiguous** option off. Unfortunately, similarly colored areas of the house were removed along with the road.

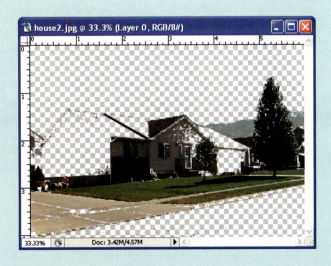

28. Select the **Eraser Tool**.
29. In the options bar, select **Brush** from the **Mode:** drop-down list.
30. Change the brush diameter to 2 px and the **Hardness:** setting to 100%.
31. Use the brush to erase any leftover bits of sky showing through the tree leaves.
32. Erase other items until your house looks like the example in **Figure T7-24**. Use different brush sizes as needed.
33. Zoom in on the driveway, as shown in **Figure T7-25**.
34. Select the **Polygonal Lasso Tool**.
35. Click at the location shown in Figure T7-25 to begin selecting the concrete driveway. Then, follow these guidelines:
    - Click every time you change direction.
    - To finish the selection border, hold the polygonal lasso over the exact point that you began. When you see a small circle appear next to the **Polygonal Lasso Tool** cursor, click to finish the selection.
36. When you have selected the driveway as shown, press [Delete].
37. Use the **Move Tool** to drag the house over to the 06hillside.psd image.

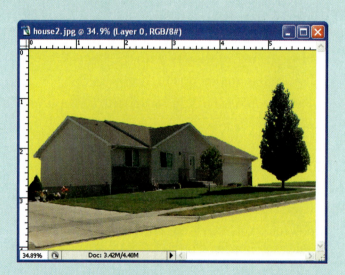

Figure T7-24.
This is how the house should look after you use the **Eraser Tool** to delete unwanted portions of the image.

Figure T7-25.
Select the driveway with the **Polygonal Lasso Tool** and press [Delete].

Click here to begin and end the selection

Chapter 7   Erasing, Deleting, and Undoing

38. Move the house to the location shown in **Figure T7-26**.
39. Close the house2.jpg file. Do *not* save the changes.
40. Choose **File > Save**, but leave the 06hillside.psd image open after saving it.
41. Open the house3.jpg file.
42. Press [Ctrl][A] to select the entire image.
43. Choose **Edit > Transform > Flip Horizontal**.
44. Delete the background and the road until the house looks like the example in **Figure T7-27**.
45. If you added a colored layer to help you identify garbage pixels, delete it now.
46. Use the **Move Tool** to drag the house over to the 06hillside.psd image.
47. Choose **Edit > Transform > Scale** and enter 300% in the **W:** and **H:** boxes.

> **Note**   When you make an image larger, you will start to see individual pixels unless the image has a high-quality resolution. The house3.jpg image has a resolution high enough to allow it to be enlarged by 300% without a *noticeable* loss in quality.

Figure T7-26. _____
Drag the house to 06hillside.psd image and position it as shown.

Figure T7-27. _____
Flip the house horizontally, and then erase the background using a variety of methods. The final result should look like this. Note that a colored layer has been added to help spot garbage pixels.

48. Click the **Commit** button in the options bar to end the scale command.
49. Move the house to the location shown in **Figure T7-28**.
50. Choose **Edit > Transform > Skew**.
51. Find the middle handle (square) on the right side of the bounding box. Hold the mouse cursor near the middle handle until the double arrow cursor appears.
52. Click and drag upward until the sidewalk appears to be running parallel to the road.

    Making the road and sidewalk *appear* to be parallel is *not* the same as making their edges parallel in the image. See **Figure T7-29**. The road and sidewalks should converge at a point in the distance, called the *vanishing point*. If the road were straight and level, the centerline of the sidewalk and the centerline of the road would converge at the horizon. However, in your image, the road changes direction and elevation slightly, making the lines of convergence dog-legged.

53. Click the **Commit** button in the options bar to end the **Skew** command.
54. Make sure that the layer containing the house closest to the viewer is at the top of the stack in the **Layers** palette. The layer containing the middle house should be next in the stack, followed by the layer containing the farthest away house, and, lastly, the background layer.
55. Choose **Layer > Flatten Image**.

    Because this file is so large, you flatten your image at this point to save file space.

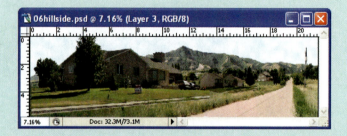

Figure T7-28.
Scale the house to 300% and move it to roughly the location shown here.

Figure T7-29.
Skew and reposition the house(s) as needed to make the sidewalk and road appear to run parallel to each other.

56. Choose **File > Save As...** and name the file 07hillside.psd. Close this file when you are done.

    You will work on this scene again later.

57. Close the house3.jpg file. Do not save the changes.

Key Terms

asymmetrical	erase	state
balance	extract	symmetrical design
delete	snapshot	vanishing point

Review Questions

Answer the following questions on a separate sheet of paper.

1. Briefly describe the difference between erasing and deleting, as explained by the author.
2. How can you use the selection tools to delete part of an image?
3. The **Eraser Tool**'s options bar is almost identical to what other tool's options bar?
4. What does the **Eraser Tool** do if you use it on a locked layer?
5. What does the **Eraser Tool** do if you use it on an unlocked layer?
6. What brush **Hardness:** setting is recommended when using the **Eraser Tool**?
7. What does the **Eraser Tool**'s **Erase to History** option do?
8. What does the **Background Eraser Tool**'s **Tolerance:** setting control?
9. What is the difference between the **Background Eraser Tool**'s **Sampling : Continuous** and **Sampling : Once** sampling options?
10. Describe the difference between the **Background Eraser Tool**'s **Contiguous** and **Discontiguous** options.
11. How do you check for garbage pixels after deleting an area with the **Background Eraser Tool** or **Magic Eraser Tool**?
12. How does the **Contiguous** option affect the **Magic Eraser Tool**?
13. How many states does the **History** palette remember (unless you change the setting)?
14. When referring the **History** palette, what is the difference between a snapshot and a state?
15. What command resets your file to its condition the last time you saved it?
16. What does the **History Brush Tool** do?
17. How is the **Art History Brush** different from the **History Brush Tool**?
18. Describe how you should apply highlighting to the edges of an object when extracting it from an image with the **Extract** filter. Focus on the relationship between the highlighting and the edge rather than the tools and mechanics used.
19. What does the **Extract** filter's **Smart Highlighting** option do?
20. What two tools become active when you switch to preview mode when using the **Extract** filter?

21. How do you change the brush pressure of the **Extract** filter's tools?
22. In the **Extract** dialog box, when is it not a good idea to use the **Edge Cleanup Tool** to go over the edges of an object before extracting it?
23. What does the **Reveal All** command do?
24. When using the **Trim** command, explain what happens when you choose either the **Top Left Pixel Color** or the **Bottom Right Pixel Color** option in the **Based On** section of the **Trim** dialog box.
25. Describe the function of the four check boxes in the **Trim Away** section of the **Trim** dialog box.

8 Restoring and Retouching Photos

Learning Objectives

After completing this chapter, you will be able to:
- Discuss the differences between restoring and retouching a photo.
- Explain what happens to a photo when it is sharpened.
- Sharpen a photo using the **Unsharp Mask** or **Smart Sharpen** filter.
- Sharpen or blur a small part of a photo using the **Sharpen Tool** and **Blur Tool**.
- Define the term "noise" as it applies to an image.
- Compare and contrast the four filters that remove noise from an image.
- Remove blemishes from an image with the **Spot Healing Brush Tool**.
- Describe the differences between the **Spot Healing Brush Tool**, **Healing Brush Tool**, and **Patch Tool**.
- Correct red eye problems in a photo with the **Red Eye Tool**.
- Explain how the **Clone Stamp Tool** is used to remove unwanted objects in a photo.
- Use the **Clone Stamp Tool** to retouch and manipulate photos.
- Use the **Vanishing Point** filter to maintain the proper perspective while retouching images that contain rectangular objects.

Introduction

Photos that have been ripped or damaged by sunlight, dirt, or grime can be scanned on a flatbed scanner, restored with Photoshop's tools, and printed. The term *restoring* refers to returning a photo to its original condition. The term *retouching* means to alter a photo from its original appearance. This could be a slight adjustment, like removing a pimple or a stray wisp of hair from a portrait—or a significant overhaul, such as completely removing a person from a group photo.

Photos that need to be restored or retouched should be scanned at a resolution of 300 spi (dpi) or higher. The smaller the pixels are in an image, the easier it is to repair problem areas. For accuracy, you should also zoom in on your image (at least 200%) when restoring or retouching it.

Photoshop has some amazing tools and techniques that are used to restore and retouch photos. We will begin with a simple retouching technique that many photos need—sharpening.

Sharpening an Image

Photoshop has several sharpening filters that can improve the appearance of images that are *slightly* out of focus. Unfortunately, Photoshop cannot sharpen an image that is considerably blurry.

When Photoshop sharpens an image, it causes dark pixels to get even darker, while light pixels become lighter. Most of the seashells shown in **Figure 8-1** have clearly defined edges that are slightly shadowed. When this image is sharpened, the edges become easier to see, or *sharper*, because the shadows get darker and the bright parts of the edges get even brighter. However, sharpening does not just affect the *edges* of objects—it can affect *all* of the detail in an image.

The Unsharp Mask Filter

The **Unsharp Mask** filter was used to sharpen the image in Figure 8-1B. One advantage of this filter is it lets you control the amount of sharpening. When you choose **Filter > Sharpen > Unsharp Mask…**, the **Unsharp Mask** dialog box appears, **Figure 8-2**. A preview of how the settings affect your image is displayed in the large window inside the dialog box. You can adjust this view using the zoom buttons (**+** and **−**) and the **Hand Tool**, which appears automatically when you click and drag the view of your image. To help you see how the sharpening settings affect your image, each time you click on the preview of your image with the **Hand Tool**, your image is displayed in its original condition. When you release the mouse button, the sharpening settings are applied to the preview again.

> **Note** The controls and techniques used to move around the preview window of the **Unsharp Mask** dialog box are common to many filter dialog boxes, including most of the dialog boxes described later in this chapter.

Figure 8-1.
Sharpening can bring out the details in an image. **A**—The original image is slightly blurry. **B**—Applying the **Unsharp Mask** filter causes light pixels to become lighter and dark pixels to become darker, causing the edges of objects to appear crisper.

A B

Figure 8-2.
A preview window in the **Unsharp Mask** dialog box shows how the current settings would affect the image.

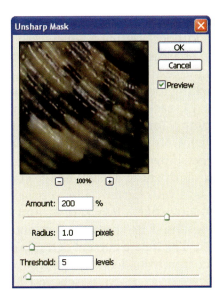

In addition to the preview window, the dialog box also has a **Preview** check box. When this check box is checked, the current settings are temporarily applied to the actual image. The effect on the image is updated every time the settings change. However, if you cancel out of the dialog box, the image is automatically restored to its original condition.

The **Amount:** slider setting determines how much darker the dark pixels become and how much lighter the light pixels become. Adjust this setting higher or lower depending on your personal preference, but a setting between 150 and 300 works well in most cases.

The **Radius:** slider setting determines the width of the effect. The higher the **Radius:** setting, the wider the sharpening effect appears along the object edges in your image. This setting is often best left between .5 and 1.5 pixels. A higher **Radius:** setting creates more extreme edges when the image is sharpened. Settings above 2 are usually not recommended, unless a special effect is desired.

The **Threshold:** slider setting tells Photoshop how sensitive it should be when searching for "edges" in an image. A low **Threshold:** setting causes Photoshop to sharpen almost all of the pixels in the image. A higher setting will sharpen only *high-contrast* edges, such as a bright, colorful object with a very dark shadow along its edge.

A recommended way to begin using the **Unsharp Mask** filter is to keep the **Radius:** slider set at 1.0 pixels. Then, jump back and forth between the **Amount:** setting and **Threshold:** setting until the effect looks good to you. Remember, lower **Threshold:** settings cause details in the entire image to become sharper; higher **Threshold:** settings cause obvious edges to become sharper.

The Smart Sharpen Filter

The **Smart Sharpen** filter is more complex than the **Unsharp Mask** filter. It is "smart" because it can help correct more than one kind of blur, such as *Gaussian blur* (a slight blur that is evenly distributed across the entire image) and *motion blur* (caused by camera movement or subject movement when the photo was captured).

When you select **Filter > Sharpen > Smart Sharpen...**, the **Smart Sharpen** dialog box appears. You can navigate around the preview window of this dialog box the same way you navigate the preview window in the **Unsharp Mask** dialog box. This dialog box also uses the same **Amount:** and **Radius:** settings that are used with the **Unsharp Mask** filter, plus several additional settings, **Figure 8-3**.

After you sharpen an image by adjusting the **Amount:** and **Radius:** settings, you can fine-tune the results by separately adjusting either the shadows or highlights. This is done by clicking the **Advanced** radio button, which causes the **Shadow** and **Highlight** tabs to appear. On each of these tabs is yet another **Amount:** (**Fade Amount:**) and **Radius:** slider, along with a **Tonal Width:** slider, which is similar to a tolerance control. The **Tonal Width:** slider controls how many closely-related colors found in the shadows (or highlights) are affected by the other two sliders.

If you are sharpening several images that have very similar blur problems, it may be helpful to save your current filter settings by clicking the **Save current filter settings** button, which looks like a floppy disk, and then naming the settings in the **New Filter Settings** dialog box. Filter settings that you have saved are available in the **Settings:** drop-down list. The **Delete current settings** button, which looks like a trash can, is used to delete the currently loaded settings from the **Settings:** drop-down list.

The **Remove:** drop-down list lets you select the type of blur to remove. The default setting is **Gaussian Blur**, which is the same blur setting used automatically by the **Unsharp Mask** filter. Try the **Lens Blur** option when sharpening images with lots of fine detail—you may get slightly better results. If the camera or the subject moved slightly when the image was captured, try correcting the problem with the **Motion Blur** option. When you choose the **Motion Blur** method, the **Angle:** setting becomes active. Enter a new value in the **Angle:** text box, or click and drag the compass icon to match the direction that the camera was jerked while shooting the picture.

Placing a check mark in the **More Accurate** check box causes Photoshop to take more time when calculating the sharpening effect. On some images, you may not be able to see a difference between using this option and leaving it off.

Other Sharpening Filters

There are several other filters in the **Filter** menu. The **Sharpen**, **Sharpen Edges**, and **Sharpen More** filters do not have any settings—they just apply an automatic dose of sharp-

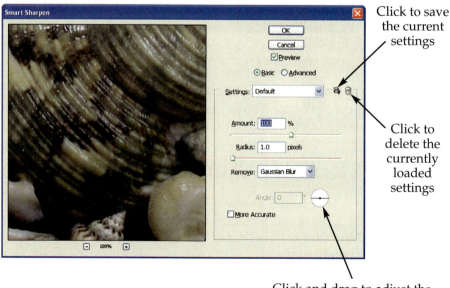

Figure 8-3.
The **Smart Sharpen** filter gives you the most control when sharpening an image.

ening to an image. It is recommended that you use the **Unsharp Mask** filter or the **Smart Sharpen** filter so you can view the results of your adjustments before clicking **OK**.

Sharpening Tips

Sharpening can be applied to only one layer at a time. If you want your entire image to be sharpened, save an unflattened copy of your file and then flatten it. After flattening the image, you can apply a sharpening filter to the entire image at once.

It is important to remember that sharpening will correct only *minor* blur problems. If an image is too blurry, do not use it—obtain another image.

As a general rule, sharpening your image should be the *last* thing you do before printing. For example, if you sharpen your image and then scale it to a larger size, the edge detail will become exaggerated. Professional Photoshop users do not sharpen until they know what type of printing device will be used to print the image. Images used in a newspaper ad, for example, need to be sharpened more than images that will appear in a high-quality magazine. Occasionally, trial and error is necessary when learning how much sharpening is ideal for a particular printing medium.

The Sharpen Tool vs the Blur Tool

When you only need to sharpen a small area of an image, you can create a selection around the area and use one of the sharpen filters. A feathered selection causes the filter effect to gradually blend into the surrounding areas of the image.

You can also sharpen a small area using the **Sharpen Tool**. The **Sharpen Tool** is found in Photoshop's **Toolbox**, just below the eraser tools, **Figure 8-4**. The **Sharpen Tool**'s options bar contains a **Brush Picker** and a **Mode** drop-down list, which should be familiar to you from your study of the brush tools. It also contains a **Strength:** slider, which controls how much sharpening is applied when you click and drag over the image. The final control in the **Sharpen Tool**'s options bar is the **Sample All Layers** check box. When this option is active, the **Sharpen Tool** will simultaneously sharpen the current layer and all layers *below* it in the **Layer Palette**'s layer stack.

Figure 8-4.
The **Sharpen Tool** and **Blur Tool** are found below the eraser tools in the **Toolbox**.

The **Blur Tool** is grouped with the **Sharpen Tool** in the **Toolbox**. The way the **Blur Tool** is used and its available options are exactly the same as those for the **Sharpen Tool**. However, as its name suggests, the tool blurs an image instead of sharpens it.

Filters That Remove Dust, Scratches, and Noise

If you have ever developed photographic prints in a darkroom, you know it can be difficult to keep dust from getting on your negatives and appearing on your prints. Another problem you may experience if you are a photographer is *noise*, inappropriate pixels that appear all over your image. These pixels may be too bright, too dark, an inappropriate color, or a combination of these problems. Noisy images are often described as "grainy" images. Noise is caused by increasing the ISO setting on a digital camera or by using "fast" film speeds in traditional photography. Both of these techniques allow you to capture photos in low light conditions. Some lower-quality digital cameras produce images with noise, too. The image in **Figure 8-5** has both dust and noise problems—dust on the negative caused the larger white specks to appear, and the tiny gray specks that cover the entire image is noise.

When you choose **Filter > Noise**, you will see several filters listed. The first filter, **Noise**, *adds* noise to an image as a special effect. The other filters in the **Noise** category *remove* unwanted specks and noise from an image and are described in the following sections.

The Despeckle Filter

The **Despeckle** filter removes noise by blurring an image slightly. Similar to the **Sharpen** filters, this filter finds edges of objects in the image and avoids blurring those areas so that edges remain sharp. The **Despeckle** filter was applied to the image in **Figure 8-6**.

The **Despeckle** filter has no settings to adjust. Other noise-removing filters have sliders that control both the blurring and sharpening effects. So, in cases where you need more precise control, use those instead of the **Despeckle** filter.

Figure 8-5.
When this image was developed, there was dust on the negative, which caused the white specks to appear. The tiny gray specks over the entire image are called noise, and were caused because the photographer used film with a high speed rating.

Figure 8-6.
The **Despeckle** filter removed much of the noise from this image, but the large white dust specks are too large to be removed by the filter.

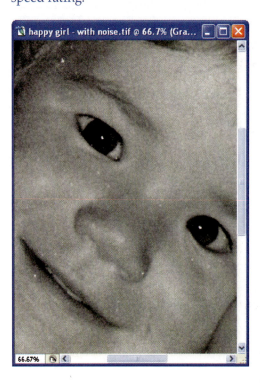

The Dust & Scratches and Median Filters

The **Dust & Scratches** and **Median** filters are very similar. Selecting **Filter > Noise > Dust & Scratches...** opens the **Dust & Scratches** dialog box, and selecting **Filter > Noise > Median...** opens the **Median** dialog box, Figure 8-7. Both dialog boxes have a preview window and preview controls, which should be familiar to you from your study of the **Unsharp Mask** filter's dialog box. In addition, both dialog boxes have a **Radius:** slider, which controls how intense the blurring effect will be to remove the noise. A **Radius:** setting greater than 2 is *not* recommended for most images.

The **Dust & Scratches** filter has a control that the **Median** filter does not have, the **Threshold:** slider. If this slider is set to 0, all pixels in the image will be blurred. This is what occurs automatically if you use the **Median** filter. As the **Threshold:** setting is increased, only the most obvious specks are eliminated. After setting the **Radius:** setting to 1 or 2, use the highest **Threshold:** setting that makes your image look good. Usually, **Threshold:** values above 128 are not used.

Figure 8-7.
Both the **Dust & Scratches** and **Median** filters let you control the blurring effect with the **Radius:** slider. **A**—The **Dust & Scratches** filter adds a **Threshold:** setting, which controls how much noise is blurred. **B**—The **Median** filter does not have the **Threshold:** setting. Instead, it automatically blurs all of the pixels in the image.

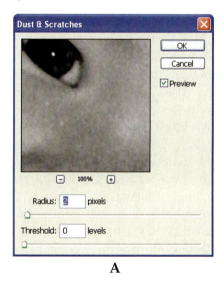
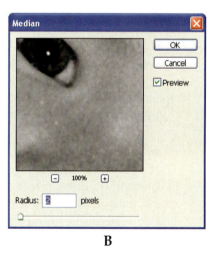

A   B

The Reduce Noise Filter

The **Reduce Noise** filter gives you the most precise control when removing noise from an image. When you choose **Filter > Noise > Reduce Noise...**, the **Reduce Noise** dialog box opens, Figure 8-8. This dialog box has the familiar preview window, zoom buttons, and **Preview** check box. It also has a number of other controls not found in the other noise filter dialog boxes.

At the top of the dialog box are two radio buttons, **Basic** and **Advanced**. When the **Advanced** radio button is selected, tabs labeled **Overall** and **Per Channel** appear under the **Settings:** drop-down list. If you select the **Per Channel** tab, you can adjust the noise-reduction setting on one *channel* at a time. This is helpful because occasionally, a particular channel may contain more noise than other channels. Select the appropriate channel from the **Channel:** drop-down list, adjust the **Strength:** slider to provide the desired level of noise reduction, and adjust the **Preserve Details:** slider to retain an

Figure 8-8.
The **Reduce Noise** filter gives you the most flexibility when attempting to clean up noise in an image.

acceptable level of edge detail in the image. Channels are discussed further in Chapter 10, *Advanced Color Correction Techniques*.

When the **Overall** tab is selected, the dialog box is configured the same way it is when the **Basic** radio button is selected instead of the **Advanced** radio button. All of the basic controls are available, and changes to the settings affect the entire image, not just one channel.

Beneath the **Basic** and **Advanced** radio buttons are the **Settings:** drop-down list, the **Save current filter settings** (floppy disk) button, and the **Delete current settings** (trash can) button. If you are working with several images that have the same noise problem, you can use these controls to save filter settings and then easily apply them again to another image.

The **Strength:** and **Preserve Details:** sliders are the first sliders you should adjust. These controls serve the same functions as their counterparts in the **Per Channel** tab, but apply the filter to the entire image instead of a single channel. You should start adjusting the filter effect by moving both of these sliders until you find a combination that removes the most noise. The higher the **Strength:** setting, the more noise is eliminated. The higher the **Preserve Details:** setting, the greater preservation of edges and textured areas in your image. If *color noise* (speckles or blotches of inappropriately colored pixels) is still visible after adjusting the first two sliders, adjust the **Reduce Color Noise** slider.

The **Sharpen Details:** slider serves the same function as a sharpening filter. You can use this slider to sharpen the image, or ignore it and use one of the sharpen filters instead.

The **Remove JPEG Artifact** option removes noisy pixels that appear when images are saved as low-resolution JPEG files. These stray pixels, or *artifacts*, can be scattered throughout the image or appear as light-colored halos around edges in an image.

Blemish-Removing Tools

The large white dust specks that are visible in the image of a smiling little girl are too large to be effectively removed by any of the noise filters. The blurring techniques simply do not hide such large specks. However, Photoshop has several tools in the **Toolbox** that will easily remove these large blemishes.

The Spot Healing Brush Tool

The **Spot Healing Brush Tool** is used to fix *blemishes* (small imperfections, such as dust specks) in a photo. It does this by automatically sensing where the blemish is when you click on it. Then, the pixels that surround the blemish are analyzed. The "undamaged" pixels are blended into the problem area, causing the area to "heal."

This tool works best if the area around the blemish is *not* highly detailed. Sometimes, it takes two or three clicks to completely fix a blemish with this tool. There are other situations where this tool will not fix the problem at all. However, because it is such an easy tool to use, it is worth trying first. You can also drag with this tool (over a scratch, for example), but you will get the best results by clicking in a single area at a time. If you make a mistake while using this tool, an easy way to correct it is to use the **History Brush Tool** to paint the area back to its original state. Then, try again.

Like many of Photoshop's tools, the **Spot Healing Brush Tool** has a **Brush Picker** and **Mode:** setting in its options bar, Figure 8-9. You should choose a brush size that is a bit larger than the area you want to fix.

The two radio buttons in the **Type:** area of the options bar determine how the **Spot Healing Brush Tool** fills in the blemish. The **Proximity Match** option tells the tool to fill the blemish with a blend of pixels that appear around the blemish and are contained within the limits of the brush. The **Create Texture** option fills in the area you click on with a blend of all of the pixels (including the blemish), creating a more textured look. Try using this option if the **Proximity Match** option does not produce good results.

Unless the **Sample All Layers** option is checked, the **Spot Healing Brush** will only sample a source point from a single, active layer.

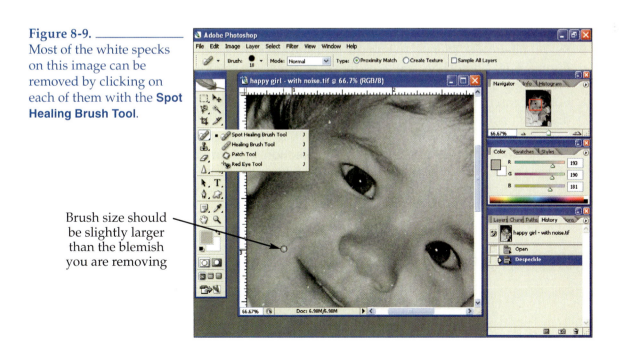

Figure 8-9. Most of the white specks on this image can be removed by clicking on each of them with the **Spot Healing Brush Tool**.

Brush size should be slightly larger than the blemish you are removing

The Healing Brush Tool

The **Healing Brush Tool** is similar to the **Spot Healing Brush Tool**. The main difference is that instead of clicking on the problem area, you first take a sample by choosing a *source point*, an area that Photoshop will refer to when fixing the problem.

To use the **Healing Brush Tool**, you set the brush size to be slightly larger than the area you are going to clean up. Then, you press [Alt] (or [Option] for Mac) and click on a source point—an area that the blemished area *should* look like. Photoshop will analyze the area you sampled as you click on (or drag over) the blemish. To hide the blemish, Photoshop creates a blend of the sampled area and the blemish area. The lighting and texture of the area you sample will be recreated over the problem area, so choose your sampling area carefully.

The **Healing Brush Tool**'s options bar has a **Source:** area containing two radio buttons, **Sampled** and **Pattern:**. See Figure 8-10. So far, you have read how this tool works with the **Sampled** option active. If the **Pattern:** option is selected instead, you do *not* choose a source point to begin the process. Instead, you begin by selecting a pattern from the **Pattern Picker**. As you click in the image with the **Healing Brush Tool**, Photoshop blends the selected pattern with the area in the brush radius. This creates a *textured* effect.

When the **Aligned** check box is checked and the **Pattern:** option is selected, a *tiled* pattern is created as you use the **Healing Brush Tool**. If the **Aligned** option is turned off, clicking the mouse occasionally as you paint creates a pattern that is *not tiled*. If the **Sampled** option is selected, the **Aligned** check box determines whether the sample area is continuous or resets every time the mouse is clicked.

The Patch Tool

The **Patch Tool** is similar to the **Healing Brush Tool**. However, the procedures for hiding a blemish are quite different. The technique used to hide a blemish with the **Patch Tool** depends on the radio button that is selected in the **Source** area of the options bar. When the **Source** radio button is selected, you begin by drawing a selection around the problem area. Then, you drag the problem area to a good area and release the mouse, Figure 8-11. Photoshop analyzes the good area and blends it with the problem area, preserving the shadows and texture of the problem area. Clicking the **Destination** radio button causes the tool to work in the opposite manner. A good area is selected first and dragged on top of the problem area.

The **Patch Tool** creates selections just like the **Lasso Tool**. If necessary, you can use the **Add to selection**, **Subtract from selection**, and **Intersect with selection** buttons on the options bar to fine-tune a selection before dragging it. When you want to add or subtract an area from the **Patch Tool** selection, make sure you start your additional

Figure 8-10.
The **Healing Brush Tool**'s options bar is shown here.

Figure 8-11.
When the **Patch Tool**'s **Source** option is active, a selection is drawn around the blemish and then dragged to a good area of the image. The selected area around the blemish is automatically updated as the selection is moved.

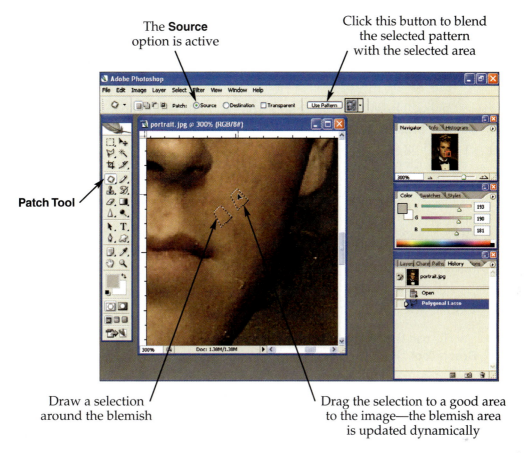

selection outside of the existing selection. Otherwise, you will adjust the contents of the patch rather than alter the shape of the selection.

The **Transparent** option, when on, causes the finished patch to end up being a bit lighter than it would be if this option were not checked. This option could be useful if you wanted to combine two features. However, you will want to leave this option off in most cases.

If you click the **Use Pattern** button, the pattern selected in the **Pattern Picker** is blended with the selected area, resulting in a *textured* look.

The Red Eye Tool

Red eye is caused when a camera's flash bounces off of the inside of the eyeball and reflects back toward the camera. The light reflects off of blood vessels in the back of the eye, causing a person's pupils to appear bright red.

The **Red Eye Tool** is one of Photoshop's easiest tools to use. It automatically senses the red area of the eye when you click on it, and changes all the red and pink pixels to black (since most people's pupils are nearly black). Shiny spots (highlights) in the eye are preserved, maintaining a realistic appearance.

The options bar of this tool has only two settings, **Figure 8-12**. There are no brush sizes to set with this tool. The **Pupil Size:** setting determines how large of a pupil area Photoshop attempts to create. That area is changed to black. The remainder of the red/pink area is changed to a dark gray, which helps blend the pupil area into the rest of the eye. The **Darken Amount:** setting controls how dark the grays and blacks appear in the pupil area.

The Clone Stamp Tool

Before discussing the **Clone Stamp Tool**, think of how similar the **Patch Tool**, **Healing Brush Tool**, and **Spot Healing Brush Tool** are. Each of these tools fix a problem by blending or "healing" the problem area.

The **Clone Stamp Tool** works differently. The term *clone* means to "create an exact copy of" something. The **Clone Stamp Tool** copies pixels from one area to another in an image, using any brush size and style that you select. This tool is used to remove unwanted areas from a photo by copying desirable areas on top of the unwanted areas. For example, you could remove an old, junky car from a scenic photo by cloning grass and shrubs found in other areas of the image over the old car until it completely disappears.

Using the Clone Stamp Tool

To use the **Clone Stamp Tool**, you first choose a source point. As with the **Healing Brush Tool**, the source point is selected by pressing [Alt] (or [Option] for Mac) and clicking

Figure 8-12.
To fix red eye, simply click once on the red pupil area with the **Red Eye Tool**. The **Red Eye Tool**'s options let you specify how large the pupil should be and how dark the pupil becomes.

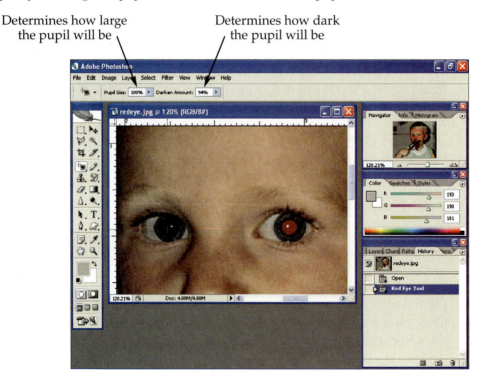

on the area you want to copy. A crosshair symbol appears, helping you click in an exact spot. Next, move the cursor to another area and start painting. The crosshair symbol remains on your screen, showing you exactly where you are copying from—it moves along with your brush that is "painting" the copied pixels. For best results, clone a little at a time, release the mouse button, and choose another source point—even if it is near the same spot as the previous source point. When you clone a little at a time, you can easily undo a mistake without losing a lot of your work.

Usually, you choose a source point and clone on the same layer, but in situations where you want to keep layers separate, you can sample from one layer and clone to another layer. Use the **Layers** palette to make the layer you sample from active first, then make the layer you are cloning to active after choosing a source point. You can also open two different images and clone from one image to another.

The Clone Stamp Tool's Options Bar

The **Clone Stamp Tool**'s options bar contains the same settings as the **Brush Tool**'s options bar, plus two more, Figure 8-13. When the **Aligned** option is turned off, the **Clone Stamp Tool** starts over every time the mouse is clicked. This is useful if you want to reproduce the same small area of the source image multiple times in the target image. If the **Aligned** option is active, the **Clone Stamp Tool** continues cloning based on the first location you clicked, even if you have jumped to a different location. In essence, the **Clone Stamp Tool** continues painting the same "big picture." This is useful if you want to reproduce different areas of the source image, but you want them to keep their spatial relationship. In most cases, you will need to click on several different source points as you clone, so it does not matter whether this option is off or on.

The **Sample All Layers** option, when enabled, causes the **Clone Stamp Tool** to copy pixels from all visible layers instead of from the single layer that was active when the source point was selected.

To get realistic results when cloning, you must pay attention to the lighting and shadows that help define an object. A correct and incorrect source point selection are shown in Figure 8-14. The fingers all have similar shadows. The top of each finger is well-lit. The sides of the fingers are somewhat in shadow, and toward the bottom of each finger, the shadows are darker still. To successfully remove the ring from the finger, you must clone the right skin color over the ring.

There are other ways you can adjust the **Clone Stamp Tool** to match the brightness and darkness of the areas you are retouching. You may try lowering the **Opacity:** setting in the options bar to help create a blended look. You may also try experimenting with the blending modes available in the **Mode:** drop-down list, especially the **Darken** and **Lighten** modes.

Figure 8-13.
The **Clone Stamp Tool** has the same options as the **Brush Tool**, plus the **Aligned** and **Sample All Layers** options.

Figure 8-14.
You must choose your source point carefully when using the **Clone Stamp Tool**. **A**—A light area of the finger is being cloned to an area that should be somewhat shaded. This results in unacceptable mismatch between the original skin tone and the cloned areas. **B**—The ring can be removed successfully by cloning the correct shade of skin over it. Note that the source point and the brush are at the same horizontal level.

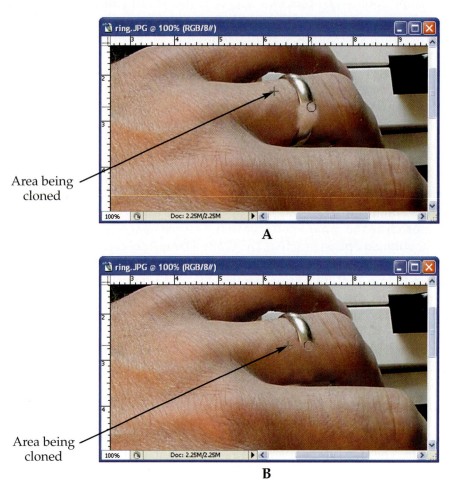

The Vanishing Point Filter

The term *vanishing point* refers to the point at which parallel receding lines of rectangular object, such as a box or a building, converge (or *would* converge if they were extended) in a perspective drawing. A ***perspective drawing*** is a drawing that creates the illusion of depth.

The **Vanishing Point** filter is used to help you retouch images in the proper perspective. For example, long ago, someone started painting the barn shown in **Figure 8-15**, but never finished. Suppose you are working on a project that requires an image of an old red barn, but this is the best image you have been able to come up with. You can use the **Vanishing Point** filter to help you finish painting all of the walls, including the upper wall that is shaded and slants away from the front of the barn.

> **Note**
> You can use any method to select an area of your image *before* choosing **Filter > Vanishing Point...**. Changes made with the **Vanishing Point** filter will only affect the area that you selected.

Figure 8-15. _____
The **Vanishing Point Filter** can be used to alter this image so that the barn appears to be completely painted. It could also be used to copy windows to the shaded wall.

Creating and Adjusting Planes

Choosing **Filter > Vanishing Point...** opens the **Vanishing Point** dialog box. Your first task is to help Photoshop recognize the different sides of this barn. This is done by creating planes on your image. The **Create Plane Tool** is the second tool from the top of the dialog box toolbar. It looks like a slanted rectangular grid. Use this tool to create a plane by clicking four corners of the most obvious surface of the barn. In this case, the front wall of the barn is the most obvious surface. When you have clicked to establish four corners, a grid-covered plane is created. Click on the corner points of the plane with the **Edit Plane Tool** (the first tool in the dialog box toolbar) to adjust the plane, if necessary. You can also move the plane by clicking and dragging it with the **Edit Plane Tool**. If desired, you can change the **Grid Size** setting to change the number of grid lines. In the Figure 8-16, the first corner of the plane was placed at the intersection of the barn's wall and roof. The bottom of the plane was lined up with the barn's foundation and the sides were lined up with the edges of the walls. The final corner was adjusted so that the top

Figure 8-16. _____
The first step when using the **Vanishing Point** filter is to create a plane on the most obvious surface of the structure. Once the proper place has been established, you can grab the center handles to resize the plane without changing its perspective.

Drag the center handles to resize the plane

Drag the corner handles to change the plane's perspective

line of the plane was parallel to the bottom of the hayloft door and intersected the roof at the same place on both sides.

Correctly-drawn planes are blue. If a plane is red or yellow, Photoshop cannot analyze it. Correct the problem by adjusting the corner points with the **Edit Plane Tool** until the plane turns blue.

The dialog box toolbar includes **Zoom Tool** and **Hand Tool** so you can adjust your view until you can easily see the area you are working on. You can also *temporarily* zoom in by pressing [X].

To help Photoshop recognize a structure, you must create additional planes that are *perpendicular* (at a 90° angle) to the first plane. To do this, click the **Create Plane Tool** again. Hold down [Ctrl] (or [Command] for Mac), and grab a side handle (not a corner handle) of the first plane you created. Drag the handle in the desired direction to create an additional plane. This process is called "tearing off" another plane. In **Figure 8-17**, the plane was dragged along the upper, shadowed wall of the barn. Then, the **Edit Plane Tool** was used to adjust the corners of the plane until it followed the barn's roof line.

At this point, Photoshop can calculate where two different barn walls are located and how they relate to each other. You are now ready to retouch this image, using several familiar-looking tools—although in the **Vanishing Point** filter, these tools behave differently than what you might expect.

The Vanishing Point Filter's Marquee Tool

The **Vanishing Point** filter's **Marquee Tool** can be used to select an area, which can then be moved, transformed, or copied and pasted. This tool can also function like the **Patch Tool**. Its options include some familiar controls, **Figure 8-18**.

The **Show Edges** option displays the borders of planes and the marching ants of selections in the dialog box's preview window. When this option is deselected, any selections you have made and planes you have created are temporarily hidden. This is useful if those features get in the way.

Increasing the **Feather:** setting creates a selection with a feathered edge instead of a crisp edge. You can adjust this setting before or after creating a selection. The **Opacity:** setting controls the transparency of an area that you copy and paste or drag to a new location.

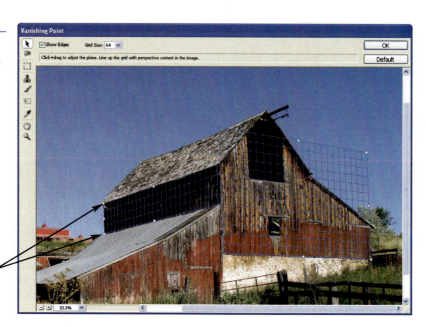

Figure 8-17. Create additional planes (by dragging side handles from the first plane) until you have defined all of the surfaces you will be working with.

Drag the corner handles to adjust the perspective

Figure 8-18.
The **Vanishing Point** filter's **Marquee Tool** is a combination of a selection tool and a version of the **Patch Tool**.

The **Marquee Tool** draws a selection in the same perspective as the plane

Using the Marquee Tool to Patch an Area

When using this tool to patch an area, **Luminance** (a lighter blending mode) or **On** (a darker blending mode) must be selected in the **Heal:** drop-down list. The **Move Mode:** drop-down list becomes available just after you create a selection. As with the **Patch Tool**, this option can either be set to **Destination** or **Source**.

The **Destination** mode is straightforward—you press [Alt], click, and drag the selected area to a new destination. If you drag from one plane to another, the selection adjusts to the proper perspective. A blended area will result if the **Heal:** option is set to **On** or **Luminance**. Once you have placed the patch, the **Transform Tool** becomes available in the toolbar of the dialog box, **Figure 8-19**. With this tool, you can scale or rotate your selection by dragging handles that appear around it. You can also flip or flop (a vertical version of flip) the selected area.

The **Source** mode is more complicated. When this mode is active, you cannot move the selected area elsewhere. Instead, the selected area is filled with the area under the

Figure 8-19.
The **Transform Tool** becomes available when you copy and paste or press [Alt] (or [Option] for Mac) and drag a selected area.

Once the patch is placed, the **Transform Tool** becomes available

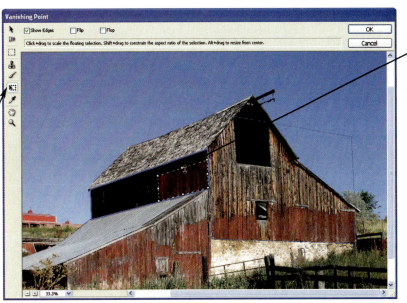

The selected area is blended with the existing image

cursor. The pixels inside the selection are updated as you drag the cursor around your image. Again, a blended effect results if the **Heal:** option is set to **On** or **Luminance**.

> **Note** Pressing [Ctrl], and dragging is the shortcut to selecting **Source:** mode.

The Vanishing Point Filter's Stamp Tool

When the **Heal** option is off, the **Vanishing Point** filter's **Stamp Tool** works just like Photoshop's **Clone Stamp Tool**. When **Heal:** is set to **Luminance** or **On**, it works like the **Healing Brush Tool**.

To begin cloning an area, first select the source point by pressing [Alt] (or [Option] for Mac) and clicking the desired area. Next, set the brush controls for the **Stamp Tool** to the desired values. Then, click and drag to reproduce the sampled area with the **Stamp Tool**.

Green crosshairs mimic the movements of the cursor, continually showing you the area being sampled. If the **Aligned** check box is checked, the crosshairs follow the cursor even when the mouse button is released. This allows you to continue painting the same image with multiple strokes. When this check box is unchecked, the crosshairs remain stationary every time the mouse button is released, essentially resetting the tool.

If you clone in a different plane, the cloning adjusts to the proper perspective. In Figure 8-20, a rectangular selection was created on the upper, unpainted barn wall. Then, the **Stamp Tool** was used to sample a painted area on the front of the barn. The painted area is being cloned within the selection border, which protects the two roofs from being edited. Because the **Heal:** option is set to **On**, the cloned area will blend somewhat with the shadowed unpainted area behind it when the mouse button is released.

The Vanishing Point Filter's Brush Tool

The **Vanishing Point** filter's **Brush Tool** applies color that you select in the options bar of the dialog box. You can specify how transparent the paint appears by adjusting

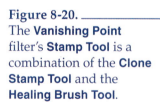

Figure 8-20.
The **Vanishing Point** filter's **Stamp Tool** is a combination of the **Clone Stamp Tool** and the **Healing Brush Tool**.

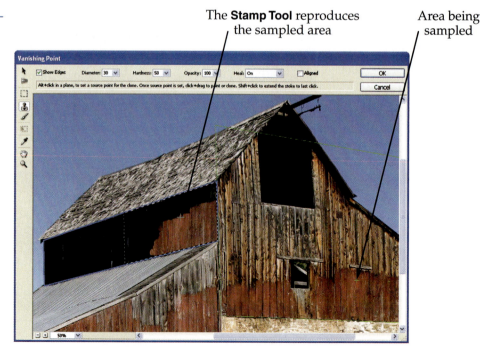

The **Stamp Tool** reproduces the sampled area

Area being sampled

the value in the **Opacity:** slider. If you set the **Heal:** option to **Luminance** or **On**, the **Brush Tool** will blend the paint into the existing image. If the **Heal:** option is set to **Off**, the paint replaces the image. To select a color, click the **Brush Color:** box or double-click on the **Brush Tool** itself. Or, you can use the **Vanishing Point** filter's **Eyedropper Tool** to sample a color in the image you are editing.

For the example of the barn, a very effective way to make it appear freshly painted is to draw a selection around the areas you want to paint and then use the **Eyedropper Tool** to select the red paint color. Next, use the **Brush Tool**, with the opacity lowered, to paint the bare wood on the front wall. The opacity should be lowered yet again to paint the shadowed wall. The texture of the wood and the shadows show through the paint that is applied, giving the barn a realistic appearance. The advantage of doing this in the **Vanishing Point** filter is that it allows you to quickly create selections in perspective, protecting the areas that you do not want to paint, **Figure 8-21**.

Another benefit of painting in the **Vanishing Point** dialog box, is that the brush shape and size are automatically adjusted for the perspective. As the brush moves over areas of the image that are farther away from the viewer, the brush size automatically shrinks. As the brush moves from one plane to another, its shape changes accordingly.

Other Tips for Working with the Vanishing Point Filter

The following are some other points to consider before you experiment with the **Vanishing Point** filter:

- The **Vanishing Point** dialog box does not have menu commands. If you want to copy something from another image and paste it into the **Vanishing Point** dialog box, copy it to the clipboard (choose **Edit > Copy** or press [Ctrl][C]) before you open the image you want to edit in the **Vanishing Point** filter. When you are ready to paste, press [Ctrl][V].

- Create a new layer before choosing **Filter > Vanishing Point**. All of your work done with the **Vanishing Point** filter will be saved on this new layer, and your original image will be preserved.

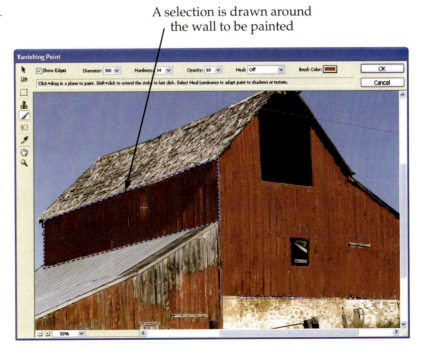

Figure 8-21.
The **Brush Tool** is being used to paint one side of the barn. Note that the brush shape is adjusted for the perspective. Also, a selection protects the surrounding areas from accidental painting. In addition to applying color, the **Vanishing Point** filter's **Brush Tool** can blend color if the **Heal:** option is set to **Luminance** or **On**.

A selection is drawn around the wall to be painted

- When you close the **Vanishing Point** dialog box by clicking **OK**, the changes are applied to your image. The planes that you defined to establish the perspective of your image are saved to memory. If you select the **Vanishing Point** filter again in the same session, the grids will already be there. If you save the image after modifying it with the **Vanishing Point** filter, the grids you defined are saved with the image. That means that you can use the **Vanishing Point** filter on the image again in a completely different session, and the planes will already be defined.

GRAPHIC DESIGN:
Using a Grid

Another way to create a sense of balance, especially in multiple-page designs such as magazine articles or brochures, is to use a grid. To use this approach, the design area is divided up horizontally and vertically, forming a grid of rectangular shapes. Then, design elements are shaped and placed according to the grid. When a designer uses the same grid as a guide when designing each page, a consistent look is created throughout the entire document.

Refer to the sample grid shown in **Figure 8-22** as you consider the following guidelines:

- Do not create the grid where page margins should appear.
- Leave channels of white space between each grid area so design elements are not crowded together when placed on the grid.
- There are many possible grid configurations. The horizontal and vertical areas can be spaced equally as shown in Figure 8-22, but grid styles can vary. Elaborate grid systems can be used, but the design will most likely

Figure 8-22.
Grids are extremely useful for designing a document. **A**—A simple grid containing three equally-spaced horizontal and vertical areas has been created on an 8.5" × 11" document. **B**—The grid is then used as a guide when placing elements in the design.

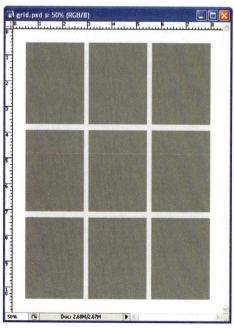

A   B

appear overcrowded if a grid containing more than seven horizontal and seven vertical areas is used.

- Photoshop's rulers and guides or rectangular shapes can be used to create a grid.

Figure 8-23 shows two slightly different page designs based on the same grid. When placing design elements according to a grid, consider these tips:

- Text areas and photographs can occupy more than one grid area, as long as they do not partially cover any grid area.
- Care should be taken when breaking text up into sections. For maximum readability, text should be placed in columns.

Grids can be created and stored as templates and brought out later to help a designer create a quick design. Using grids is also a good practice when a team of designers is assigned to a project. Consistency is easier to obtain when each team member refers to the same grid.

Figure 8-23.
This two-page article was based on the same grid pattern.

Summary

The restoring and retouching tools discussed in this chapter can help you improve the appearance of almost any photo. However, your best choice may be to obtain another image if your image is extremely blurry, damaged, or has severe lighting problems (large areas of dark shadows or bright highlights that completely drown out the details). Of course, if you are restoring old photographs, you must use the image you have—just do the best you can.

Remember that if you scan an image to restore or retouch it, set the scan resolution to a minimum of 300 spi for best results.

Chapter Tutorials

These tutorials will provide opportunities for you to practice sharpening images, manipulating photos with the **Clone Stamp Tool**, removing red eye, and retouching portraits and old photos, including one old photograph that is very difficult to restore.

Tutorial 8-1: Sharpening (and Blurring) an Image

In this tutorial, you will use the **Unsharp Mask** filter to bring out detail in the foreground object of an image. You will also apply a **Gaussian Blur** filter to the background of the image, to add emphasis to the object in the foreground. This technique is useful when you want to draw attention to one object in an image.

1. Open the quarter.jpg file.
2. The entire image (canvas), needs to be rotated. Choose **Image > Rotate Canvas > 90° CCW**.
3. Select the **Elliptical Marquee Tool** in the **Toolbox**.
4. Hold down [Alt] (or [Option] for Mac) and click in the center of the quarter. Drag to create a selection around the quarter, **Figure T8-1**.

   As you drag, hold down [Shift], if necessary, to force a perfect circle. Press [Spacebar] to drag the selection as you are creating it.

5. When you have created a selection around the quarter, choose **Filter > Sharpen > Unsharp Mask…**. See **Figure T8-2**.
6. In the **Unsharp Mask** dialog box, set the **Amount:** slider to 200%, the **Radius:** slider to 1.2 pixels, and the **Threshold:** slider to 6 levels. When the settings are adjusted, Click **OK**.
7. Choose **Select > Deselect**.
8. The **Elliptical Marquee Tool** should still be active. In the options bar, enter 150 px in the **Feather:** box.

Elliptical Marquee Tool

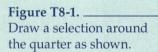

Figure T8-1. Draw a selection around the quarter as shown.

Figure T8-2. _____
The **Unsharp Mask** filter brings out detail on the quarter.

9. Create another circular selection around the quarter as shown in **Figure T8-3**.

   Because of the large feather setting, your circle will shrink after you create it, showing you the halfway mark of the feather effect. To compensate for the feathering, make your selection 1/2" larger in *diameter* than the selection shown in the figure.

10. Choose **Select > Inverse**.
11. Choose **Filter > Blur > Gaussian Blur**.
12. In the **Gaussian Blur** dialog box, set the **Radius:** slider to 3.5 pixels.
13. Click **OK**.
14. Choose **Select > Deselect**.

    Because of the feather setting you entered, the blur effect gradually blends into the area of the image that is in focus.

15. Choose **File > Save As...** and name this file 08quarter.psd.
16. Close the 08quarter.psd file.

Figure T8-3. _____
After drawing a new, larger selection around the quarter and inverting it, apply a **Gaussian Blur** filter to the selection.

Tutorial 8-2: Retouching a Damaged Portrait

In this tutorial, you will use the **Spot Healing Brush Tool**, the **Healing Brush Tool**, and the **Patch Tool** to remove blemishes from a photo.

1. Open the file named portrait.jpg.
2. Zoom in as shown.
3. Click the **Healing Brush Tool**.

Healing Brush Tool

4. Set the brush **Diameter:** to 15 px and the **Hardness** to 50%.
5. Hold down [Alt] (or [Option] for Mac) and click on a clear area of skin that is the same color and lighting as the area surrounding the blemish. See **Figure T8-4**.
6. Release [Alt].
7. Click on the most prominent pimple in the image.

The blemish area is blended with the sampled area, hiding the pimple.

Spot Healing Brush Tool

8. Click the **Spot Healing Brush Tool** in the **Toolbox**.
9. Improve the image by clicking on pimples, dust, and scratch marks with the **Spot Healing Brush Tool**. Continually adjust the brush size as needed.

If the **Spot Healing Brush Tool** fails to fix an area after clicking on it twice, switch to the **Healing Brush Tool** and follow steps 5–7 to fix the area. Do not worry about fixing the background. You will fix that with a different tool.

10. Zoom into the upper left corner of the portrait.jpg image, as shown in **Figure T8-5**.
11. Click the **Patch Tool** in the **Toolbox**.

Patch Tool

12. In the options bar, click the **Destination** radio button. Make sure the **Transparent** check box is not checked.

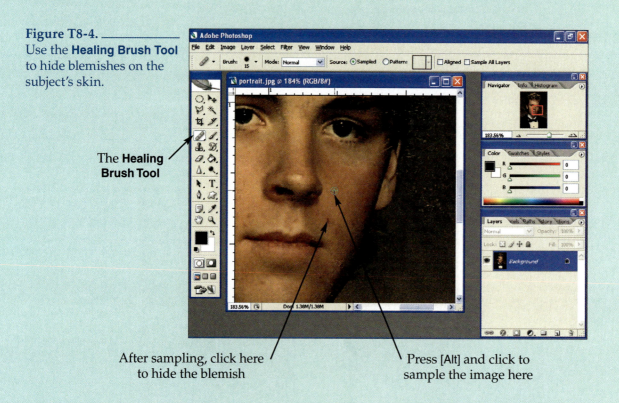

Figure T8-4.
Use the **Healing Brush Tool** to hide blemishes on the subject's skin.

The **Healing Brush Tool**

After sampling, click here to hide the blemish

Press [Alt] and click to sample the image here

Figure T8-5.
Use the **Patch Tool** to repair speckles from background.

Activate the **Destination** option

Draw a selection border with the **Patch Tool**

Click and drag the selection to a speckled area of the background

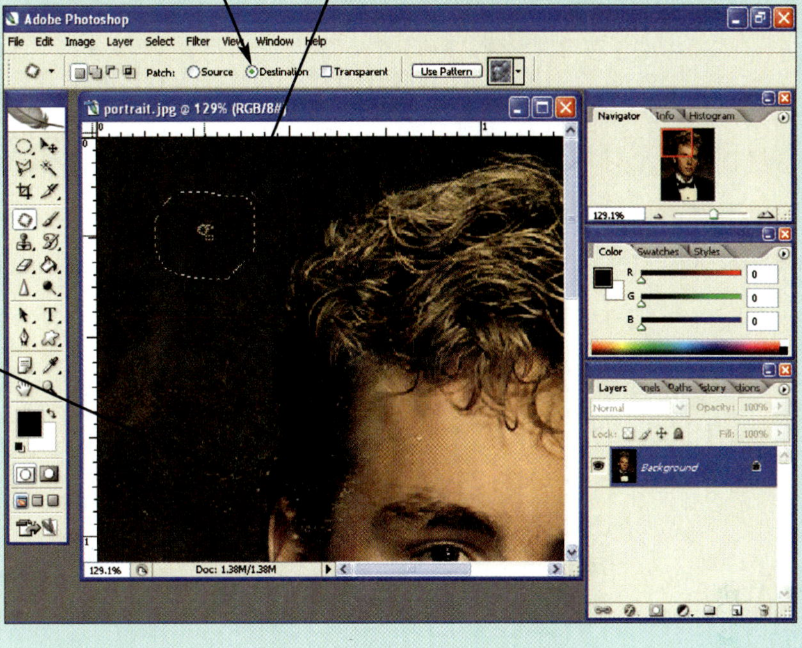

13. Use the **Patch Tool** to draw a small selection border on the background, where there are no dust specks.
14. Move the cursor inside of the selected area and drag the selection border on top of some dust specks. Then, release the mouse button.
15. Drag the selection border over another area with dust specks.
16. Continue using the **Patch Tool**, the **Healing Brush Tool**, and the **Spot Healing Brush Tool** to remove all of the dust specks and scratches from the entire photo.
17. Choose **File > Save As...** and name this file 08portrait.jpg.
18. Close the 08portrait.jpg file.

Tutorial 8-3: Manipulating Photos with the Clone Tool

In this tutorial, you will use the **Clone Stamp Tool** to remove unwanted objects in the image. You will also carefully draw selections and use the **Clone Stamp Tool** to create new features in the image based on existing features. These techniques are used extensively in the creation of photo simulations.

1. Open the 07hillside.psd file that you edited in the last chapter.
2. Close all palettes except for the **Layers** palette and the **Navigator** palette. Arrange the windows on your screen as shown in **Figure T8-6**.
3. Zoom in on the utility pole.
4. Click the **Clone Stamp Tool** in the **Toolbox**.

Clone Stamp Tool

5. In the options bar, set the brush **Master Diameter:** to 100 px and the **Hardness:** to 0.
6. Hold down [Alt] (or [Option] for Mac) and click a portion of the sky near the pole.
7. Release the [Alt] key.

Figure T8-6. Use the **Clone Stamp Tool** to hide the top of the pole by painting over it with sky.

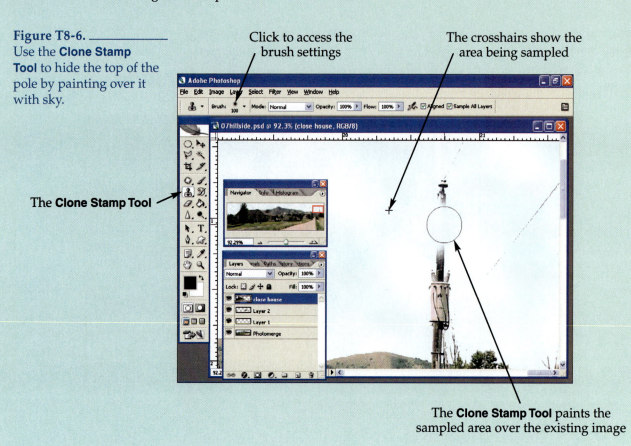

8. Paint a small area of the utility pole.

   The crosshairs symbol (+) shows where you are cloning (copying) from.

9. Hold down [Alt] and click in a different place in the sky.
10. Release the [Alt] key.
11. Clone (paint) sky over another small area of the pole.

    Whenever you use the **Clone Stamp Tool**, you should only do a little bit at a time. That way, you will not lose too much work if you need to undo any of it. You should also be aware of the crosshairs. They show you exactly where you are copying from.

12. Continue cloning sky over the pole until you get to the horizon (where the mountains meet the sky), **Figure T8-7**.

    You may need to reduce the size of the brush as you begin to work closer to the horizon. Also, make sure you clone out the wires.

13. Hold down [Alt] and click an area of the tree to the right of the pole.
14. Change the brush size to 50 pixels.
15. Paint tree leaves over a small area of the utility pole.
16. Hold down [Alt] and click in a different place on the tree.
17. Release the [Alt] key.
18. Clone (paint) trees over another small area, as shown in **Figure T8-8**.

    When you clone from different areas, you avoid creating tree branches that look exactly the same, something you would never see in nature.

19. In the options bar, set the brush size to 3 pixels and the **Hardness:** to 100%.

Figure T8-7.
Sample from different areas as you clone out the pole.

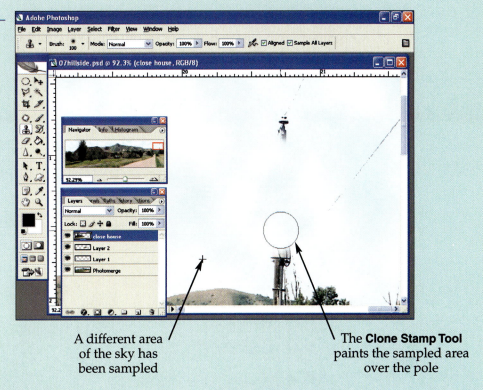

A different area of the sky has been sampled

The **Clone Stamp Tool** paints the sampled area over the pole

Figure T8-8.
After you sample an area from the original tree, paint a small area of the pole, and then sample a new area. Choose your sample areas carefully. For example, sample the areas from the middle of the tree to cover the middle of the pole, and from the top of the tree to cover the top of the pole.

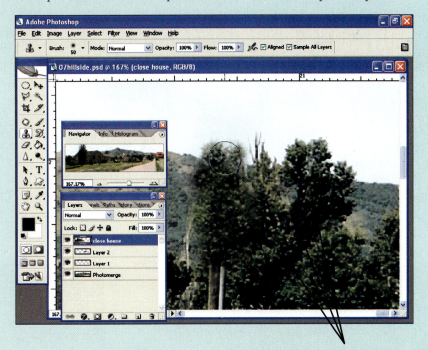

Sample from different areas of the tree to avoid obvious duplications

20. Clone the sky over the fuzzy edges of the tree. See **Figure T8-9**.
21. Continue to remove the utility pole with the **Clone Stamp Tool**. Use **Figure T8-10** as a guide.

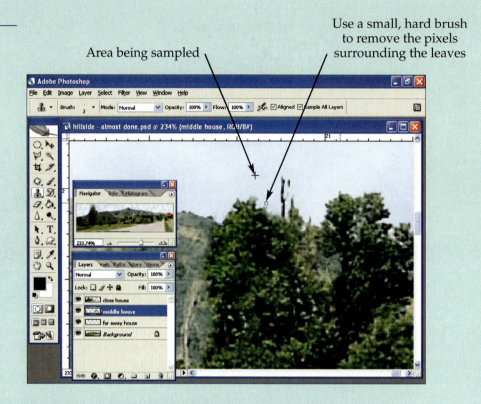

Figure T8-9. Use a small, hard brush to clone sky around the edges of the tree.

Area being sampled

Use a small, hard brush to remove the pixels surrounding the leaves

Figure T8-10. With careful sampling and proper use of the **Clone Stamp Tool**, you can effectively hide the pole. **A**—The pole in the original image. **B**—The pole has been effectively hidden by cloning the background.

A

B

Chapter 8   Restoring and Retouching Photos

Polygonal Lasso Tool

22. Use the **Clone Stamp Tool** to remove three other utility poles that are farther up the road (zoom in to find them).
23. Choose **File > Save**.
24. Zoom in on the front lawn of the middle house.
25. Use the **Polygonal Lasso Tool** to create a selection border like the one shown in **Figure T8-11**.
26. Click the **Clone Stamp Tool**.
27. Press [Alt] (or [Option] for Mac) and click on the road. Then, clone the road inside the selection border.
28. Choose **Select > Deselect**.
29. The concrete curb needs to be longer. Create another selection border like the one shown in **Figure T8-12**, and clone from the curb next to it.
30. Continue using the **Clone Stamp Tool** and careful selections to create natural-looking curbs, driveways, and sidewalks.
31. Clone trees and shrubs to help blend the houses with their surroundings.

Figure T8-11.
Draw a selection like the one shown here. This selection will be used to extend the road to the curbside.

Figure T8-12.
Use the **Clone Stamp Tool** to widen the road. Then, draw a selection to use for lengthening the curb.

The road has been widened with the **Clone Stamp Tool**

Draw a selection to extend the curb

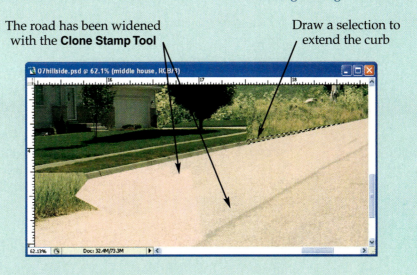

32. Check for bits of blue sky around the tree indicated in **Figure T8-13**. Use the **Clone Stamp Tool** to cover any blue spots with leaves.
33. Zoom in close and check around each house for other bits of color that do not belong.
34. Choose **Window > Workspace > Reset Palette Locations**.
35. Choose **Layer > Flatten Image**.
36. Choose **File > Save As...** and name this file 08hillside.psd.
37. Close the 08hillside.psd file.

Tutorial 8-4: Using the Clone Stamp Tool to Remove an Object from an Image

In this tutorial, you will use the **Clone Stamp Tool** to remove a person's ring in a photo. By cloning areas with the same light conditions, you will ensure that your alterations will blend well with the original image and look completely natural. This is a common photo touch-up technique.

1. Open the file named ring.jpg.
2. Zoom in closer to the ring, as shown in **Figure T8-14**.
3. Click the **Clone Stamp Tool**. In the options bar, select a soft round brush and make it 10 pixels wide.
4. Start by cloning the lightest part of the finger over upper part of the ring.
5. Clone the darker parts of the finger over the lower part of the ring.

   The finger will look real if you pay attention to the lighting and shadows as you clone.

6. Use the **Clone Stamp Tool** to remove the rest of the ring, **Figure T8-15**.

   Use the bracket keys ([,]) to change brush sizes as you work.

7. Choose **File > Save As...** and name this file 08ring.jpg.
8. Close the 08ring.jpg file.

Figure T8-13. Check the tree in front of the middle house for remnants of blue sky. Taper the ends of the curbs and flare the end of the driveway. Clone bushes to hide elements that look out of place.

Clone shrubs to blend the houses with their surroundings

Look for and clone out bits of blue sky around this tree

Figure T8-14. Sample an area that is directly across from the area you will be brushing. By sampling a spot that is right next to the area you will be brushing, you ensure that the lighting will be very similar.

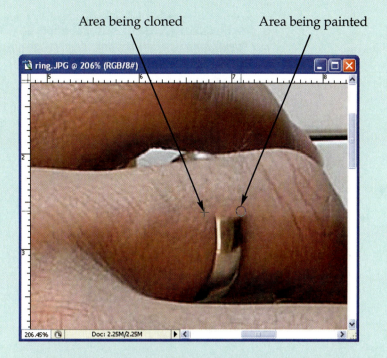

Figure T8-15. If the **Clone Stamp Tool** is properly applied, the alteration is nearly undetectable.

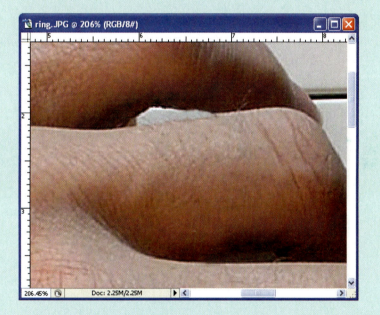

Tutorial 8-5: Fixing Red Eye

In this tutorial, you will use the **Red Eye Tool** to remove red eye from an image taken by flash photography. Red eye is caused when a camera's flash illuminates blood vessels in the back of the eye. The **Red Eye Tool** makes it extremely easy to correct red eye.

1. Open the redeye.jpg file.
2. Zoom in as shown in **Figure T8-16**.
3. Click the **Red Eye Tool**.

Red Eye Tool

Figure T8-16. Zoom in on the eyes before using the **Red Eye Tool**.

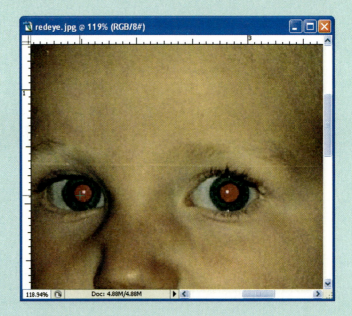

4. In the options bar, set the **Pupil Size:** slider to 90% and the **Darken Amount:** slider to 92%.
5. Click on the red area of each eye once.
6. Choose **File > Save As…** and name this file 08redeye.jpg.
7. Close the 08redeye.jpg file.

Tutorial 8-6: Restoring a Damaged Photo

In this tutorial, you will restore a photo that had previously been ripped in half. The two pieces were placed on a scanner and scanned at a resolution of 300 dpi. Unfortunately, the two halves were not properly lined up before the image was scanned. You will select one half of the photo and move it into proper alignment. You will then use the **Spot Healing Brush Tool** and the **Clone Stamp Tool** to hide the tear and repair the defects in the photo.

1. Open the buggy.jpg file.
2. Zoom in on the tear as shown in **Figure T8-17**.
3. Select the **Magnetic Lasso Tool** in the **Toolbox**. In the options bar, set the **Width:** to 4 px, the **Edge Contrast:** to 75%, and the **Frequency:** to 40.
4. Use the **Magnetic Lasso Tool** to select the right half of the photo as shown in Figure T8-17.

   Magnetic Lasso Tool

   Press the [Spacebar] to temporarily activate the **Hand Tool** and pan the image as you work. With the **Magnetic Lasso Tool**, carefully follow the tear in the *emulsion* (the top, glossy part that contains the image) of the photo rather than the tear in the paper backing (called the *substrate*).

   Do not worry too much about cleanly selecting the top, bottom, and right edges of the photo at this point. In the following steps, you will use the **Rectangular Marquee Tool** to clean up the other edges of your selection.

5. Zoom out so the full image is displayed in the window.

Figure T8-17. Carefully follow the edge of the emulsion with the **Magnetic Lasso Tool**.

Follow the right side of the tear with the **Magnetic Lasso Tool**

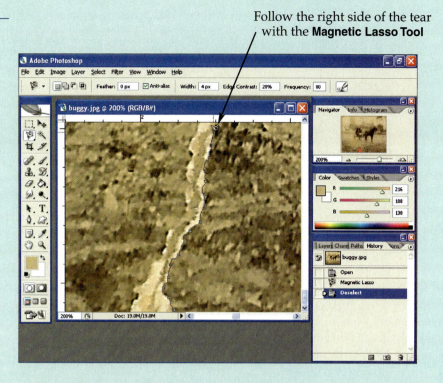

Rectangular Marquee Tool

Add to selection

Lasso Tool

Subtract from selection

6. Select the **Rectangular Marquee Tool** in the **Toolbox**.
7. Click the **Add to selection** button in the options bar.
8. Use the **Rectangular Marquee Tool** to add to the selection until the entire right half of the ripped photo is selected, **Figure T8-18**.
9. Zoom in and carefully check your selection. Use the **Lasso Tool** and the **Add to selection** and **Subtract from selection** options to fine tune the selection, if necessary.
10. When you are happy with your selection, choose the **Move Tool** in the **Toolbox**.

Figure T8-18. Select the top, right, and bottom sides of the image with the **Rectangular Marquee Tool** with the **Add to selection** option active.

The **Add to selection** button

The **Rectangular Marquee Tool**

Move Tool

11. Use the arrow keys on your keyboard to precisely position the right half of photo.

    As you position the photo half, keep your eye on the features of the photo that span across both halves, such as the buggy's rear wheel, leaf springs, and axle, as well as the reins and whip higher in the image. See **Figure T8-19**. You will need to move the selection approximately 17 pixels to the left, and 1 pixel down.

    There will be a few large holes in the image. These are areas where the emulsion flaked away from the substrate. You will use the **Clone Stamp Tool** to correct these areas.

12. When the image is properly positioned, choose **Select > Deselect**.

    You will notice that there is still a very thin rift between the two halves of the photo. You will use the **Spot Healing Brush Tool** to fix the areas of the rift that are surrounded by less detail or are very thin, and the **Clone Stamp Tool** to fix the larger problem areas and areas that require a higher degree of detail.

13. Select the **Spot Healing Brush Tool** in the **Toolbox**.
14. In the options bar, set the brush size to 10 pixels, and the **Hardness:** to 50%.
15. Use the **Spot Healing Brush Tool** to fix the thin white tear line in the sky of the image, **Figure T8-20**.
16. Select the **Clone Stamp Tool** in the **Toolbox**.
17. Using a soft, small brush, fix the rest of the photo with the **Clone Stamp Tool**, **Figure T8-21**.

    As you work, remember to change your sampled areas frequently to prevent a noticeable repeating pattern. When you use the clone tool to fix the buggy, sample areas that are adjacent to the area being fixed. If you choose your sampled areas carefully, your repairs should be nearly undetectable.

18. Choose **File > Save As...** and name the file 08buggy.psd.
19. Close the 08buggy.psd file.

Figure T8-19.
Line up the two halves of the image. Pay close attention to horizontal lines that stretch across both halves of the image.

Missing emulsion

Chapter 8 Restoring and Retouching Photos 349

Figure T8-20. Use the **Spot Healing Brush Tool** to hide the thin line separating the two halves of the image. Also, fix only the top third of the image with the **Spot Healing Brush Tool**. Because the remaining areas that need to be fixed contain more detail and harder edges, you will use the **Clone Stamp Tool** to fix them.

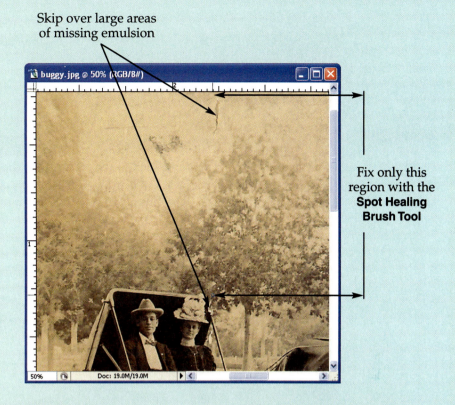

Skip over large areas of missing emulsion

Fix only this region with the **Spot Healing Brush Tool**

Figure T8-21. When you are finished restoring the photo, your repairs should be undetectable.

Tutorial 8-7: Using the Vanishing Point Filter

In this tutorial, you will use the **Vanishing Point** filter to copy a set of speakers from one side of a speaker box to another side. If you make a mistake while working on this tutorial, press [Ctrl][Z].

1. Open the speaker.tif file.

2. Choose **Filter > Vanishing Point…**.

   The **Vanishing Point** dialog box opens, and the **Create Plane Tool** should be automatically selected.

Edit Plane Tool

3. Click the four corners of the front of the speaker to create a plane, as shown in **Figure T8-22**.

   If necessary, use the **Edit Plane Tool** to adjust the corner handles until the plane fits perfectly over the front of the speaker.

Create Plane Tool

4. Make sure the **Create Plane Tool** is selected in the dialog box toolbar.
5. Press [Ctrl] and drag handle A (the middle left handle) to the left and slightly upward to "tear off" a new plane. See **Figure T8-23**.
6. Press [X] and the [Spacebar].

   Use the **Edit Plane Tool** to adjust the corner handles until the grid fits as closely as possible to the two sides of the speaker. Make sure you switch back to the **Create Plane Tool** when you are finished adjusting the grid.

Figure T8-22.
Create a plane that matches the front face of the speaker box.

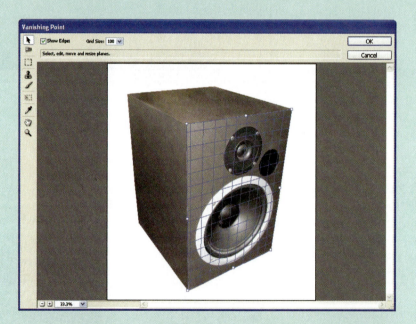

Figure T8-23.
Create a plane that matches the side of the box by dragging the handle A to the left and slightly upward.

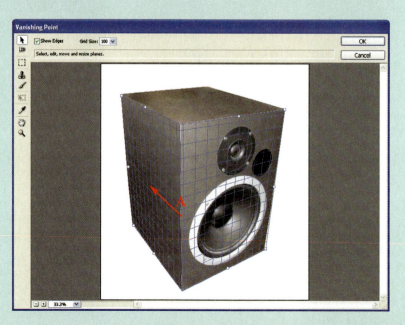

Chapter 8   Restoring and Retouching Photos   351

Marquee Tool

7. Click the **Vanishing Point** filter's **Marquee Tool**.
8. In the dialog box's options bar, set **Feather:** to 3 and **Heal:** to On.
9. Create a rectangular selection around the speaker components, as shown in **Figure T8-24**.
10. In the options bar, select **Destination** in the **Move Mode:** drop-down list.
11. Press [Alt] (or [Option] for Mac) and drag the selected area to the side of the speaker, as shown in **Figure T8-25**.

   Pressing [Alt] and dragging creates a selection that is floating, or separate, from the rest of the image.

Transform Tool

12. Click the **Transform Tool** in the dialog box toolbar.
13. In the options bar of the dialog box, place a check mark in the **Flip** check box.

Figure T8-24. Drag a rectangular selection around the speakers.

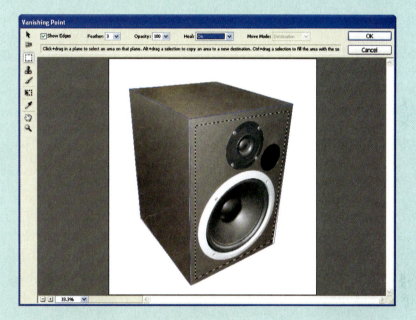

Figure T8-25. Press [Alt] (or [Option] for Mac) and drag the selection to the side of the box. Select the **Vanishing Point** filter's **Transform Tool** and place a check mark in the **Flip** check box.

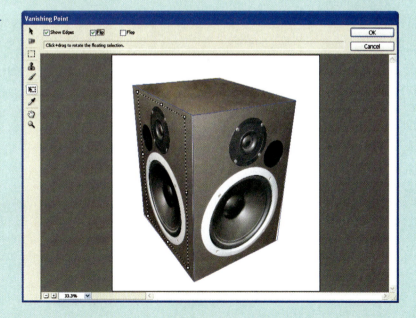

14. Click the **OK** button in the top right corner of the **Vanishing Point** dialog box.
15. Choose **File > Save As...** and name this file 08speaker.tif.
16. Close the 08speaker.tif file.

Tutorial 8-8: Restoring a Damaged Photo (Advanced Level of Difficulty)

In this tutorial, you will restore a photo that has been damaged by pencil marks and a rip. The photo is also faded. Parts of the photo are out of focus, making this a difficult restoration project.

1. Open the 03bball.psd file that you cropped in an earlier chapter.
2. Before continuing, read the following tips:
    - When you repair damaged photos, stay zoomed in (at least 200%) for best results.
    - You will need to use the **Clone Stamp Tool** to make most repairs to this photo.
    - When necessary, change the **Opacity:** setting of the **Clone Stamp Tool** to create the most blended look possible.
    - Use the **History Brush Tool**, the **History** palette, or the **Undo** command if you make any mistakes.
    - Be patient, it will take at least an hour to do a high-quality job.

History Brush Tool

3. Select (with a slight feather) a portion of the bottom-middle boy's jersey and patch it over the top of the ripped area of the bottom-right boy's torso.
4. Use the **Clone Stamp Tool** and the **Spot Healing Brush Tool** to remove the pencil marks and any other blemishes from the entire photo. See **Figure T8-26**.

    Because sharpening should be the last edit you make before printing, you will sharpen this photo in a later chapter, after you adjust its color and brightness.

5. Choose **File > Save As...** and name this file 08bball.psd.
6. Choose **File > Close**.

Figure T8-26. _____
This photograph is challenging to restore.
A—The original photograph has missing emulsion and is marred with pencil marks.
B—Using the **Clone Stamp Tool**, **Spot Healing Brush Tool**, and **Patch Tool**, you should be able to restore the photo as shown here.

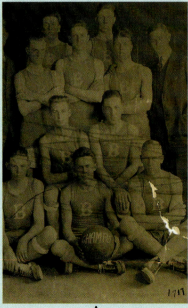
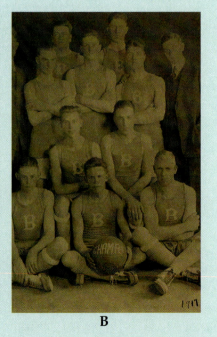

A   B

Key Terms

artifacts	motion blur	retouching
blemishes	noise	sharper
clone	perpendicular	source point
color noise	perspective drawing	substrate
emulsion	red eye	vanishing point
Gaussian blur	restoring	

Review Questions

Answer the following questions on a separate sheet of paper.

1. What is the difference between restoring a photo and retouching a photo?
2. What resolution should a scanned image be if it is going to be restored or retouched?
3. When restoring or retouching an image, you should zoom in at least _____%.
4. Briefly describe what happens when Photoshop sharpens an image.
5. When using the **Unsharp Mask** filter, what does the **Threshold:** setting do?
6. Why is it recommended to use the **Unsharp Mask** filter instead of the **Sharpen** or **Sharpen More** filters?
7. When using the **Smart Sharpen** filter, in what situation would you select the **Motion Blur** option?
8. If your image is made of several layers, what must you do to sharpen the entire image at the same time?
9. As a general rule, at what point in the Photoshop session should you sharpen an image?
10. What is image noise, and what causes it?
11. How does the **Despeckle** filter work?
12. What does the **Dust & Scratches** filter's **Threshold:** setting do?
13. What filter gives you the most precise control when removing noise from an image?
14. What are JPEG artifacts?
15. How does the **Spot Healing Brush Tool** repair a blemish?
16. What is the difference between the **Spot Healing Brush Tool**'s **Proximity Match** and **Create Texture** options?
17. What is the main difference between the **Spot Healing Brush Tool** and the **Healing Brush Tool**?
18. When using either of the healing brush tools, how large should you set the brush size?
19. What is the main difference between the **Patch Tool** and the healing brush tools?
20. How is the **Clone Stamp Tool** significantly different from the **Patch Tool**, **Healing Brush Tool**, and **Spot Healing Brush Tool**?
21. What is a source point?

22. Why is it a good idea to clone a little at a time, release the mouse button, and then do a little more cloning?
23. Can you use the **Clone Stamp Tool** to clone from one image to another?
24. When using the **Vanishing Point** filter, what do you need to do before using the filter's retouching tools?
25. How do you copy something from another image and paste it into an image being edited with the **Vanishing Point** filter?

Introduction to Color Correction

Learning Objectives

After completing this chapter, you will be able to:
- Describe three ways to preserve your original image before adjusting it.
- Adjust color, contrast, or brightness with the **Variations** command.
- Explain the difference between shadows, midtones, and highlights.
- Discuss how to use an RGB/CMY color wheel to determine how to correct a color cast.
- Differentiate between brightness and contrast.
- Recognize the difference between hue and saturation.
- Use the **Hue/Saturation** command to change the colors of an image.
- Explain how the **Replace Color** command is similar to the **Hue/Saturation** command.
- Use the **Color Replacement Tool** to change colors of objects in an image.
- Remove or intensify color in an image using the **Sponge Tool**.
- Use the **Dodge Tool** to lighten colors in an image.
- Use the **Burn Tool** to darken colors in an image.
- Edit the shadows and/or highlights in an image with the **Shadow/Highlight** command.
- Adjust the color in an image using gradients and blending modes.
- Adjust the color in an image with Photoshop's one-step color correction tools.
- Explain how the **Photo Filter**, **Gradient Map**, **Match Color**, and **Color Balance** commands can be used to adjust color in an image.
- Explain the purpose of the **Threshold** command.
- Describe how adjustment layers are used to correct color in an image.

Introduction

You are the judge of how the colors in your image should look. If the sky looks too light in one of your favorite scenery shots, you must decide how blue to make it as you correct the color. See **Figure 9-1**. To make good decisions about color correction, you

Figure 9-1.
Which shade of blue best represents the sky? You must make decisions such as this one as you adjust the color of images.

must have a good sense for color as it appears in the natural world. This awareness will strengthen with careful observation and experience.

Photoshop offers more than twenty color correction commands, all of which are listed in the **Image > Adjustments** submenu. Some of these commands are very simple to use. Others are quite sophisticated and require some background knowledge before they can be used effectively. You will find that there is a lot of overlap—settings associated with some color correction commands are also associated with others. There are so many different commands to choose from that you will probably never use all of them.

In this chapter, several color correction techniques used by beginning- to intermediate-level Photoshop users will be explained. In Chapter 10, *Advanced Color Correction Techniques*, more-advanced color topics and tools will be discussed, including channels, levels, and curves.

Before You Read On…

As you read about correcting color in digital images, keep the following tips in mind:
- Color correction commands will affect only the layer that is currently active.
- If your image is contained on one layer, and only one area of the image needs to be adjusted, consider *feather-selecting* the area, so the color correction will blend into the rest of the image. You can also apply a layer mask using soft brushes (discussed in Chapter 11, *Additional Layer Techniques*) to protect the area of the image you do not want to change.

Chapter 9 Introduction to Color Correction

- Always preserve your original image, in case your color-correction efforts do not work out. You can use one of three methods to protect your original image:
  1. Use adjustment layers, which are explained near the end of this chapter.
  2. Create a duplicate layer and adjust it instead of the original layer. Delete the original layer when you are fully satisfied with the color correction.
  3. Create a duplicate file as a backup before making any color adjustments.

The Variations Command

One of Photoshop's simplest color correction tools to use, but not necessarily its most precise tool, is the **Variations** command. The **Variations** command is introduced first in this chapter because it gives you a quick, visual explanation of several different ways that Photoshop can adjust color. Read this section carefully. You will see many of these terms again and again when reading about Photoshop's other color-adjustment tools.

To use the **Variations** command, open an image and choose **Image > Adjustments > Variations...**. This opens the **Variations** dialog box, Figure 9-2. The **Original** image thumbnail is displayed in the upper left corner of the dialog box. This thumbnail shows you what your image looked like before you made any modifications, and clicking it returns the image to its original condition. The **Current Pick** thumbnail is displayed to

Figure 9-2.
The **Variations** command provides a user-friendly interface for making color adjustments.

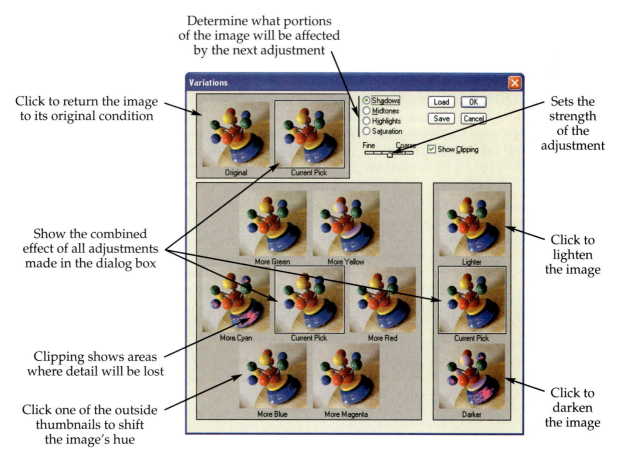

the immediate right of the **Original** thumbnail. It shows you how all of the changes you have made will affect your image. Clicking this thumbnail has no effect.

The **Fine/Coarse** slider controls how powerful each adjustment is. Each time the slider is moved up a notch, the adjustment effect is doubled the next time a thumbnail is clicked. When the **Show Clipping** check box is checked, areas that will be *over-adjusted* (so bright or dark that image detail is being lost), are shown in a solid, contrasting color in the thumbnails. It is important to realize that the colors that indicate clipping in the thumbnails will *not* appear in the actual image when it is adjusted.

> **Note** Since clipping shows areas that are becoming too light or too dark, it is not displayed when midtones are being adjusted.

Once you have adjusted the variation settings to your liking, you can click the **Save** button and save the settings to a file. Then, you can click the **Load** button and reload saved settings at a later time, or even in a different session. This allows you to apply the same variation adjustments to different images.

Adjusting Shadows, Highlights, and Midtones

To begin using the **Variations** tool, you must first choose what areas of your image you want to adjust. This is done by selecting one of the radio buttons in the top right section of the dialog box. If the **Shadows** radio button is selected, only *shadows* (the darkest areas in an image) are adjusted. Selecting the **Highlights** radio button causes only the *highlights* (the brightest areas in an image) to be adjusted. Highlights include places where light is reflecting off a shiny surface, objects that are pure white, and other bright, vivid colors. *Midtones*, areas of an image that are not shadows or highlights, make up the largest percentage of most images. Selecting the **Midtones** radio button causes only these areas to be adjusted.

Adjusting the Hue and Fixing a Color Cast

When the **Shadows**, **Midtones**, or **Highlights** radio button is selected, seven thumbnails appear in one section in the lower part of the dialog box. The **Current Pick** (center) thumbnail shows the combined effects of all of the adjustments made in the dialog box. The six thumbnails that form a circle around the **Current Pick** thumbnail offer different options for changing the hue of the image. These thumbnails show you what your image will look like once the adjustment is made. To adjust the color in your image, simply click on one or more of these thumbnails. The same thumbnail can be clicked more than once.

If your image has a *color cast* (an unnatural tint, usually caused by bad lighting when the image was captured), a different color cast can be applied to correct the problem. An RGB/CMY color wheel, **Figure 9-3**, can be used to figure out how to correct a color cast. For example, suppose you have an image with a slight *blue* color cast, such as the color cast caused by fluorescent lighting. Find the color on the RGB/CMY color wheel that is *opposite* of blue. In this case, the color is yellow. Clicking the **More Yellow** thumbnail in the **Variations** dialog box once or twice will help correct a blue color cast. The color-correcting thumbnails in the **Variations** dialog box are arranged in the same order as the colors on a RGB/CMY color wheel.

Figure 9-3.
Cyan is directly opposite red on a RGB/CMY color wheel.

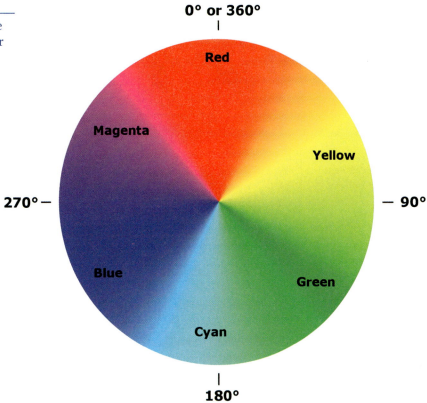

Lightening and Darkening an Image

At the right edge of the dialog box is another section that contains a column of three thumbnails. These thumbnails can be used to help correct problems caused by the lighting conditions under which the image was captured. In other words, they can be used to make the image lighter or darker. The degree of lightness of an image is referred to as *brightness*, or *luminosity* in other areas of Photoshop. Again, the center thumbnail is the **Current Pick** thumbnail, which shows the combined effects of the adjustments previously made in the dialog box. Clicking the **Lighter** thumbnail lightens the image, and clicking the **Darker** thumbnail will darken it.

Adjusting Saturation

The term *saturation* refers to how intense colors appear. When the **Saturation** radio button is selected at the top of the **Variations** dialog box, three thumbnails appear in the bottom section of the dialog box, **Figure 9-4**. Again, the **Current Pick** thumbnail appears in the center. If the **Less Saturation** thumbnail is clicked, the intensity of colors in the image is diminished. If it is clicked several times, the image will become desaturated (grayscale). Clicking the **More Saturation** thumbnail increases the intensity of colors in the image. When the **Saturation** radio button is selected, you cannot choose to affect only shadows, highlights, or midtones. Instead, the entire image is adjusted, Figure 9-4.

Figure 9-4.
The **Variations** command can also be used to adjust saturation in the image.

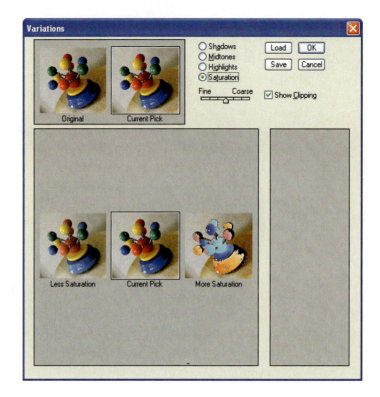

The Brightness/Contrast Command

Images captured indoors by a digital camera are often a bit too dark, so increasing the brightness of images is a common task. Also, many images captured by a digital camera or scanner can use a slight boost in *contrast*, or the tonal range of the image. An image with good contrast (a full tonal range) would have a few shadows that are perfectly black, a few highlights that are pure white, and a full range of midtones in between. For example, a black and white image that does not have enough contrast will have gray shadows (instead of near-black) and light gray highlights (instead of near-white), causing it to appear murky. Images that have too much contrast have the white highlights and black shadows, but not enough different midtones in between. This decreases the detail in the image.

The **Variations** command you read about in the previous section can be used to adjust the brightness of an image, but not its contrast. The **Brightness/Contrast** command provides a simple way to adjust both the brightness and contrast of an image, **Figure 9-5**. To use this command, choose **Image > Adjustments > Brightness/Contrast…**. This opens the **Brightness/Contrast** dialog box.

The **Contrast:** slider controls the range of luminosities in the image. Dragging the **Contrast:** slider to the right increases the contrast of the image. The highlights in the image become brighter and the shadows become darker. In other words, colors stand out more in the image. However, you want to make sure you do not increase the contrast too much, or you will lose details in the shadow and highlight areas of the image.

The **Brightness:** slider performs the same function as the **Lighter** and **Darker** thumbnails in the **Variations** dialog box, but it applies the changes to the entire image rather than just the highlights, midtones, or shadows. Dragging the **Brightness:** slider to the left decreases the overall brightness of the image, and dragging the slider to the right increases it.

Figure 9-5.
As its name suggests, the **Brightness/Contrast** command can be used to adjust both the brightness and the contrast of an image. **A**—The original image appears a bit dull and dark. **B**—The colors in the image appear much richer and vivid after adjusting the **Contrast:** slider. Because the original image was a bit dark, the **Brightness:** slider was also adjusted.

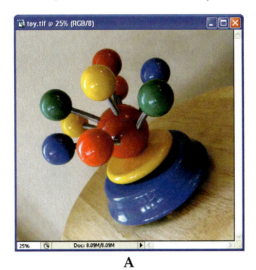
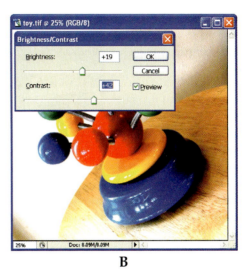

A   B

As you adjust the brightness and contrast, keep an eye on the fine details in the image, such as the textured wall behind the toy in Figure 9-5. If details start to disappear, or if colors become wildly different, you have adjusted the image too much.

The Hue/Saturation Command

The **Hue/Saturation** command is a more precise color-adjustment tool than the **Variations** command. The term *hue* means "a particular color," such as blue, orange-red, or sea green. And, as you learned earlier, saturation is how intense or vivid a particular hue appears. When you choose **Image > Adjustments > Hue/Saturation…**, the **Hue/Saturation** dialog box opens. From this dialog box, you can adjust the hues used in your image, and their level of saturation.

> **Note**
> You should be aware that "hue" is not the only term people use to describe a particular color. You may hear these closely-related terms used instead: "tone," "shade," and "tint." These terms, when used in technical contexts, usually describe other color qualities. However, they are often used as synonyms for hue in nontechnical situations.

The **Variations** command, discussed earlier in the chapter, requires that you choose to adjust either the shadows, midtones, or highlights in an image. The **Hue/Saturation** command is different—it breaks down your image according to pixel color. For example, if you select **Blues** from the **Edit:** drop-down list, any adjustments you make will only affect the blue hues (and nearly-blue hues) in your image. You can adjust one hue by selecting the appropriate color in the **Edit:** drop-down list, or all of the hues simultaneously by selecting **Master**. In **Figure 9-6**, the **Hue/Saturation** dialog box has been used to change the parts of the toy that used to be blue to a light green.

Figure 9-6.
Because **Blues** was chosen from the **Edit:** drop-down menu, all blue colors in the image were changed to a different hue by dragging the **Hue:** slider.

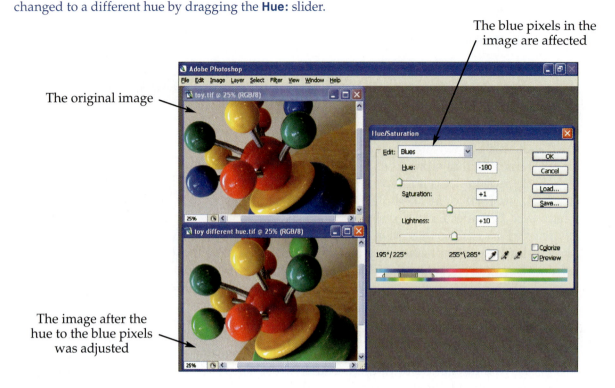

The original image

The blue pixels in the image are affected

The image after the hue to the blue pixels was adjusted

There are three sliders in the **Hue/Saturation** dialog box, and they allow you to change the hue, saturation, and lightness of particular colors in the image. Below the sliders are two color bars, which are basically color wheels that have been stretched out into a line. The top color bar represents the original colors in the image. As you drag the sliders, the bottom bar shows how colors are shifting, or changing. You can look at the top bar, identify a color, and then look at the same location on the bottom bar to determine how that color has changed.

In **Figure 9-7**, **Blues** has been selected from the **Edit:** drop-down menu, causing small triangles and a small, double-ended slider to appear between the color bars. You can adjust how many different hues of blue will be edited by changing the width of the double-ended slider. On each side of the double-ended slider is a small triangle. These two triangles are also adjustable; they show additional hues that will be *slightly* edited.

Using the **Eyedropper Tool**, **Add to Sample**, and **Subtract from Sample** buttons is an optional way to select the colors you want to edit. However, the eyedropper buttons are not available until a specific color is chosen from the **Edit:** drop-down menu. If necessary, click the **Eyedropper Tool** button, and then click a different hue in the image. Then, use the **Add to Sample** and **Subtract from Sample** buttons to add or remove additional hues from your selection. As you pick hues in the image with these tools, the double-ended slider and small triangles change accordingly.

Adding a Tint to an Image

The **Colorize** check box is used to add a color tint to a grayscale image. It can also be used on a color image, in which case it strips existing color information from the image, turning it into a grayscale image, and then adds an overall tint to the image. This technique

Figure 9-7.
Two color bars at the bottom of the **Hue/Saturation** dialog box show what colors will be affected.

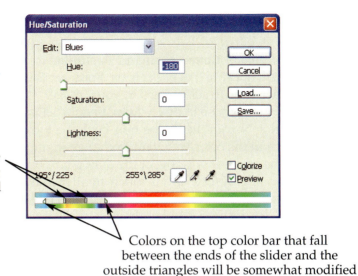

Colors on the top color bar that fall between the slider ends will be fully modified

Colors on the top color bar that fall between the ends of the slider and the outside triangles will be somewhat modified

is very useful for replicating the popular tinting effects produced by conventional photographic printing, such as sepia prints, cyanotypes, and Van Dyke Brown prints.

To use this feature, begin by assigning a color mode to the image. To do this, choose **Image > Mode** and then pick one of the available color modes in the submenu: **Indexed Color**, **RGB Color**, **CMYK Color**, or **Lab Color**. The color mode you choose will depend on what you intend to do with the final image. This step can be skipped if you are already working with a color image, or a grayscale image that has been saved in a color mode. (Color modes will be discussed in detail in the next chapter.)

Next, choose **Image > Adjustments > Hue/Saturation…**. This opens the **Hue/Saturation** dialog box. Place a check mark in the **Colorize** check box, and adjust the **Hue:** slider to produce the tint you want. Adjust the **Saturation:** slider until you reach the desired intensity of the tint. To lighten or darken the image, adjust the **Lightness:** slider as needed. See **Figure 9-8**.

Figure 9-8.
A tint can be added to a grayscale image by checking the **Colorize** check box in the **Hue/Saturation** dialog box.

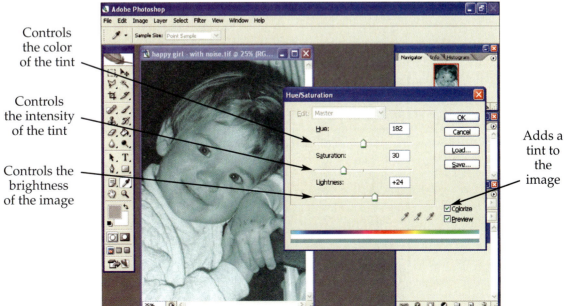

Controls the color of the tint

Controls the intensity of the tint

Controls the brightness of the image

Adds a tint to the image

The Replace Color Command

The **Replace Color** command is similar to the **Hue/Saturation** command, except instead of choosing hues, such as **Reds** or **Blues**, from a drop-down list, you use eyedropper tools to select hues in your image.

To begin, choose **Image > Adjustments > Replace Color...**. This opens the **Replace Color** dialog box. In the dialog box, click the **Eyedropper Tool** button in the dialog box. Then, *click* on the color you want to change in the image window. You can also select the color in the preview window of the dialog box, but this is not recommended because the preview is in grayscale and is much smaller than the actual image.

Next, drag the **Fuzziness:** slider (which is really a *tolerance* setting) to select additional hues that are closely related to the first color you clicked on. The **Preview** window of the dialog box shows, in white, what areas of the image you have selected. You can use the **Add to Sample** and **Remove from Sample** buttons to add hues to or remove hues from your selection. Once you have selected the hues of color you want to adjust, tweak the **Hue:**, **Saturation:**, and **Lightness:** sliders to produce the effect you want. See **Figure 9-9**.

The Color Replacement Tool

With the commands described in this chapter so far, you must use eyedroppers and sliders to change colors in an image. The **Color Replacement Tool** lets you *paint* an area to change its color. You do not need to be absolutely accurate with this tool, because only the color under the brush's crosshairs will be changed within the brush area. This allows you to use a brush that is larger than the area you want to change.

Figure 9-9.
The eyedropper tools and the **Fuzziness:** slider were used to select the blue shades. Then, the **Hue:** and **Saturation:** sliders were adjusted. The result was that the blues in the image were changed to purples.

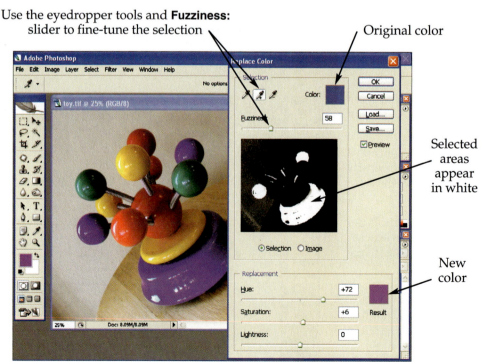

This tool is grouped with the **Brush Tool** and **Pencil Tool** in the **Toolbox**, **Figure 9-10**. The **Color Replacement Tool** is *almost* identical to the **Background Eraser Tool** you learned about in Chapter 7, *Erasing, Deleting, and Undoing*. However, instead of deleting color from an image, this tool replaces colors with the foreground color shown in the **Toolbox**. Most of the settings on the options bar are the same as those for the **Background Eraser Tool**, **Figure 9-11**. The two exceptions are the **Mode:** settings and the **Anti-alias** option. The **Anti-alias** option smoothes the edges of the brush stroke and should be left on in most cases.

Figure 9-10. _____
The **Color Replacement Tool** is grouped with the **Brush Tool** and **Pencil Tool** in the **Toolbox**.

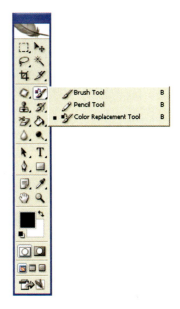

The **Mode:** drop-down list offers four choices:
- The **Hue** option is similar to adjusting the **Hue** slider in the **Hue/Saturation** dialog box. When you paint over a color with this option active, only the color's hue is changed. The hue is adjusted to match the hue of the foreground color selected in the **Toolbox**, but the luminosity (lightness) and saturation (intensity) of the color remain unchanged.
- The **Saturation** option is similar to adjusting the **Saturation** slider in the **Hue/Saturation** dialog box. When you paint over a color with this option active, only the saturation of that color is changed. The hue and luminosity of the color are *not* altered.
- The **Color** option is similar to adjusting both the **Hue** slider and the **Saturation** slider in the **Hue/Saturation** dialog box. When you paint over a color with this option active, the color's hue and saturation are adjusted to match those of the foreground color selected in the **Toolbox**. This is the best option in most situations.
- The **Luminosity** is not often used. This option is similar to adjusting the **Brightness** slider in the **Hue/Saturation** dialog box. If the selected foreground color is light, your image will be lightened when you paint over it. The opposite is true if a dark foreground color is selected.

If you need a reminder about how the other options in the **Color Replacement Tool**'s options bar work, review *The Background Eraser Tool* section in Chapter 7. Remember, these tools work the same, except the **Background Eraser Tool** *deletes* color and the **Color Replacement Tool** *replaces* color.

Figure 9-11. _____
The **Color Replacement Tool**'s options bar is similar to the options bar of the **Background Eraser Tool**.

The Sponge Tool

The **Sponge Tool** could also be called "the saturation tool" because it alters the color saturation level within the brush area. See Figure 9-12. If the **Mode:** setting in the **Sponge Tool**'s options bar is set to **Desaturate,** color is removed from the image as you paint over it. If you paint long enough, you will cause your image to be grayscale. If **Mode:** setting is set to **Saturate**, colors in the image will intensify as you paint over them. The **Flow:** slider controls how quickly the image is altered as you paint over it. The **Airbrush** option is available with the **Sponge Tool**, as it is with most tools that use brushes.

The Dodge Tool and Burn Tool

The **Dodge Tool** and **Burn Tool** are named after traditional darkroom printing techniques used by photographers. In the darkroom, dodging and burning techniques involve changing the *exposure* (amount of light applied to the photosensitive paper) to lighten or darken parts of a photograph so the overall image appears more balanced. In Photoshop, the **Dodge Tool** *lightens* areas of an image by adjusting luminosity. The **Burn Tool** does just the opposite—it *darkens* colors in an image.

The options bar settings for both tools are the same, Figure 9-13. The options bar for both tools has the **Brush Picker**, **Range:** drop-down list, **Exposure:** slider, and the

Figure 9-12.
The **Sponge Tool** can be used to intensify or diminish the color in an image.

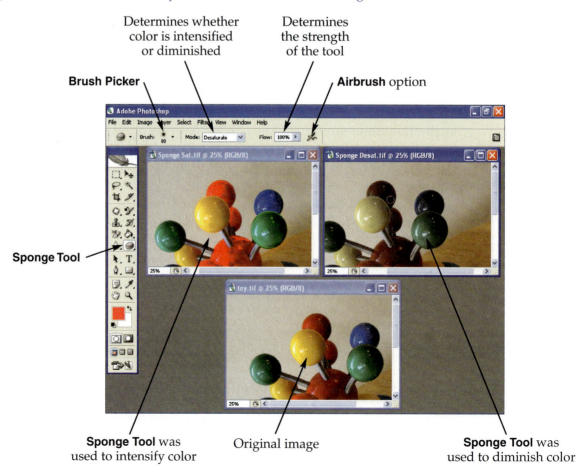

Figure 9-13.
The **Dodge Tool** is used to lighten areas in an image, and the **Burn Tool** is used to darken them. The two tools have identical options bars.

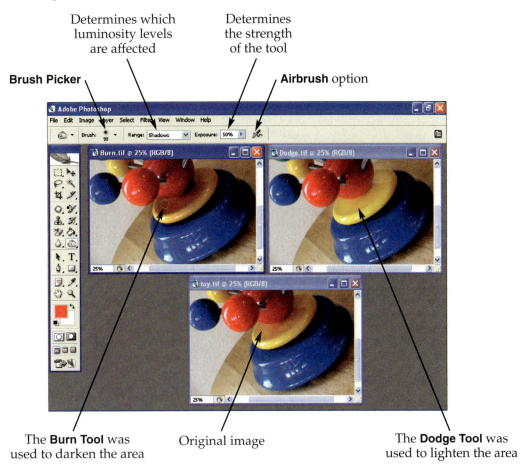

Airbrush option. The **Range:** drop-down list lets you choose what portions of your image will be affected as you paint with these tools. The available options are **Shadows**, **Midtones**, or **Highlights**. The **Exposure:** setting controls how drastically your image is lightened or darkened as you paint over it. You can activate the **Airbrush** button to change the behavior of the brush, if desired.

For colored images, these tools are best used to touch up small areas. They can leave undesirable shades of color if used too heavily. The **Dodge Tool** and **Burn Tool** work very well on grayscale images, however.

The Shadow/Highlight Command

The **Shadow/Highlight** command is an excellent choice if your image contains shadows that are too dark or highlights that are too light. Choosing **Image > Adjustments > Shadow/Highlight...** opens the **Shadow/Highlight** dialog box. From this dialog box, you can change the characteristics of shadows and/or highlights in the image. See **Figure 9-14**.

Figure 9-14.
The **Shadow/Highlight** command is useful for correcting problems in an image's shadow or highlight areas. **A**—The original image contains dark shadows. **B**—The settings needed to correct the vase are made in the **Shadow/Highlight** dialog box. **C**—After adjusting the shadows and applying a small amount of color correction, the vase looks better.

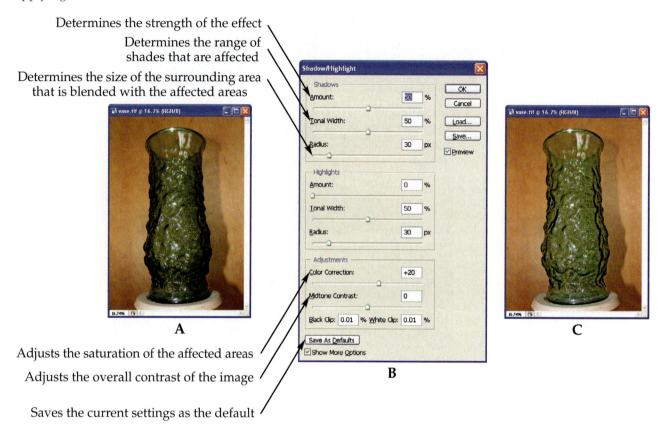

Adjust the appropriate **Amount:** slider first as desired. In the **Shadows** section of the dialog box, the **Amount:** slider lightens the shadow areas. In the **Highlights** section of the dialog box, the **Amount:** slider darkens the highlights. The **Tonal Width:** slider in each section controls how many different luminosity levels are affected. The **Radius:** slider in each section controls how much the changed areas of the image blend with the rest of the image.

At the bottom of the dialog box is the **Show More Options** check box. When this check box is checked, the **Adjustments** section is added to the dialog box. From this section, you can adjust the color of the affected shadow or highlight areas by dragging the **Color Correction:** slider. The contrast of the midtones in the image can be tweaked by adjusting the **Midtone Contrast:** slider. In effect, this changes the overall contrast in the image.

The **Black Clip:** and **White Clip:** text boxes control how much of your image turns pure white or pure black. Higher settings in the **White Clip:** text box, for example, will result in greater amounts of highlight areas turning pure white.

A button at the bottom of the dialog box allows you to save the current settings as the default settings. The original default settings, shown in Figure 9-14B, were designed for correcting images in which detail is lost in shadow because of excessive backlighting.

Blending Modes

In Chapter 6, *Painting Tools and Filters*, you learned about using blending modes with the **Brush Tool**. You probably recall that you can adjust the color in an image by using a painting tool and one of the blending modes. Several tools that are not considered painting tools can be used with blending modes, as well. Refer back to Chapter 6 for a visual review of how blending modes interact with an image.

The color of the image in **Figure 9-15** was adjusted using a purple-and-transparent gradient. The **Gradient Tool** was used in this example because only part of the image needed color correction. The purple portion of the gradient blended with and enhanced the image, and the transparent portion had no effect on the image. Most importantly, the blend between the corrected and non-corrected portions of the image is gradual enough to be unnoticeable.

To create the effect in Figure 9-15, the **Eyedropper Tool** was used to select a purple color from one of the flowers. Next, the **Gradient Tool** was selected and the **Color Dodge** blending mode was chosen from the options bar. The **Opacity:** setting was lowered to 30% in the options bar so the **Color Dodge** blending effect would not be too overpowering. A duplicate layer was created in the **Layers** palette to preserve the original image. Last, a gradient was dragged from the bottom right corner (because the purple color appears first in the gradient) to the upper left corner of the image. The **Color Dodge** blending mode caused the purple paint to blend with and enhance the colors in the area of the flowers. The transparent portions of the gradient had no effect on the remainder of the image.

There are endless ways to adjust color with gradients and blending modes. Remember that the longer you drag a line with the **Gradient Tool**, the more gradual the transitions are between colors in the gradient—and gradual gradients tend to give you the smoothest results.

The **Brush Tool**, **Paint Bucket Tool**, and the **Edit > Fill** command can also be used with blending modes to adjust the color in an image.

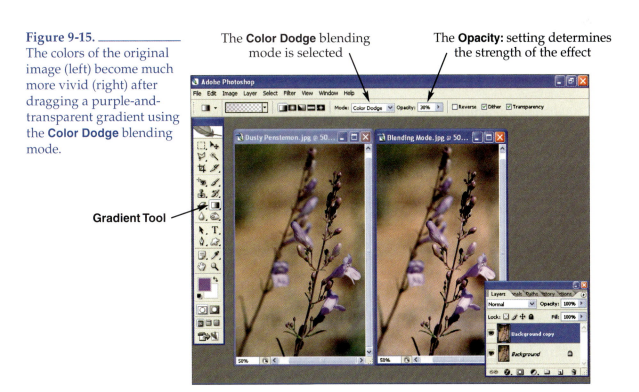

Figure 9-15. The colors of the original image (left) become much more vivid (right) after dragging a purple-and-transparent gradient using the **Color Dodge** blending mode.

One-Step Color Correction Tools

Some of Photoshop's simplest color correction tools have no settings to adjust. These commands are useful for adjusting color quickly, but do not offer the advanced capabilities offered by the tools already discussed.

The Auto Color Command

The **Auto Color** command is executed by choosing **Image > Adjustments > Auto Color**. When this command is executed, Photoshop makes a quick automatic guess about the changes that are required to correct the image's color or contrast. This command can remove some color casts effectively.

The Auto Contrast Command

The **Auto Contrast** command is accessed by choosing **Image > Adjustments > Auto Contrast**. When this command is executed, the contrast of an image is automatically increased. Highlights become a bit lighter, and shadows become a bit darker. You can change the amount of contrast that is applied by this command by clicking the **Options…** button in the **Levels** dialog box or the **Curves** dialog box, and then selecting new options and entering new values in the **Auto Color Correction Options** dialog box. The **Levels** command and **Curves** command are discussed in the next chapter.

The Auto Levels Command

To run the **Auto Levels** command, choose **Image > Adjustments > Auto Levels**. This command automatically adjusts the brightness and contrast in an image. It is better to adjust levels manually. This will be explained in the next chapter.

> **Note** Occasionally, the three automatic adjustments that were just described are effective, but using non-automatic color correction tools is recommended for best results.

The Desaturate Command

The **Desaturate** command, which is run by choosing **Image > Mode > Desaturate**, removes color from an image. The result is a grayscale image. It should be noted that although the image appears in grayscale, the image file is still in a color mode, meaning that color can be added to it later.

The Invert Command

The **Invert** command changes each color in the image to the opposite color on the color wheel, called the *complementary color*. The effect that is created resembles a photographic negative, **Figure 9-16**. You can run the **Invert** command by choosing **Image > Adjustments > Invert**.

The Equalize Command

The **Equalize** command adjusts the brightness of an image, often drastically. The command equally distributes brightness levels throughout the image. If the majority

Figure 9-16.
The **Invert** command is used to swap colors in the image with their complementary colors. The result is an image that resembles a film negative. **A**—The original image. **B**—The inverted image.

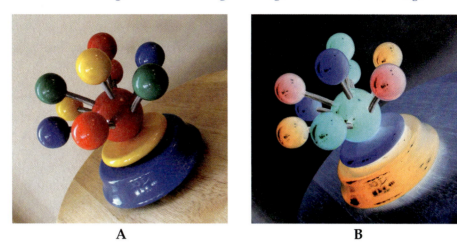

A   B

of colors are bright, the command has a darkening effect on the image. If the majority of the colors are dark in the image, the command lightens the image. For this reason, the command does not work well for images with a light background. However, the command can improve the appearance of some images that are too dark.

Other Easy-to-Use Color-Adjustment Commands

The following sections will describe several other color-adjustment commands that are not difficult to use. All of these tools are found in the **Image > Adjustments** submenu. An adjusted version of Figure 9-17 is shown after the description of each tool so you can see the tool's effect.

Figure 9-17.
The stop sign image is shown here in its original condition. Modified examples are shown in the following sections.

The Photo Filter Command

If you have ever used lens filters with a camera, you will enjoy this tool. Traditional *photo filters* are colored translucent lenses that are placed at the end of the camera lens. The filter allows light of the same color to pass freely to the film, but absorbs light of different colors. The filters can be used to correct for lighting problems, to increase contrast, or for artistic effect. The **Photo Filter** command in Photoshop emulates the effect of these powerful tools.

Choosing **Image > Adjustments > Photo Filter...** opens the **Photo Filter** dialog box. If you activate the **Filter:** radio button, you can choose one of twenty different predefined filters from the drop-down list to the right of the radio button. The predefined filters include warming, cooling, and several other different-colored filters. If you activate the **Color:** radio button, you can use any color you desire for the filter. To create your own color filter, simply click the color box next to the **Color:** button and choose a color from the **Color Picker**.

The **Density:** slider determines how much light the filter blocks. Remember that light that is the same color as the filter passes through it freely, so only dissimilarly colored light is blocked. Therefore, as the filter density increases, more of the image takes on the hue of the filter, and other colors disappear from the image. See **Figure 9-18**.

Since filters block light, increasing the density of a filter darkens the image. You can overcome this by checking the **Preserve Luminosity** check box. When this check box is checked, the luminosity (lightness) of the image remains constant even if the filter density or color changes.

> **Note**
> When you use a filter in conventional photography, the whites in the image take on some of the filter color. In Photoshop, however, pure white is unaffected by the filter when the **Preserve Luminosity** option is active.

Figure 9-18.
The **Photo Filter** command was used to apply a cooling filter with a density of 33% to the image. The colors in the image are shifted to the blue range.

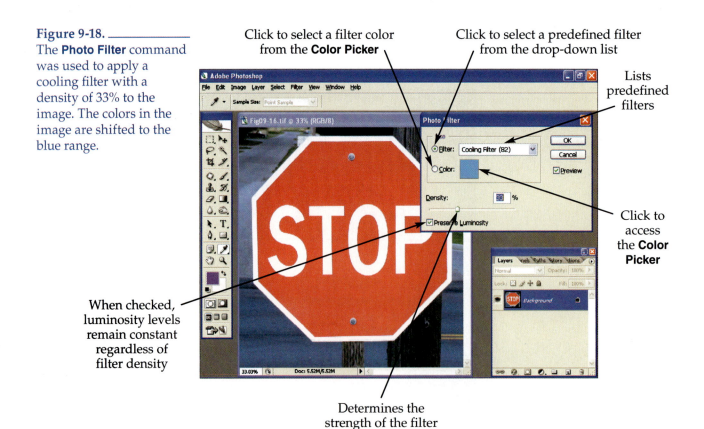

The Gradient Map Command

The **Gradient Map** command provides a quick way to apply a wild color scheme to an image. This command analyzes the image as if it were a grayscale image, and then assigns the colors of a selected gradient to the grayscale image. The shadows (darkest colors) in the image are replaced with the colors at the left end of the gradient while the highlights (lightest colors) in the image are replaced with the colors at the right of the gradient. The midtones are replaced with the colors in the middle of the gradient. However, the order in which the colors are assigned can be reversed.

To run this command, choose **Image > Adjustments > Gradient Map**. This opens the **Gradient Map** dialog box, **Figure 9-19**. Next, select a gradient from the drop-down list at the top of the dialog box. If you want to use your own gradient, you must create it using the **Gradient Editor** before choosing **Gradient Map**. As you may recall, the **Gradient Editor** is accessed through the options bar of the **Gradient Tool**. If you need to review the **Gradient Tool**, refer to Chapter 6, *Painting Tools and Filters*.

Placing a check mark in the **Dither** check box causes Photoshop to add noise to the image to smooth out the transitions from one color to the next. Placing a check mark in the **Reverse** check box reverses the order in which the gradient colors are assigned to the image.

The Posterize Command

The **Posterize** command is used to reduce the number of tonal values (brightness levels) allowed for each color in the image. This results in an image that is simplified and typically has large areas of uniform color. This command is typically used to create a special effect rather than actually adjust an image's color.

To run this command, choose **Image > Adjustments > Posterize…**. This opens the **Posterize** dialog box. Enter a value in the **Levels** text box. The value entered in the text

Figure 9-19.
A purple-red-yellow gradient has been applied to this image. Purple replaced the shadows, red replaced the midtones, and yellow replaced the highlights.

box determines the maximum number of shades allowed for each color in the image, Figure 9-20. For example, if a color image is posterized and 4 is entered in the **Levels** text box, there will be a maximum of four shades of each color in the image. If the image is grayscale, there would simply be four shades of gray in the image.

The Match Color Command

This command is fairly versatile. It is used to match colors between a *target image* (the image that will be adjusted) and a *source image* (the image that provides the colors). The **Match Color** command can also be used to adjust color in a single image, match colors between layers of an image, or match colors between selections.

When you use this command to match colors between images, the command "borrows" colors from one image and applies them to another image. This technique is useful when trying to create a consistent look and feel between several images, such as creating the same vivid look between several images of sunsets, for example. It can also be a fun and creative way to adjust the color scheme of an entire image.

To match colors between images, choose **Image > Adjustments > Match Color…**. This opens the **Match Color** dialog box, Figure 9-21. The target image, the image to which the new colors are applied, is the image that was active when you chose the **Match Color** command. Select an image in the **Source:** drop-down list to open as the source of the new colors. If the source image has several layers and you want to use a specific layer as the color source, select the layer in the **Layer:** drop-down list. Then, click **OK**. The colors in the target image are matched to the colors in the source image. You can fine-tune the color match by experimenting with the **Luminance**, **Color Intensity**, and **Fade** sliders, found in the **Image Options** section of the dialog box. See Figure 9-22.

If you would like to attempt to match the color between selected areas on both images, make sure both check boxes at the top of the **Image Statistics** section of the **Match Color** dialog box are checked. Also, make sure the **Ignore Selection when Applying Adjustment** check box at the top of the dialog box is *unchecked*. Photoshop will consider

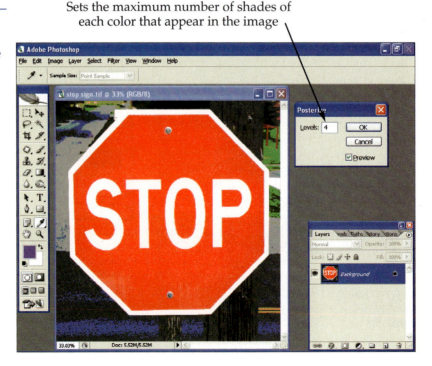

Figure 9-20. The **Posterize** command lessens the variety of colors in your image (note the background behind the stop sign), depending on the amount set in the **Levels:** text box.

Sets the maximum number of shades of each color that appear in the image

Figure 9-21. When matching colors between images, you choose the source of the new colors and fine-tune the command's effect in the **Match Color** dialog box.

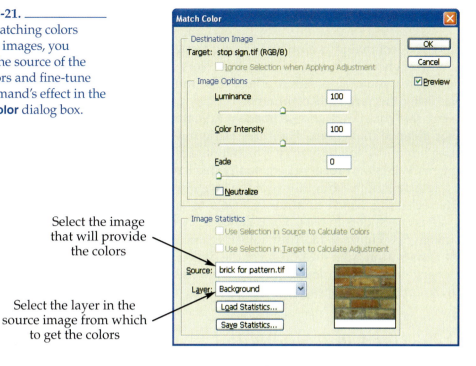

Select the image that will provide the colors

Select the layer in the source image from which to get the colors

Figure 9-22. The **Match Color** command has been used to apply the colors from the brick image to the stop sign image. **A**—The brick image is the source of new colors. **B**—The stop sign is the target image and takes on the color of the bricks.

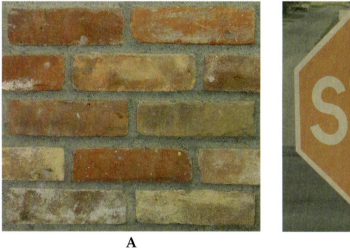

A   B

only the selected area of the source image and will attempt to match the color in only the selected area of the target image. Matching color between selections can be tricky. You will get different results depending on how many shadows, midtones, and highlights are contained in the selected areas of both images.

You can also use this command to adjust a single image. When **None** is selected in the **Source:** drop-down list, the sliders in the **Image Options** section of the dialog box will fine-tune the appearance of a single image.

The Color Balance Command

Using this command is similar to using the **Variations** command to correct color casts. You can choose whether to shift the colors of the shadows, midtones, or highlights. However, you drag sliders to adjust color rather than click on thumbnails, as you do when using the **Variations** command.

To run this command, choose **Image > Adjustments > Color Balance...**. This opens the **Color Balance** dialog box. The three radio buttons in the **Tone Balance** section of the dialog box allow you to specify which tonal areas of your image are affected by the adjustments. When the **Preserve Luminosity** check box is checked, the adjustments made do not affect the original brightness of the image while the colors are being adjusted.

After selecting which luminosity levels to adjust (shadows, midtones, or highlights), adjust the sliders in the **Color Balance** section of the dialog box to shift the colors in the image. See Figure 9-23. After adjusting one range of luminosities, you can select another radio button from the bottom of the dialog box and repeat the process to adjust another range of luminosities. Once you have the colors adjusted the way you want, click **OK** to apply the changes to the image.

The Selective Color Command

The **Selective Color** command allows you to choose and adjust a single color component in an image. This tool is especially useful for adjusting images that will be printed on commercial printing presses, because cyan, magenta, yellow, and black inks are used. You will learn more about CMYK color mode in the next chapter.

To use this command, choose **Image > Adjustments > Selective Color...**. In the **Selective Color** dialog box, choose the range of colors you want to affect in the **Colors:** drop-

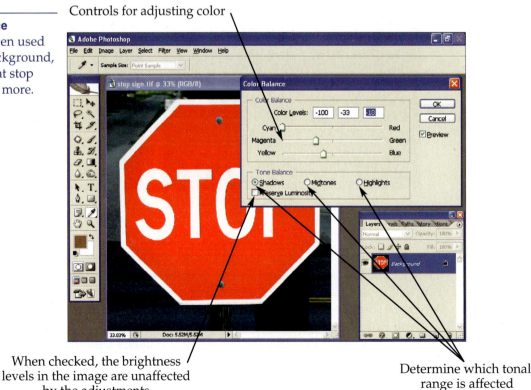

Figure 9-23.
The **Color Balance** command has been used to darken the background, causing the bright stop sign to stand out more.

Controls for adjusting color

When checked, the brightness levels in the image are unaffected by the adjustments

Determine which tonal range is affected

down list. Your choices are **Reds**, **Yellows**, **Greens**, **Cyans**, **Blues**, **Magentas**, **Whites**, **Neutrals**, or **Blacks**. Drag the **Cyan:**, **Magenta:**, **Yellow:**, and **Black:** sliders to adjust the selected colors. See **Figure 9-24**. Two radio buttons at the bottom of the dialog box determine how the adjustments are applied to the image.

If the **Relative** radio button is active, colors are adjusted based on how much of the component color (cyan, yellow, magenta, or black) they already contain. In other words, if you choose to adjust the blues in the image and then increase their yellow levels by dragging the **Yellow:** slider to the right, the blues that have more yellow in them to begin with are affected to a greater extent than those that begin with less yellow. Pure whites are not affected at all.

If the **Absolute** radio button is active, the component makeup of the color does *not* affect the extent to which it is adjusted. In the example of the blues in an image being adjusted, the same amount of yellow would be added to all colors within the blue range, regardless of how much yellow they had to begin with. Generally speaking, this option provides more dramatic (but less natural) color shifts than the **Relative** option.

After making the adjustments to the selected color range, you can select a new color range in the **Colors:** drop-down list and repeat the process to change a different range of colors. Once you have made all of the desired changes, click **OK** to apply them to the image.

Adjustment Layers

Now that you have learned about several of Photoshop's color-adjustment commands, you should know that some of them are available as an adjustment layer. If you use the color-adjustment commands on a regular layer, the changes become part of the image. An *adjustment layer* is a special type of layer that will apply a color-adjustment

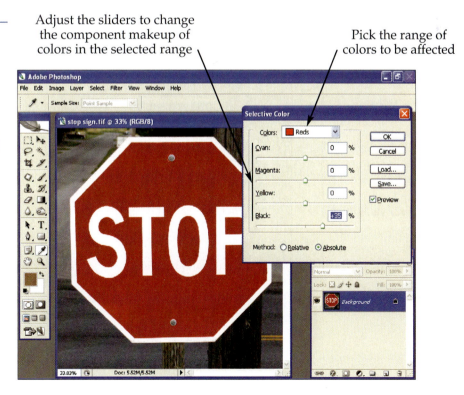

Figure 9-24.
The **Selective Color** command was used to make the red stop sign a darker, deeper red. **Reds** was chosen in the **Colors:** drop-down list and the **Black:** slider was dragged to the right until the desired color was achieved.

Adjust the sliders to change the component makeup of colors in the selected range

Pick the range of colors to be affected

command to the image, but keeps the corrections you make separate from your image. The adjustment layer is added to the **Layers** palette, and it affects all layers that appear beneath it in the **Layers** palette stack.

Only twelve of Photoshop's color-adjustment commands can be used with adjustment layers. To add an adjustment layer, choose **Layer > New Adjustment Layer** and then select the desired color-adjustment command from the submenu, **Figure 9-25**. The same menu can also be accessed from the **Layers** palette by clicking the **Create new fill or adjustment layer** (small black and white circle) button at the bottom of the palette. Some of the commands listed in this menu will be discussed in the next chapter.

You can hide any changes you made to your image by clicking the **Layer visibility** (eye) toggle next to the adjustment layer in the **Layers** palette, **Figure 9-26**. You can change your adjustment settings any time by double-clicking the icon just to the right of the **Layer** visibility toggle. Also, you can permanently remove the color adjustment by deleting the adjustment layer.

Figure 9-25.
In the **Layer > New Adjustment Layer** submenu, you can choose from twelve color-adjustment tools that can be used as adjustment layers.

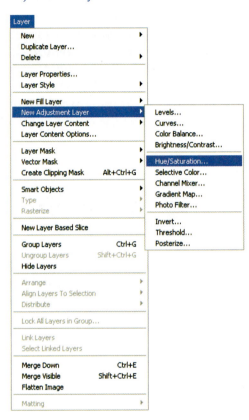

Figure 9-26.
When a color adjustment layer is added to an image, it appears in the **Layers** palette. You can temporarily hide the effects of the adjustment layer by clicking its **Layer visibility** toggle, or adjust its settings by double clicking the icon to the right of the **Layer visibility** toggle.

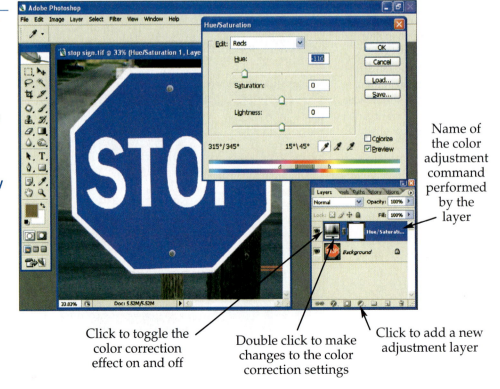

Name of the color adjustment command performed by the layer

Click to toggle the color correction effect on and off

Double click to make changes to the color correction settings

Click to add a new adjustment layer

GRAPHIC DESIGN:
Color and Mood

Warm, Cool, and Neutral Colors

Colors can be grouped into three basic categories: warm, cool, and neutral. See **Figure 9-27**. Warm colors are those associated with fire and heat: yellows, oranges, reds, and pinks. Other colors are perceived as cooler by the viewer. These cool colors are shades of blue, green, and purple. Shades of brown and gray are considered neutral—they seem neither warm or cool.

Advancing and Retreating Colors

Warm colors in a design seem to jump out toward the viewer, creating an energetic mood. Cool colors do just the opposite—they retreat from the viewer, creating a more placid feeling. See **Figure 9-28**.

Figure 9-27.
Colors can be divided into three categories: warm colors (top), cool colors (middle), and neutral colors (bottom).

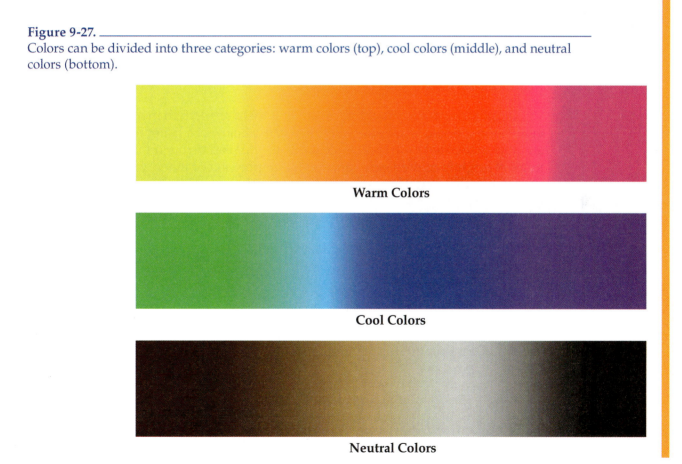

Figure 9-28.
The types of colors (warm, cool, or neutral) influence the way the viewer perceives a design. **A**—Warm colors, such as the yellow sun shape in this design appears to advance towards the viewer. **B**—Blue colors appear, like the blue sun shape in this design, seem to move away from the viewer.

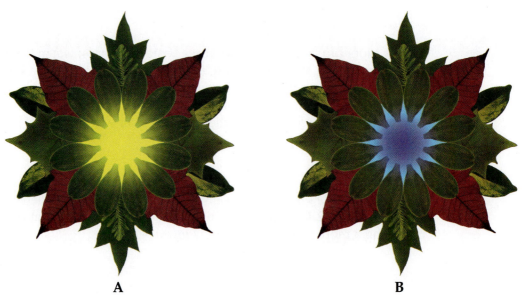

Impressions Inspired by Colors

Graphic designers should be aware that there are certain moods and qualities associated with each individual color. Below is a list of moods and qualities associated with common colors. As you read through the list below, think of brightly colored new cars and the impression or mood you feel when you see one drive by. Then, see if you agree with the impressions listed below. Perhaps you can add to the list.

- **Blue:** strong, peaceful, stable, loyal, determined.
- **Green:** refreshing, invigorating, calm, natural.
- **Purple:** imaginative, noble, unpredictable.
- **Red:** powerful, attention-getting, angry, aggressive.
- **Yellow:** happy, vigorous, vibrant, comfortable.
- **Orange:** creative, spunky, warm, energetic.
- **Gray and Brown:** neutral, drab.

Brightness and Saturation

When any of these colors are at full saturation and brightness, they appear more energetic. Lower brightness and saturation settings appear less energetic and more subdued, traditional, dignified, or even neutral. See **Figure 9-29**.

You can tell if a color is at full saturation and brightness as you select a color with the **Color Picker**. The saturation and brightness settings are at full strength when 100% appears in the text boxes next to the **S:** and **B:** radio buttons, **Figure 9-30**.

Figure 9-29.
Compare the shades of yellow in these two designs. **A**—The brighter shade of yellow causes the entire design to appear more energetic and dynamic. **B**—The less intense shade of yellow makes the design appear dull and unenergetic.

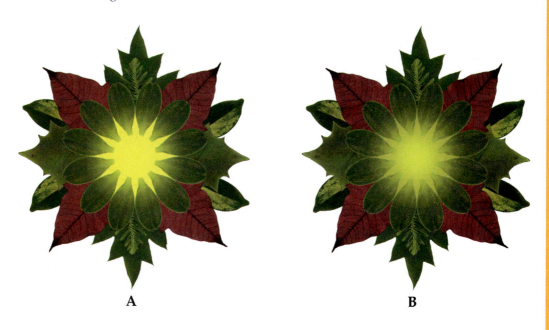

Figure 9-30.
Check the **S:** and **B:** settings in the **Color Picker** to determine if a particular shade has full-strength saturation and brightness.

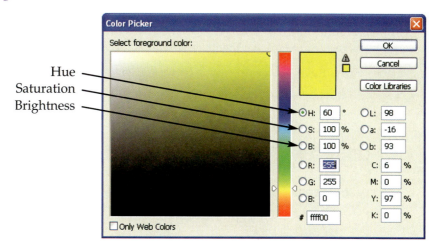

Summary

Using the tools and commands discussed in this chapter, you can improve the appearance of most images. However, more powerful color-correction commands are discussed in the next chapter.

CHAPTER TUTORIALS

In the tutorials that follow, you will correct the color of a few images that you have previously worked on. During the process, you will get a chance to try out many of the tools discussed in this chapter.

Tutorial 9-1: Using a Hue/Saturation Adjustment Layer

In this tutorial, you will use a **Hue/Saturation** adjustment layer to make one object change color in an image. This technique is frequently used to draw attention to particular objects in a scene.

1. Open the 06peppers.psd file.

   You used the **Brush Tool** with the **Hue** blending mode to paint one of the peppers in an earlier chapter.

Magnetic Lasso Tool

Lasso Tool

2. Zoom in and use the **Magnetic Lasso Tool** and **Lasso Tool** to select the pepper directly above the one that is already painted. Do *not* include the stem. See **Figure T9-1**.

3. Because the **Hue/Saturation** command is available as an adjustment layer, choose **Layer > New Adjustment Layer > Hue/Saturation…**.

4. Click **OK** in the **New Layer** dialog box to accept the default settings for the new adjustment layer.

5. In the **Hue/Saturation** dialog box, drag the **Hue:** slider so −114 appears in the **Hue:** text box. See **Figure T9-2**.

   The color adjustment you just created is separate from the other layers. It can be readjusted, if desired, by double-clicking the icon to the right of the adjustment layer's **Layer visibility (eye)** toggle in the **Layers** palette.

6. Choose **File > Save As…** and name this file 09peppers.psd.

7. Close the 09peppers.psd file.

Figure T9-1.
Use the lasso tools to select the pepper as shown.

Figure T9-2.
Adjust the **Hue:** slider until the pepper turns purple.

Adjust the hue of the pepper by moving this slider

Double click to re-adjust the hue and saturation settings

Tutorial 9-2: Replacing Color

In this tutorial, you will use the **Color Replacement Tool** and the **Hue/Saturation** command to change the colors of objects in an image. Unlike the **Hue/Saturation** command, the **Color Replacement Tool** allows you to select an existing color to match, taking the guess work out of adjusting the color settings. Also, it is applied with a brush, which allows for greater control. On the other hand, the **Hue/Saturation** command affects all similarly colored objects in the image, so a careful selection must be created before the command is used.

1. Open the toy.tif file.
2. Choose **Layer > Duplicate Layer....** In the **Duplicate Layer** dialog box, click **OK** to accept the default settings for the new layer.

   You will do all of your color correction on this layer. That way, if you make a mistake, the original layer will be preserved.

Eyedropper Tool

3. Zoom in on the green sphere at the left side of the photo, as shown in **Figure T9-3**.
4. Click the **Eyedropper Tool** in the **Toolbox**.
5. With the **Eyedropper Tool**, click on a midrange (not too dark or light) shade of blue on the blue sphere.

   This sets the foreground color to blue.

Color Replacement Tool

6. Click the **Color Replacement Tool**, found behind the **Brush Tool** in the **Toolbox**.
7. Change the following settings in the options bar:
   - Set the brush **Diameter:** to 60 px.
   - Set the **Mode:** to Color.
   - Click the **Sampling: Continuous** button.
   - Set the **Limits:** to Find Edges.
   - Set the **Tolerance:** to 50%.

Sampling: Continuous

Figure T9-3. Create a copy of the Background layer, and then select a midtone blue with the **Eyedropper Tool**.

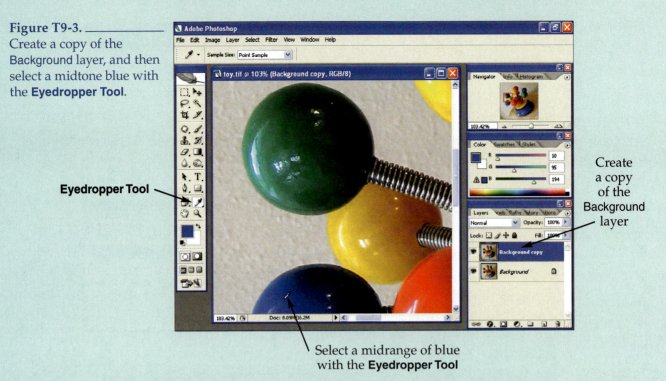

8. Zoom in further on the green sphere, as shown in **Figure T9-4**.
9. Paint the sphere to replace the color. As you paint, do *not* allow the crosshairs to touch anywhere outside of the green sphere.
10. Zoom in on the other green sphere in the image, as shown in **Figure T9-5**.
11. Use the **Color Replacement Tool** to change this sphere to blue, also.
12. Choose **View > Fit on Screen**.

In the following steps, you will adjust the yellow spheres using the **Hue/Saturation** command. Before doing so, notice that the wooden table beneath the toy contains some hints of yellow. Since you want the table to remain the same color, you need to exclude it from the effects of the **Hue/Saturation** command by deselecting it.

Figure T9-4. Use the **Color Replacement Tool** to change the ball from green to blue. Do *not* stray outside the edges of the ball.

Figure T9-5.
Use the **Color Replacement Tool** to change the sphere on the right side of the image from green to blue.

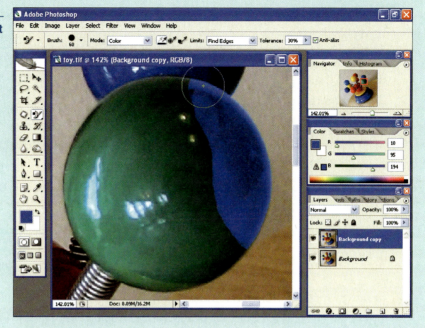

Subtract from selection

Add to selection

13. Choose **Select > All**.
14. Click on your choice of the lasso tools in the **Toolbox**. Click the **Subtract from selection** button in the options bar. Then, draw a selection border around the wooden table.

    You may need to zoom in on the table and use additional selection tools and the **Add to selection** and **Subtract from selection** buttons to clean up the selection border around the table.

15. Once you have subtracted the wooden table from the selection, choose **Image > Adjustments > Hue/Saturation….** See **Figure T9-6**.

Figure T9-6.
Make sure everything but the table is selected before using the **Hue/Saturation** command.

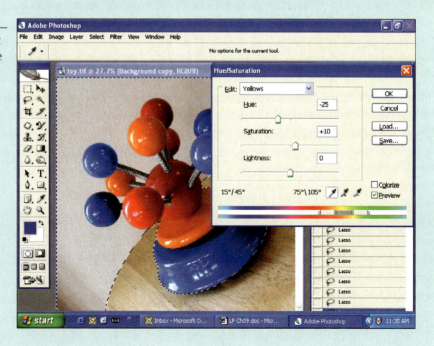

16. In the **Hue/Saturation** dialog box, choose **Yellows** from the **Edit** drop-down menu.
17. Drag the **Hue:** slider to –23.
18. Drag the **Saturation:** slider to +10 to boost the intensity of the new orange colors.
19. Pick the **OK** button in the **Hue/Saturation** dialog box to accept the changes.
20. Choose **Image > Adjustments > Brightness and Contrast…**.
21. In the **Brightness/Contrast** dialog box, drag the **Contrast:** slider to +18. Click **OK**.

    This intensifies the toy's colors even further and causes it to stand out from the background, **Figure T9-7**.

22. Choose **File > Save As…** and name this file 09toy.tif in the **Save As** dialog box.
23. Close the 09toy.tif file.

Figure T9-7.
Use the **Brightness/Contrast** command to increase the contrast in the image.

Tutorial 9-3: Adjusting Shadows and Highlights

In this tutorial, you will use the **Shadow/Highlights** command to correct excessively heavy shadows in an image.

1. Open the vase.tif file.
2. Choose **Layer > Duplicate Layer…**. In the **Duplicate Layer** dialog box, click **OK** to accept the default settings for the new layer.
3. Choose **Image > Adjustments > Shadow/Highlight…**.
4. If the **Show More Options** check box at the bottom of the **Shadow/Highlight** dialog box does not have a check in it, check it now.
5. Set the **Color Correction:** slider to 61 and the **Midtone Contrast:** slider to 24. See **Figure T9-8**.
6. Click **OK**.

    This closes the **Shadow/Highlight** dialog box and applies the settings to the image. You will notice that the vase is lightened and brightened, and the shadows are better defined.

Figure T9-8.
The **Shadow/Highlight** command is used to decrease the shadows in the image of the vase. **A**—The original image. **B**—The **Shadow/Highlight** dialog box. **C**—The adjusted image.

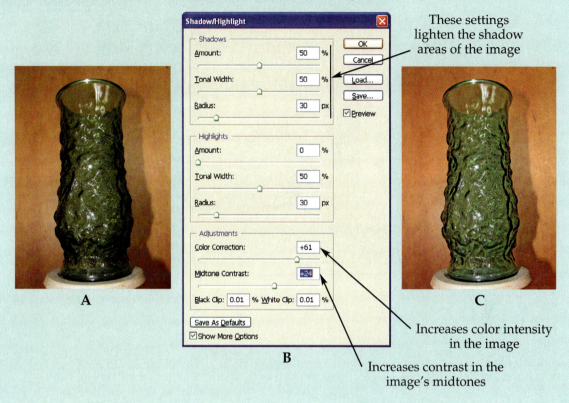

7. Choose **File > Save As…** and name this file 09vase.tif.
8. Close the 09vase.tif file.

Tutorial 9-4: Use Blending Modes and Painting Tools to Adjust Color

In this tutorial, you will use the **Gradient Tool** with the **Color Dodge** blending mode to enhance the colors in an image. Similar effects can be achieved with the other painting tools and blending modes.

1. Open the penstemon.jpg file.
2. Choose **Layer > Duplicate Layer** and click **OK** in the **New Layer** dialog box to accept the default settings.
3. Zoom in on the flowers as shown in **Figure T9-9**.
4. Click on the **Eyedropper Tool** in the **Toolbox**.
5. Use the **Eyedropper Tool** to sample the darker purple area of the flower.
6. Choose **View > Fit on Screen**.
7. Click the **Gradient Tool** in the **Toolbox**.

Gradient Tool

8. In the options bar, click the down arrow next to the gradient sample to open the **Gradient Picker**. Choose the second gradient on the top row, which should be a blend of the dark purple color you chose and a transparent area. See **Figure T9-10**.

Figure T9-9.
Sample a dark purple area of the flower with the **Eyedropper Tool**.

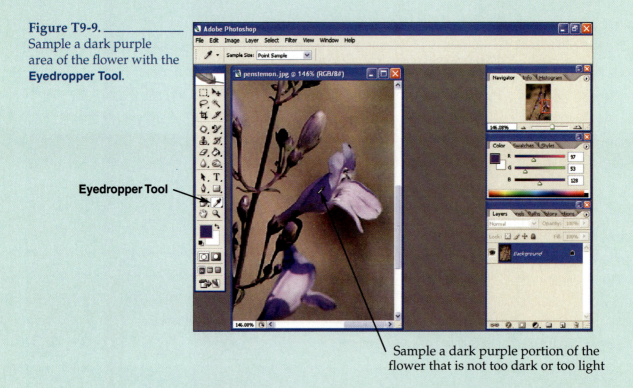

Sample a dark purple portion of the flower that is not too dark or too light

Figure T9-10.
Click the **Gradient Tool** and select the purple-to-transparent gradient in the **Gradient Picker**.

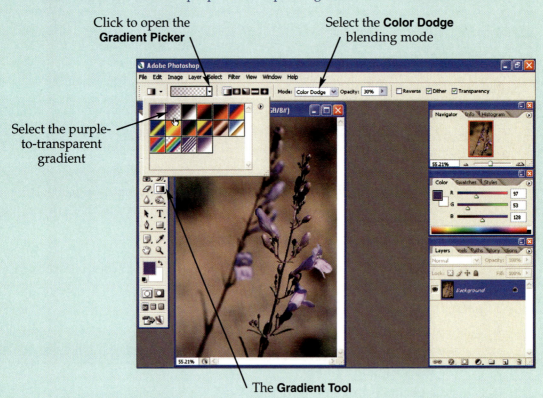

Click to open the **Gradient Picker**

Select the **Color Dodge** blending mode

Select the purple-to-transparent gradient

The **Gradient Tool**

Chapter 9   Introduction to Color Correction   389

9. In the options bar, choose **Color Dodge** in the **Mode:** drop-down list and set the **Opacity:** to 30%.

   This selects the blending mode that will be used with the Gradient Tool and determines how visible the effect will be.

10. Beginning in the lower right corner of the image, drag the gradient to the upper left corner of the image. See **Figure T9-11**.

Brush Tool

11. Choose **Edit > Undo Gradient** and use this image to experiment with different gradients and blending modes. You should also try out the **Brush Tool** on this image using different blending modes.

12. After experimenting, choose **File > Revert** and apply the gradient described in steps 7 through 10 of this tutorial.

13. Choose **File > Save As...** and name the file 09penstemon.jpg.

14. Close the 09penstemon.jpg file.

Figure T9-11. Begin the gradient in the lower right corner of the image and drag it to the upper left corner.

Tutorial 9-5: The Dodge Tool

In this tutorial, you will use the **Dodge Tool** to lighten an area in an image in order to make the text stand out from the background.

1. Open the 05ostrichville.psd file that you edited in a previous chapter.
2. Zoom in on the large ostrich's neck, as shown in **Figure T9-12**.
3. Click the **Dodge Tool** in the **Toolbox**.

Dodge Tool

4. In the options bar, select a soft brush with a size of 125 px. Set the **Exposure:** slider to 25%.

Figure T9-12. Select the **Dodge Tool** and lighten the area on the ostrich's neck directly behind the text.

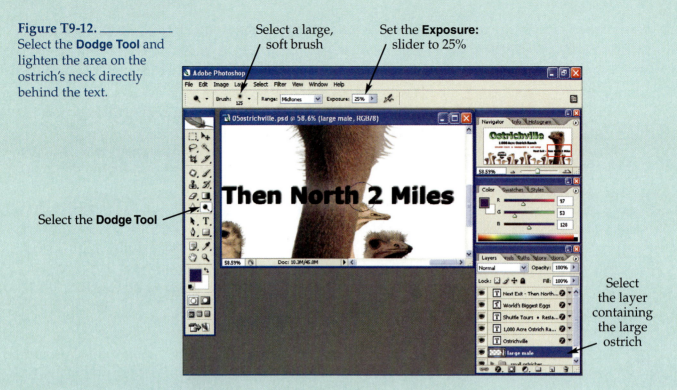

5. In the **Layers** palette, click the layer that contains the large male ostrich.
6. Use the **Dodge Tool** to softly lighten the ostrich in the area behind the text. This will help the text stand out a bit more.
7. Choose **File > Save As…** and name this file 09ostrichville.psd.
8. Close the 09osterichville.psd file.

Tutorial 9-6: The Sponge Tool and Burn Tool

In this tutorial, you will use the **Sponge Tool** to remove an unnatural tint from the road by desaturating it. You will also use the **Burn Tool** to darken one of the houses so that it more closely matches the other houses in the image.

1. Open the 08hillside.psd file that you edited in a previous chapter.
2. Choose **Layer > Duplicate Layer…**.
3. Zoom in on the road.
4. Most of the road has a pinkish-orange color cast that looks unnatural.
5. Click the **Sponge Tool** in the **Toolbox**.
6. In the options bar, enter the following settings:
   - Select a soft round brush, and set the **Master Diameter:** to 200 px.
   - Set the **Mode:** to Desaturate.
   - Set the **Flow:** to 100%.
7. Bit by bit, drag the **Sponge Tool** over the entire road until it is gray. For accuracy, use a smaller brush on the edges of the road. See **Figure T9-13**.

Use the **Navigator** palette or the **Hand Tool** to move around as you work.

8. Zoom in on the farthest house, as shown in **Figure T9-14**.
9. Click the **Burn Tool**.

Burn Tool

Figure T9-13.
Use the **Sponge Tool** to remove the pinkish cast from the road. Change brush sizes as needed.

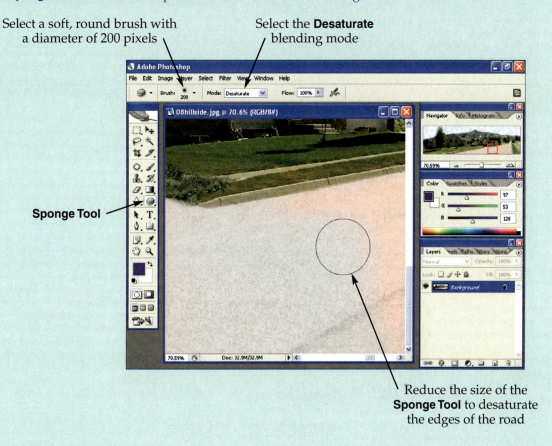

Figure T9-14.
Use the **Burn Tool** to darken the farthest house in the image. Be careful to apply the **Burn Tool** evenly.

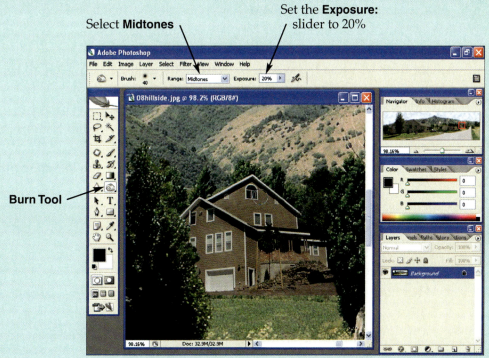

10. In the options bar, enter the following settings:
    - Select a soft round brush, and set the **Master Diameter:** to 40 px.
    - Set the **Range:** to Midtones.
    - Set the **Exposure:** to 15%.
11. Darken the house with the **Burn Tool**. For best results, do *not* release the mouse button until you are finished burning the entire house.
    Be careful to darken the house uniformly.
12. Choose **Layer > Flatten Image**.
13. Choose **File > Save As…** and name this file 09hillside.jpg. Then, close it.

Key Terms

adjustment layer
brightness
color cast
complementary color
contrast
exposure

highlights
hue
luminosity
midtones
over-adjusted

photo filters
saturation
shadows
source image
target image

Review Questions

Answer the following questions on a separate sheet of paper.

1. Which of Photoshop's submenus contains the color correction commands?
2. If an image contains more than one layer, which layer will be affected when using Photoshop's color correction commands?
3. If only a portion of an image needs to be adjusted, what must be done to ensure that the color correction will blend in with the rest of the image?
4. List three ways you can protect your original image before attempting to adjust its color.
5. List the four radio buttons in the **Variations** dialog box, which allow you to select the color qualities of your image that are to be adjusted.
6. What is the **Fine/Coarse** slider in the **Variations** dialog box used for?
7. How can an RGB/CMY color wheel be used to determine how to correct a color cast?
8. Briefly describe how some of the thumbnails found in the **Variations** dialog box are similar to a color wheel.
9. If an image has a blue color cast, what color will help correct it?
10. What is saturation?
11. What happens to an image if the contrast is boosted?
12. What is the definition of the term *hue*?
13. What do the two colored bars found at the bottom of the **Hue/Saturation** dialog box represent?
14. How do you choose colors in an image when using the **Replace Color** command?

15. What does the **Fuzziness:** slider in the **Replace Color** dialog box do?
16. The **Color Replacement Tool** shares many of the same options with what other tool?
17. In what two ways can the **Sponge Tool** affect the colors in an image?
18. What does the **Dodge Tool** do?
19. What does the **Burn Tool** do?
20. In this chapter, you learned that painting tools (such as the **Gradient Tool**) can be used to adjust the color in an image. What feature of the painting tools allows color adjustment?
21. What one-step command removes color from an image, causing it to become grayscale?
22. Which color-adjustment command reduces the number of brightness levels of each color in the image, resulting in large areas of uniform color?
23. Which command lets you "borrow" colors from one image and instantly apply them to another image?
24. What are two advantages of using an adjustment layer when correcting an image's color?
25. If an adjustment layer is above four other layers in the **Layers** palette, how many of those layers will be affected by the adjustment layer?

The image in the upper left corner has good color and tone. The other five images suffer from common image problems.

Good Color, Contrast, and Brightness

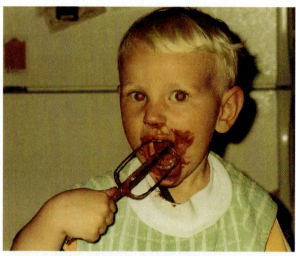
Color Cast from Incandescent Light

Not Enough Contrast

Too Much Contrast

Too Light

Too Dark

10 Advanced Color Correction Techniques

Learning Objectives

After completing this chapter, you will be able to:
- Explain how a computer monitor displays color.
- Describe how color is created in the printing industry.
- Differentiate between an additive and subtractive color system.
- Understand the purpose of Photoshop's color modes.
- Explain how Photoshop measures both RGB and CMYK color.
- Describe the various settings on the **Color Picker**.
- Explain what out-of-gamut colors are.
- Use the **Channels** palette to view color information or save a selection.
- Describe what a histogram is.
- Use the **Threshold** command to find highlights in an image.
- Mark highlights in an image with the **Color Sampler** tool.
- Adjust an image with the **Levels** command.
- Adjust an image with the **Curves** command.
- Explain bit depth.
- Explain the purpose of the **Info**, **Color**, and **Swatches** palettes.
- Describe the recommended sequence you should follow when adjusting color in an image.
- Be familiar with the basic steps of color management.

Introduction

The previous chapter focused on color correction tools and techniques that are not too difficult to use. Before introducing you to some of Photoshop's more advanced color correction tools, this chapter will provide you with some background knowledge about color.

You have learned that Photoshop can be used to create projects that will be displayed either on a computer screen or in printed form. There are some significant differences between the manner in which a computer monitor and a printing press produce color, and Photoshop users must understand these differences.

Different Shades of Color

Computer monitors and television screens create color by shining light at our eyes. Most of these display screens are capable of producing millions of shades of colors, an impressive number. Some video displays, such as certain high-end plasma-screen televisions, are even capable of producing billions of different shades of color!

Printers and printing presses use inks to create color on a page. By mixing four different shades of ink, printing presses are able to produce as many as 6,000 different shades of color. This number may seem insignificant when compared to the millions (or billions) of colors that monitors or televisions can display, but think about it—a printing press can produce hundreds of different shades of red, hundreds of different shades of blue, and so on. This level of color detail is more than enough to produce printed materials that contain photo-realistic images.

Red, Green, and Blue Light (RGB Color)

A computer monitor or television screen is made of thousands of tiny, glowing squares. Each of these squares is capable of displaying a different color. How is this done? Within each tiny square, there are actually three different elements that emit light—a red, green, and blue element. Using different combinations of red, green, and blue light, each tiny square on a typical computer monitor or television screen can display over 16 million different shades of color.

Using light to create colors is called an *additive color system*, simply because wavelengths of light are added together to create color. *White light* is created when red, green, and blue light are added together at full strength. You can begin to see how additive color works by placing a red, green, and blue light source so that their beams overlap. See **Figure 10-1**.

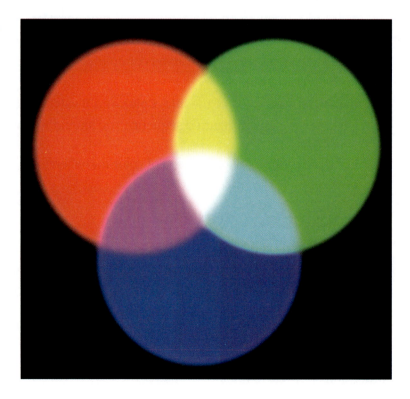

Figure 10-1.
When red, green, and blue light mix, other colors are created.

Cyan, Magenta, Yellow, and Black (CMYK Color)

Color is created differently in the printing industry. If you are creating color by applying inks to white paper, you must use cyan (a light blue), magenta (a purplish-pink), and yellow. Mixing cyan, magenta, and yellow ink does not create black (instead, a dark brown color is produced), so black ink must be added to the other three colors to properly reproduce dark areas in an image.

> **Note** The letter K in CMYK represents black, because the letter B is used to represent blue in RGB.

Using CMYK inks, around 6,000 different colors can be created on a printed page. Next time you change the printing cartridges in your inkjet printer, you will notice that CMYK inks are used, Figure 10-2. Many consumer-level printers use more than the four standard CMYK inks so that more shades of color can be produced.

In the professional printing industry, if a project requires a color that cannot be represented by CMYK inks (such as fluorescent orange or metallic silver), a separate, premixed ink called a *spot color* is used. Spot colors must be added separately during the printing process. An additional printing plate must be created for the spot color and each page with spot color must pass through the printing press again. This causes a printing project to become more expensive.

Creating color by applying inks to paper is called a *subtractive color system*, because of the way our eye perceives color when we look at an object. For example, when you look at a red apple (either a picture of an apple or a real apple), the apple's color causes the red wavelengths of light to be reflected back into your eyes. Other wavelengths of light, such as blue and green, are absorbed (or *subtracted*) by the color of the apple and they do not reflect into your eye. As a result, your eye sees red.

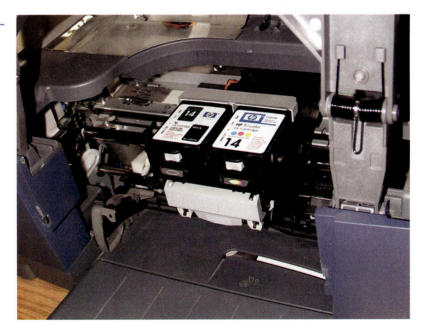

Figure 10-2. Consumer-level and professional-level printers both use CMYK inks.

Color Modes

In Photoshop, you can create files in different *color modes*. Color modes determine which shades of color are available for your image. As a general rule, if you are a beginning or intermediate-level Photoshop user and you wish to create a full-color project, it is recommended that you create it in RGB color mode.

As mentioned earlier, the *RGB color mode* creates color by combining red, green, and blue. This color mode is capable of producing all shades of color that a computer monitor can display. If your project was created in RGB color mode but will be printed on a commercial printing press, it can be converted to CMYK mode before printing.

The *CMYK color mode* produces color by combining cyan, magenta, yellow, and black. These are the same four colors that are used by most printing presses. Since this color mode is primarily used for projects that are intended to be printed, it permits the image to contain only those colors that are reproducible by a printing press. If an image was created in RGB mode and converted to CMYK, Photoshop will locate any colors in the image that cannot be printed and substitute the closest printable color instead. Furthermore, the **Color Picker** will warn you if a color cannot be printed. See the "Non-Web-Safe and Out-of-Gamut Colors" section later in this chapter.

The *grayscale color mode* uses only combinations of black and white to create numerous shades of gray. If your project is black-and-white or grayscale, it should be created in (or converted to) grayscale color mode to minimize file size. While in grayscale color mode, you can choose from only white, black, and shades of gray when selecting a color.

Color modes are assigned to images in one of two ways. When creating a new image file, you can select a color mode from the **Color Mode:** drop-down list in the **New** dialog box, Figure 10-3. You can also convert an existing file to a different color mode by choosing a color mode from the **Image > Mode** submenu. When you change color modes in your image, Photoshop automatically adjusts the colors in the image. So, to preserve as much color detail as possible, you should only change color modes when absolutely necessary.

In addition to the RGB, CMYK, and grayscale color modes already discussed, you will find several additional color modes in the **Image > Mode** submenu, Figure 10-4. Most of these are used in specialized printing situations.

All of Photoshop's tools and features work in RGB mode. When an image has been converted to another color mode, you will find there are a few tools that will not work, simply because the technology does not allow them to. This is especially true

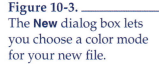

Figure 10-3.
The **New** dialog box lets you choose a color mode for your new file.

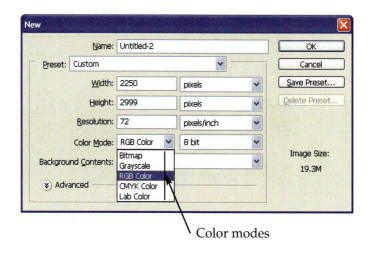

Figure 10-4.
These color modes are not used as frequently as RGB, CMYK, or grayscale.

Color Mode	Brief Description
Bitmap	Converts a file in grayscale mode to black and white dots. All shades of gray are replaced by either black or white.
Duotone	The duotone mode is used for projects that will be printed in 2 colors. However, once the duotone mode is selected, the **Duotone Options** dialog box opens. From this dialog box, you can choose to convert the image to monotone format (for printing with 1 color), tritone format (for printing with 3 colors), or quadtone format (for printing with 4 colors). You also specify the ink colors in this dialog box.
Indexed Color	Limits the colors in an image to 256. Used in situations where file space must be small, such as multimedia projects and web pages. When an image in indexed color mode is active, a color table (that shows all 256 colors) can be displayed by choosing **Image > Mode > Color Table**.
LAB Color	An alternative to RGB and CMYK color modes, this mode separates an image into three channels: a lightness/darkness channel (L), a red-green channel (A), and a blue-yellow channel (B). Its gamut (see next section) is more expansive than the gamuts of RGB and CMYK modes.
Multichannel	Used to create spot channels for specialized printing situations.

of tools and commands in the color correction category. If you need to use a certain color correction command that is unavailable in the current color mode, and you cannot think of another way to accomplish the same task, you will need to convert your image back to RGB mode to use the tool.

Identifying and Matching Colors in Photoshop

As a graphic artist, you will often be called upon to use a specific color in your designs. For example, you might be asked to use a client's corporate colors in a marketing brochure or use the colors specified by an architect in a rendering of a new building. "Eyeballing" colors is not a good enough method for matching colors in many professional situations. You must be able to *precisely* reproduce the colors requested by the client.

Fortunately, Photoshop has a strong set of tools for matching and identifying colors. These tools provide a means for precisely matching desired colors and communicating color specifications to others.

How Photoshop Measures Color

To understand how Photoshop measures color, we will use Photoshop's **Color Picker** to choose white. A few of the **Color Picker**'s settings were discussed in Chapter 1, *The Work Area*. The remainder of them will be introduced here. Remember, the **Color Picker** is displayed by clicking the foreground or background color box in the **Toolbox**. One way to choose white in the **Color Picker** is to click in the extreme upper left corner of the color field, **Figure 10-5**.

Figure 10-5.
When white is selected in the **Color Picker**, RGB values are at their maximum, and CMYK values are at their minimum.

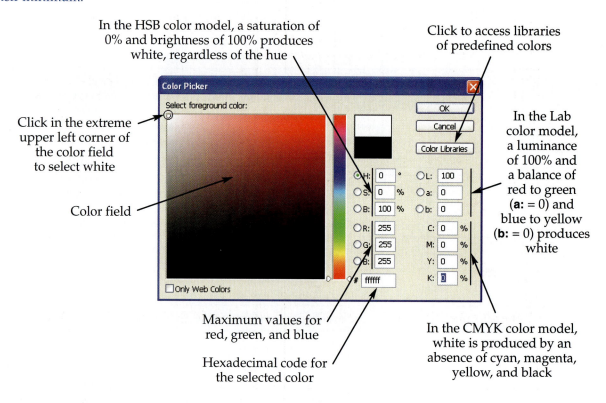

Reading RGB and CMYK Values in the Color Picker

After selecting white, look at the RGB values in the **Color Picker**. They show that white is represented by a value of 255 for each color: red, green, and blue. A value of 255 is the *maximum* setting for RGB values. In other words, when red, green, and blue light are each at maximum strength, white light is created.

The CMYK values are to the immediate right of the RGB settings in the **Color Picker**. These color values are shown in percentages (0%–100%), representing how much of each of the four inks is applied to the paper to create a certain color. These values show that to create white, *no* ink is used. Since no ink is applied, blank paper is visible in those areas.

The opposite is true if black is chosen in the **Color Picker**. RGB values would each be 0, meaning no light is emitted by the monitor. CMYK values, on the other hand, would show values between 65% and 90% for each color—a combination of inks that prints a deep black.

Reading H, S, and B Values in the Color Picker

The **H:**, **S:**, and **B:** settings in the **Color Picker** represent the hue, saturation, and brightness of the selected color. As you learned in the previous chapter, these qualities can be adjusted to shift the color in an image. The same qualities can also be used to define a specific color.

The **H:** (hue) value describes the color's position on a color wheel or the linear color bar in the **Color Picker**. Red appears at both ends of the **Color Picker**'s color bar, equating to the positions of 0° and 360° on a color wheel. As you know, the RGB color mode divides the spectrum into three primary colors, and those colors are located 120° apart on the color wheel (a complete circle of 360° divided by 3). Red is at 0° (or 360°), green is at 120°, and blue is at 240°.

Cyan, magenta, and yellow are the complementary colors for red, green, and blue, and are located directly across (or 180°) from them on the color wheel. Cyan, which is the complement of red, is located at 180° (0°+180°) on the color wheel. Magenta, which is the complement of green, is located at 300° (120°+180°). Yellow, which is the complement of blue, is located at 60° (240°–180°).

The **S:** (saturation) setting determines the intensity of a color. The minimum value of 0% indicates that the color is a shade of gray, with no trace of the hue specified by the **H:** setting. As the saturation increases, so does the percentage of hue in the color. The maximum value of 100% produces a color with the maximum amount of hue.

The **B:** (brightness) setting determines how light or dark the color is. When this value is set to 0%, the minimum, the color is black, regardless of the other settings. As the brightness increases, the level of black in the color decreases. When this value is set to its maximum, the color has no black in it.

Reading L, A, and B Values

The **L:**, **a:**, and **b:** settings allow you to see color values in Lab color mode, a mode more complex than RGB or CMYK. One benefit of the Lab color mode is that it has a larger gamut (range of colors) than RGB or CMYK mode. Sometimes, images are converted to Lab mode, adjusted, and converted back to RGB mode.

The **L:** (luminance) setting determines how light a color is. This setting is basically the same as the brightness setting in the HSB color model. The **a:** setting determines how much red and green are in the color, and the **b:** setting determines the amount of blue and yellow.

Locating the Hexadecimal Code in the Color Picker

A text box simply labeled with a number sign (#) appears at the bottom of the **Color Picker**. This box displays a *hexadecimal code* (alphanumeric code using characters 0–f) for the selected color. If a new color is selected in the color field or the current color's settings are altered, the hexadecimal code is automatically updated. This code is especially useful for web designers, who have to use hexadecimal codes to specify colors in HTML code.

Using Color Libraries

Clicking the **Color Libraries** button opens **Color Libraries** dialog box. This dialog box gives you access to a vast collection of spot colors. The spot colors are organized into groups according to color matching books, such as those from Pantone® and TRUMATCH®. See **Figure 10-6**. Scroll through the choices and select a spot color, which becomes the selected color in the **Color Picker**. Click **OK** to accept the color, close the dialog box, and return to the image window. If you would rather return to the **Color Picker**, click the **Picker** button.

Using the Color Settings to Specify and Match Colors

All of the **Color Picker** settings described so far make it possible to exactly match colors, or to provide exact color specifications when creating colors. After you have created a color that you want to share with others, all you need to do is record and

Figure 10-6.
The **Color Libraries** dialog box gives you access to collections of predefined colors. When you select a library from the **Book:** drop-down list, proprietary names and color samples are displayed in the left side of the dialog box. Also, a CMYK equivalent is displayed for the selected color.

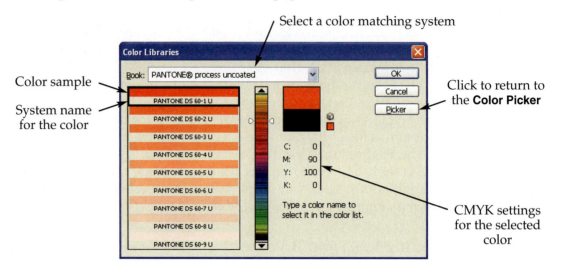

provide the appropriate set of color specifications. For example, if you have designed a sign in Photoshop and want to have it mounted in frame that is the same color as the background, you would select the sign's background color with the **Eyedropper Tool**, open the **Color Picker**, click the **Color Libraries** button, and select a color matching book like **Pantone® solid coated**. The Pantone equivalent of the background color would be automatically selected. Then, you would simply write down the name of the Pantone color so you could take it with you to the paint shop.

If you clicked the **Picker** button in the **Color Libraries** dialog box, you would see the RGB, CMYK, Lab, HSB, and hexadecimal settings for the selected Pantone color displayed in the **Color Picker**. If you were working with a web designer instead of a painter, the designer may request HSB, RGB, or hexadecimal specifications instead of a Pantone number for the color. A printer may request the CMYK specifications.

If you are on the receiving end of a color specification, all you need are one of the following: the RBG values, the CMYK values, the HSB values, the Lab color values, the hexadecimal value, or the color matching system number for the color. See **Figure 10-7**.

Figure 10-7.
There are many ways to specify a color. The best way to identify a color depends largely on how it is going to be output.

Values Used to Describe or Create the Color
PANTONE® process uncoated: PANTONE DS 6-4 U
CMYK color model: C: 0, M: 10, Y: 100, K: 5
RGB color model: R: 245, G: 209, B: 0
HSB color model: H: 51, S: 100, B: 96
Lab color model: L: 85, a: 2, b: 85
Hexadecimal (HTML): f5d100

In the **Color Picker**, simply enter the values in the appropriate text boxes or access the appropriate color library and select the desired color.

> **Note** If you want to see a better visual representation of what each color setting does in the **Color Picker**, try activating the radio button next to the setting as you adjust it. The color field and color bar change to give you a better idea of how to adjust the setting to get the desired result.

Non-Web-Safe and Out-of-Gamut Colors

Remember, millions of color shades can be created by using red, green, and blue light (RGB). Unfortunately, not all web browsers can display the full range of colors that can be created in RGB mode. If a color is chosen in the **Color Picker** that will not display properly in *all* web browsers, a small cube icon appears next to the color sample. See **Figure 10-8**. This is a warning for anyone developing content for the web, indicating that the color is not web-safe. The most similar web-safe color is displayed in a color box under the icon. Clicking on the icon (or the color box under it) replaces the currently selected color with the web-safe color in the color box.

Similarly, a printing press using CMYK inks cannot produce anywhere near the number of color shades that can be defined in RGB mode. If you use the **Color Picker** to select a color that cannot be produced on a four-color printing press, a triangular out-of-gamut icon appears. The term *gamut* means "the range of colors that can be produced." Just underneath the out-of-gamut icon is a color box that displays the closest in-gamut color. You can choose the suggested in-gamut color by clicking on the out-of-gamut icon (or color box below it), or you can pick a different shade in the color field.

Most images captured with a camera or scanner contain out-of-gamut colors. To see the colors that are out-of-gamut, open any image and choose **View > Gamut Warning**. All out-of-gamut pixels are temporarily covered with gray, **Figure 10-9**. To hide the gamut warning, choose **View > Gamut Warning** again.

Out-of-gamut colors may seem like a significant problem until you consider these facts:

- Even though consumer-level printers (like inkjets and photo printers) use CMYK inks, they are designed to print RGB files. The printer driver software converts the colors from RGB to CMYK automatically. You only need to worry about using Photoshop's CMYK color mode if your project will be printed commercially. Your print service provider can help if you encounter problems.

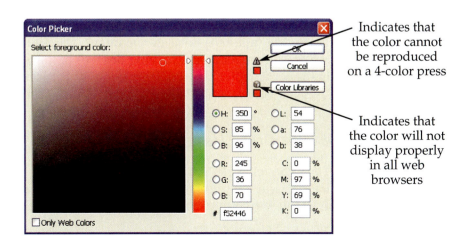

Figure 10-8. If the selected color is not web-safe, a small icon appears next to the color sample. Similarly, an out-of-gamut icon appears if you choose a color that cannot be printed using CMYK inks.

Indicates that the color cannot be reproduced on a 4-color press

Indicates that the color will not display properly in all web browsers

Figure 10-9.
A—This RGB image, captured with a digital camera, contains many out-of-gamut colors.
B—Choosing **View > Gamut** warning reveals the out-of-gamut colors in the image by replacing them with gray pixels.

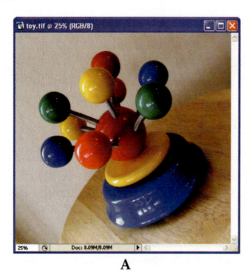
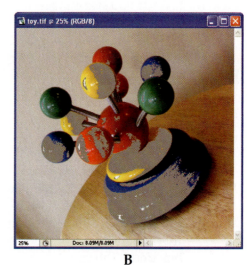

A   B

- When you use Photoshop to convert a file from RGB mode to CMYK mode, out-of-gamut colors are automatically replaced with the nearest possible match. The image usually looks very close to (but less vibrant than) the original.
- Photoshop users can force the colors on their monitor to match what comes out of their printer. This advanced-level process is called *color management*, and is briefly described at the end of this chapter.

Channels

As described earlier, images are created by mixing primary colors to create other colors. *Color channels* show the distribution of the primary colors throughout an image, and use grayscale versions of the image to represent the amount of distribution, Figure 10-10. For example, if a pixel is black in a color channel, it means that pixel contains none of that primary color in the image. Pixels containing a higher percentage of the primary color are a lighter shade of gray in the color channel.

Alpha channels are special channels that store information about selections and masks. Like color channels, alpha channels are grayscale versions of the image. However, the shades of gray in an alpha channel record selection, or masking, information instead of color information. By default, the black areas in an alpha channel represent the unselected (masked) areas of the image, the white areas are selected (unmasked), and the gray areas represent varying degrees of masking.

In the next chapter, you will learn about layer masks, which are used to hide portions of a layer. The **Channels** palette also stores layer mask information.

The Channels Palette

The **Channels** palette displays thumbnails of the image's channels, which look just like layer thumbnails. You can select the channel thumbnails to display the channels in the image window. You may wonder why the channels are grayscale instead of the

Figure 10-10.
The three color channels and composite channel of an RGB image are shown here. Notice the difference in tones from channel to channel.

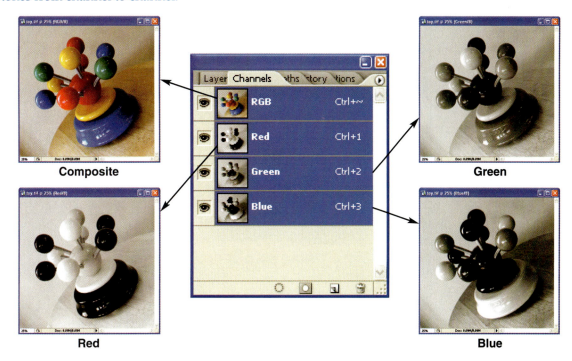

primary color they represent. This is done because it is often easier to judge the density of gray than the density of some of the lighter primary colors, like yellow or cyan.

If you click on one of the channels in the **Channels** palette, that channel is displayed in the image window. Once a channel is selected, you can edit it using Photoshop's tools and filters. You can hide the effects of each channel by clicking its **Channel visibility** (eye) toggle.

> **Note** Although color channels are displayed individually in grayscale, selecting two or more color channels in the **Channels** palette displays those channels in their actual color in the image window. By toggling the visibility of channels on and off, you can easily see the interaction of specific color channels.

Imagine you have an RGB image open and are looking at the Red channel in the **Channels** palette. The white and gray areas in the Red channel's image window and thumbnail preview show where red light is needed to create the image on a computer monitor. The black areas show where no red light is required. If the image you have open is in CMYK mode, the channels represent how much of each ink is necessary to produce the image.

The channel at the top of the list in the **Channels** palette is called the *composite channel*. This channel is really a shortcut you can click to select all *color* channels and make their combined effects visible in the image window. Alpha channels, layer masks, and spot channels are listed after the color channels in the **Channels** palette. See **Figure 10-11**.

> **Note** If you want to see a grayscale representation of an alpha channel, layer mask, or spot channel in the image window, you must turn on visibility for that channel and then turn off visibility for all color channels.

Figure 10-11.
The **Channels** palette displays color information about an image. It can also be used to save selections.

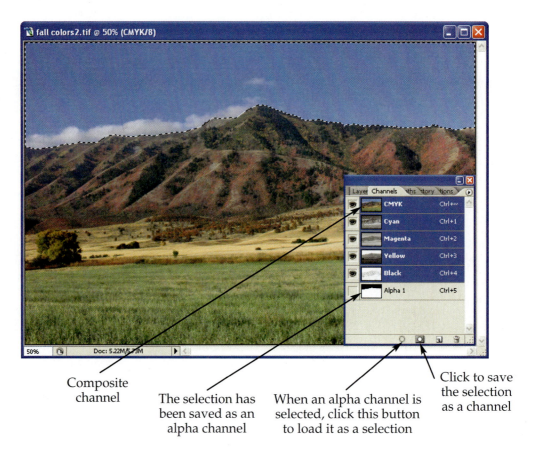

Saving a Selection as a New Channel

A selection made with Photoshop's selection tools disappears when you save and close the image file unless you save the selection as an alpha channel. After making the selection in the image window, you can save the selection by choosing **Select > Save Selection…**. The **Save Selection** dialog box appears, allowing you to name the selection and choose an existing alpha channel (or create a new alpha channel) in which to save it, **Figure 10-12**.

If you choose to save the selection to a new channel, the selection can be saved as either a simple selection or as a layer mask. A *layer mask* is a special type of mask that makes part of a layer transparent, but keeps the image information so the hidden area can be restored at any time. To save the selection as a layer mask, choose the **Layer X Mask** option in the **Channel:** drop-down list and click **OK**. Layer masks are discussed further in Chapter 11, *Advanced Layer Techniques*.

If you want to save the selection as a new alpha channel without turning it into a layer mask, choose the **New** option in the **Channel:** drop-down list. You can then type a new name for the alpha channel in the **Name:** text box, if you wish. Click the **OK** button to create the new alpha channel. You can also save selections as a new alpha channel directly from the **Channels** palette. To do this, simply open the **Channels** palette when the selection is made, and click the **Save selection as channel** button at the bottom of the palette. This saves the current selection as a new alpha channel.

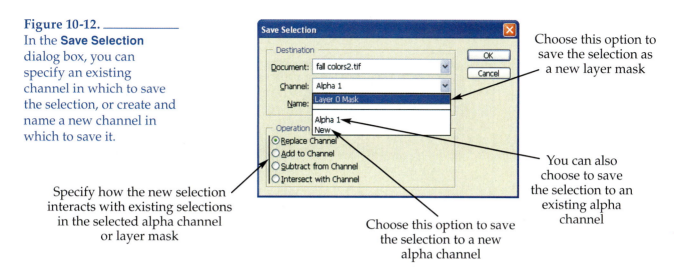

Figure 10-12.
In the **Save Selection** dialog box, you can specify an existing channel in which to save the selection, or create and name a new channel in which to save it.

If you wish to save the selection to an existing alpha channel or layer mask, select the existing channel in the **Channel:** drop-down list of the **Save Selection** dialog box. In the **Operation** section of the dialog box, select a radio button to specify how the new selection should interact with the existing selection in the channel, and then click **OK**.

When you save a selection as an alpha channel or layer mask, the new channel appears in the **Channels** palette. By default, selected pixels appear as white, and unselected pixels appear black. As long as you save the file after adding the alpha channel or layer mask, you can retrieve the selection at any time by choosing **Select > Load Selection**. You can also load the selection from the **Channels** palette by selecting the channel containing the selection and clicking the **Load channel as selection** button at the bottom of the palette.

Spot Channels

Spot channels are special channels that indicate where spot color is to be applied to the image. Creating spot color channels is relatively easy. To create a new spot channel, make a selection of the area you want to fill with spot color. Then, open the **Channels** palette. Click the small arrow button in the top right corner of palette to open the **Channels** palette menu. Choose **New Spot Channel…** from the menu. This opens the **New Spot Channel** dialog box. See **Figure 10-13**.

> **Note**
> You can also create a new spot channel by pressing [Ctrl] ([Command] for Mac) and clicking the **Create new channel** button at the bottom of the **Channels** palette.

In the **New Spot Channel** dialog box, click the **Color:** box to open the **Color Picker**. It is recommended that you select a spot color from a color library rather than select a color in the **Color Picker**. This will make it easier for the printer to match the ink. As soon as you pick a color, the image window is updated with the spot color applied to the selection. If the color is satisfactory, close the **Color Picker** by clicking **OK**.

Back in the **New Spot Channel** dialog box, enter a percentage in the **Solidity:** text box. This setting has no effect on the separations that will be prepared for the image, but can be used to simulate onscreen the ink that will be used in the printing process. If a predefined color was selected from a color library, the default name of the spot

Figure 10-13.
You can add a spot color channel to an image through the **Channels** palette menu.

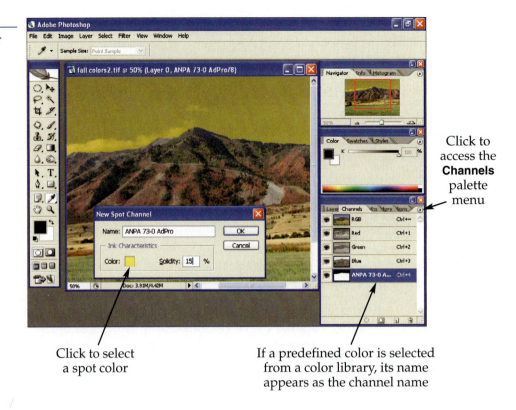

Click to select a spot color

If a predefined color is selected from a color library, its name appears as the channel name

Click to access the **Channels** palette menu

channel is the same as the color that was picked. Otherwise, the channel is named **Spot Color** followed by a number. You can rename the channel by typing a new name in the **Name:** text box if you like. When you are happy with the settings, click **OK** to create the spot channel.

The new spot channel appears in the **Channels** palette. Spot colors can be hidden or displayed in the image window by clicking the **Channel visibility** (eye) toggles next to the spot channel thumbnails. If spot colors are being used for a professional print job, a spot channel can be created for each spot color. Photoshop supports up to 56 channels, including color channels, spot channels, and alpha channels.

The Channel Mixer

The **Channel Mixer** command allows you to adjust images by changing the amount of color information that displays on each channel. However, this command is probably used more often to convert an RGB color image into grayscale. It is much better to use the **Channel Mixer** to do this instead of simply choosing **Image > Adjustments > Desaturate**, because you are given a lot of creative control over manipulating the contrast when using the **Channel Mixer**'s sliders.

To convert a color RGB image into grayscale, choose **Layer > New Adjustment Layer > Channel Mixer...** (or **Image > Adjustments > Channel Mixer...**, if the layer is unlocked). Place a check mark in the **Monochrome** check box at the bottom of the **Channel Mixer** dialog box. This changes the **Output Channel:** setting to **Gray**.

Next, do a little experiment. Enter 100 in the **Red:** setting and make sure the **Green:** and **Blue:** settings are set to 0. Observe the contrast of your image. Next, enter 100 in the **Green:** setting and set the other two settings to 0. Last, try the **Blue:** setting at 100 and the others at 0. Return to the settings that looked the best. In **Figure 10-14**, the barn and sky look best when the **Green:** channel is set 100%.

Figure 10-14.
Using the **Channel Mixer** dialog box to change a color image into a grayscale image gives you extra control over contrast in the image.

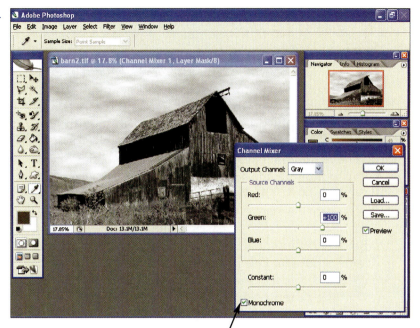

When checked, converts the image to grayscale

After determining which channel looks best at 100%, carefully start nudging each slider a bit while noticing the effect on the image. Keep two tips in mind as you experiment with different settings. First, try to end up with the total percentage amounts in all three boxes equaling 100%. This is a good rule of thumb; however, you may end up with slightly different results. In this example, it makes sense to keep the **Green:** setting high, since it looked the best initially. Second, do not forget that you can select (sometimes feather-selecting is best) portions of your image, and only those portions will be affected by your adjustments. This way, you can adjust the contrast differently in different areas of your image.

> **Note** If your image is in CMYK color mode, the same process still applies, but you will have four channels to adjust instead of three.

After adjusting the sliders, you can easily add a color tint (such as a sepia tone) to your grayscale image. To do this, turn off the **Monochrome** check box and experiment with adjusting each slider. For some more exaggerated color effects, experiment with also changing the channel selected in the **Output Channel:** drop-down list. In addition, you can adjust the **Constant:** slider. If the **Monochrome** check box is checked at the bottom of the dialog box, this slider is used to add more black or more white to your image, depending on which way the slider is dragged. If the **Monochrome** check box is unchecked, this slider is used to change the hue of color that is applied.

After clicking **OK** in the **Channel Mixer** dialog box, your image appears in grayscale, with any tints you added. Although the image may look like a grayscale image, it is actually still in its original color mode.

The Histogram Palette

A *histogram* is a graph that shows you how balanced an image is. In other words, a histogram shows you whether the image has a good mixture of shadows, midtones, and highlights. The extreme left side of the graph shows how much pure black is in an image. As you move farther right, the graph represents brighter and brighter shades. The extreme right side of the histogram represents how much of the image is pure white.

The **Histogram** palette shows you how shades of color are distributed in an image. The histogram for the stop sign image, **Figure 10-15**, shows a tall spike toward the left side of the graph. This represents the *red* shades in the image. The red shades found on the stop sign are nearly all the same brightness, that is why there is such a large spike in the histogram. The increases in the middle of the histogram represent the midtones in the background behind the stop sign. There is another spike in the histogram at the extreme right side. This means that there are a lot of white and near-white shades in this image (the lettering and edges of the stop sign). However, notice that the graph fades away at the extreme left side of the histogram, indicating that the image contains very few black or near-black shades.

The Histogram Palette Menu

The **Histogram** palette menu gives you access to other display options. Click the small arrow button in the upper right corner of the **Histogram** palette to open the **Histogram** palette menu. The first option available in the menu is **Dock to Palette Well**. This option moves the palette to the palette well, which is only available if your monitor's display resolution is set to 1024 × 768 or higher.

Figure 10-15.
The **Histogram** palette displays a graph that represents how darker and lighter shades of color are distributed in an image.

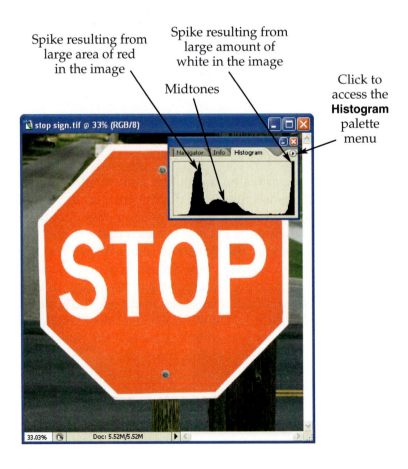

Refreshing the Histogram

As you work with an image, its histogram will be derived from cached information rather than the actual image information. This allows for quicker updates, but results in less accurate graphs. When the graph is being calculated from cached information rather than current image information, a small triangular warning icon appears in the upper right corner of the graph. The second option in the **Histogram** palette menu, **Uncached Refresh**, recalculates and updates the graph based on the actual image information rather than cached information. The same thing can be accomplished by clicking the small **Uncached Refresh** button in the **Histogram** palette.

Compact View, Expanded View, and All Channel View

The **Compact View** option in the **Histogram** palette menu is the default way of displaying the **Histogram** palette. It shows only the histogram. The **Expanded View** and **All Channel View** options in the palette menu display a **Channel:** drop-down list, **Source:** drop-down list, and **Uncached Refresh** button in addition to the histogram. The **All Channel View** option offers all of the features as the **Expanded View** option, but adds separate histograms for each of the color channels. See **Figure 10-16**.

By default, the histogram displays the combined luminosities from all color channels. You can display information about a particular channel by choosing it from

Figure 10-16.
Through the **Histogram** palette menu, you can choose to display an expanded version of the **Histogram** palette. You can also choose to add displays of the individual color channel histograms and color statistics for the image.

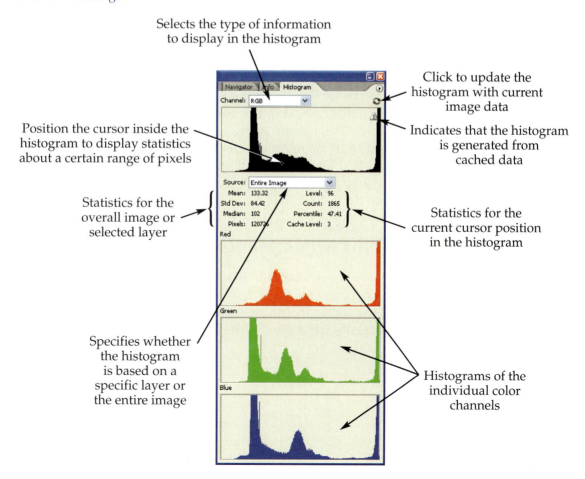

the **Channel:** drop-down list. Selecting **Luminosity** in the drop-down list causes the histogram to display information about the composite channel, which is different than the combined information displayed by default. When **RGB** or **CMYK** is selected in the **Channel:** drop-down list, the components that make up a color are considered. For example, in the stop sign image, the red is made up of one part midtone red, one part dark green, and one part dark blue. The result is a spike toward the left (dark) side of the histogram when **RGB** is selected in the **Channel:** drop-down list. When **Luminosity** is selected in the **Channel:** drop-down list, the histogram does not take the component parts into consideration, only the final result. In the case of the stop sign, the red is simply a midtone red. As a result, the histogram is shifted more toward the center. The **Colors** option in the **Channel:** drop-down list displays histograms of all of the color channels superimposed over one another.

The **Source:** drop-down list appears under the histogram when the **Expanded View** or **All Channels View** option is selected for the **Histogram** palette. If the image has more than one layer, you can use this drop-down list to specify whether the histogram is to be calculated from a specific layer or from the entire image.

The Show Statistics and Show Color Options

When the **Show Statistics** option is selected in the **Histogram** palette menu, two columns of statistics are displayed beneath the **Source:** drop-down list in the **Histogram** palette. The left column displays some statistics for the entire image, including the total number of pixels used to calculate the histogram (**Pixels:**) and the mathematical average of their luminosities (**Mean:**). Half the pixels in the image have luminosity levels higher than the **Median:** value and half have luminosity values that are lower. The **Std Dev:** (standard deviation) value is a measure of how luminosity values are distributed throughout the pixels.

As you place the cursor in the histogram and move it through the full range of luminosity levels (0 at the far left to 255 at the far right), the right column of statistics displays information about the number of pixels in each luminosity level. As you move the cursor in one direction, the **Count:** value shows you how many pixels in the image fall into each luminosity level, and the **Percentile:** value shows you the percentage of pixels in the image that have lower luminosity values, or are darker.

When the **Show Channels in Color** option is selected in the **Histogram** palette menu, the histograms of color channels are displayed in the color of the channel. When this option is turned off, color channel histograms are displayed in black. This option does not affect the histogram that is displayed when **Colors** is selected in the **Histogram** palette's **Channel:** drop-down list.

Viewing Color Adjustments in the Histogram Palette

If you display the **Histogram** palette while adjusting an image with any of Photoshop's color-correction tools, the **Histogram** palette will display the modified histogram over the top of the ghosted-out original histogram. This allows you to see how your adjustments affect the distribution of shadows, midtones, and highlights in the image.

The Threshold Command

The **Threshold** command, which is activated by choosing **Image > Adjustments > Threshold...**, opens the **Threshold** dialog box. This dialog box shows a histogram of your image and a slider directly underneath the histogram. As you move the slider, a higher or lower luminosity level (displayed in the **Threshold Level:** text box) is selected in the histogram. All of the pixels in the image with a luminosity value lower than the **Threshold Level:** value are changed to black. All pixels with luminosity levels higher than the **Threshold Level:** value remain white.

The **Threshold** command can be used for two purposes. First, you can drag the slider and turn your image into a simple-looking black and white image. You will probably never need to do that, unless a special effect is your goal.

You can also use **Threshold** command to locate the brightest highlights and darkest shadows in an image. Finding highlights, for example, can help you set the white point when using the **Levels** command and **Curves** command, explained later in this chapter. To find the brightest highlights, drag the slider underneath the histogram almost all the way to the right. Then, slowly keep dragging to the right until just before the last black dots appear, Figure 10-17. The remaining white spots are the brightest areas in your image.

> **Note** In some cases, the brightest highlights are a only handful of pixels scattered throughout the image. In such cases, you may need to lower the threshold by dragging the slider to the left until there are enough white pixels to accurately mark and sample.

To help you remember where the brightest and/or darkest areas of your image are, *color sampler marks* can be placed on your image. With the **Threshold** dialog box open,

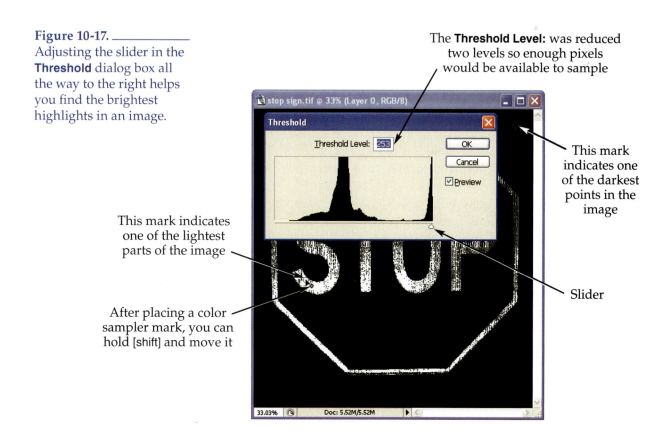

Figure 10-17.
Adjusting the slider in the **Threshold** dialog box all the way to the right helps you find the brightest highlights in an image.

press [Shift] to activate the **Color Sampler Tool**. This tool can also be found behind the **Eyedropper Tool** in the **Toolbox**. Click on an area of highlight or shadow to mark it so you can find it again if you use the **Levels** command or **Curves** command (discussed later in this chapter) to adjust the image. After placing a color sampler mark, you can move it by pressing [Shift], clicking on the marker, and dragging it to the desired location. You can remove color sample marks after closing the **Threshold** dialog box, by choosing the **Color Sampler Tool** in the **Toolbox** and clicking on the **Clear** button in the options bar. Color sampler marks cannot be removed while the **Threshold** dialog box is open.

If you are using the **Threshold** command to locate highlights and shadows in your image, click the **Cancel** button to close the **Threshold** dialog box after marking the light and dark points. If you *want* to change your image into a black and white image, click the **OK** button to close the **Threshold** dialog box.

The Levels Command

The **Levels** command allows you to adjust the shadows, midtones, and highlights in an image, **Figure 10-18**. If desired, the **Levels** command can adjust a single channel. This provides an alternative way to remove color casts or enhance the color in an image. The **Levels** command is especially useful when adjusting grayscale images or line art (drawings). Levels is one of Photoshop's color correction tools that is available as an adjustment layer by choosing **Layer > New Adjustment Layer > Levels…**. When this is done, any image correction is kept separate from the image, even though the image appears to have been permanently changed. This makes it possible to edit the **Levels** adjustment again later, if necessary.

To run the **Levels** command, choose **Image > Adjustments > Levels…**. This opens the **Levels** dialog box. The **Levels** dialog box displays a histogram of your image, Figure 10-18C. At the bottom of the histogram are three sliders. When adjusting your image, the first sliders you should move are the white and black sliders under the histogram. These sliders are used to set the image's *white point* (lightest pixels) and *black point* (darkest pixels). As the black slider is adjusted to the right, all of the shades to the left of the black slider become *pure* black. In other words, the dark areas of the image become even darker until they reach pure black. The white slider works the same way—all the tones represented in the histogram that are on the right side of the white slider will become *pure* white. This can enhance the contrast of an image considerably, but keep in mind that subtle details in an image (such as textures or wood grain) are lost when areas become too dark or light. As you move these sliders, the gray slider is automatically adjusted to maintain its relative position between the black and white sliders.

You can view what areas of your image are turning pure white or black as you adjust the sliders. To do this, press [Alt] or [Option] as you drag the white or black slider. If you press [Alt] or [Option] and drag the black slider, a low-resolution view of your image appears. Any black areas you see as you adjust the slider will become pure black, and all other tones in the image are represented by white in the preview. If you press [Alt] or [Option] while dragging the white slider, the white areas in the preview represent areas that will be pure white in the image. All areas of the image that will be shadows or midtones are represented by black in the preview.

You can also set the black and white point using the eyedropper tools on the right side of the **Levels** dialog box. Before doing this, you may want to use the **Threshold** command to determine where the darkest and lightest pixels in your image are located. Use the **Set Black Point** eyedropper to select the part of your image that should be pure black. The black slider moves automatically when this is done. Use the **Set White Point** eyedropper to select the part of the image that should be pure white.

Figure 10-18.
You can increase the tonal range and contrast in an image using the **Levels** command. **A**—The original image is somewhat flat, meaning that it has a limited range of tones. **B**—The image is improved after adjusting the black point and gray sliders. The white point needed no adjustment in this image. **C**—The settings in the **Levels** dialog box darken the shadows and midtones in the image.

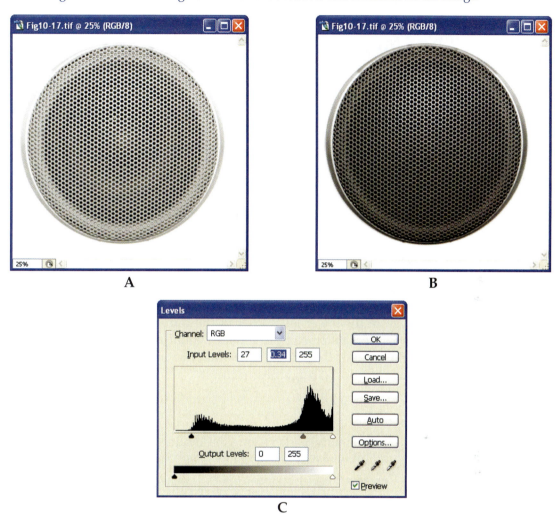

When adjusting color images, the **Set Gray Point** eyedropper can be used to remove a slight color cast in the image. To use this feature, locate an area of the image that should be true gray (have a saturation of 0) in your image and click on it with the **Set Gray Point** eyedropper. When you click on the pixel, Photoshop shifts the saturation and hue of all the colors in the image so that the selected pixel becomes gray, with a saturation of 0. If you click on any pixel that already has a saturation of 0 (middle gray, white, or black, it does not matter), the **Set Gray Point** tool has no effect on the image. Only if the selected pixel has a saturation above 0, does the tool work.

> **Note** The **Set Gray Point** eyedropper is used only to compensate for minor color casts created by common lighting problems. Selecting a vivid color with the tool creates unpredictable results.

After setting the black and white points, use the gray slider under the histogram to adjust the overall brightness of the image, if necessary. Dragging the slider to the right darkens the image, and dragging it to the left lightens the image.

The **Output Levels:** section of the **Levels** dialog box consists of a gradient bar with two sliders and two text boxes. These controls are used to keep the shadows from being too dark and the highlights from being too light for different types of print jobs. Printing a newspaper will require different **Output Levels:** setting than printing a magazine, so consult with your print service provider for the actual settings to use.

The Curves Command

The **Curves** command is Photoshop's most complicated color-adjustment command. This command allows you to fine-tune your image by adjusting tonal values at up to 16 points along the tonal range for each of the image's color channels. Theoretically, the **Curves** command provides Photoshop users the most control over correcting an image. However, in many cases, images can be adjusted just as effectively with simpler color-correction tools.

You can run the **Curves** command by choosing **Image > Adjustments > Curves…**. You can also use a **Curves** adjustment layer, which is the recommended method. After running the command or creating the adjustment layer, the **Curves** dialog box appears, Figure 10-19. A graph in the dialog box represents the image in its current state.

Clicking in the image causes a temporary symbol to appear on the graph, showing you the darkness or lightness of the pixel you clicked on. Move your eye straight down (see the dashed arrow in Figure 10-19) to the gradient bar below the diagonal line to see how dark or light the sampled shade is. The actual tonal value of the sampled pixel is displayed in the lower left corner of the **Curves** dialog box. The value following the **Input:** label refers to the sampled shade's tonal value on a scale of 0–255 (if your image is in RGB mode) or 0–100% (if your image is in CMYK mode). You can think of this number as the color's "brightness rating."

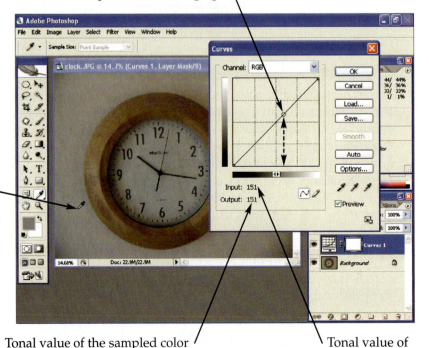

Figure 10-19.
When you have opened the **Curves** dialog box, you can click on a pixel in the image to see its initial tonal value and the effect that any changes to the graph line will have on it.

Click in the image to select a color to display in the **Curves** dialog box

Temporary marker shows the location of the sampled tone on the graph

Tonal value of the sampled color that will result from the changes made to the graph line

Tonal value of the sampled pixel

Adjusting Color in the Curves Dialog Box

The horizontal gradient bar is the scale representing the image's current tonal range. The vertical scale represents the tonal range in the adjusted image. Before you make any adjustments, these values are identical, resulting in a straight diagonal graph line. By changing the graph line, you change the way the colors in the original image relate to colors in the adjusted image.

To adjust an image in the **Curves** dialog box, begin by selecting a channel to affect from the **Channel:** drop-down list. In most cases, you will want to adjust the RGB or CMYK channel, which affects the entire image. If your image has a color cast, you may want to adjust a specific color channel instead.

Next, locate the tonal level you want to adjust on the bottom gradient bar. Then, click the point on the graph line that is directly above that shade. You can [Alt] click in the graph to add more gridlines, making it easier to see the spot on the graph line that lies directly above the tone you want to adjust. When you have located the point on the graph line, click there to add an editing point.

Then, look at the gradient bar on the left side of the graph. Determine whether you want the selected tone to be lighter or darker, and drag the editing point up or down until it is straight across from the desired tone. See **Figure 10-20**. If you move the editing point right or left instead of up or down, you are actually selecting a different tone in the original image to edit. To make sure you are moving the editing point up and down but not left and right, watch the **Input:** and **Output:** numbers below the horizontal gradient bar. Only the **Output:** number should change; the **Input:** number should remain constant.

> **Note** When you move an editing point in the graph line to change a tone, all non-white and non-black tones in the image are adjusted. However, the amount the tones are adjusted depends on how close they are to the selected tone. The closest tones are affected the most, and the farthest tones are affected least.

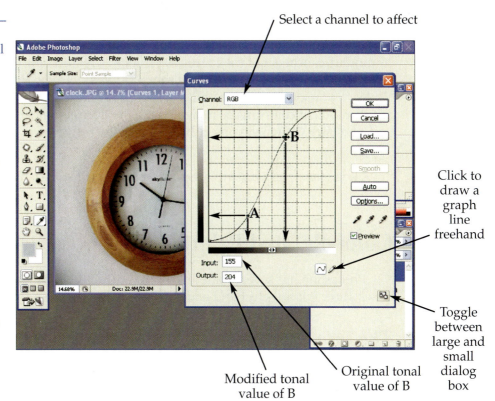

Figure 10-20.
You can see what an editing point's initial tonal value was by looking straight down from it. By looking straight to the left of the editing point, you can see what its tonal value will be after applying the adjustments in the **Curves** dialog box. In this example, the lighter midtones have been lightened further by moving B up, and the darker midtones have darkened further by moving A down. This increases the tonal range and contrast in the image.

If the image you are working with is flat, meaning that it lacks a full range of tones, you will need to adjust two or more points along the graph. Notice in Figure 10-19 that editing point A on the graph was moved down to a darker tone, and that editing point B was moved up to a higher tonal value. The result is a darkening of some of the midtone grays, a lightening of some of the midtone grays, and an increase in the contrast of the image.

Instead of (or in addition to) clicking points to create editing points to shape the graph line, you can click the **Pencil** button under the bottom right corner of the graph and then use the cursor to draw the graph line (or just sections of it) freehand. Position the cursor at the point where you want to start drawing freehand, click and hold, and drag the mouse to draw the desired line. You do not have to begin drawing on the existing line; you can begin anywhere in the graph. As you drag the mouse left or right, the line segment you draw replaces the corresponding section of the existing graph line.

You can click the **Enlarge/Reduce** toggle at the bottom right corner of the **Curves** dialog box to increase the size of the **Curves** dialog box, or to make it smaller if it is already enlarged. Clicking the double arrow button in the middle of the horizontal gradient bar reverses the direction of both (horizontal and vertical) scales. Reversing the direction of the scales causes the graph line to be rotated 180°.

Adjusting Curves with the Eyedropper Tools

An alternative way to adjust an image is to use the eyedropper tools near the bottom of the column of buttons in the **Curves** dialog box. Use the **Set Black Point** eyedropper to sample the darkest pixels in the image and the **Set White Point** to sample the lightest pixels in the image (as was done in the **Levels** command). For color images, the **Set Gray Point** eyedropper works the same as the **Set Gray Point** eyedropper in the **Levels** dialog box. It changes the hue and saturation of the image's colors until the selected pixel becomes gray. The tool is not available for grayscale images.

Using the Luminosity Blending Mode to Limit the Curve Command's Effects

If the colors in an image change too much when adjusting it with the **Curves** command, cancel out of the current operation. Create a new **Curves** adjustment layer by choosing **Layer > New Adjustment Layer > Curves…**. In the **New Layer** dialog box, set the **Mode:** to **Luminosity**, which will allow only brightness values be adjusted, not the hue or saturation of colors in the image. Make the desired adjustments in the **Curves** dialog box, and click **OK** when you are happy with the results.

> **Note** Remember, adjustment layers affect all layers beneath them in the **Layers** palette.

Color-Related Palettes

Photoshop has several palettes that are directly related to image color. These dialog boxes allow you to select and adjust color and review color and tool information.

The Info Palette

Regardless of what tool you are currently using in the image window, the **Info** palette, **Figure 10-21**, displays information about the pixel directly underneath your

Figure 10-21.
The **Info** palette displays information that includes tips about the currently selected tool, image color under the cursor, cursor location, selections, and image file size.

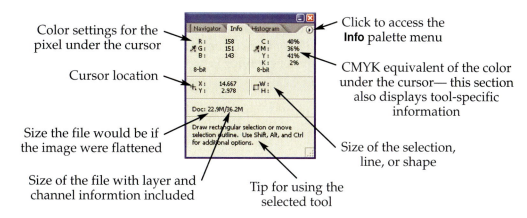

cursor. The **RGB** and **CMYK** sections show color information about the pixel. The other sections in the palette show other information relating to the tool being used and the cursor's location.

Bit Depth and Other Color Information

Two sections at the top of the **Info** palette display color information about the pixel under the cursor. The pixel's color composition (its RGB, CMYK, or Lab values) is displayed in the left section. The equivalent CMYK values are displayed in the right section. However, the CMYK information in this section may be replaced with other types of information when certain tools are used. The bit depth of the image is displayed at the bottom of these sections.

Bit depth is a measurement of how many different shades of color a Photoshop file can display. A *bit* is a tiny scrap of computer data that has two possible values: a one or a zero. In Photoshop, each pixel in a 1-bit image is strictly black or white.

In an 8-bit-per-channel image, a combination of eight bits is used to describe one pixel. Because an RGB image is divided into three channels (red, green, and blue), each pixel in the image is capable of displaying 2^8 (or 256) possible color values on each channel. Therefore, an 8-bit image can actually produce well over 16 million different color values ($256 \times 256 \times 256$, $2^{8 \times 3}$, or 2^{24}) as the different channels mix together to form other colors. That is generally considered a greater number of unique colors than human vision is capable of distinguishing. It also far exceeds the number of distinct colors that can be printed.

So why are some images captured with 16-bit or 24-bit color depths? The answer is that the greater number of colors allows more flexibility and reliability in editing. By increasing the initial number of colors in the image, you increase the mathematical precision used to calculate edits and decrease the risk that an edit or adjustment will produce an undesirable result.

Often an image is referred to by the number of its color channels times its bit depth. This can be confusing if you are not aware of it. For example, an RGB image with a bit depth of 8-bits per channel will often be referred to as a 24-bit RGB image (8-bit color depth times 3 color channels). If the same image were in CMYK mode, it would be referred to as a 32-bit CMYK image (8-bit color depth times 4 color channels).

For advanced-level high-end photo retouching, images can be converted into a 16-bit-per-channel image (and in some cases, a 32-bit-per-channel image) by choosing the appropriate color depth from the **Image > Mode** submenu. This increases the number of different shades of color that can be produced. In most cases, images you work with in Photoshop will be 8-bits per channel. Not all of Photoshop's tools work with 16-bit-per-channel images, and only a few tools can be used with 32-bit-per-channel images. 16-bit-per-channel images have up to 65,536 (or 2^{16}) shades for each color channel. 32-bit-per-channel HDR (or high dynamic range) images can contain more shades of color than a typical computer monitor is capable of displaying.

> **Note**
>
> The title bar of an image window displays the color mode and per-channel bit depth of the image.

Location and Selection Size

Beneath the color information sections, you will find two sections that display cursor location and selection measurements. In the section on the left, the **X:** and **Y:** values show exactly where your cursor is. The **Y:** value is the cursor's distance from the bottom of the image, and the **X:** value is the cursor's distance from the left side of the image. Photoshop's **Measure Tool**, grouped with the **Eyedropper Tools** in the **Toolbox**, also displays this information, along with distance data if the cursor is dragged.

The right section displays **W:** (width) and **H:** (height) values if you are dragging a shape, line, or selection with your cursor. In addition, the upper right section of the dialog box, which displays CMYK color settings by default, will display different information when certain tools are selected or commands are run. This information may include anchor point location, change in position (Δ**X:** and Δ**Y:**), angle (**A:**), and distance (**D:**). The exact types of information displayed in this section depend on the tool or command that is selected, and usually match the info displayed in the tool's options bar.

Other Information

Beneath the location and measurement sections in the **Info** palette, you will see a section that displays the *document size*, or file size. The number on the left represents the size the image file would be if it were flattened. The number on the right is the file size of the image with all layer and channel information included. If the image has only a single layer and only color channels, these numbers will be the same. Beneath the document size section is a section that displays tips about using the currently selected tool.

You can change the information that is displayed in the **Info** palette by opening the palette menu and selecting **Palette Options…**. This opens the **Info Palette Options** dialog box. From this dialog box, you can choose new or additional types of information to display in the **Info** palette. You can also use this dialog box to change the units that certain information is displayed in.

The Color Palette

The **Color** palette, Figure 10-22, can be used instead of the **Color Picker** to choose a foreground color. From the **Color** palette menu, you can select from several different slider configurations that will produce RGB, CMYK, and other color mode combinations. The sliders work the same as the sliders in the **Color Picker**.

Colors can also be chosen from the spectrum (the colored bar at the bottom of the palette). This is essentially the same as picking a color by clicking in the color field of

Figure 10-22.
You can use the **Color** palette to select a new foreground color.

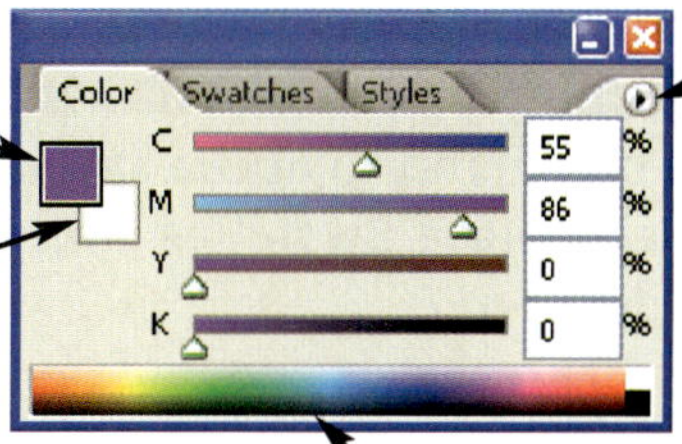

the **Color Picker**. You can change the spectrum by selecting a different option in the **Color** palette menu.

To set a foreground color with the **Color** palette, simply adjust the sliders to produce the desired color, or select it from the spectrum. The foreground color is automatically updated as you adjust the settings. If you want to select a new background color, you must first switch the foreground and background colors. Then, make the desired changes. When you have the color you want, switch the foreground and background colors again.

The Swatches Palette

Clicking on a color in the **Swatches** palette, Figure 10-23, is yet another way to choose the foreground color. *Swatches* are a collection of color samples, like you might find at a paint store.

In its default state, the **Swatches** palette displays six RGB colors on the top row: red, yellow, green, cyan, blue, and magenta. These colors are at full brightness (values of 255). The next row displays the same colors in CMYK mode, using maximum ink settings. Various shades of gray are also included on the top two rows. The next row in the default **Swatches** palette is a collection of light, pastel colors. The four rows that follow are increasingly dark versions of the same colors. The final row of the default **Swatches** palette is a collection of brown colors.

The **Swatches** palette menu displays a long list of colors that can be loaded into the palette, including spot colors. When you select one of these other collections of swatches, a dialog box appears asking if you want to append the existing swatches with the new swatches or replace them. If, after loading a new set of swatches, you want to restore the default swatches, select **Reset Swatches...** from the **Swatches** palette menu.

Perhaps the most useful feature of this palette is that you can store your own commonly-used colors by selecting **New Swatch...** in the **Swatches** palette menu. This command saves the current foreground color as a swatch and saves it to the swatches palette. You can store your customized collections of swatches using the **Save Swatches** command in the palette menu. If you want your collection of swatches to be available to

Figure 10-23.
Colors can also be selected using the **Swatches** palette.

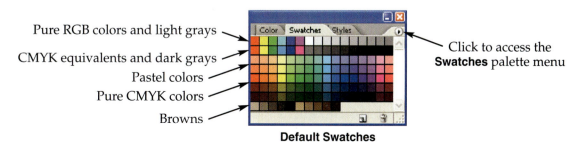

Default Swatches

other Adobe CS2 applications, use the **Save Swatches for Exchange** command instead of the **Save Swatches** command. After saving a collection of swatches, you can use the **Load Swatches** command to add a saved collection of swatches to the current swatch collection, or the **Replace Swatches** command to replace the current swatch collection with a saved collection.

Recommended Sequence for Color Correction

Now that you have been introduced to Photoshop's color correction tools, you may wonder if there are certain steps you should follow as you correct color in an image. According to information found in Photoshop's help file, the following is the recommended sequence for correcting color in an image.

Use tools of your choosing to accomplish the following tasks in the specified order:

1. Correct any color casts first.
2. Correct oversaturated (too intense) or undersaturated (too weak) problem areas.
3. Adjust highlight and shadow areas as needed.
4. Set overall tonal range of the image by adjusting white and black points.
5. Make other color adjustments that please your eye.
6. Sharpen the image.

Color Management

Think of the last time you were in a store that sold TVs. Did you notice that each TV displays color and brightness in a slightly different way? Computer monitors are the same—they all display color differently. Most likely, the image you see on your monitor will not look exactly the same when printed. If you look closely, there will be differences in the color.

Steps can be taken to ensure that the colors you view on your computer monitor match the results you get when you print. This can be controlled through a process called color management. Color management is a highly technical procedure. Entire books have been written about the subject. Because many readers of this text are not professional Photoshop users yet, color management procedures will be briefly introduced here, but not thoroughly explained. If you are a beginning-level Photoshop user, you may want to skip this section.

Color management requires you to do the following:

- *Calibrate* your monitor. This means that you set your monitor to display colors using certain brightness and contrast settings, etc. Information on how to calibrate a monitor can be found in Photoshop's help file.

- Choose an RGB color workspace. An *RGB color workspace* is a generic setting that controls how your monitor will display RGB colors. You can view the different choices by choosing **Edit > Color Settings...** (or **Photoshop > Color Settings...** for Mac) and then clicking the **RGB:** drop-down list in **Working Spaces** section of the **Color Settings** dialog box. **Adobe RGB** is a highly recommended all-purpose setting.

- Create ICC profiles of your monitor, printer, and image capture devices. *ICC profiles* are small computer files that describe how your monitor, printer, and other devices display or capture color in terms of standards set by the International Color Consortium.

The most accurate ICC profiles are created using third-party hardware and software, such as Colorvision's Spyder2 Plus bundle. This hardware and software will analyze your devices and create ICC profiles. Another option is to hire someone to do this for you. Your print service provider may be able to recommend a qualified individual. There are also online companies that provide color-management services.

- After ICC profiles have been created and stored in the proper folders on your hard drive, you must assign profiles and convert from one profile to another as you work. These commands are found under Photoshop's **Edit** menu. For example, after scanning an image, you can choose **Edit > Assign Profile...** and choose the ICC profile you created for your scanner. Because of the scanner's ICC profile, Photoshop understands how your scanner captures color and adjusts the colors in your image appropriately, although the differences may be subtle. If you want to apply color correction to your image, you will next need to convert the image to working RGB mode (the RGB color workspace you chose previously). When you are ready to print, choose **File > Print with Preview...**. In the **Print** dialog box, select the printer's profile in the **Options** section. You may need to click the **More Options** button first.

GRAPHIC DESIGN:
Color Harmony and Contrast

As you create various combinations of color in a design, be aware that different moods can be created by placing particular colors next to each other. Color combinations can be grouped into two basic categories. *Analogous colors* are colors that look good together, creating a sense of harmony and tranquility. *Complementary colors* are extremely different from each other and cause each other to stand out.

As you read this section, refer to the RYB (red-yellow-blue) color wheel shown in **Figure 10-24**. This traditional color wheel is slightly different than

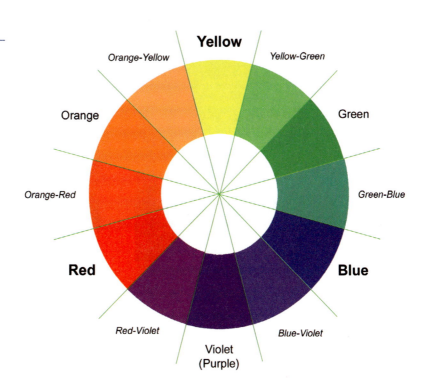

Figure 10-24. A traditional (RYB) color wheel can be used to determine whether colors are analogous or complementary.

the RGB/CMY color wheel you were introduced to in Chapter 9, because it represents a subtractive color system (such as different shades of paint). In a traditional color wheel, red, yellow, and blue are **primary colors**. When two primary colors are mixed, a **secondary color** is created. Secondary colors are orange, green, and violet. When a primary and secondary color are mixed, a **tertiary color** is created (such as red-violet or yellow-green). For your information, *cyan* is near in color to green-blue on the traditional color wheel and *magenta* is near in color to red-violet.

Analogous colors are next to each other (or very near to each other) on a color wheel. They blend well together and can help create a calm, peaceful mood in a design. Using a color combination such as blue and violet is an example of an analogous color scheme. See **Figure 10-25**.

Complementary colors are opposite from each other (or near-opposite) on a color wheel. Complementary colors, when used together, cause each other to stand out vividly. Examples of such color combinations are blue and orange or red and green.

The CD liner design in Figure 10-25B uses a combination of red and blue; these colors are *almost* opposite from each on a color wheel. Red and blue contrast vividly and are much more complementary than analogous, so they create a sense of energy when used together.

Graphic designers should use good judgment when using complementary colors. If designs are too attention-grabbing, some viewers might be repelled by the design instead of attracted to it.

When text is placed on a design, it must contrast sharply with the background so it can be easily read. In most cases, black or white text stands out better than colored text. Even if black or white text is used, consider using layer styles such as drop shadows to help the text contrast more with the background.

Figure 10-25.
The color combination used in a design affects the mood of the design. **A**—When analogous colors are used in a design, a calmer mood is created. **B**—The original design uses contrasting colors, red and blue, to create a more energetic feeling.

A   B

Examine the versions of the Farmer's Market poster in **Figure 10-26**. This design is extremely varied and colorful—and busy. When text is added without any layer styles, none of the colors stand out well from the multi-colored background. In the second example, a drop shadow has been added to each text entry. In the last example, both a drop shadow and a stroked border have been added to each text entry. Which text example is easiest to read? Do you agree that the easiest text to read is white with both a drop shadow and a stroked border added?

Figure 10-26.
Which of these text examples most effectively contrasts with the background colors? **A**—Plain text of various colors. **B**—Various colors of text with drop shadows. **C**—Various colors of text with stroked borders and drop-shadows.

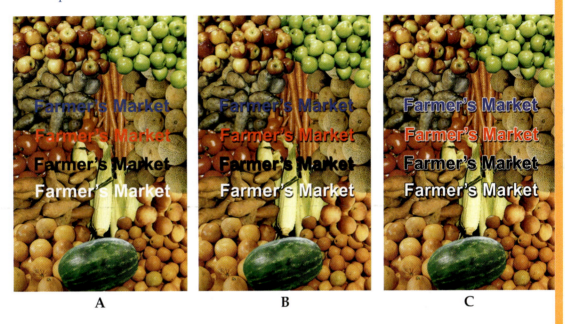

Summary

In the last two chapters, you learned about Photoshop's color correction tools and palettes. Because many of these tools and palettes are closely related, it is seldom necessary to use *all* of them. Think about different ways to accomplish the same color adjustment, and choose the color correction tools that help you get the best results.

In this chapter, you have been introduced to some of the deeply technical issues that advanced Photoshop users must be familiar with. With practice, experience, and further training, you will become more comfortable with these topics. For Photoshop users who are preparing projects for commercial printing presses, remember to seek the advice of knowledgeable staff at printing companies with whom you do business.

Chapter Tutorials

In the tutorials that follow, you will use the **Levels** command and **Curves** command to adjust some images. You will also correct an image using the sequence recommended in this chapter.

Tutorial 10-1: Adding a Levels Adjustment Layer

In this tutorial, you will add a **Levels** adjustment layer to darken an area of the design behind text. This will help the text to stand out and make it more legible.

1. Open the 05cardfront.psd file you edited in an earlier chapter.
2. Choose **Edit > Preferences > Guides, Grid & Slices**.
3. In the **Preferences** dialog box, make sure the controls in the **Grid** section are set up to display a gridline every 1" with 4 subdivisions. Click **OK** when finished.
4. Turn on the grid by choosing **View > Show > Grid**.
5. Choose **View > Snap To** and, in the submenu, make sure there is a check mark next to **Grid**.
6. Use the **Rectangular Marquee Tool** to select the area shown in **Figure T10-1**.

   The selection border snaps to the gridlines.

7. Choose **View > Snap** to turn off snap.
8. Choose **View > Show > Grid** to turn off the grid.
9. In the **Layers** palette, click the layer that contains the yellow flowers to make it active.
10. Choose **Layer > New Adjustment Layer > Levels…**.
11. In the **New Layer** dialog box, accept the default name of Levels 1 by clicking **OK**.
12. In the **Levels** dialog box, drag the midtones slider at the bottom of the histogram until the middle text box above the histogram reads .55. See **Figure T10-2**.

    You can accomplish the same thing by entering .55 in the middle text box.

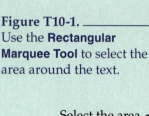

Figure T10-1. Use the **Rectangular Marquee Tool** to select the area around the text.

Select the area around the text with the **Rectangular Marquee Tool**

Figure T10-2.
Darken the midtones in the selection by moving the gray slider in the **Levels** dialog box to the right.

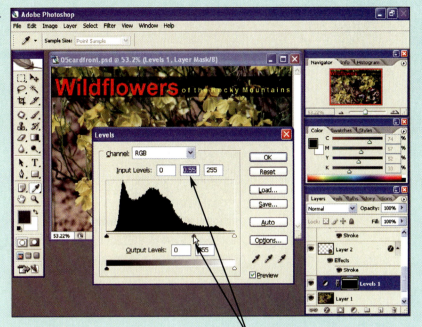

Adjust the midtones slider, or enter the new value in the text box

Move Tool

13. Click **OK** to close the **Levels** dialog box and apply the adjustment.
14. If necessary, use the **Move Tool** to position the text so it fits attractively in the area you just darkened.
15. Choose **File > Save As…** and name this file 10cardfront.psd. Close the file after you have saved it.

Tutorial 10-2: Correcting an Image Using Levels

In this tutorial, you will add a **Levels** adjustment layer and use it to set a new black point. The result is better contrast and an increase in the tonal range of the image.

1. Open the speaker2.jpg file.
2. Choose **Layer > New Adjustment Layer > Levels…**.
3. In the **New Layer** dialog box, click **OK** to accept Levels 1 as the name of the adjustment layer.

Set Black Point

4. Click the **Set Black Point** button and then click on an area inside the speaker grille that is dark gray. Do not click on the grille itself. See **Figure T10-3**.

Notice that the image and histogram are adjusted automatically when the gray is sampled.

> **Note** When using the **Eyedropper Tool** to sample a color, make sure the bottom left tip of the eyedropper cursor is positioned over the pixel you want to sample.

5. Drag the white slider at the right corner of the **Output Levels:** gradient bar until the amount in the corresponding **Output Levels:** text box is 245.
6. Choose **File > Save As…** and name this file 10speaker2.tif.
7. Close the 10speaker2.tif file.

Figure T10-3.
With the **Levels** dialog box open, set the black point of the image by clicking on the darkest gray in the image with the **Eyedropper Tool**.

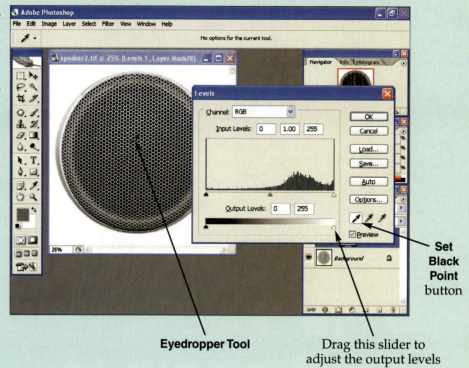

Tutorial 10-3: Correcting an Image Using Curves

In this tutorial, you will convert an image to grayscale color mode. You will use the **Threshold** command to determine the lightest and darkest portions of the image, which you will then set as the white point and black point of the image. You will improve contrast and expand the tonal range of the image using a **Curves** adjustment layer. You will remove heavy shadows from one subject using a **Levels** adjustment layer, and finally sharpen the image using the **Unsharp Mask** command.

1. Open the 08bball.psd file that you began restoring in an earlier chapter.

   This image has a heavy, brownish-yellow color cast. Because it is an old photo, you will turn it into a grayscale image.

2. Choose **Image > Mode > Grayscale**. Click **OK** when asked if you want to discard color information.

3. Choose **Image > Adjustments > Threshold**.

4. In the **Threshold** dialog box, drag the slider to the right until only the lightest areas remain.

   A value of 135 in the **Threshold Level:** text box is about right.

5. Hold down [Shift] and click on the white area in the image, as shown in **Figure T10-4**.

   This places a color sampler mark on one of the brightest spots in the image. If you need to adjust the position of the color sampler mark, hold [Shift] and then click and drag the mark to the correct location.

6. In the **Threshold** dialog box, drag the slider to the left until only the darkest areas of the image are visible.

   A value of 43 in the **Threshold Level:** text box is about right.

7. Hold down [Shift] and click on a dark area of the image to place a color sampler mark. See **Figure T10-5**.

Figure T10-4. Place a color sampler mark on the brightest highlights in the image.

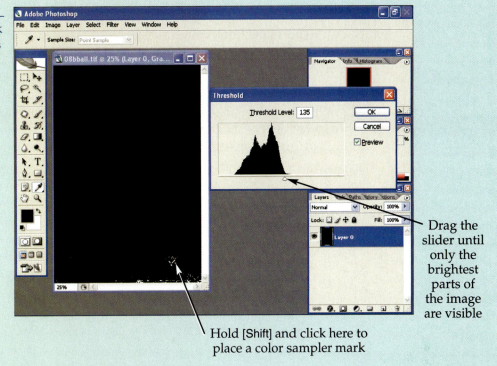

Drag the slider until only the brightest parts of the image are visible

Hold [Shift] and click here to place a color sampler mark

8. Click the **Cancel** button in the **Threshold** dialog box.
9. Choose **Window > Histogram**.

   The current histogram in the Histogram palette shows that most of the grays in this image are dark midtones. There are no bright highlights or black shadows.

10. Choose **Layer > New Adjustment Layer > Curves…**.
11. In the **New Layer** dialog box, click **OK** to accept Curves 1 as the name of the adjustment layer.

Figure T10-5. Place a color sampler mark on the darkest shadows in the image. When you are done, cancel out of the **Threshold** dialog box.

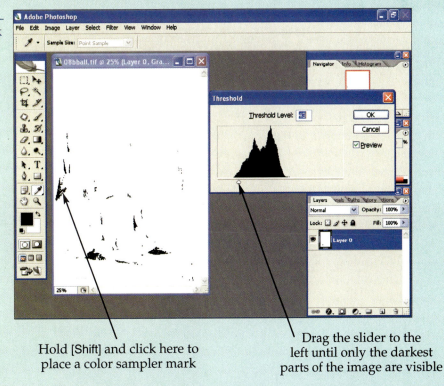

Hold [Shift] and click here to place a color sampler mark

Drag the slider to the left until only the darkest parts of the image are visible

Set White Point

12. In the **Curves** dialog box, click the **Set Black Point** button.
13. Use the **Eyedropper Tool**, which automatically appears when you position the cursor over the image, to click inside the color sampler mark you placed over the darkest part of your image.
14. Click the **Set White Point** button in the **Curves** dialog box, and then click on the color sampler mark you placed over the brightest part of your image.
15. If necessary, click and drag the editing points on the **Curves** graph line horizontally until there are no spikes in the histogram on the extreme right or left side.

    An example of a desirable histogram is shown in Figure T10-6.

16. In the **Curves** dialog box, click to place another point in the middle of the graph line. Click and drag the center editing point slightly to adjust the contrast of the image, as desired. See Figure T10-7.
17. Click **OK** to accept the adjustments and close the **Curves** dialog box.
18. Now that you can see the image more clearly, you will most likely need to retouch a few blotchy areas that are distracting.

    Since the adjustment layer is active, you will need to select the image layer before making your adjustments. The following are the suggested tools to use:

Figure T10-6.
This histogram shows a good distribution of tones. Note that there are no spikes at the ends of the histogram.

Figure T10-7.
After setting the black point and white point, add an editing point representing the image midtones to the graph line and adjust it to improve contrast.

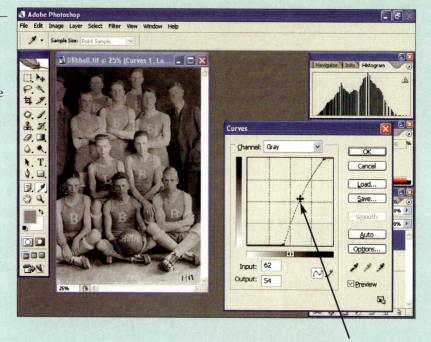

Add an additional editing point and adjust it to get the desired contrast

Chapter 10   Advanced Color Correction Techniques   431

Patch Tool

Dodge Tool

Burn Tool

Lasso Tool

- Use the **Patch Tool** to create more consistent skin textures.
- Use the **Dodge Tool** with soft brushes and a low **Exposure:** setting to lighten dark blotches in the image.
- Use the **Burn Tool** with soft brushes and a low **Exposure:** setting.

19. Zoom in on the face of the boy shown in **Figure T10-8**.
20. Click the **Lasso Tool** and enter 10 in the **Feather:** text box.
21. Create a selection around the dark shadows on the boy's face.
22. Choose **Layer > New Adjustment Layer > Levels…**.
23. In the **New Layer** dialog box, click **OK** to accept Levels 1 as the name of this layer.
24. Drag the midtones (gray) slider as shown in **Figure T10-9** to lighten the dark gray shadows on the boy's face.

Figure T10-8. _____
Carefully select the shadows on this player's face. Because of the **Feather:** setting, the selection will appear rounded off.

Figure T10-9. _____
Adjust the sliders in the **Levels** dialog box to fix the deep shadows on the player's face.

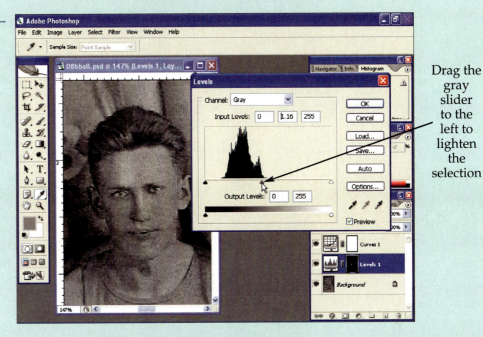

Drag the gray slider to the left to lighten the selection

25. Once you are happy with the adjustment, click the **OK** button to apply the changes and close the **Levels** dialog box.
26. Choose **View > Fit on Screen**.
27. Select the Background layer and then choose **Filter > Sharpen > Unsharp Mask…**.
28. In the **Unsharp Mask** dialog box, set the **Amount:** slider to 40%, the **Radius:** slider to 1.5 pixels, and the **Threshold:** slider to 10 levels. Then, click **OK**.

    The sharpening settings improve most of the image. However, two of the basketball players and one of the coaches are so out of focus that no amount of sharpening can improve them. See Figure T10-10. Those subjects were probably moving as the camera exposed this image.

29. Zoom in and make one final check for areas that need retouching.
30. If possible, print this image at a high-quality setting so you can accurately see the results of your efforts.
31. Flatten the image, and then choose **File > Save As...** and name this file 10bball.tif. Then, close the file.

Figure T10-10. You can dramatically clean up an image using the color-correction tools and techniques described in this chapter. **A**—The original image is flat and has a strong color cast. **B**—The adjusted image has an improved tonal range and is sharper. The color cast has been removed.

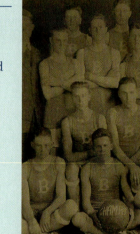
A

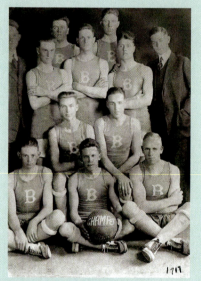
B

Key Terms

additive color system
alpha channels
analogous colors
bit
bit depth
black point
calibrate
CMYK color mode
color channels
color management
color modes

color sampler marks
complementary colors
composite channel
document size
gamut
grayscale color mode
hexadecimal code
histogram
ICC profiles
layer mask
primary colors

RGB color mode
RGB color workspace
secondary color
spot channels
spot color
subtractive color system
swatches
tertiary color
white light
white point

Review Questions

Answer the following questions on a separate piece of paper.

1. Which can contain a greater number of colors, an image printed on a printing press or an image displayed on a typical computer monitor?
2. An additive color system uses _____ to create color.
3. How is white created in an additive color system?
4. What are the four colors represented by CMYK?
5. What is a spot color?
6. Briefly describe how a subtractive color system (used to create a printed page) is different than an additive color system (used to create an onscreen image).
7. As a general rule, what color mode should new, full-color documents be created in?
8. What color mode should black-and-white projects be created in?
9. How do you convert an image to a different mode?
10. In RGB color mode, red light at maximum strength would be represented by an **R:** value of _____.
11. In CMYK color mode, what value would appear in each of the **C:**, **M:**, **Y:**, and **K:** boxes to represent white?
12. In the **Color Picker**, what button do you click to select a spot color?
13. What is an "out-of-gamut" color?
14. How do you temporarily view out-of-gamut colors in Photoshop?
15. What happens when you print a RGB file to a consumer-level inkjet printer?
16. When an image in RGB color mode is converted to CMYK color mode, what happens to the out-of-gamut colors in the image?
17. What is a color channel?
18. How do you store selection data in the **Channels** palette?
19. What is a histogram?
20. How do you delete color sampler marks?
21. What does the gray slider in the **Levels** dialog box do?
22. In the **Curves** dialog box, what do the horizontal and vertical gradient bars represent?
23. If the hue and saturation of colors in your image change undesirably when the **Curves** command is used, how can you limit the effect so that only the brightness of colors will be changed?
24. List two palettes that can be used instead of the **Color Picker** to select the foreground color.
25. What is the purpose of color management?

Six less-common color modes are shown here. The appearance of images in these modes will vary depending on the settings chosen.

Bitmap Mode

Grayscale Mode

Duotone Mode (Black/Green)

Tritone Mode (Black/Green/Yellow)

Quadtone Mode (Black/Green/Yellow/Red)

Indexed Color Mode (System/Windows)

11 Additional Layer Techniques

Learning Objectives

After completing this chapter, you will be able to:
- Apply blending modes to a layer.
- Use the **Fade** command to apply blending modes after applying a filter or color adjustment.
- Blend layers together by applying a layer mask to a layer.
- Blend layers together by applying a vector mask to a layer.
- Combine layers in creative ways using clipping masks.
- Mask dark or bright portions of an image using layer style blending options.
- Describe how to permanently delete masked areas of an image.
- Use layer comps to store multiple versions of a design.
- Line up multiple layers with the **Align** commands.
- Create equal amounts of space between layers with the **Distribute** commands.

Introduction

In Chapter 4, *Introduction to Layers*, you learned how to create, organize, and manage layers. In this chapter, you will learn about other useful layer techniques that allow you to blend layers together in creative ways. You will also learn about layer comps, a feature that helps designers quickly save multiple versions of a design. Lastly, you will learn how to line up objects on various layers and distribute equal amounts of space between each object using the **Align** and **Distribute** commands.

Blending Modes

You were introduced to blending modes in Chapter 6, *Painting Tools and Filters*. In that chapter, you learned that blending modes control how colors applied with a painting tool (such as the **Brush Tool**) blend with colors that already exist in the image.

Using Blending Modes with Layers

Blending modes can also be used to blend entire layers with each other. A blending mode can be assigned to any layer that appears above another layer in the **Layers** palette. This causes the colors in the top layer to blend with, and change, the appearance of the colors in all layers beneath it, Figure 11-1.

To use a blending mode on a layer, begin by accessing the **Layers** palette. Select the layer that you want to affect that is uppermost in the layer stack. If the stack includes layers that you do *not* want to affect, you may need to reorganize your image to ensure that those layers are listed above the selected layer. Then, select the desired blending mode from the pop-up menu in the upper right corner of the **Layers** palette.

As shown in Figure 11-1, the **Soft Light** mode is a good choice when blending a layer with another layer containing an object with shiny surfaces, such as the drum. The

Figure 11-1.
Blending modes are used to change the way layers blend with one another. **A**—Gravel. **B**—Drum. **C**—These two images were combined by dragging the gravel image over to the drum image, creating a new layer. The **Soft Light** blending mode was then assigned to the gravel layer, resulting in the blend of the two images.

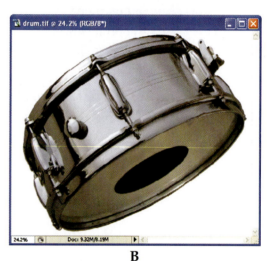

Soft Light blending mode causes the contents of the blending layer to blend with and lighten the lighter colors in the layer(s) beneath it. At the same time, it blends with and darkens the darker colors in the layer(s) beneath it. The white background around the drum was not affected by this particular blend because pure white cannot be lightened any further.

There are endless creative possibilities when using blending modes with layers. For example, photographers can intentionally underexpose and overexpose the same image with their camera, combine both layers within a single file, and then blend the two layers to create unique lighting effects in the image. Blending modes can even be used for color correction.

To review the basic characteristics of each of the blending modes, refer to the "Brush Tool Blending Modes" section in Chapter 6, *Painting Tools and Filters*.

Using Blending Modes with Filters and Color Adjustment Tools

It is also possible to add a blending mode when using any of the following: a filter, a color-adjustment tool or command, a painting tool, or an eraser tool. *Immediately* after applying one of these tools, choose **Edit > Fade (*previous command or tool*)....** You can then choose a blending mode from the **Mode:** drop-down list to adjust the filter or tool you just used. Or, you can adjust the **Opacity:** setting to fade the previous filter or tool used. The lower the **Opacity:** setting, the less influence the filter, tool, or command has on the image. See Figure 11-2.

For example, suppose you use the **Levels** command to adjust the colors in an image and the results are close to what you want, but a bit too extreme. You can mellow (or intensify) the color adjustment by using the **Edit > Fade** command and experimenting with different blending modes and **Opacity:** settings.

Layer Masks

A *layer mask* is a special area that is created on a layer to hide (or mask) part of that layer. When you create a layer mask, it looks like you have deleted part of the layer. However, the entire layer is still there, and the hidden portions can easily be made visible again. Layer masks are particularly useful when two or more images need to be blended together.

Before creating a layer mask, the layer that will have a mask applied to it must be selected in the **Layers** palette. If necessary, the layer transparency must be unlocked, using techniques described in Chapter 4, *Introduction to Layers*.

After selecting the layer and ensuring that layer transparency is unlocked, click the **Layer Mask** button at the bottom of the **Layers** palette. The same command is found

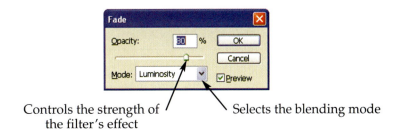

Figure 11-2.
The **Fade** command lets you apply a blending mode or change the opacity of a filter, painting tool, erasing tool, or color adjustment.

Controls the strength of the filter's effect

Selects the blending mode

by choosing **Layer > Layer Mask > Reveal All.** This causes a layer mask thumbnail to appear in the **Layers** palette. If part of your image is selected just before you create a layer mask, the selected area becomes a mask. If you need to return to a layer mask and edit it, the layer mask thumbnail must be clicked in the **Layers** palette (causing a thick, white borderline to appear around it). See **Figure 11-3**.

The layer mask can then be created using the painting and eraser tools and the following colors: black, white, and various shades of gray. When you paint on the masked layer with black as the foreground color, the mask is actually created, causing the painted portions of the layer to be hidden. As you paint, the layer mask thumbnail is automatically updated to show any changes to the masked areas. See **Figure 11-4**.

When you paint on the masked layer with white as the foreground color (or erase with white as the background color), the mask is removed. Painting with various shades of gray creates various levels of opacity in the layer mask. An easy place to choose various shades of gray is from the top two rows of the **Swatches** palette. Gradients made from black, white, and gray can also be used to create layer masks that "fade out."

The effect of the layer mask is also affected by the transparency of the opacity of the paint being used to create it. For example, if you use pure black paint to create the layer mask, but drop the **Opacity:** setting of the **Brush Tool**, the effect is the same as painting with a lighter shade of gray.

Displaying Layer Masks

So far, you have only been able to see the effects of a layer mask rather than the mask itself. However, there is a way you can display the mask on screen. When you open the **Channels** palette, a thumbnail of any layer mask assigned to the currently selected layer is displayed below the color channels in the channel list. If you double click on the layer mask thumbnail, the **Layer Mask Display Options** dialog box opens. In this dialog box, click in the color box to use the **Color Picker** to assign a color to the layer mask. In some cases, you may want to make the layer mask easier or harder to see

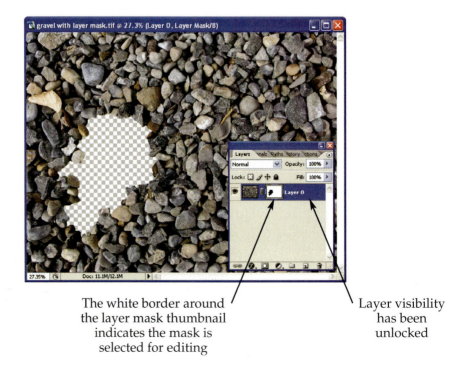

Figure 11-3.
A layer mask has been created on this layer, hiding (but not deleting) some of the rocks.

The white border around the layer mask thumbnail indicates the mask is selected for editing

Layer visibility has been unlocked

Figure 11-4.
A layer mask is used to hide parts of a layer. **A**—Areas of the layer containing the gravel image are hidden by applying a layer mask. **B**—The layer mask fully reveals the metal frame of the drum, resulting in a drum that looks as if it contains the rocks.

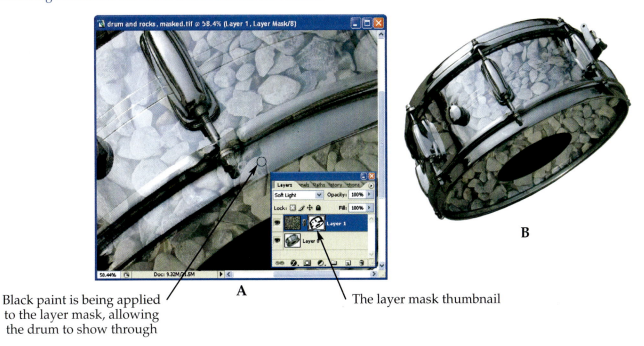

through. To do this, enter the desired value in the **Opacity:** text box. Click **OK** to close the **Layer Mask Display Options** dialog box when you have entered the settings you want. In the **Channels** palette, click the layer mask channel's **Visibility** toggle to turn the layer mask display on or off. See **Figure 11-5**.

Figure 11-5.
Visibility for the layer mask has been turned on. The masked areas are reddish.

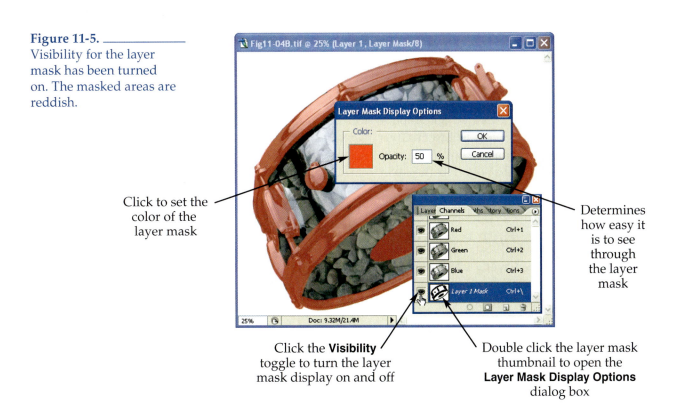

Linking Layer Masks and Layers

In the **Layers** palette, a chain (linking) icon appears between the layer mask thumbnail and the layer thumbnail. This icon indicates that the layer mask is linked to the layer. In other words, if you use the **Move Tool** to move the layer in the image window, the mask will move with it. Linking can be turned on or off by clicking on the linking icon. When linking is off, the layer mask and layer can be moved independently of each other in the image window.

The Layer Mask Shortcut Menu

Right clicking on the layer mask thumbnail opens a shortcut menu that provides a number of options for working with the layer mask. Some of these commands are also available in the **Layer > Layer Mask** submenu, which will be discussed shortly.

Deleting, Applying, and Temporarily Disabling Layer Masks

Layer masks are deleted by right-clicking on the layer mask thumbnail and choosing **Delete Layer Mask** from the shortcut menu. This permanently deletes the layer mask, meaning that a new layer mask will have to be created to restore the effect. To temporarily turn off the effect of the layer mask rather than permanently delete it, choose **Disable Layer Mask** from the shortcut menu. When a layer mask is disabled, a red X appears in the layer mask thumbnail. If you temporarily disable the layer mask, you can restore it later by right clicking on the layer mask thumbnail and selecting **Enable Layer Mask** from the shortcut menu. You can also press [Shift] and click the layer mask thumbnail to enable or disable it.

If you are happy with the effect of the layer mask, and want to make it a permanent part of the layer, choose **Apply Layer Mask** from the shortcut menu. However, you should note that the masked part of the image will be permanently deleted. For this reason, you should not use the **Apply Layer Mask** option until you are absolutely sure the mask or masked area will require no further changes.

Modifying Selections with a Layer Mask

You can also use a layer mask to modify a selection. To do this, make a selection on the layer, and then right click on the layer mask thumbnail. In the shortcut menu, select **Add Layer Mask To Selection** to add the area covered by the layer mask to the current selection. Select **Subtract Layer Mask From Selection** to remove any areas covered by the layer mask from the current selection. If you want to keep only those areas of the selection that overlap the layer mask, choose the **Intersect Layer Mask With Selection** option in the shortcut menu.

The Layer > Layer Mask Submenu

The **Layer > Layer Mask** submenu contains commands that let you create new layer masks, and work with existing layer masks, **Figure 11-6**. Some of these commands are identical to those found in the layer mask shortcut menu described in the previous section.

Figure 11-6.
The **Layer Mask** submenu contains a number of commands for working with layer masks.

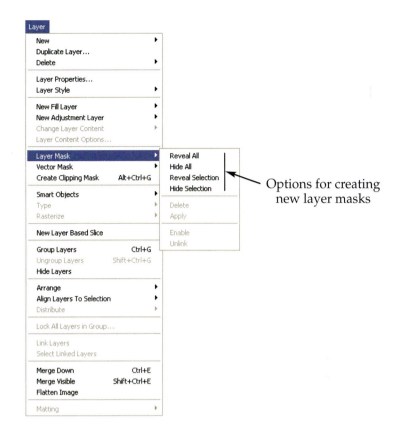

Creating New Layer Masks

The first group of commands in the **Layer Mask** submenu offer different options for creating new layer masks. The **Reveal All** command, which was mentioned earlier in the chapter, creates a new layer mask that is completely empty. When you select this option, no parts of the selected layer are masked. In order to hide areas of the selected area, you must paint the areas with black or gray paint as described earlier. This is the best option if you have only a few objects on the layer that you want to hide.

The **Hide All** command is the exact opposite. This command creates a new layer mask that is completely filled, and therefore hides all of the content on the selected layer. If you use this option to create a layer mask, you must then erase areas of the mask (or paint them with white) in order to reveal objects on the layer. This option works best if you only want to keep a few objects on the layer visible and hide the rest.

The next two commands in the **Layer Mask** submenu are only available if there is currently a selection made in the image window. If you choose the **Reveal Selection** command, a layer mask is created in which the selected area is visible, but the unselected portion of the layer is hidden. If you choose the **Hide Selection** command, a new layer mask is created that hides the selected area, but displays everything else in the layer.

Other Commands in the Layer Mask Submenu

The remaining commands in the **Layer Mask** submenu are only available if the selected layer already contains a layer mask. These commands can also be accessed through the **Layers** palette, as described earlier.

The **Delete** command permanently removes the layer mask on the selected layer. This command is identical to the **Delete Layer Mask** command in the layer mask shortcut menu. The **Apply** command removes the layer mask by permanently deleting the masked areas from the layer. This command is the same as the **Apply Layer Mask** command in the layer mask shortcut menu. The **Disable** command temporarily turns off the effect of the layer mask. If the layer mask is already disabled, this command is replaced with the **Enable** command, which turns on the layer mask effect. These commands are the same as the **Disable Layer Mask** and **Enable Layer Mask** commands in the shortcut menu.

The final commands in the **Layer Mask** submenu are the **Link** and **Unlink** commands. These commands perform the same functions as clicking the linking icon in the **Layers** palette.

Adjusting Layer Masks with Filters

Layer masks can be further adjusted by applying filters to the mask. For example, the boundaries of a layer mask can be expanded or contracted by using the **Maximum** or **Minimum** filters, located in the **Filter > Other...** submenu. In another example, the edge of a layer mask can be softened by applying the **Gaussian Blur** filter.

Before applying a filter, you must make sure that the layer mask and not the layer itself is selected in the **Layers** palette. If the layer mask is selected, a white border appears around the layer mask thumbnail in the **Layers** palette. You can select a layer mask by simply clicking on its thumbnail in the **Layers** palette.

Creating Layer Masks with the Paste Into Command

You can also create layer masks automatically as you paste content into your image. To do this, begin by opening the **Layers** palette and selecting the layer on which you want to be able to see the new content; this will be referred to as the target layer. Then, draw a selection on the target layer that represents the exact area where you want new content to appear.

Next, activate the layer or image that contains the content you want to copy. This will be referred to as the source. Draw a selection around the portion of the source image that you want to copy. In most cases, you will want the source to be larger than the target selection. This will allow you to move the content around behind the layer mask, making different parts of it visible. Once you have made the selection, use the **Edit > Copy** command to copy the selected content.

After you have copied the selected content in the source, activate the target layer again and choose **Edit > Paste Into**. This copies the material to a new layer, just like normal pasting. However, it also creates a layer mask on the new layer that matches the selection made on the target layer. Only this portion of the copied content is visible. You can then move the copied content around in the new layer so that different parts of it appear through the layer mask.

Vector Masks

Vector masks accomplish the same thing as layer masks—they are used to hide portions of a layer. However, vector masks are *not* created with painting tools. Instead, they are created with the same tools that create vector paths—most notably, the shape tools and pen tools. As you learned in Chapter 5, *Text, Shapes, and Layer Styles*, vector paths are not made of pixels. They are lines that are controlled by mathematical formulas. Therefore, they always have a clean, crisp edge, even in low-resolution images.

Creating a Vector Mask

To begin creating a vector mask, choose **Layer > Vector Mask > Reveal All**. This creates an empty vector mask on the layer, and adds a vector mask thumbnail to the **Layers** palette. Next, choose one of the shape or pen tools to draw the boundaries of the layer mask. When using the pen tools or shape tools, make sure the **Paths** button is selected in the options bar. Remember, you can use the shape tool's **Add to path area**, **Subtract from path area**, **Intersect path areas**, and **Exclude overlapping path areas** buttons to create complex shapes. As long as the vector mask is selected (a white border appears around the vector mask thumbnail), you can refine it. In **Figure 11-7**, a custom shape is used to create a vector mask on the drum layer, causing the side of the drum to appear damaged.

Converting a Path into a Vector Mask

You can also convert a path into a vector mask. To do this, draw the desired boundaries with the shape tools or pen tools or select the desired path in the **Paths** palette. Next, open the **Layers** palette and select the layer on which you want to create the new vector mask. Finally, choose **Layer > Vector Mask > Current Path**.

Figure 11-7.
This image now has a layer mask and a vector mask. The vector mask is hiding part of the drum layer, causing it to appear damaged.

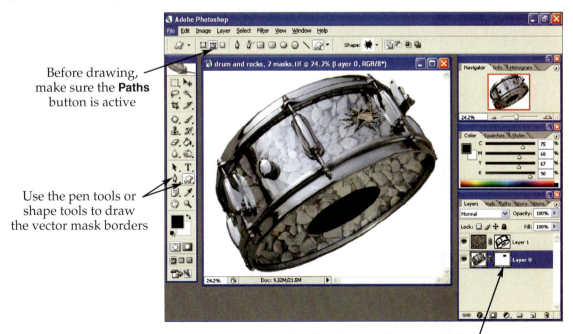

Setting the Areas to Display and Hide

If the **Subtract from path area** button is active in the options bar when you begin drawing the vector mask boundaries with a pen or shape tool, the area inside the boundaries will be hidden. If the **Add selection to path, Intersect path areas**, or **Exclude overlapping path areas** button is active when you first begin to draw the vector mask boundaries, the areas inside the boundaries will be displayed, and the rest of the layer will be hidden. After drawing the mask boundaries, you can change the effect of the vector mask by activating a different selection button in the options bar.

When you draw paths that you intend to convert into vector masks at a later time, they need to be handled the same way. If you want the resulting vector mask to hide the area inside the boundaries, you must draw the path with the **Subtract from path** area option active. If you want to show the area inside the boundaries and hide the rest of the layer with the layer mask, you should select the **Add to path area** option.

The path thumbnails in the **Paths** palette and the vector mask thumbnails in the **Layers** palette show you what areas of the layer are hidden and which areas are displayed. The dark areas represent those parts of the image that are hidden and the white areas are the areas that show.

Converting a Selection into a Vector Mask

Because a selection can be converted into a path, you can also convert any selection, including text created with the type masking tools, into a vector mask. To do this, create the selection, then open the **Paths** palette. In the **Paths** palette, click the **Make work path from selection** button. In the **Layers** palette, choose the layer on which to create a mask. Finally, choose **Layer > Vector Mask > Current Path** to create a layer mask from the existing path. See **Figure 11-8**.

> **Note** To quickly select all visible (unmasked) areas of a layer, press [Ctrl] and click a layer mask thumbnail. Press [Command] and click for Mac.

Working with Vector Masks

You can permanently delete a vector mask by right-clicking on the vector mask thumbnail in the **Layers** palette. In the shortcut menu that appears, select **Delete Vector Mask**. You can also delete the vector mask by highlighting the vector mask thumbnail in the **Layers** palette and clicking the **Delete layer** (trash can) button, or by dragging the vector mask thumbnail over the **Delete layer** button and releasing the mouse button, or by choosing **Layer > Vector Mask > Delete**.

If you want to temporarily turn off the effect of the vector mask, right click on the vector mask thumbnail and select **Disable vector mask** from the shortcut menu. This turns off the vector mask, but does not delete it. To turn the vector mask back on, right click on the vector mask thumbnail and select **Enable layer mask** from the shortcut menu, or choose **Layer > Vector Mask > Enable**.

Figure 11-8.
A gradient layer was created on top of the gravel background. Then, a selection was made using the **Horizontal Type Mask Tool**. The selection was converted into a working path. Then, the working path was changed into a vector mask by selecting **Layer > Vector Mask > Current Path**. The result is gradient text on top of the gravel layer.

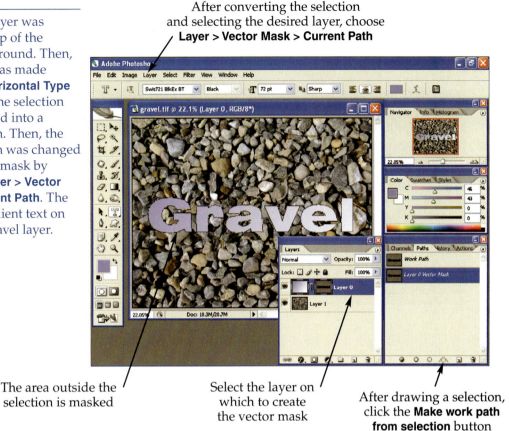

After converting the selection and selecting the desired layer, choose **Layer > Vector Mask > Current Path**

The area outside the selection is masked

Select the layer on which to create the vector mask

After drawing a selection, click the **Make work path from selection** button

You can quickly and easily convert a vector mask into a layer mask by right-clicking on the vector mask thumbnail and selecting **Rasterize Vector Mask** from the shortcut menu. The same thing can be accomplished by highlighting the vector mask thumbnail in the **Layers** palette and then choosing **Layer > Rasterize > Vector Mask**.

As with layer masks, vector masks are initially linked to the layers they are created on. This means that the mask and the layer cannot be moved independently. However, you can unlink the mask and layer by clicking the linking (chain) icon between the layer thumbnail and the vector mask thumbnail. You can also unlink the layer and vector mask by choosing **Layer > Vector Mask > Unlink**. The link between the layer and vector mask can be restored by clicking the space between the layer and vector mask thumbnails in the **Layers** palette, or by choosing **Layer > Vector Mask > Link**.

Clipping Masks

Instead of using painting tools or paths to create masks, *clipping masks* use the entire contents of a layer to mask another layer, **Figure 11-9**. In the **Layers** palette, the layer you want to use as a mask must be *just below* the layer that will have the mask applied to it. Then, select the layer you want to be visible through the mask and choose **Layer > Create Clipping Mask**. In the **Layers** palette, the masked layer becomes indented, reminding you that a clipping mask has been created.

Figure 11-9.
Clipping masks are easy to apply. **A**—A text layer was created on top of the Background (gravel) layer. **B**—The Background layer was unlocked by renaming it. Then, the gravel layer was positioned above the text, allowing the text layer to become a clipping mask by choosing **Layer > Create Clipping Mask**.

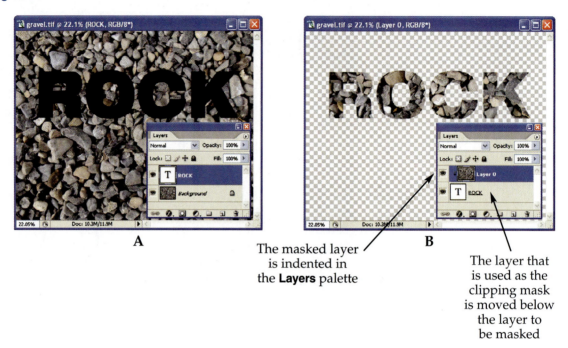

A

B

The masked layer is indented in the **Layers** palette

The layer that is used as the clipping mask is moved below the layer to be masked

After adding the clipping mask to one layer, you can repeat the procedure to add it to the layer directly above that layer. Continue the process until you have assigned the clipping mask to all of the layers that you want to trim. See **Figure 11-10**.

Figure 11-10.
A clipping path can be applied to multiple layers. Here, five different images on five separate layers were trimmed by the same clipping mask.

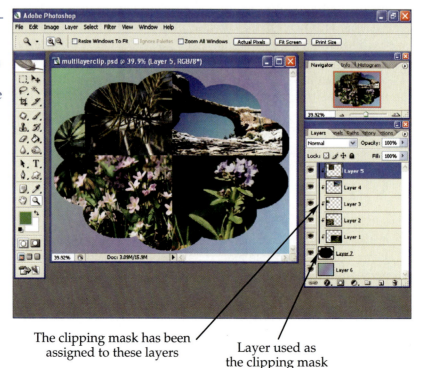

The clipping mask has been assigned to these layers

Layer used as the clipping mask

Controlling the Visible and Hidden Areas of a Clipping Mask

Controlling the transparent and opaque areas created by clipping masks is similar to controlling them in a layer mask. As you recall, when you create a layer mask, the shades of gray you use determine how much or how little you can see through the masked area. Where the mask is black, the layer is transparent. Where the mask is white, the layer is completely opaque. The opacity level of the paint also plays a role. As the opacity of the paint increases, the paint's effect on the layer mask also increases.

Unlike a layer mask, the tonal level of the paint used to draw a clipping mask does not influence how much of the layer can be seen through the mask. For clipping masks, the visibility of the masked layer depends entirely on the *opacity* of the paint used to create the clipping mask. In other words, gray paint will have the same effect on a clipping mask as white paint or black paint. The masked layer will be completely visible in areas where the clipping mask is completely transparent. Areas of the clipping mask that are more opaque will create areas on the masked layer that are more transparent.

Releasing Clipping Masks

The clipping mask can be disabled by selecting the appropriate layer and choosing **Layer > Release Clipping Mask** or by right clicking on the layer in the **Layers** palette and selecting **Release Clipping Mask**. When you release the clipping mask on a layer, the clipping mask is also released on all layers above that layer in the **Layers** palette stack.

> **Note** Be aware that clipping masks can become accidentally deleted when rearranging the stacking order of layers in the **Layers** palette.

Using Blending Options to Hide Portions of a Layer

In addition to the layer mask, vector mask, and clipping mask techniques already discussed, you can use the blending controls in the **Layer Style** dialog box to hide portions of the different layers in your image. These settings are found by choosing **Layer > Layer Style > Blending Options…** or by selecting a layer in the **Layers** palette, right clicking, and selecting **Blending Options…** from the shortcut menu. Either method opens the **Layer Style** dialog box.

General Blending

The controls in the **General Blending** section of **Layer Style** dialog box are identical to the **Blending Mode** drop-down list and **Opacity:** slider found at the top of the **Layers** palette. With these controls, you can assign a blending mode to the selected layer, and adjust the visibility of the entire layer. This is useful if you want to blend an entire layer with the layers beneath it in the **Layers** palette. See **Figure 11-11**.

To use this technique, select the layer you want to alter in the **Layers** palette and open the **Layer Style** dialog box. Select a blending mode in the **Blend Mode:** drop-down list. Adjust the **Opacity:** slider until the layer has the desired level of transparency.

Creating a Knockout

The term *knockout* refers to an area of an image that is removed so a layer below it can show through. In Photoshop, knockouts are similar to clipping masks. Knockouts

Figure 11-11.
The **General Blending** section of the **Layer Style** dialog box allows you to apply a blending mode to an entire layer and adjust the layer's opacity. **A**—The controls in this section of the dialog box are identical to the controls found at the top of the **Layers** palette. **B**—A **Dissolve** blending mode has been applied to Layer 0, and the **Opacity:** setting has been dropped to allow some of the Background layer to show through. The result looks like paint spatter on the image.

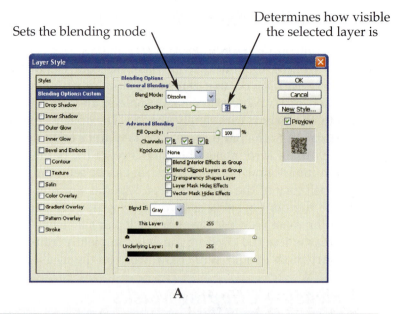

A

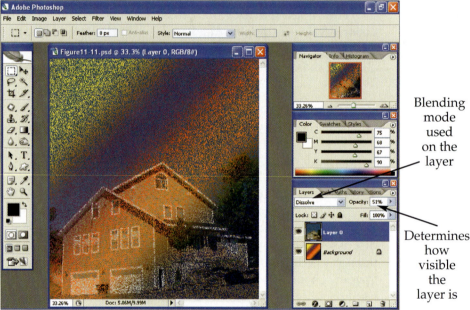

B

use one layer to create transparent areas in another layer, like clipping masks. Also like clipping masks, knockouts can be applied to numerous layers. In this section, you will learn how to create the simplest type of knockouts. There are several other ways that layers can be arranged and knockouts set up that make the technique even more versatile. You are encouraged to review Photoshop's help files to learn about alternative ways to set up knockouts.

To create a knockout in an image, begin by arranging your layers in the **Layers** palette. The layer that is going to create the knockout must be above all of the layers that are going to be affected in the layer stack. The layer that is going to show through the knockout must be a background layer, otherwise, all of the layers beneath the knockout layer (including the bottom layer) will have a knockout, and transparency will show through. If you need to convert a layer to a background, select the layer in the **Layers** palette and choose **Layer > New > Background From Layer**.

Once you have the layers set up as needed, select the layer that will create the knockout in the **Layers** palette, right click on the layer, and select **Blending Options...**

from the shortcut menu. In the **Advanced Blending** section of the **Blending Options** dialog box, place check marks in the **Channels:** check boxes to specify what color channels you want to use to create the knockout. Next, select the style of knockout to create from the **Knockout:** drop-down list. With the setup that is being explained here, both the **Shallow** option and the **Deep** option hide the image all the way to the background. However, if you use one of the alternative setups described in the Photoshop help files, the **Shallow** option will only knockout to the first possible stopping point and the **Deep** option will knockout all the way to the background. After selecting a knockout style, adjust the **Fill Opacity:** slider to produce the desired effect. See **Figure 11-12**. A setting of 0% makes the knockout completely transparent.

Underneath the **Fill Opacity:** slider are five check boxes that allow you to adjust the knockout further. If you position the cursor directly over one of these check boxes, a tool tip appears that explains the function of the check box.

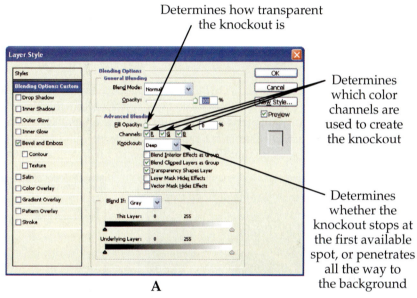

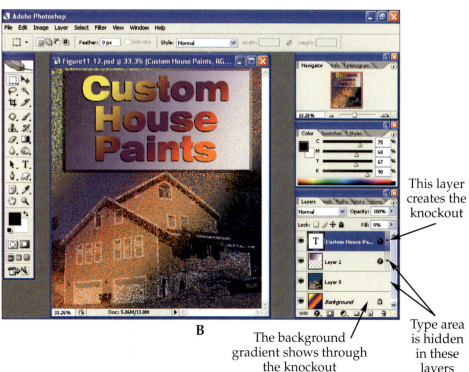

Figure 11-12. Knockouts create similar effects to clipping masks. **A**—The controls in the **Advanced Blending** section of the **Layer Style** dialog box allow you to apply a knockout to an image. **B**—The knockout in this image hides portions of two layers to reveal the gradient background in the knockout area.

Using Layer Style Blending Options to Mask a Layer

In images where there is a stark difference between the brightness of the subject and the background, layer style blending options can be used to mask dark or light parts of a layer. To use this technique, begin by selecting the layer that you want to mask in the **Layers** palette and opening the **Layer Style** dialog box.

In the bottom section of the dialog box are a set of controls that will allow you to mask the layer based on luminosity values. Dragging the black or white **This Layer:** sliders will hide dark or light areas in your layer. The tonal range between the sliders remains visible while the tonal range outside the sliders is masked. See **Figure 11-13**.

Each slider can be split apart by holding down [Alt] (or [Option] for Mac) and dragging half of the slider to the desired setting. The tonal range between the two halves of the slider is partially masked. This allows you to soften the appearance of the mask edges.

The **Blend If** drop-down list lets you isolate a particular channel before adjusting the sliders. The **Gray** option in this drop-down list represents the composite channel. Remember that the colors in the image are composed of a mixture of the primary colors found in the color channels. Therefore, adding masking based on one of the color channels may have a farther-reaching effect than you might expect.

Figure 11-13.
The bottom section of the **Layer Styles** dialog box contains controls that can be used to quickly mask extremely dark or light areas in an image. **A**—This image has a strongly contrasting background and subject. **B**—The **This Layer:** sliders can be split in half to set tonal ranges that will be partially masked. **C**—Note that the darkest tones in the layer are completely masked (hidden).

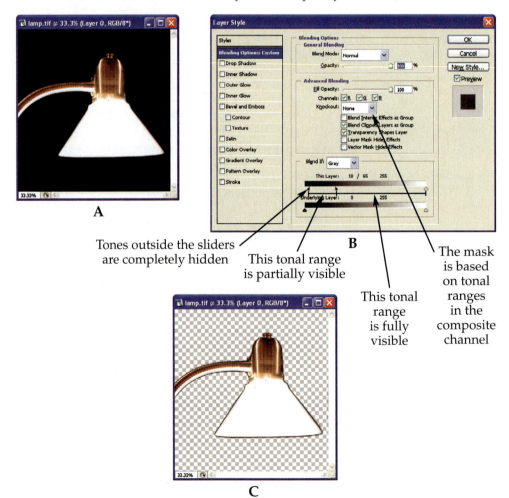

You can also use the controls in this section of the **Layer Style** dialog box to mask the selected layer based on the colors and tonal values of the layer *underneath* it. The **Underlying Layer:** sliders control what portions of the layer below the active layer will be used to mask the active layer. This slider is useful if you have an object that stands out against its background on the layer below the current layer and you want to be able to see that object through the current layer. By selecting the necessary channels in the **Blend If** drop-down list and carefully adjusting the sliders, you can make the object or areas on the lower layer visible through the current layer. See **Figure 11-14**.

Unlike the other methods used to mask a layer, the blending options method does not create a layer mask thumbnail in the **Layers** palette. The only way to cancel this effect is to choose the menu command again and reset the blending sliders to their original positions. Or, if you have not performed other tasks since changing the blending options setting, you can undo the **Blending Options** command or delete it from the **History** palette.

Figure 11-14. The blending options can also use the tonal ranges of a layer to mask the layer above it. **A**—You can select a channel to use from the **Blend If:** drop-down list and set the tonal range to use for masking using the **Underlying Layer:** sliders. **B**—Through careful selection of channels and tonal ranges on Layer 0, all areas but the blue sky were masked on Layer 1.

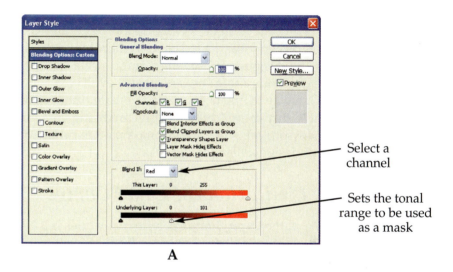

Select a channel

Sets the tonal range to be used as a mask

A

The areas of this layer that cover the blue sky remain visible, but all other areas have been hidden

B

The colors and tones on this layer determine the shape of the mask on the layer above

Deleting the Masked Area of a Layer

When using layer masks, vector masks, or clipping masks, the masked area becomes hidden, but not deleted. To *permanently delete* the masked area, you must merge the layers that create the masked effect. The masked portion of the image is discarded in this process.

When using layer style blending options to hide a portion of an image, an extra step is necessary to make the change permanent. Create a new layer and, in the **Layers** palette, drag it below the layer that has been adjusted with the blending options. Finally, merge the two layers.

> **Note** Photoshop allows you to have more than one type of mask on a single layer.

Layer Comps

As graphic designers work on a project, they usually create more than one version of their design ideas, called *comps* (short for *compositions*), to show to their client. This helps the designer and client communicate more effectively, and allows the client to make decisions about the design as it evolves.

One way to create comps is to create duplicate files and make changes to each file. When highly complicated designs are being created, this may be the best method. But for many projects, the **Layer Comps** palette can help you to save more than one version of your design *within the same file*.

The Limitations of Layer Comps

What the **Layer Comps** palette really does is let you save various states of the **Layers** palette. However, there are some limitations. Layer comps can only keep track of the following information:

- The *position* of each layer on the canvas.
- The *visibility* of each layer.
- The *blending mode* of each layer.
- Any *layer styles* that have been added to a layer.

If you make changes to your image other than those listed above, the changes are applied to all layer comps you have created. For example, if a layer is added or deleted from an image, the same layer will be added or deleted from all layer comps. Similarly, any change to the content of a layer will also be made to all of the layer comps. As mentioned previously, only the position, visibility, layer styles, and blending modes of the layers can vary from layer comp to layer comp.

You can sometimes work around these limitations by duplicating the layer, turning off visibility for the original layer, making the desired changes to the content of the layer, and then saving the layer comp.

Creating a New Layer Comp

The **Layer Comps** palette is simple to use. When the layers are adjusted the way you want them, within the limits described above, choose **Window > Layer Comps**. This opens the **Layer Comps** palette. Next, click the **New Layer Comp** button at the bottom of the palette. The **New Layer Comp** dialog box appears, **Figure 11-15**. Enter a name for the

Figure 11-15.
The **Layer Comps** palette can be used to store different versions of a design. **A**—The original design is saved as a layer comp. The layers are then adjusted as desired, and the **New Layer Comp** dialog box is opened again. In this dialog box, you name the layer comp and specify what types of information it will store. **B**—After saving a layer comp, you can quickly toggle between the various layer comps by clicking their names in the **Layer Comps** palette. The palette shown here has two layer comps.

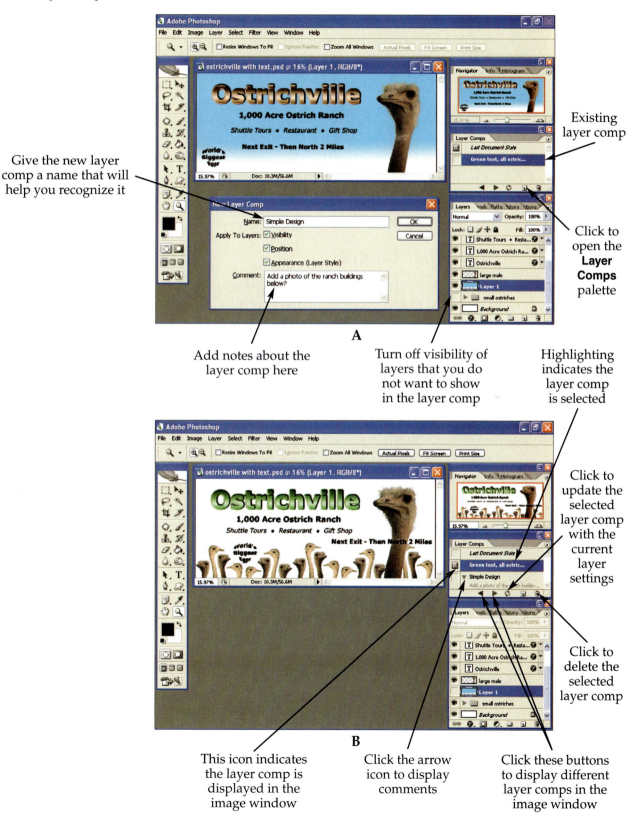

layer comp in the **Name:** text box. You may find it useful to assign a name that will help you remember which design variation is saved in the layer comp.

The three check boxes in the **Apply To Layers:** section, **Visibility**, **Position**, and **Appearance (Layer Style)**, do not affect *what is saved* in a layer comp. Instead, they control *what is displayed* when a layer comp is selected. You can turn on or off layer visibility, position, or appearance data for a particular comp by right-clicking on that comp in the **Layer Comps** palette, choosing **Layer Comp Options...** from the shortcut menu, and adjusting the check boxes. Any feature that is turned off will not change when the layer comp is selected; it will continue to look the same as it did in the previously selected layer comp.

Comments, such as questions for the client, can be added in **Comments:** text box and saved with the layer comp. The comments can be displayed by clicking the small arrow icon next to the layer comp in the **Layer Comps** palette, or accessed and edited by right-clicking on the layer comp and choosing **Layer Comp Options...** from the shortcut menu.

Once you have made the desired settings in the **New Layer Comp** dialog box, click **OK** to save the layer comp and close the dialog box. The new layer comp is added to the bottom of the list in the **Layer Comps** palette. To create another comp, make adjustments to your design and repeat this process.

Editing Layer Comps

If you want to make changes to a comp, select the layer comp in the **Layer Comps** palette, make the changes to your image, and then click the **Update Layer Comp** button. The arrow buttons at the bottom of the palette can be clicked to view different comps, or you can click the icon at the left of each comp to view it. You can delete an unwanted layer comp by selecting it and clicking the **Delete Layer Comp** (trash can) button at the bottom of the palette.

You can access these and other functions in the **Layer Comps** palette menu by clicking the arrow button in the upper-right corner of the palette. This menu provides all of the functions available in the buttons at the bottom of the dialog box, plus a few others.

Choosing the **Duplicate Layer Comp** command in the palette menu creates a copy of the currently selected layer comp, and makes it active. This is a useful option if you want to make slight modifications to an existing layer comp, and save it as a new comp. The **Apply Layer Comp** command simply makes the selected comp active, and displays it in the image window. Choosing the **Restore Last Document State** command is the same as clicking the box to the left of the **Last Document State** entry in the **Layer Comps** palette. Choosing the **Layer Comp Options** command opens the **Layer Comp Options** dialog box, which is identical to the **New Layer Comp** dialog box. From this dialog box, you can rename the layer comp, change the type of information stored in the layer comp, and change the comments associated with the layer comp.

> **Note**   It is possible to select a layer comp in the **Layer Comps** palette while displaying a different layer comp in the image window. For this reason, you want to make sure that the layer comp is both selected and displayed before making changes to it. The selected layer comp is highlighted in the **Layer Comps** palette, and a small icon appears next to the layer comp that is currently displayed in the image window.

Presenting Layer Comps

There are a number of different ways to show clients layer comps. If your client is nearby, you can show the comps on your computer by opening the file, opening the **Layer Comps** palette, and clicking the icon to the left of each layer comp. If your client is far away, you can quickly convert layer comps into various types of files and send them to the client on CD or electronically.

Comps can be saved as individual documents in PSD, JPEG, TIFF, and other image formats. File formats will be discussed further in the next chapter. Comps can also be converted to PDF files or even WPG (web photo gallery) format.

Saving Layer Comps as Individual Image Files

To save the layer comps in an image as individual image files, choose **File > Scripts > Layer Comps To Files**. This opens the **Layer Comps To Files** dialog box, Figure 11-16. Enter the path to the target folder (folder in which to save the images) in the **Destination:** text box, or by clicking the **Browse...** button and selecting the folder in the Explorer-style dialog box. In the **File Name Prefix:** text box, enter any text that you want to appear at the beginning of each file name. By default, the prefix is set to the filename of the image containing the layer comps. If you want to save only the layer comps that are currently selected in the **Layer Comps** palette, put a check mark in the **Selected Layer Comps Only** check box. Otherwise, all layer comps in the image will be saved. Select an image file type from the **File Type:** drop-down list. The advantages and disadvantage of each file type are discussed in Chapter 12, *File Management and Automated Tasks*. The section beneath the **File Type:** drop-down list contains settings for the specific type of image file selected.

Once you have made the desired settings, click the **Run** button. This executes a script (a series of commands that run automatically) that converts the layer comps into individual image files without altering the original. Depending on the number of comps being converted, this process could take a while. A dialog box appears when the script is finished running, and notifies you whether the process succeeded or failed. The procedures for saving layer comps as PDF files or WPG files are very similar, but have settings relating to those specific file types.

Figure 11-16.
In the **Layer Comp To Files** dialog box, you specify the folder in which to save the image files generated from the layer comps, and the image file type they should be saved as.

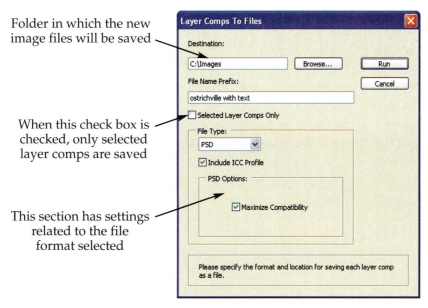

Aligning and Distributing Layers

The term *align* means "to arrange in a straight line," and the term *distribute* means "to spread out evenly over a given distance." In Chapter 4, *Introduction to Layers*, you learned that one way to align layers is to drag them with the **Move Tool**, using Photoshop's rulers, grid or guides to help you line everything up. When the **Snap** command is active, objects jump into place next to a gridline or guide line as you drag them with the **Move Tool**.

Using Photoshop's **Align** and **Distribute** commands is an alternative way to line up objects without displaying Photoshop's guides or grid. Furthermore, the **Align** and **Distribute** commands allow you to do something else—line up objects *in relation to each other*. If your goal is to straighten a row (or column) of objects (such as photos or shapes) and place equal amounts of space between each object, then using the **Align** and **Distribute** commands may be the quickest way to accomplish this. When the **Align** and **Distribute** commands are used, a selection (usually rectangular or square) can be used as a reference for layers to align to.

The Align Commands

The **Layer** pull-down menu has a submenu that contains six **Align** commands. The name of the submenu and the function of its commands changes depending on whether there is a selection made in the image or not.

If no selection is made in the image and at least two layers are selected in the **Layers** palette, the **Align** submenu appears in the **Layers** menu. The commands in this submenu align the layer(s) relative to each other. The reference point used to align the layers depends on which command is used. If the command aligns the layers to an edge, the outermost edge on the outermost layer in the given direction becomes the reference point. For example, if left edges are aligned, all of the selected layers will align with the left edge of the leftmost layer. If the layers are aligned by vertical centers, they align at the midpoint between the topmost layer and the bottommost layer. If they are aligned by horizontal centers, they are aligned at the midpoint between the layer at the farthest left and the layer at the farthest right.

If a selection has been made in the image and at least one *non-background* layer is selected in the **Layers** palette, the **Align To Selection** submenu appears in the **Layers** menu. The commands found in this submenu align the selected layers to a reference point on the selection. For example, the following steps were used to align the small red squares in a column at the exact center of the image in **Figure 11-17**:

- The red squares were dragged to their approximate desired location.
- The entire image was selected by choosing **Select > All**.
- All layers (except the Background layer) were selected in the **Layers** palette by holding down [Ctrl] and clicking on each layer.
- The **Layer > Align Layer to Selection > Horizontal Center** command was chosen, aligning the layers to the center of the square-shaped selection that surrounds the entire image.

Note Layers can also be aligned to the top, bottom, right side, left side, or horizontal centers of a selection.

Figure 11-17.
The layers in this image are being aligned to a selection. **A**—A selection border was created around the entire file. **B**—Then, the square shapes were aligned to the center of the selection.

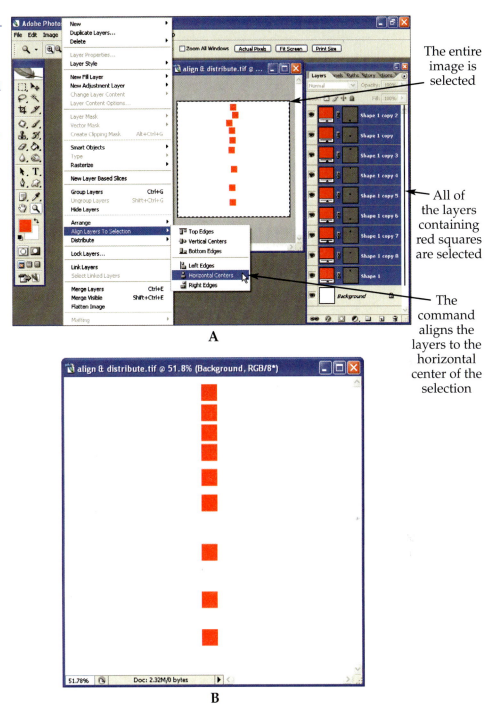

The Distribute Commands

In the example shown, the red squares are aligned in the center of the image, but they are not evenly spaced. The **Distribute** commands are used to create equal spacing between layers. Since the **Distribute** commands place objects at equal intervals over a given distance, three or more layers must be selected in the **Layers** palette before these commands will become available. The two layers farthest away from each other in the direction selected determine the distance through which the remaining layers will be distributed. For example, if the selected layers are being distributed in relation to top or bottom edges or vertical center points, the uppermost selected layer and the bottommost determine the distance. If the layers are being distributed in relation to left or right edges or horizontal centers, the leftmost and rightmost layers determine the distance. The two layers that determine the distance of the distribution are *not* moved by the command. In **Figure 11-18**, the red squares were equally distributed by following these steps:

- Because the selection was no longer needed, it was removed by choosing **Select > Deselect**.
- The layer containing the top square shape was selected in the **Layers** palette. The rest of the layers were unselected.

Figure 11-18. Now that the squares are centered in the file, they need to be spaced evenly. **A**—The top and bottom squares are moved to their desired location. **B**—All of the shapes are evenly distributed between the top and bottom squares when **Layer > Distribute > Vertical Centers** is chosen.

This command evenly distributes the selected layers between the top and bottom square, creating equal space between their vertical centers

The top and bottom squares are positioned manually

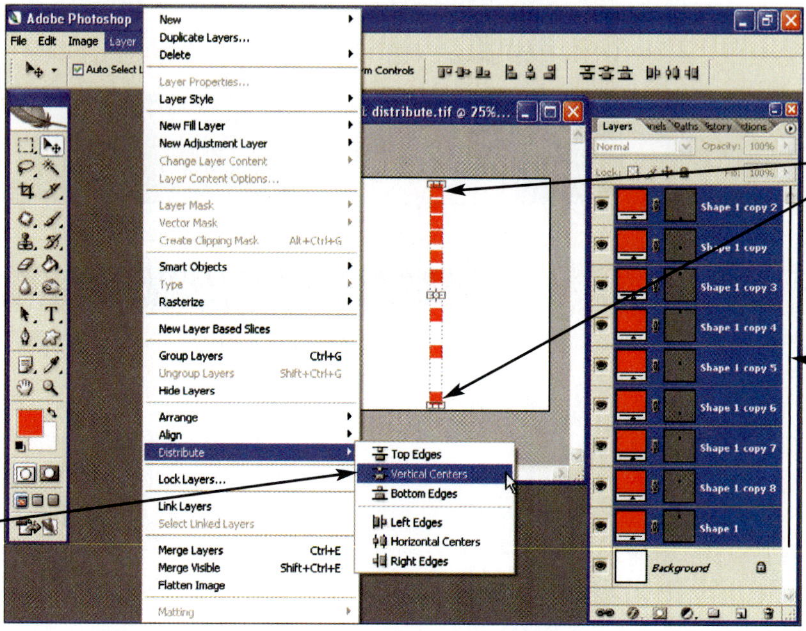

All layers containing red squares are selected

A

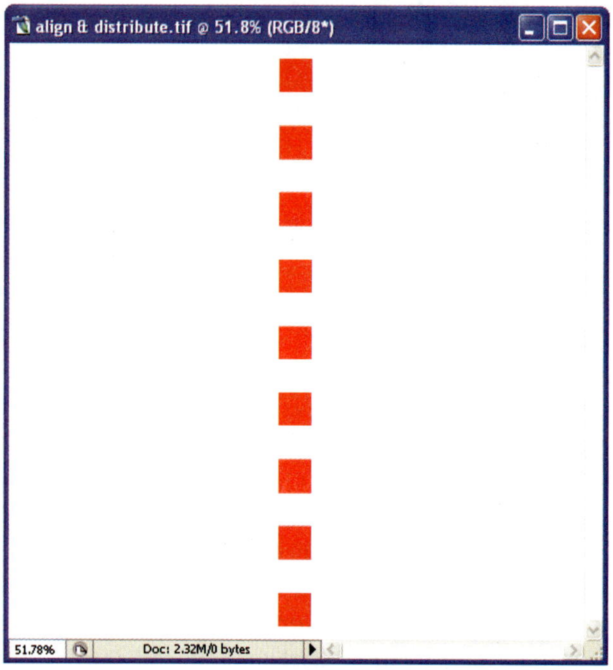

B

- The top square was moved to its desired final position using the up and down arrow keys. Using only the up and down arrow keys preserved the center alignment of the square.
- The previous two steps were repeated for the bottom square.
- All of the layers containing red squares were then selected in the **Layers** palette.
- **Layer > Distribute > Vertical Centers** was chosen. This command causes Photoshop to analyze where the center of each square is and evenly distribute those center points between the first and last shapes in the column.

Note   For best results, remember to first arrange the layers approximately where you want them to end up. Then, use the **Align** and **Distribute** commands to adjust them perfectly.

The Align and Distribute Buttons on the Options Bar

The **Move Tool**'s options bar contains **Align** and **Distribute** buttons that provide the same functionality as the commands discussed in the previous sections, **Figure 11-19**. The **Align** buttons only become available if two or more layers are selected in the **Layers** palette, and the **Distribute** commands only become available if three or more layers are selected.

When using the **Move Tool** to align or distribute layers, select the layers that you want to adjust in the **Layers** palette. Then, click the appropriate button on the options bar. The layers are aligned to the outside edge of the outermost layer in the direction of alignment. Because this method can be confusing, it is recommended that you use square or rectangular selections to align layers, as explained earlier.

Artwork Created in Other Applications and Smart Objects

Readers who plan on inserting artwork created in other applications such as Adobe Illustrator® should research the following topics in Photoshop's help files: *To place a file in Photoshop* and *Smart Objects*. Think of **smart objects** as layers that can also behave like a separate file, allowing a designer to edit the smart object separately, if desired. Layers are converted to smart objects and edited using the commands found in the **Layer > Smart Objects...** submenu.

Figure 11-19.
The **Move Tool**'s options bar contains the same **Align** and **Distribute** commands found in the **Layer** menu.

Align buttons   **Distribute** buttons

GRAPHIC DESIGN:
The Prepress Process—Preparing Documents for Print

Complex printed projects, such as a brochure, can be many pages in length and contain various graphics, images, and text. Such projects need to be created in a page layout application such as Adobe InDesign® or QuarkXPress®. These programs allow you to create multi-page documents at a page size you specify. Then, you can easily place images created in other programs (such as Photoshop) and sections of text exactly where they will appear when printed. Page layout applications have many tools that allow you to enhance the look of your documents with decorative borders and graphics. They also provide precise typography and general layout controls.

Before you prepare any kind of document for print, consult with your print service provider to be sure you are using a compatible page layout program. If you plan on using an old version of Adobe PageMaker® for example, chances are your provider no longer uses the old software and may not be able to open your file.

When you have finished creating a document in your page layout program, your next step is to package the project. When you use the package command, all necessary fonts and graphic files that are linked to your document are copied into separate folders. You submit this package of folders along with your multi-page document to your print service provider.

Page layout programs have a built-in feature called a *preflight check* that makes sure that all necessary support files are packaged. After receiving your package, a prepress professional at your print service provider uses the same software to run a preflight check to ensure the document is ready to print. Because images that you placed in your document are actually linked to the document rather than embedded in it, all of these links are checked to be sure there are no missing graphic files. Preflight also checks all of the fonts used in the document, and makes sure no font files are missing. The most common problems encountered by prepress professionals are missing image files and missing fonts. See Figure 11-20.

For simpler projects that are not multi-paged, you may need only Photoshop to create a file that will be delivered to your print service provider. In these cases, be sure to send a flattened image (this ensures no guesswork is required at the printing company) and submit the file in a format preferred by the printer. Some print service providers recommend that if you use Photoshop to create a project that includes small text, create the project at up to 600 dpi to ensure that even the smallest text characters have crisp edges. In most situations, however, 300 dpi documents are acceptable.

Figure 11-20. These are InDesign's preflight check screens. Other programs have similar screens. **A**—The summary screen indicates how many fonts are missing, how many images are missing, and how many images are in RGB mode. **B**—A detailed screen lists information about the fonts that are missing. **C**—Another page lists detailed information about the images in design, including images that are missing or are in RGB color mode.

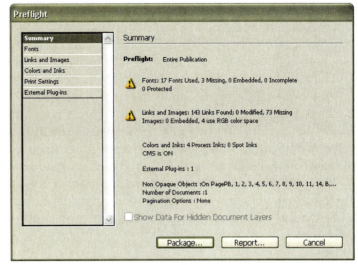

A

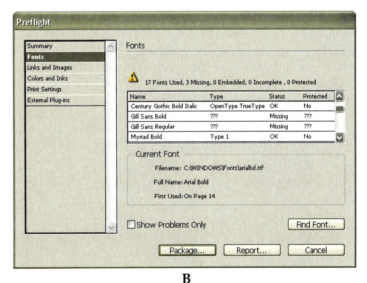

B

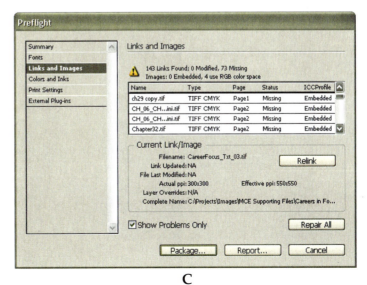

C

After the print service provider does a preflight check, further preparations must be made if the document will be printed on a 4-color offset press. First, software is used to create *color separations*, separate files that show what portions of the image will be cyan, magenta, yellow, and black. Then, these files are printed onto plates. Each plate is loaded into a 4-color press. The plates apply ink to the paper in turn as the paper moves through the press. See Figure 11-21.

For certain low-quantity or specialty printing runs, many print service providers are moving toward using digital printing processes, which do not require color separations. Rather, files can be sent directly to the digital printer. Think of digital printers as much larger and more powerful versions of the desktop printer you probably have at your desk, Figure 11-22. Such printers are becoming more common as the need for publishing-on-demand increases.

Figure 11-21.
Printing is a multi-step process. **A**—A printing plate is made for each of the colors to be printed. The machine shown here prints each color in the separation directly to a printing plate, simplifying and speeding the process. **B**—A completed printing plate is shown here. **C**—The printing plates are loaded into a press, like this 4-color offset press. **D**—In offset lithography, which is used for the majority of commercial printing, the printing plate transfers ink to a rubber cylinder that, in turn, applies ink to the paper.

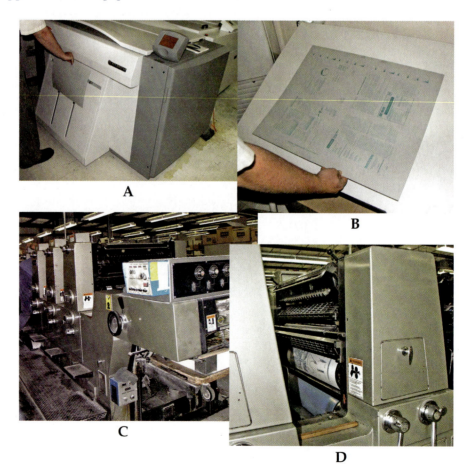

Figure 11-22.
Digital presses, like the iGen3 Digital Production Press from Xerox, offer high-speed full color printing and a variety of finishing options, such as collating, hole-punching, stapling, laminating, and various binding methods. (Image courtesy of Xerox Corporation)

Summary

When should you use masks to hide parts of a layer, and when should you delete parts of a layer instead? Use masks if there is any chance that, at a later time, you may want to change the amount or portion of the layer that is hidden. You should only *erase* portions of a layer when you are absolutely sure you never want to see those portions again.

In your spare time, experiment with blending modes, using different layer combinations. You will probably find techniques that are appealing to you and complement your design tastes. Keep a watchful eye for tips about blending modes found on the web and in other publications.

Chapter Tutorials

In the tutorials that follow, you will be guided through the process of creating the drum and rocks blend shown in this chapter. You will also create a clipping mask and use the **Align** and **Distribute** commands to further refine the CD liner you created in an earlier chapter.

Tutorial 11-1: Blending Modes and Layer Masks

In this tutorial, you will use blending modes and layers to make a gravel look as if it is contained inside a drum. You will add a layer mask so that the gravel cannot be seen behind the metal frame of the drum, but is still visible through the sides and skins of the drum. Lastly, you will add a vector mask to make the drum appear ruptured at one location.

Move Tool

1. Open the drum.tif and the gravel.tif files.
2. Use the **Move Tool** to drag the gravel.tif image over to the drum's image window.
3. Use the **Move Tool** and arrow keys to move the new gravel layer so the drum image is completely covered, as shown in **Figure T11-1**.
4. Close the gravel.tif image window.

Figure T11-1.
The gravel image is dragged and dropped on the drum image.

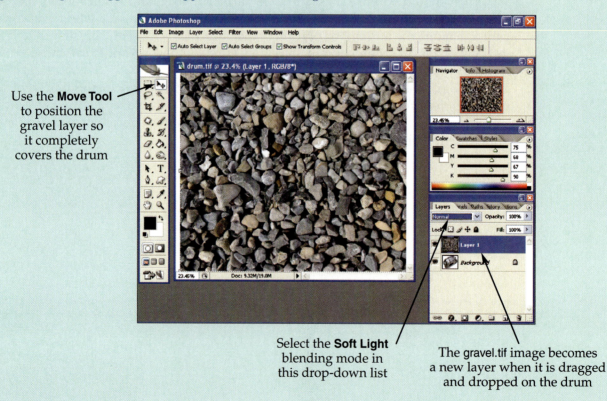

Chapter 11 Additional Layer Techniques 465

5. With the gravel layer active, choose **Soft Light** from the **Mode:** drop-down list at the top left of the **Layers** palette.
6. Begin the process of creating a mask on the gravel layer by choosing **Layer > Layer Mask > Reveal All**.
7. In the **Toolbox**, click the **Default Foreground and Background Colors** button to reset the colors to black and white.
8. In the **Toolbox**, click the **Switch Foreground and Background Colors** button so that black is the foreground color.

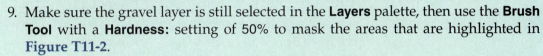
Brush Tool

9. Make sure the gravel layer is still selected in the **Layers** palette, then use the **Brush Tool** with a **Hardness:** setting of 50% to mask the areas that are highlighted in **Figure T11-2**.

   If you need to erase part of the mask, switch the colors so white is the foreground color. This will cause the **Brush Tool** to remove the mask. As you paint the mask, adjust the brush size as needed using the left bracket ([ ) and right bracket ( ]) keys.

10. Double-click the Layer 0 and, in the **New Layer** dialog box, click **OK** to accept Layer 0 as the new name.

    This unlocks the layer transparency for the Background layer. Notice that the padlock icon is gone. Unlocking transparency allows you to add a mask.

11. With Layer 0 (which contains the drum) still active, choose **Layer > Vector Mask > Reveal All**.

Custom Shape Tool

    This adds an empty vector mask to the layer.

12. Click the **Custom Shape Tool** in the **Toolbox**.

    The **Custom Shape Tool** may be hidden behind another shape tool in the **Toolbox**. In the options bar, notice that the **Paths** option is automatically selected.

Figure T11-2.
Mask the areas of the drum shown in red.

Click the **Switch Foreground and Background Colors** button to make black the foreground color

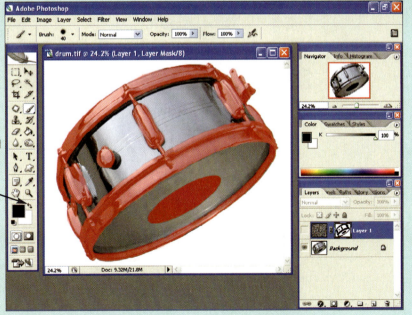

Subtract from path area

13. Make sure the **Subtract from path area** button is selected in the options bar.
14. In the options bar, click the **Shape:** icon or the arrow button next to it to open the **Custom Shape Picker**.

    If you hold your cursor over the shape icons in the **Custom Shape Picker**, a tool tip appears with the name of the shape.

15. Select the Starburst shape.
16. Draw the shape on the side of the drum, as shown in **Figure T11-3**.
17. In the **Layers** palette, click the vector mask thumbnail to hide the outline of the path.
18. Choose **File > Save As…** and name this file 11rockdrum.tif.
19. Close all open image windows.

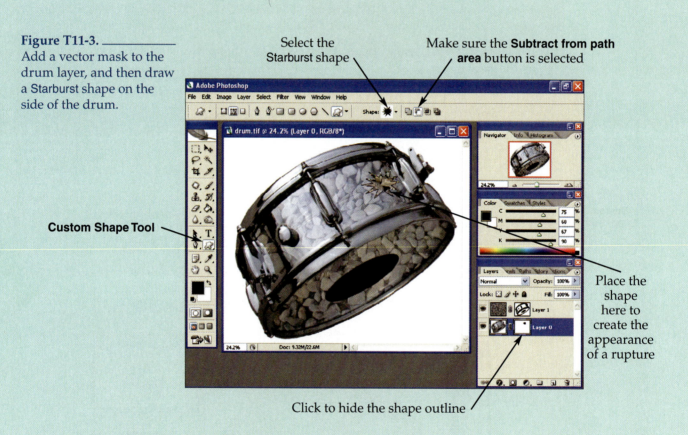

Figure T11-3. Add a vector mask to the drum layer, and then draw a Starburst shape on the side of the drum.

Tutorial 11-2: Create a Clipping Mask

In this tutorial, you open the same gravel image used in the previous tutorial. You will then add a text layer to the image, and apply that layer as a clipping mask to the gravel image. Then, you will merge the layers and stroke the text, to create the finished filled text.

Horizontal Type Tool

1. Open the gravel.tif file.
2. Click the **Horizontal Type Tool** in the **Toolbox**.

3. In the options bar, enter the following settings:
   - **Font:** Tahoma
   - **Font Style:** Bold
   - **Font Size:** 140 pt

Commit

4. Click at the left side of the gravel image and enter this text: ROCK. Click the **Commit** (check mark) button in the options bar when finished.
5. If necessary, click the **Move Tool** and center the text in the image window. See **Figure T11-4**.
6. Unlock transparency for the Background layer by double-clicking on it. Then, in the **New Layer** dialog box, click **OK** to accept Layer 0 as the layer name.

   In order to apply a clipping mask to a layer, the layer must be unlocked.

7. In the **Layers** palette, drag the text layer below the gravel layer.

   The layer that is going to be used as the clipping mask must be below the layer(s) that are going to be clipped.

8. Make sure the gravel layer is active in the **Layers** palette.
9. Choose **Layer > Create Clipping Mask**.
10. Combine the two layers by choosing **Layer > Merge Visible**.

    This permanently applies the clipping mask by eliminating any hidden parts of the layers. The layers must be merged to achieve the desired effect when the text is stroked in the step that follows.

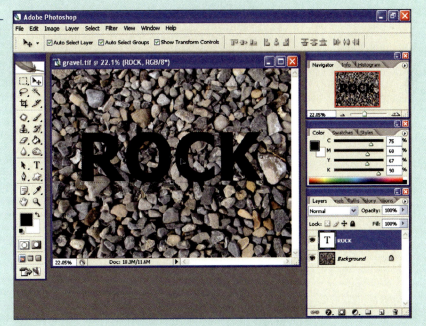

Figure T11-4. Create text in the center of the gravel image.

11. Choose **Edit > Stroke…**. This is similar to choosing **Layer > Layer Style > Stroke…**. In the **Stroke** dialog box, enter the following settings and click the **OK** button:
    - **Width:** 4 px
    - **Color:** Black
    - **Location:** Outside

    This creates a black outline 4 pixels wide around the text, helping it to stand out. See Figure T11-5.

12. Choose **File > Save As…**. Name this file 11rocktext.tif, and then close it.

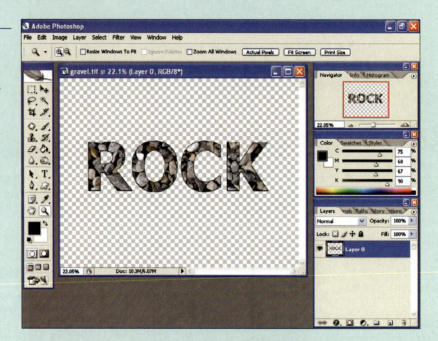

Figure T11-5. After the layers are merged, the **Stroke** command is used to add a thin outline around the text.

Tutorial 11-3: The Align and Distribute Commands

In this tutorial, you will a create a small, semitransparent circle. Then, you will make two copies of the circle with decreasing opacities. You will align the circles with the centerline of the text, equally space them, and then merge the new layers. You will create a copy of the merged layer for each song title, and then use the **Align** command to properly align the sets of circles with the song titles.

1. Open the 07CDback.psd file you edited in an earlier chapter.
2. Choose **File > Save As…** to create a copy of this file. Name the new file 11CDback.psd. Click **Save**.

    The 07CDback.psd file is closed automatically and the 11CDback.psd file is now open on your screen.

Shape layers

3. Choose **Layer > Flatten Image**.
4. Click the **Custom Shape Tool** in the **Toolbox**.
5. In the options bar, make sure the **Shape layers** button is clicked.

Chapter 11 Additional Layer Techniques 469

Ellipse Tool

Create new shape layer

6. Click the **Ellipse Tool** button in the options bar, and make sure the **Create new shape layer** button is active.
7. Click the **Color:** box in the options bar and choose white in the **Color Picker**.
8. In the options bar, click the **Geometry options** button and click the **Circle** radio button in the box that appears. See **Figure T11-6**.
9. Zoom in on the first song title, select the **Ellipse Tool** in the **Toolbox**, and create a circle to the right of the song title, as shown in **Figure T11-7**. Make the circle not quite as tall as the text.

Figure T11-6.
Select the **Ellipse Tool** and set it up to create a white circle on a new layer.

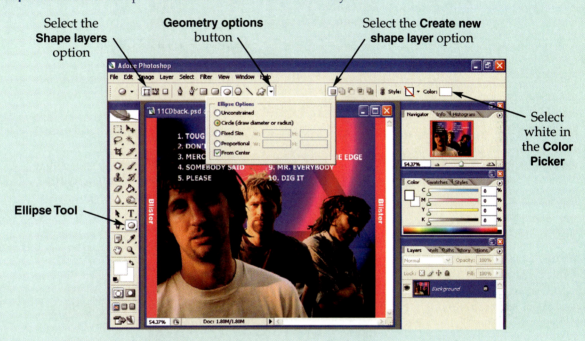

Figure T11-7.
Create the first circle in approximately the location shown. Duplicate it twice, reducing the opacity of each copy, and move the copies to the right of the original.

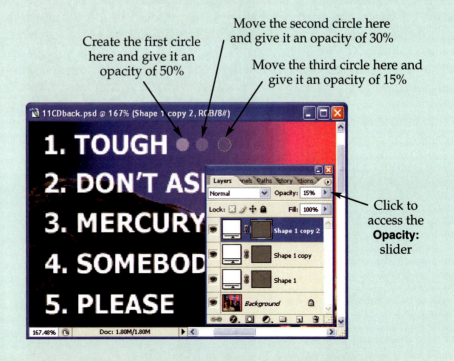

10. In the **Layers** palette, set the **Opacity:** slider of this new shape layer to 50%.
11. Choose **Layer > Duplicate Layer....** In the **Duplicate Layer** dialog box, click **OK** to accept Shape 1 copy as the layer name.
12. Set the **Opacity:** slider of this layer to 30% and move the circle to the right of the first circle, as shown in Figure T11-7.
13. Repeat the step 11 to create a third shape layer. Set the **Opacity:** slider of this shape layer to 15%. Move it to the location shown in Figure T11-7.
14. Click the **Rectangular Marquee Tool** in the **Toolbox**.
15. In the options bar, make sure **Feather:** is set to 0 px.
16. Create a rectangular selection snugly around the text and the circles, as shown in **Figure T11-8**.
17. In the **Layers** palette, make all three shape layers active by holding down [Ctrl] while clicking them.
18. Choose **Layer > Align Layers To Selection > Vertical Centers**.

    The circles are aligned using the center of the vertical sides of the selection as a reference point.

19. Choose **Layer > Distribute > Horizontal Centers**.

    This spaces the circles equally apart without moving the first and last circles.

20. Choose **Select > Deselect**.
21. Make sure all the three shape layers are selected in the **Layers** palette and the Background layer is not selected. Then, choose **Layer > Merge Layers**.

Rectangular Marquee Tool

Figure T11-8. Draw a rectangular selection around the title, and align the circles to the vertical center of the selection.

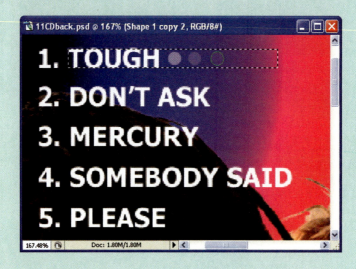

Chapter 11 Additional Layer Techniques

22. Finish the design as shown by duplicating layers, moving them to their approximate locations, creating a selection around the text, and aligning the shapes to the vertical center of the selection.

    Make sure that when you prepare to align a set of the circles, you have the appropriate layer selected in the layer palette. You may want to align the sets of circles in pairs to speed up the process. See **Figure T11-9.**

23. Delete the circle that overlaps the red sidebar on the right.
24. Save changes and close the 11CDback.psd file.

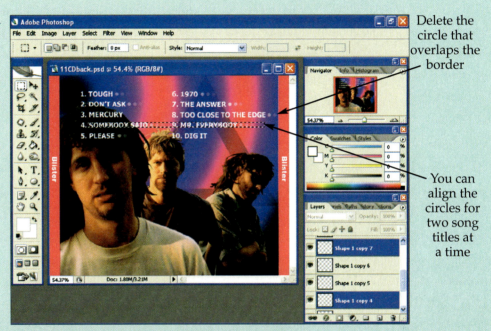

Figure T11-9. After the circles have been evenly distributed, merge the circle layers to create a single layer with three circles. Then, duplicate the layer and move a copy next to each song title. Lastly, align the dots to the vertical center of the text.

Delete the circle that overlaps the border

You can align the circles for two song titles at a time

Key Terms

align
clipping masks
color separations
compositions
comps
distribute
knockout
layer mask
preflight check
smart objects
vector masks

Review Questions

Answer the following questions on a separate piece of paper.

1. If a blending mode is assigned to a layer, what other layer(s) are affected by the blending mode?
2. What blending mode is a good choice when blending an image with another layer that contains a photo of a shiny surface?
3. Name four different types of tools that can have a blending mode applied to them when **Edit > Fade (*previous command or tool*)…** is chosen immediately after using the tool.

4. Can a layer mask be applied to a layer that has transparency locked?
5. What tools can be used to apply a layer mask?
6. How are parts of a layer mask deleted?
7. How are parts of a layer mask made to be partially transparent?
8. How is an entire layer mask deleted?
9. What tools are used to create vector masks?
10. How is a clipping mask different from layer masks or vector masks?
11. Layer style blending options can be used effectively to mask areas on what kind of images?
12. How do you permanently delete the masked (hidden) area of a layer?
13. When the **Layer Comps** palette is used to create different versions of a project, what four layer characteristics can be adjusted and saved in the layer comps?
14. Describe two techniques for aligning layers using the **Align** commands.
15. When you use the **Distribute** commands to distribute layers, which two layers do not move?

12 File Management and Automated Tasks

Learning Objectives

After completing this chapter, you will be able to:
- Explain what happens to an image when it is compressed.
- Describe the difference between saving a JPEG image with high-quality and low-quality compression settings.
- Differentiate between lossy and lossless compression.
- Recognize commonly used file formats used to save image files.
- Recognize commonly used file formats used to save other types of graphic files.
- Explain what happens when a Camera RAW image is opened in Photoshop.
- Differentiate between scripts and actions.
- Use the **Actions** palette to record an action.
- Describe the tools that are available in the **File > Automate** menu.
- Explain the features of Bridge that make it easy to organize and sort files.
- Use the **Notes Tool** or **Audio Annotation Tool** to add comments to a project.

Introduction

This chapter wraps up your exploration of Photoshop's many features and tools. Several important topics are discussed in this chapter, including file formats and compression. You will also be introduced to actions and scripts, which let you program Photoshop to accomplish specific tasks. Finally, you will take a look at Bridge, Photoshop's file browser, and several powerful tools found in the **File > Automate** menu.

File Formats

When you save an image, the file format you choose to save it in can make a big difference in the quality of the image, the file size of the image, and other image characteristics. There are numerous file formats available in Photoshop. Knowing a little bit about the various options will help you choose the option that gives you the quality level and characteristics that you need, while minimizing file size.

JPEG Images and Compression

You have probably noticed that many digital cameras and scanners save images in the JPEG file format by default. This is because the JPEG format compresses image files, making them smaller. For digital camera users, this means that more images will fit on a memory card.

To *compress* a file means to reorganize the file data in a more efficient way. When an image is compressed, the computer does not keep track of each pixel anymore. Instead, the computer records groups or patterns of similarly-colored pixels. Because the image file now keeps track of "clumps" of pixels instead of each individual pixel, there is less information to keep track of, resulting in smaller file sizes.

When you save a JPEG image in Photoshop, a dialog box appears, allowing you to choose between varying degrees of compression quality. High-quality compression settings leave you with an almost unnoticeable decrease in the quality of the image, and the image's file size becomes smaller than it would be without any compression. When low-quality compression settings are chosen, the file size becomes *much* smaller, but the quality of the image worsens considerably. This is because the effects of compression become so intense that some pixels actually change color, allowing them to be more easily grouped into patterns. This is referred to as *lossy* compression, because some of the original colors of the image become lost. Heavy compression results in distracting square patterns in the image. See **Figure 12-1**.

When you save a JPEG image and choose a level of compression, you will not see the effects of your settings until you close and reopen the image. Every time a JPEG image is re-saved, a bit more of the original image quality is lost.

Other file formats (such as TIFF) are capable of compressing images using a *lossless* method. In other words, some compression takes place, but colors in the image are not sacrificed during the process. As you might expect, file sizes do not become as small after using lossless compression, but the quality of the image is not compromised.

If you are after the highest image quality possible, consider these tips:

- If your digital camera only captures files in the JPEG format, use the highest quality JPEG compression setting available. Then, save the image as a TIFF immediately after importing it into Photoshop. After editing the image, you can then resave it as a JPEG to reduce the file size.

Figure 12-1.
Compression quality makes a big difference in the appearance of images. **A**—This is a close-up of an image saved with high-quality JPEG compression. **B**—When the same image is saved with low-quality compression, the image becomes blocky.

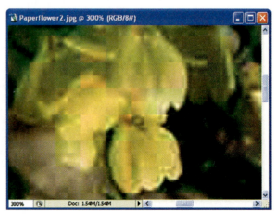

A B

- Check your scanner software to see if you can capture images in TIFF format instead of JPEG.
- Avoid saving any file as a JPEG until you are completely done editing it in Photoshop.
- If your digital camera uses the Camera RAW format (discussed later in this chapter), you can use that setting to capture images without any further processing from the camera.

Common File Formats

When saving a Photoshop file for the first time, or when choosing **File > Save As...**, you have probably noticed that there are many different file formats to choose from, **Figure 12-2**. Here is a quick breakdown of the most commonly used file formats:

Commonly used formats for photographic image files:

- *PSD* (Photoshop Document): This is the *default* file format used to save Photoshop projects. Layers and other data are all preserved. These files are intended to be opened within Photoshop.
- *TIFF* (Tagged Image File Format): This is the industry standard for saving images that will be printed commercially. This format is also used for high-quality archival (storage) purposes. The TIFF format saves layer information, so an image does not need to be flattened before being saved in this format.
- *JPEG* (Joint Photographers Experts Group): This is the most popular format for lowering file sizes of photographic images, especially for use on the web. *JPEG 2000* is an improved version of JPEG (available as a Photoshop plug-in). The JPEG format does not save layer information.

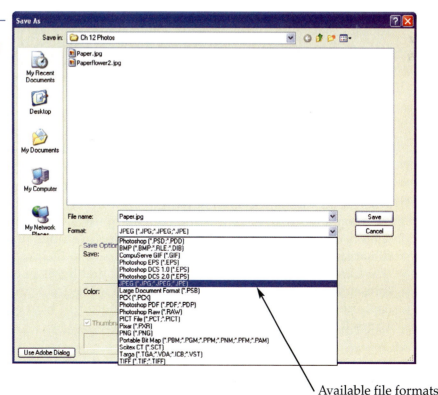

Figure 12-2. After **File > Save As...** is chosen, a file can be saved in many different file formats.

Available file formats

Commonly used file formats for web graphics (other than photos):
- *CompuServe GIF* (Graphics Interchange Format): This format converts images to indexed color (256 colors) and is commonly used in web design. It also compresses images to create very small file sizes.
- *PNG* (Portable Network Graphics): This format is similar to GIF, but is newer and contains more features and flexibility.

Commonly used formats for printing/publishing (check with your print service provider to determine the most appropriate choice):
- *Photoshop PDF* (Photoshop Portable Document Format): This is a version of Adobe's popular PDF format. Photoshop PDF can save Photoshop data such as layers, spot color information, and alpha channels. Other advanced options are available that prepare files for large commercial printing presses.
- *EPS* (Encapsulated PostScript): Almost any page-layout, illustration, or graphics program can open a graphic file saved in this format. A PostScript printer must be used to correctly print EPS files.
- *DCS 1.0 and 2.0* (Desktop Color Separations): When saving CMYK images, the DCS formats (which are versions of the EPS format) can save each color channel as a separate file. The DCS 2.0 format can save spot color channel information.

Camera RAW

Some digital cameras can capture images in a high-quality format called *Camera RAW* in addition to the JPEG format. When images are saved as Camera RAW files, the image is saved exactly as the camera saw it. Even though a slight amount of high-quality *(lossless)* compression is applied to RAW files, they still take up considerably more file space than images in JPEG format.

When you open a Camera RAW image in Photoshop, the Camera RAW dialog box appears, **Figure 12-3**, enabling you to quickly and easily adjust an image with a variety of settings. For example, if a RAW image has been underexposed or overexposed as it was captured, you can correct the problem with the **Exposure** slider. Other settings such as **White Balance:**, **Temperature**, and **Tint** can quickly adjust RAW images to remove color casts caused by varying lighting conditions. There are many other settings that are similar to commands you have already learned about, but they will not be explained in this text. Entire books have been written about adjusting Camera RAW files in Photoshop.

If you own a digital camera that can capture both RAW and JPEG formats, you may be wondering in what situations you should use each format. The **Camera Raw** dialog box makes it very easy to correct common problems with images, and this is certainly an argument for shooting in RAW mode. However, RAW images take up much more space on a memory card. It is the opinion of this author that amateur photographers should use their camera's highest-quality JPEG settings unless they find themselves dissatisfied over time with how the colors appear in their captured images. It is argued that Camera RAW format tends to represent highlights in an image better than JPEG format. If you are the type of photographer who evaluates the color quality of their captured images very closely, you should experiment with both formats and decide for yourself in what situations you will use each format.

Figure 12-3.
The Camera RAW dialog box appears when a RAW file is opened in Photoshop.

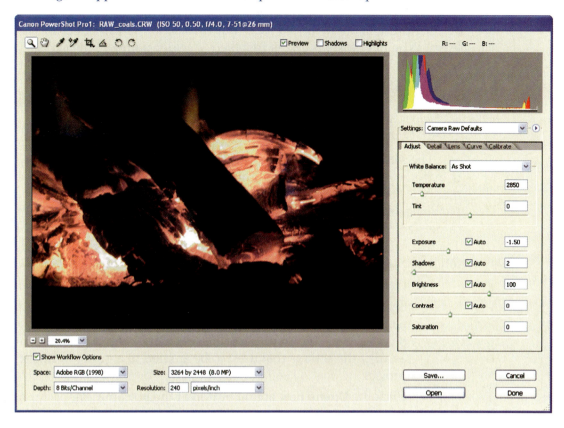

Scripts and Actions

Occasionally, you might be required to use Photoshop for a repetitive task. For example, imagine you have been asked to place a decorative border around 500 image files. Rather than do one file at a time, you can use actions or scripts to do this task automatically for you. The terms *scripts* and *actions* both refer to a programmed series of commands that accomplish a particular task. The difference between the two is that actions are a series of Photoshop commands that can be recorded using simple techniques, while scripts are typically commands created with a programming language, such as Visual Basic, AppleScript, or JavaScript. Scripts are more flexible than actions, because they are not limited to using only commands found within Photoshop. Scripts can process images using more than one application (such as Photoshop and Illustrator). Furthermore, scripts can be written so that different outcomes occur, based on particular conditions being met.

Using Scripts

Photoshop's **File > Scripts** submenu provides a few scripts that have already been created. In the previous chapter, you learned that three of these scripts can be used to convert layer comps into separate files in various formats. The **Export Layers To Files** script, which is similar to the layer comp conversion scripts, can be used to convert any number of layers selected in the **Layers** palette to separate files.

Another script is named **Image Processor**. Running this script opens an interface similar to a wizard, Figure 12-4, allowing you to convert a folder of images into JPEG, PSD, or TIFF format, at various sizes.

Scripting is an advanced skill, but instruction is provided for those who wish to learn. When Photoshop CS2 is installed, a folder named Scripting Guide is placed with the rest of Photoshop's program files. This folder contains guides that explain how to create scripts, as well as sample scripts and their descriptions.

Recording and Using Actions

The **Actions** palette can be used to record a series of Photoshop commands. This is extremely useful when using Photoshop to edit numerous files in exactly the same manner. For example, suppose you are assigned to prepare images to display on a particular website. The website's design requires that all images need to be exactly the same size. The images also need to be sharpened slightly and saved in JPEG format. To create an action that will run these commands automatically, these steps should be followed:

- Open an image.
- Optional: Create a new set by clicking the **Create New Set** button. Enter a new name in the **New Set** dialog box and click **OK**. The set is added to the **Actions** palette. Sets are basically folders in which you can group related actions, such as all of the actions that need to be applied to a group of images in a particular project.
- Click the **Create new action** button at the bottom right of the **Actions** palette.
- In the **New Action** dialog box, name the action. Use the **Set** drop-down list to select a set in which to save the action. If desired, assign a hot key combination to execute the action using the **Function Key:** drop-down list and the **Shift** and **Control** check boxes. Click the **Record** button when you are done.

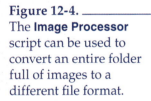

Figure 12-4.
The **Image Processor** script can be used to convert an entire folder full of images to a different file format.

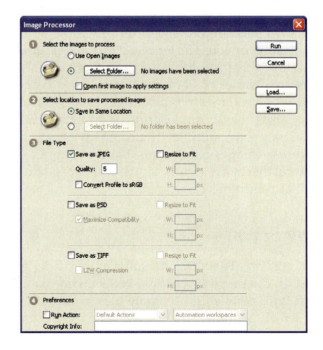

- Edit the image using the **Image Size** command and add the desired sharpening filter.
- Use the **Save As...** command to save the file in JPEG format with desired compression settings. Select a different folder in which to save the image and click **OK**. Do *not* rename the file, or the action will automatically rename all files with the same name, and they will overwrite one another.
- Click the **Stop playing/recording** button in the **Actions** palette.
- Open another image, make sure the desired action is selected in the **Actions** palette, and then click the **Play selection** button. This automatically runs all of the commands recorded in the action.

Once you have recorded an action, it is added to the **Actions** palette and is available for all images that you open in the future. You can also go back and edit the action at any time. Clicking the arrow next to the action reveals all of the steps in it. If any of the steps has an arrow next to it, you can click that arrow and reveal further details about that step. See **Figure 12-5**.

If you want to disable, but not permanently remove, steps in the action, click on the check mark next to the step in the **Actions** palette. Clicking the check box again turns the step back on. Clicking the check mark toggle at the action or set level turns all of the steps in the action on or off at the same time.

Clicking a box just to the right of the check mark toggle will cause the dialog box related to that step to appear when you play the action. This is a good feature to enable if the files you are processing need to be handled differently. For example, if some of your images need to be resized to 3″ × 4″ and some need to be resized to 5″ × 7″, you should enable the **Image Size** dialog box so you can manually enter the different sizes when the action is played back. Clicking the box again disables the dialog box for that step.

Figure 12-5.
The **Actions** palette records Photoshop commands, which can be replayed at any time, and in any image, by selecting the action in the palette and pressing the **Play selection** button.

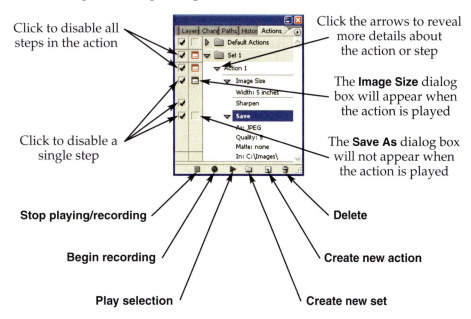

If you want to permanently remove steps from the action, simply highlight the step(s) to be removed in the **Actions** palette and click the **Delete** button at the bottom of the palette. If you want to add a step, select the step in the action that you want to come right before the step you are about to add. Then, click the **Begin recording** button in the palette and perform the task. Click the **Stop playing/recording** button as soon as you are done. The new task is added to the action just below the selected step.

You have been shown just one example of the many types of tasks that can be automated using the **Actions** palette. With some practice, you will find this feature very useful for processing large batches of images.

The Automate Menu

The **Automate** menu contains several powerful, action-based commands. To run any of these commands, choose **File > Automate** and select the command. After entering your desired settings, Photoshop uses actions to create the final result. The following are brief explanations of the commands found in the **File > Automate** menu. The commands that are most user-friendly are listed first.

The Fit Image Command

The **Fit Image** command is used to quickly resize an image to fit within the pixel dimensions you specify. The values entered represent a maximum size of the image for each dimension. Photoshop will *not* change the aspect (width-to-height) ratio of the image to fill the area specified, but will change the image size until one dimension matches maximum value, and the other is equal to or less than the maximum value. The image is resampled during the process, so the resolution of the image remains the same. See **Figure 12-6**.

The PDF Presentation Command

The **PDF Presentation** command saves one or more images in PDF format either as a multi-page PDF document or a PDF slide show that can play automatically. See **Figure 12-7**. The PDF format is popular because anyone can view a PDF file as long as they have Adobe Reader® (formerly Adobe Acrobat Reader) installed on their computer.

The Contact Sheet II Command

The **Contact Sheet II** command creates small thumbnails of the images in the selected folder and arranges them on a new Photoshop file that is ready to print. The result is similar to a contact sheet made from 35 mm negatives. See **Figure 12-8**.

Figure 12-6.
The **Fit Image** dialog box allows you to set maximum values for the image's dimensions. Photoshop will automatically resize the image, but maintain its proportions, until it is as large as possible without exceeding either of the dimensional limits that were set.

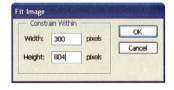

Figure 12-7.
The **PDF Presentation** command creates either a multi-page document or a slide show from a selected group of images. **A**—The **PDF Presentation** command's dialog box allows you to specify the images to use in the presentation, determine the type of presentation, and if a slide show is chosen, set up slide transitions and delays. **B**—This multi-page PDF document was created from images in one of the Student CD folders.

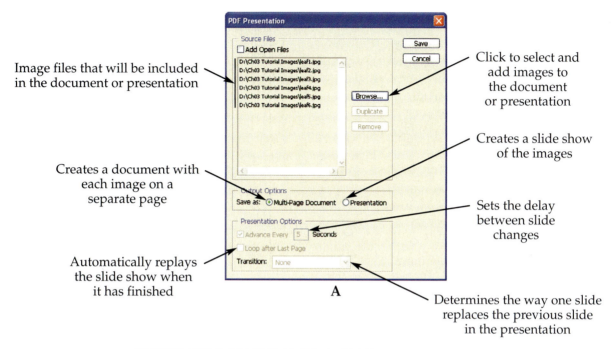

Figure 12-8.
The **Contact Sheet II** command can be used to create single-page images made up of the thumbnails of numerous images. **A**—The **Contact Tool II** dialog box has controls for selecting images to include on the contact sheet, and numerous predefined layouts for arranging the image thumbnails. **B**—A contact sheet with the default layout is shown here. Thumbnail size will vary depending on the layout specified.

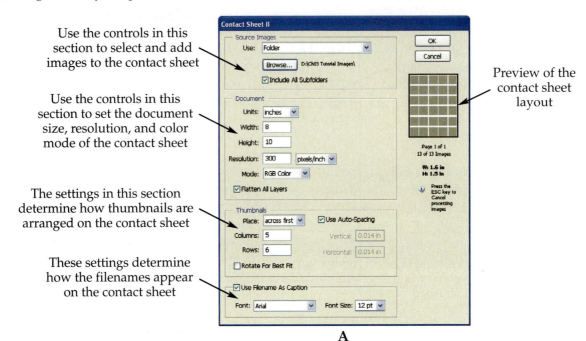

A

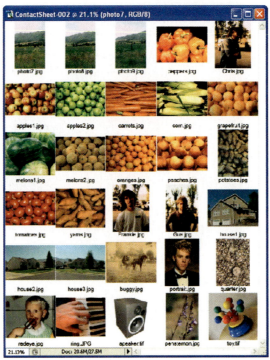

B

The Crop and Straighten Photos Command

When a group of photos have been placed crookedly on a scanner and scanned, the **Crop and Straighten Photos** command can be used to separate and straighten them. First, the image to be straightened is surrounded with a selection. Sometimes your selection will need to slightly overlap another image in order to completely select the desired image. This is alright. If the overlap area is small and there is white space between the images, Photoshop will disregard the small portion of the second image that is selected, and crop and straighten only the desired image. If the overlap area is larger, Photoshop will crop and straighten the selected areas of both images separately.

After the selection is made, choosing **Automate > Crop and Straighten Photos** automatically rotates the cropping box to create a straight-edged image. A new image containing the result is automatically created. The process can be repeated for other images in the group. See **Figure 12-9**.

The Picture Package Command

The **Picture Package** command creates a multi-picture layout of a single image. There are a number of different configurations, called layouts, to choose from. These layouts are similar to the way a portrait photographer packages school photos. The layouts that are available depend on the size of the document you want to create. Also, a combination of images can be arranged as a single picture package, if desired. See **Figure 12-10**.

Figure 12-9.
Straightening and cropping an image is a relatively easy task. **A**—One of the crookedly scanned photos is selected. Do not worry if the selection slightly overlaps the image you want to crop. **B**—The **Crop and Straighten Photos** command automatically creates a new file containing the straight-edged result.

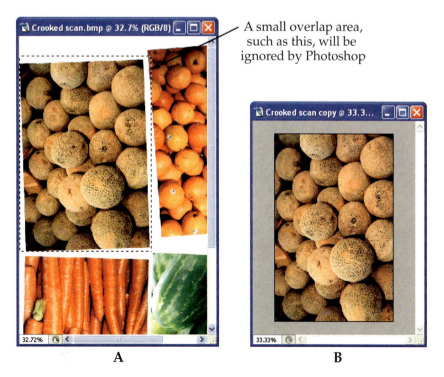

A small overlap area, such as this, will be ignored by Photoshop

A   B

Figure 12-10.
This is one of several possible picture packages that can be created from a single image. Two or more images can also be used to create a picture package.

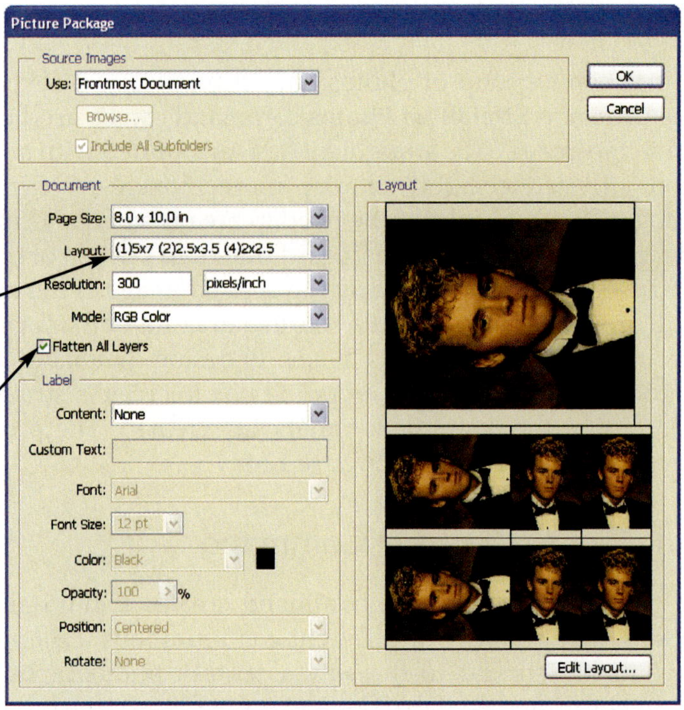

You can choose from a number of document sizes and layouts

Indicates that all images will be placed on the same layer

When the **Flatten All Layers** check box is checked, the individual images in the package are all placed on the same layer. When this option is unchecked, each image is placed on a separate layer. It is suggested that you leave this option checked unless you want to adjust the images individually after the package is created.

The Web Photo Gallery Command

For web designers who wish to create a photo gallery of images, the **Web Photo Gallery** command can save a lot of time. First, all images that will appear in a particular gallery must be placed in a folder. Then, a new folder must be created. This new folder, called the destination folder, is selected in the **Web Photo Gallery** dialog box. The destination folder will contain all of the optimized images and linking information required for the photo gallery to function properly on the web. The content in the destination folder is then ready to be edited further if desired and uploaded to a website. There are twenty different photo gallery formats to choose from. See **Figure 12-11**.

The Photomerge Command

Photomerge is the command that directs Photoshop to stitch together a group of photos to create a panoramic view. When capturing photos that will be used to create a panoramic image, overlap each photo by 25–30% as you take different shots from the same location. You already learned how to use the **Photomerge** command in Tutorial 6-7 in Chapter 6, *Painting Tools and Features*.

Figure 12-11.
This is one of 20 different web photo gallery formats that can be selected.

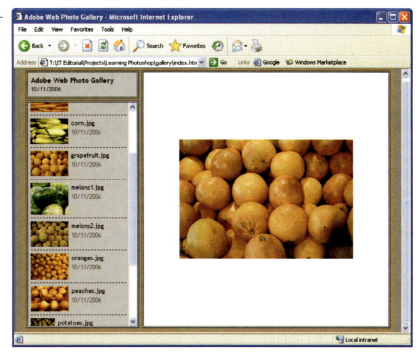

Other Action-Based Commands in the Automate Menu

The **Merge to HDR** command is used to combine multiple images into a single *HDR image*. HDR stands for high dynamic range. HDR images are created by capturing the same image at different exposures with a camera, resulting in different shadows and highlights in each image. Then, the images can be combined with the **Merge to HDR** command, resulting in a single image with a greater range of shadows and highlights.

Use the **Batch** command when you have multiple images that require the same action. The **Batch** dialog box lets you choose the source folder (where the images are), the destination folder, and the action.

Have you ever opened Photoshop by dragging an image file on top of the Photoshop icon on your desktop? The **Create Droplet** command creates a droplet, which works the same way. The droplet looks like an application icon, and it runs an action when you drag an image (or images) onto it. The **Create Droplet** dialog box is similar to the **Batch** dialog box. You must choose where the droplet icon appears (the desktop is a good place), a destination folder in which the edited image will be placed, and what action will be performed.

The **Conditional Mode Change** command needs to be used when recording actions that involve converting images in various color modes to another color mode. See Photoshop Help for more information if you record an action that contains a task such as this.

Organizing Files with Bridge

Photoshop has a built-in file browser, called Bridge, that is activated when you choose **File > Browse....** Using Bridge is optional. However, you may prefer to use Bridge's features instead of organizing files using traditional methods, especially if you need to keep a large number of image files and folders well organized.

When you use Bridge, you can easily create new folders using the **File** menu. You can also move images by dragging and dropping them into different folders, or by cutting, copying, and pasting them into new folders using the **Edit** menu. Image files can be renamed by clicking on the filename under the appropriate thumbnail and entering a new name, and you can open an image in Photoshop by double-clicking on its thumbnail.

Viewing Options

The slider at the bottom of the **Bridge** dialog box allows you to change the size of the image thumbnails. See **Figure 12-12**. When you drag the slider to the right, the thumbnails get larger. This allows you to see the details of the image without actually opening it in Photoshop. Four buttons in the bottom right corner of the **Bridge** dialog box let you view the thumbnails in different ways.

Figure 12-12.
Bridge, Photoshop's file browser, offers many ways to organize and sort files.

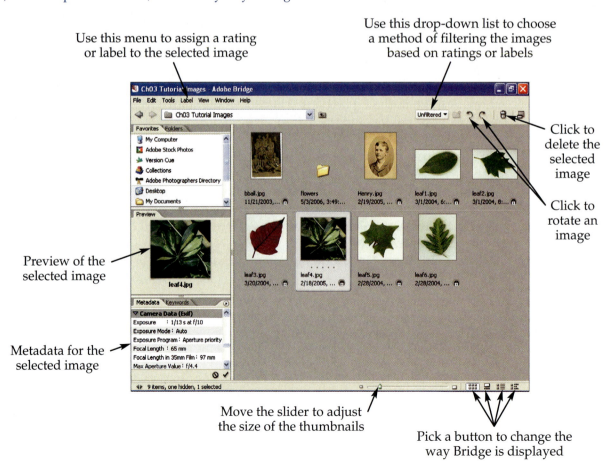

You can also choose to display certain information panels in the **Bridge** dialog box by selecting the panel type from the **View** pull-down menu. The **Favorites** panel allows you to quickly locate images stored in folders you have marked as favorite places. The **Folders** panel allows you to browse for images using a File Explorer–style window. The **Preview** panel displays a preview of the selected image. The **Metadata** panel displays detailed information about the image. The **Keywords** panel allows you to assign new keywords and displays the assigned keywords.

Metadata

Details about each image, called *metadata*, can be entered and viewed at any time by choosing **File > File Info...** in the **Bridge** dialog box. Some metadata is automatically created and attached to the file when it is captured. This includes file size and resolution information. If the image was captured with a digital camera, information about the camera settings can be automatically recorded, depending on the camera. If you capture RAW images, you may notice a file with the exact same name as one of your images, but with an XMP file extension and very small in size. This is the metadata file. Other metadata can be added manually by choosing **File > File Info...** and entering information such as copyright notes and author (photographer) information.

Sorting

Bridge lets you assign labels to images, and then sort the images by their assigned labels. This is also called *flagging*. Labels can be a color-coded bar that appears underneath the image thumbnail or a rating of one to five stars that appears in the same area. Using either (or a combination) of these two labeling methods, you can organize your photos in any way you desire. At any time, you can instantly filter (sort) images according to their labels.

The **Label** menu in the **Bridge** dialog box is used to assign labels, and the drop-down list at the top-right of the dialog box is used to view images according to the labels you have assigned. You can also select all labeled or all unlabeled images by using commands in the **Edit** menu of the dialog box.

Rotating Images without Opening Them

You can rotate an image by right-clicking an image thumbnail in the **Bridge** dialog box and choosing from three different rotate commands. You can also rotate an image by clicking on its thumbnail, and then clicking one of the two **Rotate** buttons at the top right of the dialog box. The next time you open the image it will be rotated.

Audio Annotation and Notes

Busy designers can attach important notes (in text or audio format) to a Photoshop file. In the **Toolbox**, just above the **Hand Tool**, is the **Notes Tool**, Figure 12-13. When this tool is used to click anywhere in an open file, a small text-entry window appears. After entering notes and closing the text-entry window, a small icon remains visible in the file. You can reposition the note icon by dragging and dropping it in the desired location.

Figure 12-13.
The **Notes Tool** or **Audio Annotation Tool** can be used to easily add comments to a Photoshop project.

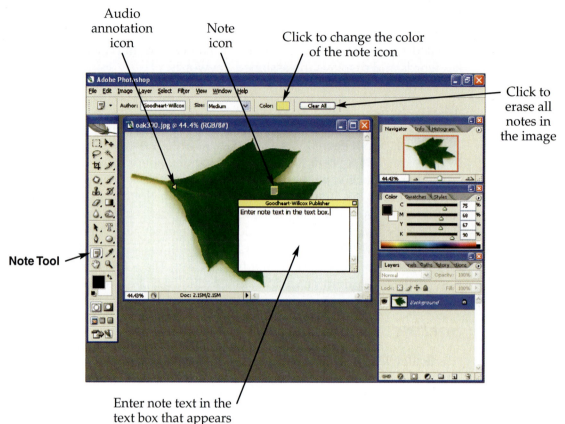

This icon can be double-clicked anytime to reveal the text. The note can be deleted by clicking the icon to select it (the center of the icon turns grey) and then pressing [Delete]. You can delete all of the notes in the image by clicking the **Clear All** button in the options bar.

Using the controls in the options bar, you can change the color of the note icon and change the size of the text in the note. If multiple people are working on or reviewing the image, each can leave individualized notes by changing the name in the **Author:** text box and the color of the note icon.

Audio notes can be added to a file if a microphone is connected to your computer. The **Audio Annotation Tool** is found in the **Toolbox** behind the **Notes Tool**, and works much the same way, with one exception. Instead of a text-entry window, the **Audio Annotation** dialog box appears, which contains **Start...** and **Stop** buttons. Click the **Start...** button to begin recording the note and the **Stop** button when you have finished. You can play the annotation by right clicking on the audio annotation icon and selecting **Play** from the shortcut menu.

Note Annotations can only be saved for images in the PSD, PSB, PDF, and TIFF file formats.

GRAPHIC DESIGN:
FAQ—Graphic Design Careers

What kinds of designs do graphic designers create?

Most design work is published either in printed form or on the Internet, **Figure 12-14**. The following are some examples from both categories:

Internet-Based
- Graphics for web pages.
- Web-based animations.
- Overall layout schemes for websites.
- Site navigation strategies.

Print-Based
- Business cards.
- Company and product logos.
- Stationery.
- Posters.
- Brochures.
- Book and periodical covers.
- Illustrations (artistic and technical).
- Product packaging.
- Large banners.
- Car wraps.
- Photography.
- Any other type of printed advertising.
- Outdoor signs and billboards.
- Signage systems (such as the directional signs found in grocery stores, corporate buildings, and cultural centers).

Figure 12-14.
A graphic designer must be able to present information in a visually alluring package. These tri-fold brochures are typical of the types of materials a graphic designer might be asked to develop. (Courtesy of the Xerox Corporation)

What kinds of companies employ graphic designers?

A wide range of businesses and organizations employ graphic designers, **Figure 12-15**. The following are a few of the more common places where graphic designers find employment:

- Graphic design agencies.
- Advertising agencies.
- Printing and publishing companies (magazines, newspapers, etc.).
- Any other company that produces graphic designs in-house, such as manufacturers and companies that create packaging materials.
- Television, video, and movie industries.
- Educational institutions (teachers of graphic design).
- Some graphic designers are self-employed and work on a contract basis.

What experience do I need to be hired as a graphic designer?

The graphic design field can be competitive. The more education and experience you have, the greater your advantage will be when you go in for an interview. The following are a few tips to keep in mind as you prepare for a career in the graphic design field.

Earning a bachelor's degree in Graphic Design from a college, university, or design school is strongly recommended. While there, you will study a variety of different art mediums, both traditional and computer-based.

A well-rounded general education is also important. Good language skills will help you when your designs involve text. Nothing is more embarrassing than a misspelled word or grammatical error in six-foot-tall letters on a billboard. Mathematics and geometry can come in handy for such things as sizing designs, locating centers of design elements, and creating geometric elements in a design.

Employers are always on the lookout for designers who are well-versed in various software packages, including image-editing programs (such as Photoshop), illustration software (such as Adobe Illustrator), and page layout

Figure 12-15. _____
This graphic designer is developing a cover for a new textbook.

programs (such as InDesign or QuarkXpress). Designers who have website design skills, especially experience with web programming languages, will have advantages over designers without these skills.

The graphic design field attracts many artistically talented people. You must have a strong *portfolio* (samples of the best artwork you have created) to stand out from other job seekers. When you interview for jobs, carry the portfolio with you. Your portfolio will likely be one of the most influential factors that a potential employer will consider during the interview process.

How much do graphic designers earn?

The salaries earned by graphic designers vary depending on a number of factors, including the region where the artist is employed and the type of work the designer is doing. The U.S. Department of Labor's website, www.dol.gov, is a good place to find information about the latest salary statistics and other information about any career. Click the **Occupational Outlook Handbook** link, and then look for graphic designers in the **Professional > Art and design occupations** category.

What personal qualities are employers looking for?

Doing well in school can only make you look better in the eyes of your employers. Employers are aware that good study skills translate into good work habits. However, in addition to a good education and work history, there are certain personal qualities that will make you more desirable to employers. The following are qualities that employers look for in employment candidates. The same qualities are important for promotion and, ultimately, supervisory and leadership roles:

- Artistic ability—A strong portfolio will best communicate your abilities to a potential employer.
- A personality that is flexible and personable—A designer must be able to respond appropriately to constructive criticism. Many first attempts at a design must be reworked at the client's or supervisor's request.
- Ability to work well in team situations—Be aware of the impact (both positive and negative) that your actions and words have on others, and be sensitive to cultural and physical differences.
- Hard-working—Be willing to work extra time when necessary to meet deadlines.
- Willingness to learn—A designer must continually update their technology skills as new versions of software are released. Attending conferences, reading trade magazines, or taking classes are a few ways to stay current. Designers should also stay informed about current practices and trends in the design industry.
- Good interview skills—Learn all you can about how to prepare for and successfully participate in a job interview.

Once you are employed, how do you continue to grow professionally?

In many cases, productivity is one of the most important measures of job performance. With the pressures of looming deadlines, you may feel like you no longer have time to experiment with new tools and techniques. However, continued growth is essential for job satisfaction and for staying competitive in the workplace. Only by increasing your knowledge and skill set can you push beyond your current limitations. There are a number of things you can do to help you continue learning throughout your career.

You may want to obtain professional certification. Some employers encourage their employees to prove their understanding of design-related software by passing an industry-standard test. For example, Adobe offers such a test for Photoshop users called the Adobe Certified Expert (ACE) Exam. Successfully passing such an exam requires a thorough knowledge of the software. Designers who pass this test can place the ACE logo on their business cards or other publications that advertise their services.

You can also do volunteer work to give something back to the community. You may want to volunteer to visit schools and offer practical advice to students. You can donate your time and talents to worthy causes, such as designing banners for a community event or fliers for a youth organization. This is not only personally rewarding, but gives you an opportunity to experiment with new design techniques away from the pressures and restrictions of your daily job.

You may also want to consider becoming a member of a trade association. Typically, a yearly fee is required. In return for the annual fee, you can enjoy benefits like the following:

- Association with other professionals who share your interests.
- Subscriptions to trade magazines, journals, or newsletters that offer information on the latest trends and technology.
- Use of the association's name on your business cards.
- The opportunity to attend association-sponsored conferences that focus on graphic design trends and issues.
- The chance to enter association-sponsored design contests.
- Access to design-related Internet forums, where you can ask questions and share information with your peers.

How difficult would it be to start my own graphic design business?

An *entrepreneur* is a person who operates his or her own business. It takes a great deal of energy, initiative, patience, and stamina to take a business from a small beginning to a successful enterprise. A graphic designer who wishes to start an entrepreneurship faces the challenging task of finding clients. If the designer does excellent work and deals with clients in a highly professional manner, the client may seek the designer's services for future projects. Building up a client base to keep a successful designer busy full-time may take a year or two or more.

Summary

In this chapter, you learned that an image can be saved in a variety of file types, each with specific strengths and weaknesses. This knowledge will help you choose the best format to save your image in, so that you get the quality level and features you need with the smallest possible file size.

You learned that scripts are small programs that run a preprogrammed string of commands with a single click. You also found that actions, while similar to scripts, can be recorded by the user and played back at any time.

In addition, you were introduced to Bridge, a powerful tool for browsing and organizing images. In the **Bridge** dialog box, you can move files around, edit an image's metadata, and rotate images without opening them.

Now that you have read this entire book and completed the tutorials, you have been exposed to most of Photoshop's tools, palettes, and menu commands. With this knowledge and a further experience using what you have learned, you can consider yourself an intermediate-level Photoshop user.

Key Terms

actions
Camera RAW
compress
CompuServe GIF
entrepreneur
flagging
HDR image
JPEG
lossless
lossy
metadata
PNG
portfolio
PSD
scripts
TIFF

Review Questions

Answer the following questions on a separate piece of paper.

1. Why do many digital cameras and scanners save captured images as JPEG files by default?
2. Briefly explain what it means to compress an image file.
3. If a JPEG image has distracting square patterns all over it, what likely caused the patterns to appear?
4. When saving a JPEG image, you will not see the effects of the JPEG compression settings until you do what?
5. What is the difference between lossy and lossless compression?
6. Why should you avoid unnecessarily re-saving a JPEG image?
7. If your camera can capture an image in only the JPEG format, what step should you take to preserve the quality of the image?
8. What file formats discussed in this chapter are capable of saving layer information?
9. What is the difference between scripts and actions?
10. What is the **Actions** palette used for?
11. What do all of the commands in the **Automate** menu have in common?
12. List three advantages of using Bridge to manage image files.
13. What are the two kinds of labels you can apply to organize and sort image thumbnails in Bridge?
14. What two tools can be used to place notes at specific locations in an image?
15. If two people are working on the same image, how can each person leave notes in the image that will not be confused with their coworker's notes?

Glossary

A

actions: A series of Photoshop commands recorded to accomplish a particular task.

active: An image or area of an image that is selected and ready to work on.

additive color system: Adding wavelengths of light together to create colors.

adjustment layer: A special type of layer that will apply a color-adjustment command to the image, but keeps the corrections you make separate from your image.

align: To arrange in a straight line.

alpha channels: Special channels that store information about selections and masks.

analogous colors: Colors that look good together, creating a sense of harmony and tranquility.

anti-aliasing: A selection tool option that creates a slight smoothing effect around the edges of the selection.

artifacts: Noise that appears when images are saved as low-resolution JPEG files.

asymmetrical: Not symmetrical.

B

background color: Color that is revealed by the **Eraser Tool** when it is used on a layer that has transparency locked.

balance: The equal distribution of visual elements.

bit: A tiny scrap of computer data that has two possible values, one or zero.

bit depth: A measurement of how many different shades of color a Photoshop file can display.

bitmap graphic: An image that is captured by a digital camera or scanner and is made up of pixels. Also called *raster graphic.*

black point: The darkest pixels in an image.

blemishes: Small imperfections, such as dust specks, in a photo.

body text: Complete sentences and paragraphs.

bounding box: A box that appears around all of the pixels in the active layer when the **Show Transform Controls** option is on.

brightness: The degree of lightness of an image.

brush marks: The individual patterns of paint created by the brush.

C

calibrate: Set the monitor to display colors using certain brightness and contrast settings, etc.

Camera RAW: High-quality format in which the image is saved exactly as the camera captured it.

canvas: In Photoshop, the entire area of an image.

capture: To cause data to be stored in computer memory.

clients: Businesses or individuals that hire outside services.

clipboard: Temporary computer memory that makes cut, copy, and paste operations possible.

clipping masks: Masks that use the entire contents of a layer to mask another layer.

clone: To create an exact copy of something.

closed paths: Fully enclosed shapes.

CMYK color mode: Color mode that produces color by combining cyan, magenta, yellow, and black.

color cast: An unnatural tint, usually caused by bad lighting when the image was captured.

color channels: Show the distribution of the primary colors throughout an image, and use grayscale versions of the image to represent the amount of distribution.

color depth: The total number of colors that can be used in the image. This is expressed as the number of bits of data used to describe each color.

color management: Advanced-level process in which Photoshop users can force the colors on their monitor to match what comes out of their printer.

color modes: The different ways Photoshop creates colors in images.

color noise: Speckles or blotches of inappropriately colored pixels.

color sampler marks: Can be placed on the image to help you remember where the brightest and/or darkest areas are.

color separations: Separate files that show what portions of the image will be cyan, magenta, yellow, and black.

color stops: Color stops appear along the bottom of the sample gradient box in the **Gradient Editor**. They each represent one color in the gradient and indicate where the color shifts begin and end within the gradient.

complementary colors: Pairs of colors that are opposite of one another on the color wheel and cause each other to stand out.

composite channel: A shortcut you can click to select all *color* channels and make their combined effects visible in the image window.

compositions: Graphic designers' versions of their design ideas, which are prepared to show clients.

compress: To reorganize file data in a more efficient way.

comps: Short for *compositions*.

CompuServe GIF (Graphics Interchange Format): Format that converts images to indexed color (256 colors) and is commonly used in web design. It also compresses images to create very small file sizes.

contiguous: Pixels that are touching or bordering each other.

contrast: The tonal range of the image.

crop: To cut off.

D

DCS 1.0 and 2.0 (Desktop Color Separations): Versions of EPS format that can save each color channel in a separate file when saving CMYK images.

decorative fonts: Fonts that are non-traditional in appearance.

default: How a computer program looks before any settings are changed.

delete: Pressing a key or choosing a menu command to remove something.

deselected: Selection border is removed.

design elements: Images, graphics, text, colors, and empty space on the page used to create different feelings or moods.

destination image: The image to which you want to copy a selection.

digital: A format that a computer can recognize.

digital camera: Camera that converts an image to a format a computer can recognize.

distribute: To spread out evenly over a given distance.

document bounds: The edges of an image.

document size: File size.

dots per inch (dpi): Scale for measuring the resolution of a printed image.

drag a box: Click and hold the mouse button and drag the cursor to the opposite corner of a desired area before releasing the mouse button.

E

ellipses: Ovals.

emulsion: The top, glossy part of a photo that contains the image.

entrepreneur: A person who operates his or her own business.

EPS (Encapsulated PostScript): A file format used for printing/publishing. This format can be opened by almost any page-layout, illustration, or graphics program.

erase: Using a tool to remove pixels.

exposure: The amount of light applied to photosensitive paper.

extract: To remove carefully.

F

fastening points: Points created by the **Magnetic Lasso Tool** that hold the selection border to edges in the image.

feathering: A fading-out effect created at the edges of a selection.

filters: Special effects that can be applied to all or part of file.

flagging: Assigning labels to images and sorting the images by their assigned labels.

flatten: Merge all layers in an image using a single command.

flip: To mirror an image so it appears as if you were looking at it from the other side.

font: A named set of text and numeric characters that share the same look and feel.

font family: A group of fonts that share the same name and characteristics, yet vary slightly from one another.

foreground color: The color applied by painting tools in Photoshop.

G

gamut: The range of colors that can be produced.

Gaussian blur: A slight blur that is evenly distributed across the entire image.

gradient: Two or more colors that gradually blend together.

graphic designer: Individual who arranges images, illustrations, and text to effectively and creatively communicate a message.

grayscale color mode: Color mode that uses only combinations of black, white, and numerous shades of gray.

grid: A pattern of horizontal and vertical lines that appears on your screen but does not print.

H

halftone: Type of printing done by laser printers and commercial printing presses. Creates rows of tiny dots that can be square, diamond-shaped, circular, and even cross-shaped, and are often printed at an angle.

handles: Small squares that appear around the selected area when cropping an image or transforming a layer.

HDR image: High dynamic range image, created by capturing the same image at different exposures with a camera and then combining those versions.

headings: Titles and subtitles.

hexadecimal code: Alphanumeric code using characters 0–f.

highlights: The brightest areas in an image.

high resolution: An image with pixels so small that the human eye cannot make out the individual pixels when printed.

histogram: A graph that shows the mixture of shadows, midtones, and highlights in an image.

hue: A particular color, such as blue, orange-red, or sea green.

I

ICC profiles: Small computer files that describe how your monitor, printer, and other devices display or capture color in terms of standards set by the International Color Consortium.

icon: A picture or symbol that represents the selected tool.

image capture device: Device that converts an image to a format that can be stored in computer memory.

inkjet printers: Printers that create an image by spraying microscopic dots of ink on paper.

inverse: The opposite of.

J

jitter: Random fluctuation.

JPEG (Joint Photographers Experts Group): The most popular format for lowering file sizes of photographic images, especially for use on the web.

JPEG 2000: An improved version of the JPEG image format.

justification: The way the words in the paragraph align with the edges of the document.

Glossary

K

knockout: An area of an image that is removed so a layer below it can show through.

L

layer group: A folder that can be created in the **Layers** palette. By clicking on the group, all layers within that group become active, allowing you to move or transform them simultaneously.

layer mask: A special type of mask that makes part of a layer transparent, but keeps the image information so the hidden area can be restored at any time.

layers: Parts of a Photoshop file that keep different parts of the design separate from each other.

layer styles: Special effects such as drop shadows, beveled edges, and colorful outlines that can quickly be applied to an entire layer.

ligatures: The blending of two letters together.

linking: A way of grouping layers without organizing them into folders.

lists: Bulleted or numbered groups of items.

lock: Protect a layer from being changed.

lossless: Type of compression in which colors in the image are not sacrificed during the process.

lossy: Type of compression in which low-quality compression settings are chosen, resulting in the loss of some of the original colors of the image.

low-resolution: Image with pixels large enough to be visible when printed.

luminosity: The degree of lightness of an image.

M

marquee: A large sign surrounded by blinking lightbulbs. Also refers to a set of Photoshop selection tools that create selections with fixed shapes.

megapixel: One million pixels.

menu bar: Area at the top of the work area in which Photoshop's menus are located.

menus: Lists of commands that are related to each other.

merging: Combining two or more layers into one.

mesh: A grid that helps you see how the image was changed with the **Liquefy Filter** tools.

metadata: Details about the image that are saved in the image file and can be viewed.

midtones: Areas of an image that are not shadows or highlights.

motion blur: Blur caused by camera movement or subject movement when the photo was captured.

N

noise: Inappropriate pixels that appear all over an image.

O

open path: A path that is not closed, such as a zig-zag line.

options bar: Located just below the menu bar. When you click on any tool in the **Toolbox**, the tool's options (or settings) appear here.

ordinals: The small, raised letters found in 1st, 2nd, etc.
over-adjusted: So bright or dark that image detail is lost.

P

palette: Small window that contains a variety of related settings.
path: An adjustable outline of a shape.
perpendicular: At a 90° angle.
perspective drawing: A drawing that creates the illusion of depth.
photo filters: Colored translucent lenses that are placed at the end of the camera lens. The filter allows light of the same color to pass freely to the film, but absorbs light of different colors.
Photoshop PDF (Photoshop Portable Document Format): A version of Adobe's PDF format. Photoshop PDF can save Photoshop data such as layers, spot color information, and alpha channels.
pixel aspect ratio: Description of how wide a pixel is compared to how tall it is.
pixelated: An image in which individual pixels are visible.
pixels: Tiny, colored squares that make up a digital image.
pixels per inch (ppi): Scale used for measuring the resolution of a digital image. Measured by counting a single row of pixels along one inch.
PNG (Portable Network Graphics): A format for web graphics similar to GIF, but newer and containing more features and flexibility.
point: A tiny unit of measure—1/72 of an inch.
portfolio: Samples of the best artwork a graphic designer has created.
preflight check: Built-in feature in page layout programs that makes sure all necessary support files are packaged.
primary colors: Red, yellow and blue.
printing resolution: The quality level that a printer is capable of producing.
PSD (Photoshop Document): The *default* file format used to save Photoshop projects.

R

raster graphic: An image that is captured by a digital camera or scanner and is made up of pixels. Also called *bitmap graphic.*
rasterize: To convert a vector graphic into a bitmap graphic.
red eye: Undesirable photographic effect in which a camera's flash reflects off of blood vessels in the back of the subject's eye, making the pupils appear bright red.
resampling: Changing the total number of pixels in an image.
resolution: Quality level of an image.
restoring: Returning a photo to its original condition.
retouching: Altering a photo from its original appearance.
RGB color mode: Color mode that creates color by combining red, green, and blue.
RGB color workspace: A generic setting that controls how your monitor will display RGB colors.
rulers: Graduated measuring devices that can be displayed along the edges of an image window.

S

sample: To choose a pixel or group of pixels on which to base settings.

samples per inch (spi): Technical term for scanner resolution.

sans serif fonts: Fonts that have no serifs.

saturation: Term that refers to how intense colors appear.

scale: To make larger or smaller.

scanner: A digital copy machine that shines a strong light on an image and analyzes the image with its sensors. A digital version of the image is created, which can be saved into computer memory.

scripts: A series of commands created with a programming language to accomplish a particular task.

scroll bars: Sliders that allow you to reposition the image in the window.

secondary color: Color created when two primary colors are mixed.

separated: A palette that has been removed from a stack by dragging its tab clear of the other palettes' window.

serifs: Small flares or "tails" that decorate text characters.

shadows: The darkest areas in an image.

shapes: Vector graphics.

sharper: Easier to see.

skew: To slant at an angle.

slices: Invisible boundaries that are placed on web images.

smart guides: Temporary guides that automatically appear as you use the **Move Tool** to adjust the position of a layer or move a selection in the image.

smart objects: Layers that can also behave like a separate file, allowing a designer to edit the smart object separately, if desired.

snapshot: A temporarily-saved version of your file.

source image: The image that provides the colors when using the **Match Color** command.

source point: An area that a blemished area *should* look like. Photoshop will refer to this area when fixing the problem.

spot channels: Special channels that indicate where spot color is to be applied to the image.

spot color: A separate, premixed ink used when a project requires a color that cannot be represented by CMYK inks.

stacked palette: Dragging a palette's tab just to the right of another palette's tab.

state: Each action listed in the **History** palette.

steps: The regular intervals at which brush marks are created when a painting tool is being used.

stock photo agencies: Companies that keep large libraries of images, usually categorized by subject, that can be purchased for use.

stretched: Making a palette taller by dragging its bottom-right corner to resize its window.

styles: A variety of effects, such as drop shadows and beveled edges, applied to text or shapes.

subpaths: Unconnected path fragments.

substrate: The paper backing of a photo.

subtractive color system: Creating color by applying inks to paper.

swatches: A collection of color samples, like you might find at a paint store.

symbol fonts: Fonts used in special circumstances in design work.

symmetrical design: A design in which both sides appear equal.

T

tab: A small tag at the top of the palette window that displays the palette name.

target image: The image that will be adjusted when using the **Match Color** command.

tertiary color: Color created when a primary and secondary color are mixed.

thumbnails: Small pictures of what is contained on the layers.

TIFF (Tagged Image File Format): The industry standard for saving images that will be printed commercially. This format is also used for high-quality archival (storage) purposes.

tileable: Able to blend together seamlessly when placed edge to edge.

tiled: Pattern which repeats itself over and over, side by side, as you paint it.

toggle: Turn on and off.

tooltip: A brief description of each option.

type: A word referring to individual text characters that were set by hand, inked, and pressed against paper in the early days of the printing industry.

V

vanishing point: The point at which parallel receding lines of rectangular object, such as a box or a building, converge (or *would* converge if they were extended) in a perspective drawing.

vector graphics: Graphics composed of lines that are controlled by mathematical formulas.

vector masks: Masks that hide portions of a layer. They are created with the same tools that create vector paths.

visual hierarchy: The order in which design elements are presented from the greatest amount of visual weight to the least.

visual weight: Emphasis of a design element.

W

white light: Light created when red, green, and blue light are added together at full strength.

white point: The lightest pixels in an image.

Z

zipped shut: When a palette or group of palettes is zipped shut, its window is minimized and only the palette tab(s) are visible.

zoom percentage: Value between .01–1600% shown in the title bar when an image is open. It compares the size of the pixels in the image to the size of the glowing dots on the computer screen.

Index

A

actions, 477–480
Actions palette, 478–480
active, 65
Actual Pixels button, 38–39
Add Anchor Point Tool, 183, 187
additive color system, 396
Add to selection button, 66
adjustment layer, 377–378, 418
Adobe Help Center dialog box, 24
advancing colors, 379
Again command, 122
Align commands, 456
aligning layers, 456
All command, 82
alpha channel, 404
    saving a selection as a new channel, 406–407
analogous colors, 423–424
anchor points, adding and deleting, 186–187
angle jitter effect, 225–226
anti-aliasing, 69
Apply command, 442
Apply Layer Comp command, 454
Apply Layer Mask command, 442
arrowheads, 178–179
Arrowheads dialog box, 178–179
Art History Brush Tool, 285, 287
artifact, 322
asymmetrical design, 293–294
audio annotation, 487–488
Audio Annotation Tool, 488

Auto Add/Delete option, 183
Auto Color command, 370
Auto Contrast command, 370
Auto Levels command, 370
Automate menu, 480–485
Auto Resolution dialog box, 45

B

background color, 14–15
    switching, 16
Background Color button, 14–15
Background Eraser Tool, 278–282, 365
    Contiguous option, 281
    Discontiguous option, 281
    Tolerance: setting, 279–280
balance, 293–294
Batch command, 485
bit, 419
bit depth, 419–420
bitmap graphic, 161
black point, 414
blemishes, 323
blemish-removing tools, 322–327
blending modes, 218, 220–222, 369
    luminosity, 418
    using with color adjustment tools, 437
    using with filters, 437
    using with layers, 436–437
blending options, 447–451
Blending Options command, 451
Bloat Tool, 245
Blur filter, 244

Blur Tool, 319
body text, 140
Border command, 84
bounding box, 114
    transforming with, 116–123
Bridge dialog box, 486–487
Bridge, organizing files with, 486–487
brightness, 359, 380
Brightness/Contrast command, 360–361
Brightness/Contrast dialog box, 360–361
Bring Forward command, 131
Brushes palette, 223–231
    Brush Tip Shape section, 223–224
    Color Dynamics section, 229–230
    Dual Brush section, 229
    Other Dynamics section, 230
    other options, 231
    scattering settings, 227
    Shape Dynamics section, 224–226
    Texture section, 227–228
brush marks, 224
Brush Picker, 276
Brush Preset Picker, 218–220
brush strokes, 188–189
brush tip, creating, 231
Brush Tool, 80–81, 188, 218–231
    blending modes, 218, 220–222
    Flow: setting, 219
    Opacity: setting, 218–219
    options bar, 218
Brush Tool button, 14–15
Burn Tool, 366–367

C

calibrating monitor, 422
Camera RAW, 476
Camera Raw dialog box, 476–477
Cancel button, 121
canvas, 242
Canvas Size command, 242
Canvas Size dialog box, 242–243
capture, 35
careers, 489–492
Cascade command, 22
Change Text Orientation command, 169
Channel Mixer command, 408–409

Channel Mixer dialog box, 408–409
Channels palette, 404–408
Character palette, 140, 165–170
    menu, 169–170
    OpenType submenu, 169–170
Cleanup Tool, 289
clients, 26
clipboard, 123
clipping masks, 445–447
Clone Stamp Tool, 326–327
closed path, 182
CMYK
    color, 397
    color mode, 398
    values, 400
Color Balance command, 376
Color Balance dialog box, 376
color cast, 358
color channels, 404–409
    saving a selection as a new channel, 406–407
color correction, 355–381
    advanced techniques, 395–425
    one-step tools, 370
    recommended sequence for, 422
color depth, 113
Color Dodge blending mode, 369
Color Libraries button, 401
Color Libraries dialog box, 401–402
color management, 404, 422–423
color matching books, 401
color modes, 398–399
color noise, 322
Color palette, 420–421
Color Picker, 15, 174–175, 372, 380, 399–403
    H, S, and B values, 400–401
    hexadecimal code, 401
    L, A, and B values, 401
    using color settings to specify and match colors, 401–403
Color Range command, 83
Color Replacement Tool, 14–15, 364–365
colors
    and mood, 379–380, 424
    harmony and contrast, 423–425

how Photoshop measures, 399–403
identifying and matching in Photoshop, 399–404
resetting to black and white, 16
shades of, 396
switching foreground and background, 16
color sampler marks, 413–414
Color Sampler Tool, 414
color separations, 462
color stops, 236–237
Commit button, 121, 164
complementary colors, 370, 423–424
composite channel, 405
composition, 88
compression, JPEG images, 474–475
comps, 452–455
CompuServe GIF format, 476
Conditional Mode Change command, 485
Constrain Proportions option, 42
Contact Sheet II command, 480
contiguous, 79, 238
Contract command, 85
contrast, 360–361, 423–425
Convert Point Tool, 186
cool colors, 379
Copy command, 123–124, 132
Create Droplet command, 485
Create New Tool Preset button, 19
Create Plane Tool, 329–330
crop, 72
Crop and Straighten Photos command, 483
cropping an image, 73–74
Crop Tool, 72–74, 242
cropping an image, 73–74
initial options, 72
Perspective check box, 74–75
secondary options, 74
Curves command, 413–414, 416–418
Curves dialog box, 416–418
adjusting color in, 417–418
eyedropper tools, 418
Custom Shape Picker, 179–181
Custom Shape Tool, 177, 179–181
Cut command, 123–124, 132

D

darkening an image, 359
DCS 1.0 format, 476
DCS 2.0 format, 476
decorative font, 195
Default Foreground and Background Colors icon, 16
default work area, 13
Defringe command, 87
delete, 275
Delete Anchor Point Tool, 183, 187
Delete command, 442
Delete Layer button, 132
Delete Layer Mask command, 442
Desaturate command, 370
Deselect command, 82
deselected, 65
design elements, 50–51
Despeckle filter, 320
destination image, 116
digital, 35
digital camera, 35
tips, 47
Direct Selection Tool, 185
Disable command, 442
Disable Layer Mask command, 442
Distort command, 122
Distribute commands, 457–459
distributing layers, 457–459
Dock to Palette Well command, 138, 169, 410
document bounds, 127
document size, 420
Dodge Tool, 366–367
dots per inch (dpi), 46
drag a box, 39
Duplicate Layer Comp command, 454
Dust & Scratches filter, 321

E

Edge Highlighter Tool, 288
Edge Touchup Tool, 289
Edit in ImageReady button, 17–18
Edit in Quick Mask Mode button, 80
Edit in Standard Mode button, 80
Edit Plane Tool, 329–330
Edit > Transform submenu, 122–123

ellipses, 69
Elliptical Marquee Tool, 71, 127
e-mail, images for, 47–50
Enable command, 442
Enable Layer Mask command, 442
entrepreneur, 492
EPS format, 476
Equalize command, 370–371
erase, 275
Eraser Tool, 188, 276–278
eraser tools, 276–283
Expand command, 84–85
Extract dialog box, 288
Extract filter, 251, 287–289
extracting an image, 288–289
Eyedropper Tool, 83–84, 236, 240–241, 280, 402

F

Fade command, 437
fastening points, 76
Feather command, 84
feathering, 68
File > Automate menu, 480–484
file formats, 473–476
    common, 475–476
Fill command, 240
Fill pixels button, 175–176
Fill Tool, 288
Filter Gallery, 244–245
Filter menu, 243–244
filters, 218, 242–251
    dust, scratch, and noise removal, 320
    multiple, 245
Fit Image command, 480
Fit Image dialog box, 480
Fit Screen button, 38–39
flagging, 487
Flatten All Layers check box, 484
flattening an image, 136
flip, 123
Flip Canvas Horizontal command, 123
Flip Canvas Vertical command, 123
Flip Horizontal command, 123
Flip Vertical command, 123

flip x jitter effect, 226–227
focal point, 251–252
focus, 88
font family, 195
fonts
    categories, 194–195
    sizes, 141
foreground color, 14–15
    switching, 16
Foreground Color button, 14–15
Forward Warp Tool, 245
Freeform Pen Tool, 184, 188
    Magnetic option, 184
Freeze Mask Tool, 246
fringe, removing, 87
Full Screen Mode button, 16–17
Full Screen Mode with Menu Bar button, 16–17

G

gamut, 403
garbage pixels, 282–283
Gaussian blur, 317
Gaussian Blur filter, 442
Generate button, 248–249
Geometry Options menu, 177–179
gradient, 233
    editing, 236–237
    styles, 234–235
Gradient Editor, 236–237, 373
Gradient Map command, 373
Gradient Map dialog box, 373
Gradient Picker, 233–234
Gradient Tool, 233–237, 373
graphic design
    balance in designs, 293
    careers, 489–492
    color harmony and contrast, 423–425
    prepress process, 460–462
    text basics, 140
graphic designer, 25
    education and experience needed, 490–491
    professional growth, 492
grayscale color mode, 398

grid, 125–126, 334–335
grouping layers, 133–134
Grow command, 85
guides, 126–127

H

halftone printing, 44
Hand Tool, 39–40, 288, 330
    Scroll All Windows option, 40
handles, 73
HDR image, 485
headings, 140
Healing Brush Tool, 324
Help menu, 22, 24
hexadecimal code, 401
highlights, 358, 413
high resolution, 36
histogram, 410
    refreshing, 411
Histogram palette, 410–412
    viewing color adjustments, 412
History Brush Tool, 285
History palette, 283–285
Horizontal Type Mask Tool, 81–82
Horizontal Type Tool, 19, 162–165
HSB color model, 237
hue, 361
    adjusting, 358
Hue/Saturation command, 361–363
Hue/Saturation dialog box, 361–363
    Colorize check box, 363

I

ICC profiles, 422–423
icon, 18
Ignore Palettes option, 38
image capture devices, 34–35
Image Processor, 478
ImageReady, 17–18
Image Size command, 479
Image Size dialog box, 41–42, 479
Info palette, 418–420
inkjet printer, 44
Intersect with selection button, 66
Inverse command, 83
Invert command, 370

J

jitter, 224–226
JPEG 2000, 475
JPEG format, 475
JPEG images, and compression, 474–475
justification, 140

K

keyboard shortcuts, 20–21
    lasso selection tools, 78
knockout, 447–449

L

LAB color model, 237
labels, 487
Lasso Tool, 74–78
lasso tools, keyboard shortcuts, 78
layer comp
    creating, 452, 454
    editing, 454
    presenting, 455
Layer Comps palette, 452–455
    limitations, 452
Layer Comp to Files dialog box, 455
layer group, 133–134
Layer > Layer Masks submenu, 440–442
layer masks, 406–407, 437–442
    applying, 440
    creating, 441
    creating with **Paste Into** command, 442
    deleting, 440
    displaying, 438–439
    linking with layers, 440
    modifying selections with, 440
    shortcut menu, 440
    temporarily disabling, 440
Layer Masks Display Options dialog box, 439
Layer Palette Options dialog box, 138–139
Layer Properties dialog box, 130
Layer Style dialog box
    Advanced Blending section, 449
    blending options, 447–451

General Blending section, 447–448
layer styles, 190–193
Layer visibility toggle, 130, 378
layers, 111–141, 435–463
    aligning and distributing, 456–459
    changing the stacking order, 131–132
    creating new, 132
    deleting, 132
    deleting masked areas, 452
    distributing, 457–459
    duplicating, 129–130
    flattening an image, 136
    grouping, 133–134
    linking, 134
    locking, 138
    making active, 128
    menu, 138–139
    merging, 135–136
    opacity, 136
    renaming and color-coding, 130–131
    right clicking on, 139
    selecting the content, 128
    transparency, 136, 138
    using blending modes, 436–437
    using blending options, 447–451
    visibility, 132
Layers palette, 112, 128–139, 378, 436–438
Levels command, 413–416
Levels dialog box, 414–416
ligatures, 169
lightening an image, 359
lighting, 88
Line Tool, geometry options, 177–179
Link command, 442
linking layers, 134
Liquify dialog box
    mask options, 247
    reconstruct options, 247
    tool options, 247
    view options, 248
Liquify filter, 245–248
lists, 140
Load Swatches command, 422
locking layers, 138

lossless compression, 474
lossy compression, 474
low resolution, 36
luminosity, 359

M

Magic Eraser Tool, 282–283
Magic Wand Tool, 79–80
    Contiguous check box, 79
Magnetic Lasso Tool, 76–78
marquee, 69
marquee selection tools, 69–71
Marquee Tool, 330–332
    patching an area, 331–332
Match Color command, 374–375
Match Color dialog box, 374–375
Maximum filter, 442
Median filter, 321
megapixel, 47
menu bar, 18
menus, 18
merging layers, 135–136
Merge to HDR command, 485
mesh, 247
metadata, 487
midtones, 358
Minimum filter, 442
Mirror Tool, 246
Modify submenu, 84–85
mood
    and color, 379–380, 424
    and design, 51–52
motion blur, 317
Move Backward command, 131–132
Move Tool, 114–116, 124, 126–127, 164
    Align and **Distribute** buttons, 459
multimedia, images for, 47–50
multiple image windows, 22–24

N

neutral colors, 379
New dialog box, 112–114, 398
new file, creating, 112–114
New Layer button, 129
New Layer command, 112
New Layer Comp dialog box, 452–454
New Path button, 187–188

Index

New Selection button, 66
New Spot Channel dialog box, 407–408
noise, 320
noise-type gradient, 237
non-web-safe colors, 403
Notes Tool, 487–488

O

opacity, 136
open path, 182, 189
options bar, 18
ordinals, 169
out-of-gamut colors, 403–404
over-adjusted, 358

P

Paint Bucket Tool, 238–239
    All Layers option, 238–239
painting tools, 217–242
Palette Options command, 139
palettes, 21–22
    arranging, 21–22
Palette Well, 21–22
Paragraph palette, 140, 170–172
    menu, 171–172
Paste command, 124, 132
Paste Into command, 442
patching an area, 324–325, 331–332
Patch Tool, 324–325
paths, 181–182
    converting into a selection, 189
    converting into brush strokes, 188–189
    converting into filled shape, 189
    creating with **Freeform Pen Tool,** 184
    creating with **Pen Tool,** 182–183
    modifying with **Path Selection Tool,** 184–185
    modifying with **Pen Tool,** 186–187
    text on, 190
Paths button, 175–176
Path Selection Tool
    modifying a path, 184–185
    options bar, 185–186
Paths palette, 187–189
Pattern Maker dialog box, 248–250
    Preview Settings section, 250
    Tile Generation section, 248–250
    Tile History section, 250
Pattern Maker filter, 248
Pattern Picker, 238
patterns, creating, 233
Pattern Stamp Tool, 232–233
PDF Presentation command, 480
PDF Presentation dialog box, 481
Pencil Tool, 14–15, 231–232
Pen Tool
    creating a path, 182–183
    modifying paths with, 186–187
    options bar, 183
Pen Tool button, 176–177
pen tools, 181–182
personal qualities, 491
Perspective command, 122
perspective drawing, 328
Photo Filter command, 372
photo filters, 372
Photomerge command, 484
Photoshop PDF format, 476
Picture Package command, 483
pixel aspect ratio, 50
pixels, 33–34
    and resolution, 36
    finding extra, 290
pixels per inch (ppi), 40
pixilated, 36
planes, creating and adjusting, 329–330
Play selection button, 479
PNG format, 476
point, 141
Polygonal Lasso Tool, 67, 75–76
Polygon Tool, geometry options, 177–179
portfolio, 491
Posterize command, 373–374
Preferences dialog box
    Grid section, 125–126
    Guides section, 127
    Units section, 126
preflight check, 460
prepress process, 460–462
Preset Manager command, 220
primary color, 424
print size, 37

Print Size button, 38–39
printing resolution, 44
PSD format, 475
Pucker Tool, 245
Push Left Tool, 246

Q

quick mask mode, 80
Quick Mask Options dialog box, 80–81

R

raster graphic, 161
rasterizing text, 172
Reconstruct Tool, 245
Rectangle Tool, geometry options, 177
Rectangular Marquee Tool, 70, 127, 248
red eye, 325
Red Eye Tool, 325–326
Reduce Noise dialog box, 321–322
Reduce Noise filter, 321–322
reference point coordinate text boxes, 117–118
reference point locator, 117
Replace Color command, 364
Replace Color dialog box, 364
Replace Swatches command, 422
Resample Image option, 42
resampling, 42–43
Reselect command, 83
Reset Tool, 18
Resize Image Wizard, 45
Resize Windows to Fit check box, 38
resizing images, 42–43
    for printing, 44–45
resolution, 33–51
    image resolution and size, 40–45
    printing, 44
Restore Last Document State command, 454
restoring, 315
retouching, 315
retreating colors, 379
Reveal All command, 290, 441
Reverse command, 132
RGB
    color, 396
    color mode, 398
    color model, 237
    color workspace, 422
    values, 400
RGB/CMY color wheel, 358–359
Rotate 90° CCW command, 123
Rotate 90° CW command, 123
Rotate 180° command, 123
rotating images, without opening them, 487
Rounded Rectangle Tool, 177, 179
roundness jitter effect, 225–226
Rubber Band option, 183
rulers, 40, 126
RYB color wheel, 423–424

S

sans serif font, 195
saturation, 359, 380
Save As... command, 479
Save As dialog box, 479
Save For Web dialog box, 47–50
    2-Up tab, 48
    4-Up tab, 48
    Color Table tab, 49
    image properties settings, 49
    Image Size tab, 50
    Optimized tab, 48
    Original tab, 48
    Preview button, 48
Save Selection dialog box, 86, 406–407
Save Swatches command, 421–422
Save Swatches for Exchange command, 422
scale controls, 118–119
Scale Styles option, 42
scanner, 35
scanning tips, 46
screen modes, 16
scripts, 477–478
Scroll All Windows option, 40
scroll bars, 39
secondary color, 424
Select menu, 82–87
selection border, 65–66, 128
selection tools, 65–89
    crop, 72–74
    fine-tuning selections, 66–68

Index

fringe removal, 87
lasso, 74–78
magic wand, 79–80
marquee, 69–71
options, 65–69
quick mask mode, 80
saving and loading a selection, 86–87
Select menu, 82–87
temporarily hiding a selection, 87
type masking, 81–82
Selective Color command, 376–377
Selective Color dialog box, 376–377
Send to Back command, 131
serifs, 194
Set rotation text box, 119
Shadow/Highlight command, 367–368
Shadow/Highlight dialog box, 367–368
shadows, 358
Shape layers button, 174
shapes, 173
shape tools, 173–181
    Custom Shape Tool, 177, 179–181
    Fill pixels button, 175–176
    Geometry Options menu, 177–179
    options bar, 173–181
    Paths button, 175–176
    Pen Tool button, 176–177
    Shape layers button, 174
    shape tool buttons, 177
    tool-specific options, 179
Sharpen Edges filter, 318–319
Sharpen filter, 318–319
sharpening an image, 316–319
sharpening tips, 319
Sharpen More filter, 318–319
Sharpen Tool, 319
Similar command, 85
Single Column Marquee Tool, 71–72
Single Row Marquee Tool, 71
Skew, 119–120
slices, 127
smart guides, 127
smart objects, 459
Smart Sharpen dialog box, 317–318
Smart Sharpen filter, 317–318
Smooth command, 84

Smudge Tool, 240
Snap command, 127
snapshot, 284
Snap To submenu, 127–128
Soft Light blending mode, 436–437
solid-type gradient, 237
source image, 374
source point, 324
special text characters, 165
Sponge Tool, 366
spot channels, 407–408
spot color, 397
Spot Healing Brush Tool, 323
stacking order of layers, 131–132
Standard Roman Alignment toggle, 169
state, 284
Step Backward command, 25
steps, 224
stock photo agencies, 88
straightening scanned images, 483
styles, 161
Styles palette, 190, 192–193
Subtract from selection button, 66–67
subtractive color system, 397
swatches, 421
Swatches palette, 421–422, 438
Switch between free transform and warp modes button, 121
Switch Foreground and Background Colors icon, 16, 280
symbol font, 195
symmetrical design, 293

T

tab, 21
target image, 374
tertiary color, 424
text, 162–172
    basics, 140
    entering and editing, 163–164
    inserting special text characters, 165
    on a path, 190
    rasterizing, 172
    special characters, 165
Thaw Mask Tool, 246
Threshold command, 413–414

Threshold dialog box, 413–414
thumbnails, 128, 139
    changing size with Bridge, 486
    rotating images, 487
TIFF format, 474–475
Tile Horizontally command, 22
Tile Vertically command, 22
tileable pattern, 248
tiled pattern, 233
tint, adding to an image, 362–363
toggle, 48
Tool Preset dialog box, 18–19
Toolbox, 14–18, 173, 365
    hiding, 16
Tools palette, 14
tooltip, 18
Transform icon, 117
Transform options bar, 117–121
Transform Selection command, 85–86
Transform Tool, 331
transparency, 136, 138
Trim command, 291–292
Turbulence Tool, 246
Twirl Clockwise Tool, 245
type, 162
type masking tools, 81–82, 164–165
type (text) tools, 140
type tool options bar, 162–163

U

Undo command, 25
Unlink command, 442
Unsharp Mask dialog box, 316–317
Unsharp Mask filter, 316–317

V

vanishing point, 328
Vanishing Point dialog box, 329, 333–334
Vanishing Point filter, 251, 328–334
    Brush Tool, 332–333
    Eyedropper Tool, 333
    Marquee Tool, 330–332
    Stamp Tool, 332
    tips for working with, 333–334
Variations command, 357–359
Variations dialog box, 357–359
vector graphics, 161
vector masks, 442–445
    converting a selection into, 444
    converting paths into, 443
    creating, 443
    setting areas to display and hide, 444
    working with, 444–445
Vertical Type Mask Tool, 81–82
Vertical Type Tool, 162
video, creating images
View menu, 18, 20
visual hierarchy, 251–252
visual weight, 251

W

warm colors, 379
Warp Text dialog box, 163
Web Photo Gallery command, 484
Web sites, images for, 47–50
Welcome Screen, 14
white light, 396
white point, 414
Window menu, 21–22, 24
    working with multiple image windows, 22–24
work area, 13–26
workspace arrangement, saving, 22

Z

zipped shut, 21
Zoom All Windows option, 38
Zoom In button, 38
Zoom Out button, 38
zoom percentage, 37
Zoom Tool, 37–39, 330